ANNUAL REVIEW OF PSYCHOLOGY

EDITORIAL COMMITTEE (1977)

ANNUAL REVIEW OF PSYCHOLOGY

MARK R. ROSENZWEIG, *Editor*
University of California, Berkeley

LYMAN W. PORTER, *Editor*
University of California, Irvine

VOLUME 28

1977

ANNUAL REVIEWS INC.   4139 EL CAMINO WAY   PALO ALTO, CALIFORNIA 94306

ANNUAL REVIEWS INC.
Palo Alto, California, USA

International Standard Book Number: 0–8243–0228–1
Library of Congress Catalog Card Number: 50–13143

Annual Reviews Inc. and the Editors of its publications assume no
responsibility for the statements expressed by the contributors to this Review.

REPRINTS

The conspicuous number aligned in the margin with the title of each article in this
volume is a key for use in ordering reprints. Available reprints are priced at the
uniform rate of $1 each postpaid. The minimum acceptable reprint order is 10
reprints and/or $10.00, prepaid. A quantity discount is available.

PRINTED AND BOUND IN THE UNITED STATES OF AMERICA

PREFACE

At its 1976 meeting the Editorial Committee decided to simplify the Master Plan to a set of main headings which should remain relatively stable; these are listed below. In the past the subheadings have been revised rather often, so there is little purpose in publishing them, but no area formerly covered is being dropped from consideration. Since a number of readers have expressed interest or concern about the frequency of coverage of one or another topic, we show for each of the headings the number of chapters for the five most recent volumes, as well as chapters projected for the next two volumes. More detail is given in the cumulative indexes at the back of the book, where we list the chapter titles and authors. It should, of course, be understood that a few of the planned chapters may not appear, for reasons beyond our control. In the table below, a few chapters are listed under more than one heading, so that for some volumes the entries exceed by one or two the total number of chapters in the volume.

	Year: Volume:	1973 24	1974 25	1975 26	1976 27	1977 28	1978 29	1979 30
Biological Psychology		1	2	2	1	1	3	3
Receptor Processes		2	2	1	1	1	1	2
Perception		1	—	1	—	—	2	—
Cognitive Processes		—	1	1	—	1	2	1
Learning and Memory		1	1	2	1	2	2	1
Motivation		1	1	1	—	—	2	—

Comparative Psychology,
  Ethology, and Animal
  Behavior
		—	—	—	1	—	—	—

Development		1	1	2	1	2	1	1
Personality		1	1	1	1	1	1	3
Psychopathology		—	1	1	1	—	1	1
Clinical Psychology: Diagnosis and Treatment		1	2	2	2	1	2	2
Social Psychology		3	—	1	1	1	2	1
Personnel—Organizational Psychology		1	1	2	3	2	1	1
Education and Counseling		1	1	1	1	1	1	1
Research Methodology		1	1	—	2	—	1	1
Other		1	—	1	1	—	—	1
Special Timely Topics		—	—	2	2	3	2	3
Total Chapters in Volume:		16	15	21	19	15	22	22

It will be seen that about half of the main headings are represented by at least one chapter per volume, and most of the other headings average a chapter every other year. Most chapters are selective within their areas, so that no one volume can review all of the recent progress in psychology. Over a span of a few years, however, the volumes offer wide representation and scholarly evaluation of the main findings and conceptual advances.

In 1975 we began to include special chapters on timely topics that are not in the Master Plan. These articles are prepared to shorter deadlines than the other chapters so that they can be particularly up to date. This year we offer three such chapters: "Psychological and Physiological Mechanisms of Pain," by John C. Liebeskind and Linda A. Paul, "Psychological Perspectives on Death," by Robert Kastenbaum and Paul T. Costa, Jr., and "Twenty Years of Experimental Gaming," by Dean G. Pruitt and Melvin J. Kimmel. We would appreciate receiving comments from readers as to whether such chapters should be included as a regular feature of succeeding volumes.

In 1976 we welcomed the appointment of Norman Sundberg to the Editorial Committee. When his sabbatical year abroad kept him from attending the Committee meeting, we were happy that we could prevail upon Leona Tyler to extend her notable service on the Committee for another year after the expiration of her five-year term. Warren Norman's term on the Committee ended with the 1976 meeting; we will miss his wide-ranging knowledge of psychology and psychologists and his penetrating formulations. We welcome Lewis R. Goldberg as his successor.

M.R.R.

L.W.P.

CONTENTS

ANNUAL REVIEWS INC. is a nonprofit corporation established to promote the advancement of the sciences. Beginning in 1932 with the *Annual Review of Biochemistry,* the Company has pursued as its principal function the publication of high quality, reasonably priced Annual Review volumes. The volumes are organized by Editors and Editorial Committees who invite qualified authors to contribute critical articles reviewing significant developments within each major discipline.

Annual Reviews Inc. is administered by a Board of Directors whose members serve without compensation.

Annual Reviews are published in the following sciences: Anthropology, Astronomy and Astrophysics, Biochemistry, Biophysics and Bioengineering, Earth and Planetary Sciences, Ecology and Systematics, Energy, Entomology, Fluid Mechanics, Genetics, Materials Science, Medicine, Microbiology, Nuclear Science, Pharmacology and Toxicology, Physical Chemistry, Physiology, Phytopathology, Plant Physiology, Psychology, and Sociology. The *Annual Review of Neuroscience* will begin publication in 1978. In addition, two special volumes have been published by Annual Reviews Inc.: *History of Entomology* (1973) and *The Excitement and Fascination of Science* (1965).

Ann. Rev. Psychol. 1977. 28:1–39
Copyright © 1977 by Annual Reviews Inc. All rights reserved

BEHAVIORAL DECISION THEORY[1]

❖265

Paul Slovic, Baruch Fischhoff, and Sarah Lichtenstein[2]

Decision Research, Eugene, Oregon 97401

Behavioral decision theory has two interrelated facets, normative and descriptive. The normative theory is concerned with prescribing courses of action that conform most closely to the decision maker's beliefs and values. Describing these beliefs and values and the manner in which individuals incorporate them into their decisions is the aim of descriptive decision theory.

This review is organized around these two facets. The first section deals with descriptive studies of judgment, inference, and choice; the second section discusses the development of decision-aiding techniques.

As we reviewed the literature, several trends caught our attention. One is that decision making is being studied by researchers from an increasingly diverse set of disciplines, including medicine, economics, education, political science, geography, engineering, marketing, and management science, as well as psychology. Nevertheless, the importance of psychological concepts is increasing, in both the normative and descriptive work. Whereas past descriptive studies consisted mainly of rather superficial comparisons between actual behavior and normative models, research now focuses on the psychological underpinnings of observed behavior. Likewise, the prescriptive enterprise is being psychologized by challenges to the acceptability of the fundamental axioms of utility theory (140, 188, 256).

[1]This is the fourth survey of this topic to appear in the *Annual Review of Psychology*. Its predecessors were articles by Edwards (78), Becker & McClintock (24), and Rapoport & Wallsten (226). The present review covers publications appearing between January 1, 1971, and December 31, 1975, with occasional exceptions.

[2]Support for this review was provided by the Advanced Research Projects Agency of the Department of Defense and was monitored by the Office of Naval Research under Contract No. N00014-76-0074 (ARPA Order No. 3052) under subcontract to Oregon Research Institute from Decisions and Designs, Inc.

We wish to thank Barbara Combs, Robyn Dawes, Lewis R. Goldberg, and Jerry LaCava for their comments on an early draft of the manuscript.

Nancy Collins and Peggy Roecker have earned our gratitude and respect for handling an arduous secretarial job with competence and good humor.

1

Second, increasing effort is being devoted to the development of practical methods for helping people cope with uncertainty. Here psychological research provides guidance about how to elicit the judgments needed for decision-aiding techniques. Third, the field is growing rapidly, as evidenced by the numerous reviews and bibliographies produced during the past 5 years. Slovic & Lichtenstein (254) reviewed the literature on Bayesian and regression approaches to studying information processing in decision making and judgment; Dillon (73) covered utility theory with a view towards its application in agricultural contexts; MacCrimmon (187) examined work in management decision making; Shulman & Elstein (247) discussed the implications of judgment and decision making research for teachers; Nickerson & Feehrer (209) searched for studies relevant to the training of decision makers (since there aren't many, they settled for a general review); Beach (21a) reviewed research about experts' judgments under uncertainty; Vlek & Wagenaar (292) surveyed the entire field, and Kozielecki (157) and Lee (165) have provided its first textbooks.

A selective and annotated bibliography on Behavioral Decision Theory has been compiled by Barron (18). Kusyszyn (161, 162) has provided bibliographies covering the psychology of gambling, risk-taking, and subjective probability. Houle (124) has accumulated a massive bibliography on Bayesian statistics and related behavioral work, which by 1975 included 106 specialized books, 1322 journal articles, and about 800 other publications. By the time you read this, Kleiter, Gachowetz & Huber (153) will have assembled the most complete bibliography ever in this field. They generously supplied us with more than 1000 relevant references, all produced between 1971 and 1975.

To ease cognitive strain (and stay within sight of our page allotment), we have focused on psychological aspects of individual judgment and decision making. Thus we omit group and organizational decision making, Bayesian statistics, and much of the work on the axiomatic formulations of decision theory. Game theory is reviewed elsewhere in this volume. Even with this narrow focus, we have had to limit our coverage severely, concentrating on those references to which our prejudices have led us.

DESCRIPTIVE RESEARCH

Probabilistic Judgment

Because of the importance of probabilistic reasoning to decision making, considerable effort has been devoted to studying how people perceive, process, and evaluate the probabilities of uncertain events. Early research on "intuitive statistics" led Peterson & Beach (218) to an optimistic conclusion:

> . . . man gambles well. He survives and prospers while using . . . fallible information to infer the states of his uncertain environment and to predict future events (p. 29). Experiments that have compared human inferences with those of statistical man show that the normative model provides a good first approximation for a psychological theory of inference. Inferences made by subjects are influenced by appropriate variables in appropriate directions (pp. 42–43).

MODEL-BASED PARADIGMS   One result of this high regard for our intellectual capability has been a reliance on normative models in descriptive research. Thus Barclay, Beach & Braithwaite (15) proposed beginning with a normative model and adjusting its form or parameters to produce a descriptive model. This approach is best exemplified by the study of conservatism—the tendency, when integrating probabilistic information, to produce posterior probabilities nearer the prior probabilities than those specified by Bayes' theorem. In 1971, conservatism was identified as the primary finding of Bayesian information integration research (254). Reports of the phenomenon have continued to appear, in tasks involving normally distributed populations (75, 290, 305), and in that old favorite, the binomial (book-bag and poker chip) task (3, 196). Even filling the bookbags with male and female Polish surnames fails to lessen the effect (261). Donnell & DuCharme's (75) subjects became optimal when told the normative response, but when the task changed, their learning failed to generalize. As the next section shows, conservatism occurs only in certain kinds of inference tasks. In a variety of other settings, people's inferences are too extreme.

Cascaded inference   Real-life problems often have several stages, with inferences at each stage relying on data which are themselves inferences from unreliable observations or reports. For example, a physician who uses the condition of the patient's lungs as a cue for diagnosis must first infer that condition from unreliable data (e.g. the sound of a thumped chest). Several normative models for such cascaded or multistage inference tasks have been developed in recent years (217, 238). Schum (239) has shown the relevance of cascaded inference models to the judicial problem of witness credibility and the probative value of witness testimony.

Descriptive studies of cascaded inference, comparing subjects' responses in the laboratory with a normative model, have consistently shown a result just the opposite of conservatism: subjects' posterior probabilities are more extreme than those prescribed by the model (100, 217, 266). The extremity of subjects' responses has been traced to their use of a simple, but inappropriate, "best-guess" strategy (103, 137, 257, 266), which is insensitive to data unreliability.

HEURISTICS AND BIASES   In these recent studies of conservatism and cascaded inference, one can see an increasing skepticism about the normative model's ability to fulfill its descriptive role, and the view of humans as good intuitive statisticians is no longer paramount. A psychological Rip van Winkle who dozed off after reading Peterson & Beach (218) and roused himself only recently would be startled by the widespread change of attitude exemplified by statements such as "In his evaluation of evidence, man is apparently not a conservative Bayesian: he is not Bayesian at all" (138, p. 450), or ". . . man's cognitive capacities are not adequate for the tasks which confront him" (114, p. 4), or ". . . people systematically violate the principles of rational decision making when judging probabilities, making predictions, or otherwise attempting to cope with probabilistic tasks" (252, p. 169).

Van Winkle would be further surprised to see Hammond (114) and Dawes (69) putting information-processing deficiencies on a par with motivational conflicts as causes of the ills that plague humanity, and to see financial analysts, accountants, geographers, statisticians, and others being briefed on the implications of these intellectual shortcomings (14, 121a, 248, 249, 253, 282).

In 1971, when reviewing the literature on probabilistic inference, Slovic & Lichtenstein (254) found only a handful of studies that looked at subjects' information-processing heuristics. Since then, rather than simply comparing behavior with normative models, almost every descriptive study of probabilistic thinking has attempted to determine how the underlying cognitive processes are molded by the interaction between the demands of the task and the limitations of the thinker.

Much of the impetus for this change can be attributed to Tversky & Kahneman's (138, 139, 284–286) demonstrations of three judgmental heuristics—representativeness, availability and anchoring—which determine probabilistic judgments in a variety of tasks. Although always efficient, and at times valid, these heuristics can lead to biases that are large, persistent, and serious in their implications for decision making.

Judgment by representativeness   What is the probability that object B belongs to class A? Or what is the probability that process A will generate event B? Kahneman & Tversky (138) hypothesized that people answer such questions by examining the essential features of A and of B and assessing the degree of similarity between them, the degree to which B is "representative" of A. When B is very similar to A, as when an outcome is highly representative of the process from which it originates, then its probability is judged to be high.

Several lines of evidence support this hypothesis. Tversky & Kahneman (284) demonstrated a belief in what they called "the law of small numbers," whereby even small samples are viewed as highly representative of the populations from which they are drawn. This belief led their subjects, research psychologists, to underestimate the error and unreliability inherent in small samples of data. Kahneman & Tversky (138) showed that both subjective sampling distributions and posterior probability estimates were insensitive to sample size, a normatively important but psychologically nonrepresentative factor. In a subsequent paper, Kahneman & Tversky (139) demonstrated that people's intuitive predictions violate normative principles in ways that can be attributed to representativeness biases. For one, representativeness causes prior probabilities to be neglected. For another, predictions tend not to be properly regressive, being insensitive to considerations of data reliability.

Judgment by availability   Other judgmental biases are due to use of the "availability" heuristic (285) whereby an event is judged likely or frequent if it is easy to imagine or recall relevant instances. In life, instances of frequent events are typically easier to recall than instances of less frequent events, and likely occurrences are usually easier to imagine than unlikely ones. Thus availability is often a valid cue for the assessment of frequency and probability. However, since availability is also affected by subtle factors unrelated to likelihood, such as familiarity, recency, and emotional saliency, reliance on it may result in systematic biases.

Judgment by adjustment   Another error-prone heuristic is "anchoring and adjustment." With this process, a natural starting point or anchor is used as a first approximation to the judgment. The anchor is then adjusted to accommodate the implications of additional information. Typically, the adjustment is imprecise and insufficient (248). Tversky & Kahneman (286) showed how anchoring and adjustment could cause the overly narrow confidence intervals found by many investigators (175) and the tendency to misjudge the probability of conjunctive and disjunctive events (16, 57, 317).

Related work   Numerous studies have replicated and extended the Kahneman & Tversky studies, and others have independently arrived at similar conclusions. The representativeness heuristic has received the most attention. Wise & Mockovak (310), Bar-Hillel (17), and Teigen (278, 279) have documented the importance of similarity structures in probability judgment. Like Kahneman & Tversky (138), Marks & Clarkson (191, 192) and Svenson (271) observed that subjects' posterior probabilities in binomial bookbag and poker chip tasks were predominantly influenced by the most representative aspect of the sample, the proportion of red chips. Contrary to the normative model, population proportion and sample size were relatively unimportant. Leon & Anderson (166) did find an influence of these two characteristics and, as a result, claimed that Kahneman & Tversky's subjects must have misunderstood the task. Ward (302), however, argued that the conflicting results were most likely due to differences in the tasks, rather than to misinterpretation of instructions. Hammerton (113), Lyon & Slovic (184), Nisbett & Borgida (210), and Borgida & Nisbett[3] have replicated Kahneman & Tversky's finding that subjects neglect population base rates when judging the probability that an individual belongs to a given category. Nisbett & Borgida argued that this neglect stems in part from the abstract, pallid, statistical character of base-rate information. They found that concrete, case-specific information, even from a sample of one, may have much greater importance, a rather dramatic illustration of the law of small numbers. Additional evidence for representativeness comes from studies by Brickman & Pierce (45), Holzworth & Doherty (123), Bauer (20, 21), and Lichtenstein, Earle & Slovic (173).

Availability and anchoring have been studied less often. Evidence of availability bias has been found by Borgida & Nisbett[3] and Slovic, Fischhoff & Lichtenstein (252). Anchoring has been hypothesized to account for the effects of response mode upon bet preferences (176, 177), and it has been proposed as a method that people use to reduce strain when making ratio judgments (106). Pitz (219) gave the anchoring heuristic a key role in his model describing how people create subjective probability distributions for imperfectly known (uncertain) quantities.

Overconfidence   The evidence presented above suggests that the heuristic selected, the way it is employed, and the accuracy of the judgment it produces are all highly problem-specific; they may even vary with different representations of the same

---

[3]E. Borgida & R. E. Nisbett. *Abstract vs. concrete information: The senses engulf the mind.* Unpublished, University of Michigan, 1976.

problem. Indeed, heuristics may be faulted as a general theory of judgment because of the difficulty of knowing which will be applied in any particular instance.

There is, however, one fairly valid generalization that may be derived from this literature. Except for some Bayesian inference tasks, people tend to be overconfident in their judgments. This may be seen in their nonregressive predictions (139), in their disregard for the extent of the data base upon which their judgments rest (138), or its reliability (217), and in the miscalibration of their probabilities for discrete and continuous propositions (175). Howell (128) has repeatedly shown that people overestimate their own abilities on tasks requiring skill (e.g. throwing darts). Langer (163) dubbed this effect "the illusion of control" and demonstrated that it can be induced by introducing skill factors (such as competition and choice) into chance situations.

In a task that had people estimate the odds that they had been able to select the correct answer to general knowledge questions, Slovic, Fischhoff & Lichtenstein (251) found that wrong answers were often given with certainty. Furthermore, subjects had sufficient faith in their odds that they were willing to participate in a gambling game that punished them severely for their overconfidence.

How do we maintain this overconfidence? One possibility is that the environment is often not structured to show our limits. Many decisions we make are quite insensitive to errors in estimating what we want (utilities) or what is going to happen (probabilities)—so that errors in estimation are hard to detect (294a). Sometimes we receive no feedback at all. Even when we do, we may distort its meaning to exaggerate our judgmental prowess, perhaps convincing ourselves that the outcome we got was what we really wanted. Langer & Roth (164) found that subjects who experienced initial successes in a repetitive task overremembered their own past successes. Fischhoff & Beyth (93) found that people asked to recall their own predictions about past events remembered having assigned higher probabilities to events that later occurred than was actually the case. Fischhoff (89) also found that people (*a*) overestimate the extent to which they would have been able to predict past events had they been asked to do so, and (*b*) exaggerate the extent to which others should have been able to predict past events. These hindsight biases are further evidence of overconfidence for they show that people have inordinately high opinions of their own predictive abilities.

Descriptive theories   Most of the research on heuristics and biases can be considered pretheoretical. It has documented the descriptive shortcomings of the normative model and produced concepts such as representativeness and anchoring that may serve as the bases for new descriptive theories. Although theory development has been limited thus far, efforts by Wallsten (300, 301) and Shanteau (243, 244) to produce descriptive algebraic models are noteworthy. Shanteau's approach is based upon the averaging model of Anderson's integration theory (7). Wallsten's model, formulated and tested within the framework of conjoint measurement, assumes that limited capacity causes people to process dimensions of information sequentially and weight them differentially, according to their salience.

Choice

In their introduction to two volumes on contemporary developments in mathematical psychology, Krantz et al (159) explained their exclusion of the entire area of preferential choice as follows:

> There is no lack whatever of technically excellent papers in this area but they give no sense of any real cumulation of knowledge. What are established laws of preferential choice behavior? (Since three of the editors have worked in this area, our attitude may reflect some measure of our own frustration) (p. xii).

This sense of frustration is understandable when one reviews recent research on choice. The field is in a state of transition, moving away from the assumption that choice probability is expressable as a monotone function of the scale values or utilities of the alternatives. Present efforts are aimed at developing more detailed, molecular concepts that describe choice in terms of information-processing phenomena. Researchers appear to be searching for heuristics or modes of processing information that are common to a wide domain of subjects and choice problems. However, they are finding that the nature of the task is a prime determinant of the observed behavior.

ELIMINATION BY ASPECTS   One major new choice theory is Tversky's (280, 281) elimination-by-aspects (EBA) model. The model describes choice as a covert sequential elimination process. Alternatives are viewed as sets of aspects (e.g. cars described by price, model, color, etc). At each stage in the choice process an aspect is selected with probability proportional to its importance; alternatives that are unsatisfactory on the selected aspect are eliminated. Tversky showed that the EBA model generalizes the models of Luce (183) and Restle (228) while avoiding some of the counter-examples to which these earlier models are susceptible. Searching for even broader applicability, Corbin & Marley (62) proposed a random utility model that includes the EBA model as a special case. Other models built around the concept of successive elimination of alternatives have been developed by Hogarth (121, 122) and Pollay (220).

PROCESS DESCRIPTION   Most recent empirical research has been concerned with describing the decision maker's methods for processing information before choosing. Whereas earlier work focused on external products (e.g. choice proportions and rankings) and used rather simple methods, process-descriptive studies must employ more complex procedures for collecting and analyzing data. Thus we find a return to introspective methods (28, 199, 272) in which subjects are asked to think aloud as they choose among various multiattribute alternatives. Bettman & Jacoby (31) and Payne (214) supplemented the think-aloud procedure by requiring subjects to seek information from envelopes on an "information board." Russo & Rosen (231) used eye-movement data conjointly with verbal protocols. One goal of these studies is to represent the choice process graphically as a tree or network (discrimination net) of successive decisions. Swinth, Gaumnitz & Rodriguez (275) developed a method of controlled introspection that enables subjects to build and validate their own discrimination nets. Bettman (27) showed how to describe such nets via graph-theoretical concepts. Uneasy about the subjectivity of introspective techniques, Hogarth (121) used an ingenious blend of theory and empiricism to develop a computer algorithm that builds the tree without recourse to subjective inputs.

Can introspective methods be trusted? Nisbett & Wilson[4] reopened an old debate by arguing that people lack awareness of the factors that affect their judgments. After documenting this claim with results from six experiments, they concluded that "Investigators who are inclined to place themselves at the mercy of such [introspective] reports . . . would be better advised to remain in the armchair" (p. 35). While important, this criticism may be overstated. Students of choice have in many instances validated their introspective reports against theoretical predictions (199) and data from other sources[5] (see also 214).

What do these methodologies tell us about choice? First they indicate that subjects use many rules and strategies enroute to a decision. These include conjunctive, disjunctive, lexicographic and compensatory rules, and the principle of dominance (274). A typical choice may involve several stages, utilizing different rules at different junctures. Early in the process, subjects tend to compare a number of alternatives on the same attribute and use conjunctive rules to reject some alternatives from further consideration (26, 214, 245, 272). Later they appear to employ compensatory weighting of advantages and disadvantages on the reduced set of alternatives (214). Features of the task that complicate the decision, such as incomplete data, incommensurable data dimensions, information overload, time pressures, and many alternatives seem to encourage strain-reducing, noncompensatory strategies (214, 255, 313, 314). Svenson (272) and Russo & Rosen (231) found subjects reducing memory load by comparing two alternatives at a time and retaining only the better one for later comparisons. Russo & Dosher[5] observed simple strategies, such as counting the number of dimensions favoring each alternative or ignoring small differences between alternatives on a particular dimension. In some instances, these strategies led to suboptimal choices.

In general, people appear to prefer strategies that are easy to justify and do not involve reliance on relative weights, trade-off functions, or other numerical computations. One implication of this was noted by Slovic (250), whose subjects were forced to choose among pairs of alternatives that were equal in value for them. Rather than choose randomly, subjects consistently followed the easy and defensible strategy of selecting the alternative that was superior on the more important dimension.

SCRIPT PROCESSING   Abelson's (1) new approach to explaining decisions warrants further study. It is based on the concept of a "cognitive script," which is a

---

[4] R. E. Nisbett & T. D. Wilson. *Awareness of factors influencing one's own evaluations, judgments, and behavior.* Unpublished, University of Michigan, 1976.

[5] J. E. Russo & B. A. Dosher. *Dimensional Evaluation: A heuristic for binary choice.* Unpublished, University of California, Santa Barbara, 1975.

coherent sequence of events expected by the individual on the basis of prior learning or experience. When faced with a decision, individuals are hypothesized to bring relevant scripts into play. For example, Candidate Y's application for graduate school may be rejected because Y reminds the decision maker of Candidate X who was accepted and failed miserably. Another script might assimilate the candidate into a category (He's one of those shy types who does well in courses, but doesn't have enough initiative in research). Script theory, though still in a highly speculative stage, suggests a type of explanation for choice that has thus far been overlooked.

CONSUMER CHOICE   Much research on choice has been done within the domain of consumer psychology. Comprehensive reviews of this research have been provided by Jacoby (134, 135). Although some of this work is application of multiple regression, conjoint measurement, and analysis of variance to describe consumers' values (30, 107, 312), many other studies have investigated basic psychological questions. For example, one major issue has been the effect of amount and display of information on the optimality of choice. Jacoby and his colleagues have argued that more information is not necessarily helpful, as it can overload consumers and lead them to select suboptimal products. Russo, Krieser & Miyashita (230) observed that subjects had great difficulty finding the most economical product among an array of different prices and packages. Even unit prices, which do the arithmetic for the consumer, had little effect on buyer behavior when posted on the shelf below each product. However, when prices per unit were listed in order from high to low cost, shoppers began to buy less expensive products.

Models of Risky Choice

Decision making under conditions of risk has been studied extensively. This is probably due to the availability of (a) an appealing research paradigm, choices among gambles, and (b) a dominant normative theory, the subjectively expected utility (SEU) model, against which behavior can be compared. The SEU model assumes that people behave as though they maximized the sum of the products of utility and probability.

Early studies of the model's descriptive adequacy produced conflicting results. Situational and task parameters were found to have strong effects, leading Rapoport & Wallsten (226) to observe that a researcher might accept SEU with one set of bets and reject it with another, differently structured set. Proponents of the SEU model point out that it gives a good global fit to choice data, particularly for simple gambles.[6] In addition, certain assumptions of the model, like the independent (multiplicative) combination of probabilities and payoffs, have been verified for simple gambles (244, 299).

However, during the past 5 years, the proponents of SEU have been greatly outnumbered by its critics. Coombs (60) has argued that risky choice is determined not by SEU, but by a compromise between maximization of expected value (EV)

---

[6]B. Goodman, M. Saltzman, W. Edwards & D. Krantz. *Prediction of bids for two-outcome gambles in a casino setting.* Unpublished, 1976.

and optimization of risk. He proposed an alternative to SEU, "portfolio theory," in which risk preferences play a central role. That role is illustrated in a study by Coombs & Huang (61) in which gamble B was constructed as a probability mixture of two other gambles, A and C. Many subjects preferred gamble B (with its intermediate risk level) to gambles A and C, thus violating a fundamental axiom of SEU theory.

Zagorski (318) demonstrated a result that appears to violate SEU and many other algebraic models as well. Zagorski's subjects were shown pairs of gambles (A, B) and were asked to judge the amount of money (A-B) that would induce them to trade the better gamble (A) for the worse gamble (B). He demonstrated that one can construct quadruples of gambles A, B, C, and D such that

$$(A-B) + (B-C) \neq (A-D) + (D-C)$$

In other words, path independence is violated. The difference between gambles A and C depends on whether the intermediate gamble is B or D.

A favorite approach of SEU critics is to develop counterexamples to the fundamental axioms of the theory. The paradoxes of Allais (4) and Ellsberg (85) are two of the most famous, both designed to invalidate Savage's (232) independence principle. Until recently, few theorists were convinced. MacCrimmon (185) showed that business executives who violated various axioms could easily be led, via discussion, to see the error of their ways. However, Slovic & Tversky (256) challenged Mac-Crimmon's discussion procedure on the grounds that it pressured the subjects to accept the axioms. They presented subjects with arguments for and against the independence axiom and found persistent violations, even after the axiom was presented in a clear and presumably compelling fashion. Moskowitz (200) used a variety of problem representations (matrix formats, trees, and verbal presentations) to clarify the principle and maximize its acceptability, yet still found that the independence axiom was rejected. Even MacCrimmon's faith in many of the key axioms has been shaken by recent data (see 188), leading him to suggest that reevaluation of the theory is in order.

Kahneman & Tversky (140, 283) attempted this sort of reevaluation, presenting evidence for two pervasive violations of SEU theory. One, the "certainty effect," causes consequences that are obtained with certainty to be valued more than uncertain consequences. The Allais paradox may be due to this effect. The second, labeled the "reference effect," leads people to evaluate alternatives relative to a reference point corresponding to their status quo, adaptation level, or expectation. By altering the reference point, formally equivalent versions of the same decision problem may elicit different preferences. These effects pose serious problems for the normative theory and its application.

Payne (213) proposed replacing the SEU model with information processing theories that describe how probabilities and payoffs are integrated into decisions. He presented a "contingent process" model to describe the sequential processes involved in choice among gambles. For support, he cited a number of display and response-mode effects that are due to processing difficulties (176, 177, 179, 215).

Kozielecki's (158) discussion of the internal representation of risky tasks carried a similar message. Kunreuther (160) has argued that utility theory would be of little value to a policy maker trying to predict how people would respond to various flood or earthquake insurance programs. First, the theory makes predictions that are not borne out by actual behavior—for example, that people will prefer policies with high deductibles or that subsidizing premiums will increase insurance purchasing. Second, it gives no guidance about the social, situational, and cognitive factors that are likely to influence insurance purchase. Like Payne, Kunreuther called for an alternative theory, founded on the psychology of human information processing, and presented a model of his own to support his case.

Readers interested in additional attacks on the staggering SEU model should consult Barron & MacKenzie (19), Davenport & Middleton (66), Fryback, Goodman & Edwards (99), Ronen (229), and Svenson (273).

Regression Approaches

The regression paradigm uses analysis of variance, conjoint measurement, and multiple regression techniques to develop algebraic models that describe the method by which individuals weight and combine information.

INTEGRATION THEORY   Working within the framework of "information integration theory," Anderson and his colleagues have shown that simple algebraic models describe information use quite well in an impressive variety of judgmental, decision making, attitudinal, and perceptual tasks (6, 7). These models typically have revealed stimulus averaging, although some subtracting and multiplying has been observed. Particularly relevant to decision making are studies of risk taking and inference (244), configurality in clinical judgment (5), intuitive statistics (167, 168), preference for bus transportation (210a), and judgment in stud poker (181). There is no doubt that algebraic models derived from Anderson's techniques provide good surface descriptions of judgmental processes. However, as Graesser & Anderson (106) have observed, establishment of an algebraic model is only the first step towards disclosing the underlying cognitive mechanisms, which may be rather different from the surface form of the model.

POLICY CAPTURING   Another form of the regression paradigm uses correlational statistics to provide judgmental models in realistic settings. The most systematic development of these procedures has been made by Hammond and his colleagues (117) within "social judgment theory." This theory assumes that most judgments depend upon a mode of thought that is quasi-rational, that is, a synthesis of analytic and intuitive processes. The elements of quasi-rational thought are cues (attributes), their weights, and their functional relationships (linear and nonlinear) to both the environment and the judge's responses. Brunswik's lens model and multiple regression analysis are used to derive equations representing the judge's cue utilization policy. Judgmental performance is analyzed into knowledge and "cognitive control," the latter being the ability to employ one's knowledge consistently (118).

By 1971 it was evident that linear models could describe college students' cue-weighting policies in a wide variety of laboratory tasks (254). During the past 5 years, such models have been used with similar success to analyze complex real-world judgments. Judges in these studies have included business managers (119, 193, 201, 202), graduate admissions committees (68, 237), auditors, accountants, and loan officers (13, 172, 315), military officers (277), literary critics (84), and trout hatchery employees (182), as they attempted to predict business failures and stock market performance, select graduate students, plan work force and production schedules, evaluate accounting procedures, Air Force cadets, and theatrical plays, and recommend trout streams. Even United States senators have been modeled and their roll-call votes predicted (298). As in the laboratory studies, linear equations have accounted for most of the predictable variance in these complex judgments. The coefficients of these equations have provided useful descriptions of the judges' cue-weighting policies and have pinpointed the sources of interjudge disagreement and nonoptimal cue use.

While policies were being captured in the field, other researchers were deepening our understanding of the models. Dawes & Corrigan (70) observed that linear models have typically been applied in situations in which (a) the predictor variables are monotonically related to the criterion (or can be easily rescaled to be monotonic), and (b) there is error in the independent and dependent variables. They demonstrated that these conditions insure good fits by linear models, regardless of whether the weights in such models are optimal. Thus the linearity observed in judges' behaviors may be reflecting only a characteristic of linear models, not a characteristic of human judgment.

In other work, theoretical and methodological refinements of the lens model have been developed by Castellan (52, 53) and Stenson (267). Cook (59) and Stewart & Carter (268) have worked towards developing interactive computer programs for policy capturing. Mertz & Doherty (195) and Brehmer (37) examined the influence of various task characteristics on the configurality and consistency of policies. Miller (197) demonstrated that improper cue labels could mislead judges despite the availability of adequate statistical information about cue validities. Lichtenstein, Earle & Slovic (173) and Birnbaum (32) showed that even though regression equations can be used to describe cue-combination policies, subjects often average cues, in violation of the additivity inherent in the equations. Wiggins (306) discussed the problems of identifying and characterizing individual differences in judgmental policies, and Ramanaiah & Goldberg (222) explored the stability and correlates of such differences. McCann, Miller & Moskowitz (193) examined the problems of capturing policies in particularly complex and dynamic tasks such as production planning.

MULTIPLE CUE PROBABILITY LEARNING   Considerable effort has been invested in studying how people learn to make inferences from several probabilistic cues. Most of this work goes under the label "multiple-cue probability learning" (MCPL) and relies on the lens model for conceptual and analytic guidance. Typically, the cues are numerical and vary in their importance and in the form (linear or nonlinear) of their relationship to the criterion being judged. The criterion usually contains error, making perfect prediction impossible. Because these tasks embody the essential features of diagnostic inference, they are studied for their potential applied significance as well as their contributions to basic knowledge.

Slovic & Lichtenstein (254) reviewed MCPL studies published prior to 1971. They concluded that: (a) subjects can learn to use linear cues appropriately; (b) learning of nonlinear functions is slow, and especially difficult when subjects are not forewarned that relations may be nonlinear; (c) subjects are inconsistent, particularly when task predictability is low; (d) subjects fail to take proper account of cue intercorrelations; and (e) outcome feedback is not very helpful.

Research during the past half decade has confirmed and extended these conclusions. Difficulties people have in coping with intercorrelated cues have been documented in numerous studies (8, 9, 178, 236). Hammond and his colleagues (115) used the MCPL paradigm to analyze the effects of psychoactive drugs on cognition. They found that some drugs that are used to enhance emotional control interfered with learning and communication in ways that may be detrimental to therapy. Bjorkman (33) and Castellan (54) reviewed results from studies using nonmetric cues and criteria.

Other research has worked towards developing a theory to explain MCPL results in terms of erroneous intuitions about probabilistic tasks, the manner in which individuals acquire and test hypotheses, and their cognitive limitations. For example, Brehmer (38, 40, 41) has studied how subjects formulate and test hypotheses as they search for rules that will produce satisfactory inferences. Hypotheses about the functional rule relating cues and criterion appear to be sampled from a hierarchical set based on previous experience and dominated by the positive linear rule. Testing of hypotheses about rules shows inadequate appreciation of the probabilistic nature of the task. Subjects keep searching for deterministic rules that will account for the randomness in the task; since there are none, they change rules frequently (i.e. become inconsistent) and eventually resample rules they had previously discarded.

Even when subjects are informed of the correct rules, they have trouble applying them consistently (31, 36, 42, 118). Nonlinear rules are particularly hard to apply. Brehmer, Hammond, and their colleagues have thus conceptualized inference as a skill analogous to motor behavior: with both, we can know what we want to do without necessarily being able to do it.

Dynamic Decision Making

At the time of Rapoport & Wallsten's review, one active research area was dynamic decision making (DDM), the study of tasks in which "decisions are made sequentially in time; the task specifications may change over time, either independently or as a result of previous decisions; information available for later decisions may be contingent upon the outcomes of earlier decisions; and implications of any decision may reach into the future" (224, p. 345). The present half-decade began promisingly with Rapoport & Burkheimer's (225) explication of formal models for deferred decision making and the manner in which they might be utilized in psychological experiments. Shortly thereafter, Ebert (77) reported finding no difference between stochastic and deterministic versions of a task which Rapoport (223) earlier had found to differ. After that, relative silence.

Several possible reasons for this decline in interest come to mind. The mathematical sophistication of DDM may deter some researchers, as may the on-line computer and long start-up time often required. Furthermore, DDM models are so complex and require so many assumptions that the interpretation of experimental results is typically ambiguous—witness the morass of explanations facing Ebert (77) for why his experiment and Rapoport's produced different results. Kleiter (151) noted particular problems with creating cover stories that induce subjects to accept the assumptions underlying the model and with ascertaining that subjects understood the task. He also questioned "the metahypothesis that human behavior is optimal" (p. 374), which limits psychological theories to variations on the optimal model, (e.g. using subjective probability estimates rather than "objective" relative frequencies or assuming a reduced planning horizon). In his own work, Kleiter (152) has assessed people's planning horizons and has used a non-normative variance-preference model to predict betting behavior in a multistage game (154). These predictions relied on the assumption that people were perfect Bayesian information processors.

A more active area of DDM research deals with sequential information purchasing or sampling. Levine & Samet (169) allowed subjects to purchase information from three fallible sources until they could decide which of eight possible targets was the object of an enemy advance. They found that information seeking was greater and accuracy was lower in low reliability conditions. Similar results were obtained by Snapper & Peterson (259), whose subjects appeared to be relatively unresponsive to changes in information quality because of a policy of purchasing "intermediate" amounts of information.

Another sequential task that has attracted some attention is optional stopping: the decision maker must choose between accepting a currently available outcome versus sampling further outcomes that may be of greater or lesser worth. Although earlier research (see 225a) found that subjects performed well when options were generated by a random but stationary process, Brickman (44) found very poor performance with options that tended to increase or decrease in value. In particular, subjects persisted much longer in sampling options with a descending than with an ascending sequence. Brickman likened this behavior to "throwing good money after bad." His subjects' "take the money and run" strategy with ascending series was similar to that found by Corbin, Olson & Abbondanza (63). Their subjects seem to have called it quits as soon as an option appeared that was a good bit better than its predecessors. Ölander (212), too, described satisficing (rather than maximizing) principles that may guide subjects' decisions about searching further.

Are Important Decisions Biased?

A coherent picture emerges from research described so far. Because of limited information-processing capacity and ignorance of the rules for optimal information processing and decision making, people's judgments are subject to systematic biases. Can these results be generalized from the lab to the real world?

A number of critics are doubtful. Edwards (80) argued that experimenters, by denying subjects necessary tools and providing neither the time nor the guidance to find them, have exaggerated human intellectual limitations. Winkler & Murphy (309) criticized laboratory experiments for being overly simplified and too well structured when compared with the real-world situations they are meant to model. They suggested that people may perform poorly in the lab because of improper generalization from their real-world experiences. For example, because real-world information tends to be redundant and unreliable, people may naturally devalue the reliable information provided in experiments, producing conservatism. In addition, experimental subjects may be poorly motivated and forced to deal with unfamiliar tasks and substantive areas without adequate training—even in the meaning of the response mode (121a).

In rebuttal, one could argue that laboratory studies may show subjects at their best. Use of unfamiliar substantive topics may free them from preconceived notions that could prejudice their judgments. Provision of all information necessary for an optimal decision (and little else) is, as noted by Winkler & Murphy (309), a boon seldom offered by the real world. It may create demand characteristics forcing subjects toward optimal responses (90, 97, 302). An alternative rebuttal is that there are many real-life situations which are quite like the laboratory, forcing people to make a decision without the benefit of training and experience. People typically buy cars and houses and decide to marry and divorce under such circumstances, functioning as their own best approximation to experts.

Perhaps the best way to resolve this argument is to look at the evidence.

EXPERTS IN THE LABORATORY   The robustness of biases is shown in formal experiments using experts as subjects. As examples: Tversky & Kahneman's (284) "law of small numbers" results were obtained with statistically savvy psychologists. Las Vegas casino patrons showed the same irrational reversals of preferences for gambles as did college students (176, 177). Bankers and stock market experts predicting closing prices for selected stocks showed substantial overconfidence and performed so poorly that they would have done better with a "know nothing" strategy (264). Lichtenstein & Fischhoff (174) found that the probability assessments of psychology graduate students were no better for questions within their area of expertise than for questions relating to general knowledge.

The "experts" in these studies were selected on the basis of what they knew about the subject area, not what they knew about judgment and decision making (i.e. they were substantive rather than normative experts). Can normative experts be created in the laboratory by proper training? The evidence is mixed, suggesting either that some biases are robust or that we have failed to understand the psychology of our subjects well enough to assist them.

OUT IN THE FIELD   With the exception of some well-calibrated weather forecasters (described below), similar biases have been found in a variety of field studies. For example, Brown, Kahr & Peterson (49, p. 431) observed overconfidence in the probability assessments of military intelligence analysts. Kidd (149) found that engineers for the United Kingdom's Central Electricity Generating Board consistently underestimated repair time for inoperative units. Bond (34) observed suboptimal play among 53 blackjack players at four South Lake Tahoe casinos. "By wagering small bets in a sub-fair game, [these] blackjack gamblers practically guaranteed loss of their betting capital to the casinos" (p. 413). Flood plain residents misperceive the probability of floods in ways readily explained in terms of availability and representativeness (253). Surveying research published in psychological and educational journals, Cohen (56) and Brewer & Owen (43) found that investigators regularly design experiments with inadequate statistical power, reflecting a belief in the "law of small numbers" (284). Misinterpretation of regression toward the mean appears to be as endemic to some areas of psychology (101) as to Kahneman & Tversky's (139) subjects.

A major legal debate concerns the incarceration of individuals for being "dangerous." What little evidence there is regarding the validity of dangerousness judgments indicates substantial "over-prediction," incarceration of people who would not have misbehaved had they been set free (72, 242). Although this bias may reflect a greater aversion to freeing someone who causes trouble than to erring in the other direction, some observers have attributed it to judgmental problems such as failure to consider base rates, ignorance of the problems of predicting rare events, perception of nonexistent correlations, and insensitivity to the reliability of evidence (198a).

Jurors appear to have great difficulty ignoring first impressions of the accused's personality, pretrial publicity, and other forms of inadmissible evidence (46, 270), tendencies which may represent both hindsight and anchoring biases (92). The vagaries of eyewitness testimony and witnesses' overconfidence in erroneous knowledge are quite well known (51, 180).

Zieve (319) has described at length the misinterpretation and abuse of laboratory test results by medical clinicians. Although some of these errors are due to ignorance, others reflect naive statistical reasoning. A classic case of the "law of small numbers" is Berkson, Magath & Hurn's (25) discovery that aspiring lab technicians were expected by their instructors to show greater accuracy in performing blood cell counts than was possible given sampling variation. These instructors would marvel that the best students (those who would not cheat) had the greatest difficulty in producing acceptable counts. In a phenomenological study of orthopedic surgeons, Knafl & Burkett (155) found a variety of simplifying heuristics, some of them in the form of general treatment philosophies (e.g. "don't cut unless you absolutely have to").

The immense decisions facing our society (e.g. nuclear power) have prompted the development of formal analytic techniques to replace traditional, error-prone, "seat of the pants" decision making. Fischhoff (91) reviewed a variety of cost-benefit analyses and risk assessments performed with these techniques and found them liable to omissions of important consequences reflecting availability biases. In case studies of policy analyses, Albert Wohlstetter (311) found that American intelligence analysts consistently underestimated Soviet missile strength, a bias possibly due to anchoring. Roberta Wohlstetter's (311a) study of American unpreparedness at Pearl Harbor found the U.S. Congress and military investigators guilty of hindsight bias in their judgment of the Pearl Harbor command staff's negligence.

Even if policy analyses are performed correctly, they still must be explained (sold?) to the public. In the area of natural hazard management, well-founded government policies have foundered because people do not perceive flood hazards the way policy makers expect them to (253). For example, the National Flood Insurance Program has had only limited success because the endangered people will not buy the highly subsidized and normatively very attractive insurance offered them (160).

THE ULTIMATE TEST   "If behavioral decision theory researchers are so smart, why aren't they rich?"

"They're not in business."

"Then why aren't people who are in business falling over themselves to utilize their results?"

Well, although psychological research has not swept the world's decision makers like wildfire, it has kindled some nonnegligible interest. The concern weather forecasters and decision analysts have shown for research in probability assessment is described elsewhere in this review. The Department of Defense is developing sophisticated decision aids to relieve military commanders of the need to integrate information in their heads (148). United States intelligence analysts have shown interest in the use of Bayesian approaches for processing of intelligence information (79a, 147). Researchers in accounting[7] (see also 14) have advocated considering information-processing limits in designing financial reports. The American College of Radiology has launched a massive "Efficacy Study" to see how radiologists use the probabilistic information from X rays. Bettman (29), Armstrong, Kendall & Ross (10), and others have argued that legislation intended to provide consumers with necessary information (e.g. unit pricing, true interest rates) must consider how those consumers do in fact process information.

DECISION AIDS

"What do you do for a living?"

"Study decision making."

"Then you can help me. I have some big decisions to make."

"Well, actually . . ."

That sinking feeling of inadequacy experienced by many of us doing psychological research in decision making is probably *not* felt by most experts in decision analysis, multiattribute utility theory, or other decision aiding techniques. Proponents of these approaches have remedies for what ails you—techniques to help users make better decisions in any and all circumstances.

Most of these decision aids rely on the principle of divide and conquer. This "decomposition" approach is a constructive response to the problem of cognitive overload. The decision aid fractionates the total problem into a series of structurally related parts, and the decision maker is asked to make subjective assessments for

[7]T. A. Climo. *Cash flow statements for investors.* Unpublished, University of Kent at Canterbury, 1975.

only the smallest components. Such assessments are presumably simpler and more manageable than assessing more global entities. Research showing that decomposition improves judgment has been reported by Armstrong, Denniston & Gordon (11), Gettys et al (104), and by Edwards and his colleagues (254, pp. 717–21).

Critics of the decomposition approach would argue that many of the aids require assessments of quantities the decision maker has never thought about, and that these apparently simple assessments may be psychologically more complex than the original decision. In some situations, people may really know what they want to do better than they know how to assess the inputs required for the decision aid.

Decision aids which do not rely on decomposition, but instead require the decision maker to state preferences among whole, nonfractionated alternatives, are here called "wholistic." The models in these aids are used to smooth or correct the wholistic judgments and to partial them into components.

Since several of the decision aids rely on assessments of probability, we start this section with a review of probability elicitation techniques.

Assessing Probabilities

What's the best way to assess probabilities? Spetzler & Stäel von Holstein (260) have written an excellent description of how the Decision Analysis Group at Stanford Research Institute approaches this problem. They recommended (a) carefully structuring the problem with the client ("mental acrobatics should be minimized", p. 343), (b) minimizing biases that might affect the assessor, (c) using personal interviews rather than computer-interactive techniques with new clients, and (d) using several different elicitation methods, both direct and indirect. Their favorite elicitation technique is a reference bet involving a "probability wheel," a disk with two differently colored sectors whose relative size is adjustable. The assessor is offered two bets, each with the same payoff. One bet concerns the uncertain quantity (you win if next year's sales exceed $X); the other bet concerns the disk (you win if the pointer lands in the orange sector after the disk is spun). The relative size of the two sectors is varied until the assessor is indifferent between the two bets. The proportion of the disk which is orange is taken as the probability of the event stated in the other bet.

Despite the appeal of this method (it is formally justified within axiomatic models of subjective probability, does not require the assumption that the utility of money is linear with money, and requires no numerical response from the assessor), we have been unable to find any research on its use.

DISCRETE EVENTS   Comparisons among several direct methods for assessing the probabilities of discrete events (probabilities vs odds vs log odds) have failed to identify one clearly preferable response mode (35, 73a, 105). Beach (22) found a mean within-subject correlation of only 0.49 between probabilities assessed directly and indirectly (via bids for bets). DuCharme & Donnell (76) found equally conservative inferences using odds, probabilities, and an indirect method similar in concept to, but more complicated than, the reference bet method discussed by Spetzler & Stäel von Holstein (260).

These studies focused on the assessment of middle-range probabilities; even less is known about assessing very large or very small probabilities. Slovic, Fischhoff & Lichtenstein (251) have shown that subjects grossly misuse odds of greater than 50:1. Selvidge (241) has made some common-sense suggestions for assessing very small probabilities. She advised first structuring and decomposing the problem, then ranking various unlikely events, and finally attaching numbers to those events with the help of reference events (like dying in various rare accidents).

Once you have assessed a probability, how good is it? When there is an agreed-upon "true probability"—as with bookbag and poker chip tasks—the assessed probability may be compared with the "truth." But more often the assessed probability states a degree of belief in some proposition, so that no criterion "true" probability value exists. One test of such probabilities is coherence, that is, do they abide by the axioms of probability? (290, 316). A second kind of validity, called calibration, may be examined if one collects a large number of assessments for which the truth of the associated propositions is known. For discrete propositions, calibration means that for every collection of propositions assigned the same numerical probability, the hit rate or proportion which actually is true should be equal to the assessed probability. The research on calibration has recently been reviewed extensively (175), so only a summary of findings will be given here: (a) Experienced weather forecasters, when performing their customary tasks, are excellently calibrated. (b) Everybody else stinks. (c) People are overconfident except with very easy tasks.

UNCERTAIN QUANTITIES   The most common technique for assessing probability density functions across uncertain quantities is the fractile method. An assessor who names a value of an uncertain quantity as its 0.25 fractile, for example, is saying that there is just a 25% chance that the true value will be smaller than that specified value. Stäel von Holstein (263) and Vlek (290) have studied the consistency between the fractile method and other elicitation methods. Stäel von Holstein found that even after four sessions most subjects were inconsistent. Vlek's subjects showed greater consistency.

Continuous probability density functions can also be tested for calibration. Assessors are calibrated when, over many such assessments, the proportion of true answers falling below a given fractile is equal to that fractile. The evidence on calibration (175) may be summarized as follows: (a) A strong and nearly universal bias exists: the assessed distributions are too tight, so that from 20% to 50% of the true values, instead of 2%, fall outside of the 0.01 to 0.99 range of the distributions. (b) Training improves performance.

SCORING RULES   Scoring rules are functions which assign a score to an assessed probability (or a vector of probabilities) as a function of both the true outcome of the event being assessed and the size of the probability associated with the true outcome. Such rules are strictly proper if and only if the only strategy for maximizing one's expected score is to tell the truth—to state one's true belief without hedging. Usually the only rules considered are those which reward expertise: given that one tells the truth, the more one knows, the larger the score [an exception is Vlek's (291) fair betting game]. Scoring rules have recently been discussed by Murphy & Winkler (205, 206) and by Shuford & Brown (50, 246).

Scoring rules may be used for three purposes. The first use is as an indirect method for measuring probabilities. A list of bets is generated from the scoring rule. Each bet gives two numbers, how much the assessor wins if the event in question occurs and how much is lost if it does not. The assessor selects his or her preferred bet from the list; this choice implies a probability. Jensen & Peterson (136) and Seghers, Fryback & Goodman (240) found this method unsatisfactory; their subjects were apparently using other strategies rather than trying to maximize winnings.

The second use of scoring rules is to educate assessors about probability assessments made with other methods. Several studies have used scoring rule feedback (246, 262, 308) without reporting whether it helped. Hoffman & Peterson (120) reported that subjects who received such feedback improved their scores on a subsequent task, but Vlek (290) found no such improvement. Scoring rules are now widely used by weather forecasters, and this may be why they are so well calibrated (175). Murphy & Winkler (207) reported that a majority of 689 weather forecasters (a) described themselves as being uncomfortable thinking in probabilistic terms (though their job is to report probabilities and they do it well), and (b) rejected the idea that their forecasts can be properly evaluated by a single quantitative measure like a scoring rule (though many had had experience with such feedback).

The third use for scoring rules is to evaluate assessors. When all assessors are working in the same situation, the assessor with the highest score is the best assessor. However, not all situations are equal; there is more uncertainty in forecasting rain in Chicago than in Oregon. Thus Oregon forecasters will earn higher scores simply because of where they work. Murphy (203) has shown that the Brier scoring rule (the one used in meteorology) may be partitioned into three additive components, measuring (a) the inherent uncertainty in the task, (b) the resolution of the assessor (i.e. the degree to which the assessor can successfully assign probabilities different from the overall hit rate), and (c) the assessor's calibration. None of the components is itself a proper scoring rule, but the difference between the total score and the inherent uncertainty component is proper, and this difference could be used to compare assessors in different situations (204).

The astute reader will note that the research does not provide an adequate answer to the question asked at the start of this section: What is the best way to assess probabilities? In addition, the research has yielded few theoretical ideas. Only Pitz (219) has speculated on the cognitive processes underlying probability assessment. Finally, although a few studies have noted that training improves performance in eliciting probabilities, a definitive long-range learning study is still needed.

Multiattribute Utility Theory

Suppose you must choose one object or course of action from a set. Each object or action is describable in terms of a number of dimensions or attributes of value to you, and the outcomes of your choice are certain. Then multiattribute utility theory

(MAUT) prescribes that you compute, for each object j, the following weighted utilities, summed across the attributes i:

$$MAU_j = \sum_i w_i u_{ij}$$

where w_i is the relative importance of the ith attribute and u_{ij} is the utility of the jth object on the ith attribute. For example, when choosing a car, w_i might be the importance of design, and u_{ij} would indicate how beautifully designed car j is. The theory prescribes that you choose the car with the largest MAU. While this model is the most common, variants exist which incorporate additional features such as uncertainty, multiplicativity (rather than additivity) of the weighted utilities, time factors, and the possibility that your choice will affect others (293).

MAUT is a decision aid strongly grounded in theory. The axioms of the theory lead to the models, to methods for measuring the utilities and weights, and to specified tests that show which of the models is applicable. MAUT models have been developed extensively in the last 5 years (94–96, 141, 143, 233, 234). If these sources are too technical, the review papers by MacCrimmon (186), Fischer (86, 88), von Winterfeldt & Fischer (296), Humphreys (131), and Huber (129a) may be helpful.

ASSESSMENT TECHNIQUES   The first step in constructing a MAU is to list the attributes. Techniques for doing this are rarely discussed. Among those who have faced the problem, some have used the Delphi technique (e.g. 102, 211). Humphreys & Humphreys (132) suggested using George Kelly's repertory grid technique. Dalkey, Lewis & Snyder (65) proposed evaluating diverse problems (e.g. job choice, modes of transportation) not on the basis of their apparent attributes but on a common set of attributes reflecting quality of life (e.g. security, fun, freedom). Beach et al (23) described an extensive interviewing technique, involving several interactions with different decision makers, to arrive at a list of attributes.

It seems obvious that the omission of an important attribute can seriously alter the results of a MAUT application. However, Aschenbrenner & Kasubek (12) found reasonably similar results for preferences among apartments from MAU analyses based on two different, only partially overlapping sets of attributes.

Weights and utilities can be assessed either directly or indirectly. Direct approaches, which are simple but not theoretically justified, include ranking or rating scales, or just asking the assessor for the relevant numbers. For utilities, the assessor may be presented with graph paper and asked to sketch a curve. Utility functions may also be derived by constructing indifference curves for pairs of variables (189, 190); these methods are lengthy, tedious, and clearly impractical when there are many variables. After two indifference curves for the same pair of variables are assessed, a "staircase" method can be used by the analyst to uncover the utility curves for each of the variables, assuming that the variables are value independent (see 156, p. 57–61).

Indirect methods are justified within the theory, but are exceedingly complex. They rely on a comparison between a gamble and a sure thing, and thus introduce probabilities into an otherwise riskless situation. For example, to assess the weight of one attribute from a set of 14 attributes describing apartments (such as number of bedrooms, general cleanliness, etc), the analyst says, "Apartment A has the best (most preferred) level of all 14 attributes. Apartment B has the worst level of all 14 attributes. Apartment C has the best level on one attribute and the worst level on each of the other 13. State a probability p such that you are indifferent between receiving C for sure versus receiving a gamble wherein you will obtain A with probability p and B with probability $(1-p)$. What is the value of p that makes you indifferent?" The value of p that you name is the weight; such a question must be asked for each attribute.

The two indirect methods for assessing utilities are similar to the indirect method for assessing weights, except that "Apartment C" now has an *intermediate* level for one alternative, and the worst level for all others. In the variable-probability method, as with assessing weights, the task is to name a probability that makes the sure thing (Apartment C) indifferent to the gamble. In the fixed-probability method, the probabilities associated with the gamble are held constant at (1/2, 1/2), and the assessor must name that intermediate value on one attribute of the sure thing which leads to indifference. In either case, one answer gives only one point on the utility curve, so that several responses are required to estimate its shape, for each attribute.

Kneppreth et al (156) have written an excellent review of the methods for assessing utilities, explaining each method in detail, noting advantages and disadvantages, and referencing relevant research. That research has been unsystematic and allows no clear conclusions. Perhaps future researchers should model their work on a study by Vertinsky & Wong (289). Comparing an indifference curve method with the indirect fixed-probability method, they looked at test-retest reliability and a host of other indices, including the acceptance of particular rationality axioms, realism of the task, confidence in the method, bias in the interpretation of probability, and a measure of the width of an indifference band across the variables. They found that the indirect method was more reliable and easier for the subjects, while the indifference curve technique predicted more subsequent choices.

ISSUES   In MAUT, two issues are paramount. The first is: Is it valid? Early research in the use of MAUT frequently involved correlating the results of the model with unaided wholistic judgments of the same situations made by the same subjects (e.g. 130, 132, 294, and earlier papers referenced in the reviews mentioned above). A high correlation between the model and the wholistic judgments, the usual result, was taken as evidence that the model was valid. This conclusion seems faulty to us. If unaided wholistic preferences are good enough to constitute criteria for a decision aid like MAUT, who needs the decision aid? Furthermore, a decade or more of research has abundantly documented that humans are quite bad at making complex unaided decisions (248); it could thus be argued that high correlations with such flawed judgments would suggest a *lack* of validity. More sophisticated approaches have been taken by Fischer (87), who showed greater agreement among three different decomposition procedures than among three different wholistic procedures, and by Newman (208), who proposed applying Cronbach's (64) theory of generalizability to the problem of validating MAUT techniques.

But most practitioners and theorists approach the validity question as follows: the theory specifies the models, the assessment procedures, and the tests for choosing which model applies. Thus if you accept the axioms (yes, I do want my choices to be transitive; I should not be swayed by irrelevant alternatives, etc) and pass the tests, then you can be assured that you are doing the right thing. There is no remaining validity question.

The second issue concerns error. Indirect elicitation techniques for both weights and utilities are, as previously noted, quite complex, but theoretically justifiable. The direct methods, in contrast, seem easier, but are theoretically unjustified. If one assumes that the decision maker has underlying weights, utilities, and preferences, which approach, direct or indirect, elicits these underlying values with least error? Von Winterfeldt (293) discussed but did not resolve this issue. Practitioners can (and often do) perform sensitivity analyses (how much can I change this parameter before the decision changes?). Such sensitivity analyses will identify potential problems of measurement but not solve them.

The tests which are used to determine which MAUT model is applicable are equally complex. The test for additivity uses the weights derived from the indirect method. If the weights across all the attributes sum to 1.0, an additive model may be used. Otherwise, a multiplicative model is used. No error theory is available to tell you whether a sum of, say, 1.4 is "close enough" to 1.0 to justify an additive model. An alternative, and seemingly easier, test is available for additivity (see 296, p. 70). Unfortunately, no alternatives are available for two other necessary tests. These tests are for two kinds of utility independence [called "preferential independence" and "utility independence" by Keeney (142), and "WCUI" and "SCUI" by others (see 296)]. The following question, with reference to the location of the Mexico City airport (142), is just the starting point for these tests: "How many people seriously injured or killed per year, call that number x, makes you indifferent between the option: [x injured or killed and 2500 persons subjected to high noise levels] and the option: [one person injured or killed and 1,500,000 subjected to high noise level]?" Several such questions must be asked for each attribute and for all pairs of attributes. The frequent avoidance of these tests may not reflect laziness, but a genuine suspicion that using an unjustified model may lead to fewer errors than choosing a model on the basis of confused responses to complex questions such as these. As von Winterfeldt (293) has noted, "even after you go through the process of model elimination and selection, you will still have to make up your mind about the possible trade-offs between assessment error and modeling error" (p. 65).

The flavor of the indirect assessment methods and the three tests mentioned above may be appreciated by reading 54 pages of dialogue between an analyst (Keeney) and an expert as they evaluate alternatives for the production of electrical energy (144).

RECENT RESEARCH The "new look" in MAUT research is to explore its uses. Can it be done? What problems are encountered? What can be learned from applying MAUT? Gardiner & Edwards (102) showed that in a highly controversial issue (coastal land development) two groups of experts (developers and conservationists) showed notably less disagreement about the evaluation of proposed apartment buildings in their MAUT evaluations than in their wholistic evaluations. O'Connor (211) reported the difficulties in getting many experts to agree on evaluations of water quality while trying to (a) minimize the amount of experts' time needed for the evaluation, (b) eliminate redundant or strongly interrelated attributes, and (c) cope with possible noncompensatory factors (if the water is loaded with arsenic, nothing else matters). Guttentag & Sayeki (110) used a MAUT technique to illuminate the cultural differences in values and beliefs about peace issues between Japanese and Americans. In one of two reports of real applications (i.e. working with clients who paid for the advice), Keeney observed the changes in a MAUT system after 2 years of use (145). In the second report, he described the complexities of deciding where and when to build a new airport in Mexico City (142). Additional proposals for applications of MAUT, without relevant data, have been made for the development of social indicators (258), military system effectiveness (287), and solid waste management (150). Finally, computer programs to aid elicitation of MAUT have been written (146).

Decision Analysis

The most general approach for systematically evaluating alternative actions is decision analysis, an approach developed largely at the Harvard Business School (221, 235) and two private contract research firms, the Stanford Research Institute (125), and Decisions and Designs, Inc. (49). In facing a new problem, the analyst lists the decision alternatives, constructs a model of their interrelations, assesses the probabilities of relevant contingencies, finds out what the decision maker wants, and finally, assays the expected value or utility of each alternative. To do this, decision analysts use a bag of tricks drawn from crafts such as operations research, Bayesian statistics, SEU and MAUT, which allow the analyst to "in principle, address any decision problem with unimpeachable rigor" (49, p. 64). A common tool is the decision tree which diagrams the uncertain consequences arising from a decision.

Among the problems that have been given full-dress decision analyses are whether to seed hurricanes in hopes of reducing their intensity (126), how to establish planetary quarantine requirements for trips to Mars and Jupiter (127), what value nuclear power generating plants have for Mexico (265), and how to design export controls on computer sales to the Soviet Bloc (71). Many environmental impact statements, cost-benefit analyses, and risk assessments constitute variants on decision analytic-methodology (55, 91, 198, 216).

Although many of these analyses are already highly sophisticated, the basic methodology is still developing—often in response to specific problems. Work in the last 5 years has increased our ability to evaluate decision trees efficiently (288), assess the value of decision flexibility (194), and understand how models approximate the processes they are intended to describe (276).

Some awareness of psychological issues can be found in decision analysis. One example attempts to use the best psychological scaling techniques for eliciting probability judgments (260). Another emphasizes communicating effectively with decision makers; the analyst is encouraged to develop a role "not too dissimilar to that of a psychoanalyst" (49, p. 9). Brown (48) raised a cognitive problem that warrants further examination. He noted that decision analyses often fail to model responses to future events. As a result, when those future events actually occur, they are responded to in totally unanticipated ways, because in the flesh they look different than they did at the time of the analysis.

Man/Machine Systems

For years, one of the most promising areas in decision aiding has been the development of computerized aids for helping decision makers cope with complex problems. Systems designed to elicit MAUT appraisals fall into this category, as do the approaches described below.

REGRESSION APPROACHES   Research within the regression paradigm has shown that people have difficulty both applying the judgmental policies they wish to implement and describing the policies they actually are implementing. Hammond and colleagues have developed computer-graphics systems to combat both of these problems (113a, 117). Since these techniques can describe the policies of several participants in a given situation, they have been used to resolve interpersonal and intergroup conflicts (39) and to facilitate policy formation at the societal level (2, 116).

Another major decision-aiding technique is bootstrapping, which replaces judges with algebraic models of their own weighting policies. Recent research has continued to demonstrate that these models perform as well as or better than the judges themselves (14, 68, 119, 202, 237, 307). Additional work promises to further enhance the usefulness of bootstrapping. Einhorn (81, 82) showed how expert judgment and statistical techniques can incorporate poorly defined and hard to measure variables into judges' models. Dawes & Corrigan (70) demonstrated that in most situations the criterion being judged could be predicted well by models with unit weights (see also 83, 297). These unit-weighting results suggest that in many decision settings, all the judge needs to know is what variables to throw into the equation, which direction (+ or −) to weight them, and how to add. Actually, Benjamin Franklin had this insight about unit weighted linear models back in 1772 (186, p. 27).

PIP   One of the earliest proposals for sharing the decision-making load between the machine and the decision maker was (79) the Probabilistic Information Processing System (PIP). In situations where judges must revise their probabilities upon receipt of new information, the PIP system accepts the judges' subjective assessments of prior probabilities, and of the probability of each datum conditional on each hypothesis, and then aggregates them according to Bayes' theorem in order to produce posterior probabilities of the hypotheses. A review in 1971 (254) revealed an abundance of research on PIP; since then, however, the flood has receded. A few recent studies have discussed what to do when the data are not conditionally independent of one another and have examined how well subjects handle such data (74, 129, 266). A couple of interesting medical applications have been proposed (21a, 108, 109).

DYNAMIC SYSTEMS   Some of the most ambitious interactive man/machine systems have been developed to handle dynamic decision-making situations. The problems studied by researchers in this area are extremely varied and the systems developed to solve them tend to be highly specific. However a pattern of conceptualizing the task, developing the mathematics and software to handle it, and then validating the system in one or a series of experiments is common. As an example, a team at Perceptronics, Inc. has developed a highly sophisticated system to assist naval officers tracking "the elements of a simulated fishing fleet [one trawler and one iceberg] as it moves about in an expanse of ocean," a task that vaguely resembles a futuristic version of Battleships (67, sect. 3, p. 1). The system tracks the decision maker's responses continuously and uses utilities inferred from them to recommend maximum expected utility decisions (98). From an experiment testing the system with 12 Naval Reserve NCOs during four 90-minute sessions, Davis et al (67) concluded that it worked in realistic decision-making situations, was accepted by experienced operators, and markedly improved performance.

Such systems may be designed either as products that will actually work in some field situation or as research tools. Perhaps because of their expense, most products have been designed to solve specific military problems with no civilian analog [although readers concerned about the possible presence of Soviet frogpersons in their bathtub or swimming pool might want to consult Irving (133)]. It is difficult for the nonexpert to judge the validity of these systems and the acceptability of their advice.

With systems designed for research purposes, a critical issue is the tradeoff between realism and generality. One strategy is to design systems whose complexity begins to approach that found in the real world—at the risk of investing too much of available resources in the machine and too little in understanding how people use it. Some human factors questions worth studying are (a) how do variations in the basic system (e.g. different instructions or information displays) affect people's performance? (b) how do person and machine errors interact? (c) how should machine output be adjusted to different decision makers' cognitive styles and work paces (170, 171)? and (d) when do people heed the machine's advice (111, 112)?

Another problem with these systems is that their very complexity makes it difficult to compare results from one research context to the next. Perhaps the only way to do that is to interpret the results in terms of basic psychological (judgmental) phenomena. If that tack is taken, then one might ask whether the development of general behavioral principles would not be served best by using a number of simpler, cheaper, and more flexible systems, such as the tactical and negotiations game used by the Streuferts and colleagues (e.g. 269). Research showing why man/machine systems should be adopted might provide a more convincing case than the demonstration in a complex simulation that decision makers do better with the machine's help. The skeptic may argue that such demonstrations merely show that one can design a simulated task in which it helps to have machine assistance.

Using Decision Aids

Do decision makers use these sophisticated techniques? Bootstrapping is now being applied for a variety of repeated decisions. On the other hand, apparently few, if any,

PIP systems are operational today despite the mass of research refining its methodology. For most aids, a clear picture is hard to come by. In the scientific literature one can find demonstration projects showing a procedure's viability. However, when a technique passes the test of getting someone to pay for it, the result typically becomes proprietary. For reasons of national or industrial security, the details of such projects are not divulged, nor are the decision makers' responses to them. Most overviews by those in the decision aiding business understandably tend to be quite optimistic.

Brown (47, 49), however, has presented an insightful discussion of factors that may limit decision makers' receptiveness to decision analysis and presumably to other techniques as well. One is the fact that decision makers often employ an analyst to reduce the uncertainty in a problem situation, not to acknowledge and quantify it. Another source of resistance is the absence of top-level decision makers familiar with the technique; a third is the bad experiences of decision makers who try to solo on the technique without proper training. Brown, Kahr & Peterson (49) suggested that decision analysis is a clinical skill that should only be practiced after internship with an expert.

Another problem is that decision makers may, even after careful coaching, reject the basic conception (e.g. the axioms) on which the aids are based. Protocols of conversations between analysts and decision makers leave the impression that decision makers are under considerable pressure to adopt the analyst's perspective. It is debatable whether satisfaction with the results of such an analysis show that the analyst has really answered the decision maker's needs. Conrath (58) and Reeser (227) found that decision makers reject decision analysis (and related techniques) for being both overly complicated and divorced from reality. Individuals who may accept the assumptions of such analysis may still reject their logical implications if they are unintuitive or too difficult to explain and justify to others.

A problem discussed earlier is whether decision makers can provide the required probability, utility, and modeling judgments. Because of the vagaries of such judgments, the decision aider runs the risk of grinding through highly sophisticated analyses on inputs of very little value. Certainly "garbage in—garbage out" applies to decision aiding—with the particular danger that undue respect may be given to garbage produced by high-powered and expensive grinding. Relatively little is known about the sensitivity of decision aids to errors in elicitation and problem structuring. Von Winterfeldt & Edwards (294a) have proved that under very general conditions probability and utility estimates can be somewhat inaccurate without leading to appreciably suboptimal decisions. Their proof is applicable to the case where decision options are continuous (e.g. invest X dollars). However, Lichtenstein, Fischhoff & Phillips (175) have shown how a moderate error in probability estimation can lead to a substantial decrease in expected utility when the decision options are discrete (e.g. operate vs don't operate). Von Winterfeldt & Edwards (295) have identified a large class of errors which can lead to large expected losses and are extremely difficult to detect. They arise from the selection of dominated decision alternatives as the result of inappropriately modeling the decision problem.

How much is a decision aid worth? This difficult question is typically answered with arguments why aids should, in principle, be worth the resources invested in them. Recently Watson & Brown (303) provided enlightenment with a formal model for performing a decision analysis of a decision analysis. The model is accompanied by three case studies (304) that highlight the difficulties of performing a hindsightful analysis. Ironically, the greatest value of two of these analyses came from their contribution to organizational processes (reduction of controversy and improvement of communication), considerations that were left out of the formal model for the sake of simplicity.

CONCLUSION

One reason for the vitality of the research described here is the increased importance of deliberative decision making in our daily lives. In a nontraditional society individuals must rely on their analytical resources rather than habit in guiding their affairs. A rapidly changing and interrelated world cannot allow itself the luxury of trial and error as it attempts to cope with problems like nuclear power and natural hazard management. Economists, engineers, operations researchers, decision analysts and others are developing sophisticated procedures for these problems. It is our job as psychologists to remind them of the human component in implementing these techniques and explaining their conclusions to the public—in particular to point out the errors that may arise from judgmental biases. We must help the public to make its private decisions and to develop a critical perspective on those decisions made in its behalf.

Literature Cited[1]

1. Abelson, R. P. 1976. Script processing in attitude formation and decision making. In *Cognition and Social Behavior*, ed. J. S. Carroll, J. W. Payne. Hillsdale, NJ: Erlbaum. In press
2. Adelman, L., Stewart, T. R., Hammond, K. R. 1975. A case history of the application of social judgment theory to policy formulation. *Policy Sci.* 6:137–59
3. Alker, H. A., Hermann, M. G. 1971. Are Bayesian decisions artificially intelligent? The effect of task and personality on conservatism in processing information. *J. Pers. Soc. Psychol.* 19:31–41
4. Allais, P. M. 1953. The behavior of rational man in risk situations—A critique of the axioms and postulates of the American School. *Econometrika* 21:503–46
5. Anderson, N. H. 1972. Looking for configurality in clinical judgment. *Psychol. Bull.* 78:93–102
6. Anderson, N. H. 1974. Algebraic models in perception. In *Handbook of Per-*

ception, ed. E. C. Carterette, M. P. Friedman, pp. 215–98. New York: Academic. 556 pp.
7. Anderson, N. H. 1974. Information integration theory: A brief survey. In *Measurement, Psychophysics, and Neural Information Processing*, ed. D. H. Krantz, R. C. Atkinson, R. D. Luce, P. Suppes, 2:236–305. San Francisco: Freeman. 468 pp.
8. Armelius, B., Armelius, K. 1974. Utilization of redundancy in multiple-cue judgments: Data from a suppressor variable task. *Am. J. Psychol.* 87:385–92
9. Armelius, K., Armelius, B. 1976. The effect of cue-criterion correlations, cue intercorrelations and the sign of the cue intercorrelation on performance in suppressor variable tasks. *OBHP.* In press
10. Armstrong, G. M., Kendall, C. L., Russ, F. A. 1975. Applications of consumer information processing research to public policy issues. *Commun. Res.* 2:232–45

[1]To conserve space, frequently cited sources have been abbreviated as follows: JEP (*Journal of Experimental Psychology*); OBHP (*Organizational Behavior and Human Performance*).

11. Armstrong, J. S., Denniston, W. B. Jr., Gordon, M. M. 1975. The use of the decomposition principle in making judgments. *OBHP* 14:257–63

12. Aschenbrenner, K. M., Kasubek, W. 1976. Convergence of multiattribute evaluations when different sets of attributes are used. In *Proceedings of the Fifth Research Conference on Subjective Probability, Utility, and Decision Making*, ed. H. Jungermann, G. de Zeeuw. In press

13. Ashton, R. H. 1974. Cue utilization and expert judgments: A comparison of independent auditors with other judges. *J. Appl. Psychol.* 59:437–44

14. Ashton, R. H. 1975. User prediction models in accounting: An alternative use. *Account. Rev.* 50:710–22

15. Barclay, S., Beach, L. R., Braithwaite, W. P. 1971. Normative models in the study of cognition. *OBHP* 6:389–413

16. Bar-Hillel, M. 1973. On the subjective probability of compound events. *OBHP* 9:396–406

17. Bar-Hillel, M. 1974. Similarity and probability. *OBHP* 11:277–82

18. Barron, F. H. 1974. Behavioral decision theory: A topical bibliography for management scientists. *Interfaces* 5:56–62

19. Barron, F. H., Mackenzie, K. D. 1973. A constrained optimization model of risky decisions. *J. Math. Psychol.* 10: 60–72

20. Bauer, M. 1971. Accuracy and congruence in estimations of probabilities and odds from binomial distributions. *Umeå Psychol. Rep. 36.* Umeå, Sweden: Univ. Umeå

21. Bauer, M. 1973. Inference strategies in Bayesian tasks not requiring high scale-level responses. *Umeå Psychol. Rep. 61.* Umeå, Sweden: Univ. Umeå

21a. Beach, B. H. 1975. Expert judgment about uncertainty: Bayesian decision making in realistic settings. *OBHP* 14:10–59

22. Beach, L. R. 1974. A note on the intrasubject similarity of subjective probabilities obtained by estimates and by bets. *OBHP* 11:250–52

23. Beach, L. R., Townes, B. D., Campbell, F. L., Keating, G. W. 1976. Developing and testing a decision aid for birth planning decisions. *OBHP* 15:99–116

24. Becker, G. M., McClintock, C. G. 1967. Value: Behavioral decision theory. *Ann. Rev. Psychol.* 18:239–86

25. Berkson, J., Magath, T. B., Hurn, M. 1940. The error of estimate of the blood cell count as made with the hemocytometer. *Am. J. Physiol.* 128:309–23

26. Berl, J., Lewis, G., Morrison, R. S. 1976. Alternative models of choice in important and nonrepetitive situations. See Ref. 1

27. Bettman, J. R. 1971. A graph theory approach to comparing consumer information processing models. *Manage. Sci.* 18:114–28

28. Bettman, J. R. 1974. Toward a statistics for consumer decision net models. *J. Consum. Res.* 1:71–80

29. Bettman, J. R. 1975. Issues in designing consumer information environments. *J. Consum. Res.* 2:169–77

30. Bettman, J. R., Capon, N., Lutz, R. 1975. Multiattribute measurement models and multiattribute attitude theory: A test of construct validity. *J. Consum. Res.* 1:1–15

31. Bettman, J. R., Jacoby, J. 1975. Patterns of processing in consumer information acquisition. *Papers in Consumer Psychol. No. 150.* West Lafayette, Ind: Purdue Univ.

32. Birnbaum, M. H. 1976. Intuitive numerical prediction. *Am. J. Psychol.* In press

33. Björkman, M. 1973. Inference behavior in nonmetric ecologies. In *Human Judgment and Social Interaction*, ed. L. Rappoport, D. A. Summers, pp. 144–68. New York: Holt, Rinehart & Winston. 403 pp.

34. Bond, N. A. Jr. 1974. Basic strategy and expectation in casino blackjack. *OBHP* 12:413–28

35. Braithwaite, A. 1974. A note comparing three measures of subjective probability, their validity and reliability. *Acta Psychol.* 38:337–42

36. Brehmer, B. 1971. Subjects' ability to use functional rules. *Psychon. Sci.* 24:259–60

37. Brehmer, B. 1973. Note on clinical judgment and the formal characteristics of clinical tasks. *Umeå Psychol. Rep. 77.* Umeå, Sweden: Univ. Umeå

38. Brehmer, B. 1974. Hypotheses about relations between scaled variables in the learning of probabilistic inference tasks. *OBHP* 11:1–27

39. Brehmer, B. 1976. Social judgment theory and the analysis of interpersonal conflict. *Psychol. Bull.* In press

40. Brehmer, B., Kuylenstierna, J., Liljergren, J. 1974. Effects of function form and cue validity on subjects' hypotheses in probabilistic inference tasks. *OBHP* 11:338–54

41. Brehmer, B., Kuylenstierna, J., Lil-jergren, J. 1975. Effects of information about the probabilistic nature of the task on learning of uncertain inference tasks. *Umeå Psychol. Rep. 90.* Umeå, Sweden: Univ. Umeå
42. Brehmer, B., Quarnstrom, G. 1976. Information integration and subjective weights in multiple-cue judgments. *OBHP.* In press
43. Brewer, J. K., Owen, P. W. 1973. A note on the power of statistical tests in the *Journal of Educational Measurement. J. Educ. Meas.* 10:71–4
44. Brickman, P. 1972. Optional stopping on ascending and descending series. *OBHP* 7:53–62
45. Brickman, P., Pierce, S. M. 1972. Estimates of conditional probabilities of confirming versus disconfirming events as a function of inference situation and prior evidence. *JEP* 95:235–37
46. Brooks, W. N., Doob, A. N. 1975. Justice and the jury. *J. Soc. Issues* 31:171–82
47. Brown, R. V. 1971. Marketing applications of personalist decision analysis. *MSI Field Res. Proj. Rep. P-55.* Cambridge: Manage. Sci. Inst.
48. Brown, R. V. 1975. Modeling subsequent acts for decision analysis. *DDI Tech. Rep. 75-1.* McLean, Va: Decisions & Designs
49. Brown, R. V., Kahr, A. S., Peterson, C. 1974. *Decision Analysis for the Manager.* New York: Holt, Rinehart & Winston. 618 pp.
50. Brown, T. A., Shuford, E. H. 1973. Quantifying uncertainty into numerical probabilities for the reporting of intelligence. *RAND Rep. 1185-ARPA.* Santa Monica: Rand Corp.
51. Buckhout, R. 1974. Eyewitness testimony. *Sci. Am.* 231:23–31
52. Castellan, N. J. Jr. 1972. The analysis of multiple criteria in multiple-cue judgment tasks. *OBHP* 8:242–61
53. Castellan, N. J. Jr. 1973. Comments on the "lens model" equation and the analysis of multiple-cue judgment tasks. *Psychometrika* 38:87–100
54. Castellan, N. J. Jr. 1976. Decision making with multiple probabilistic cues. In *Cognitive Theory,* ed. N. J. Castellan Jr., D. B. Pisoni, G. R. Potts, Vol. 2. Hillsdale, NJ: Erlbaum. In press
55. Coates, J. F. 1976. The role of formal models in technology assessment. *Tech. Forecasting Soc. Change.* In press
56. Cohen, J. 1962. The statistical power of abnormal-social psychological research. *J. Abnorm. Soc. Psychol.* 65:145–53
57. Cohen, J., Chesnick, E. I., Haran, D. 1972. A confirmation of the inertial-ψ effect in sequential choice and decision. *Br. J. Psychol.* 63:41–6
58. Conrath, D. W. 1973. From statistical decision theory to practice: Some problems with the transition. *Manage. Sci.* 19:873–83
59. Cook, R. L. 1974. An interactive and iterative approach to computer-aided policy capturing. *Prog. Res. Hum. Judgment Soc. Interaction Rep. 64.* Boulder: Inst. Behav. Sci., Univ. Colorado
60. Coombs, C. H. 1975. Portfolio theory and the measurement of risk. In *Human Judgment and Decision Processes,* ed. M. F. Kaplan, S. Schwartz. pp. 64–83. New York: Academic. 325 pp.
61. Coombs, C. H., Huang, L. C. 1974. Tests of the betweenness property of expected utility. *MMPP Rep. 74-13.* Ann Arbor: Univ. Michigan
62. Corbin, R. M., Marley, A. A. 1974. Random utility models with equality: An apparent but not actual generalization of random utility models. *J. Math. Psychol.* 11:274–93
63. Corbin, R. M., Olson, C. L., Abbondanza, M. 1975. Context effects in optional stopping decisions. *OBHP* 14:207–16
64. Cronbach, L. J., Gleser, G., Nanda, H., Rajaratnam, N. 1972. *The Dependability of Behavioral Measurements: Theory of Generalizability for Scores and Profiles.* New York: Wiley
65. Dalkey, N. C., Lewis, R., Snyder, D. 1970. Measurement and analysis of the quality of life: With exploratory illustrations of applications to career and transportation choices. *RAND RM-6228-DOT.* Santa Monica: Rand Corp.
66. Davenport, W. G., Middleton, M. A. 1973. Expectation theories of decision making for duplex gambles. *Acta Psychol.* 37:155–72
67. Davis, K. B., Weisbrod, R. L., Freedy, A., Weltman, G. 1975. Adaptive computer aiding in dynamic decision processes: An experimental study of aiding effectiveness. *Tech. Rep. PTR-1016-75-5.* Woodland Hills, Calif: Perceptronics
68. Dawes, R. M. 1971. A case study of graduate admissions: Applications of three principles of human decision making. *Am. Psychol.* 26:180–88
69. Dawes, R. M. 1976. Shallow psychology. See Ref. 1

70. Dawes, R. M., Corrigan, B. 1974. Linear models in decision making. *Psychol. Bull.* 81:95–106
71. Decisions & Designs, Inc. 1973. Computer sale to the Soviet bloc. *Tech. Rep. 73-4*
72. Dershowitz, A. M. 1968. Psychiatry in the legal process: "Knife that cuts both ways." *Judicature* 51:370–77
73. Dillon, J. L. 1971. An expository review of Bernoullian decision theory. *Rev. Mark. Agric. Econ.* 39:3–80
73a. Domas, P. A., Goodman, B. C., Peterson, C. R. 1972. Bayes's theorem: Response scales and feedback. *Eng. Psychol. Lab. Tech. Rep. 037230-5-T.* Ann Arbor: Univ. Michigan
74. Domas, P. A., Peterson, C. R. 1972. Probabilistic information processing systems: Evaluation with conditionally dependent data. *OBHP* 7:77–85
75. Donnell, M. L., DuCharme, W. M. 1975. The effect of Bayesian feedback on learning in an odds estimation task. *OBHP* 14:305–13
76. DuCharme, W. M., Donnell, M. L. 1973. Intrasubject comparison of four response modes for "subjective probability" assessment. *OBHP* 10:108–17
77. Ebert, R. J. 1972. Human control of a two-variable decision system. *OBHP* 7:237–64
78. Edwards, W. 1961. Behavioral decision theory. *Ann. Rev. Psychol.* 12:473–98
79. Edwards, W. 1962. Dynamic decision theory and probabilistic information processing. *Hum. Factors* 4:59–73
79a. Edwards, W. 1972. Application of research on cognition to man-machine system design. *Eng. Psychol. Lab. Rep. 010342-1-F.* Ann Arbor: Univ. Michigan
80. Edwards, W. 1975. Comment. *J. Am. Stat. Assoc.* 70:291–93
81. Einhorn, H. J. 1972. Expert measurement and mechanical combination. *OBHP* 7:86–106
82. Einhorn, H. J. 1974. Cue definition and residual judgment. *OBHP* 12:30–49
83. Einhorn, H. J., Hogarth, R. M. 1975. Unit weighting schemes for decision making. *OBHP* 13:171–92
84. Einhorn, H. J., Koelb, C. 1976. Psychometric study of literary critical judgment. *Grad. Sch. Bus. Work. Pap.* Univ. Chicago Press
85. Ellsberg, D. 1961. Risk, ambiguity, and the Savage axioms. *Q. J. Econ.* 75: 643–49
86. Fischer, G. W. 1975. Experimental applications of multi-attribute utility models. In *Utility, Probability, and Human Decision Making,* ed. D. Wendt, C. A. J. Vlek, pp. 7–46. Dordrecht, The Netherlands: Reidel. 418 pp.
87. Fischer, G. W. 1972. Four methods for assessing multi-attribute utilities: An experimental validation. *Eng. Psychol. Lab. Tech. Rep. 037230-6-T.* Ann Arbor: Univ. Michigan
88. Fischer, G. W. 1976. Multidimensional utility models for risky and riskless choice. *OBHP.* In press
89. Fischhoff, B. 1975. Hindsight ≠ foresight: The effect of outcome knowledge on judgment under uncertainty. *JEP: Hum. Percept. Performance* 1:288–99
90. Fischhoff, B. 1976. Attribution theory and judgment under uncertainty. In *New Directions in Attribution Research,* ed. J. H. Harvey, W. J. Ickes, R. F. Kidd, pp. 419–50. Hillsdale, NJ: Erlbaum.
91. Fischhoff, B. 1976. Cost-benefit analysis and the art of motorcycle maintenance. *ORI Res. Monogr. 16(1).* Eugene: Oregon Res. Inst.
92. Fischhoff, B. 1976. Perceived informativeness of factual information. *ORI Res. Bull. 16(3).* Eugene: Oregon Res. Inst.
93. Fischhoff, B., Beyth, R. 1975. "I knew it would happen"—remembered probabilities of once-future things. *OBHP* 13:1–16
94. Fishburn, P. C. 1970. *Utility Theory for Decision Making.* Publ. in Oper. Res. Ser. 18, ed. D. B. Hertz. New York: Wiley. 234 pp.
95. Fishburn, P. C. 1974. von Neumann-Morgenstern utility functions on two attributes. *Oper. Res.* 22:35–45
96. Fishburn, P. C., Keeney, R. L. 1974. Seven independence concepts and continuous multiattribute utility functions. *J. Math. Psychol.* 11:294–327
97. Fontaine, G. 1975. Causal attribution in simulated versus real situations: When are people logical, when are they not? *J. Pers. Soc. Psychol.* 32:1021–29
98. Freedy, A., Weisbrod, R., Davis, K., May, D., Weltman, G. 1974. Adaptive computer aiding in dynamic decision processes: Adaptive decision models and dynamic utility estimation, Part I. *Tech. Rep. PTR-1016-74-5(1).* Woodland Hills, Calif: Perceptronics
99. Fryback, D. G., Goodman, B. C., Edwards, W. 1973. Choices among bets by Las Vegas gamblers: Absolute and contextual effects. *JEP* 98:271–78

100. Funaro, J. F. 1975. An empirical analysis of five descriptive models for cascaded inference. *OBHP* 14:186–206
101. Furby, L. 1973. Interpreting regression toward the mean in developmental research. *Dev. Psychol.* 8:172–79
102. Gardiner, P. C., Edwards, W. 1975. Public values: Multiattribute-utility measurement for social decision making. See Ref. 60, pp. 1–37
103. Gettys, C. F., Kelly, C. W. III, Peterson, C. R. 1973. The best guess hypothesis in multistage inference. *OBHP* 10:364–73
104. Gettys, C. F., Michel, C., Steiger, J. H., Kelly, C. W. III, Peterson, C. R. 1973. Multiple-stage probabilistic information processing. *OBHP* 10:374–87
105. Goodman, B. C. 1973. Direct estimation procedures for eliciting judgments about uncertain events. *Eng. Psychol. Lab. Tech. Rep. 011313-5-T.* Ann Arbor: Univ. Michigan
106. Graesser, C. C., Anderson, N. H. 1974. Cognitive algebra of the equation: Gift size = generosity X income. *JEP* 103:692–99
107. Green, P. E., Wind, Y. 1975. New way to measure consumers' judgments. *Harvard Bus. Rev.* 53:107–17
108. Greist, J. H., Gustafson, D. H., Stauss, F. F., Rowse, G. L., Laughren, T. P., Chiles, J. A. 1973. A computer interview for suicide-risk prediction. *Am. J. Psychiatry* 130:1327–32
109. Gustafson, D. H., Kestly, J. J., Greist, J. H., Jensen, N. M. 1971. Initial evaluation of a subjective Bayesian diagnostic system. *Health Serv. Res.* 6:204–13
110. Guttentag, M., Sayeki, Y. 1975. A decision-theoretic technique for the illumination of cultural differences. *J. Cross-Cult. Psychol.* 6:203–17
111. Halpin, S. M., Johnson, E. M., Thornberry, J. A. 1973. Cognitive reliability in manned systems. *IEEE Trans. Reliab.* R-22:165–70
112. Halpin, S. M., Thornberry, J. A., Streufert, S. 1973. The credibility of computer estimates in a simple decision making task. *ONR Tech. Rep. 5.* West Lafayette, Ind: Purdue Univ.
113. Hammerton, M. 1973. A case of radical probability estimation. *JEP* 101:252–54
113a. Hammond, K. R. 1971. Computer graphics as an aid to learning. *Science* 172:903–8
114. Hammond, K. R. 1974. Human judgment and social policy. *Prog. Res. Hum. Judgment Soc. Interaction Rep. 170.*

Boulder: Inst. Behav. Sci., Univ. Colorado
115. Hammond, K. R., Joyce, C. R. B., eds. 1975. *Psychoactive Drugs and Social Judgment.* New York: Wiley. 278 pp.
116. Hammond, K. R., Stewart, T. R., Adelman, L., Wascoe, N. E. 1975. Report to the Denver city council and mayor regarding the choice of handgun ammunition for the Denver police department. *Prog. Res. Hum. Judgment Soc. Interaction Rep. 179.* Boulder: Inst. Behav. Sci., Univ. Colorado
117. Hammond, K. R., Stewart, T. R., Brehmer, B., Steinmann, D. O. 1975. Social judgment theory. See Ref. 60, pp. 271–312
118. Hammond, K. R., Summers, D. A. 1972. Cognitive control. *Psychol. Rev.* 79:58–67
119. Hamner, W. C., Carter, P. L. 1975. A comparison of alternative production management coefficient decision rules. *Dec. Sci.* 6:324–36
120. Hoffman, J., Peterson, C. R. 1972. A scoring rule to train probability assessors. *Eng. Psychol. Lab. Tech. Rep. 037230-4-T.* Ann Arbor: Univ. Michigan
121. Hogarth, R. M. 1974. Process tracing in clinical judgment. *Behav. Sci.* 19:298–313
121a. Hogarth, R. M. 1975. Cognitive processes and the assessment of subjective probability distributions. *J. Am. Stat. Assoc.* 70:271–94
122. Hogarth, R. M. 1975. Decision time as a function of task complexity. See Ref. 86, 321–38
123. Holzworth, R. J., Doherty, M. E. 1974. Inferences and predictions: normative vs. representative responding. *Bull. Psychon. Soc.* 3:300–2
124. Houle, A. 1973. *Bibliography: Bayesian Statistics.* Supplemented 1974–75. Ste-Foy, Quebec: Univ. Laval
125. Howard, R. A., Matheson, J. E., Miller, K. E. 1976. *Readings in Decision Analysis.* Menlo Park: Stanford Res. Inst.
126. Howard, R. A., Matheson, J. E., North, D. W. 1972. The decision to seed hurricanes. *Science* 176:1191–1202
127. Howard, R. A., North, D. W., Pezier, J. P. 1975. A new methodology to integrate planetary quarantine requirements into mission planning, with application to a Jupiter orbiter. *SRI Final Rep. NAS7-100.* Menlo Park: Stanford Res. Inst.
128. Howell, W. C. 1972. Compounding un-

certainty from internal sources. *JEP* 95:6-13

129. Howell, W. C., Gettys, C. F., Martin, D. W. 1971. On the allocation of inference functions in decision systems. *OBHP* 6:132-49

129a. Huber, G. P. 1974. Multi-attribute utility models: A review of field and field-like studies. *Manage. Sci.* 20:1393-1402

130. Huber, G. P., Daneshgar, R., Ford, D. L. 1971. An empirical comparison of five utility models for predicting job preferences. *OBHP* 6:267-82

131. Humphreys, P. 1976. Applications of multiattribute utility theory. See Ref. 12

132. Humphreys, P., Humphreys, A. 1975. An investigation of subjective preference orderings for multi-attributed alternatives. See Ref. 86, pp. 119-33

133. Irving, G. W. 1975. Alternative man/machine interface designs for swimmer defense systems. *Integrated Sci. Corp. TM-75-36.* Point Mugu, Calif: Pacific Missile Test Cent.

134. Jacoby, J. 1975. Perspectives on a consumer information processing research program. *Commun. Res.* 2:203-15

135. Jacoby, J. 1976. Consumer psychology: An octennium. *Ann. Rev. Psychol.* 27:331-58

136. Jensen, F. A., Peterson, C. R. 1973. Psychological effects of proper scoring rules. *OBHP* 9:307-17

137. Johnson, E. M., Cavanagh, R. C., Spooner, R. L., Samet, M. G. 1973. Utilization of reliability measurements in Bayesian inference: Models and human performance. *IEEE Trans. Reliab.* R22:176-83

138. Kahneman, D., Tversky, A. 1972. Subjective probability: A judgment of representativeness. *Cogn. Psychol.* 3:430-54

139. Kahneman, D., Tversky, A. 1973. On the psychology of prediction. *Psychol. Rev.* 80:237-51

140. Kahneman, D., Tversky, A. 1975. *Value Theory: An Analysis of Choices Under Risk.* Presented at Conf. on Public Economics, Jerusalem, Israel

141. Keeney, R. L. 1971. Utility independence and preferences for multiattributed consequences. *Oper. Res.* 19:875-93

142. Keeney, R. L. 1973. A decision analysis with multiple objectives: The Mexico City Airport. *Bell J. Econ. Manage. Sci.* 4:101-17

143. Keeney, R. L. 1974. Multiplicative utility functions. *Oper. Res.* 22:22-34

144. Keeney, R. L. 1975. Energy policy and value tradeoffs. *IIASA Res. Memo RM-75-76.* Schloss Laxenburg, Austria: Int. Inst. Appl. Syst. Anal.

145. Keeney, R. L. 1975. Examining corporate policy using multiattribute utility analysis. *Sloan Manage. Rev.* 17:63-76

146. Keeney, R. L., Sicherman, A. 1975. An interactive computer program for assessing and analyzing preferences concerning multiple objectives. *IIASA Res. Memo 75-12.* Schloss Laxenburg, Austria: Int. Inst. Appl. Syst. Anal.

147. Kelly, C. W. III, Peterson, C. R. 1971. Probability estimates and probabilistic procedures in current-intelligence analysis. *IBM Rep. 71-5047.* Gaithersburg, Md: Int. Bus. Mach.

148. Kelly, C. W. III, Peterson, C. R. 1975. Decision theory research. *DDI Tech. Rep. DT/TR 75-5.* McLean, Va: Decisions & Designs

149. Kidd, J. B. 1970. The utilization of subjective probabilities in production planning. *Acta Psychol.* 34:338-47

150. Klee, A. J. 1971. The role of decision models in the evaluation of competing environmental health alternatives. *Manage. Sci.* 18B:52-67

151. Kleiter, G. D. 1975. Dynamic decision behavior: Comments on Rapoport's paper. See Ref. 86, pp. 371-80

152. Kleiter, G. D. 1975. Estimating the planning horizon in a multistage decision task. *Psychol. Res.* 38:37-64

153. Kleiter, G. D., Gachowetz, H., Huber, D. 1976. *Bibliography: Decision Making.* Salzburg, Austria: Psychol. Inst., Univ. Salzburg

154. Kleiter, G. D., Wimmer, H. 1974. Information seeking in a multistage betting game. *Arch. Psychol.* 126:213-30

155. Knafl, K., Burkett, G. 1975. Professional socialization in a surgical specialty: Acquiring medical judgment. *Soc. Sci. Med.* 9:397-404

156. Kneppreth, N. P., Gustafson, D. H., Leifer, R. P., Johnson, E. M. 1974. Techniques for the assessment of worth. *Tech. Paper 254.* Arlington, Va: Army Res. Inst.

157. Kozielecki, J. 1975. *Psychologiczna Teoria Decyzji (Behavioral Decision Theory).* Warszawa, PWN 352 pp. (Table of contents in English and Russian)

158. Kozielecki, J. 1975. The internal representation of risky tasks. *Pol. Psychol. Bull.* 6:115-21

159. Krantz, D. H., Atkinson, R. C., Luce, R. D., Suppes, P., eds. 1974. *Contemporary Developments in Mathematical Psy-*

chology, Vol. 1. San Francisco: Freeman
160. Kunreuther, H. 1976. Limited knowledge and insurance protection. *Public Policy* 24:227–61
161. Kusyszyn, I. 1972. Psychology of gambling, risk-taking, and subjective probability: A bibliography. J. Suppl. Abstr. Serv., *Cat. Sel. Doc. Psychol.* 2:7
162. Kusyszyn, I. 1973. Gambling, risk-taking and personality: A bibliography. *Int. J. Addict.* 8:173–90
163. Langer, E. J. 1975. The illusion of control. *J. Pers. Soc. Psychol.* 32:311–28
164. Langer, E. J., Roth, J. 1975. Heads I win, tails it's chance: The illusion of control as a function of the sequence of outcomes in a purely chance task. *J. Pers. Soc. Psychol.* 32:951–55
165. Lee, W. 1971. *Decision Theory and Human Behavior.* New York: Wiley. 352 pp.
166. Leon, M., Anderson, N. H. 1974. A ratio rule from integration theory applied to inference judgments. *JEP* 102:27–36
167. Levin, I. P. 1974. Averaging processes and intuitive statistical judgments. *OBHP* 12:83–91
168. Levin, I. P. 1976. Information integration in numerical judgments and decision processes. *JEP:Gen.* 104:39–53
169. Levine, J. M., Samet, M. G. 1973. Information seeking with multiple sources of conflicting and unreliable information. *Hum. Factors* 15:407–19
170. Levine, J. M., Samet, M. G., Brahlek, R. E. 1975. Information seeking with limitations on available information and resources. *Hum. Factors* 17:502–13
171. Levit, R. A., Alden, D. G., Erickson, J. M., Heaton, B. J. 1974. Development and application of a decision aid for tactical control of battlefield operations. *ARI DAHC 19-73-C-0069,* Vol. 2. Minneapolis: Honeywell
172. Libby, R. 1975. The use of simulated decision makers in information evaluation. *Account. Rev.* 50:475–89
173. Lichtenstein, S. C., Earle, T., Slovic, P. 1975. Cue utilization in a numerical prediction task. *JEP:Hum. Percept. Performance* 104:77–85
174. Lichtenstein, S. C., Fischhoff, B. 1976. Do those who know more also know more about how much they know? *ORI Res. Bull. 16(1)* Eugene: Oregon Res. Inst.
175. Lichtenstein, S. C., Fischhoff, B., Phillips, L. 1976. Calibration of probabilities: The state of the art. See Ref. 12

176. Lichtenstein, S. C., Slovic, P. 1971. Reversals of preference between bids and choices in gambling decision. *JEP* 89:46–55
177. Lichtenstein, S. C., Slovic, P. 1973. Response-induced reversals of preference in gambling: An extended replication in Las Vegas. *JEP* 101:16–20
178. Lindell, M. K., Stewart, T. R. 1974. The effects of redundancy in multiple-cue probability learning. *Am. J. Psychol.* 87:393–98
179. Lindman, H. R. 1971. Inconsistent preferences among gambles. *JEP* 89:390–97
180. Loftus, E. 1974. The incredible eyewitness. *Psychol. Today* 8:116–19
181. Lopes, L. 1976. Model based decision and judgment in stud poker. *JEP:Gen.* In press
182. Louviere, J. J. 1974. Predicting the evaluation of real stimulus objects from abstract evaluation of their attributes: The case of trout streams. *J. Appl. Psychol.* 59:572–77
183. Luce, R. D. 1959. *Individual Choice Behavior.* New York: Wiley
184. Lyon, D., Slovic, P. 1976. Dominance of accuracy information and neglect of base rates in probability estimation. *Acta Psychol.* In press
185. MacCrimmon, K. R. 1968. Descriptive and normative implications of the decision theory postulates. In *Risk and Uncertainty,* ed. K. Borch, J. Mossin, pp. 3–32. New York: St. Martin's. 455 pp.
186. MacCrimmon, K. R. 1973. An overview of multiple objective decision making. In *Multiple Criteria Decision Making,* ed. J. L. Cochrane, M. Zeleny, pp. 18–44. Columbia, SC: Univ. South Carolina Press. 816 pp.
187. MacCrimmon, K. R. 1974. Managerial decision making. In *Contemporary Management: Issues and Viewpoints,* ed. J. W. McGuire, pp. 445–95. Englewood Cliffs, NJ: Prentice-Hall
188. MacCrimmon, K. R., Larsson, S. 1976. Utility theory: Axioms versus "paradoxes." In *Rational Decisions Under Uncertainty,* special volume of *Theory and Decision,* ed. M. Allais, O. Hagen. In press
189. MacCrimmon, K. R., Siu, J. K. 1974. Making trade-offs. *Decis. Sci.* 5:680–704
190. MacCrimmon, K. R., Wehrung, D. A. 1975. Trade-off analysis: Indifference and preferred proportion. *Fac. Commer. Bus. Admin. Work. Pap. 323.* Vancouver, BC: Univ. British Columbia

191. Marks, D. F., Clarkson, J. K. 1972. An explanation of conservatism in the bookbag-and-pokerchips situation. *Acta Psychol.* 36:145–60

192. Marks, D. F., Clarkson, J. K. 1973. Conservatism as non-Bayesian performance: A reply to DeSwart. *Acta Psychol.* 37:55–63

193. McCann, J. M., Miller, J. G., Moskowitz, H. 1975. Modeling and testing dynamic multivariate decision processes. *OBHP* 14:281–303

194. Merkhofer, M. W. 1975. Flexibility and decision analysis. *Decis. Anal. Program Res. Rep. EES-DA-75-1.* Stanford Univ. Press

195. Mertz, W. H., Doherty, M. E. 1974. The influence of task characteristics on strategies of cue combination. *OBHP* 12:196–216

196. Messick, D. M., Campos, F. T. 1972. Training and conservatism in subjective probability revision. *JEP* 94:335–37

197. Miller, P. M. 1971. Do labels mislead? A multiple cue study, within the framework of Brunswik's probabilistic functionalism. *OBHP* 6:480–500

198. Mishan, E. J. 1972. *Cost-Benefit Analysis.* New York: Praeger

198a. Monahan, J., Cummings, L. 1974. Prediction of dangerousness as a function of its perceived consequences. *J. Crim. Justice* 2:239–42

199. Montgomery, H. 1976. A study of intransitive preferences using a think aloud procedure. See Ref. 12

200. Moskowitz, H. 1974. Effects of problem representation and feedback on rational behavior in Allais and Morlat-type problems. *Decis. Sci.* 5:225–42

201. Moskowitz, H. 1974. Regression models of behavior for managerial decision making. *OMEGA, Int. J. Manage. Sci.* 2:677–90

202. Moskowitz, H., Miller, J. G. 1972. Information and decision systems for production planning: An inter-disciplinary perspective. *Inst. Res. Behav. Econ. Manage. Sci. paper 373.* West Lafayette, Ind: Purdue Univ.

203. Murphy, A. H. 1973. A new vector partition of the probability score. *J. Appl. Meteorol.* 12:595–600

204. Murphy, A. H. 1974. A sample skill score for probability forecasts. *Mon. Weather Rev.* 102:48–55

205. Murphy, A. H., Winkler, R. L. 1970. Scoring rules in probability assessment and evaluation. *Acta Psychol.* 34:273–86

206. Murphy, A. H., Winkler, R. L. 1971. Forecasters and probability forecasts: Some current problems. *Bull. Am. Meteorol. Soc.* 52:239–47

207. Murphy, A. H., Winkler, R. L. 1974. Probability forecasts: A survey of national weather service forecasters. *Bull. Am. Meteorol. Soc.* 55:1449–53

208. Newman, J. R. 1975. Assessing the reliability and validity of multi-attribute utility procedures: An application of the theory of generalizability. *SSRI Res. Rep. 75-7.* Los Angeles: Univ. South. Calif.

209. Nickerson, R. S., Feehrer, C. E. 1975. Decision making and training: A review of theoretical and empirical studies of decision making and their implications for the training of decision makers. *Tech. Rep. 73-C-0128-1.* Orlando, Fla: Nav. Train. Equip. Cent. 210 pp.

210. Nisbett, R. E., Borgida, E. 1975. Attribution and the psychology of prediction. *J. Pers. Soc. Psychol.* 32:932–43

210a. Norman, K. L., Louviere, J. J. 1974. Integration of attributes in bus transportation: Two modeling approaches. *J. Appl. Psychol.* 59:753–58

211. O'Connor, M. F. 1973. The application of multiattribute scaling procedures to the development indices of water quality. *Cent. Math. Stud. Bus. Econ. Rep. 7339.* Univ. Chicago Press

212. Ölander, F. 1975. Search behavior in non-simultaneous choice situations: Satisficing or maximizing. See Ref. 86, pp. 297–320

213. Payne, J. W. 1973. Alternative approaches to decision making under risk: Moments versus risk dimensions. *Psychol. Bull.* 80:439–53

214. Payne, J. W. 1976. Task complexity and contingent processing in decision making: An information search and protocol analysis. *OBHP.* In press

215. Payne, J. W., Braunstein, M. L. 1971. Preference among gambles with equal underlying distributions. *JEP* 87:13–18

216. Peskin, H. M., Seskin, E. P. 1973. *Cost Benefit Analysis and Water Pollution Policy.* Washington, DC: Urban Inst. 325 pp.

217. Peterson, C. R., ed. 1973. Special Issue: Cascaded inference. *OBHP* 10:315–432

218. Peterson, C. R., Beach, L. R. 1967. Man as an intuitive statistician. *Psychol. Bull.* 68:29–46

219. Pitz, G. F. 1974. Subjective probability distributions for imperfectly known quantities. In *Knowledge and Cognition,*

ed. L. W. Gregg, pp. 29–41. New York: Wiley. 321 pp.

220. Pollay, R. W. 1970. The structure of executive decisions and decision times. *Admin. Sci. Q.* 15:459–71

221. Raiffa, H. 1968. *Decision Analysis: Introductory Lectures on Choice Under Uncertainty.* Reading, Mass: Addison Wesley. 309 pp.

222. Ramanaiah, N. V., Goldberg, L. R. 1976. Stylistic components of human judgment: The generality of individual differences. *Appl. Psychol. Meas.* In press

223. Rapoport, A. 1966. A study of human control in a stochastic multistage decision task. *Behav. Sci.* 11:18–32

224. Rapoport, A. 1975. Research paradigms for studying dynamic decision behavior. See Ref. 86, pp. 349–69

225. Rapoport, A., Burkheimer, G. J. 1971. Models for deferred decision making. *J. Math. Psychol.* 8:508–38

225a. Rapoport, A., Tversky, A. 1970. Choice behavior in an optimal stopping task. *OBHP* 5:105–20

226. Rapoport, A., Wallsten, T. S. 1972. Individual decision behavior. *Ann. Rev. Psychol.* 23:131–75

227. Reeser, C. 1971. The use of sophisticated analytical methods for decision making in the aerospace industry. *MSU Bus. Top.* 19:63–69

228. Restle, F. 1961. *Psychology of Judgment and Choice.* New York: Wiley

229. Ronen, J. 1973. Effects of some probability displays on choices. *OBHP* 9:1–15

230. Russo, J. E., Krieser, G., Miyashita, S. 1975. An effective display of unit price information. *J. Mark.* 39:11–19

231. Russo, J. E., Rosen, L. D. 1975. An eye fixation analysis of multialternative choice. *Mem. Cogn.* 3:267–76

232. Savage, L. J. 1954. *The Foundations of Statistics.* New York: Wiley. 294 pp.

233. Sayeki, Y. 1972. Allocation of importance: An axiom system. *J. Math. Psychol.* 9:55–65

234. Sayeki, Y., Vesper, K. H. 1973. Allocation of importance in a hierarchical goal structure. *Manage. Sci.* 19:667–75

235. Schlaifer, R. 1969. *Analysis of Decisions Under Uncertainty.* New York: McGraw-Hill. 729 pp.

236. Schmitt, N., Dudycha, A. 1975. A reevaluation of the effect of cue redudancy in multiple-cue probability learning. *JEP* 104:307–15

237. Schmidt, F. L., Marshall, R. L. 1973. Construction and use of a paramorphic representation of departmental policies in graduate admissions decision making. J. Suppl. Abstr. Serv., *Cat. Sel. Doc. Psychol.* 3:92

238. Schum, D. A. 1975. Contrast effects in inference: On the conditioning of current evidence by prior evidence. *Res. Rep. Ser. 75-05.* Houston, Tex: Rice Univ.

239. Schum, D. A. 1975. On the behavioral richness of cascaded inference models: Examples in jurisprudence. *Res. Rep. Ser. 75-1.* Houston, Tex: Rice Univ.

240. Seghers, R. C., Fryback, D. G., Goodman, B. C. 1973. Relative variance preferences in a choice-among-bets paradigm. *Eng. Psychol. Lab. Tech. Rep. 011313-6-T.* Ann Arbor: Univ. Michigan

241. Selvidge, J. 1975. A three-step procedure for assigning probabilities to rare events. See Ref. 86, pp. 199–216

242. Shah, S. A. 1975. Dangerousness and civil commitment of the mentally ill: Some public policy consideration. *Am. J. Psychiatry* 132:501–5

243. Shanteau, J. 1972. Descriptive versus normative models of sequential inference judgment. *JEP* 93:63–68

244. Shanteau, J. 1975. An information-integration analysis of risky decision making. See Ref. 60, pp. 110–34

245. Sheridan, J. E., Richards, M. D., Slocum, J. W. 1975. Comparative analysis of expectancy and heuristic models of decision behavior. *J. Appl. Psychol.* 60:361–68

246. Shuford, E., Brown, T. A. 1975. Elicitation of personal probabilities and their assessment. *Instr. Sci.* 4:137–88

247. Shulman, L. S., Elstein, A. S. 1975. Studies of problem solving, judgment, and decision making: Implications for educational research. In *Review of Research in Education,* ed. F. N. Kerlinger, 3:3–42. Itasca, Ill: Peacock Publ. 305 pp.

248. Slovic, P. 1972. From Shakespeare to Simon: Speculations—and some evidence—about man's ability to process information. *ORI Res. Monogr. 12(2).* Eugene: Ore. Res. Inst.

249. Slovic, P. 1972. Psychological study of human judgment: Implications for investment decision making. *J. Finance* 27:779–99

250. Slovic, P. 1975. Choice between equally-valued alternatives. *JEP:Hum. Percept. Performance* 1:280–87

251. Slovic, P., Fischhoff, B., Lichtenstein, S. C. 1976. The certainty illusion. *ORI*

Res. Bull. 16(4). Eugene: Ore. Res. Inst.

252. Slovic, P., Fischhoff, B., Lichtenstein, S. C. 1976. Cognitive processes and societal risk taking. See Ref. 1

253. Slovic, P., Kunreuther, H., White, G. F. 1974. Decision processes, rationality and adjustment to natural hazards. In *Natural Hazards, Local, National and Global,* ed. G. F. White, pp. 187–205. New York: Oxford Univ. Press. 288 pp.

254. Slovic, P., Lichtenstein, S. C. 1971. Comparison of Bayesian and regression approaches to the study of information processing in judgment. *OBHP* 6:649–744

255. Slovic, P., MacPhillamy, D. J. 1974. Dimensional commensurability and cue utilization in comparative judgment. *OBHP* 11:172–94

256. Slovic, P., Tversky, A. 1974. Who accepts Savage's axiom? *Behav. Sci.* 19:368–73

257. Snapper, K. J., Fryback, D. G. 1971. Inferences based on unreliable reports. *JEP* 87:401–4

258. Snapper, K. J., O'Connor, M. F., Einhorn, H. J. 1974. Social indicators: A new method for indexing quality. *Soc. Res. Group Tech. Rep. 74-4.* Washington DC: George Washington Univ.

259. Snapper, K. J., Peterson, C. R. 1971. Information seeking and data diagnosticity. *JEP* 87:429–33

260. Spetzler, C. S., Staël von Holstein, C.-A. S. 1975. Probability encoding in decision analysis. *Manage. Sci.* 22:340–58

261. Stachowski, R. 1974. Effect of predecisional information integration strategy on cognitive conservatism. *Pol. Psychol. Bull.* 5:17–23

262. Staël von Holstein, C.-A. S. 1971. An experiment in probabilistic weather forecasting. *J. Appl. Meteorol.* 10:635–45

263. Staël von Holstein, C.-A. S. 1971. Two techniques for assessment of subjective probability distributions—an experimental study. *Acta Psychol.* 35:478–94

264. Staël von Holstein, C.-A. S. 1972. Probabilistic forecasting: An experiment related to the stock market. *OBHP* 8:139–58

265. Stanford Research Institute 1968. Decision analysis of nuclear plants in electrical system expansion. *SRI Proj. 6496 Final Rep.*

266. Steiger, J. H., Gettys, C. F. 1972. Best-guess errors in multistage inference. *JEP* 92:1–7

267. Stenson, H. H. 1974. The lens model with unknown cue structure. *Psychol. Rev.* 81:257–64

268. Stewart, T. R., Carter, J. E. 1973. POLICY: An interactive computer program for externalizing, executing, and refining judgmental policy. *Prog. Res. Hum. Judgment Soc. Interaction Rep. 159.* Boulder: Univ. Colorado Inst. Behav. Sci.

269. Streufert, S. C. 1973. Effects of information relevance on decision making in complex environments. *Mem. Cogn.* 1:224–28

270. Sue, S., Smith, R. E., Caldwell, C. 1973. Effects of inadmissible evidence on the decisions of simulated jurors: A moral dilemma. *J. Appl. Soc. Psychol.* 3:345–53

271. Svenson, O. 1973. Analysis of strategies in subjective probability inferences as evidenced in continuous verbal reports and numerical responses. *Psychol. Labs. Rep. 396.* Sweden: Univ. Stockholm

272. Svenson, O. 1974. A note on think aloud protocols obtained during the choice of a home. *Psychol. Labs. Rep. 421.* Sweden: Univ. Stockholm

273. Svenson, O. 1975. A unifying interpretation of different models for the integration of information when evaluating gambles. *Scand. J. Psychol.* 16:187–92

274. Svenson, O., Montgomery, H. 1976. On decision rules and information processing strategies for choices among multiattribute alternatives. *Scand. J. Psychol.* In press

275. Swinth, R. L., Gaumnitz, J. E., Rodriguez, C. 1975. Decision making processes: Using discrimination nets for security selection. *Decis. Sci.* 6:439–48

276. Tani, S. N. 1975. Modeling and decision analysis. *Decis. Anal. Prog. Res. Rep. EES-DA-75-3.* Stanford Univ.

277. Taylor, R. L., Wilsted, W. D. 1974. Capturing judgment policies: A field study of performance appraisal. *Acad. Manage. J.* 17:440–49

278. Teigen, K. H. 1974. Overestimation of subjective probabilities. *Scand. J. Psychol.* 15:56–62

279. Teigen, K. H. 1974. Subjective sampling distributions and the additivity of estimates. *Scand. J. Psychol.* 15:50–55

280. Tversky, A. 1972. Choice by elimination. *J. Math. Psychol.* 9:341–67

281. Tversky, A. 1972. Elimination by aspects: A theory of choice. *Psychol. Rev.* 79:281–99

282. Tversky, A. 1975. Assessing uncertainty. *J. R. Stat. Soc.* 36B:148–59

283. Tversky, A. 1975. *On the Elicitation of Preferences: Descriptive and Prescriptive Considerations.* Presented at Workshop on Decision Making with Multiple Conflicting Objectives, IIASA, Schloss Laxenburg, Austria

284. Tversky, A., Kahneman, D. 1971. The belief in the "law of small numbers." *Psychol. Bull.* 76:105–10

285. Tversky, A., Kahneman, D. 1973. Availability: A heuristic for judging frequency and probability. *Cogn. Psychol.* 5:207–32

286. Tversky, A., Kahneman, D. 1974. Judgment under uncertainty: Heuristics and biases. *Science* 185:1124–31

287. Turban, E., Metersky, M. L. 1971. Utility theory applied to multivariate system effectiveness evaluation. *Manage. Sci.* 17B:817–28

288. Ulvila, J. W. 1975. A pilot survey of computer programs for decision analysis. *DDI Tech. Rep. 75-2.* McLean, Va: Decisions & Designs

289. Vertinsky, I., Wong, E. 1975. Eliciting preferences and the construction of indifference maps: A comparative empirical evaluation of two measurement methodologies. *Socio-Econ. Plan. Sci.* 9:15–24

290. Vlek, C. A. J. 1973. Coherence of human judgment in a limited probabilistic environment. *OBHP* 9:460–81

291. Vlek, C. A. J. 1973. The fair betting game as an admissible procedure for assessment of subjective probabilities. *Br. J. Math. Stat. Psychol.* 26:18–30

292. Vlek, C. A. J., Wagenaar, W. A. 1975. *Judgment and Decision Under Uncertainty.* Leiden, The Netherlands: Univ. Leiden. 82 pp.

293. von Winterfeldt, D. 1975. An overview, integration, and evaluation of utility theory for decision analysis. *SSRI Res. Rep. 75-9.* Los Angeles: Univ. South. Calif.

294. von Winterfeldt, D., Edwards, W. 1973. Evaluation of complex stimuli using multi-attribute utility procedures. *Eng. Psychol. Lab. Tech. Rep. 011313-2-T.* Ann Arbor: Univ. Michigan

294a. von Winterfeldt, D., Edwards, W. 1973. Flat maxima in linear optimization models. *Eng. Psychol. Lab. Tech. Rep. 011313-4-T.* Ann Arbor: Univ. Michigan

295. von Winterfeldt, D., Edwards, W. 1975. Error in decision analysis: How to create the possibility of large losses by using dominated strategies. *SSRI Res.*

Rep. 75-4. Los Angeles: Univ. South. Calif.

296. von Winterfeldt, D., Fischer, G. W. 1975. Multi-attribute utility theory: Models and assessment procedures. See Ref. 86, pp. 47–86

297. Wainer, H. 1976. Estimating coefficients in linear models: It don't make no nevermind. *Psychol. Bull.* 83:213–17

298. Wainer, H., Zill, N., Gruvaeus, G. 1973. Senatorial decision making: II. Prediction. *Behav. Sci.* 18:20–26

299. Wallsten, T. S. 1971. Subjectively expected utility theory and subjects' probability estimates: Use of measurement-free techniques. *JEP* 88:31–40

300. Wallsten, T. S. 1972. Conjoint-measurement framework for the study of probabilistic information processing. *Psychol. Rev.* 79:245–60

301. Wallsten, T. 1975. Using a conjoint measurement model to develop theory about probabilistic information processing. *Psychometric Lab. Rep. 127* (revised). Chapel Hill, NC: Univ. North Carolina

302. Ward, W. M. 1975. Heuristic use or information integration in the estimation of subjective likelihood? *Bull. Psychon. Soc.* 6:43–46

303. Watson, S. R., Brown, R. V. 1975. Issues in the value of decision analysis. *DDI Tech. Rep 75-9.* McLean, Va: Decisions & Designs

304. Watson, S. R., Brown, R. V. 1975. Case studies in the value of decision analysis. *DDI Tech. Rep. 75-10.* McLean, Va: Decisions & Designs

305. Wheeler, G. E., Edwards, W. 1975. Misaggregation explains conservative inference about normally distributed populations. *SSRI Res. Rep. 75-11.* Los Angeles: Univ. South. Calif.

306. Wiggins, N. 1973. Individual differences in human judgments: A multivariate approach. See Ref. 33, pp. 110–42

307. Wiggins, N., Kohen, E. S. 1971. Man versus model of man revisited: The forecasting of graduate school success. *J. Pers. Soc. Psychol.* 19:100–6

308. Winkler, R. L. 1971. Probabilistic prediction: Some experimental results. *J. Am. Stat. Assoc.* 66:675–85

309. Winkler, R. L., Murphy, A. H. 1973. Experiments in the laboratory and the real world. *OBHP* 10:252–70

310. Wise, J. A., Mockovak, W. P. 1973. Descriptive modeling of subjective probabilities. *OBHP* 9:292–306

311. Wohlstetter, A. 1974. Legends of the strategic arms race, Part I: The driving machine. *Strategic Rev.* pp. 67–92

311a. Wohlstetter, R. 1962. *Pearl Harbor: Warning and Decision.* Stanford Univ. Press. 422 pp.

312. Wright, P. L., 1973. Use of consumer judgment models in promotion planning. *J. Mark.* 37:27–33

313. Wright, P. 1974. The harassed decision maker: Time pressures, distractions and the use of evidence. *J. Appl. Psychol.* 59:555–61

314. Wright, P. 1974. The use of phased, noncompensatory strategies in decisions between multiattribute products. *Grad. Sch. Bus. Res. Pap. Ser. 223.* Stanford Univ.

315. Wright, W. F. 1975. Cognitive information processing models: An empirical study. *Grad. Sch. Bus. Res. Paper Ser. 246.* Stanford Univ.

316. Wyer, R. S. 1974. *Cognitive Organization and Change: An Information Processing Approach.* Potomac, Md: Erlbaum. 502 pp.

317. Wyer, R. S. 1976. An investigation of the relations among probability estimates. *OBHP* 15:1–18

318. Zagorski, M. A. 1975. Risky decision: attention effects or masking effects? *Acta Psychol.* 39:487–94

319. Zieve, L. 1966. Misinterpretation and abuse of laboratory tests by clinicians. *Ann. NY Acad. Sci.* 134:563–72

Ann. Rev. Psychol. 1977. 28:41–60

PSYCHOLOGICAL AND ♦266
PHYSIOLOGICAL MECHANISMS
OF PAIN

John C. Liebeskind and Linda A. Paul

Department of Psychology, University of California, Los Angeles, California 90024

INTRODUCTION

The Recent Development of Interest in Pain Research

The past decade has witnessed a remarkable expansion of interest in the scientific study of pain. Theoretical developments have generated and in turn been generated or shaped by an outpouring of empirical findings from a wide variety of experimental and clinical disciplines. Many factors could be identified as providing major impetus for this growth spurt. Probably the most important was the appearance in 1965 of the gate control theory of pain by Melzack & Wall (103). This theory, acknowledged by its authors to be heavily indebted to earlier conceptions of Noordenbos (111) and others, and now generally held to be incorrect in at least some of its fundamental details, has nonetheless, and like none before it, proved enormously heuristic. It continues to inspire basic research and clinical applications.

Reflecting and greatly reinforcing the development of interest in pain scholarship has been a series of conferences, symposia, and reviews on this topic (e.g. 24, 26, 74, 165, 167). In 1973, an international pain symposium was held in Seattle (24) at which the International Association for the Study of Pain (IASP) was conceived. IASP now includes over 1500 members and sponsors publication of a journal, *Pain*, covering 14 different disciplines, including psychology. The pace of such scholarly and professional activity seems not to be abating. The laboratory and the clinic have found it increasingly useful to communicate, and this discourse has already begun to enrich pain scholarship and improve pain therapy.

Problems in the Measurement of Pain

The problem of measurement has been particularly difficult for the pain research worker. The origins of the problem seem largely definitional. Pain means many different things; and the variables which correlate with, inhibit or enhance one kind of pain, and the neural mechanisms which underlie it, may not be associated with or influence other kinds. Thus one must distinguish between the normal perception

41

of noxious stimuli and pain of pathological origin, and between acute pathological pain and chronic, intractable pain conditions. Among chronic pain states, for example, trigeminal neuralgia is thought to result from hyperexcitability in the trigeminal nucleus and may be treated with anticonvulsant drugs (21), whereas postherpetic neuralgia is thought to result from diminished afferent excitability due to a preferential loss of large diameter sensory fibers and may be treated with transcutaneous electrical stimulation (110). Then again, neither anticonvulsant drugs nor skin stimulation may affect greatly the normal pain response to pin prick or noxious heat.

While it is often useful to distinguish between various aspects of pain experience [e.g. "sensory-discriminitive" versus "motivational-affective" components (cf 36)], other dichotomous terms used in an attempt to specify the origin of pain ("physiological" versus "psychological," "organic" versus "functional") connote a Cartesian dualism and should have been discarded long ago. The use of such terms promotes an unfortunate division of pain patients into those seen to have "real" versus those seen to have "imagined" pain and may lead to inappropriate or insufficient treatment offered the latter. It serves little purpose (except perhaps to reduce the physician's frustration at failing to help many patients) to label pain patients with a strong affective component as "quacks" or "crocks." When considering the source of pain, therefore, it seems to us more reasonable to distinguish only between pains of peripheral, central, or unknown origin.

In measuring human pain, verbal report is naturally relied upon heavily to provide the most direct access to subjective experience; yet it is occasionally forgotten that even verbal report is only behavior from which we infer the internal state, sometimes incorrectly. A dramatic example of the dissociation possible between overtly reported and covertly felt pain is provided by the elegant work of Hilgard (60) with hypnotized subjects (see below). Similarly in studying laboratory animals, insufficient attention is paid to the fact that the different pain behaviors measured are organized in different ways and at different levels in the nervous system. Thus a treatment failing to affect a spinal reflex manifestation of pain may, for example, powerfully alter pain measured by vocalization (31). The evident solution to this problem is the use of a battery of tests which differ from each other by the nature of the pain behavior measured.

The physiologist too is hampered in measuring pain-evoked neural activity when making surgical interventions which require administration of anesthetic drugs or use of a "reduced" preparation (e.g. spinal or decerebrate). Naturally, anesthetics alter markedly the normal pain responsiveness of neurons, as do surgical transections (e.g. 19, 152). Here the solution lies in the development of chronic preparations where the animal can be studied either without restraint or with painless restraint and where necessary surgical procedures are performed under anesthesia well in advance of the data collection period. Such procedures are often difficult, however, as for example those needed to study the spinal cord in the awake, intact animal. More work of this sort is badly needed.

Aims of This Review

Our primary objective is to call to the attention of psychologists some fascinating recent developments in the field of pain research. Inevitably reflecting the authors' limitations of competence and their personal views of what is fascinating, some topics will be treated in more detail than others and some, regrettably, not at all. We hope this chapter will provide at least a convenient entrée to the current literature. The main sections of the chapter are the following: (a) Studies of pain in human beings, (b) Research on physiological mechanisms of pain, and (c) Some speculative concluding remarks on pain and on the effectiveness of various analgesic procedures. The literature search made in preparation for this writing ended in April 1976.

HUMAN PAIN

The philosophical and experimental complexities of assessing human pain have been well documented (e.g. 16, 97, 106, 111, 138). In evaluating this literature, it is essential to keep in mind *what* is measured (e.g. pain threshold, tolerance, or magnitude), as well as *how* it is measured (e.g. reaction time or verbal rating). Thus one treatment may affect pain tolerance but not threshold, and one measure may uncover significant differences when another does not.

The placebo effect is an important component of all the treatments to be discussed. It has been shown to be part of the analgesic effect of hypnosis (95) and drugs (16), and some authors report pain attenuation following acupuncture at placebo loci (49). On the other hand, the placebo effect has been experimentally dissociated from suggestibility and hypnotizability and should be understood as a powerful tool in its own right, especially in the clinical situation (cf 47, 63). It is but one example of the extent to which higher-level factors can influence the human pain experience.

Pain Control Through Psychological Strategies

The subject of hypnotic analgesia has been extensively reviewed in the past few years (e.g. 12, 61–63). The mechanisms underlying the impressive reductions which have been reported in normal and pathological pain remain unknown, and no consistent relation between extent of pain relief and physiological indicators has been found (63). Orne has called hypnotic analgesia a form of "negative hallucination" (117). The discovery that certain highly hypnotizable subjects who overtly report analgesia can, on occasion, reveal a covert aspect of their pain equal to waking pain levels but lacking most of the distress component normally present led Hilgard to formulate a "neo-dissociation" theory of hypnotic analgesia (60). He suggests that hierarchically arranged cognitive systems may become rearranged under hypnosis to alter the significance and awareness of the pain message.

The work of Hilgard's group represents what Spanos & Barber (137) have called the "state theory" of hypnosis. Alternative explanations for analgesia induced through experimenter-subject verbal interaction do not consider hypnotic induction per se as adding to the analgesia attainable without it. Thus Barber's group reports equivalent decreases in pain intensity ratings to finger pressure in subjects given suggestions to utilize certain cognitive strategies, whether or not they had been hypnotized prior to receiving the suggestion (12). Hilgard (62), on the other hand, reports that subjects do demonstrate more analgesia to cold pressor pain following hypnosis with suggestion of analgesia than after suggestion alone ("waking analgesia"). It should be noted, however, that differences in design and in wording of instructions in the two cases could have produced important differences in analgesic levels following hypnosis (62, 63, 68). Analgesia has also been reported following expectation of reduced pain and distraction and, to a lesser degree, after hypnotic induction without suggestion and after relaxation (cf 12, 63). In sum, although the "state-nonstate" controversy remains unresolved, all would agree that significant pain reductions in many people, and very powerful reductions in a few, are attainable with a variety of psychological approaches, the relative efficacies of which may depend more upon the particular experimenter-subject interaction than upon any inherent differences among these techniques.

Pain Control Through Peripheral Stimulation

The phenomenon of acupuncture analgesia has been received by Western experimentalists with some skepticism due to the unpredictability of its effect on individual subjects or patients. In fact, in China only 15–20% of surgical candidates are selected to receive acupuncture as the only analgesic (69). Induction times, locus of stimulation points, and methods of analgesic evaluation vary enormously across studies; and it can be argued that in studies where the characteristic, somewhat unpleasant paresthesia known as Teh Ch'i is not elicited, acupuncture is not being performed at all. When methodology is carefully attended to and attempts are made to follow classical guidelines, some studies report strong (49, 86) and others weak (44, 79) effects.

Although acupuncture points have been described as a locus of decreased GSR (28), and reports in this country as early as 1952 indicated a special effect from dry needling certain trigger zones (145), it has yet to be shown rigorously that traditional acupuncture methodology and sites result in stronger analgesia than electrical stimulation from cutaneous electrodes placed over or near the painful area. For example, the substantial elevation in threshold to tooth pain following electric stimulation to the cheek (nontraditional acupuncture point) and the hand (traditional acupuncture point) was not duplicated if the hand alone was stimulated (7). Lynn & Perl (85) have thrown this issue further into doubt by their demonstration that stimulation at certain acupuncture loci produces equivalent small reductions in pain ratings over wide areas of the body surface.

A small group of recent studies with laboratory animals has shown neurophysiological (37, 84) and behavioral (150) alterations following electric stimulation of supposed acupuncture points. These authors contend that the effects are frequency- and intensity-dependent. Human studies also indicate the importance of stimulation parameters. It has been shown, for example, that acute pain in normal subjects is blocked better by low-frequency cutaneous stimulation, whereas chronic pain is better relieved by stimulation at high frequencies (7, 8). In both cases, pain attenuation often required stimulation intensities which elicited powerful muscle contractions and which were near the threshold of tolerance (9). On the basis of these and other findings, it seems reasonable to state that the parameters of stimulation may be more important than the locus of stimulation points, and that different kinds of pain are differentially sensitive to these parameters.

It is difficult to draw any firm conclusions from the extensive literature on peripheral stimulation. Attempts to relate acupuncture and hypnotic analgesia yield unclear results (70, 79), although the fact that the former is partially reversed by a narcotic antagonist drug (naloxone) (93), whereas the latter is not (52, 93), has suggested at least some differences in their mechanisms of action. As with all treatments applied to human beings, it is impossible to create identical conditions in the laboratory across subjects when each person comes with his or her unique history of experience. In China, acupuncture treatment is part of an entire approach involving the establishment of rapport, explanation, and expectations, which is not duplicated in Western culture or medical practice.

Personality and Sociocultural Factors

Individual variability in pain responding has been approached in at least two major ways: from the standpoint of personality variables, and from that of cultural determinants. Regarding the former, the pain patient has emerged as an important subject of psychological study (120, 138), reflecting the modern view of pain as a clinical entity rather than as merely a symptom of disease process (22, 25). Merskey in England (106) and Sternbach in the United States (138) have been the most prolific contributors to this literature. A number of studies has attempted to establish a personality profile for the chronic pain sufferer. Thus several authors (23, 140, 162) have reported elevations in scales measuring neuroticism on standardized personality tests (MMPI or EPI) in pain patients, as well as a shift toward normality following surgery (140). It also seems that the longer patients suffer, the more emotionally disturbed they become as measured by these tests (15). However, it is possible that personality variables are different for people with problems treatable by surgery, and that there is a predisposition for certain personality types to become chronic pain patients.

Presence or absence of organic impairment has been reported to yield no differences on personality measures (141), although some differences in physiological measures among patients with and without an organic basis for their pain have been found (e.g. 77). The extent to which pain for the chronic sufferer is seen as psychogenic is being increasingly deemphasized. Sternbach prefers to describe pain phenomena in neurological, physiological, behavioral, and affective terms (138). Although some studies have found correlations between personality variables and acute pain responding, these correlations have not held up when more than one type of pain measure was used (cf 29).

The cultural approach to pain has viewed an individual's reaction as but one of many behavior patterns he or she has been taught by family, ethnic, and sex groups. Although early studies often revealed strong ethnic differences (cf 157 for discussion), more recent, better controlled work attempts to distinguish between a learned component (reflected in tolerance), and an unlearned component (threshold) of pain perception. Thus, in one recent study (158) anxiety was higher for Puerto Ricans, blacks, and females although no differences appeared in the amount of pain the patients had overall. Significant differences were also found in a pressure pain tolerance test for age, sex, and ethnicity (163); and among whites of different ethnic origins (146), autonomic changes to pain were found to differ, reflecting the different implicit sets of these subjects. A summary of work in this area has recently been published (156). Current awareness about the effects on pain of experimental conditions and situational variables should result in more accurate information about the importance of social determinants of the pain response.

New Techniques of Pain Assessment

Obtaining a meaningful, objective, and reliable measure of clinical pain has long been a problem for experimentalist and health professional alike. Several new developments in this area, however, appear quite promising. Sternbach (139) has modified the submaximum tourniquet technique (135) to allow a patient to match the intensity of his chronic pain to the ischemic pain experienced while wearing a blood pressure cuff and squeezing a hand exerciser. The patient's latency to reach a level of tourniquet pain equal to his self-evaluated level of clinical pain is divided by his latency to reach tourniquet pain tolerance threshold, resulting in a tourniquet pain ratio score. Sternbach finds the ratio score to be a valid and reliable means of describing clinical pain intensity. He has demonstrated, for example, that this ratio declines following successful pain surgery (140).

A number of attempts has been made to organize into meaningful categories the words with which patients describe their pain (e.g. 2, 102). The most extensive instrument of this sort so far developed is the McGill Pain Questionnaire (98), which provides information on sensory, affective and evaluative dimensions of pain. The questionnaire is reported to possess internal consistency and test-retest reliability, and patients with a given pain syndrome have been shown to group together on some measures. In addition, the questionnaire has been found sensitive enough to detect differences among pain-relieving treatments (98).

An important new contribution to the assessment of experimental pain has been the application of Sensory Decision Theory. With this approach, two determinants of threshold performance are separately identified: a measure of "sensory discriminability," and a measure of affective and motivational factors reflecting "response bias." Recent discussions have appeared of the special applications of this method to psychological research (142) and to the measurement of pain in particular (42). Clark (41) was the first to employ this method in assessing the effectiveness of an analgesic treatment. He has now shown that the analgesic effects of placebo (41) and suggestion (42) result only from a change in response bias. On the other hand, Chapman et al (39) found that nitrous oxide alters both bias and discriminability. Recent applications of Sensory Decision Theory to the study of acupuncture analgesia have been controversial, and issue was taken on both methodological (38) and conceptual (58) grounds with Clark & Yang's (43) original finding of a change in bias only.

PHYSIOLOGICAL MECHANISMS

Peripheral Nociceptors

Zotterman (166) is generally credited with being the first to provide direct neurophysiological evidence of the special and probably unique importance for pain of thinly myelinated (A$_\delta$) and unmyelinated (C) fibers in peripheral nerve. Although several others subsequently confirmed his observation in a small fraction of fibers studied, it was only very recently, following development of appropriate dissection and recording techniques, that Perl and his associates (20, 30, 118) found a significant proportion of both A$_\delta$ and C fibers in cutaneous nerve in cat and monkey to be specifically (that is, uniquely) responsive to injurious or near-injurious intensities of peripheral stimulation. Still more recently, several groups have succeeded in applying microelectrode techniques to recording from single cutaneous C fibers of normal human subjects (143, 144, 147). These and related studies (123, 144) have permitted the correlation of A$_\delta$ activation with the experience of "first" or fast, sharp, well-localized pain, and of selective C-fiber activation with the experience of "second" or slow, aching or burning, long-duration and poorly localized pain.

In general, three classes of nociceptors are encountered: high threshold mechanoreceptors, heat nociceptors, and so-called "polymodal" nociceptors responsive both to noxious mechanical and noxious thermal stimuli. Polymodal and heat nociceptors show the interesting property of sensitization after repeated or prolonged noxious stimulation or during regeneration following nerve section, whereby the threshold for their activation can diminish to levels of intensity which are ordinarily innocuous (20, 46). This characteristic may help to explain the hyperpathia commonly observed in man following burns or nerve injury (20, 46). Similarly, Wall & Gutnick (154) recently showed with experimental sciatic nerve section in the rat that a neuroma may form comprising regenerated small fiber filaments. By recording more proximally from these fibers it was found that they have an unusual degree of spontaneous activity as well as a low threshold for activation, once again suggestive of a role in spontaneous pain states following nerve injury in man, including phantom pain. The fact that activity in these fibers could be blocked for long periods of time by a brief volley of antidromic stimulation further suggests that at least some of the pain relief afforded by transcutaneous nerve stimulation in certain human pathological pain conditions may have a peripheral origin (154).

These discoveries have revitalized conceptions of pain as a specific sensory event (119). It is now clear that information about pain is carried to the central nervous system over a morphologically discrete subset of A$_\delta$ and C fibers. The question of how far into the CNS specificity is maintained, however, remains an open one. In any case, pain appreciation cannot simply be attributed to the activation of nociceptors but surely depends upon the complex central connections of these fibers.

The Spinal Cord Dorsal Horn

The role of the spinal cord dorsal horn in nociception has been the subject of a large and fascinating literature during the past decade. From direct observation with microelectrode recording techniques, two general classes of dorsal horn, sensory interneurons have been identified with a certain, if not altogether clearly understood, relation to pain mechanisms. Class 1 nociceptive cells, described first by Christensen & Perl (40), share with peripheral nociceptors the property of specific responsiveness to noxious or near-noxious stimuli. These are chiefly located in the most superficial layer or marginal zone of the dorsal horn (lamina 1). Class 2 nociceptive cells respond clearly to activation of low-threshold inputs, but as the intensity of the peripheral stimulus is increased to noxious levels these cells respond with an increasingly vigorous and prolonged discharge (cf, for example, 18, 64, 125, 152, 161). Cells characterized by this wide dynamic range of responsiveness have been located principally in the deeper layers of the dorsal horn, laminae 4–6, especially lamina 5.

Class 2 interneurons receive a convergence of information from somatic and visceral inputs suggestive of a role in visceral referred pain (122). These cells show "windup" or temporal summation with repetitive C-fiber activation which might account for the appearance of hyperpathic states in such clinical pain syndromes as causalgia and postherpetic neuralgia in which there is a selective loss of large fibers (105, 128). Long duration afterdischarges to the application of noxious heat also characterize Class 2 cells (57). Interestingly, the properties of temporal summation and prolonged afterdischarge have been shown to be associated with second pain in psychophysical experiments on normal human subjects following temporary nerve compression resulting in a preferential block of A fibers (123, 124).

The axons of many Class 1 and 2 cells project directly to the brain, others form propriospinal connections and ascend multisynaptically or contribute to reflex paths (cf 73). Important interspecific differences are evident in the spinal projection pathways and final destinations of these axons (73). In primates (including man), we know from a confluence of anatomical and physiological evidence that a large proportion of both cell types ascend in the contralateral anterolateral quadrant and terminate in the thalamus (73, 96). Projections to the lower brain stem via the anterolateral path and to the thalamus via the dorsolateral spino-cervical tract characterize the central distribution of these cells in the cat (cf 27). Recent evidence suggests that the distribution of ascending fibers of Class 1 and 2 cells in the rat resembles more that of the primate than the cat (51).

In a fascinating and important series of papers, Mayer et al (91) and Price & Mayer (127) have recently provided strong presumptive evidence that adequate activation of Class 2 dorsal horn cells in man is a sufficient condition for the experience of pain. Information concerning the current threshold and optimal stimulation frequency for eliciting reports of pain as well as refractory period data indicative of fiber diameter were collected by directly stimulating the anterolateral columns in conscious patients undergoing cordotomy for pain relief (91). These findings were compared with similar data collected in a study on monkeys of Class 1 and 2 dorsal horn cells identified by antidromic activation as projecting in the anterolateral columns (127). Refractory periods and electrical thresholds of Class 2 cells in the monkey more closely resembled the values of these parameters found optimal for eliciting pain in man than did those of Class 1 cells. While these findings, as the authors point out, do not exclude the possibility that Class 1 dorsal horn cells participate importantly in the perception of pain, they do strongly suggest that cells of the Class 2 type are alone able to mediate at least certain kinds of human pain experience. These experiments exemplify the value of intelligent collaboration among laboratory and clinical scientists; we hope they will serve to inspire additional comparative and interdisciplinary studies of this genre.

The gate control theory of pain described in 1965 by Melzack & Wall (103) was based largely upon some well-established clinical observations and the anatomy and physiology of the dorsal horn as it was understood at that time. The theory proposed a dynamic interaction among large and small afferent fibers mediated through the small cells of the substantia gelatinosa (laminae 2 and 3 of the dorsal horn). It was suggested that substantia gelatinosa (SG) cells exerted presynaptic inhibition on both large and small fiber terminals as they synapsed on larger dorsal horn (central transmission) cells whose axons project to the brain. Large fibers were thought to excite the SG thereby enhancing presynaptic inhibition (closing the gate), small fibers to inhibit the SG thereby reducing presynaptic inhibition (opening the gate). Pain perception resulted when a critical level of firing was attained by central transmission cells. It was further supposed that the gate was influenced by fibers descending from the brain. In this way, higher centers could affect transmission through the centrally projecting spinal cord cells.

Since 1965, gate theory has undergone various modifications (e.g. 36, 97, 104) and has been subjected to a variety of criticisms on the grounds of anatomical (73), physiological (e.g. 48), psychophysical (e.g. 109), and theoretical (119) considerations. On the other hand, a wide assortment of clinical and experimental findings has been interpreted as generally supporting the theory or at least certain aspects of it (59, 94, 134, 151, 152, 155). To assess adequately the current status of gate theory would be an undertaking well beyond the scope of this review. Moreover, there are still crucial gaps in our knowledge of dorsal horn synaptology and in our understanding of the interactions among different fiber types and dorsal horn cells. These gaps stem from the anatomical complexities of the dorsal horn and an inability to record from many of the smaller spinal cord cells (e.g. SG cells) assumed to be involved in pain integration.

Viewed broadly, gate theory has made an enormous and enduring contribution to our thinking about processes of nociception by focusing attention on the afferent interactions and descending controls operating in the dorsal horn. The theory's central theme, which views the plasticity of pain experience in terms of these centripetal and centrifugal influences, seems today as compelling and salient a conceptualization as it did in 1965.

Supraspinal Structures

Several nuclear regions of the brain known to receive input from the anterolateral columns (96) have been the subject of electrophysiological analysis in relation to nociception. Among these, the most extensively studied has been the *nucleus gigantocellularis* (NGC) of the bulbar reticular formation. In an excellent series of experiments, Casey and co-workers have examined NGC in the chronically implanted, unanesthetized rat and cat with microelectrode, electrical brain stimulation, and behavioral techniques (33–35, 108). They found that many cells in this region respond maximally to activation of A_δ and C fibers or to intense natural stimuli of the skin. For example, it was shown that a majority of NGC cells in the cat responded best at intensities of peripheral nerve shock which led to rapid escape behavior (35). Electrical stimulation through the microelectrode was seen to elicit escape at lowest threshold with placements in the exact area where escape-related cells were found (34). It has also been reported that spontaneous activity in a high proportion of NGC cells is significantly affected by intra-arterial injection of the pain-producing substance, bradykinin, into the limb (54). Interestingly, Morrow & Casey (108) recently showed that midbrain central gray stimulation in the rat, known to produce powerful pain inhibition (see below), not only blocked pain behavior but also inhibited NGC units responsive to noxious stimuli without affecting NGC units responsive only to innocuous stimuli.

It should be noted that little evidence is available to suggest the existence of any substantial number of specifically nociceptive units in NGC. On the contrary, the vast majority of cells tested with natural stimuli in the awake animal show response properties similar to Class 2, not Class 1 dorsal horn cells; that is, they respond maximally, not uniquely, to noxious stimuli (33). NGC cells are characterized, moreover, by very large peripheral receptive fields (33) [once again more similar to Class 2 than Class 1 cells (cf 10, 126)], and hence would not alone qualify for a role in the sensory-discriminitive aspects of pain perception. From these facts it would appear that NGC cells are concerned more with the affective component of nociception (34). In this regard it is interesting to note a recent study by Vertes & Miller (148) showing a small number of reticular formation cells in the rat which increased their activity to a conditioned stimulus (CS) paired with noxious foot shock but not to a neutral CS nor to one paired with positive reinforcement. The possibility that activity in these cells signals or underlies a pain-related emotional reaction such as fear, as suggested by these authors, is an intriguing one.

Most electrophysiological studies of more rostral brain regions in relation to nociception have been performed in anesthetized animals and hence shed little light on the problem of brain mechanisms of nociception. An early investigation by Poggio & Mountcastle (121), for example, showed that nearly 60% of the neurons studied in the thalamic posterior nuclear group (PO) of the anesthetized cat were activated specifically by noxious stimuli. However, Casey (32) later found in the unanesthetized preparation that whereas a few PO units were specifically nociceptive during slow-wave sleep, none were during wakefulness. On the other hand, many cells widely distributed throughout the diencephalon and rostral midbrain did respond differentially to noxious and innocuous stimuli. Most of these, like NGC cells, had wide peripheral receptive fields.

In sum, those portions of the brain which have been adequately studied in relation to pain respond, if at all, maximally, not specifically, to noxious stimuli and encode perhaps the intensive and qualitative features of pain, but surely not well its spatial or temporal characteristics. Because these same structures are thought to participate in pain-related affective and motivational behaviors as well as in autonomic nervous system functions, it seems likely that they play their major role in informing the organism that a threatening stimulus has occurred and in preparing the organism for an integrated response. It is always possible that a substantial number of nociceptive cells will yet be found, in some heretofore inadequately researched brain region, which encode the sensory-discriminative aspects of pain. It appears to us more likely, however, that these spatiotemporal properties of pain are encoded by lemniscal neurons located within the specific somatosensory path and perhaps *not* themselves responsive to noxious stimuli per se. Consistent with the views of a number of workers (cf, for example, 5, 6), it is suggested that pain perception results from the concurrent activation of such lemniscal (sensory-discriminative) and extralemniscal (emotional-motivational) elements.

Behavioral Deficits Following Lesions

Attempts to eliminate normal pain appreciation or pain of pathological origin have been made, employing the full gamut of available techniques. Perhaps least fruitful among these approaches has been that of making restricted lesions within putative pain tracts or relays of the central nervous system. The results of these attempts, while instructive, have been only occasionally, partially, and/or transiently successful, and this conclusion can be drawn both from the extensive clinical literature (160) and from a relatively scant literature on experimental animals.

Within this body of work, certainly the most satisfactory results demonstrating pain attenuation derive from selective spinal cord lesions (72, 73, 92, 149). Important interspecific differences are evident, however, regarding the role in nociception played by the various ascending paths (73). In man, a critical role in pain conduction can be ascribed to fibers ascending in the anterolateral quadrant (159). It has been suggested that short-fiber, multisynaptic systems (13) and dorsal and dorsolateral paths (72, 149) may be as or more important in infra-human species. A cautionary note should be sounded, however, in view of the finding by Vierck et al (149) that dorsal column lesions in monkeys diminished pain reactivity as measured by the force and latency but not the threshold of an escape response. The apparent role of the dorsal columns in sensory-motor interactions (153) and in the rapid sequencing of behavior (100) casts in some doubt the specific relationship of these findings to pain mechanisms.

Surprisingly few systematic attempts have been made to assess the antinociceptive effects of intracerebral lesions in experimental animals. Most studies have focused on brain regions known to receive fibers from the anterolateral quadrant, known to contain cells differentially responsive to noxious stimuli, and known to yield aversive effects upon electrical stimulation. In some studies, deficits in avoidance but not escape or nociceptive reflexes have been observed following lesions in such structures, for example, intralaminar thalamus (45) and midbrain central gray matter (83); but lesions in some brain areas not known on other grounds to be clearly involved in nociception also cause avoidance deficits. Even when escape deficits are found with central gray (56, 101), medial thalamic (107), or bulbar reticular (55) lesions, it may be that the deficit is due more to a loss of emotionality (for example, fear, which is normally elicited by noxious stimulation and no doubt serves to energize escape responding) than to an analgesic effect per se (cf discussion in 83). In this regard it is interesting that central gray lesions failed to affect performance in a shock-titration procedure (71), where, because the well-trained animal controls the amount of shock he receives, fear might be assumed to play a rather minimal role. Unfortunately, in the majority of such studies only a single pain test is employed, and by consequence the results are very difficult to interpret.

In sum, the lesion literature is replete with failures to excise pain appreciation, especially when the lesions are made at supraspinal levels. From these failures, however, we may draw an important conclusion: As fibers carrying the pain message ascend to progressively higher stations, considerable divergence occurs, and this divergence makes it unlikely that focal destruction will ever seriously or permanently interrupt the sensory-discriminative (36) aspects of nociception. On the other hand, there is reason to believe that brain regions receiving this sensory inflow play a role in affective, attentional, cognitive, motivational and/or visceromotor phenomena associated with pain and that these factors can importantly and differentially influence various components of pain behavior. In fact, we now know that descending controls from some of these same brain regions powerfully modulate both spinal reflexes and sensory interneurons in the cord involved in nociception (see below). Thus even spinally mediated components of pain behavior are not immune from influence by supraspinal centers and the "higher" functions they mediate. Lesion deficits, therefore, must always be evaluated with a diversity of measures if we are to understand intimately the underlying nature of the functional loss.

Descending Controls: Endogenous Mechanisms of Pain Inhibition

There has been a particularly rapid development of interest during the past few years in central mechanisms of antinociception (cf 80, 81, 90). A spate of recent papers employing focal brain stimulation suggests the existence within the mammalian medial brain stem of endogenous and extremely potent centrifugal mechanisms of pain inhibition (e.g. 89, 94, 99, 114, 129, 136). Stimulation-produced analgesia (SPA) has been measured behaviorally using a wide assortment of pain tests and species ranging from rat to man (1, 11, 50, 53, 89, 99, 116, 131, 132, 136). SPA can be equi-analgesic to large doses of morphine (89) and can totally block all manifestations of nociception from spinal reflexes to higher-order, learned escape reactions (89, 94, 136). After only several seconds of stimulation, the analgesic effect may last up to several hours (89). Importantly, the peripheral field of analgesia is frequently subtotal, such that the animal completely ignores strong pinch to one limb while responding normally to pinch applied elsewhere (11, 89, 94, 136). Thus the analgesic effect cannot be attributed to interference with general affective or response mechanisms (94). In fact, during central stimulation many animals appear normally reactive to other modalities of stimulation and can occasionally be seen to engage in such normal behaviors as feeding (94, 136).

SPA has been reported to result from stimulation of medial brain stem structures from the rostral medulla (*nucleus raphe magnus*), through the midbrain central gray matter, to the caudal diencephalon (11, 53, 89, 94, 115, 130–132, 136). Although at certain sites both analgesia and self-stimulation are found, at others the central stimulation that produces analgesia is itself aversive (11, 89, 94, 136). In the latter case, analgesia can be measured only after the central stimulus and the aversive behaviors elicited by it have terminated. At still other sites, self-stimulation but not analgesia may be found (89, 94, 136).

SPA results in and, in part at least, seems able to be understood in terms of a powerful descending inhibitory effect on nociceptive mechanisms in the spinal cord (80–82, 90, 94, 114). For example, SPA causes suppression of various spinal reflexes (94). Moreover, analgesic stimulation in the cat can arrest totally the pain-evoked discharges of Class 2 dorsal horn cells, often without affecting responsiveness of these or other spinal cord cells to innocuous stimuli (114). Interestingly, Basbaum et al (14) recently reported that the analgesic effect of central gray stimulation measured in the rat tail-flick test was blocked by selective destruction of the spinal cord dorsolateral funiculus in which the serotonin-containing fibers originating in *nucleus raphe magnus* are known to descend.

A series of studies has disclosed some remarkable parallels between morphine's site and mechanism of analgesic action and the site and mechanism of action of SPA. SPA has been found susceptible to many of the same pharmacological manipulations as morphine. Thus drugs that alter cerebral concentrations of monoamine neurotransmitters are seen to alter SPA and morphine analgesia in a similar fashion (3). Moreover, naloxone, a specific morphine antagonist, has been shown to reverse SPA partially (1, 4, 115), and Mayer & Hayes (88) reported both that tolerance develops with repeated SPA trials and that cross-tolerance between SPA and morphine can occur. That an important site of morphine's analgesic action is the central gray matter is indicated by several lines of investigation. Morphine when applied directly to the central gray through microinjection cannulae exerts more powerful analgesia than when applied elsewhere within the brain or ventricular system (e.g. 67, 133, 164); also, stereospecific opiate binding sites have been found in central gray as well as elsewhere in the brain (76). Several reports indicate that SPA and morphine have similar electrophysiological effects in the brain and spinal cord. For example, morphine, like SPA, selectively suppresses nociceptive responding in dorsal horn cells (75, 78); and both morphine and SPA selectively inhibit pain-evoked responses in the brain stem (113) while augmenting spontaneous multiple unit activity in many of the same areas, including the *nucleus raphe magnus* (112).

In a dramatic new development, Hughes discovered an endogenous, morphine-like factor in the brain (termed "enkephalin"), described its peptidic nature, and synthesized it (65, 66). Stein and co-workers have now shown both that intraventricular microinjections of this substance yield analgesia (17) and that central gray stimulation releases this substance or a peptide very similar to it (personal communication). Similarly, E. Wei has found that slow infusions of enkephalin into the central gray matter of the rat lead to dependence (personal communication).

In sum, these findings suggest, as we have previously concluded (3, 4, 80–82, 89, 94), that an endogenous substrate of antinociception exists within the medial brain stem. It may be that morphine directly activates this substrate, whereas brain stem stimulation both activates it directly and also indirectly via the release of enkephalin (4, 87). An important consequence of adequate activation of the substrate is the reduction or arrest of transmission of nociceptive information through the spinal cord (80). The *nucleus raphe magnus* with its descending serotonin fibers seems to be a crucial relay in the centrifugal path (14, 80, 81, 115).

SOME SPECULATIVE CONCLUDING REMARKS

The vast majority of recent human pain studies as well as many recent studies in lower animals have dealt with the efficacy of different treatments or procedures in blocking pain perception. Logically, pain inhibition may occur in only three ways:

1. locally (passively), by damage or chemical blockage of critical portions of the pain path peripherally or centrally; 2. centripetally (actively), by interactions among first-order sensory nerve fibers or among central neurons in their afferent pathway; and 3. centrifugally (actively) via descending fibers from higher central structures to lower ones. Local or passive analgesic treatments clearly work well only in the peripheral nervous system, since in the central nervous system the dispersion of the ascending pain message to ever wider regions makes it impractical or impossible to interrupt pain with focally applied chemicals or discrete lesions (cf above). Centripetal interactions are known to occur both pre- and postsynaptically among primary afferents in the spinal gray matter, among propriospinal elements, and perhaps also at higher stations in the brain. We know of no evidence, however, that such interactions can more than weakly or briefly interrupt pain in normal man or animals, and even then the interfering stimulus must generally be itself quite aversive and hence of limited practical value. On the other hand, it is now clear that very powerful, centrifugal pain control systems exist in the mammalian brain, one example of which was described in the preceding section on stimulation-produced analgesia. Other centrifugal systems of pain modification may also exist, intracerebral as well as cerebrospinal, which serve either to amplify or dampen pain perception.

In the light of such considerations it is of interest to re-examine several of the analgesic procedures employed in man (as described above). We suggest that in normal human or animal subjects acupuncture and transcutaneous electrical stimulation exert at best a weak analgesic effect via centripetal mechanisms; and that when they work powerfully, they do so by activation of centrifugal controls. The centrifugal systems which they activate may also underlie other analgesic procedures which depend upon expectation, suggestion, hypnosis, and possibly helplessness (the "still reaction" readily observed in many infrahuman species); although the fact that the narcotic antagonist naloxone can partially reverse acupuncture analgesia (93) without affecting hypnotic analgesia (52, 93) clearly suggests at least a partial segregation of the analgesia substrates of these two phenomena. The enormous intersubject variability in degree of analgesia attainable by all these procedures attests principally, in our view, to the difficulties most organisms have in reliably accessing their own centrifugal pain-inhibitory systems or having them reliably accessed by these imperfect techniques.

We think it likely that all mammals possess a set of powerful and endogenous centrifugal mechanisms of pain control within the brain stem. Lower animals may have little access to these systems except under the most dire circumstances, such as during strong appetitive, aggressive, or self-protective drive states, and especially during the goal-directed behaviors associated with these states. In man, however, it may be that there are better developed pathways of access (perhaps of telencephalic origin) to these brain stem systems. Thus our cognitive capacities to think, to believe, and to hope enable us, probably all of us under the appropriate conditions, to find and employ our pain inhibitory resources. The important challenge in the years to come for behavioral scientists involved in pain research will be to explore and ultimately bring under control those precise circumstances and techniques that will reliably enable people to make use of these resources when needed.

ACKNOWLEDGMENTS

Preparation of this chapter was supported by NIH grant NS 07628. The authors gratefully acknowledge the assistance of Glenn J. Giesler Jr. and Judy A. Turner with certain portions of this review. We appreciate as well the helpful comments provided by Dr. David J. Mayer.

Literature Cited

1. Adams, J. E. 1976. Naloxone reversal of analgesia produced by brain stimulation in the human. *Pain* 2:161–66
2. Agnew, D. C., Merskey, H. 1976. Words of chronic pain. *Pain* 2:73–81
3. Akil, H., Liebeskind, J. C. 1975. Monoaminergic mechanisms of stimulation-produced analgesia. *Brain Res.* 94:279–96
4. Akil, H., Mayer, D. J., Liebeskind, J. C. 1976. Antagonism of stimulation-produced analgesia by naloxone, a narcotic antagonist. *Science* 191:961–62
5. Albe-Fessard, D. 1968. Central nervous mechanisms involved in pain and analgesia. In *Pharmacology of Pain*, ed. R. K. S. Lim, pp. 131–68. Oxford:Pergamon
6. Albe-Fessard, D., Besson, J. M. 1973. Convergent thalamic and cortical projections—the non-specific system. In *Handbook of Sensory Physiology.* ed. A. Iggo, 2:489–560. Berlin:Springer
7. Andersson, S. A., Ericson, T., Holmgren, E., Lindqvist, G. 1976. Analgetic effects of peripheral conditioning stimulation. I. General pain threshold effects on human teeth and a correlation to psychological factors. *Acup. & Electro-Ther. Res.* In press
8. Andersson, S. A., Hansson, G., Holmgren, E., Renberg, O. 1976. Evaluation of the pain suppressive effect of different frequencies of peripheral electrical stimulation in chronic pain conditions. *Acup. & Electro-Ther. Res.* In press
9. Andersson, S. A., Holmgren, E. 1976. Analgetic effects of peripheral conditioning stimulation. III. Effect of high frequency stimulation; segmental mechanisms interacting with pain. *Acup. & Electro-Ther. Res.* In press
10. Applebaum, A. E., Beall, J. E., Foreman, R. D., Willis, W. D. 1975. Organization and receptive fields of primate spinothalamic tract neurons. *J. Neurophysiol.* 38:572–86
11. Balagura, S., Ralph, T. 1973. The analgesic effect of electrical stimulation of the diencephalon and mesencephalon. *Brain Res.* 60:369–79
12. Barber, T. X., Spanos, N. P., Chaves, J. F. 1974. *Hypnosis, Imagination, and Human Potentialities.* Elmsford, NY: Pergamon
13. Basbaum, A. I. 1973. Conduction of the effects of noxious stimulation by short-fiber multisynaptic systems of the spinal cord in the rat. *Exp. Neurol.* 40:699–716
14. Basbaum, A. I., Marley, N., O'Keefe, J. 1976. Effects of spinal cord lesions on the analgesic properties of electrical brain stimulation. See Ref. 26
15. Beals, R. K., Hickman, N. W. 1972. Industrial injuries of the back and extremities. *J. Bone Joint Surg.* 54A:1593–1611
16. Beecher, H. K. 1959. *Measurement of Subjective Responses. Quantitative Effects of Drugs.* New York:Oxford Univ. Press
17. Belluzzi, J. D., Grant, N., Garsky, V., Sarantakis, D., Wise, C. D., Stein, L. 1976. Analgesia induced in vivo by central administration of enkephalin in rat. *Nature* 260:625–26
18. Besson, J. M., Conseiller, C., Hamann, K. F., Maillard, M. C. 1972. Modifications of dorsal horn cell activities in the spinal cord after intra-arterial injection of bradykinin. *J. Physiol. Lond.* 221:189–205
19. Besson, J. M., Guilbaud, G., LeBars, D. 1975. Descending inhibitory influences exerted by the brain stem upon the activities of dorsal horn lamina V cells. *J. Physiol. Lond.* 248:725–41
20. Bessou, P., Perl, E. R. 1969. Response of cutaneous sensory units with unmyelinated fibers to noxious stimuli. *J. Neurophysiol.* 32:1025–43
21. Black, R. G. 1974. A laboratory model for trigeminal neuralgia. See Ref. 24, pp. 651–58
22. Black, R. G. 1975. The chronic pain syndrome. *Surg. Clinics N. Am.* 55:999–1011

23. Bond, M. R. 1973. Personality studies in patients with pain secondary to organic disease. *J. Psychosom. Res.* 17: 257–63

24. Bonica, J. J., ed. 1974. *Advances in Neurology*, Vol. 4. New York: Raven

25. Bonica, J. J. 1974. General clinical considerations (including organization and function of a pain clinic). In *Recent Advances on Pain*, ed. J. J. Bonica, P. Procacci, C. A. Pagni, pp. 274–98. Springfield, Ill: Thomas

26. Bonica, J. J., Albe-Fessard, D., eds. 1976. *Recent Advances in Pain Research and Therapy: Proceedings of the First World Congress on Pain.* New York: Raven. In press

27. Brown, A. G. 1973. Ascending and long spinal pathways: dorsal columns, spinocervical tract and spinothalamic tract. In *Handbook of Sensory Physiology*, ed. A. Iggo, 2:321–31. Berlin:Springer

28. Brown, M. L., Ulett, G. A., Stern, J. A. 1974. Acupuncture loci: techniques for location. *Am. J. Chin. Med.* 2:67–74

29. Brown, R. A., Fader, K., Barber, T. X. 1973. Responsiveness to pain: stimulus-specificity versus generality. *Psychol. Rec.* 23:1–7

30. Burgess, P. R., Perl, E. R. 1967. Myelinated afferent fibres responding specifically to noxious stimulation of the skin. *J. Physiol. Lond.* 190:541–62

31. Carroll, M. N. Jr., Lim, R. K. S. 1960. Observations on the neuropharmacology of morphine and morphinelike analgesia. *Arch. Int. Pharmacodyn.* 125:383–403

32. Casey, K. L. 1966. Unit analysis of nociceptive mechanisms in the thalamus of the awake squirrel monkey. *J. Neurophysiol.* 29:727–50

33. Casey, K. L. 1971. Responses of bulboreticular units to somatic stimuli eliciting escape behavior in the cat. *Int. J. Neurosci.* 2:15–28

34. Casey, K. L. 1971. Escape elicited by bulboreticular stimulation in the cat. *Int. J. Neurosci.* 2:29–34

35. Casey, K. L. 1971. Somatosensory responses of bulbo-reticular units in awake cat: relation to escape-producing stimuli. *Science* 173:77–80

36. Casey, K. L., Melzack, R. 1967. Neural mechanisms of pain: A conceptual model. In *New Concepts in Pain and Its Clinical Management*, ed. E. L. Way, pp. 13–31. Philadelphia:Davis

37. Chang, H. 1973. Integrative action of thalamus in the process of acupuncture for analgesia. *Scientica Sin.* 16:25–60

38. Chapman, C. R., Gehrig, J. D., Wilson, M. E. 1975. Acupuncture, pain, and signal detection theory. *Science* 189:65

39. Chapman, C. R., Murphy, T. M., Butler, S. H. 1973. Analgesic strength of 33 percent nitrous oxide: a signal detection theory evaluation. *Science* 179:1246–48

40. Christensen, B. N., Perl, E. R. 1970. Spinal neurons specifically excited by noxious or thermal stimuli: marginal zone of the dorsal horn. *J. Neurophysiol.* 33:293–307

41. Clark, W. C. 1969. Sensory-decision theory analysis of the placebo effect on the criterion for pain and thermal sensitivity (d'). *J. Abnorm. Psychol.* 74: 363–71

42. Clark, W. C. 1974. Pain sensitivity and the report of pain: an introduction to sensory decision theory. *Anesthesiology* 40:272–87

43. Clark, W. C., Yang, J. C. 1974. Acupunctural analgesia? Evaluation by signal detection theory. *Science* 184: 1096–98

44. Day, R. L., Kitahata, L. M., Kao, F. F., Motoyama, E. K., Hardy, J. D. 1975. Evaluation of acupuncture anesthesia: a psychophysical study. *Anesthesiology* 43:507–17

45. Delacour, J., Alexinsky, T. 1969. Rôle spécifique d'une structure thalamique médiane dans le comportement conditionné du Rat blanc. *C. R. Acad. Sci. Paris* 268:569–72

46. Dickhaus, H., Zimmermann, M., Zotterman, Y. 1976. Neurophysiological investigations of the development of nociceptors in regenerating cutaneous nerves of the cat. See Ref. 26

47. Evans, F. J. 1974. The placebo response in pain reduction. See Ref. 24, pp. 289–96

48. Franz, D. N., Iggo, A. 1968. Dorsal root potentials and ventral root reflexes evoked by nonmyelinated fibers. *Science* 162:1140–42

49. Gaw, A. C., Chang, L. W., Shaw, L.-C. 1975. Efficacy of acupuncture on osteoarthritic pain. *New Engl. J. Med.* 293:375–78

50. Giesler, G. J. Jr., Liebeskind, J. C. 1976. Inhibition of visceral pain by electrical stimulation of the periaqueductal gray matter. *Pain* 2:43–48

51. Giesler, G. J. Jr., Menetrey, D., Guilbaud, G., Besson, J. M. 1976. Lumbar cord neurons at the origin of the spinothalamic tract in the rat. *Fed. Proc.* 35:483

52. Goldstein, A., Hilgard, E. R. 1975. Lack of influence of the morphine antagonist naloxone on hypnotic analgesia. *Proc. Natl. Acad. Sci.* 72:2041–43

53. Goodman, S. J., Holcombe, V. 1976. Selective and prolonged analgesia in monkey resulting from brain stimulation. See Ref. 26

54. Guilbaud, G., Besson, J. M., Oliveras, J. L., Wyon-Maillard, M. C. 1973. Modifications of the firing rate of bulbar reticular units (nucleus gigantocellularis) after intra-arterial injection of bradykinin into the limbs. *Brain Res.* 63:131–40

55. Halpern, B. P., Halverson, J. D. 1974. Modification of escape from noxious stimuli after bulbar reticular formation lesions. *Behav. Biol.* 11:215–29

56. Halpern, M. 1968. Effects of midbrain central gray matter lesions on escape-avoidance behavior in rats. *Physiol. Behav.* 3:171–78

57. Handwerker, H. O., Iggo, A., Zimmermann, M. 1975. Segmental and supraspinal actions on dorsal horn neurons responding to noxious and non-noxious skin stimuli. *Pain* 1:147–65

58. Hayes, R. L., Bennett, G. J., Mayer, D. J. 1975. Acupuncture, pain, and signal detection theory. *Science* 189:65–66

59. Higgins, J. D., Tursky, B., Schwartz, G. E. 1971. Shock-elicited pain and its reduction by concurrent tactile stimulation. *Science* 172:866–67

60. Hilgard, E. R. 1973. A neodissociation interpretation of pain reduction in hypnosis. *Psychol. Rev.* 80:396–411

61. Hilgard, E. R. 1975. Hypnosis. *Ann. Rev. Psychol.* 26:19–44

62. Hilgard, E. R. 1975. The alleviation of pain by hypnosis. *Pain* 1:213–31

63. Hilgard, E. R., Hilgard, J. R. 1975. *Hypnosis in the Relief of Pain*. Los Altos, Calif:Kaufmann

64. Hillman, P., Wall, P. D. 1969. Inhibitory and excitatory factors influencing the receptive fields of lamina 5 spinal cord cells. *Exp. Brain Res.* 9:284–306

65. Hughes, J. 1975. Isolation of an endogenous compound from the brain with pharmacological properties similar to morphine. *Brain Res.* 88:295–308

66. Hughes, J., Smith, T. W., Kosterlitz, H. W., Fothergill, L. A., Morgan, B. A., Morris, H. R. 1975. Identification of two related pentapeptides from the brain with potent opiate agonist activity. *Nature* 258:577–79

67. Jacquet, Y. F., Lajtha, A. 1974. Paradoxical effects after microinjection of morphine in the periaqueductal gray matter in the rat. *Science* 185:1055–57

68. Johnson, R. F. Q. 1974. Suggestions for pain reduction and response to cold-induced pain. *Psychol. Rec.* 24:161–69

69. Kaada, B., Hoel, E., Leseth, K., Nygaard-Φstby, B., Setekleiv, J., Stovner, J. 1974. Acupuncture analgesia in the People's Republic of China. *Tidsskr. Nor. Laegeforen.* 94:417–42

70. Katz, R. L., Kao, C. Y., Spiegel, H., Katz, G. J. 1974. Pain, acupuncture, hypnosis. See Ref. 24, pp. 819–25

71. Kelly, D. D., Glusman, M. 1968. Aversive thresholds following midbrain lesions. *J. Comp. Physiol. Psychol.* 66:25–34

72. Kennard, M. A. 1954. The course of ascending fibers in the spinal cord of the cat essential to the recognition of painful stimuli. *J. Comp. Neurol.* 100:511–24

73. Kerr, F. W. L. 1975. Neuroanatomical substrates of nociception in the spinal cord. *Pain* 1:325–56

74. Kerr, F. W. L., Casey, K. L. 1976. *Neurosci. Res. Progr. Bull.* In press

75. Kitahata, L. M., Kosaka, Y., Taub, A., Bonikos, K., Hoffert, M. 1974. Lamina-specific suppression of dorsal-horn unit activity by morphine sulfate. *Anesthesiology* 41:39–48

76. Kuhar, M. J., Pert, C. B., Snyder, S. H. 1973. Regional distribution of opiate receptor binding in monkey and human brain. *Nature* 245:447–50

77. Lascelles, P. T., Evans, P. R., Merskey, H., Sabur, M. A. 1974. Plasma cortisol in psychiatric and neurological patients with pain. *Brain* 97:533–38

78. LeBars, D., Menetrey, D., Conseiller, C., Besson, J. M. 1975. Depressive effects of morphine upon lamina V cells activities in the dorsal horn of the spinal cat. *Brain Res.* 98:261–77

79. Li, C. L., Ahlberg, D., Lansdell, H., Gravitz, M. A., Chen, T. C., Ting, C. Y., Bak, A. F., Blessing, D. 1975. Acupuncture and hypnosis: effects on induced pain. *Exp. Neurol.* 49:272–80

80. Liebeskind, J. C. 1976. Pain modulation by central nervous system stimulation. See Ref. 26

81. Liebeskind, J. C., Giesler, G. J. Jr., Urca, G. 1976. Evidence pertaining to an endogenous mechanism of pain inhibition in the central nervous system. See Ref. 167

82. Liebeskind, J. C., Mayer, D. J., Akil, H. 1974. Central mechanisms of pain inhibition: studies of analgesia from focal brain stimulation. See Ref. 24, pp. 261–68

83. Liebman, J. M., Mayer, D. J., Liebeskind, J. C. 1970. Mesencephalic central gray lesions and fear-motivated behavior in rats. *Brain Res.* 23:353–70

84. Linzer, M., Van Atta, L. 1974. Effects of acupuncture stimulation on activity of single thalamic neurons in the cat. See Ref. 24, pp. 799–811

85. Lynn, B., Perl, E. R. 1976. Failure of acupuncture to produce localized changes in subjective cold pain ratings. See Ref. 26

86. Mann, F., Bowsher, D., Mumford, J., Lipton, S., Miles, J. 1973. Treatment of intractable pain by acupuncture. *Lancet* 2:57–60

87. Mayer, D. J. 1975. Pain inhibition by electrical brain stimulation: comparison to morphine. *Neurosci. Res. Progr. Bull.* 13(1):94–99

88. Mayer, D. J., Hayes, R. L. 1975. Stimulation-produced analgesia: development of tolerance and cross-tolerance to morphine. *Science* 188:941–43

89. Mayer, D. J., Liebeskind, J. C. 1974. Pain reduction by focal electrical stimulation of the brain: an anatomical and behavioral analysis. *Brain Res.* 68:73–93

90. Mayer, D. J., Price, D. D. 1976. Central nervous system mechanisms of analgesia. *Pain.* In press

91. Mayer, D. J., Price, D. D., Becker, D. P. 1975. Neurophysiological characterization of the anterolateral spinal cord neurons contributing to pain perception in man. *Pain* 1:51–58

92. Mayer, D. J., Price, D. D., Becker, D. P., Young, H. F. 1975. Threshold for pain from anterolateral quadrant stimulation as a predictor of success of percutaneous cordotomy for relief of pain. *J. Neurosurg.* 43:445–47

93. Mayer, D. J., Price, D. D., Rafii, A., Barber, J. 1976. Acupuncture hypalgesia: evidence for activation of a central control system as a mechanism of action. See Ref. 26

94. Mayer, D. J., Wolfle, T. L., Akil, H., Carder, B., Liebeskind, J. C. 1971. Analgesia from electrical stimulation in the brainstem of the rat. *Science* 174:1351–54

95. McGlashan, T. H., Evans, F. J., Orne, M. T. 1969. The nature of hypnotic analgesia and placebo response to ex-perimental pain. *Psychosom. Med.* 31:227–46

96. Mehler, W. R., Feferman, M. E., Nauta, W. J. H. 1960. Ascending axon degeneration following anterolateral cordotomy. *Brain* 83:718–50

97. Melzack, R. 1973. *The Puzzle of Pain.* New York:Basic Books

98. Melzack, R. 1975. The McGill Pain Questionnaire: major properties and scoring methods. *Pain* 1:277–99

99. Melzack, R., Melinkoff, D. F. 1974. Analgesia produced by brain stimulation: evidence of a prolonged onset period. *Exp. Neurol.* 43:369–74

100. Melzack, R., Southmayd, S. E. 1974. Dorsal column contributions to anticipatory motor behavior. *Exp. Neurol.* 42:274–81

101. Melzack, R., Stotler, W. A., Livingston, W. K. 1958. Effects of discrete brainstem lesions in cats on perception of noxious stimulation. *J. Neurophysiol.* 21:353–67

102. Melzack, R., Torgerson, W. S. 1971. On the language of pain. *Anesthesiology* 34:50–59

103. Melzack, R., Wall, P. D. 1965. Pain mechanisms: a new theory. *Science* 150:971–79

104. Melzack, R., Wall, P. D. 1970. Psychophysiology of pain. *Int. Anesthesiol. Clinics* 8:3–34

105. Mendell, L. 1966. Physiological properties of unmyelinated fiber projections to the spinal cord. *Exp. Neurol.* 16:316–32

106. Merskey, H., Spear, F. G. 1967. *Pain: Psychological and Psychiatric Aspects.* London:Bailliere, Tindall & Cassell

107. Mitchell, C. L., Kaelber, W. W. 1967. Unilateral vs. bilateral medial thalamic lesions and reactivity to noxious stimuli. *Arch. Neurol.* 17:653–60

108. Morrow, T. J., Casey, K. L. 1976. Analgesia produced by mesencephalic stimulation: effect on bulboreticular neurons. See Ref. 26

109. Nathan, P. W., Rudge, P. 1974. Testing the gate-control theory of pain in man. *J. Neurol. Neurosurg. Psychiatry* 37:1366–72

110. Nathan, P. W., Wall, P. D. 1974. Treatment of post-herpetic neuralgia by prolonged electric stimulation. *Br. Med. J.* 3:645–47

111. Noordenbos, W. 1959. *Pain.* Amsterdam:Elsevier

112. Oleson, T. D., Liebeskind, J. C. 1975. Relationship of neural activity in the raphe nuclei of the rat to brain stimula-

tion-produced analgesia. *Physiologist* 18:338

113. Oleson, T. D., Liebeskind, J. C. 1976. Modification of midbrain and thalamic evoked responses by analgesic brain stimulation in the rat. See Ref. 26

114. Oliveras, J. L., Besson, J. M., Guilbaud, G., Liebeskind, J. C. 1974. Behavioral and electrophysiological evidence of pain inhibition from midbrain stimulation in the cat. *Exp. Brain Res.* 20: 32–44

115. Oliveras, J. L., Redjemi, F., Guilbaud, G., Besson, J. M. 1975. Analgesia induced by electrical stimulation of the inferior centralis nucleus of the raphe in the cat. *Pain* 1:139–45

116. Oliveras, J. L., Woda, A., Guilbaud, G., Besson, J. M. 1974. Inhibition of the jaw opening reflex by electrical stimulation of the periaqueductal gray matter in the awake, unrestrained cat. *Brain Res.* 72:328–31

117. Orne, M. T. 1974. Pain suppression by hypnosis and related phenomena. See Ref. 24, pp. 563–72

118. Perl, E. R. 1968. Myelinated afferent fibres innervating the primate skin and their response to noxious stimuli. *J. Physiol. Lond.* 197:593–615

119. Perl, E. R. 1971. Is pain a specific sensation? *J. Psychiat. Res.* 8:273–87

120. Pilowsky, I., Spence, N. D. 1976. Illness behavior syndromes associated with intractable pain. *Pain* 2:61–71

121. Poggio, G. F., Mountcastle, V. B. 1960. A study of the functional contributions of the lemniscal and spinothalamic systems to somatic sensibility. *Bull. Johns Hopkins Hosp.* 106:266–316

122. Pomeranz, B., Wall, P. D., Weber, W. V. 1968. Cord cells responding to fine myelinated afferents from viscera, muscle and skin. *J. Physiol. Lond.* 199:511–32

123. Price, D. D. 1972. Characteristics of second pain and flexion reflexes indicative of prolonged central summation. *Exp. Neurol.* 37:371–87

124. Price, D. D. 1976. Modulation of first and second pain by peripheral stimulation and by psychological set. See Ref. 26

125. Price, D. D., Browe, A. C. 1973. Responses of spinal cord neurons to graded noxious and nonnoxious stimuli. *Brain Res.* 64:425–29

126. Price, D. D., Mayer, D. J. 1974. Physiological laminar organization of the dorsal horn of *M. mulatta*. *Brain Res.* 79:321–25

127. Price, D. D., Mayer, D. J. 1975. Neurophysiological characterization of the anterolateral quadrant neurons subserving pain in *M. mulatta*. *Pain* 1:59–72

128. Price, D. D., Wagman, I. H. 1970. Physiological roles of A and C fiber inputs to the spinal dorsal horn of *Macaca mulatta*. *Exp. Neurol.* 29:383–99

129. Reynolds, D. V. 1969. Surgery in the rat during electrical analgesia induced by focal brain stimulation. *Science* 164: 444–45

130. Rhodes, D. L. 1975. *A behavioral investigation of pain responsiveness following electrical stimulation of the rostral brain stem of the rat.* PhD thesis. Univ. Calif., Los Angeles, Calif.

131. Richardson, D. E., Akil, H. 1976. Stimulation-produced analgesia: acute study of effective periaqueductal and periventricular sites in the human. *J. Neurosurg.* In press

132. Richardson, D. E., Akil, H. 1976. Stimulation-produced analgesia: chronic self-administration in periventricular gray sites in intractable pain patients. *J. Neurosurg.* In press

133. Sharpe, L. G., Garnett, J. E., Cicero, T. J. 1974. Analgesia and hyperreactivity produced by intracranial microinjections of morphine into the periaqueductal gray matter of the rat. *Behav. Biol.* 11:303–13

134. Shealy, C. N., Mortimer, J. T., Hagfors, N. R. 1970. Dorsal column electroanalgesia. *J. Neurosurg.* 32:560–64

135. Smith, G. M., Egbert, L. D., Markowitz, R. A., Mosteller, F., Beecher, H. K. 1966. An experimental pain method sensitive to morphine in man: The submaximum effort tourniquet technique. *J. Pharmacol. Exp. Ther.* 154:324–32

136. Soper, W. Y. 1976. Effects of analgesic midbrain stimulation on reflex withdrawal and thermal escape in the rat. *J. Comp. Physiol. Psychol.* 90:91–101

137. Spanos, N. P., Barber, T. X. 1974. Toward a convergence in hypnosis research. *Am. Psychol.* 29:500–11

138. Sternbach, R. A. 1974. *Pain Patients: Traits and Treatment.* New York: Academic

139. Sternbach, R. A., Murphy, R. W., Timmermans, G., Greenhoot, J. H. Akeson, W. H. 1974. Measuring the severity of clinical pain. See Ref. 24, pp. 281–88

140. Sternbach, R. A., Timmermans, G. 1975. Personality changes associated with reduction of pain. *Pain* 1:177–81

141. Sternbach, R. A., Wolf, S. R., Murphy, R. W., Akeson, W. H. 1973. Traits of pain patients: the low back "loser". *Psychosomatics* 14:226–29

142. Swets, J. A. 1973. The relative operating characteristic in psychology. *Science* 182:990–1000

143. Torebjörk, H. E., Hallin, R. G. 1973. Perceptual changes accompanying controlled preferential blocking of A and C fibre responses in intact human skin nerves. *Exp. Brain Res.* 16:321–32

144. Torebjörk, H. E., Hallin, R. G. 1974. Identification of afferent C units in intact human skin nerves. *Brain Res.* 67:387–403

145. Travell, J., Rinzler, S. H. 1952. The myofascial genesis of pain. *Postgrad. Med.* 11:425–34

146. Tursky, B., Sternbach, R. A. 1967. Further physiological correlates of ethnic differences in responses to shock. *Psychophysiology* 4:67–74

147. Van Hees, J., Gybels, J. M. 1972. Pain related to single afferent C fibers from human skin. *Brain Res.* 48:397–400

148. Vertes, R.P., Miller, N. E. 1976. Brain stem neurons that fire selectively to a conditioned stimulus for shock. *Brain Res.* 103:229–42

149. Vierck, C. J. Jr., Hamilton, D. M., Thornby, J. I. 1971. Pain reactivity of monkeys after lesions to the dorsal and lateral columns of the spinal cord. *Exp. Brain Res.* 13:140–58

150. Vierck, C. J., Lineberry, C. G., Lee, P. K., Calderwood, H. W. 1974. Prolonged hypalgesia following "acupuncture" in monkeys. *Life Sci.* 15:1277–89

151. Wagman, I. H., Price, D. D. 1969. Responses of dorsal horn cells of *Macaca mulatta* to cutaneous and sural nerve A and C fiber stimuli. *J. Neurophysiol.* 32:803–17

152. Wall, P. D. 1967. The laminar organization of dorsal horn and effects of descending impulses. *J. Physiol. Lond.* 188:403–23

153. Wall, P. D. 1970. The sensory and motor role of impulses travelling in the dorsal columns towards cerebral cortex. *Brain* 93:505–24

154. Wall, P. D., Gutnick, M. 1974. Ongoing activity in peripheral nerves: the physiology and pharmacology of impulses originating from a neuroma. *Exp. Neurol.* 43:580–93

155. Wall, P. D., Sweet, W. H. 1967. Temporary abolition of pain in man. *Science* 155:108–9

156. Weisenberg, M., ed. 1975. *Pain: Clinical and Experimental Perspectives.* St. Louis:Mosby

157. Weisenberg, M. 1976. Cultural and racial reactions to pain. In *The Control of Pain,* ed. M. Weisenberg, New York: Psychol. Dimensions. In press

158. Weisenberg, M., Kreindler, M. L., Schachat, R., Werboff, J. 1975. Pain: anxiety and attitudes in black, white, and Puerto Rican patients. *Psychosom. Med.* 37:123–35

159. White, J. C. 1965. Cordotomy: assessment of its effectiveness and suggestions for its improvement. *Clin. Neurosurg.* 13:1–9

160. White, J. C., Sweet, W. H. 1972. *Pain and the Neurosurgeon.* Springfield, Ill: Thomas

161. Willis, W. D., Trevino, D. L., Coulter, J. D., Maunz, R. A. 1974. Responses of primate spinothalamic tract neurons to natural stimulation of the hindlimb. *J. Neurophysiol.* 37:358–72

162. Woodforde, J. M., Merskey, H. 1972. Personality traits of patients with chronic pain. *J. Psychosom. Res.* 16:167–72

163. Woodrow, K. M., Friedman, G. D., Siegelaub, A. B., Collen, M. F. 1972. Pain tolerance: differences according to age, sex, and race. *Psychosom. Med.* 34:548–56

164. Yaksh, T. L., Yeung, J. C., Rudy, T. A. 1976. Systematic examination in the rat of brain sites sensitive to the direct application of morphine: observation of differential effects within the periaqueductal gray. *Brain Res.* In press

165. Zimmermann, M. 1976. Neurophysiology of nociception. In *International Review of Physiology,* ed. R. Porter, Vol. 10, *Neurophysiology* 11, pp. 179–221. Baltimore: Univ. Park Press

166. Zotterman, Y. 1939. Touch, pain and tickling: an electrophysiological investigation in cutaneous sensory nerves. *J. Physiol. Lond.* 95:1–28

167. Zotterman, Y., ed. 1976. *Sensory Functions of the Skin in Primates, with Special Reference to Man.* Oxford:Pergamon. In press

Ann. Rev. Psychol. 1977. 28:61–84
Copyright © by Annual Reviews Inc. All rights reserved

AUDITORY COMMUNICATION ♦267
IN LOWER ANIMALS: ROLE OF
AUDITORY PHYSIOLOGY

Johann Schwartzkopff
Lehrstuhl für Allgemeine Zoologie der Ruhr-Universität Bochum,
Federal Republic of Germany

INTRODUCTION AND DEFINITIONS

Some distinctions should be made before reviewing the ample field of comparative studies in the physiology of hearing. In this paper, we use "hearing" to designate a certain level of sensory achievement for which particular organs have differentiated to receive specifically air- or waterborne sound within the acoustic far field. This involves the "auditory" parts of the vertebrate labyrinth as well as the tympanic organs of certain insects. Correspondingly, information exchange is termed "auditory communication" when particular organs produce acoustic signals which match the receiving sensory structures and processes. In the lower animals, such communication systems are based almost exclusively upon codes which are (*a*) organized intraspecifically and (*b*) transferred by inherited mechanisms. The contribution of individual learning or cultural tradition appears weak, if any, exists.

The increasing number and weight of contributions about bioacoustics, animal communication systems, and the special neurophysiology of hearing in animals has recently induced an increasing number of reviews, proceedings of meetings, and other summarizing papers, as well as handbook articles of high quality (e.g. 28, 64, 81, 104, 177, 204). Therefore, only a very restricted selection of research tendencies can be considered here. Attempting to survey the comparative aspects of our theme, we have chosen an arrangement in which the presentation of material follows roughly the zoological system:

A. Arthropoda (restricted to some orders of insects)
B. Anamnia (fishes, amphibians)
C. Sauropsida (reptiles, birds)
D. Mammalia (excluding man)

Though arthropods are opposed hereby to the vertebrate groups as a whole, they do not differ very much in their auditory performance from fishes and amphibians, and the levels of the communication systems are comparable too. Reptiles and birds have been studied with special emphasis on phylogenetic development (102, 163). In mammals, there has been interest, on the one hand, in the multifold adaptations by which defined morphological and functional types meet various ecological requirements (ultrasound hearing, communication in air or water, etc). On the other hand, intensive research work in certain laboratory mammals is leading from different directions toward understanding the significant role of the human ear in the origin of language and culture.

A. ARTHROPODA

General

The morphological and physiological basis of auditory communication could not emerge among all invertebrate groups but only within some orders of insects. Independently, tympanic hearing organs have originated several times from the tracheal respiratory system (see 165).[1] Communicative sounds are produced by stridulatory mechanisms that are connected with locomotion. By the discrimination of simple sounds, partners are recognized and localized, territories defended, fights between rivals provoked, and copulation initiated (28, 91, 97, 126, 205). The transfer of auditory information is based exclusively upon sounds and responsive behavior coded genetically. Estraspecific signals or abiotic acoustic stimuli are involved only secondarily.

The relation between the echo-guided bats and some of their prey, certain nocturnally flying moths provided with simple tympanic organs, constitutes an interesting exception from the rule, since a highly adaptive communication system has developed across the borders of species (Roeder and co-workers, cf 165). Hearing, e.g. in the Noctuidae, seems to be prepared exclusively for the identification of the hunting enemy and the control of evasive flight. The information needed is provided by the bats' sonar cries and received by two receptor neurons within the hearing organs of the moth. It is processed further through the thoracic and the supraesophageal ganglia, central auditory stations homologous in all insects. There is an overwhelming advantage in natural selection for "hearing" moths as compared with other insects flying at night and "probed" by bats without being alarmed. Therefore, atypical hearing devices have developed several times, as in the hawk moth, where a hearing mechanism developed from the mouth parts (141).

Bioacoustics of Insect Sounds

The various species-specific communication systems dealt with by recent research are to be introduced here by the most intensively studied orthopteres. Both sexes do hear, but singing is restricted to the males in most cases. Behaviorally, the

[1]Numbers preceded by "see" indicate references to secondary rather than primary literature.

production of acoustic signals may be combined with visual display (84, 97, 174). The central nervous programs of stridulation are organized hierarchically and coincide largely with those of general locomotion (24–27). Since many of the neurons and muscles which supply the legs or wings are bifunctional, a smaller number of motor units is required than would be needed for separate systems of sound production and locomotion. This illustrates an economic principle, detectable also within the auditory system of insects.

While the influences upon song activities through extrinsic acoustical and optical stimuli have been corroborated in many cases (84, 125), and quantitative studies on the interactions and the cybernetics have been conducted (60, 97, 126, 171), it is not known whether intrinsic control devices participate. So far, no case of direct regulation of the stridulation by hearing of the individual's voice has been reported. Muscular proprioceptors may influence slightly the bilateral phase relations of the stridulating extremities (24).

Besides biotic factors, climatic conditions influence communicative behavior. Sound production depends essentially upon the temperature, to which signal frequency is related almost linearly. This indicates rather complex nervous functions, since simple chemical reactions show exponential temperature dependency (188).

Auditory Pathway in Insects

The participation of a limited number of neurons with particular histochemical properties provides favorable material for morphological and physiological studies of the auditory pathway. In insects extracellular nerve impulses can be recorded and the fiber studied can be marked simultaneously by cobalt ions (136). By combining such experiments with classical methods of nerve degeneration or subvital sectioning of fiber tracts (73, 75, 135), a complete description of the system involved can be achieved. In all insects studied so far, the primary receptor axons of the tympanic organ terminate ipsilaterally within one of the thoracic ganglia of the ventral cord. Secondary and higher ranking interneurons decussate and/or ascend to upper centers after synaptic or ephaptic contacts within defined neuropiles. Additional ascending and descending giant fibers (called T-neurons) integrate and distribute the nervous information (73, 78, 139). Besides some recurrent connections and networks formed by the branches of several types of acoustic neurons, a defined sensorimotor transfer appears possible between the uppermost hearing center located within the protocerebrum and the song center found close by at a medial position. Furthermore, nervous wiring has been found within the thoracic ganglia by which acoustic sensory and motor centers are linked up at lower levels (75, 76).

Sensory Transduction and Coding

The primary events of mechanosensory transduction are performed by rather uniform receptors, the scolopidia, found in all insects. Recent electronmicroscopic studies disclose their intimate structure (see 165, 206). The sensory dendrite of the receptor neuron is coupled to the sound collecting chitinous membrane. Mechanical resonance of the latter determines the most efficient stimulus frequency (8, 109–111,

137). Also the mass or the spatial distribution of the scolopidia may influence the resonating vibrations of the segments of the tympanic membrane (118). The coupling to the tympanic system dampens the vibrations or shifts the preferential frequency (158).

The tympanic nerves entering the ventral cord contain less than 100 unmyelinated fibers which differ in their preferential frequencies (109, 137, 140), absolute thresholds, slope of intensity functions, and directionality (73, 77, 111, 140). From these characteristics, corresponding variations of the respective sensory transduction can be derived.

Central Nervous Processing

The evaluation of the perceived bioacoustic information seems to follow rather similar physiological principles in the moths, locusts, katydids, crickets, and cicades studied so far (see 165, 166; 73, 74, 118, 125, 126, 205).

Experiments using microelectrodes have demonstrated that sound intensity and its modulation are evaluated before other parameters by the central neurons. In the periphery, the absolute sensitivities are found between 20–40 dB SPL (sound pressure level) for the species, and differences of 40–50 dB exist within the bundle of one tympanic nerve (see 165; 1, 73, 137, 140). A single receptor neuron exhibits a dynamic range of 20–40 dB within which a 10 dB increment of sound strength enhances pulse rate two- to fivefold. The peripheral coding of intensity, which is rather uniform, on the whole, is followed by increasing diversification within the ascending auditory pathway (73, 75, 137). At the subesophageal level a few neuronal types are found which are less sensitive to intensity changes (flat slope of intensity function or on-response), while other types show enhanced sensitivity combined with a restriction of the dynamic range. Still other neurons develop nonlinearities, mostly optimum functions, thus coding a particular level of intensity (137). Roeder could demonstrate how such intensity-detecting neurons control specific behavior patterns, e.g. in the moth, the change from directed evasive flight away from the hunting bat to undirectional diving (see 165).

The evaluation of sound intensities is connected closely with phonotactic movements. The distance to the chirping mate is calculated from the loudness of the signals and translated into running velocity (125). The directional information is extracted from nervous interaction of bilateral intensity differences. The discharges of all primary fibers studied in various insects disclose directionality (see 165; 75, 77, 111, 137). In the locust, variation of the preferential direction was found within the fibers of one tympanic organ (140). Normally, sound impinging asymmetrically generates bilateral intensity differences of nerve discharges. The aspects employed in further physiological processing are still unresolved; the critical aspects may be the differences of neuronal latency or the height of excitation, or cooperation of both. In any case, the bilateral contrast is enhanced (lateral inhibition) (73, 75–77).

The contribution of frequency discrimination to insect communication is still controversial (109, 110, 165). The spectra of species-specific sounds, the reactions to auditory stimuli, and the threshold curves derived from electrophysiological studies correspond in general within one species. Moreover, in many cases single receptor fibers have been shown to be sensitive for a special range of frequencies.

This, however, does not prevent song of sympatric living species or surrounding noise to be received and transmitted to the CNS (74, 126). It is a most remarkable finding that the peripheral frequency selectivity is not improved at the ascending auditory stations, but appears frequently to be damped. This contrasts sharply to the improved differentiation of intensity information at the higher stations.

The hypothesis was suggested (137) that the peripheral frequency selectivity, depending on resonance (2, 110, 111, 118), is instrumental in improving the signal-to-noise ratio; this would allow the very small receptor organ, in spite of exposure to thermic noise, to attain lower thresholds than would otherwise be possible. During central processing, most of the frequency selectivity would be integrated in favor of the general sensitivity. It is interesting that the concept of peripheral sound analysis by partial resonance of the tympanic segments—the theory of hearing originally proposed by von Helmholtz for mammals—seems to be realized in insects.

Neurophysiological findings as well as behavioral studies [phonotaxis in crickets (208)] demonstrate excellent performance in the evaluation of temporal patterns in species-specific sounds (see 165; 91, 125, 126, 137, 138). The precise rhythmicity of motor command fiber discharges to the stridulatory organs (24–27) correspond with the coding of acoustic patterns by the neurosensory elements.

B. ANAMNIA

General

The hearing organ of higher vertebrates (Amniota), its sensory and neurophysiological performance, and the auditory communication are derived from precursory stages appearing in the bioacoustic behavior of lower vertebrates. The phylogenetic context is equivocal, however, in questions of detail. The Anamnia as a whole may as well be compared with the "hearing" orders of insects as with higher vertebrates, since both Anamnia and insects depend upon only a small number of discernible acoustic signals and since auditory communication is closely connected with orientation.

The involvement in sound reception of different labyrinthine maculae (sacculus, utriculus, lagena, papilla amphibiorum, papilla basilaris) varies in fishes and amphibians (16, 36, 124, 148). Though all fishes can hear, only a few species have developed systems of communication. In contrast, sound production is common at least among anuran amphibians.

Bioacoustic Behavior of Fishes

The older bioacoustic studies have shown that many fish species generate several sound signals in the course of their reproductive activities and especially in territorial behavior (114, 177). Such fish sounds may inhibit the aggressive behavior of conspecific males more efficiently than the playback of biotope noise (162). *Eupomacentrus partitus,* a reef fish of the Bahamas and southern Florida, lives sympatrically with several closely related species. Responding to the playback of "chirps," *Eupomacentrus* prefers its own signals, the temporal pattern being the most efficient parameter in recognition, especially the pulse interval (115). Similarly, species of

Myripristis orient preferentially toward the source of species-specific sound [however, within the near field only (130)].

Behavioral studies have shown, paradoxically, that those fish species that have the most sensitive hearing and rather good frequency discrimination capacity do not produce sound signals of their own (178), and do not depend therefore upon intraspecific communication (for discussion see 129, 167, 177).

Auditory Physiology of Fishes

Receptor problems prevail in recent research on fish hearing which can be dealt with here only cursorily (see 129). Sound oscillations of the surrounding fluid are perceived by the polarized receptors of the lateral line organ as well as by the hair cells of the inner ear, loaded by otoliths (39, 40). The lateral line organ is supposed to respond exclusively to the acoustic near field in which particle displacement (or velocity) is the efficient stimulus parameter (see 129, 167). The sensory endings of the inner ear seem to react to the near field and also to the far field which is characterized by periodic pressure changes. However, sound pressure too is transformed eventually into relative displacement of the oscillating inner ear structures through their different impedances (30, 129). The swimbladder, intercalated in sound transmission, improves the sensitivity and extends the higher frequency range of the ear in some species (14, 15, 127, 146, 147). But vibrations applied directly to the head may generate sensitive reactions of the microphonic potentials or the auditory nerve discharges (35, 145, 148).

The capacity of fishes to orient toward a source of sound was doubted throughout the older literature. More recent attempts to explain controversial findings by referring to the vectorial component of the near field (see 129, 130) do not reconcile behavioral results proving that fishes can locate a far field sound source (116, 156, 157). It was shown at the same time that the cochlear microphonics (CM) of the inner ear follow directional changes of vibrations applied to the head, or of waterborne sound in the transmission of which the swimbladder and tissue-conduction through the head are involved (30, 145, 146, 148). It is of special interest that the excitatory events within the inner ear are influenced not only by the direction of the sound oscillations but at the same time by its frequency, both parameters being interdependent. This may be related to variations of impedance and/or directional polarization within the hair cell population by which the divergent acoustic parameters are analyzed simultaneously.

Experiments testing single auditory nerve fibers have established tuning curves, though of rather broad shape (29, 148). The assumption is thereby supported that separate endorgans within the fish labyrinth receive certain frequencies preferentially and that within one macula some additional differentiation may take place. This concept of sound analysis by a place principle does not exclude that analysis by the periodicity of oscillations may also occur (time principle). This is emphasized by the phase-locking of nerve discharges up to the highest auditory center in the midbrain, as well as by the interpretation of psychometric studies (see 129; 33, 128, 166, 167).

The auditory thresholds of fishes can be masked by noise of varying bandwidths and center frequencies. Although this suggests interesting ecological implications, some comparative conclusions drawn from these data have been criticized (34, 59, 129, 178), since the psychometric concepts of "critical ratio" and "critical bandwidth," derived originally from auditory mechanisms in higher vertebrates (e.g. integrative action of the basilary membrane), were applied to quite different structures and functions in fishes.

Bioacoustic Behavior of Anurans

The performance of the anuran ear as presented by neurophysiology corresponds with the communication system as shown by behavioral studies. But almost nothing is known about the hearing in the larval stages (tadpoles) or in the urodeles. The mating partners are often brought together by calls coming from a considerable distance. The auditory isolation of species enhances phyletic differentiation since communication systems are encoded genetically. Sympatric species differ from each other by their calls, and this prevents hybridization. Allopatric populations of one species show geographic variation of their sounds as a first step towards genetic isolation [in Australian call-races of Limnodynastes (92)]. The variation of the calls is correlated with the distribution of "best frequencies" of auditory neurons [in races of Acris crepitans from New Jersey and South Dakota (13)]. Frogs, treefrogs, toads, etc (93, 154, 155, 198) can be compared with locusts, katydids, crickets, or cicades (125, 126) in regard to geographic variation and the modest number of acoustic signals available [e.g. six signals in Discoglossus (190)]. Furthermore, synchronized or alternating chorus songs improve communication over long distances in both groups. The amphibians too, as poikilothermic animals, depend upon environmental factors, mainly upon temperature which significantly modulates the call rate (122). The anurans differ essentially from insects in being controlled by sexual hormones in the production of and the reaction to sound signals, together with integrative reproductive behavior (120, 121, 152, 153). Both sexes of anurans have some sounds in common, but they also have some sex-specific signals (190). The mating call characterizes the males, while the females produce typical release calls (90).

Auditory Physiology of Anurans

The spectra of sound production show, in general, two center frequencies. Neighboring or sympatric species differ at least in one of these frequencies which is correlated with sensitivity peaks of hearing. This was shown by studies of single auditory neurons (94) or of evoked potentials at several levels (90, 96). The two sensitivity peaks are related to separate sensory epithelia, namely the papilla basilaris and the papilla amphibiorum. Auditory nerve fibers of the bullfrog transmitting low and medium range frequencies could be ascribed after electrophysiological criteria to the p. amphibiorum and high frequency fibers to the p. basilaris, as shown in transsection experiments (36).

Nevertheless, the spectral distribution of frequencies is probably not the crucial parameter in auditory communication of frogs but rather a predisposition for the sensory perception of messages. Experiments in which both the frequency composition and the temporal patterns of acoustic stimuli have been varied systematically demonstrate the outstanding role of repetition rate in the discrimination of call types (8, 41, 175). The differences in rhythmicity are minimized by the conventional sonagraphic display of sounds, but they are emphasized by oscillographic recording (93, 154, 155).

The central nervous mechanism which controls chorus song in frogs must not only recognize its species-specific quality but must, in addition, coordinate the rhythm. The sounds of individual frogs contributing to the chorus vary in their rates and duration if the animals are isolated. Laboratory experiments have demonstrated how sound production is influenced by the presentation of simulated songs. The general outline of a pacemaker mechanism influencing duration and period of the calls has been presented (95). The underlying reflex mechanism is probably located in the midbrain where senso-acoustic and moto-acoustic centers are arranged adjacently. The actual control of vocalization is combined with respiration, the nervous connections of which originate from medullary centers (153). The midbrain, on the other hand, is subordinated to parts of the preoptic nucleus upon which the input of other sensory systems and hormonal influences converge (152).

The anuran midbrain structures seem to organize the reflex orientation toward a source of sound as their third function after the recognition of messages and the initiation of acoustic responses. Though behavioral studies prove the capacity for auditory localization, the corresponding sensory mechanism is not yet clear. It seems that binaural differences are utilized, more probably of intensity than of time. Within the torus semicircularis, auditory neurons react to ipsilateral, contralateral, or bilateral stimuli. They are distributed in relations similar to those in mammals (80).

C. SAUROPSIDA

General

The phylogenetic relations of reptiles and birds are based essentially upon morphology, e.g. the middle ear structures where only the columella serves sound transmission. Auditory physiology seems to correspond essentially to these morphological dispositions, but it is also modulated by secondary differences of inner ear structures, metabolic intensity, and of bioacoustic behavior (67, 100, 102, 131, 132, 163, 164.) Auditory communication is preeminent only in certain avian orders, while vision contributes strongly in social contacts of other birds and of most reptiles, or hearing plays a negligible role at all (e.g. turtles or snakes).

Physiology of the Reptilian Ear

In reptiles (and birds) the perception of higher frequencies is limited by the sound transmission properties of the middle ear (falling off above 2 kHz), as demonstrated by Mössbauer methods (151). However, impedance matching for lower frequencies is performed as efficiently by the columella system as by the mammalian ossicles (194–196). In some species, adapted especially to the evaluation of substrate sound (Amphisbaena,[2] snakes), the columella may pick up vibrations directly, without an eardrum (42, 57).

[2]Spelled "Amphisbaenia" in Ref. 42.

Crocodiles and the nocturnal geckos, both communicating by sound (44, 193), come close to birds in the delicate structure of the inner ear (21, 102, 112, 113). The sensory transduction by the hair cells is accompanied by the same bioelectric phenomena in reptiles as it is in higher vertebrates, although the endocochlear DC-potential does not surpass 5 mV and is thus weaker than found in birds. Its physiological influence is supposed to be negligible (79). Cochlear microphonics can always be recorded, and they provide routine methods for the tests of hearing capacities (e.g. 42, 196). They depend upon metabolic activity and temperature in a complex way. In some cases, the influence of temperature is quite weak [Amphisbaena (43), caiman (79)]. In others, auditory sensitivity is shifted to higher frequencies by moderate increases of temperature [Iguanidae (192); evoked midbrain potentials of snakes (58)]. Among the various reptiles, only in the caiman have most stations of the auditory pathway been studied. The level of differentiation is not much inferior to that of birds. This finding is surprising since the biological significance of hearing seems to be limited; at least auditory communication remains on a very low level (44). But physiological performance is good enough, the CM responding sensitively to a broad band of frequencies [lowest threshold 0.2–2 kHz (195)]. The elongated papilla basilaris is represented by tonotopic organization of the cochlear nuclei (nucleus angularis and nucleus magnocellularis), comparable to the case in birds (50, 84, 99). In the gecko, where males and females communicate acoustically (112, 193) and the basilary membrane bearing 2000 hair cells is also rather long, the neuronal representation in the cochlear nuclei resembles that of the caiman. In both species, tuning curves of single auditory neurons can be compared with those of birds; they differ from other reptiles with less developed basilary membrane by the representation of higher frequencies, sharper tuning, lower thresholds (100, 102).

Also the mesencephalic torus semicircularis of the caiman is organized tonotopically, i.e. along a vertical axis; the lowest frequencies are represented on the surface (101). From there, according to degeneration studies (131, 132), the auditory fibers ascend through the intercalated nucleus reuniens pars centralis to the telencephalic field G which can be compared with field L in birds. Here neurons activated by acoustic stimuli have been found, but no tonotopic organization has yet been discovered (191). Also the course of the efferent connections descending from the superior olive of the cochlea corresponds closely in crocodiles and birds (see 164).

Auditory Communication in Birds

There is no other class of animals in which the differentiation of species is so closely connected with auditory communication as in birds. Correspondingly, vocalization is studied as instrumental behavior as well as for indications of evolution. Research on bird behavior is either derived from evolutionary questions or from problems of social organization and vocal communication is fundamental in both of these areas (64, 105, 106).

The ontogeny of vocalization, which begins before hatching, has raised multifold problems of behavioral maturation, of hormonal effects, and of auditory control (52–55, 84). Many acoustic signals, the model of which is inherited, need control by the ear to achieve final performance through exercise. Songs are demarcated from such sounds since they are acquired partially or completely by imitation or learning, and can be subject to tradition. The information transferred by avian vocalization is utilized for general species identification, in eliciting different behavior patterns, or for individual recognition, the latter especially by "learned" songs (9, 10, 64, 119).

The neurological aspect of vocalization has led to the question of how far motor output is regulated by auditory input. Electrical stimulation of nucleus intercollicularis, part of the torus semicircularis, induces the production of typical sounds (119). Chicken are rendered mute by the destruction of the rostral intercollicular area (18). Nucleus mesencephalicus lateralis is located adjacently, and is an important center of the ascending auditory pathway (119, 187). Further nervous structures qualified for control connections have been described at the telencephalic level.

For the precise sensomotor processing of sound production, the duet-song serves as an example. In some species the pair bonds are reinforced by duetting. The mates combine their consecutive contributions without delay thus achieving one integrated song (180). In *Cossypha heuglini* the speed of the respective song segments is coordinated either by changing the motif (in the male) or by variation of the tempo (of the female) (197).

Many song bird species and parrots are distinguished by the variability of their songs, and identification of the partner or the neighboring rival is achieved by this means (see 64; 9, 10). The recombination patterns of song elements [for example, in blackbird, nightingale, parrot (181–183)] have been analyzed and quantified, thus allowing for the design of a computer model describing the control mechanism of the communicative system. The degree of spontaneity as well as the interdependence of the vocalizations and of sensomotor interactions can be demonstrated by this model (172, 184).

Auditory communication of bird orders other than song birds or parrots is also integrated primarily into reproductive behavior; in *Alca torda* (razorbill), the parents identify the young after they have left the nesting site on the cliff and are swimming on the sea (68). Yodel sounds are part of ritual aggression in the common loon (*Gavia imme,* 143). General intraspecific recognition is based upon vocal signals in *Pediocoetes phasianellus* (83).

In all kinds of birds, sexual hormones influence development of the vocal mechanisms and the acquisition and production of song and other sounds (119; see also 3, 4, 170).

The auditory control of vocalization shows ample interspecific variation, especially in song birds, because of the outstanding proportion of song learned or "exercised under auditory control" (104, 119). On the other hand, pigeons or fowl and their relatives show little or no vocal disorder after destruction of the ears in early youth (see 119). After all, the reactions to so-called inherited signals are also subject to habituation; this is the case with the alarm call of the chaffinch (209). Such habituation does not occur under natural conditions, however, because of the continual renewal of the internal and external predisposition.

Ontogeny of Hearing in Birds

Since precocious birds communicate acoustically with each other and with the mother bird, the maturation of auditory capacities and corresponding behavior raises special questions. Auditory stimuli heard by chicken embryos between the thirteenth and eighteenth day of incubation influence vocalization frequency after hatching (134). Shortly before hatching, embryos of the wood duck *(Aix sponsa)* discriminate their mother's voice from that of the mallard *(Anas platyrhynchos)*, as indicated by bill-clapping activity within the egg (59a). Prenatal sensory experience may not only regulate later behavior, but corresponding sensory deprivation leads to perceptual deficits, as was shown by studies of the reaction of ducklings incubated normally, or isolated without external stimulation, or devocalized by embryonic surgery (52–55). Varying alterations appear in the following reaction that is activated by sounds: after complete auditory deprivation, frequency sensitivity is shifted corresponding with the loss of perception of the animal's own voice. The deficit can be repaired by artificial auditory stimuli, applied within 3 days after hatching. The sensitive period is correlated with the imprinting of social reactions towards the mother duck. Prenatal auditory experience has been shown to be effective in other precocious birds too, preparing social relations [e.g. quail (32)].

The behavioral findings on early sensory development are supplemented by neurophysiology: in embryonic ducklings neurons activated acoustically and arranged in tonotopic order have been found within the cochlear nuclei after 20 days of incubation. The representation of frequencies below 1 kHz appears first. A distribution of neurons corresponding with the normal audiogram is achieved no earlier than 2 days after hatching which takes place after 28 days of incubation (84). The evoked potentials of the brainstem in one-day-old chickens and ducklings show maximum sensitivity, respectively around 800 or 1500 Hz, corresponding with the differences of the maternal voices of the two species (150). In chickens one day and 3 weeks of age, or adult fowl, the audiogram as derived from CM extends to progressively higher frequencies with age (45).

Morphology and Physiology of the Avian Ear

Studies of the anatomical relations, the ultrastructures of the inner ear, the afferent and efferent nerve connections, and the general auditory physiology in birds (together with reptiles) have revealed a rather puzzling problem: the actual performance of the avian ear and its contribution to behavioral activities equal or are sometimes even superior to that of the mammals, in contrast to the less elaborate level of morphological differentiation (for discussion see 164; 151).

Only the adaptive structures of the external ear of birds clearly surpass those of the reptiles. In most birds, a screen of feathers covers the auditory orifice; this screen is permeable to sound and adapted to aerodynamic requirements. The most elaborate structures are found in the various species of owls which depend upon auditory localization of their prey. Correspondingly, the differentiation of ear flaps and the sensitivity of CM vary and are correlated with ecology (186). Other bird species, living on fish which they catch at various depths, have developed protective ear flaps in adaptive competition between the requirements of water pressure and auditory sensitivity (67).

The middle ear of birds equals the performance of that of mammals in the lower and medium frequency range. The impedances of air and inner ear fluids are matched, and thereby an undistorted sound transmission over 100 dB is provided (151). The (single) tympanic muscle seems to function like the (two) mammalian, at least in principle (51, 123), showing reflex activation by sound and damping of higher intensities.

Stimulation of the ear by filtered noise of narrow bandwidth raises thresholds almost solely within the applied band of frequencies, unlike the case in mammals. This suggests the possibility of differences in the peripheral auditory mechanisms of birds and mammals (149). In contrast, similarity in the damping of the basilary membrane (144) has been derived from the discharge pattern of auditory nerve fibers.

The primary process of sensory transduction as studied by experimental manipulation of the inner ear potentials in birds corresponds with that of other vertebrates and especially of the homeothermic mammals in its particular metabolic sensitivity (72, 163). The subsequent nervous transmission of auditory information differs in details from the mammalian auditory pathway. In the pigeon's auditory nerve fibers the discharge rate of spontaneous activity and of maximum response exceeds that found in the cat (144). Tuning curves, however, are of comparable selectivity and parallel the audiogram. Phase-locked discharges have been found up to at least 4 kHz.

Two-tone inhibition becomes more pronounced ascending from the auditory nerve to higher centers (65, 87). A clear tonotopic organization exists within nucleus angularis and nucleus magnocellularis, the medullary centers corresponding with the mammalian cochlear nuclei (85). In the higher diencephalic and telencephalic centers an orderly arrangement of frequency representation has not been detected so far (88). Phase-locked responses have been found occasionally even within field L of the caudal neostriatum, the uppermost auditory station in birds. The variations of the neuronal response pattern as seen in the peristimulus-time histograms follow the same general principles in the starling as described for the cat (87). Frequency- and intensity-modulation, laterality, and more complex species-specific sounds are efficient parameters, among others (88, 89). However, the efforts of many students have not yet been successful in searching for selective detector-systems of communicative signals that would not also be activated by other stimuli (166, 204).

Audiometry of Avian Hearing

Older findings about hearing in birds (see 164) have been corroborated by studies in which improved methods have been applied on additional species. Birds equal human auditory sensitivity within a restricted band of frequencies, centering around their vocalizations (1–3 kHz), but they are inferior in perceiving lower and higher notes [turkey (98), canary (19), parakeet (20)]. Frequency discrimination in the owl is a trifle superior to that in the cat [$DF/F = 0.005$–0.007 between 3 and 10 kHz

(133)]. In the parakeet too, a Weber-fraction of 0.007 was found between 1 and 4 kHz (20). In man, DF/F values are 2–3 times lower, which may be due to methodological difficulties in animal psychophysics. In the parakeet, masked thresholds have been measured (20) but, in contrast to man, a constant critical ratio has not been established. An optimum was found around 2 kHz, corresponding with auditory sensitivity and vocalization. The concept of critical bandwidth and the interpretation of the underlying mechanism in non-mammalian vertebrates is discussed in this context.

D. MAMMALIA

Mammalian Vocal Behavior

Bioacoustic research in mammals that is directed at understanding human language is not dealt with here. In primitive mammals as well as in other vertebrates, the ear is involved preferentially in securing social contacts. This was demonstrated by the functional analysis of 8 vocalizations in the house mouse [*Mus musculus* (23)]. In 5 species of *Microtus* (17), the neonates produce ultrasonic signals when the nest is exposed and the pups are cooled. The mother responds by approaching. The juvenile vocalization deteriorates drastically after the tenth day of life. At this age the direct dependency on the mother comes to an end, and the young might endanger themselves by calling outside of the nest. Correspondingly, neonate kittens begin with signalizing unspecifically their "need of care," when cooled, by ultrasonic sounds. The mother (sensibilized hormonally) reacts by nursing. Further vocalizations together with mother-related behavior are differentiated during the growing-up period of the young (56).

Only the primates among mammals surpass most bird species in the efficiency of their auditory communication system (104, 105). In the squirrel monkey *(Saimiri sciureus)*, which has been the subject of studies in auditory physiology and communication as well, the acoustic parameters of 26 separate types of vocalization have been analyzed thoroughly (200, 201). Since the variation of the single types shows normal distributions, each vocalization is considered homologous in morphology and function, which suggests having a defined communicative significance. Free ranging *Saimiri* groups emit the same signals in comparable situations as enclosed groups do. Young squirrel monkeys, raised by mothers which were rendered mute by denervation, or growing up in complete auditory isolation after surgical destruction of the ear, do not differ from normal fellows of the same age in the inventory of available vocalizations. The communicative sounds must be transferred therefore by inheritance, as is true for the calls of birds in contrast to parts of their songs (203). Though deafened adult squirrel monkeys produce the same sounds as hearing ones do, their overall behavior is louder and individual ranking seems to influence vocalization (176).

Audiometry in Mammals

The influence of methodological procedures on the results in the determination of auditory thresholds has been analyzed critically in the mouse (103). The data of older studies differ by 60 dB. Conforming results could be obtained by using either electroshock or reward methods: lowest threshold was found between 5 and 20 kHz (0–5 dB SPL) and the upper frequency limit of hearing at 100 kHz. In aging mice —as in man—auditory sensitivity is reduced mainly for higher frequencies, and before histological disturbances of the inner ear can be detected (22, 23).

The pinnipeds and cetaceans have achieved a high level of auditory communication and partially (Odontoceti) echo-orientation in their extreme adaptation to the aquatic life. The auditory system also is prepared for an efficient information exchange with the human, utilized in psychometry, for example, by conditioned vocalization (161) or instrumental methods (6, 62, 159, 160). In mammals in general, as well as in other vertebrates, center frequencies of vocalization and highest sensitivity of hearing are correlated, but the upper limit of hearing has frequently been found at considerably higher frequencies [chinchilla (66), raccoon (63), cat (169), lemur (49), owl monkey (7), cercopithecinae (173), sea lion (161), ringed seal (179), fresh water dolphin (70)]. Frequency discrimination, essential in communication and in orientation, is excellent in the porpoise which achieves DF/F-values of 0.003–0.004 [12–40 kHz (69)] or even (61) 0.002 (1–36 kHz) respectively 0.001 (27 kHz). Compared with the extremely cooperative behavior of the porpoise, the pinnipeds seem inferior (harbor seal: DF/F 0.013). The porpoise surpasses man in the discrimination of sound duration under water (9 or 25 kHz: 0.3–1.2 sec) where DT/T values of 0.06–0.08 were found (207). In general, the performance of the porpoise in learning auditory discrimination tasks reaches the level of primates, in correspondance with the cortical differentiation (62).

Behavioral results and auditory physiology have been compared, utilizing evoked potentials from the inferior colliculus of the California sea lion [*Zalophus californianus* (12)] and the porpoise [*Tursiops truncatus* (11)]. While the sea lion too can perceive ultrasound, its echo-orientation capacity is disputed, although this ability is well known in the porpoise. The midbrain can be activated by sounds up to 35 kHz with best sensitivity at 3–6 kHz. No peculiarities have been observed in comparison of the evoked potentials with those of other mammals used routinely in laboratories. In contrast, certain structures of the porpoise midbrain respond most sensitively to ultrasonic signals of very short duration and steep slope. Also the latencies and recovery periods of such responses are remarkably short and can thus be compared with findings in bats. The evoked potentials derived from other region of the inferior colliculi respond best to stimuli of longer duration and frequencies below 5 kHz which come close to the communicative whistle sound of the porpoise.

Auditory Physiology of Mammals

Mammalian hearing functions have been the subject of recent handbook volumes (81, 82). In this review, only few new findings can be dealt with. In the juvenile development of the mongolian gerbil *(Meriones unguiculatus)*, the morphological differentiation of the external, the middle, and the inner ear comes to an end at about the sixteenth day of life (38). This is correlated with the gradual beginning of auditory functions. Auditory reflexes and CM appear 12–14 days after birth and improve subsequently, achieving their final level between the twenty-third and ninetieth day. In the rat, the development of inner ear potentials is paralleled by increasing enzymatic activity (Na-, K-ATPase), responsible for active ion transport (86). The histological differentiation of the stria vascularis in which most of the ion pump mechanism is located also coincides with the generation of the endocochlear potential (EP). This reaches its final level in the kitten at the twenty-seventh to twenty-ninth day of life (37). Intercellular junctions (zonulae occludentes) have been studied by freeze etch techniques; these junctions tighten the cochlear duct in the guinea pig and thus the endolymphatic/perilymphatic barrier (71). The integrity of the ultrastructures at the molecular level is prerequisite for inner ear functions.

The waveform of the basilar membrane displacement can be observed, even at the moderate stimulation of 40 dB SPL by refined methods [subminiature capacity probe, Mössbauer techniques (199)]. However, the mechanical tuning thereby observed is still insufficient to account for the peripheral frequency analysis as derived from tuning curves in auditory nerve fibers. The threshold sensitivity of the latter, and therefore frequency selectivity, is reduced by hypoxia or by drugs which interfere with metabolism (31). This indicates the participation of a "second filter" based upon biochemical mechanisms. The rapid and reversible course of the impairment supports the assumption of this author that the electrogenic pump of the endocochlear potential is involved (168, 181, 185). This also would fit into a concept of the functions performed by the efferent olivocochlear bundle (46, 47). This is thought to control ion currents passing through the hair cells and thereby the spike generation at the afferent synapse. The tuning curves of auditory nerve fiber discharges (in the squirrel monkey) can be described partially as transformation of the basilar membrane waveform, but additional input was postulated; it is probably suppressive (48).

Another research group (142) has drawn conclusions from the distribution of phase-locked discharges concerning the displacement pattern of the basilar membrane. The discharge intensity functions reveal nonlinearities of the membrane displacement, when activation is by complex low frequency oscillations. The reciprocal damping results in effective amplitudes which become measurable by the phase-locked nerve signals. By the same mechanism, subthreshold displacement of the basilar membrane can become effective in nervous coding.

Detection of Auditory Messages

The further central nervous filtering of acoustic parameters and parameter combinations is based essentially upon the wiring of the activated neurons and, in particular, their tonotopic organization. The linear projection of frequencies along the cochlear duct is rearranged repeatedly within the ascending auditory pathway. A laminated representation of frequency has been demonstrated within the central nucleus of the inferior colliculus in cat (107), high-tone neurons being found in the center of the nuclear mass. The number of laminae corresponds with that of critical bands which leads to assumptions of neuronal cooperation and interaction within the lamina. The two-dimensional projection of the basilar membrane upon the primary auditory cortex area shows a disproportionate increase of high frequency representation (calculated from the bandwidth at the cochlear level and the cortical surface covered by the corresponding band). Frequency representation normal to the surface shows columnar organization (108).

The conventional studies of the auditory pathway by which variations of quantified acoustic parameters have been applied have been supplemented recently by tests with species-specific sounds which elicit selective neuronal reactions. Filtering processes that predispose to feature extraction were detected by this procedure. In the cat, single unit responses of the auditory nerve, of the cochlear nucleus, the inferior colliculus, the medial geniculate body, and of the primary auditory cortex show increasing selectivity when stimulated by the cat's voice or a filtered modification of it (189). The reaction of the auditory nerve fibers can be considered as due to a simple addition of the frequency components of the sound. Beginning at the cochlear nucleus level, inhibitory interaction can be observed, and this increases at higher stations. Inhibition depends in various ways upon the modulation pattern of the vocalization. Accordingly, the final feature extraction is thought to be based upon increasing inhibitory interaction between auditory neurons, initiated by the specific patterns of the natural sounds.

Auditory physiology approaches the correlates of recognition when studying feature extraction (204). Recognition can be defined as adequate motor response (166), but it remains difficult to relate the compound pattern of auditory neuron discharges to specific activities of motor command centers that initiate the responsive behavior. The whole of the neuronal filters, detector systems, etc involved at a time cannot be analyzed by procedures available or even conceivable today. But proof of highly specialized detector neurons is demonstrated increasingly. Single cortical elements of the squirrel monkey discharge selectively to certain components of the calls, but do not react, in general, to nonspecific acoustic stimuli (202). In other experiments (117), detector elements were found which react to several types of calls, while others recognize the common features of varying modulations of the isolation call. Finally, some neurons respond exclusively to a certain subcategory of the isolation call (117).

Literature Cited

1. Adams, W. B. 1971. Intensity characteristics of the noctuid acoustic receptor. *J. Gen. Physiol.* 58:562–79
2. Adams, W. B. 1972. Mechanical tuning of the acoustic receptor of *Prodenia eridania* (Cramer) (Noctuidae). *J. Exp. Biol.* 57:297–304
3. Arnold, A. P. 1975. The effects of castration on song development in zebra finches (*Poephila guttata*). *J. Exp. Zool.* 191:261–78
4. Arnold, A. P. 1975. The effects of castration and androgen replacement on song, courtship and aggression in zebra finches (*Poephila guttata*). *J. Exp. Zool.* 191:309–26
5. Deleted in proof

6. Beach, F. A. III, Hermann, L. M. 1972. Preliminary studies of auditory problem solving and intertask transfer by the bottlenose dolphin. *Psychol. Rec.* 22: 49–62
7. Beecher, M. D. 1974. Hearing in the owl monkey (*Aotus trivirgatus*): I. Auditory sensitivity. *J. Comp. Physiol. Psychol.* 86:898–901
8. Bibikov, N. G. 1971. The reaction of single neurons in the auditory system of the frog *Rana ridibunda* to pulsed tonal stimuli. *Zh. Evol. Biokhim. Fiziol.* 7:178–85
9. Brooks, R. J., Falls, J. B. 1975. Individual recognition by song in white-throated sparrows: I. Discrimination of

songs of neighbors and strangers. *Can. J. Zool.* 53:879–88
10. Brooks, R. J., Falls, J. B. 1975. Individual recognition by song in whitethroated sparrows. III. Song features used in individual recognition. *Can. J. Zool.* 53:1749–61
11. Bullock, T. H., Ridgway, S. H. 1972. Evoked potentials in the central auditory system of alert porpoises to their own and artificial sounds. *J. Neurobiol.* 3:79–99
12. Bullock, T. H., Ridgway, S. H., Suga, N. 1971. Acoustically evoked potentials in midbrain auditory structures in sea lions (Pinnipedia). *Z. Vergl. Physiol.* 74:372–87
13. Capranica, R. R., Frishkopf, L. S., Nevo, E. 1973. Encoding of geographic dialects in the auditory system of the cricket frog. *Science* 182:1272–75
14. Chapman, C. J., Sand, O. 1974. Field studies of hearing in two species of flatfish *Pleuronectes platessa* (L.) and *Limanda limanda* (L.) (Family Pleuronectidae). *Comp. Biochem. Physiol.* 47A:371–85
15. Clarke, N. L., Popper, A. N., Mann, J. A. Jr. 1975. Laser light-scattering investigations of the teleost swimbladder response to acoustic stimuli. *Biophys. J.* 15:307–18
16. Colnaghi, G. L. 1975. Saccular potentials and their relationship to hearing in the goldfish (*Carassius auratus*). *Comp. Biochem. Physiol.* 50A:605–13
17. Colvin, M. A. 1973. Analysis of acoustic structure and function in ultrasounds of neonatal microtus. *Behaviour* 44:234–63
18. De Lanerolle, N., Andrew, R. J. 1974. Midbrain structures controlling vocalization in the domestic chick. *Brain Behav. Evol.* 10:354–76
19. Dooling, R. J., Mulligan, J. A., Miller, J. D. 1971. Auditory sensitivity and song spectrum of the common canary (*Serinus canarius*). *J. Acoust. Soc. Am.* 50:700–9
20. Dooling, R. J., Saunders, J. C. 1975. Hearing in the parakeet (*Melopsittacus undulatus*): absolute thresholds, critical ratios, frequency difference limens, and vocalizations. *J. Comp. Physiol. Psychol.* 88:1–20
21. Düring, M. V., Karduck, A., Richter, H.-G. 1974. The fine structure of the inner ear in *Caiman crocodilus. Z. Anat. Entwicklungsgesch.* 145:41–65
22. Ehret, G. 1974. Age-dependent hearing loss in normal hearing mice. *Naturwissenschaften* 61:506
23. Ehret, G. 1975. Schallsignale der Hausmaus (*Mus musculus*). *Behaviour* 52:38–56
24. Elsner, N. 1973. The central nervous control of courtship behaviour in the grasshopper *Gomphocerippus rufus* L. (Orthoptera: Acrididae). *Neurobiol. Invertebr.*, 261–87
25. Elsner, N. 1974. Neuroethology of sound production in gomphocerine grasshoppers (Orthoptera: Acrididae). I. Song patterns and stridulatory movements. *J. Comp. Physiol.* 88:67–102
26. Elsner, N. 1974. Neural economy: bifunctional muscles and common central pattern elements in leg and wing stridulation of the grasshopper *Stenobothrus rubicundus* Germ. (Orthoptera: Acrididae). *J. Comp. Physiol.* 89:227–36
27. Elsner, N. 1975. Neuroethology of sound production in gomphocerine grasshoppers (Orthoptera: Acrididae). II. Neuromuscular activity underlying stridulation. *J. Comp. Physiol.* 97:291–322
28. Elsner, N., Huber, F. 1973. Neurale Grundlagen artspezifischer Kommunikation bei Orthopteren. *Fortsch. Zool.* 22:1–48
29. Enger, P. S. 1967. Hearing in herring. *Comp. Biochem. Physiol.* 22:527–38
30. Enger, P. S., Hawkins, A. D., Sand, O., Chapman, C. J. 1973. Directional sensitivity of saccular microphonic potentials in the haddock. *J. Exp. Biol.* 59:425–33
31. Evans, E. F. 1975. The sharpening of cochlear frequency selectivity in the normal and abnormal cochlea. *Audiology* 14:419–42
32. Ewing, A. T., Ewing, R. W., Vanderweele, D. A. 1975. Imprinting in quail as a function of pre- and postnatal auditory stimulation. *Psychol. Rec.* 25:333–38
33. Fay, R. R. 1972. Perception of amplitude-modulated auditory signals by the goldfish. *J. Acoust. Soc. Am.* 52:660–66
34. Fay, R. R. 1974. Masking of tones by noise for the goldfish (*Carassius auratus*). *J. Comp. Physiol. Psychol.* 87:708–16
35. Fay, R. R., Popper, A. N. 1975. Modes of stimulation of the teleost ear. *J. Exp. Biol.* 62:379–87
36. Feng, A. S., Narins, P. M., Capranica, R. R. 1975. Three populations of primary auditory fibers in the bullfrog (*Rana catesbeiana*): Their peripheral

origins and frequency sensitivities. *J. Comp. Physiol. Sens. Neural Behav. Physiol.* 100:221–30

37. Fernández, C., Hinojosa, R. 1974. Postnatal development of endocochlear potential and stria vascularis in the cat. *Acta Otolaryngol.* 78:173–86

38. Finck, A., Schneck, C. D., Hartman, A. F. 1972. Development of cochlear function in the neonate mongolian gerbil (*Meriones unguiculatus*). *J. Comp. Physiol. Psychol.* 78:375–80

39. Flock, A. 1974. Information transfer at the synapse between hair cells and sensory nerve fibres. *Abh. Rheinisch-Westfael. Akad. Wiss.* 53:347–54

40. Flock, A., Jorgensen, M., Russell, I. 1973. The physiology of individual hair cells and their synapses. In *Basic Mechanisms in Hearing*, ed. A. R. Moller, 273–306. New York/London: Academic. 941 pp.

41. Fouquette, M. J. Jr. 1975. Speciation in chorus frogs: I. Reproductive character displacement in the *Pseudacris nigrita* complex. *Syst. Zool.* 24:16–23

42. Gans, C., Wever, E. G. 1972. The ear and hearing in Amphisbaenia (Reptilia). *J. Exp. Zool.* 179:17–34

43. Gans, C., Wever, E. G. 1974. Temperature effects on hearing in two species of Amphisbaenia. *Nature* 250:79–80

44. Garrick, L. D. 1975. Structure and pattern of the roars of chinese alligators (*Alligator sinensis* Fauvel). *Herpetology* 31:26–31

45. Gates, G. R., Perry, D. R., Coles, R. B. 1975. Cochlear microphonics in the adult domestic fowl (*Gallus domesticus*). *Comp. Biochem. Physiol.* 51A: 251–52

46. Geisler, C. D. 1974. Hypothesis on the function of the crossed olivocochlear bundle. *J. Acoust. Soc. Am.* 56:1908–9

47. Geisler, C. D. 1974. Model of crossed olivocochlear bundle effects. *J. Acoust. Soc. Am.* 56:1910–12

48. Geisler, C. D., Rhode, W. S., Kennedy, D. T. 1974. Responses to tonal stimuli of single auditory nerve fibers and their relationship to basilar membrane motion in the squirrel monkey. *J. Neurophysiol.* 37:1156–72

49. Gillette, R. G., Brown, R., Herman, P., Vernon, S., Vernon, J. 1973. The auditory sensitivity of the lemur. *Am. J. Phys. Anthropol.* 38:365–70

50. Glatt, A.-F. 1975. Comparative morphological studies on the acoustic system of several selected reptiles: A. *Cai-*

man crocodilus. *Rev. Suisse Zool.* 82:257–82

51. Golubeva, T. B. 1972. The reflex activity of the tympanal muscle in the owl *Asio otus* (Russ.) *Zh. Evol. Biokhim. Fiziol.* 8:173–81

52. Gottlieb, G. 1974. On the acoustic basis of species identification in wood ducklings (*Aix sponsa*). *J. Comp. Physiol. Psychol.* 87:1038–48

53. Gottlieb, G. 1975. Development of species identification in ducklings: I. Nature of perceptual deficit caused by embryonic auditory deprivation. *J. Comp. Physiol. Psychol.* 89:387–99

54. Gottlieb, G. 1975. Development of species identification in ducklings: II. Experiential prevention of perceptual deficit caused by embryonic auditory deprivation. *J. Comp. Physiol. Psychol.* 89: 675–94

55. Gottlieb, G. 1975. Development of species identification in ducklings: III. Maturational rectification of perceptual deficit caused by auditory deprivation. *J. Comp. Physiol. Psychol.* 89:899–912

56. Härtel, R. 1975. Zur Struktur und Funktion akustischer Signale im Pflegesystem der Hauskatze (*Felis catus L.*) *Biol. Zentralbl.* 94:187–204

57. Hartline, P. H. 1971. Physiological basis for detection of sound and vibration in snakes. *J. Exp. Biol.* 54:349–71

58. Hartline, P. H. 1971. Mid-brain responses of the auditory and somatic vibration systems in snakes. *J. Exp. Biol.* 54:373–90

59. Hawkins, A. D., Chapman, C. J. 1975. Masked auditory thresholds in the cod, *Gadus morhua* L. *J. Comp. Physiol.* 103:209–26

59a. Heaton, M. B. 1972. Prenatal auditory discrimination in the wood duck (*Aix sponsa*). *Anim. Behav.* 20:421–24

60. Heiligenberg, W. 1969. The effect of stimulus chirps on a cricket's chirping (*Acheta domesticus*). *Z. Vergl. Physiol.* 65:70–97

61. Herman, L. M., Arbeit, W. R. 1972. Frequency difference limens in the bottlenose dolphin: 1–70 KC/S. *J. Aud. Res.* 2:109–20

62. Herman, L. M., Arbeit, W. R. 1973. Stimulus control and auditory discrimination learning sets in the bottlenose dolphin. *J. Exp. Anal. Behav.* 19: 379–94

63. Hertzler, D. R., Saunders, J. C., Gourevitch, G. R., Herman, P. N. 1970. Cochlear and neural activity in the audi-

tory system of the raccoon. *J. Aud. Res.* 10:155–63
64. Hinde, R. A. 1969. *Bird Vocalizations.* Cambridge Univ. Press. 394 pp.
65. Hotta, T. 1971. Unit responses from the nucleus angularis in the pigeon's medulla. *Comp. Biochem. Physiol.* 40A: 415–24
66. Hunter-Duvar, I. M., Bredberg, G. 1974. Effects of intense auditory stimulation: hearing losses and inner ear changes in the chinchilla. *J. Acoust. Soc. Am.* 55:795–801
67. Iljichev, V. D. 1974. Adaptationsökologische Parallelismen—mosaikartige Evolution. Das Hörsystem der Vögel als Objekt der funktionellen Morphologie. *Biol. Zentralbl.* 93:165–80
68. Ingold, P. 1973. Zur lautlichen Beziehung des Elters zu seinem Küken bei Tordalken (*Alca torda*). *Behaviour* 45: 154–90
69. Jacobs, D. W. 1972. Auditory frequency discrimination in the Atlantic bottlenose dolphin, *Tursiops truncatus* Montague: A preliminary report. *J. Acoust. Soc. Am.* 52:696–98
70. Jacobs, D. W., Hall, J. D. 1972. Auditory thresholds of a fresh water dolphin, *Inia geoffrensis* Blainville. *J. Acoust. Soc. Am.* 51:530–33
71. Jahnke, K. 1975. The fine structure of freeze-fractured intercellular junction in the guinea pig inner ear. *Acta Otolaryngol.* 336:5–40
72. Jorgensen, F. O. 1975. Frequency-dependent changes in the amplitude of the cochlear microphonic potential of the pigeon ear during transient anoxia. *Acta Physiol. Scand.* 94:14–28
73. Kalmring, K. 1975. The afferent auditory pathway in the ventral cord of *Locusta migratoria* (Acrididae). I. Synaptic connectivity and information processing among the auditory neurons of the ventral cord. *J. Comp. Physiol.* 104:103–41
74. Kalmring, K. 1975. The afferent auditory pathway in the ventral cord of *Locusta migratoria* (Acrididae). II. Responses of the auditory ventral cord neurons to natural sounds. *J. Comp. Physiol.* 104:143–59
75. Kalmring, K., Rheinlaender, J. 1974. The afferent auditory system in the CNS of katydids and locustids. *Abh. Rheinisch-Westfael. Akad. Wiss.* 53: 313–23
76. Kalmring, K., Rheinlaender, J., Rehbein, H. G. 1972. Akustische Neuronen im Bauchmark der Wanderheuschrecke

Locusta migratoria. Z. Vergl. Physiol. 76:314–32
77. Kalmring, K., Rheinlaender, J., Römer, H. 1972. Akustische Neuronen im Bauchmark von *Locusta migratoria.* Der Einfluss der Schallrichtung auf die Antwortmuster *J. Comp. Physiol.* 80:325–52
78. Kalmring, K., Römer, H., Rehbein, H. G. 1974. Connections of acoustic neurons within the CNS of grasshoppers. *Naturwissenschaften* 61:454–55
79. Kauffman, G. 1974. Zur Abhängigkeit der Cochleapotentiale des Kaimans vom Stoffwechsel, von aktiven Transporten und von der Temperatur. *J. Comp. Physiol.* 90:245–73
80. Kaulen, R., Lifschitz, W., Palazzi, C., Adrian, H. 1972. Binaural interaction in the inferior colliculus of the frog. *Exp. Neurol.* 37:469–80
81. Keidel, W. D., Neff, W. D., eds. 1974. *Handbook of Sensory Physiology,* Vol. V/1. Berlin, Heidelberg, New York: Springer. 736 pp.
82. Keidel, W. D., Neff, W. D., eds. 1975. *Handbook of Sensory Physiology,* Vol. V/2. Berlin, Heidelberg, New York: Springer. 526 pp.
83. Kermott, L. H., Oring, L. W. 1975. Acoustical communication of male sharp-tailed grouse (*Pedioecetes phasianellus*) on a North Dakota dancing ground. *Anim. Behav.* 23:375–86
84. Kerr, G. E. 1974. Visual and acoustical communicative behaviour in *Dissosteira carolina* (Orthoptera: Acrididae). *Can. Entomol.* 106:263–72
85. Konishi, M. 1973. Development of auditory neuronal responses in avian embryos. *Proc. Natl. Acad. Sci. USA* 70:1795–98
86. Kuijpers, W. 1974. Na-K-ATPase activity in the cochlea of the rat during development. *Acta Otolaryngol.* 78: 341–44
87. Leppelsack, H.-J. 1974. Funktionelle Eigenschaften der Hörbahn im Feld L des Neostriatum caudale des Staren (*Sturnus vulgaris* L., Aves). *J. Comp. Physiol.* 88:271–320
88. Leppelsack, H.-J. 1974. The effect of acoustic parameters on single unit responses in higher stations of the auditory pathway of birds. *Abh. Rheinisch-Westfael. Akad. Wiss.* 53:243–49
89. Leppelsack, H.-J., Vogt, M. 1976. Responses of auditory neurons in the forebrain of a songbird to stimulation with species-specific sounds. *J. Comp. Physiol. A* 107:263–74

90. Levenko, B. A. 1973. Hearing and voice in the acoustic behavior of anurans (Russ.) *Biol. Nauki* 16:25–35
91. Lewis, D. B., Pye, J. D., Howse, P. E. 1971. Sound reception in the bush cricket *Metrioptera brachyptera* (L.) (Orthoptera, Tettigonioidea). *J. Exp. Biol.* 55:241–51
92. Littlejohn, M. J., Roberts, J. D. 1975. Acoustic analysis of an intergrade zone between two call races of the *Limnodynastes tasmaniensis* complex (Anura: Leptodactylidae) in southeastern Australia. *Aust. J. Zool.* 23:113–22
93. Loercher, K., Schneider, H. 1973. Vergleichende bio-akustische Untersuchungen an der Kreuzkröte, *Bufo calamita* (Laur.), und der Wechselkröte, *Bufo v. viridis* (Laur.). *Z. Tierpsychol.* 32:506–21
94. Loftus-Hills, J. J. 1971. Neural correlates of acoustic behavior in the Australian bullfrog *Limnodynastes dorsalis* (Anura: Leptodactylidae). *Z. Vergl. Physiol.* 74:140–52
95. Loftus-Hills, J. J. 1974. Analysis of an acoustic pacemaker in Strecker's chorus frog, *Pseudacris streckeri* (Anura: Hylidae). *J. Comp. Physiol.* 90:75–87
96. Loftus-Hills, J. J., Johnstone, B. M. 1970. Auditory function, communication, and the brain-evoked response in anuran amphibians. *J. Acoust. Soc. Am.* 47:1131–38
97. Loher, W., Chandrashekaran, M. K. 1972. Communicative behavior of the grasshopper *Syrbula fuscovittata* (Thomas) (Gomphocerinae) with particular consideration of the male courtship. *Z. Tierpsychol.* 31:78–97
98. Maiorana, V. A., Schleidt, W. M. 1972. The auditory sensitivity of the turkey. *J. Aud. Res.* 12:203–7
99. Manley, G. A. 1970. Frequency sensitivity of auditory neurons in the caiman cochlear nucleus. *Z. Vergl. Physiol.* 66:251–56
100. Manley, G. A. 1970. Comparative studies of auditory physiology in reptiles. *Z. Vergl. Physiol.* 67:363–81
101. Manley, G. A. 1971. Single unit studies in the midbrain auditory area of caiman. *Z. Vergl. Physiol.* 71:255–61
102. Manley, G. A. 1971. Some aspects of the evolution of hearing in vertebrates. *Nature* 230:506–9
103. Markl, H., Ehret, G. 1973. Die Hörschwelle der Maus (*Mus musculus*). *Z. Tierpsychol.* 33:274–86
104. Marler, P. 1965. Communication in monkeys and apes. In *Primate Behavior*, ed. I. de Vore, 544–84. New York: Holt, Rinehart & Winston
105. Marler, P. 1969. Animals and man: Communication and its development. In *Communication*, ed. J. D. Roslansky, 25–62. Amsterdam: North Holland
106. Marler, P., Mundinger, P., Waser, M. S., Lutjen, A. 1972. Effects of acoustical stimulation and deprivation on song development in red-winged blackbirds (*Agelaius phoeniceus*). *Anim. Behav.* 20:586–606
107. Merzenich, M. M., Reid, M. D. 1974. Representation of the cochlea within the inferior colliculus of the cat. *Brain Res.* 77:397–415
108. Merzenich, M. M., Knight, P. L., Roth, G. L. 1975. Representation of cochlea within primary auditory cortex in the cat. *J. Neurophysiol.* 38:231–49
109. Michelsen, A. 1971. The physiology of the locust ear. I. Frequency sensitivity of single cells in the isolated ear. *Z. Vergl. Physiol.* 71:49–62
110. Michelsen, A. 1971. The physiology of the locust ear. II. Frequency discrimination based upon resonances in the tympanum. *Z. Vergl. Physiol.* 71:63–101
111. Michelsen, A. 1971. The physiology of the locust ear. III. Acoustical properties of the intact ear. *Z. Vergl. Physiol.* 71:102–28
112. Miller, M. R. 1973. A scanning electron microscope study of the papilla basilaris of *Gekko gecko. Z. Zellforsch.* 136:307–28
113. Miller, M. R. 1974. Scanning electron microscope studies of some skink papillae basilares. *Cell Tissue Res.* 150:125–42
114. Moulton, J. M. 1969. The classification of acoustic communicative behavior among teleost fishes. In *Approaches to Animal Communication*, ed. T. A. Sebeok, A. Ramsay, 146–78. Den Haag, Paris: Mouton
115. Myrberg, A. A. Jr., Spires, J. Y. 1972. Sound discrimination by the bicolor damselfish, *Eupomacentrus partitus. J. Exp. Biol.* 57:727–35
116. Myrberg, A. A. Jr., Ha, S. J., Walewski, S., Banbury, J. C. 1972. Effectiveness of acoustic signals in attracting epipelagic sharks to an underwater sound source. *Bull. Mar. Sci.* 22:926–49
117. Newman, J. D., Wollberg, Z. 1973. Responses of single neurons in the auditory cortex of squirrel monkeys to vari-

ants of a single call type. *Exp. Neurol.* 40:821–24

118. Nocke, H. 1975. Physical and physiological properties of the tettigoniid ("Grasshopper") ear. *J. Comp. Physiol. Sens. Neurol. Behav. Physiol.* 100:25–58

119. Nottebohm, F. 1975. Vocal behavior in birds. In *Avian Biology,* ed. D. S. Farner, J. R. King, K. C. Parkes, 5:287–332. New York: Academic. 523 pp.

120. Obert, H.-J. 1974. Untersuchungen zur hormonalen Steuerung der Rufaktivität von Fröschen und Kröten der Familien Ranidae, Discoglossidae, Hylidae und Bufonidae (*Rana temporaria, Bombina variegata, Hyla arborea, Bufo bufo*). *Zool. Jahrb. Physiol.* 78:219–41

121. Obert, H.-J. 1975. Investigations into the significance of testicles and interrenal gland in the hormonal control of mating call activity in the common frog *Rana temporaria* (L.) *Zool. Jahrb. Physiol.* 79:246–61

122. Obert, H.-J. 1975. The dependence of calling activity in *Rana esculenta* Linné 1758 and *Rana ridibunda* Pallas 1771 upon exogenous factors (Ranidae, Anura). *Oecologia* 18:317–28

123. Oeckinghaus, H., Schwartzkopff, J. 1975. Elektrische Aktivierung des Mittelohrmuskels beim Staren. *Naturwissenschaften* 62:582

124. Offutt, G. C. 1974. Structures for the detection of acoustic stimuli in the atlantic codfish, *Gadus morhua. J. Acoust. Soc. Am.* 56:665–71

125. Popov, A. V. 1975. The structure of tymbals and characteristic of sound signals of singing cicadas (Homoptera, Cicadidae) from the southern regions of the USSR (Russ.). *Entomol. Obozr.* 54:258–90

126. Popov, A. V., Shuvalov, V. F., Svetlogorskaya, I. D., Markovich, A. M. 1974. Acoustic behaviour and auditory system in insects. *Abh. Rheinisch-Westfael. Akad. Wiss.* 53:281–306

127. Popper, A. N. 1974. The response of the swim bladder of the goldfish (*Carassius auratus*) to acoustic stimuli. *J. Exp. Biol.* 60:295–304

128. Popper, A. N., Clarke, N. L. 1976. The auditory system of the goldfish (*Carassius auratus*): Effects of intense acoustic stimulation. *Comp. Biochem. Physiol.* 53A:11–18

129. Popper, A. N., Fay, R. R. 1973. Sound detection and processing by teleost fishes: a critical review. *J. Acoust. Soc. Am.* 53:1515–29

130. Popper, A. N., Salmon, M., Parvulescu, A. 1973. Sound localization by the Hawaiian squirrelfishes, *Myripristis berndti* and *M. argyromus. Anim. Behav.* 21:86–97

131. Pritz, M. B. 1974. Ascending connections of a midbrain auditory area in a crocodile, *Caiman crocodilus. J. Comp. Neurol.* 153:179–97

132. Pritz, M. B. 1974. Ascending connections of a thalamic auditory area in a crocodile, *Caiman crocodilus. J. Comp. Neurol.* 153:199–214

133. Quine, D. B., Konishi, M. 1974. Absolute frequency discrimination in the barn owl. *J. Comp. Physiol.* 93:347–60

134. Rajecki, D. W. 1974. Effects of prenatal exposure to auditory or visual stimulation on postnatal distress vocalizations in chicks. *Behav. Biol.* 11:525–36

135. Rehbein, H. G. 1973. Experimentellanatomische Untersuchungen über den Verlauf der Tympanalnervenfasern im Bauchmark von Feldheuschrecken, Laubheuschrecken und Grillen. *Verh. Dtsch. Zool. Ges.* 66:184–89

136. Rehbein, H. G., Kalmring, K., Römer, H. 1974. Structure and function of acoustic neurons in the thoracic ventral nerve cord of *Locusta migratoria* (Acrididae). *J. Comp. Physiol.* 95:263–80

137. Rheinlaender, J. 1975. Transmission of acoustic information at three neuronal levels in the auditory system of *Decticus verrucivorus* (Tettigoniidae, Orthoptera). *J. Comp. Physiol.* 97:1–53

138. Rheinlaender, J., Kalmring, K. 1973. Die afferente Hörbahn im Bereich des Zentralnervensystems von *Decticus verrucivorus* (Tettigoniidae). *J. Comp. Physiol.* 85:361–410

139. Rheinlaender, J., Kalmring, K., Römer, H. 1972. Akustische Neuronen mit T-Struktur im Bauchmark von Tettigoniiden. *J. Comp. Physiol.* 77:208–24

140. Römer, H., Schwartzkopff, J. 1975. Frequenz- und richtungs-spezifische Rezeptoren der Wanderheuschrecke. *Naturwissenschaften* 62:581

141. Roeder, K. D. 1975. Acoustic interneuron responses compared in certain hawk moths. *J. Insect Physiol.* 21:1625–32

142. Rose, J. E., Kitzes, L. M., Gibson, M. M., Hind, J. E. 1974. Observations on phase-sensitive neurons of anteroventral cochlear nucleus of the cat: Nonlinearity of cochlear output. *J. Neurophysiol.* 37:218–53

143. Rummel, L., Goetzinger, C. 1975. The communication of intraspecific aggression in the common loon. *Auk* 92: 333–46
144. Sachs, M. B., Young, E. D., Lewis, R. H. 1974. Discharge patterns of single fibers in the pigeon auditory nerve. *Brain Res.* 70:431–47
145. Sand, O. 1974. Directional sensitivity of microphonic potentials from the perch ear. *J. Exp. Biol.* 60:881–99
146. Sand, O., Enger, P. S. 1973. Function of the swimbladder in fish hearing. In *Basic Mechanisms in Hearing,* ed. A. R. Moller, 893–910. New York, London: Academic. 941 pp.
147. Sand, O., Enger, P. S. 1973. Evidence for an auditory function of the swimbladder in the cod. *J. Exp. Biol.* 59:405–14
148. Sand, O., Enger, P. S. 1974. Possible mechanisms for directional hearing and pitch discrimination in fish. *Abh. Rheinisch-Westfael. Akad. Wiss.* 53:223–42
149. Saunders, J. C., Dooling, R. 1974. Noise-induced threshold shift in the parakeet *(Melopsittacus undulatus). Proc. Natl. Acad. Sci. USA* 71:1962–65
150. Saunders, J. C., Gates, G. R., Coles, R. B. 1974. Brain-stem evoked responses as an index of hearing thresholds in one-day-old chicks and ducklings. *J. Comp. Physiol. Psychol.* 86: 426–31
151. Saunders, J. C., Johnstone, B. M. 1972. A comparative analysis of middle-ear function in non-mammalian vertebrates. *Acta Otolaryngol.* 73:353–61
152. Schmidt, R. S. 1969. Preoptic activation of mating call orientation in female anurans. *Behavior* 35:114–27
153. Schmidt, R. S. 1971. A model of the central mechanisms of male anuran acoustic behavior. *Behavior* 39:288–317
154. Schneider, H. 1973. Die Paarungsrufe einheimischer Ranidae (Anura, Amphibia). *Bonn. Zool. Beitr.* 24:51–61
155. Schneider, H., Nevo, E. 1972. Bioacoustic study of the yellow-lemon treefrog, *Hyla arborea savignyi* Audouin. *Zool. Jahrb. Physiol.* 76:497–506
156. Schuijf, A. 1975. Directional hearing of cod *(Gadus morhua)* under approximate free field conditions. *J. Comp. Physiol.* 98:307–32
157. Schuijf, A., Buwalda, R. J. A. 1975. On the mechanism of directional hearing in cod *(Gadus morhua* L.) *J. Comp. Physiol.* 98:333–43
158. Schumacher, R., Houtermans, B. 1975. Vergleich des primären Rezeptor-

bereiches der tympanalen und atympanalen tibialen Skolopalorgane von 14 mitteleuropäischen Laubheuschrecken-Arten (Orthopteren: Tettigonioidea). *Entomol. Ger.* 1:97–104
159. Schusterman, R. J. 1974. Low false-alarm rates in signal detection by marine mammals. *J. Acoust. Soc. Am.* 55:845–48
160. Schusterman, R. J. 1974. Auditory sensitivity of a California sea lion to airborne sound. *J. Acoust. Soc. Am.* 56:1248–51
161. Schusterman, R. J., Balliet, R. F., Nixon, J. 1972. Underwater audiogram of the California sea lion by the conditioned vocalization technique. *J. Exp. Anal. Behav.* 17:339–50
162. Schwarz, A. 1974. The inhibition of aggressive behavior by sound in the cichlid fish, *Cichlasoma centrarchus. Z. Tierpsychol.* 35:508–17
163. Schwartzkopff, J. 1973. Inner ear potentials in lower vertebrates; dependence on metabolism. In *Basic Mechanism in Hearing,* ed. A. R. Moller, 423–52. New York, London: Academic. 941 pp.
164. Schwartzkopff, J. 1973. Mechanoreception. In *Avian Biology,* ed. D. S. Farner, J. R. King, K. C. Parkes, 3:417–77. New York, London: Academic. 573 pp.
165. Schwartzkopff, J. 1974. Mechanoreception. In *The Physiology of Insects,* ed. M. Rockstein, 2:273–352. New York: Academic. 568 pp.
166. Schwartzkopff, J. 1974. Principles of signal detection by the auditory pathways of invertebrates and vertebrates. *Abh. Rheinisch-Westfael. Akad. Wiss.* 53:331–46
167. Schwartzkopff, J. 1976. Comparative-physiological problems of hearing in fish. In *Sound Reception in Fish,* ed. A. Schuijf, A. D. Hawkins, Vol. 20. Amsterdam: Elsevier. In press
168. Sellick, P. M., Bock, G. R. 1974. Evidence for an electrogenic potassium pump as the origin of the positive component of the endocochlear potential. *Pflügers Arch.* 352:351–61
169. Sokolovski, A. 1973. Normal threshold of hearing for cat for free-field listening. *Arch. Klin. Exp. Ohren- Nasen- Kehlkopfheilk.* 203:232–40
170. Sossinka, R., Pröve, E., Kalberlah, H. H. 1975. Der Einfluß von Testosteron auf den Gesangbeginn beim Zebrafinken *(Taeniopygia guttata castanotis). Z. Tierpsychol.* 39:259–64
171. Soucek, B. 1975. Model of alternating and aggressive communication with the

example of katydid chirping. *J. Theor. Biol.* 52:399–418

172. Soucek, B., Vencl, F. 1975. Bird communicative study using digital computer. *J. Theor. Biol.* 49:147–72

173. Stebbins, W. C. 1973. Hearing of Old World monkeys (Cercopithecinae). *Am. J. Phys. Anthropol.* 38:357–64

174. Steinberg, J. B., Willey, R. B. 1974. Visual and acoustical social displays by the grasshopper *Chortophaga viridifasciata* (Acrididae: Oedipodinae). *Can. J. Zool.* 52:1145–54

175. Straughan, I. R. 1975. An analysis of the mechanisms of mating call, discrimination in the frogs *Hyla regilla* and *H. cadaverina. Copeia,* pp. 415–24

176. Talmage-Riggs, G., Winter, P., Ploog, D., Mayer, W. 1972. Effect of deafening on the vocal behavior of the squirrel monkey *(Saimiri sciureus). Folia Primatol.* 17:404–20

177. Tavolga, W. N. 1968. Fishes. In *Animal Communication,* ed. T. S. Sebeok, 271–88. Bloomington: Indiana Univ. Press

178. Tavolga, W. N. 1974. Signal/noise ratio and the critical band in fishes. *J. Acoust. Soc. Am.* 55:1323–33

179. Terhune, J. M., Ronald, K. 1975. Underwater hearing sensitivity of two ringed seals *(Pusa hispida). Can. J. Zool.* 53:227–31

180. Todt, D. 1970. Die antiphonen Paargesänge des ostafrikanischen Grassängers *Cisticola hunteri prinioides* Neumann. *J. Ornithol.* 111:332–56

181. Todt, D. 1970. Gesangliche Reaktionen der Amsel (*Turdus merula* L.) auf ihren experimentell reproduzierten Eigengesang. *Z. Vergl. Physiol.* 66:294–317

182. Todt, D. 1971. Äquivalente und konvalente gesangliche Reaktionen einer extrem regelmässig singenden Nachtigall (*Luscinia megarhynchos* L.) *Z. Vergl. Physiol.* 71:262–85

183. Todt, D. 1975. Spontaneous recombinations of vocal patterns in parrots. *Naturwissenschaften* 62:399

184. Todt, D., Wolffgramm, J. 1975. Überprüfung von Steuerungs-systemen zur Strophenanwahl der Amsel durch digitale Simulierung. *Biol. Cybern.* 17: 109–27

185. Tonndorf, J. 1975. Davis—1961 revisited. Signal transmission in the cochlear hair cell-nerve junction. *Arch. Otolaryngol.* 101:528–35

186. van Dijk, T. 1973. A comparative study of hearing in owls of the family Strigidae. *J. Zool.* 23:131–67

187. Vasilevski, N. N., Shlifer, T. P., Tel, E. Z. 1975. Vocal reactions of hens to different electrical stimulation of the midbrain (Russ.). *Zh. Evol. Biokhim. Fiziol.* 11:77–83

188. Walker, T. J. 1975. Effects of temperature on rates in poikilotherm nervous systems: evidence from the calling songs of meadow katydids (Orthoptera: Tettigoniidae: *Orchelimum*) and reanalysis of published data. *J. Comp. Physiol.* 101:57–69

189. Watanabe, T., Katsuki, Y. 1974. Response patterns of single auditory neurons of the cat to species-specific vocalization. *Jpn. J. Physiol.* 24:135–55

190. Weber, E. 1974. Vergleichende Untersuchungen zur Bioakustik von *Discoglossus pictus,* Otth 1837 und *Discoglossus sardus,* Tschudi 1837 (Discoglossidae, Anura). *Zool. Jahrb. Physiol.* 78:40–84

191. Weisbach, W., Schwartzkopff, J. 1967. Nervöse Antworten auf Schallreiz im Grosshirn von *Caiman crocodilus. Naturwissenschaften* 54:650

192. Werner, Y. L. 1972. Temperature effects on inner-ear sensitivity in six species of iguanid lizards. *J. Herpetol.* 6:147–77

193. Werner, Y. L. 1973. Auditory sensitivity and vocalization in lizards (Reptilia: Gekkonoidea, Iguanidae, Pygopodidae and Scincidae). *Isr. J. Zool.* 22:204–5

194. Werner, Y. L., Wever, E. G. 1972. The function of the middle ear in lizards: *Gekko gecko* and *Eublepharis macularius* (Gekkonoidea). *J. Exp. Zool.* 179:1–16

195. Wever, E. G. 1971. Hearing in the crocodilia. *Proc. Natl. Acad. Sci. USA* 68:1498–1500

196. Wever, E. G., Werner, Y. L. 1970. The function of the middle ear in lizards: *Crotaphytus collaris* (Iguanidae). *J. Exp. Zool.* 175:327–42

197. Wickler, W. 1974. Über die Beeinflussung des Partners im Duettgesang der Schmaetzerdrossel *Cossypha heuglini* Hartlaub (Aves, Turdidae). *Z. Tierpsychol.* 36:128–36

198. Wickler, W., Seibt, U. 1974. Rufen und Antworten bei *Kassina senegalensis, Bufo regularis* und anderen Anuren. *Z. Tierpsychol.* 34:524–37

199. Wilson, J. P., Johnstone, J. R. 1975. Basilar membrane and middle-ear vibration in guinea pig measured by capacitive probe. *J. Acoust. Soc. Am.* 57:705–23

200. Winter, P. 1969. The variability of peep and twit calls in captive squirrel monkeys *(Saimiri sciureus)*. *Folia Primatol.* 10:204–15

201. Winter, P. 1972. Observations on the vocal behaviour of free-ranging squirrel monkeys *(Saimiri sciureus)*. *Z. Tierpsychol.* 31:1–7

202. Winter, P., Funkenstein, H. H. 1971. The auditory cortex of the squirrel monkey: neuronal discharge patterns to auditory stimuli. *Proc. 3rd Int. Congr. Primates, 1970, Zurich* 2:24–28

203. Winter, P., Handley, P., Ploog, D., Schott, D. 1973. Ontogeny of squirrel monkey calls under normal conditions and under acoustic isolation. *Behaviour* 47:230–39

204. Worden, F. G., Galambos, R. 1972. Auditory processing of biologically significant sounds. *Neurosci. Res. Progr. Bull.* 10:119

205. Yinon, U., Shulov, A., Tsvilich, R. 1971. Audition in the desert locust: behavioural and neurophysiological studies. *J. Exp. Biol.* 55:713–25

206. Young, D. 1973. Fine structure of the sensory cilium of an insect auditory receptor. *J. Neurocytol.* 2:47–58

207. Yunker, M. P., Herman, L. M. 1974. Discrimination of auditory temporal differences by the bottlenose dolphin and by the human. *J. Acoust. Soc. Am.* 56:1870–75

208. Zaretsky, M. D. 1972. Specificity of the calling song and short term changes in the phonotactic response by female crickets *Scapsipedus marginatus* (Gryllidae). *J. Comp. Physiol.* 79:153–72

209. Zucchi, H., Bergmann, H.-H. 1975. Long-term habituation to species-specific alarm calls in a songbird (*Fringilla coelebs* L.) *Experientia* 31:817–18

Ann. Rev. Psychol. 1977. 28:85–112
Copyright © 1977 by Annual Reviews Inc. All rights reserved

BRAIN FUNCTIONS: NEURONAL MECHANISMS OF LEARNING AND MEMORY

♦268

E. N. Sokolov
Department of Psychophysiology, Moscow State University, Moscow, USSR

Learning and memory represent basic brain functions. Learning might be defined as a process of an actual or latent modification of the behavioral or neuronal responses specific to the external stimulation and the state of the organism. Memory is an ontogenetically induced modification of intrinsic brain mechanisms causing changes of the efficiency of the subsequent responses, identification of the previously given signal, or reproduction of the learned response.

Two main aspects might be differentiated in the study of learning and memory at the neuronal level: intercellular (how neurons interact to produce learning and memory) and intracellular (what a neuron can do as a unit in learning and memory).

Two different sequences of events in the intracellular mechanisms of learning and memory have been proposed: DNA-independent and DNA-dependent memory.

DNA-independent memory is characterized by relatively short duration and genome independent mechanisms involved in its production. Several types of the DNA-dependent memory of different duration can be differentiated.

To prove that a particular modification of neuronal events is directly related to the behavioral modification, one should combine recording of neuronal activity with observations of the behavior, using conditioning procedures worked out by Pavlov (84). A symposium volume that deals with some of these questions and with many other aspects of neural mechanisms of learning and memory has appeared recently (91a).

MEMORY AS AN ENVIRONMENTALLY DETERMINED FORMATION OF FEATURE DETECTORS

Selection from a Genetically Fixed Set of Detectors, Formation of New Detectors, or Both?

The problem of memory is directly related to the mechanism of the representation of external events in neuronal nets. Evidence that the neuronal analysis of the stimuli is realized with the participation of detectors selectively tuned to particular parameters of the stimulus (45, 60) aroused vital interest in the role which the detectors play in the process of learning and memory. Deprivation from selected sets of stimuli and induction with selected stimulation at different ages were used as the methods to study the environmentally determined modification of the detectors. The pioneering work of Hubel & Wiesel (46) demonstrated that the orientation-specific cells which are present in inexperienced kittens disappeared in the cases of eyelid closure or opaque lenses in one month. Hubel's concept might be formulated as a selection of such cells from a genetically predetermined set of detectors which correspond to afferent input. Barlow & Pettigrew (11) found a lack of specificity of the neurons in the visual cortex of kittens. This was an incentive for Pettigrew (86) to regard memory as a modification of individual neurons induced by the environment which makes it possible to extract the given stimulus during the subsequent experiences of the organism. Rejecting Hubel's concept concerning the initially specific detectors which become unresponsive due to lack of an appropriate input, Pettigrew (85) emphasized the transformation of the initially nonspecific neurons into specific detectors after exposure to a particular stimulation. New findings were added to this controversy by Blakemore and his associates (16–18). It turned out that kittens deprived of patterned visual experience by dark rearing or diffuse occlusion of the eyes have cortical neurons of little or no specificity for the orientation or axis of movement of visual stimuli. This contradicts the results of both Hubel and Pettigrew. But the presence in kittens younger than 3 weeks of numbers of orientated selective cells broadly tuned by adult standards is the key point in Blakemore's theory which proposed the recruitment of the neurons: genetically specified predominantly monocular simple neurons initially provide a conditioning input to future complex cells, recruiting them to respond to the same orientation. The process of recruitment of new orientation-specific cells is accompanied by improvement of the crude innate orientation tuning by way of development of inhibitory sharpening. There is no passive improvement of the orientation specificity with age under conditions of deprivation. Normal visual experience increases responsiveness of cells, the proportion of orientation selective cells, and columnar organization of the visual cortex.

Evidence for the formation of new detectors can be derived from data of Pettigrew (86) and Blakemore & van Sluyters (18). Exposure to an environment containing only specifically inclined stripes produces a visual cortex with all neurons selective to the orientation seen early in life. An environment of random spots causes lack of summation along the length of the receptive field leading to the specific selectivity to spots of a size close to those presented during exposure. According to Hubel & Wiesel (46), binocular interaction is present in very young kittens without visual experience. Barlow & Pettigrew (11) regard the mechanism of disparity as ontogenetically elaborated. It seems that the binocular interaction does not correspond to the elaboration of the selective disparity mechanism. Thus the cortical neurons in adult cats are binocularly driven in a way that is very selective to the retinal disparity. There is variation in optimal disparity from cell to cell essential for their role in stereoscopic vision (76).

How Long Does the Period of Susceptibility Last?

According to Blakemore (16), the period of possible modifications resulting from exposures when the cortical neurons adopt the experienced stimulus as its preferred stimulus lasts from 3 to 14 weeks in kittens. Prolonged exposure in the adult produces no such effect. During the early critical period, exposure of a single orientation for only one hour or less can produce marked modifications. The induced modifications of the detectors determine the animal's behavior. A kitten reared during its critical period in an environment consisting only of vertical lines will mature into a cat that can only detect vertical lines. Such a cat can easily move between chair legs but makes no attempt to jump onto a horizontal surface. Exposure to only horizontal stripes results in difficulties in maneuvering between vertical objects, but the ability to easily reach a horizontal surface remains. These selective modifications in the sets of detectors seem to be permanent. Human beings who grow up with astigmatism that weakens the contrast of patterns of one orientation are left with "meridional amblyopia"—reduced acuity for the orientation that was originally out of focus. This amblyopia cannot be rectified by perfect correction of the eye's optics by lenses (33, 34, 73, 76).

If one eye of the kitten of 1–2 months of age is closed, visual cortex cells become unresponsive to the closed eye. Changes take place after a 1-week monocular deprivation period. A reduction in the proportion of units responsive to the deprived eye takes place after the first few days of monocular vision. Functional abnormalities occurring after 1 day became marked after 2.5–3.5 days and complete after 10 days. The effects were identical whether kittens were dark or light reared. The cortical susceptibility to the eye closure remains stable during 2 months. Similar modifications seem to be permanent in human beings with early strabismus (cross-eyes) (33). Cynader et al (28a) have shown that cortical units retain plasticity long after the end of the critical period. These alterations can occur following deprivation periods of up to 15 months.

It is uncertain whether such formation of detectors is a basic mechanism of memory or only a precondition of the later formation of memory. This question arises from the analysis of experiments with infantile amnesia (20). Rats that were 35 days of age at the time of training remember far better than do rats that were 18 days old at training. On the other hand, the formation of detectors is closely related to the process of imprinting. The basic difference is that the detectors are formed independent of the particular reflex. Imprinting as a specific formation of response-releasing mechanism should include stable connections between the detector and the effector cells. The extreme lateral edge of the telencephalon is involved in visual discrimination learning of imprinting (94).

In the process of coordination of the detectors with the response-releasing cells, the cerebellum and hippocampus are important. Newborn rat pups irradiated with low-level X rays demonstrate failure of formation of the cerebellum and hippocampus and impairment of learning to orient toward their nests (4).

The difficulty in accepting detector formation as the basic mechanism of memory is related to the fact that in some animals all detectors are mainly genetically predetermined. Thus in rabbits selective visual experience fails to modify receptive field properties of neurons located in the striate cortex (74), although other forms of learning and memory can be demonstrated in rabbits.

It might be assumed that formation of the detectors belongs to a specific class of memory events-perceptual learning. The detectors represent the basic mechanism for analysis of the environment. Both genetically predetermined and ontogenetically formed detectors participate in learning and memory as the process of ontogenetically acquired habits. Learning and memory from this standpoint are related to the formation of connections between detectors and response-releasing neurons. One might ask, however, whether the mechanisms responsible for the exposure-induced formation of the detectors and for the formation of the connections between the detectors and response-releasing neurons are similar or even identical, and whether the critical periods for the formation of different types of connections are different, some being lifelong.

How Complex Are the Formed Detectors?

The variety of detectors available in adults is very broad. Among these, the motion-selective cells are a very important class. Cats reared in a light-proof box with a 1 msec strobe flash every 2 sec did perceive visual forms but did not perceive visual movements. In strobe-reared cats, however, both directional sensitivity and directional selectivity were reduced in area 17. Some units responded only to strobe flashes (27). Cats reared in an environment showing motion only to the left responded with a leftward preference. The ocular dominance was shifted toward the contralateral eye relative to the normal cat. Collicular neurons were unaltered (28). These experiments show a complex interaction between different aspects of stimulation and the formation of detectors which are differently modified at different levels of the visual system (15, 115).

According to Imbert & Buisseret (47), there are two processes under normal conditions of rearing: reinforcement of the initially specific units and the formation of specific detectors from nonspecific units. In continual darkness the initially specific units become nonspecific, and no new specific units are formed from the nonspecific. In normally reared kittens, all units finally become specific, whereas in dark-reared kittens, all cells finally become nonspecific.

How Is the Formation of Detectors Correlated with the Modification of Reflexes?

Optokinetic nystagmus is a sequence of slow pursuit movements in the direction of the stimulus motion alternated with saccades in the opposite direction. Optokinetic nystagmus was obtained in dark-reared kittens, too. They were able to fixate a small visual target, but lost it frequently and could not estimate the depth. The nystagmus was disorganized at high velocity of the moving stripes. Kittens exposed between 15–19 weeks of age to unidirectional visual motion, under presentation with stripes moving opposite to the experienced direction, were characterized by the initial saccades oriented in all directions. After some time the animals displayed rhythmic saccades with normal orientation. Neurons from both colliculi in unidirectional kittens were normal (113). Kittens reared in the dark from birth were exposed 1 hour a day between 4–10 weeks of age to vertical stripes moving horizontally at a constant speed and in the same direction. The optokinetic nystagmus, tested in response to the visual field displacement, was different for different directions. Displacement in the experienced direction immediately elicited the nystagmus corresponding to the speed of the moving pattern. Displacement in the opposite direction either failed to elicit it or elicited a response not adapted to the speed of the pattern (113, 114). The experiments differentiate a component built up by early visual experience (adaptive component) and the preexisting one (preprogrammed component). This is very similar to the results of Hein & Held (41), who demonstrated visual placing of the forelimbs onto a broad surface in a cat that had never seen its limbs. The precise guidance of a paw on a small target, however, requires the opportunity to view the moving limbs.

The guided reach requires an integration of the sensorimotor system. This integration is established in 18 hr after the removal of the screen resulting in guided reaching. Thus, like the permanent modification of perceptual function resulting from the lack of particular inputs at their critical period of ontogenetic development, the sensorimotor integration function remains plastic in adult cats. This is true also for primates. Infant macaques were reared from birth in an apparatus which prevented the sight of their body. After 35 days one hand was exposed to view. Visually guided reaching was poor, but it improved during 10 hr of the exposure. Little concomitant improvement occurred for the unexposed hand, however, demonstrating the selectivity of the process (42).

Can Detectors be Modified in Adults?

In adult animals all orientations in the set of detectors are equally frequent. This presents a unique opportunity to attempt to modify the set of detectors using a long-lasting exposure of a particular orientation. Cats kept in complete darkness were exposed daily over a 2 week period to vertical stripes. This resulted in a decrease of the number of cells sensitive to vertical lines. Unlike kittens, which being presented with vertical stripes have most neurons maximally sensitive to lines within 30° of the vertical, adult cats have fewer vertical detectors than normal. The changes were similar to spatial frequency adaptation resulting in the reduction of sensitivity of cortical evoked potentials to gratings of the same spatial frequency and orientation. Thus the exposure to vertical stripes can alter the visual cortex temporarily in a way similar to the perceptual aftereffect (26). This adaptation effect is opposite to the effect of the formation of detectors in kittens. The neuronal tilt effect also belongs to the adaptation phenomena. The axes and thresholds of simple receptive fields in cats' visual cortex undergo changes in respect to the longitudinal rotation of the body (44). Under dark adaptation the simple receptive fields lost their orientation selectivity. Under light adaptation the orientational specificity recovered (97).

All these effects are operations upon the established population of detectors, resulting in the modification of their efficiency; this differs from the process of formation of detectors during the critical period.

Conclusion

The formation of detectors during the critical period is both a selection from the genetically preprogrammed set and the establishment of new detectors. The period of susceptibility and the role of plasticity for various detectors are different. The formation of detectors parallels the modification of synapses and columnar organization of the cortex. The relearning of the detectors was not demonstrated. The set of detectors, however, can undergo adaptation resulting in perceptual aftereffects. The concept concerning the formation of detectors as the basic mechanism of memory meets difficulties related to the fact of infantile amnesia. The formation of detectors as the mechanism of the analysis of the environment is a precondition for selective learning. The same set of detectors can participate in different memory traces. If this were not the case, each memory trace would have to have available in the brain a reservoir of potential detectors. The integration of the detectors into some reflexes is innate, but in some other reflexes it is mostly a plastic process.

The transformation of a nonspecific neuron into a specific detector after brief exposure to particular stimuli requires the following conditions: presence at a given time of some diffusely responsive neurons collecting a variety of signals; a long-lasting facilitation of the synaptic inputs affected by the exposure, combined with a long-lasting depression of synapses not affected by the exposure.

Since protein turnover will in the course of time eliminate all temporary synaptic modifications, the observed permanent effects of the exposure are hypothesized to involve continued activation of DNA to maintain the acquired modifications in the neuron.

MEMORY AS A DISCONNECTION OF DETECTORS FROM RESPONSE-RELEASING NEURONS

Is Habituation a Form of Learning?

The existence of learning in animals having mainly genetically determined detectors (rabbit) suggests that the formation of detectors is not directly related to memory. Formation of detectors, even in cat, is not a good model because it is restricted to a critical period, whereas memory is not restricted in this way. The other possibility is that learning can be defined as a plastic convergence of the stable detectors on plastic integrating neurons. That is, even though the responses of the detectors remain relatively constant, the response of integrating neurons could be modified depending on the applied stimulus and the following reinforcement, demonstrating a selective habituation or selective facilitation. This analysis suggests two different approaches to the study of memory: habituation and conditioning (40, 107, 108).

Habituation resulting from repeated presentation of the stimulus without subsequent reinforcement is a rather simple procedure. For the effective demonstration of habituation one needs a reflex with an initially extended receptive surface, which can be modified during repeated presentation of the stimulus. The observations of the detectors and of some integrating neurons involved in the reflex arc create conditions suitable for the study of memory as a process of the disconnection of the detectors from the integrating neuron. The orienting response meets these requirements (100).

The study of responses of detectors in rabbit visual cortex demonstrated that the majority of neurons were stable under repeated presentation of clicks and single flashes (112). Similar results were obtained when the cells of the rabbit's visual cortex were studied using flashes, clicks, and light-sound combinations at various intervals. The majority of the cells did not change their responses during repeated presentation of light stimuli. Only the stabilization of the responses, their facilitation, and partial habituation of the responses were observed. In light-responsive cells 28% responded to clicks with a stable specific response pattern. In 39% of the cells the responses to light-sound combinations differed from the responses to flashes. Only 6% of the units were identified as having nonspecific habituatable light-sound interaction (87).

New types of detectors with stable responses were demonstrated. Using light flashes at different intervals, Chelidze (see 100) found in rabbit's visual cortex interval-selective neurons differing from other stable neurons with responses not influenced by intervals between stimuli. Chikhkvadze (see 100) demonstrated stable neurons in rabbit's visual cortex which were selectively tuned to a particular light intensity. These intensity detectors differ both from the gradual neurons with responses gradually rising or vanishing with increase of stimulus intensity, and from monotonic neurons retaining constant response under different stimulus intensities. The responses of cortical neurons remained constant under repeated stimulation of different intensities.

The responses of the classical orientation-selective, direction-selective, and velocity-selective detectors were also stable (16) except for the above described effect of adaptation(26).

In search of habituatable neurons, different brain structures were investigated. Lindsley et al (63) demonstrated that many reticular formation neurons respond in a dynamic way to repetitive sensory stimuli. Thus 21 of 36 reticular formation neurons showed response habituation to repetitive sciatic stimulation. The recovery of the response to the prehabituation level indicates that habituation is specifically related to stimulus repetition.

The main problem in the study of neuronal habituation is the identification of single or several loci of the response decrement. The other brain region demonstrating habituation is the superior colliculus where "newness neurons" were described in frog by Lettvin et al (60). Oyster & Takanashi (81) and Horn & Hill (43) found that direction-selective cells and modified concentric cells in the superficial layers of the superior colliculus exhibit response decrement in the rabbit when a visual stimulus is repeated. This effect has some properties of habituation: spontaneous recovery and dependence on stimulus frequency. Drager & Hubel (30) found that the chief visual cell type in the stratum opticum and intermediate gray in rat resembled the newness neurons.

Habituation of the neuronal responses under repeated presentation of stimuli of various modalities is evident in hippocampus in CA_3, while the signals arriving from sensory stimulation are constant. The basic function of the plasticity of the changes seems to depend on dentate synapses which can be potentiated for 2 days. Hippocampal habituation resulted in decrement of the responses of some reticular neurons (110). Most important for the understanding of the mechanisms of habituation is the evaluation of neuronal responses of the entorhinal cortex as a main source of afferent input to the hippocampus, projecting to CA_1–CA_3 pyramidal cells and on the neurons of the dentate fascia. The dentate neurons contact with pyramidal cells only. Thus the pyramidal cells receive two parallel inputs, from the entorhinal cortex and via dentate granular cells. The neurons of the entorhinal cortex of the rabbit were multimodal with different spike patterns in the neurons of different modalities. In 71% of the neurons, the reactions were stable or gradually increased (102). The granular neurons of the dentate fascia, having excitatory or inhibitory responses, were, however, characterized by stable or even facilitated responses. The dentate fascia, representing a parallel input from the entorhinal cortex, interact with direct signals coming to CA_3 from this area. Synaptic connections between the dentate fascia and field CA_3 are characterized by gradual building up and prolonged preservation of the potentiated state (51a). The electrical stimulation of dentate fascia results in rapid loss of responses in CA_3 hippocampal neurons to sensory stimuli (19). This interaction results in the formation of novelty detectors from the pyramidal cells. The neuronal responses in CA_3 are habituated during 10–20 presentations of the stimulus (111). Thus the hippocampal neurons have initially extended receptive fields similar to the widely spread receptive surface of the orienting response. The hippocampal neurons also have some characteristics that can be observed at the behavioral level in the orienting response: a single hippocampal pyramidal neuron showed convergence of signals of all modalities and selective habituation to a repeated stimulus similar to the behavioral manifestations of the orienting reflex. The general structure of the novelty detectors suggests that various feature detectors send their axons directly or by means of interneurons to pyramidal cells. The membrane of the pyramidal cell occupied by synapses of the feature detectors represents a receptive surface on which the plastic modifications can "draw" the pattern of repeated stimuli. The neuronal responses to these stimuli are selectively blocked, forming a learned disconnection of pyramidal cells from the reticular neurons triggering the orienting response. This similarity between the orienting response and the responses of the pyramidal CA_3 neurons shows that selective behavioral habituation as negative learning is based on the process of disconnection of the stable detectors from the integrating neurons. This disconnection results in the modification of the initially extended receptive surface of the orienting response into a selectively tuned surface in accordance with the parameters of the repeatedly presented stimulus. To emphasize this statement, consider the habituation of the orienting response selective to the time interval between stimuli. This effect demonstrated on hippocampal neurons can be explained as a result of selective disconnection of time-detectors (100).

Is the Disconnection of Detectors from the Integrating Neurons Characteristic of Other Reflexes?

A defensive withdrawal reflex of external organs is found in invertebrates as well as in vertebrates. When the siphon or the mantle shelf is touched in the mollusc *Aplysia*, the siphon, the gill, and the mantle shelf withdraw into the mantle cavity. The excitatory receptive field of the reflex involves two independent areas: the siphon and the mantle shelf. There are two main motor components: siphon withdrawal and gill withdrawal, which readily habituate to repeated tactile stimuli. Behavioral habituation correlates with the decrement of the EPSP (Excitatory Postsynaptic Potential) in the motor neuron due to the homosynaptic depression. Behavioral dishabituation corresponds to the EPSP enhancement arising from the heterosynaptic facilitation of the same synapse. Acquisition of long-term habituation involves a gradual but profound decline of the EPSP produced in the motor neuron by stimulation of the afferent nerve. These changes persist for more than 24 hr. The long-term synaptic changes resemble those found for short-term habituation.

By repeating the training sessions the habituation could be extended into a long-term form, lasting up to 3 weeks. It is not yet specified whether the locus of alterations is pre- or postsynaptic, and desensitization is not ruled out. The neuronal correlates of short-term habituation do not require protein synthesis. The role of protein synthesis in the long-term habituation is also not yet determined, as is stated in the reviews of Kandel (50), Carew & Kandel (21), Jacklet & Lukowiak (48), Davis (29), and Willows (120).

Stimulation of various parts of the body in *Helix pomatia* results in closure of the pneumostoma and withdrawal behavior. Five command neurons were identified which being stimulated initiate the stereotyped response of the pneumostoma. No connections between the command cells were revealed. Sensory stimulation, however, evoked EPSPs in each neuron. The EPSPs were accompanied by pacemaker oscillations triggering pacemaker spikes and amplifying the response (83). Behavioral habituation was accompanied by habituation of the pacemaker oscillations in each command neuron (10). Repeated tactile stimulations resulted in habituation of the withdrawal response due to the decrease of participation of the pacemaker activity before synaptic habituation was evident. The pacemaker mechanism determines the reflex properties on the behavioral level (64). The command neurons trigger a pool of motor neurons responsible for the coordinated sequence of events characteristic for withdrawal.

The habituation of the withdrawal to repeated tactile stimuli occurs in several sites: in the peripheral nervous system, at peripheral terminals of the central neurons, and at central neurons (48).

The characteristic feature of habituation at any site is the selectivity of the decrement in respect to a particular point on the skin of the animal. This is an indication of the selective disconnection of the particular input from the integrating neurons responsible for a particular type of behavior.

Similar selective habituation was found in the crayfish withdrawal. After several tactile stimulations the defensive reflex selectively habituated to this particular stimulation, but appeared again if the stimulus was presented to another area of the body. The main site of the modification of the efficiency of habituation are the terminals of sensory neurons converging on the motor neuron triggering the withdrawal response (58, 121). The habituation of the jump response in locust is elaborated selectively in respect to a particular visual signal (78, 79). Negative learning in crayfish as well as in the locust consists in the disconnection of some detectors from the reflex-releasing neurons.

Conclusion

The reflexes with an initially extended receptive surface can be selectively tuned to the appropriate environment due to the process of selective temporary disconnection of the detectors from the reflex-releasing neurons. The mechanism of the disconnection consists in the diminution of the EPSP and the decrease of the pacemaker potentials in the postsynaptic cell. The properties of the detectors remain permanent.

MEMORY AS A FORMATION OF CONNECTIONS BETWEEN DETECTORS AND RESPONSE-RELEASING NEURONS

Is Reinforcement Essential for the Establishment of Connections Between Detectors and Integrating Neurons?

Assuming that the responses of the detectors remain constant under repeated presentation, one may conclude that the detectors establish new connections with the integrating neurons. In other words, one form of elaboration of memory traces is the establishment of connections between the detectors and the command neuron. A problem arises concerning the role of reinforcement in the elaboration of such connections (35, 36).

A convenient system for the study of the role of reinforcement is the elaboration of conditioned reflex discrimination. Repeated presentation of light flashes at regular intervals revealed in the visual cortex of the rabbit a set of interval-selective neurons which might be characterized as time detectors. Another population of neurons might be called extrapolatory neurons: under repeated presentation of rhythmic stimuli they start to generate spikes before the application of the next stimulus. It was suggested that the time detectors converging on the extrapolating neurons increase their responses, resulting in time conditioning at a single unit level. At the behavioral level, temporal conditioning is studied in the eyelid closure response (100). In this case there was no reinforcement other than the light stimuli.

Evidence that the single unit conditioning can be improved due to reinforcement was presented in experiments combining sound-motor association with motivational reinforcement. Tetanic septal stimulation results in long-lasting potentiation of pyramidal neurons in rabbits. The potentiated response can be extinguished under repeated presentations of the test stimuli. This response recovers after a rest period. Such tetanic stimulation can improve conditioning between the sound and the motor response elicited by electric stimulation of the motor cortex in the same way as motivational reinforcement does (59, 116). This experiment shows that single unit conditioning elaborated an unstable association between indifferent stimuli. It is stabilized due to the motivational reinforcement or to its substitute, septal electrical stimulation.

The role of the representation of the unconditioned stimulus in the elaboration of the conditioned reflex was demonstrated in the study of cortical somatosensory neurons. Stable responses of specific tactile neurons having local receptive fields not only remained unmodified under repeated presentation of the conditioned stimulus introduced in the center of their receptive fields, but also remained unmodified under the influence of the unconditioned stimuli which were not represented in the receptive field of such an afferent neuron. If, however, the receptive field of a neuron representing a painful unconditioned stimulus was studied under tactile or auditory conditioning, the conditioned stimulus, which initially was ineffective started to evoke responses after 35–40 combinations. This indicates that the conditioned response occurs in the cortical neurons representing the unconditioned reflex. After 2–20 trials, elimination of the reinforcement results in the disappearance of the conditioned response (72). These results show that the tactile detectors, remaining unmodified, were connected with the neurons responsible for initiation of the unconditioned reflex.

Temporal conditioning was involved in formation of the conditioned reflex as soon as a conditioned and an unconditioned stimulus were presented at regular intervals. Their regular combinations result in the neuronal time conditioning with the extrapolation effect. The time patterns of temporal conditioning were correlated with the frequency of the unconditioned stimulation. This labeled frequency of spike intervals was one of the initial indications of neuronal conditioning (72).

Neuronal time conditioning was demonstrated under 1 cps rhythmic stimulation of the lateral geniculate body. This resulted in the drop of the 1 cps periodicity in cortical cells, which could be interpreted as a frequency-specific potentiation of the IPSPs occurring in the neuronal nets with an appropriate period of circulation of the nervous impulses (57).

To understand the neuronal mechanisms of the conditioned reflex, one should undertake the conditioning procedure in an isolated set of neurons. The study of conditioning in the neurally isolated cortex showed that the establishment of connections is possible. The comparison of tetanic and single stimulations of two points in the neurally isolated cortex proved that these connections result not only in the long-lasting excitation but represent true associations elaborated in a single neuron (124).

Is the Input Modified During Conditioning?

To test this, a chemically active substance instead of the unconditioned stimulus is directly applied to the neuron studied. After combination of an 800 Hz tone with the microionophoretic application of L-glutamate on the neuron in the rabbit's sensimotor cortex, in 45% of the units the sound started to initiate the response that previously was characteristic only for L-glutamate (80). This conditioned triggering of the chemically specific response in a single neuron is an indication that the establishment of connections between the detectors and the response-releasing neuron involves the modification of the conditioned input due to intraneuronal integration (5).

The neuron can "couple" the conditioned and unconditioned inputs (89, 90). Tones under normal conditions evoked no behavioral motor responses in a rabbit and were noneffective with respect to many neurons located in the motor cortex. During anodal polarization of the motor cortex, tones evoked motor responses specific to the polarized area and became effective for the previously ineffective cells. After termination of the polarization, the tones presented during polarization remained effective. The tones not used during polarization were ineffective (75, 92). Rabinovich (89), developing this approach, found that 45 neurons from the rabbit's motor cortex that were unresponsive to the tones became effective during polarization; 24 of these cells remained responsive to the tones given during the polarization for up to 46 min. The tones not systematically presented during polarization were ineffective. Later all the cells studied became unresponsive again.

Local polarization of single motor neurons showed that 22 cells out of 58 became responsive exclusively to the tones given during the polarization. The selective responsiveness of the motor cells was retained for up to 14 min. The presentation of stimuli during the polarization of the cell seems to imitate the interaction between the conditioned and unconditioned stimuli. Possibly the unconditioned stimulus produces an effect similar to polarization (89).

The interaction between the conditioned and unconditioned stimuli in a single cortical motor neuron is evident at the synaptic level. After a combination of conditioned and unconditioned stimuli, the EPSPs characteristic for the conditioned stimulus were reproduced by the conditioned stimulus alone (55, 89, 93). Thus establishment of the connections can imply the modification of the input as a result of the integration. R. F. Thompson (108a) has shown that an increase in unit activity develops in the hippocampus in a few trials of paired conditioning and grows during the training. He concludes that this might be considered as an initial process in formation of the engram.

Evidence for the complex effect of associative training was presented by Alkon (2, 3). In the nudibranch mollusc *Hermissenda crassicornis*, repeated exposures to light associated with rotation resulted in reduction of the attraction to light lasting several hours. Synaptic interaction of the statocyst with the visual pathway underlies this behavioral modification. After associated visual and rotational stimulation caused the animal to stop going to the light spot, intracellular recording from hair cells showed the following phenomena: the depolarizing response evoked by illumination of the ipsilateral eye was not present, and the hyperpolarizing wave caused by the illumination of the contralateral eye was observed less frequently than in untrained animals. These experiments demonstrate modification of the input during the procedure of association.

Is there an Alternative to Detector-Command Neuron Interaction?

A functional approach to memory is proposed by Livanov (65, 66). Regarding memory as a result of the interaction of cortical neurons, Livanov emphasizes the formation and preservation of temporary connections on the basis of functional neuronal interaction without stable morphological changes and specific molecular modifications. This is suggested by the results of experiments with rhythmical stimulation (2–5 Hz) inducing in the rabbit's brain an increase of the cross-correlation of the spike trains for cortical neurons lasting for 20 min after the presentation of the stimulus and coinciding with elevation of the conditioned responses. The spontaneous activity traveling via neuronal network is regarded as the mechanism of memory, without differentiation of detectors and command neurons as specific subsets of the neuronal population (37, 53, 54).

Conclusion

Regarding learning as the process of the establishment of connections between the stable detectors and the modifiable integrating neuron explains many aspects of behavior. The process seems to be more complex, however. The input coming from the detector can be modified in the integrating neuron in accordance with the properties of the reinforcing stimulus. Apparently the intracellular mechanism of a single neuron can be responsible for the effect.

MEMORY AND JUNCTIONAL PLASTICITY

How to Identify the Presynaptic Site of Plasticity

The difficulty of identifying the presynaptic mechanisms of plastic modification of the synapses is related to the close dependence of the pre- and postsynaptic events. The difficulty is further increased if intracellular recording from the postsynaptic cell is used as the method of evaluating plasticity. The most effective approach is evaluation of the magnitude of the miniature postsynaptic potential. Modification of the synaptic efficiency occurring under a steady value of the amplitude of the miniature postsynaptic potential is evidence of the constant sensitivity of the postsynaptic membrane, and consequently, these modifications are a result of the increase by presynaptic processes of the number of vesicles released from the presynaptic terminal (36a).

Repetitive stimulation results in the potentiation of transmitter release. Potentiation of the end-plate potential amplitudes at the frog neuromuscular junction increases during repetitive stimulation to maximum and then decays exponentially (36a). Thus, in addition to short-term potentiation, there exists an intermediate facilitatory process which decays faster than potentiation and slower than true facilitation. This potentiation results from the increased transmitter release attributed to a progressive accumulation of active intracellular Ca^{2+} or a Ca-activated complex in the nerve terminals. Exponential decay of facilitation implies exponential decay of the active Ca^{2+} (68).

How to Identify the Postsynaptic Site of Plasticity

The main procedure for identification of postsynaptic modifications of the responsiveness of the neuron is based on direct application of the transmitter to the postsynaptic membrane. Such experiments can be carried out on the neurons having widespread sensitivity all over the somatic membrane. Thus, in molluscs some neurons are sensitive to acetylcholine applied ionophoretically. Modification of responses to repeated applications of the transmitter is an indication of the postsynaptic mechanism of plasticity. The evaluation of postsynaptic plasticity is complicated by the existence of two types of receptive proteins. Thus, in gastropod brains treated with acetylcholine, muscarine-like receptors produce hyperpolarization and nicotine-like receptors result in depolarization of the neuronal membrane. Both types of receptors are found in one neuron (96).

The biphasic potentials found in the mollusc *Aplysia* (51, 61) by acytylcholine application were present under natural conditions (62). Biphasic synaptic potentials consisting of depolarization followed by hyperpolarization are chemically mediated as shown by their susceptibility to a high magnesium medium. The natural biphasic potentials are similar to the biphasic responses evoked by ionophoretic application of acetylcholine. The response was biphasic due to the concomitant permeability changes in these cells. Two types of receptors are distributed differently over the membrane surface. The great sensitivity of the inhibitory phase of the biphasic potential to small changes in the soma membrane potential suggests that these receptors are located closer to the soma than those responsible for the excitatory phase. Since different types of acetylcholine receptors are differently distributed, it is possible that purely inhibitory and purely excitatory potentials mediated by acetylcholine will be found in one neuron (62), and this is indeed the case. Purely depolarizing, purely hyperpolarizing, and biphasic potentials to acetylcholine applied on different loci of the membrane were found in a single neuron of the mollusc *Helix pomatia* (70).

A similar phenomenon is true for dopamine. A giant dopamine-containing cell situated in pedal ganglion of the snail *Planorbis corneus* generates excitatory, inhibitory, or biphasic (depolarizing-hyperpolarizing) postsynaptic potentials (12). The existence of two receptors differently related to the permeability changes of the membrane should be taken into account to correctly evaluate the modifications of the responses to direct application of the transmitter on the sensitive membrane. Such modifications are known as the desensitization-sensitization phenomena. To exclude the effects of the interaction of two different receptors, the modifications of each type of receptor protein should be studied separately.

Can Sensitization-Desensitization Occur in Vitro?

The occurrence of desensitization and resensitization in cholinergic receptors from *Torpedo marmorata* studied in vitro showed that the whole process does not require any energetic drive (88). Desensitization of receptors occurs after a prolonged bath containing the agonist. Membrane fragments having 10–30% protein carry a binding site for acetylcholine. The cholinergic agonist increases the permeability to ^{22}Na, but prolonged exposure results in the progressive decrease of the permeability, coinciding with the slow transition of the receptors from a low to a higher affinity state. Conformational changes of the receptors correspond to the opening of the channels, and their subsequent closing corresponds to desensitization (118, 119). Thus the cholinergic receptor protein can exist in several interconvertible states of affinity. In the desensitized state, when the ionophor is shut, the receptor exhibits a high affinity for agonists. The affinity state is measured indirectly by the evaluation of decrease of the initial rate of the toxin binding. The receptor protein is spontaneously present in a form when it binds the cholinergic agonist with low affinity. The cholinergic agonist stabilizes in a reversible manner the receptor protein in a high affinity state for agonists. The low affinity state of receptor protein at rest is susceptible to activation. The high affinity state corresponds to a desensitized state of the receptors in which the ionophor is shut (118, 119).

Desensitization is a progressive decline of the amplitude of the acetylcholine potential in the muscle. The rate of the desensitization onset depends on the acetylcholine dose and the frequency of application. The recovery has a constant value. The rate of the onset of desensitization in frog muscle decreases when the temperature of the muscle bath is lowered (67).

Is the Receptor Protein the Only Site for Plasticity?

The completely isolated neuron can generate spikes spontaneously. This is due to the pacemaker potential—endogenous oscillations of the membrane potential dependent on the electrogenic effect of the active ionic transport. Depolarization of the membrane potential of a pacemaker neuron results in an increase of the frequency of pacemaker oscillations; hyperpolarization results in the lowering of the pacemaker frequency, accompanied by a drop in the amplitude down to a complete elimination of pacemaker oscillations. These responses of the pacemaker neuron to injected currents can gradually habituate, resulting in the minimal response of the pacemaker mechanism to the injected current. The response recovers spontaneously with time and can be dishabituated after a stronger intracellular stimulation. Redistribution of the currents resulting in the isolation of the pacemaker locus of the membrane might be responsible for the habituation to intracellular stimulation (7, 8, 100, 122). This pacemaker plasticity is a process occurring independently from the desensitization of the receptors. The pacemaker plasticity can participate, however, in the responses of the pacemaker neuron to direct application of the transmitter. The repeated application of acetylcholine onto some loci of the membrane of a *Helix pomatia* neuron may result in a stable acetylcholine potential without any sign of desensitization. The degree in which this stable acetylcholine potential modulated the pacemaker oscillation gradually diminished. This diminution of the response in the pacemaker neuron was due to the plastic modifications of the pacemaker mechanism similar to the habituation to intracellular injection of current (70).

Can the Transmitter Directly Influence the Pacemaker Locus?

The direct ionophoretic application of acetylcholine to the pacemaker locus of molluscan neurons results in the acceleration, deceleration or acceleration-deceleration of the rate of the pacemaker potentials occurring without any shift of the membrane potential and without any change of the membrane conductance measured by constant pulses of current injected into the neuron. This acetylcholine-dependent response of the pacemaker potential mechanism seems to be due to the activation-inactivation of the ionic pump responsible for the pacemaker oscillations (8, 70, 101, 117). These responses of the pacemaker generator can be habituated by repeated applications of acetylcholine. In this case the deviations of the pacemaker frequency from the initial level gradually diminished under a constant value of the membrane potential and the membrane conductance. The role of the receptor proteins in the acceleration-deceleration responses of the pacemaker potential should be studied.

Is Plasticity a Local Property of the Neuronal Membrane?

Repeated applications of acetylcholine on the surface of the molluscan neuron have shown three different types of plastic modifications: gradual modification of the sensitivity of the receptors, gradual modification of the responsiveness of the pacemaker locus to the current caused by the stable acetylcholine response, and gradual decrease of the responsiveness of the ionic pump present in the pacemaker locus (8).

Different loci of the membrane were characterized by different responses during application of acetylcholine, but even similar responses in different points of the membrane were characterized by different plasticity. Thus the depolarizing response to acetylcholine in one locus remained stable under repeated applications. Another locus was characterized by sensitization, and some other loci demonstrated desensitization. Each of these plastic changes was very local, and the shift of the microelectrode of only 50 micra resulted in recovery of the response. Thus the membrane is heterogeneous not only with respect to different responses to the same transmitter but also with respect to plastic changes evoked in different points of the membrane (70).

Two independent pacemaker potentials and two independent spikes of different amplitudes were recorded in some neurons. Repeated current injections showed that habituation occurs independently in each pacemaker locus. The habituation found in one locus was absent in the other (70).

The data concerning selective placticity showed that a neuron changed its responses to stimuli not as a unit but as a system of heterogeneous loci which can change their responses independently.

DNA-DEPENDENT AND DNA-INDEPENDENT MEMORIES

Since the late 1950s there has been a good deal of speculation that RNA and DNA are involved in the formation of memory traces. In recent years there has been a fair amount of experimental evidence bearing on these hypotheses. It is now possible to see how synaptic impulses could lead to altered chemical synthesis in the post-synaptic cell. We will consider evidence that some examples of memory are DNA-dependent whereas others are DNA-independent.

How is the Genome Regulated?

The DNA of each cell is the same in a multicellular animal, yet each cell type performs different functions. This means that various cells use the information encoded in DNA differently. The control of the genome is performed through the activation-inactivation of its particular regions, which causes or prevents the synthesis of molecules of mRNA. The control depends on some DNA-associated proteins: basic histones and mildly acidic nonhistones. The histones act as general inhibitors of mRNA synthesis. The nonhistones apparently specifically regulate the gene transcription. Genetic regulatory proteins recognize and bind to specific sites on DNA. When the nonhistone protein and histone come together, this leads to phosphorylation of the nonhistone protein and an increase in the strength of the attraction between nonhistone and histone proteins. This results in the displacement of the histone from DNA and the initiation of mRNA synthesis (52).

Regulation of the genome can be performed by hormones and perhaps by neural transmitters. For example, two steroid hormones, estrogen and progesterone, enter the cell by passive diffusion and bind to specific cytoplasmic receptor proteins. An activation of the receptor complex occurs at the same time with the translocation to the nuclear compartment. The activated receptor binds to chromatin acceptor sites and activates specific genes; this allows transcription of new specific mRNAs which code the specific protein synthesis (77).

It is proposed that the synaptic transmitter, as an agent combining with a receptor protein, produces a complex which may result in enzyme induction at the genome level. The enzyme could be used in at least two different ways: for synthesis of the transmitter at the axonal terminals, and for synthesis of the receptor proteins at the stimulated postsynaptic site. Both effects could occur simultaneously.

Is Trans-Synaptic Enzyme Induction Possible?

An increased activity of the preganglionic cholinergic nerves evokes in adrenergic neurons of the superior cervical ganglia a selective induction of tyrosine hydroxylase and dopamine beta-hydroxylase participating in noradrenaline synthesis (104, 106). The first messenger in this neuronally mediated enzyme induction is acetylcholine acting on the nicotinic receptors. The regulation of enzyme synthesis takes place at the transcription level, and the glucocorticoids exert a modulatory action in this process (106). It is not yet clear how the changes produced by acetylcholine in the neuronal membrane are mediated to regulation at the transcriptional level. But regulation of the degree of expression of the available genetic information as trans-synaptic enzyme induction could be compared with the contact inhibition in tissue culture and with the initiation of antibody production in lymphocytes (106).

In decentralized superior cervical ganglia, carbamylcholine, acetylcholine, and nicotine elicited a selective induction of tyrosine hydroxylase and dopamine beta-hydroxylase via nicotinic receptors similar to natural stimulation. Bethanecol stimulation of muscarinic receptors produced no effect. A 4 hr pulse of carbamylcholine produced optimal induction of tyrosine hydroxylase and dopamine beta-hydroxylase 48 and 24 hr later, respectively. The other general cell enzymes remain unchanged. This selective increase was blocked by inhibitors of protein synthesis (cycloheximide) which act at the translation level, and also by actinomycin which acts earlier at the level of transcription. This indicates that the regulation occurs at the level of transcription. Convincing proof that there is an increase of the enzyme protein synthesis is a demonstration that the amount of enzyme protein competing for binding sites of specific tyrosine hydroxylase antibodies is increased parallel with in vitro activity of tyrosine hydroxylase (49). The selective trans-synaptic enzyme induction can occur without preceding changes in cAMP and cGMP. This enzyme induction was not blocked by tetrodotoxin, implying that the mechanism was independent from the formation of action potentials (104, 105).

The transcription phase is terminated after 24 hr, but an increased rate of tyrosine hydroxylase synthesis continues up to 48 hr, implying that the turnover of mRNA is slow enough to allow an enhancement of enzyme synthesis for the next 24 hr (105).

Trans-synaptic enzyme regulation involves changes in the neuronal membrane which modify the expression of the available nuclear genetic information and produce a long-lasting DNA-dependent increase in the synaptic efficiency. Such a change could represent a memory trace in a neuronal network.

Similar effects could occur in cholinergic neurons. Nervous tissue in the mollusc *Aplysia* contains both choline and acetylcholine, as in vertebrates. Choline for transmitter synthesis is derived from the blood, and cholinergic neurons show high affinity choline uptake (95). High affinity uptake of choline was reversibly abolished when all ions were replaced by isotonic sucrose, suggesting its dependence on some ions. The electrogenic Na-pump can also participate in high affinity choline uptake (32). When ^3H choline is injected into the cell body of an identified cholinergic neuron of *Aplysia*, it is converted into acetylcholine, transported down the axon, and released by nerve impulses within a few hours. Synthesis of acetylcholine occurs only in cholinergic neurons containing choline acetyltransferase—the enzyme which catalyzes the synthesis of the cholinergic transmitter (31).

Increased preganglionic activity in rats is accompanied by activation of the choline acetyltransferase in preganglionic fibers. The increase of choline acetyltransferase activity can be prevented by administration of cycloheximide, suggesting that the increase requires new protein synthesis. The increase of choline acetyltransferase can also be abolished by transecting the spinal cord, suggesting that this increase was neuronally dependent (105).

A link between the neuronal induction of enzyme synthesis and the production of antibodies was demonstrated experimentally. Rabbits immunized against either a cholinesterase or a cholinergic nicotinic receptor-rich fraction isolated from the electric organ of *Torpedo marmorata* produced antibodies. A progressive paralysis and complete relaxation of the neck muscles developed under treatment with the receptor-rich fraction. Rabbits immunized against the cholinesterase-rich fraction showed no muscular distress. Sera obtained from receptor-immunized rabbits showed a curare-like effect (against nicotinic receptors) but were not effective against muscarinic receptors (25).

It is still puzzling how the transmitter-receptor interaction is signaled to the nucleus of the cell. There are a few indications concerning the possible routes. Thus the external surface of the postsynaptic membrane of *Torpedo* electric organ is characterized by a bidimensional lattice of repeating subunits deeply penetrating the membrane leaflet and anchoring to the cytoplasmic half of the membrane. The particulate entities at the surface of the postsynaptic membrane are morphologically identical with the isolated receptor molecules. The receptor-ionophor molecules span completely the bimolecular leaflet (22). The route can be followed further. Electron microscopy in the frog motor end plate revealed patch-like aggregations of membrane-bound particles at the entrance of junctional folds directly connected via sacs or tubules of the sarcoplasmic reticulum with the cistern of the nuclei. They represent a morphological channel between postsynaptic sites of excitation and the nuclear envelope (1).

The trans-synaptic enzyme induction discussed above provides a mechanism for the amplification of the output of the neuron. The other possible DNA-dependent modification was the influence upon the input. A possible model of the process is a sensitization of the denervated muscle cells. In rats after 3-day *d*-tubocurarine treatment, extrajunctional acetylcholine receptors appear, and these parallel the binding of alpha-bungarotoxin by the extrajunctional region of muscle. The prevention of spiking in muscle also results in spread of sensitivity (13).

Is DNA Involved in the Learning Process?

In experiments on rats with motor reflexes conditioned to light, hippocampus and neocortex showed increases in the induced level of 5-methylcytosine. DNA methylation was expressed mainly during the initial period of learning. As the DNA methylation is thought to be involved in the control of transcription, this implies that conditioning may affect regulation of the process of transcription (109). The DNA-dependent processes open a door for the understanding of new structural modifications. Conditioning of a response of approaching food at an auditory signal results in greater size of the nucleus and nucleolus in the cells of auditory and motor cortex. In the nuclear membrane pores and granular material develop. The cytoplasm of the neuron is characterized by an increased number of ribosomes. The presynaptic sites are characterized by more numerous vesicles. The postsynaptic structures develop new spine apparatus. Disorders of the conditioned reflexes evoked due to strong rhythmic auditory stimulation parallel the destruction of the organelles and spine apparatus (69).

Bennett et al (12a) have suggested that while synthesis of protein is a link in long-term memory formation, this may not always require derepression of DNA. Experiments were performed in which carefully timed injections of anisomycin (a nontoxic inhibitor of protein synthesis) were given either shortly before or shortly after one-trial avoidance training in mice, and memory was tested one week later. When inhibition began by the time of the training trial, the tests showed amnesia, but if synthesis was permitted for only about 2 min after strong training, the tests demonstrated memory. Since in mammals it requires at least 15 min for synthesis of molecules of mRNA and their transport to ribosomes, it appears that, at least in cases of strong training, memory formation may employ already existing mRNA without necessitating derepression of DNA.

Beritashvili (14), discussing the structural basis of memory, emphasized that during activity pyramidal neurons produce mRNA and protein. The latter, acting on the neuronal membrane, results in the establishment of stable long-lasting connections between all cells activated by the given object. The main structural modifications of the synaptic apparatus consist in the multiplication of the presynaptic terminals and enhancement of the myelinization of the presynaptic terminals (9, 71, 91, 91a).

Some indirect evidence concerning the DNA-dependent component of memory can be obtained from genetics. Rats with hereditary galactosemia (reduced galacto-1-phosphate uridyltransferase) demonstrated impaired long-term storage in active avoidance conditioning (123). The rate of formation of food reflexes is also genetically dependent. Selection of animals for high and low rate of conditioned reflex formation resulted in significant differences of conditioning in two strains as early as the second generation. These differences persisted in subsequent generations (98, 99).

Is DNA-Dependent Memory Time Selective?

The duration of DNA-dependent memory is determined by the duration of the depression-activation of a particular operon, resulting in the duration of structural modifications in a neuronal net. Some processes in the nervous system are periodic, however. Such periodic regulation of neuronal function seems to occur at the DNA level. In addition to the structural genes determining the catalytic activity of the enzyme, Paigen et al (82) have postulated processing genes determining the cellular apparatus involved with intracellular localization, regulating genes determining the rates of enzyme synthesis and temporal genes determining the developmental programs.

Time-selective memory events can be of different duration. The short interval periodicity is characteristic of a New Guinea firefly flashing in rhythmic synchrony at a 1000 msec interval. Artificial driving showed anticipatory entrainment at periods ranging from 800 to 1800 msec. The light resets the endogenous pacemaker analogous with pacemaker potential (19a). Similar effects can be studied in the completely isolated neuron. Using trypsinization, Chen et al (24) isolated mollusc *Aplysia* neurons and proved that they preserve spontaneous pacemaker activity. Kostenko et al (56) isolated neurons in the mollusc *Limnaea stagnalis* using pronase. Isolated neurons survived in vitro for 2 weeks, maintaining electrical excitability and sensitivity to drugs. The isolated neurons were capable of synthesizing RNA as revealed by labeled uridine incorporation into the cytoplasm and the nucleus of the cell.

Such cells can be used in neuronal learning. Chaplain & von Baumgarten (23) showed that after complete isolation of *Aplysia* neurons from synaptic and ephaptic inputs they still possessed beating or bursting pacemaker activity. The interspike and interburst intervals can be modified by depolarizing pulses rhythmically presented. After 4–14 stimuli, the neuron spontaneously discharged at the interstimulus interval. The interspike learning was accompanied by a shift of pyruvate kinase which transformed into a more active form. The interbursting learning was accompanied by an increase in phosphoprotein kinase activity (24).

The time-selective modifications of neuronal activity are represented by circadian periodicity of spike discharges. There are neurons in the parietovisceral ganglion of *Aplysia* that possess circadian oscillators which can be revealed by periodogram analysis. The neurons are free running with some delay. Impulse production and synaptic transmission are not required for the expression of a circadian cycle. The eyes undergo entrainment of a sleep-waking cycle in accordance with the artificial periodicity. Specific proteins found in the circadian pacemaker neurons suggest the DNA-dependent regulation of the intracellular oscillator (103).

Conclusion

The fact that actinomycin prevents trans-synaptic enzyme induction directly demonstrates the role of DNA-dependent events in the modification of interneuronal connections. Some indirect data suggest that the postsynaptic site is also regulated by DNA-dependent mechanisms. DNA-dependent enzyme induction affords new information concerning structural modification in the process of learning.

How to Prove that Some Examples of Plasticity are not DNA-Dependent

The main principle for the identification of DNA-independent memory is to study it under conditions when any feedback is interrupted from DNA to the postsynaptic membrane and to the terminals of the axon which form synapses on the following cell. The most effective interruption might be achieved on the level of transcription, preventing the formation of mRNA. One possible approach is to eliminate RNA in the neuron, using an incubation solution containing RNase. After incubation of the neurons of *Helix pomatia* for 0.5, 1.0, or 2.0 hr in a physiological solution containing RNase, histochemical and cytochemical evaluation revealed no RNA in the neurons, glia cells, and neuropil. Spike activity, postsynaptic potentials, and pacemaker oscillations were preserved, however. Responses to the ionophoretic microapplication of acetylcholine remained unaffected. Habituation to repeated electrical stimulation of the nerve in the identified RNA-less neurons was similar to that in the intact neurons, and habituation was still found 4 hr later (6). This is evidence for the existence of DNA-independent memory, since participation of DNA was blocked.

Interruption of the link between the synaptic site and DNA can be achieved in another way. It is suggested that long-term, DNA-dependent memory requires a period of consolidation. To intervene into the consolidation process and to prevent the formation of long-term memory, electric shocks are delivered brain structures. Electric shocks introduced into the ganglia of the mollusc result in the elimination of responses to the tactile stimulus, followed after 1.5 hr by hyperactivity. The habituation elaborated before the administration of shocks remained after 24 hr of rest in the same degree as in intact animals. If, however, the electric shock was given just before the habituation procedure, memory was not elaborated, and 24 hr later no memory trace was revealed. Intracellular recording showed that inactivation of the animal after shock corresponds with disturbances in spike generation (splitting of the spike into several subcomponents) and the elimination of chemical sensitivity lasting up to 1 hr as tested by acetylcholine application. The other mechanism of disturbance of the behavior was the elimination of pacemaker activity, preventing the animal's spontaneous activity. Similar effects were observed during intracellular shocks introduced through a microelectrode into a single neuron. Recovery from the shocks included the following modifications in the dynamics of neuronal habituation: (a) Paradoxal effect when the number of trials resulting in habituation increased; the enhanced habituation was reached after 3–5 applications. (b) The normal habituation rate was recovered after 2.5 hr. The degree of preservation of previously induced habituation after 2.5 hr was also normal (38, 39). (c) Habituation was not modified after shock treatment when the neuron recovered. This means that either the habituation is independent from DNA mechanisms, or shocks do not prevent DNA involvement. Bearing in mind that RNase treatment did not prevent habituation of neuron (6), one may conclude that there exists a form of DNA-independent plastic modifications.

Conclusion

The fact that plastic modifications can occur normally in the synaptic contact and pacemaker mechanisms after blockade of the synthesis of mRNA or after RNase treatment of the neuron indicates that there exists a form of DNA-independent memory that lasts at least for 24 hr.

SUMMARY

The study of learning and memory is now approaching understanding of the intracellular mechanisms, including the participation of macromolecules in the formation of memory traces. This makes it possible to switch from phenomenological to molecular concepts of learning and memory. DNA-dependent and DNA-independent memories are apparently of different durations. Although DNA-independent memories seem to be of different durations, they all remain below the period of turnover of proteins and RNA. DNA-dependent memories include permanent (lifelong) modifications of synaptic efficiency.

DNA-dependent memory can be represented as a sequence of the following events: 1. action of the transmitter on the membrane receptor; 2. synthesis of specific DNA-directed proteins; 3. activation-inactivation of DNA loci; 4. activation-inactivation of mRNA synthesis; 5. synthesis of specific enzymes; 6. transport of specific enzymes to receptor site and/or to axon terminals; 7. structural modifications at the receptor site and/or at axon terminals.

DNA-independent memory can be represented as follows: 1. action of the transmitter on the receptor; 2. conformational changes of the receptor protein; 3. activation-inactivation of the receptor protein; 4. modification of the responsiveness of the receptor site.

By regarding the signals from synaptic sites as chemically specific agents which derepress DNA, one can bridge the gap between synaptic functions and macromolecular participation. Trans-synaptic induction of enzyme synthesis seems to be the most promising approach to the study of different types of DNA-dependent memory. The study of conditioning is also concentrated around the intracellular mechanisms. The study of temporal conditioning in a completely isolated neuron opens new horizons. The integration of conditioned and unconditioned inputs should be solved at the intracellular level as well. The similarity between neuron polarization and the effect of the unconditioned influence opens new prospects in understanding the mechanism of the modification of conditioned input under the influence of an unconditioned stimulus.

Literature Cited

1. Akert, K., Peper, K., Sandri, C., Moor, H. 1975. Relationship between postsynaptic specific membrane sites and nuclear envelope in the frog motor endplate. *Exp. Brain Res. Suppl.* 23:6
2. Alkon, D. L. 1974. Associative training of *Hermissenda*. *J. Gen. Physiol.* 62: 185–97
3. Alkon, D. L. 1975. Neural correlates of associative training in *Hermissenda*. *J. Gen. Physiol.* 65:46–56
4. Altman, J., Bulut, F. G. 1976. Ontogeny of learning and memory. See Ref. 91a
5. Anokhin, P. K. 1968. *Biology and Neurophysiology of the Conditioned Reflex*. Moscow: Nauka (in Russian)
6. Anokhin, P. K., Arakelov, G. G., Sokolov, E. N. 1972. Electrogenesis in mollusc giant neurons after RNase effect. *Neyrofisiologiya* 4:423–28 (in Russian)
7. Arakelov, G. G. 1974. Endogenous electrical potentials of the neuron as the representation of its functional-metabolic heterogeneity. *Usp. Fiziol. Nauk.* 5:52–79 (in Russian)
8. Arakelov, G. G., Sokolov, E. N. 1975. Pacemaker potential of the nerve cell. In *Pacemaker Potential*, ed. E. N. Sokolov, N. N. Tavkhelidze, pp. 14–60. Tbilisi: Metsniereba. 214 pp. (in Russian)
9. Ashmarin, I. P. 1975. *Problems and Results in the Biochemistry of Memory*. Leningrad Univ. Press. 159 pp. (in Russian)
10. Balaban, P. M., Litvinov, E. G. 1975. Participation of identified neurons in the unconditioned reflex in a snail, *Helix pomatia*. *Zh. Vyssh. Nervn. Deyat.* 25:1320–23 (in Russian)
11. Barlow, H. B., Pettigrew, J. D. 1971. Lack of specificity of neurons in the visual cortex of young kittens. *J. Physiol.* 218:98–100
12. Barry, M. S., Cottrell, G. A. 1975. Excitatory, inhibitory and biphasic synaptic potentials mediated by an identified dopamine-containing neuron. *J. Physiol.* 244:589–612
12a. Bennett, E. L., Flood, J. F., Orme, A., Rosenzweig, M. R., Jarvik, M. 1975. Minimum duration of protein synthesis needed to establish long-term memory. 5th International Meeting of the International Society for Neurochemistry, Barcelona. Abstracts: 382
13. Berg, D. K., Hall, Z. W. 1975. Increased extrajunctional acetylcholine sensitivity produced by chronic postsynaptic neuromuscular blockade. *J. Physiol.* 244:659–76
14. Beritashvili, I. S. 1974. *Memory of Vertebrates, Its Characteristic and Origin*. Moscow: Nauka. 212 pp. (in Russian)
15. Beteleva, T. G., Farber, D. A., Shurshalina, G. V. 1975. Cortico-subcortical relationships in the system of the visual analyser at different stages of ontogenesis. *Zh. Vyssh. Nervn. Deyat.* 25:576–81 (in Russian)
16. Blakemore, C. 1974. Developmental factors in the formation of feature extracting neurons. In *The Neurosciences* (Third study program), ed. F. O. Schmitt, F. G. Worden, pp. 105–13. Cambridge, London: MIT Press. 1107 pp.
17. Blakemore, C., Mitchell, D. E. 1973. Environmental modifications of the visual cortex and the neural basis of learning and memory. *Nature* 241:467–68
18. Blakemore, C., van Sluyters, R. C. 1975. Innate and environmental factors

in the development of the kitten's visual cortex. *J. Physiol.* 228:663–716

19. Bragin, A. G., Vinogradova, O. S., Yemelyanov, V. V. 1976. The influences of the dentate fascia upon sensory responses of the CA₃ hippocampal neurons. *Zh. Vyssh. Nervn. Deyat.* 26: 605–11 (in Russian)

19a. Buck, J., Case, J., Hanson, F., Buck, E. 1975. Pacemaker behavior in entrained firefly flashing. *Biophys. J.* 16:178

20. Campbell, B., Coulter, X. 1976. Ontogeny of learning and memory. See Ref. 91a

21. Carew, T. J., Kandel, E. R. 1974. Synaptic analysis of the interrelationships between behavioral modifications in *Aplysia*. In *Synaptic Transmission and Neuronal Interaction*, pp. 339–83. New York: Raven

22. Cartaud, J. 1975. Molecular organization of the excitable membrane of *Torpedo marmorata. Exp. Brain Res. Suppl.* 23:37

23. Chaplain, R. A., von Baumgarten, R. 1975. Metabolic aspects of neuronal learning. *Pfluegers Arch. Suppl.* 355:87

24. Chen, C. F., von Baumgarten, R., Takeda, R. 1971. Pacemaker properties of completely isolated neurons in *Aplysia californica. Nature* 223:27–29

25. Clementi, F., Tranconi, B. C., Berti, F., Folco, G. 1975. Biological activity of antibodies against nicotinic receptor and acetylcholinesterase. *Exp. Brain Res. Suppl.* 23:40

26. Creutzfeldt, O. D., Heggelund, P. 1975. Neural plasticity in visual cortex of adult cats after exposure to visual patterns. *Science* 188:1025–27

27. Cynader, M., Berman, N., Hein, A. 1973. Cats reared in stroboscopic illumination: effects on receptive fields in visual cortex. *Proc. Nat. Acad. Sci. USA* 70:1353–54

28. Cynader, M., Berman, N., Hein, A. 1975. Cats raised in a one-directional world: effects on receptive fields in visual cortex and superior colliculus. *Exp. Brain Res.* 22:267–80

28a. Cynader, M., Berman, N., Hein, A. 1976. Recovery of function in cat visual cortex following prolonged deprivation. *Exp. Brain Res.* 25:139–56

29. Davis, W. J. 1976. Plasticity in the invertebrates. See Ref. 91a

30. Drager, U. C., Hubel, D. H. 1975. Responses to visual stimulation and relationship between visual, auditory, and somatosensory inputs in mouse superior colliculus. *J. Neurophysiol.* 38:690–713

31. Eisenstadt, M. L., Schwartz, J. H. 1975. Metabolism of acetylcholine in the nervous system of *Aplysia californica.* III. Studies of an identified cholinergic neuron. *J. Gen. Physiol.* 65:293–313

32. Eisenstadt, M. L., Treisman, S. N., Schwartz, J. H., 1975. Metabolism of acetylcholine in the nervous system of *Aplysia californica.* II. Regional localization and characterization of choline uptake. *J. Gen. Physiol.* 65:275–91

33. Freeman, R. D., Thibos, L. N. 1975. Contrast sensitivity in humans with abnormal visual experience. *J. Physiol.* 247:687–710

34. Freeman, R. D., Thibos, L. N. 1975. Visual evoked responses in humans with abnormal visual experience. *J. Physiol.* 247:711–24

35. Gabriel, M., Wheeler, W., Thompson, R. F. 1973. Multiple-unit activity of the rabbit cortex in single-session avoidance conditioning. *Physiol. Psychol.* I:45–55

36. Gabriel, M., Wheeler, W., Thompson, R. F. 1973. Multiple-unit activity of the rabbit cerebral cortex during stimulus generalization of avoidance behavior. *Physiol. Psychol.* 1:313–20

36a. Gage, P. W. 1976. Generation of endplate potentials. *Physiol. Rev.* 56:177–258

37. Gasanov, U. G. 1975. Systemic neuronal mechanisms of conditioned reflexes. *Zh. Vyssh. Nervn. Deyat.* 25: 1159–71 (in Russian)

38. Grechenko, T. N. 1975. Intracellular mechanisms of the functional state. In *Functional State of the Brain*, ed. E. N. Sokolov, N. N. Danilova, E. D. Khomskaya, pp. 187–203. Moscow Univ. Press. 246 pp. (in Russian)

39. Grechenko, T. N., Shekhter, E. D. 1975. Effect of electric shocks on the activity of molluscan neurons. In *Functional Organization of the Brain Activity*, pp. 137–38. Moscow: Nauka. 195 pp. (in Russian)

40. Groves, P. M., Thompson, R. F. 1973. A dual-process theory of habituation: neural mechanisms. In *Habituation: Physiological Substrates*, ed. H. V. S. Peeke, M. J. Herz, 2:175–205. New York, London: Academic

41. Hein, A., Held, R. 1967. Dissociation of the visual placing response into elicited and guided components. *Science* 158: 390–92

42. Held, R., Bauer, J. A. 1966. Visually guided reaching in infant monkeys after restricted rearing. *Science* 155:718–20

43. Horn, G., Hill, R. M. 1964. Habituation of the responses to sensory stimuli of neurons in the brain stem of rabbits. *Nature* 202:296–98

44. Horn, G., Hill, R. M. 1969. Modifications of the receptive fields of cells in the visual cortex occurring spontaneously and associated with bodily tilt. *Nature* 221:186–88

45. Hubel, D. H., Wiesel, T. N. 1959. Receptive fields of single neurons in the cat's striate cortex. *J. Physiol.* 148:579–91

46. Hubel, D. H., Wiesel, T. N. 1963. Receptive fields of cells in striate cortex of very young, visually inexperienced kittens. *J. Physiol.* 26:994–1002

47. Imbert, M., Buisseret, P. 1975. Receptive field characteristics and plastic properties of visual cortical cells in kittens reared with and without visual experience. *Exp. Brain Res.* 10:389–416

48. Jacklet, J. W., Lukowiak, K. 1974 Neural processes in habituation and sensitization in model systems. *Progr. Neurobiol.* 4:1–56

49. Joh, T. H., Geghman, C., Resis, D. J. 1973. Immunochemical demonstration of increased accumulation of tyrosine hydroxylase protein in sympathetic ganglia and adrenal medulla elicited by reserpine. *Proc. Nat. Acad. Sci. USA* 70:2767–71

50. Kandel, E. R. 1974. An invertebrate system for the cellular analysis of simple behaviors and their modifications. See Ref. 16, pp. 347–70

51. Kehoe, J. S. 1972. Three acetylcholine receptors in *Aplysia* neurons. *J. Physiol.* 225:115–46

51a. Kichigina, V. F., Bragin, A. G. 1976. Functional characteristics of some hippocampal intrinsic connections. *Neyrofisiologiya* 8:259–66 (in Russian)

52. Kleinsmith, L. J. 1975. Phosphorylation of non-histone proteins in the regulation of chromosome structure and function. *J. Cell. Physiol.* 85:459–75

53. Kogan, A. B. 1972. Concerning the organization of nerve cells as neuronal ensembles. In *Contemporary Problems of Neurocybernetics,* pp. 4–20. Leningrad: Nauka (in Russian)

54. Kogan, A. B. 1975. On the cooperative principle of the cortical neuronal activity. In *Brain Mechanisms,* ed. T. N. Oniani, pp. 437–44. Tbilisi: Metsniereba. 531 pp.

55. Kopytova, F. V. 1975. Trace reactions after pairing of a sensory stimulus with polarization of the cortical visual area in rabbits. *Zh. Vyssh. Nervn. Deyat.* 25:35–44 (in Russian)

56. Kostenko, M. A., Geletyuk, V. I., Veprintsev, B. N. 1974. Completely isolated neurons in the mollusc *Limnaea stagnalis.* A new objective for nerve cell biology investigation. *Comp. Biochem. Physiol.* 49A:89–100

57. Kotlar, B. I., Mayorov, V. I., Savchenko, E. I. 1975. Correlation between different forms of trace phenomena of the rabbit visual cortex. *Zh. Vyssh. Nervn. Deyat.* 25:568–75 (in Russian)

58. Krasne, F. B. 1973. Learning in crustacea. In *Invertebrate Learning: Arthropods and gastropod molluscs,* ed. W. C. Cornig, J. A. Dyal, A. O. D. Willows, 2:49–130. New York, London: Plenum. 236 pp.

59. Kudryashov, I. E. 1975. The study of long-lasting potentiation as memory model. See Ref. 39, pp. 34–47 (in Russian)

60. Lettvin, J. Y., Maturana, H. R., Pitts, W. H., McCulloch, W. S. 1961. Two remarks on the visual system of the frog. In *Sensory Communication,* ed. W. A. Rosenblith, pp. 757–76. Cambridge: MIT Press. 844 pp.

61. Levitan, H., Tauc, L. 1972. Acetylcholine receptors: topographic distribution and pharmacological properties of two receptor types on a single molluscan neuron. *J. Physiol.* 222:537–57

62. Levitan, H., Tauc, L. 1975. Polyphasic synaptic potentials in the ganglion of the mollusc, *Navanax. J. Physiol.* 248:35–44

63. Lindsley, D. F., Rauf, S. K., Sherwood, M. J., Preston, W. G. 1973. Habituation and modification of reticular formation neuron responses to peripheral stimulation in cats. *Exp. Neurol.* 41:174–89

64. Litvinov, E. G. 1975. Pacemaker potential in the organization of the unconditioned reflex arc. See Ref. 8, pp. 130–76

65. Livanov, M. N. 1975. Some results derived from the study of memory. See Ref. 54, pp. 74–89 (in Russian)

66. Livanov, M. N. 1975. Neuronal mechanisms of memory. *Usp. Fiziol. Nauk* 6:66–89 (in Russian)

67. Magazanik, L. G., Vyskocil, F. 1975. The effect of temperature on desensitization kinetics at the post-synaptic membrane of the frog muscle fibre. *J. Physiol.* 249: 285–300

68. Magleby, K. L., Zengel, J. E. 1975. A dual effect of repetitive stimulation on post-tetanic potentiation of transmitter

release at the frog neuromuscular junction. *J. Physiol.* 245:163–82
69. Manina, A. A., Rickel, A. V., Kucherenko, R. P., Shichko, G. A. 1975. Changes in the ultrastructure of the rat cerebral cortex in the course of learning and in the case of higher nervous activity disturbance. *Zh. Vyssh. Nervn. Deyat.* 25:363–71 (in Russian)
70. Martinez-Soler, R., Shekhter, E. D. 1975. Chemical sensitivity and plasticity of the neuron. See Ref. 8, pp. 109–29
71. Matthews, H. R., Nelson, V. H. 1975. Detachment of structurally intact nerve endings from chromatolitic neurons of rat superior cervical ganglion during the depression of synaptic transmission induced by post-ganglionic axotomy. *J. Physiol.* 245:91–133
72. Menitsky, D. N., Trubachev, V. V. 1974. *Information and Problems of Higher Nervous Activity.* Leningrad: Meditsina. 231 pp. (in Russian)
73. Mitchell, D. E., Freeman, R. D., Millodot, M., Haegerstrom, G. 1973. Meridional amblyopia: evidence for modification of the human system by early visual experience. *Vis. Res.* 13:535–58
74. Mize, R. R., Murphy, E. H. 1973. Selective visual experience fails to modify receptive field properties of rabbit striate cortex neurons. *Science* 180:320–23
75. Morrell, F. 1961. Effect of anodal polarization on the firing pattern of single cortical cells. *Ann. NY Acad. Sci.* 92:860–76
76. Olson, C. R., Freeman, R. D. 1975. Progressive changes in kitten striate cortex. *J. Neurophysiol.* 38:26–32
77. O'Malkey, B. W., Woo, S. L. C., Harris, S. E., Rosen, J. M., Means, A. R. 1975. Steroid hormone regulation of specific messenger RNA and protein synthesis in eucariotic cell. *J. Cell. Physiol.* 85:343–56
78. O'Shea, M., Williams, J. L. D. 1974. The anatomy and output connection of a locust visual interneuron; the lobular giant movement detector (LGMD) neuron. *J. Comp. Physiol.* 91:257–66
79. O'Shea, M., Rowell, C. H. F., Williams, J. L. D. 1974. The anatomy of a locust visual interneuron; the descending contralateral movement detector. *J. Exp. Biol.* 60:1–12
80. Ovcharenko, Yu. S., Svechnikov, V. V. 1975. Cellular analog of learning; combination of a sound with ionophoretic application of L-glutamate. See Ref. 39, pp. 38–42 (in Russian)

81. Oyster, C. W., Takanashi, E. S. 1975. Responses of rabbit superior colliculus neurons to repeated visual stimuli. *J. Neurophysiol.* 38:301–12
82. Paigen, K., Swank, R. T., Tomito, Sh., Ganshow, E. 1975. The molecular genetics of mammalian glucoronidase. *J. Cell. Physiol.* 85:379–92
83. Pakula, A., Sokolov, E. N. 1973. Habituation in gastropoda: behavioral, interneuronal, and endoneuronal aspects. See Ref. 40, pp. 35–107
84. Pavlov, I. P. 1947. *Lektsii o Rabotye Bol'shikh Polushariy Golovnogo Mozga.* Complete collection of works, Vol. 4. Moscow, Leningrad: Izdatel'stvo Akad. Nauk. SSSR. 351 pp.
85. Pettigrew, J. D. 1976. Effects of differential experience on brain, stressing early sensory experience. See Ref. 91a
86. Pettigrew, J. D. 1974. The effect of visual experience on the development of stimulus specificity by kitten cortical neurons. *J. Physiol.* 237:49–74
87. Polyansky, V. B., Sokolov, E. N., Polkoshnikov, E. V. 1975. Light-sound interaction in the neurons of the rabbit's visual cortex. *Acta Neurobiol. Exp.* 35:51–76
88. Popot, J. L., Sugiyama, H., 1975. In vitro desensitization of *Torpedo* cholinargic receptors. *Exp. Brain Res. Suppl.* 23:163
89. Rabinovich, M. Ya. 1975. *The Closure Function of the Brain.* Moscow: Meditsina. 248 pp. (in Russian)
90. Rabinovich, M. Ya. 1975. The neurophysiological mechanisms of conditioned reflex. In *The Summaries of Science and Technology: Physiology of Man and Animals,* ed. G. A. Stepansky, 16:5–58. 118 pp. (in Russian)
91. Roitbak, A. I. 1975. Neuroglial hypothesis of the formation of temporary connections. In *Meeting of the Physiological Society of USSR,* ed. A. N. Bakuradze, pp. 63–64. Leningrad: Nauka. 340 pp.
91a. Rosenzweig, M. R., Bennett, E. L., eds. 1976. *Neural Mechanisms of Learning and Memory.* Cambridge: MIT Press
92. Rusinov, V. S. 1969. *Dominanta.* Moscow: Meditsina. 222 pp. (in Russian)
93. Rusinova, E. V., Skrebitsky, V. G. 1975. Influence of the neural discharge on the effectiveness of its synaptic inputs. *Zh. Vyssh. Nervn. Deyat.* 25:1312–15 (in Russian)
94. Salzen, E. A., Parker, D. M., Williamson, A. J. 1975. A forebrain lesion pre-

venting imprinting in domestic chicks. *Exp. Brain Res.* 24:145–57

95. Schwartz, J. H., Eisenstadt, M. L., Cedar, H. 1975. Metabolism of acetylcholine in the nervous system of *Aplysia californica*. I. Source of choline and its uptake by intact nervous tissue. *J. Gen. Physiol.* 65:225–73

96. Seimel, E. V., Ger, G. A., Voronov, I. B., Van'kin, G. I., Besnosko, B. K. 1975. Physiological role and chemical structure of synaptic receptors. See Ref. 91, 18–19

97. Shevelev, I. A., Verderevskaya, N. I., Marchenko, V. G. 1974. The complete re-adjustment of the detector properties of striate cortex neurons depending on the conditions of adaptation. *Dokl. Akad. Nauk SSSR* 217:102–4

98. Shumskaya, I. A., Korochkin, L. I. 1975. The rate of RNA synthesis in the rat hippocampus during learning. *Zh. Vyssh. Nervn. Deyat.* 25:778–83 (in Russian)

99. Shumskaya, I. A., Marchenko, N. N., Korochkin, L. I. 1975. Studies on biochemical and genetic mechanisms of learning. II. Selection for high and low rate of formation of motor conditioned responses. *Genetika* II:74–80

100. Sokolov, E. N. 1969. *Mechanisms of Memory.* Moscow Univ. Press. 175 pp. (in Russian)

101. Sokolov, E. N., Tavzarashvili, T. A. 1971. Peculiarities of biphasic postsynaptic potential (BPSP)- mediated inhibition of the pacemaker activity in *Helix pomatia. Neyrofiziologia* 3: 426–33 (in Russian)

102. Stafekhina, V. S., Vinogradova, O. S. 1975. Sensory characteristics of cortical input to hippocampus: the entorhinal cortex. *Zh. Vyssh. Nervn. Deyat.* 25:119–27 (in Russian)

103. Strumwasser, F. 1974. Neuronal principles organizing periodic behaviors. See Ref. 16, pp. 459–78

104. Thoenen, H. 1974. Trans-synaptic enzyme induction. *Life Sci.* 14:223–35

105. Thoenen, H. 1975. Trans-synaptic regulation of neuronal enzyme synthesis. *Handb. Psychopharmacol.* 3:443–75

106. Thoenen, H., Otten, U. 1975. Transsynaptic enzyme induction in adrenergic neurons as a model for neuronal plasticity. *Exp. Brain Res. Suppl.* 23:197

106a. Thompson, R. F. 1976. The search for the engram. *Am. Psychol.* 31:209–27

107. Thompson, R. F., Patterson, M. M., Teyler, T. J. 1972. The neurophysiology of learning. *Ann. Rev. Psychol.* 23:73–104

108. Thompson, R. F., Spencer, W. A. 1966. Habituation: a model phenomenon for the study of neuronal substrates of behavior. *Psychol. Rev.* 73:16–43

109. Vanyushin, B. F., Tushmalova, N. A., Gus'kova, L. V. 1974. Brain DNA methylation as indicator of the genome participation in mechanisms of individually obtained memory. *Dokl. Akad. Nauk SSSR* 219:742–44 (in Russian)

110. Vinogradova, O. S. 1975. *Hippocampus and Memory.* Moscow: Nauka. 333 pp.

111. Vinogradova, O. S., Bragin, A. G. 1975. The sensory characteristics of the cortical input of hippocampus. The dentate fascia. *Zh. Vyssh. Nervn. Deyat.* 25:410–20 (in Russian)

112. Vinogradova, O. S., Lindsley, D. F. 1964. Extinction of reactions to sensory stimuli in single neurons of visual cortex in unanesthetized rabbits. *Fed. Proc.* (transl. suppl.) 23:T241–46

113. Vital-Durant, F., Jeannerod, M. 1974. Role of visual experience in the development of optokinetic responses in kittens. *Exp. Brain Res.* 20:297–302

114. Vital-Durant, F., Putkonen, P. T. S., Jeannerod, M. 1974. Motion detection and optokinetic responses in darkreared kittens. *Vis. Res.* 14:141–42

115. Volokhov, A. A., Pigareva, Z. D. 1975. Neurophysiological and biochemical aspects of development of the rabbit visual system in conditions of light deprivation. *Zh. Vyssh. Nervn. Deyat.* 25:799–807 (in Russian)

116. Voronin, L. L., Gerstein, G. L., Kudryashov, I. E. 1975. Elaboration of a conditioned reflex in a single experiment with simultaneous recording of neural activity. *Brain Res.* 92:385–403

117. Watanabe, A., Obara, S., Akiyama, T., Yumoto, K. 1967. Electrical properties of the pacemaker neurons in the heart ganglion of stomatopod, *Squilla oratoria. J. Gen. Physiol.* 50:813–39

118. Weber, M., David-Pfeuty, T., Changeux, J. P. 1975. Regulation of binding properties of the nicotinic receptor protein by cholinergic ligands in membrane fragments from *Torpedo marmorata. Proc. Natl. Acad. Sci. USA* 72:3438–42

119. Weber, M., Popot, J. L., Grunhagen, H. 1975. Desensitization in vitro of the cholinergic receptors from *Torpedo* electric organ. *Exp. Brain Res. Suppl.* 23:215

120. Willows, A. O. D. 1974. Learning in

gastropod molluscs. See Ref. 58, pp. 187–277

121. Wine, J., Krasne, F. B., Chen, L. 1975. Habituation and inhibition of the crayfish lateral giant fibre escape response. *J. Exp. Biol.* 62:771–82

122. Yarmizina, A. L. 1975. Plasticity of the neuron. See Ref. 8, pp. 90–100 (in Russian)

123. Yeliseyeva, A. G., Soloveyva, N. A., Morozkova, T. S. 1975. Studies of higher nervous activity in rats with features of hereditary galactosemia. *Genetika* 11:72–79 (in Russian)

124. Zarkeshev, E. G., Bogoslovsky, M. M., Moroz, B. T., Silkov, V. L. 1975. On the study of conditioning mechanism in neurally isolated cortex. *Fiziol. Zh. SSSR* 61:1142–45 (in Russian)

Ann. Rev. Psychol. 1977. 28:113–40
Copyright © 1977 by Annual Reviews Inc. All rights reserved

PERSONALITY   ♦269

E. Jerry Phares and James T. Lamiell

Psychology Department, Kansas State University, Manhattan, Kansas 66506

We begin this odyssey through the year's personality literature with the usual disclaimers and caveats. We could not begin to include every worthy paper in this review. The literature cited is obviously affected by our own biases. But beyond that, we opted for a strategy of determining, almost on the basis of a frequency count of papers, the popular areas of personality research for the year 1975. Then we sampled as much as possible within these areas. As a result, many strong and heuristic papers were excluded merely because they did not readily fit the selected categories. This is a risky strategy. But page limitations require some strategy. And if they are really good papers they will survive our exclusion.

We can observe no great changes in the literature from last year to this. Therefore, since last year's reviewer provided a provocative set of observations on subject variables and methodology, we shall keep our introductory comments brief and somewhat general. This will also enable us to include more citations.

A Time of Crisis?

Many feel that social psychology is in a period of crisis. There is no reason to feel things are much different for those who study personality. For example, Elms (38) feels that we are having difficulties in our research largely because of its inherent complexities. We are reeling from the pressures of society, demands for relevance, and the voices of women and minorities who claim their "psychology" has been slighted. Some of our colleagues accuse us of abusing our research participants. And even the government is squeezing shut the horn of plenty. What is the answer? Elms (38) suggests more attention to theory coupled with theoretical pluralism. Also suggested is greater diversity in our methods, more field studies and longitudinal work, statistical innovations, and what he terms "behavioral census" studies. Finally, greater emphasis should be placed on publication of several studies in one rather than the proliferation of discrete studies as is so often the case now.

Gadlin & Ingle (47) raise some rather serious questions about the natural science methodology that has dominated the field for so long. While we remain strongly committed to the experimental method, we must admit that the pledges of progress tendered so many years ago by the experimental approach still remain promissory notes. Perhaps the time has come to widen our tolerance for diversity and encourage a greater pluralism of methods as suggested above.

Today nearly every problem is magnified to crisis proportions. However, we cannot join this chorus of crisis with a loud voice. While we can find much to criticize, it is nonetheless impressive to observe the growth, sophistication, and diversity in personality today as compared to 15 years ago. In any case, the field will surely survive despite any protestations from us.

It is our firm belief that diversity in our orientations and methods will save us all. It is constantly reassuring that not everyone sees the personality world as we do. So often in informal discussion there is much gnashing of teeth over the poor reliability of editorial and consultative judgments in our journals. But perhaps this is not all bad. We are less concerned over the potential for chaos from many babbling voices than we are over the potential for stunted growth from too much agreement.

Last year's reviewer expressed great concern over an identity crisis in personality. While we are not as bothered by what people call themselves as by seeing that the research gets done, it is true that much of what is traditionally thought of as personality research is now carried out by social psychologists. Indeed, the 1975 *Careers in Psychology* brochure published by the American Psychological Association does not specifically identify personality research as a career except incidentally in a chart where social, developmental, and personality psychology are lumped together.

A more pressing problem that may ultimately limit the quality of research in personality is related to identity issues. It has to do with the lack of clinical exposure among students of personality. This tends not only to close whole areas of experience as bases of hypothesizing, but it also creates artificial barriers among social psychology, personality, and abnormal psychology. A related point is the failure to use pathological populations, or at least populations other than college students. Some years ago academicians scorned the theoretical and empirical work of psychodynamicists or clinicians because it was almost entirely based on pathological groups—and everyone knows you cannot generalize very far from such people. But how far can we generalize from the hordes of freshmen and sophomores now employed in personality-social research?

Researchers seem to have lost touch with their subjects. Along with their students, many researchers seem sophisticated in statistics and methodology. But their lack of *sustained* contact with subject populations (particularly with abnormal groups who can highlight certain facets of behavior in a fashion analogous to what animal research can do for human research) limits their capacity to draw on the variegated and dynamic quality of human behavior.

The failure to implement systematically the Boulder model in clinical training may have hurt us all. It produces clinicians with little interest in research and indirectly produces personality-social researchers deprived of the opportunity to blend experience with clinical populations with the sophisticated methodologies of today.

So much research these days either involves routinized administration of questionnaires to groups or else unimaginative laboratory studies. Small wonder that many students now prefer to analyze data rather than run subjects. Somehow we have to get back to research that involves something other than fleeting contacts with subjects, deductions from super-ANOVA tables to the exclusion of experience with people, and the unrealities of the laboratory that may engage hierarchies of needs and cognitions wholly different from what we are trying to capture.

Interaction and Consistency

The interaction between personality and the situation along with the consistency and generality of behavior are hot topics of debate today. Some will argue that recent progress in statistical techniques has made the interactionist point of view more acceptable. Early theorists like Lewin did not need evidence from such techniques to demonstrate the utility of interactionism. Furthermore, laymen would undoubtedly blanch were they aware that psychologists were debating their own common sense.

All too often the literature seems to imply that it is necessary to prove or disprove the existence of personality and its stability, consistency, and generality. Actually the issue seems more one of utility. Is it useful to view things in this fashion and what do we gain by doing so? The value of a theoretical orientation can be of inestimable value here since a viable theory should give us insight into the manner in which personality constructs and situational variables should be weighted in each situation. Without a guiding theory we are left to thrash about with endless factor analyses, questionnaires, and correlations.

More observational studies of behavior are needed in order to better deal with questions of consistency in behavior. Maybe this will take us back to the ecology of Barker or the personality of Murray—but can that be all bad?

We also need to devote more attention to the manner in which we define consistency. And surely the definitions will turn out to be based on the pragmatics of prediction rather than on discovery of some natural principle. Do similar behaviors become similar because of their physical identity or because of the goals to which they are directed? Whatever the answer, we need a theoretical schema that will enable us to define consistency in advance of prediction and not afterward. The importance of including pathological groups is crucial here since it is highly probable that their behavior will shed a different light on issues of interactionism and consistency. Indeed, it is often the very behavioral consistency (or rigidity if you prefer) of disturbed individuals that defines their pathology.

In this same connection, we somehow need to harness the potent technologies of factor analysis, multidimensional scaling, and related methods in order to provide some beginnings in the classification of situations. Of course some guiding theory is absolutely necessary here also to impart a sense of direction to our efforts. Otherwise we shall wind up cataloging situations along some dimension of physical similarity when we should be considering situations in terms of their need satisfaction properties, cueing potential for expectancies, etc. In any case, classification is a cornerstone of science and without it we continue to drift without an anchor.

Individual Differences

Individual differences variables still do not appear as often as they should in personality studies. This is almost a contradiction in terms since many would regard personality and individual differences as one and the same. Perhaps the renewed interest in interactionism will restore individual differences to their rightful prominence. Without them (and a theory to incorporate their relationship to situational variables in a systematic way) we are left with the prospect of an endless train of studies, each representing a slight manipulation of another condition. In such popular research areas as aggression, helping, and attribution, one is especially struck by the lack of concern over personality differences. Can it be that it never matters what *kind* of kid watches Kojak on TV, or what *kind* of potentially altruistic college student is watching another drop computer cards all over the hallway, or what *kind* of Observer A is gazing at Actor B? Do we only care about Conditions X, Y, and Z?

Theory

With a few exceptions, there is little in this year's research that reflects a theoretical orientation. While it is true that investigators sometimes employ a "minitheory" to guide their work, larger behavioral theories seem little in evidence. For example, topics like locus of control and attributional processes are important determinants of behavior. But they are not the *sole* determinants. Unfortunately, without recourse to wider theories of behavior, such constructs are of limited predictive value. As a result, it is difficult to generalize from one study to another, let alone predict behavior that is simultaneously attributional, altruistic, and anxious. Because of the absence of theory or the failure to transcend the boundaries imposed by minitheories, it is easy to overestimate the importance of particular constructs or processes. It is just as easy, consequently, to pursue relentlessly more and more information about the conditions that are of minor overall importance in behavior.

There does seem to be at least a modest trend toward publishing more than one discrete study per article. This is a healthy trend that may encourage investigators to become reacquainted with theory. In their quest for relevance, many investigators seem to have given up theory. Maybe somewhere along the line they will realize that theory and relevance are not enemies but natural companions.

REVIEW OF THE LITERATURE

Locus of Control

Research on internal-external control of reinforcement (I-E) continues at a phenomenal rate. Prociuk & Lussier (131) compiled a bibliography of 277 locus of control studies published during the 2 years of 1973–1974. Thornhill, Thornhill & Youngman (168) have also constructed a computerized bibliography of over 1200 references to published and unpublished research.

A book by Phares (126) describes the origins and theoretical foundation of I-E along with the measurement, principal correlates, functions, antecedents, and methods of changing I-E beliefs. A more concise treatment also was published (Phares 127).

At least three reasons may account for this prodigious output. First, there is the recognition that individual differences in attribution of responsibility for reinforcement to self or others are a potent contributor to behavior. Second, scales for measuring I-E are objective and easy to score. Third, many researchers seem to possess an abiding compulsion to correlate a popular scale with everything in sight. Hopefully, the first reason is the most important.

In the rush to study the relationship between I-E and a variety of variables, investigators have generally paid little heed to the more theoretical aspects of the construct. In an important paper, Rotter (137) discusses the place of I-E in a social learning theory of personality. He also deals with the importance of considering the value of the goals toward which behavior is directed and not just I-E. Discussed also are issues of specificity-generality and the tendency to "automatically" attribute positive qualities to internals and negative ones to externals. He also covers problems and misconceptions of measurement, factor analysis, unidimensionality and multidimensionality, and the meaning of externality.

Several papers incorporated some of these points. For example, Naditch & DeMaio (119) found that in ninth graders, several measures of competence were related to locus of control but *only* when the incentive value of those activities was high. In a different approach, Srull & Karabanick (161) employed cheating behavior as an index of reinforcement value. Thus internals cheated more in a skill situation than in a chance situation and more than externals in the skill situation. Externals cheated more in the chance situation than the skill situation and more than internals in the chance situation. This suggests the moderating role of goal values in certain situations.

Another trend of note is the attempt to elaborate the meaning of an external locus of control. Hochreich (66) distinguished among defensive externals, congruent externals, and internals. Defensive externals are those who receive high external scores but respond in a low trusting fashion on the Interpersonal Trust Scale (Rotter 136). Congruent externals respond in a high trusting manner. Defensive externals are viewed as being essentially internal but, having a relatively lower expectancy for success, adopt an external facade in order to guard against possible failure. Hochreich (66) found, as predicted, that defensive externals were more likely than congruent externals or internals to resort to blame projection following failure on an achievement task. No differences were expected or observed following success on the task.

Prociuk & Breen (130) used Levenson's (95) Internal (I), Powerful Others (P), and Chance (C) scales. High scores on the P scale indicated defensive externality and high scores on the C scale were used to designate congruent external beliefs. They found that internals were academically superior to both defensive and congruent externals and that defensive externals achieved higher grade point averages than congruent externals.

Relationships between externality and maladjustment, diminished functioning, and symptomatology continue to be studied. While most studies show relationships between externality and anxiety, there are exceptions. For example, Lefcourt, Hogg & Sordoni (89) note that objective self-awareness is a more disruptive state for internals than for externals. Perhaps, as Phares (126) observed, the better apparent adjustment of internals is in part a function of their denial tendencies. However, one would do well to recall the previous admonition against assuming that an internal orientation will always be the "best" orientation. Naditch, Gargan & Michael (120) used a variety of paper and pencil measures to study men in Army basic training. As in previous studies, a belief in external control was associated with depression and anxiety. Also with an Army sample, Naditch (118) obtained results indicating that increasing external scores are associated with increased drinking behavior. While this result is not consistent with previous work that found internality to be a characteristic of alcoholics in treatment, it seems consistent with the observation (Phares 126) that such alcoholics may have learned to verbalize internal beliefs as part of confidence building.

Turning to a more attributional aspect of I-E, Page & Roy (125) found that in a classroom setting externals blamed the instructor more than did internals after receiving a low grade. No difference between groups was observed following receipt of high grades. Lefcourt et al (90) found that high-confident internals attributed responsibility for outcomes to themselves more than did low-confident externals—especially after failure.

Wolk & Kurtz (178) examined a noninstitutionalized elderly population. Internal beliefs related to indices of adjustment, satisfaction, and involvement. One wonders whether the same results would obtain in a lower socioeconomic group of institutionalized elderly people (conceivably an external orientation would be more serviceable in such a population). Interestingly too, Wolk & Kurtz found their elderly sample to be much more internal than current younger samples. Clearly, older groups ought to be more external, but perhaps these older groups were, as Wolk & Kurtz suggest, raised in a more "internal era." Such a finding is intriguing and offers fertile ground for further investigations of the social and cultural antecedents of I-E beliefs.

Several studies have suggested that I-E differences can alter the usual findings that interpersonal attraction is a function of similarity. Nowicki & Blumberg (123) found that, contrary to prediction, both internals and externals were more attracted to an internal stranger. Johnson & Cerretto (73) concluded that the similarity hypothesis holds for internals but not for externals. Holmes & Jackson (69) observed that internals were more attracted (and less angry) to the experimenter than were externals in conditions involving rewards and punishments. The reverse was true in a nonevaluative condition. In a within-subjects design, however, Lombardo, Steigleder & Feinberg (100) found that internals were attracted to the internal stranger and externals to the external stranger.

Research on the relationship between I-E and helping appears unsettled. Lerner & Reavy (94) conducted two studies. The first revealed helping behavior under certain conditions on the part of both internals and externals. In the second study, externals engaged in some helping, but the internals exhibited little helping behavior regardless of the experimental conditions. Phares & Lamiell (128) presented brief case histories of several people in need and asked subjects to rate their deservingness of help. In general, internals sanctioned significantly less in the way of help than did externals. Degree of ambiguity as regards responsibility in the case histories had no differential effect on help ratings. It seems clear that the relationship between I-E and helping is moderated by a number of situational variables such as the direct-indirect nature of the help, face-to-face or remote relationships, competence facets of the helper, etc.

Some other interesting correlates of internality include weight reduction (Balch & Ross 4) and "supermale" sex stereotypes (Hochreich 67). Silvern (155) observed that externality is associated with left-wing political positions. Taub & Dollinger (165) found that internal children seem to require less motivational manipulation to elicit achievement behavior than do similar externals.

A very important research area involves the search for antecedents. Unfortunately, most of the work from prior years involves correlations between subjects' I-E scores and their responses (or their parents' responses) to parent-child questionnaires. Hopefully, future research will involve *observations* of parent-child interactions so that we will not have to rely on retrospective accounts or memories with all their potential for distortion. The kind of study which has some heuristic potential is exemplified by Loeb (99). Fourth and fifth grade boys were observed while working on a task. Parents were instructed to aid their sons as little or as much as they wished. External sons more frequently had highly directive parents who intruded into the tasks. Internal sons, on the other hand, had much less directive parents.

A second critical research arena involves methods of altering locus of control beliefs. A spate of studies in 1974 linked changes to a variety of psychotherapeutic techniques. More recently, Kilmann, Albert & Sotile (77) suggest that external clients profit most from structured therapy in a spaced time format while internal clients operate best with lessened therapist control. Moser (117) argues that structured group interactions can produce internality in an adolescent population of felons. Unfortunately, these techniques are so heterogeneous that it almost seems that any group or individual therapeutic technique is capable of producing changes in the internal direction. Until research begins to identify the specific variables (patient and process) responsible for changes we shall have only limited understanding here.

SITUATIONAL ASPECTS OF LOCUS OF CONTROL   Several studies, while not involving locus of control directly, do contribute to our understanding of the conditions which may induce I-E beliefs. In the learned helplessness paradigm, Gatchel, Paulus & Maples (49) found that inescapable aversive tones led to performance decrements on an anagrams task. The learned helplessness group also reported greater anxiety, depression, and hostility. Hiroto & Seligman (65) argue that learned helplessness is an induced trait. They note that both insolubility of a problem and inescapability of punishment seem to engender expectancies that responding is independent of reinforcement. Roth & Kubal (135) obtained a curvilinear relationship between experiences of no control and helpless behavior. Seligman's (147) book relates helplessness to phenomena of depression, development, and death. What produces the illusion of control? Langer (87) feels that objective contingencies are not crucial. The introduction of competition, choice, familiarity, and active or passive involvement in chance situations leads to skill overtones. Likewise, Langer & Roth (88) found that in a coin tossing task (chance), manipulation of order of successes and failures and playing an actor or observer role significantly affected expectancies for success and evaluation of past performances. Similarly, Wortman (180) demonstrated that merely "causing" a chance outcome and having foreknowledge about the consequences induces feelings of perceived control.

At a more attributional level, Dweck (36) feels that for so-called helpless children, learning to attribute poor performance to lack of personal motivation seems better than learning to make attributions to lack of ability or to uncontrollable events.

Allowing students a choice over preferred classes as compared to assignment by chance leads to better performance and reported greater satisfaction (Liem 98). Also, perceived choice and feelings of internal control are greater when a decision involves positive options than when it involves negative ones (Harvey & Harris 63). Finally, Wortman & Brehm (181) have made an attempt to integrate reactance theory with the learned helplessness model.

Achievement Motivation

Achievement has fallen from its former level of preeminence, but it is still an area of significant interest. Kukla (85) found that subjects high in resultant achievement motivation performed better than those low in resultant achievement motivation when the task was perceived as difficult. The opposite results obtained with easy tasks. Such work is said to suggest the need for revisions in the Spence-Atkinson-Weiner approaches (86). Work by Weiner & Sierad (176) is supportive of an attributional analysis of Expectancy X Value theory. Trope (170) and Trope & Brickman (171) argue that it is the informational value rather than the affective value of performance outcomes that determine choice among tasks. Goldman (54), using females, found that subjects high in n Ach were greater risk takers on a risky problem than were low n Ach subjects. Groups in which high n achievers outnumbered low n achievers showed a greater risky shift on risky problems than did groups in which the ratio was reversed.

Much of the achievement motivation research contains two elements that are sadly lacking in many personality studies these days. The first element is the basic recognition of the importance of individual differences. The second is the exciting presence of a theoretico-deductive approach to research. Whether one agrees or disagrees with specific constructs or conclusions of n Ach research, it is worth the price of admission just to watch investigators deductively negotiate the pathways connecting theory, hypotheses, methods, and conclusions.

An intellectual descendant of achievement motivation has surfaced again this year in McClelland's (108) book on the experience of power.

A Potpourri of Individual Differences

Other than locus of control and the old standby, need for achievement, not as much work on individual differences, the traditional core of the personality area, appeared as one might like.

Interpersonal trust, typically measured by Rotter's (136) scale, continues to attract investigators. Further construct validity was provided by Wright, Maggied & Palmer (182) in a straightforward study that utilized an unobtrusive method rather than the usual laboratory studies, self-reports, or ratings by others. Garske (48) reports that low trusters show significantly more differentiated cognitions for socially distant persons than do high trusters. Socially close persons yielded significantly lower complexity scores for high trusters than low trusters and significantly greater complexity for females than males. Hochreich (67) found that "supermales" were seen by both males and females as lower in trust than "superfemales." Wright & Tedeschi (183) carried out separate factor analyses on the Trust Scale over four samples and found three orthogonal factors that cross-validated over all samples. Contrary to expectations, McAllister & Kiesler (107) found no differences between high and low trusters as regards their self-disclosing behavior. All in all, given the presumed low estate to which trust has fallen in our society, it might well behoove investigators to incorporate systematically the interpersonal trust dimension into investigations of phenomena such as helping, attraction, and attribution.

Some work on cognitive complexity appeared. For example, Press, Crockett & Delia (129) noted that an orientation to evaluate another minimizes the cognitive complexity factor while an orientation to understand facilitates the complex perceiver's impressions and use of motivational inferences. Robbins (133) found that high dogmatic and low dogmatic subjects differed on a variety of interpersonal judgments. Cravens (22) observes that those high in need for approval revealed themselves more intimately in public than in private while low and moderate subjects did the reverse.

Eysenck (41) studied activation and extraversion as they relate to category and item recall. Schwartz (146) feels that introverts focus on the physical aspects of verbal material and extraverts organize memory around semantic cues. Mehryar, Khajavi & Hekmat (111) factor analyzed two scales, and Eaves & Eysenck (37) studied extraversion in a large sample of adult twins. Harkins & Geen (62) found that introverts could better distinguish the signal from the noise in a signal detection task than could extraverts.

Personality, the Situation, and Interactionism

An issue of continuing interest is the relative importance of personality, stiuational variables, and their interaction. Reflecting this is a recent book edited by Endler & Magnusson (39).

While the espousal of situationism has given way to a more moderate interactionism, several articles this year serve to reiterate the importance of personality variables in their own right. A survey by Sarason, Smith & Diener (143) concludes that the slight superiority of situational variables hardly suggests their prepotence.

Exploring the Persons X Situations X Responses paradigm, Cartwright (20) maintains that such studies have been unjustifiably biased against discovering appreciable person variance. He then shows that by eliminating variance attributable to response modes, and by restricting the range of situations, one can increase person variance substantially.

In the midst of the debate as to whether personality or situational factors account for more of the total variance, Golding (53) suggests that the question may be academic. He argues that if consistency in personality is defined by the limits of the trans-situational generalizability of the ordering of persons on a given personality dimension, then the proper statistic for investigation is the coefficient of generalizability and not the omega-squared ratio. Mindful of the potential counterargument that the issue is not (nor at least not *only*) one of consistency in personality, but also one of determining the relative utility of personality and situational factors in accounting for criterion variance, Golding reiterates the hazards involved in assuming interval or ratio scales of measurement. While he remains as technically correct as others who have raised this issue, we still feel that omega-squared ratios may provide important information, despite possible violations of assumptions regarding scale properties. It is noteworthy that, based on Golding's calculations of coefficients of generalizability for some earlier data, the conclusions to be drawn regarding the relative importance of person and situation factors are identical to those one would draw based on omega-squared ratios.

Snyder & Monson (157) have suggested that cross-situational consistency vs inconsistency may itself be a personality dimension. They note, however, that situational factors may influence self-monitoring of appropriate behavior, which will, in turn, affect cross-situational consistency. We believe this is where we came in.

Noting that the concept of interactionism, as it was defined by early theorists, normally refers to the interaction of a person with the *meaningful* environment, Magnusson & Ekehammar (103) investigated the congruence between the *perceptions* of stressful situations and *reactions to* those situations. They found evidence for a lack of complete isomorphism between reaction data and perception data, and discussed the theoretical importance of the possibility that situation perception and situation reaction will not be the same for all individuals across different types of situations.

A factor analytic approach to the discovery of the "true" factors of personality still find favor among some personality theorists. Guilford (59) reviews some evidence in support of his factors relative to those proposed by Eysenck and by Cattell. He argues that the use of ratings in factor analysis can reveal as much about the conception of traits on the part of the raters as it can about personality dimensions.

The latter point is noteworthy because Shweder (153) has argued that Guilford's criticisms may apply to factor-derived traits in general, whether those factors are based on observers' ratings of subjects, retrospective interviews/questionnaires, or self-report inventories. Shweder presents evidence that these factors are better accounted for by the perceived similarity between behaviors comprising the factors than by the relationship between these factors and individual differences in the referent behaviors. The issue is crucial, for it strikes at the foundation of our conception of personality in terms of individual differences.

Finally, Cronbach (23) has argued that because two-way "Attitude X Treatment" interactions are themselves nearly always mediated by higher-order interactions, we might do well to abandon our search for universal, transhistorical principles of human behavior.

Aggression

Earlier reviewers have expressed some dismay about the study of aggression, pointing to such factors as the nonrepresentativeness of experimental designs and the failure to conceptualize the social nature of aggression. Several investigations this year have incorporated reasonably representative designs and cognitive factors have received systematic attention.

Current emphasis on cognitive factors seems attributable in part to inconsistencies in research based on simpler "S-R" conceptualizations. For example, in a study of the effects of movie violence on aggression, Leyens et al (97) found that Belgian boys given a week-long diet of violent films behaved more aggressively than did boys exposed to neutral films. However, in an investigation employing the standard "Buss paradigm," Manning & Taylor (104) failed to obtain this effect. In addition, although not focusing on interpersonal aggression, Milgram & Shotland (113) failed in eight experiments to demonstrate any systematic relationship between the occurrence of an antisocial act on a popular network television show and the imitation of that act by viewers.

To resolve some of the above inconsistencies, Tannenbaum & Zillmann (164) propose a two-factor model to account for the effects of media communications on aggressive behavior. Their evidence shows that arousal alone does not reliably produce aggression and that media communications differing in aggressive content do produce differences in aggressive responding. They suggest that the concepts of transfer of arousal (through time) and cognitive misattribution of the source of arousal may provide the foundation for a theoretical framework within which the effects of media communications on aggression may be understood as a function of both emotional and cognitive factors. Geen (50) found that among subjects who have been previously attacked (and thus provided with a context in which arousal could be attributed to an aggressive attack), the observation of real as opposed to fictional violence results in higher levels of emotional arousal and aggression. While Geen did not discuss his results in terms of Tannenbaum & Zillmann's model, his data do seem compatible.

The inadequacy of strict S-R theories of aggression is highlighted by studies on the effects of various forms of extraneous arousal on subsequent aggression. Thus Konecni (79) contrasted the so-called arousal-level hypothesis with a cognitive labeling hypothesis, and the data supported the latter hypothesis. Work by Baron & Bell (6) and Donnerstein, Donnerstein & Evans (34) was also inconsistent with the arousal-level hypothesis, as well as with what would be expected from the cognitive labeling view. Thus, while cognitions are as important as arousal level, their exact roles are unclear.

The cognitive focus is also present in studies based on Zimbardo's (185) deindividuation and disinhibition of aggression. In a naturalistic study, Turner, Layton & Simons (172) investigated horn-honking in response to delay at a traffic light and noted that aggressive behavior was most likely when a situational cue was present in an aggressive context *and* where victim visibility was low.

Bond & Dutton (13) note that Zimbardo had suggested anonymity as a factor bearing on the creation of a deindividuated state and thus on the subsequent occurrence of aggression. However, those authors found that the crucial mediating variable is the victim's potential for counterattack, not simply the aggressor's expectation of future interaction. In the same study, they supported Zimbardo's prediction that when deindividuation occurs, a series of aggressive responses should progressively increase in vigor. Goldstein, Davis & Herman (55) found that not only aggression but also rewarding behavior tends to escalate over trials, suggesting that disinhibition may have implications for prosocial behavior as well.

In contrast to Bond & Dutton, Diener et al (30) obtained direct measures of deindividuation and found that although the experimental manipulations produced the predicted differences in overt aggression, these manipulations did not produce differences in measured deindividuation. Moreover, the variance in deindividuation was not systematically related to variance in levels of overt aggression.

However, Bandura, Underwood & Fromson (5) were successful in linking theoretically relevant independent variables, the organismic process of disinhibition, and overt aggression. Specifically in addition to showing that subects behave more punitively when responsibility for punitiveness is diffused and that dehumanized victims are punished more than humanized victims Bandura et al showed that self-disinhibiting justifications for punitiveness increase as the victim is dehumanized and that self-disinhibited subjects are more punitive than subjects who react to their punitive role by disapproving the use of punishment.

Disinhibition also seems useful for interpreting data reported by Wilson & Rogers (177), who found that blacks delivered more intense shock and direct verbal hostility to white men than to black targets.

Several studies involve the responses of those who have been aggressed upon. Zillman et al (184) found that under conditions of moderate arousal, mitigating circumstances surrounding initial provocation reduced retaliatory aggression, while under conditions of high arousal, no such effect was observed. Sanders & Baron (141) found that when a subject is not reinforced with a passive response from the target for his first aggressive response, subsequent aggression is reduced when the victim emits high pain cues, presumably reflecting guilt feelings on the part of the aggressor. In contrast, when the target responds passively to the subject's first aggressive response, there is no difference in the subject's subsequent aggression as a function of high vs low pain cues emitted by the target; this finding is attributed to the subject's perception that he has been able to effectively control the aggressiveness of his opponent. In two studies, Borden (14) found that the sex and the inferred or explicit values (passive or aggressive) of an observer can influence subjects' aggression levels.

In a comparison of three strategies for reducing attack-instigated aggression, Dengerink & Bertilson (27) had a confederate first instigate a high level of aggression on the part of the subject, and then revert to (*a*) matching strategy, (*b*) a strategy whereby the responses of the confederate were yoked to the responses of a previously tested subject exposed to the matching strategy, and (*c*) a withdrawal strategy, where the confederate maintained the lowest possible setting. The authors found that the withdrawal condition was most effective in reducing aggression. Individual differences in locus of control and in field dependence-independence were also found to mediate aggressive responses to attack (Dengerink, O'Leary & Kasner 28).

Donnerstein & Donnerstein (33) assessed the comparative effects of potential for retaliation and attitude similarity in controlling aggressive behavior and noted that attitudinal similarity is generally more effective than retaliation.

The concept of catharsis still occupies the attention of researchers. Manning & Taylor (104) challenged the assumption of a one-to-one relationship between hostility and aggression, obtaining evidence in support of their view that hostility as an emotion is subject to a cathartic process, while aggression as overt behavior is not. The authors caution against removing all violent shows from television, as they may constitute a valuable outlet for hostility. Unfortunately, their conclusion seems premature since it is not clear why reduced hostility is valuable. They offer no evidence that lowered hostility is positively related to desirable interpersonal behaviors. Indeed, Geen, Stonner & Shope (51) report data indicating that just the opposite may be true.

Consistent with the trend noted earlier in other lines of research, Green & Murray (56) view catharsis as both an emotional and cognitive phenomenon. They found that subjects given an opportunity to express negative feelings toward an aggressive confederate, and for whom such expression appeared to result in a nonaggressive reinterpretation by the confederate of his earlier aggressiveness, exhibited less aggression toward the confederate than did subjects who were either allowed expression of negative feelings or provided the nonaggressive reinterpretation (but not both).

Women and Sex Roles

Papers on the roles, performance, and motivation of women continue at a brisk pace. They run the gamut from consciousness raising to empirical and theoretical contributions.

Shields (150) traces some of the history of the psychology of women as it existed prior to its incorporation into psychoanalytic theory. Shields (151) also details Leta Hollingworth's role in stimulating psychology to investigate social questions inherent in the psychology of women. Bernstein & Russo (11) remind us of the psychological contributions of several women psychologists.

Horner's (70) speculations regarding fear of success in women continue as a catalyst. However, several recent studies have been less than supportive. For example, Brown, Jennings & Vanik (17) studied college and high school males and females and noted that several aspects of their results were discrepant from Horner's predictions.

Sorrentino & Short (158) proposed that Horner's measure of motive to avoid success may really be a measure of ability. Presenting the same task as either a male- or a female-oriented task, they found that women performed better at a male task than at a female one, especially in the case of women high in motive to avoid success. This is opposite from the deduction that would be made from Horner's position. In an extension of earlier work, Heilbrun & Kleemeier (64) conclude that perhaps females choose not to compete in certain activities because they achieve vicarious gratification from the achievement of males.

Zuckerman & Wheeler (186) reviewed the research of Horner and others regarding the motive to avoid success. They conclude that Horner's results offer little support for the view that women who fear success perform poorly under competitive conditions. They also find no reliable age or sex differences in the motive to avoid success nor any relationship between fear of success and sex-role orientation. They argue that it is not clear whether measures of fear of success tap a motive or a cultural stereotype.

In a thoughtful paper dealing with the entire area of achievement motivation in females, Alper (2) suggests several reasons why the now-you-see-it-now-you-don't phenomena have occurred. These reasons include personality factors, sampling differences, stimulus cues, and scoring differences among various studies.

Psychological androgeny is a topic that will surely mobilize a host of researchers. Androgeny signifies that individuals may be simultaneously masculine and feminine and that highly sex-typed individuals may be seriously limited in their behavioral flexibility. Bem (8) discussed the notion and offered a scale to measure psychological androgeny, More recently she has reported two experiments to validate her Sex Role Inventory (Bem 9). She concludes that so-called androgenous individuals will behave in an effective masculine or feminine manner depending upon the demand characteristics of the situation.

While it hardly seems reasonable to dispute the point that individuals may vary reliably in their behavioral flexibility, it seems apparent that how one regards such individuals is heavily entangled with personal and social values. For example, Bem (9) repeatedly refers to nonandrogenous subjects as showing behavioral deficits, and to androgenous subjects as doing well. She describes feminine females as having "flunked" critical tasks. One implication is that the androgenous person is better adjusted than the nonandrogenous person. While the androgenous reader may agree, the nonandrogenous reader may not.

Strahan (163) criticizes Bem's use of a t ratio measure of psychological androgeny and suggests the use of the simple difference score instead. Spence, Helmreich & Stapp (159) also argue that masculinity and femininity should be construed as a duality—that each is a separate and socially desirable component that is present in both sexes (though in different degrees). They assert that androgeny is the most desirable state. Contrary to Bem, however, these investigators seem to stress not so much balance, but a *high* degree of both characteristics as the most desirable state.

Research relating sex-role variables and occupational phenomena was prominent this year and confirmed several factors inhibiting the entry of women into certain occupations (Feather 43, Feather & Simon 44, O'Leary 124, Taynor & Deaux 167).

Vogel & Rosenkratz (173), in a study of single women attending a Catholic women's college, conclude that women who have nonstereotyped sex-role self-concepts tend to prefer more innovative sex roles in their education, child bearing activities, and employment. Goldberg, Gottesdiener & Abramson (52) asked subjects to judge the attractiveness of photos of young women whose attitude toward the feminist movement had been established. There were no sex differences in the ratings, and no real differences in the attractiveness of the photos could be linked to their belonging to the feminist movement. Nevertheless, when other subjects stated who belonged to the feminist movement, they consistently chose the less attractive women. Both male and female subjects did this regardless of their own attitudes toward the movement. In a questionnaire study of black and white female college students, Gump (60) notes that the black women were more likely to define their role as wife and mother and as home-centered, while the white students were more oriented toward furthering their own development rather than fulfilling a traditional role. It is not clear, however, how far one can generalize these results beyond a college sample.

A new look at an old observation was taken by Losco & Epstein (102). In a study of cartoon humor, they observed that both sexes preferred cartoons in which the butt of the joke was a female. Apparently females have less emotional investment in female dominance than males have in male dominance. Not surprisingly, Hoffman (68) found that in white, middle class children, consideration for others is more characteristic of girls than boys. Also, moral transgressions are more likely to be associated with guilt in females. Dion (32) observed that self-esteem in women is more vulnerable to interpersonal rejection from men as compared to other women.

Attribution

Research on attributional processes is burgeoning to the point where nearly every issue of social and personality journals includes several studies. While attribution is usually considered the province of social psychologists, we have chosen to include at least a brief sample of the area under the personality heading.

Two points seem especially relevant to this research area. First, much of the work suffers from its failure to be incorporated into a larger theory of behavior. That is, while such processes as the attribution of causality, responsibility, or intent are quite important, they do not operate in isolation from other variables. An ever-present danger in the rush to learn more and more about attributions is that their role in concert with needs, expectancies, or other variables that assist us in choosing to behave one way rather than another will be ignored. While some may feel that attribution theory is theory enough, our contention is that attribution may most usefully be considered one aspect of behavior. Thus a larger, more encompassing behavior theory is required.

A second and related point involves the role of attribution as a potential mediator of a host of social and interpersonal reactions such as helping, interpersonal distance, attraction, interpersonal trust, etc. However, if this year's research is any indication, researchers are more preoccupied with the process than they are with the consequences of attributions. For example, Shaver (148), in an introductory book, devotes 124 pages to the elements, theories, and process of attribution but only 13 pages to the interpersonal and social consequences of attribution! The most frequent topic this year was actor-observer differences in attribution. Such interest is a continuing response to the earlier Jones & Nisbett (74) paper. Consistent with the latter, Gurwitz & Panciera (61) dealt with attributions of freedom and found that students perceived teachers as having greater freedom than the teachers viewed themselves as having. What is more, each subject's partner perceived the subject's behavior during the experiment as more indicative of his behavior in general than the subject did. Miller (114) also remarks on the tendency of observers to attribute more generality to the acts of others than do the actors themselves. Further support for Jones & Nisbett comes from a study by Sherrod & Farber (149), who showed that actors attribute their failure to situational factors while observers attribute in dispositional terms.

Regan & Totten (132) tested the notion that the phenomenological aspects of a situation are more salient to actors but that actor characteristics are more salient to observers. They conclude that taking the perspective of the actor leads to attributions that are more situational, while a simple observational perspective leads to dispositional attributions. Arkin & Duval (3) feel that the focus of attention is the crucial factor here. Miller & Norman (115) emphasized the active-passive set of observers but, contrary to Jones & Nisbett, actors seemed more dispositionally oriented. The influence of positive vs negative behavior is important according to Stephan (162), who noted that both actors and observers make more situational attributions to positive behavior. Taylor & Fiske (166) argue that in making causal judgments, an observer will often attribute the most salient source of information as a cause. Karaz & Perlman (75) note that when actors are consistent and successful, observers see their behavior as determined by internal factors rather than circumstances. Clearly there is no end to the experimental variants that can influence actor-observer differences in attribution.

At least one study (Batson 7) did deal with attribution as a mediator of other behavior and found that the manner in which help is offered is a function of the locus of the problem.

McGee & Snyder (109) dealt with situational-dispositional attributions as an individual differences variable. In a clever field study, they observed people in restaurants salting their food. They found that those who salt their food before eating are dispositionally oriented, while those who salt their food after tasting are situationally oriented.

Personal determinants of attribution of responsibility and causality continue to attract attention. Miller & Ross (116), in a review of the literature, conclude that there is little empirical support for viewing attributions of causality as self-serving or defensive. However, they suggest that there is some support for self-enhancement determinants of attributions. McKillip & Posavac (110), on the old issue of responsibility for an accident, conducted two experiments supportive of the notion of the defensive attribution of responsibility for serious negative outcomes. Aderman, Archer & Harris (1) had subjects role-play innocent victims, responsible victims, or harmdoing responsible victims during a five-minute ride in a wheelchair through a hospital corridor. Here subjects in the innocent victim condition tended to display compassion for the undeserved suffering by a victim. Such results seem to contradict a just world hypothesis. Finally, in another variant of the accident paradigm, Brickman, Ryan & Wortman (16) demonstrated that immediate vs prior causes and internal vs external causes can affect the attribution of responsibility.

Interpersonal Attraction

Research into the determinants, consequences, and theory of interpersonal attraction continues. Both informational and affective analyses have vocal advocates, but Byrne, Rasche & Kelley (18) suggest that both approaches may be necessary for a really comprehensive explanation of attraction.

Many have long felt that mere attitude similarity represents an oversimplification of the determinants of interpersonal attraction. In support, Leonard (92) finds that the usual relationship between similarity and attraction holds for those with a favorable self-concept, but persons with a negative self-concept do not show a preference for similar others. Furthermore, this study employed a face-to-face procedure rather than "xeroxed descriptions of others." Other work incompatible with the usual similarity-attraction findings was discussed earlier in the locus of control section.

Still other work seems to soften the relationship between attraction and similarity. Grush, Clore & Costin (58) observe that when a dissimilar trait in another is instrumental to one's achieving satisfaction, then attraction and dissimilarity will be related. While such a finding would seem but to confirm common sense, an empirical demonstration is certainly welcome. Comparing attracted and nonattracted pairs of counselors in summer camps, Wagner (174) concluded that both the compatability of people's needs and the extent to which their behavior fulfills role expectations are important. Touhey (169) confirmed the usual attraction-similarity finding but only when there is agreement between a subject's self-concept and the behavior of another person. When couples actually went on dates after computer matching, Curran & Lippold (24) found that while attitude similarity did not affect attraction in any substantial manner, physical attractiveness was related to interpersonal attraction in males in two studies and in females in one study. One wonders whether such findings would continue to hold after several dates. Sachs (140), in trying to "deconfound" belief similarity from attitude similarity, found that both attitude and belief similarity affect attraction, but more so with attitudes.

Physical attractiveness also came in for its share of study this year (Dermer & Thiel 29, Kleck & Rubinstein 78, Krebs & Adinolfi 82). Sigall & Ostrove (154) noted the biasing effects of physical attractiveness in simulated jury settings.

Helping and Altruism

This is an area that seems to cut across the traditional boundaries of personality and social psychology. In general, the research seems to be guided less by any coherent theoretical schema than by sheer common sense. If the past is any indicant of the future, we are in for a long series of helping studies, each representing a somewhat different situational or dispositional manipulation. What could result is a large catalog of possible determinants of altruistic behavior. The coherent integration of these catalog entries is something else again. If there is hope for theoretical integration in this area, it will apparently have to come from an inductive rather than a deductive process.

One highly desirable feature of several studies on helping is their tendency to be conducted in field settings. They are often quite ingenious and help meet the frequent criticism that psychological research is too laboratory-oriented. Often the investigator's ability to control variables did not seem to be seriously hampered at all. Thus one wonders whether fear of loss of ability to exert the usual laboratory control is just a rationalization for an unwillingness to break our routinized patterns of research. At the same time, there seems to be little rush to increase the incorporation of personality variables into this research area.

Effects of race were included in two studies. Katz, Cohen & Glass (76) had confederates telephone to ask for responses to a consumer product and also used a confederate to ask subjects in a subway station for change for a quarter. Minority help-seekers were favored over whites when both displayed similar socially desirable characteristics. Wegner & Crano (175) had the experimenter drop a deck of computer cards. It was observed that black bystanders helped more black than white "victims" while white bystanders helped victims of both races equally.

Mathews & Canon (106) demonstrated that subjects offer greater help under low noise levels. The interpretation offered is that noise-produced arousal leads to a restriction in attention. This may or may not be the best explanation. However, what is particularly noteworthy about this study is that the investigators first produced their results in laboratory settings. Later, in a very ingenious fashion, they conducted a similar procedure in the field, giving their results the strength of generality. Holland was the setting for a study by Korte, Ypma & Toppen (80) that suggested that greater helping occurs when environmental input is low.

Several years ago Darley & Batson (25) concluded that reading the parable of the Good Samaritan had no effect on the prosocial behavior of seminary students. Greenwald (57) reanalyzed this data using a Bayesian approach and concludes that Darley & Batson's data did, in fact, support the effects of the parable on behavior. Clark (21) carried out a field study that involved asking for directions, and concluded that being reinforced for helping increased future helping more than did being negatively reinforced and that subjects were particularly helpful to dependent persons. When playing a nonzero-sum game, subjects exposed earlier to a prosocial newscast behaved more cooperatively than those exposed to an antisocial newscast (Hornstein et al 71).

Krebs (81) showed that subjects who experience the strongest empathic reactions toward another were most willing to help even though it meant jeopardizing their own welfare. On the other side of the prosocial coin, Wolosin, Sherman & Mynatt (179) conducted a shock experiment in which amount of punishment delivered in return by a victim varied as a function of the amount of previous shock received. Also, victims delivered fewer shocks than they received. Perhaps this is another instance of the operation of empathy. Fink et al (46) studied a campus blood drive. Males but not females responded more to an appeal based on equity than to one based on the dependency of others. In both sexes, a nontraditional sex-role orientation was associated with a similar response to both types of appeals. For the traditional sex-role orientation, response to equity was greater than to dependency.

Rushton (139) found modeling to be a potent determinant of children's sharing behavior. The sharing was not confined to a short-term period nor was it exclusively specific to one situation. Johnson (72) noted that cooperation in fourth graders was related to their ability to assume the emotional perspective of another. Long & Lerner (101) either paid or overpaid children to test a toy. Given the opportunity to donate money to poor children, overpaid children tended to donate more money.

Anxiety and Stress

This research area nearly defies any attempt to impose organization. For a concept that so many psychologists are convinced they cannot live without, there is very little agreement as to its nature (Rotter & Hochreich 138). For some the concept is treated as a dependent variable. For others it is an independent variable. And for still others it is an intervening variable. At the level of individual differences it is both a state and a trait. The variety of measures used to tap anxiety is awesome indeed and spans the range from pencil marks on a test paper to electrodermal responses. The lack of agreement among measures that should yield comparable data is also awesome. To some degree or other, this year's research reflects all these comments.

Endler & Okada (40) present reliability and some validity data on a new multidimensional measure of trait anxiety. Finch et al (45) studied the State-Trait Anxiety Inventory for Children. The results did not offer much support for the test's ability to distinguish between trait and state anxiety.

A recurrent theme in this year's research was the search for conditions that will attenuate the anxiety experience. Frequently this involved some form of cognitive appraisal or reappraisal. For example, Bennett & Holmes (10) manipulated anxiety through failure or no-failure instructions. They note that asking subjects to redefine the nature or the importance of the test before getting feedback on their performance was especially effective in reducing stress, while such redefinition after onset of threat was ineffective. Newfeld (121) utilized an experimentally programmed orientation aimed at reducing stress by modifying cognitive appraisal of stressor stimuli.

Sarason (142) reported that a high test anxiety group performed more poorly on a learning task than did the low test anxiety group under an achievement set. Under neutral conditions these results tended to reverse. Interestingly, the performance of high anxious subjects was facilitated when the experimenter disclosed instances of his own anxiety and methods of coping. Levy & McGee (96), in a questionnaire study, found that women receiving no information from their mothers concerning the latter's experience in childbirth were unprepared and effected a poorer outcome in labor and delivery than women receiving information.

Two studies capitalized on surgical experiences to study anxiety. Melamed & Siegel (112) showed a control film or a film with a relevant modeling theme to children about to undergo surgery. A variety of measures of state of anxiety disclosed a significant reduction of preoperative and postoperative fear arousal in the experimental group as compared to the control group. Trait measures of anxiety did not reflect the same differences. Martinez-Urrutia (105) administered several anxiety scales to males one day prior to surgery and again 10 days later. Results suggested that surgery as a physical threat affects A-State but not anxiety as a personality disposition.

In a miscellaneous vein, Dovidio & Morris (35) found that high stress facilitates helping behavior when the potential recipient is in a less stressful situation. Boudewyns & Levis (15) observe that high ego strength (MMPI) subjects initially respond to anxiety scenes with more affect than they do to neutral scenes, but repeated presentations lead to a rapid extinction effect. Bertilson & Dengerink (12) provide further support for the fact that in unavoidable aversive situations, subjects prefer immediate rather than delayed punishment—although these preferences are manipulable. In a move toward the classification of stress situations, Farr & Seaver(42) asked subjects to rate the degree of threat to physical comfort inherent in a variety of conditions.

The range of clinical, sociological, research, and applied work in stress and anxiety is apparent in two volumes this year (Sarason & Spielberger 144, Spielberger & Sarason 160).

Intrinsic vs Extrinsic Motivation

Does behavior occur for its own sake (intrinsic) or for its consequences (extrinsic)? The deeper theoretical implications of such a distinction are not often examined, and most research is specifically tied to laboratory variables such as task performance and satisfaction. How far beyond the old notion of functional autonomy this takes us is unclear.

In a review, Notz (122) observes that usually extrinsic motivation is manipulated by rewarding or not rewarding subjects. When all rewards are withheld and subjects spontaneously participate in the activity, this is viewed as intrinsic motivation. Most of these studies (Kruglanski et al 83) indicate a negative relationship between intrinsic and extrinsic motivation. Moreover, where intrinsic and extrinsic motivation have been manipulated orthogonally (Calder & Staw 19), the evidence indicates that they do not combine additively in determining either task satisfaction or performance.

When intrinsic and extrinsic motivation are observed to be negatively related, Kruglanski et al (84) suggest the premise that a reward administered by an external agent (e.g. money) may or may not constitute extrinsic motivation, depending upon whether or not the subject perceives the reward as part of task content or as merely a consequence of performance. Another alternative is suggested by Deci, Cascio & Krusell (26). Within the framework of cognitive evaluation theory, these authors hypothesize two processes by which extrinsic rewards can affect intrinsic motivation: when they produce a change in perceived locus of causality, and in one's feelings of competence and self-determination.

Another issue of concern involves the relative effects of extrinsic rewards on intrinsic motivation. Calder & Staw (19) made the administration of extrinsic rewards expected and noncontingent. But Kruglanski et al (83, 84), Deci et al (26), and Ross (134) used expected and contingent extrinsic rewards. Lepper & Greene (93) administered contingent extrinsic rewards while varying expectancy, and found that expected extrinsic rewards result in lower intrinsic motivation than do unexpected extrinsic rewards.

Future research on intrinsic and extrinsic motivation should attempt to establish the parametric limits (with both people and tasks) within which the negative relationship between intrinsic and extrinsic motivation, the interactive effects of combining the two, and the effects of expectancies, contingencies, etc may be expected to be observed (Calder & Staw 19, Notz 122). The consideration of individual differences is a potentially important yet heretofore neglected issue. In short, investigators should heed Calder & Staw's admonition against assuming that the interaction between intrinsic and extrinsic motivation in determining such factors as satisfaction and performance is simply linear by linear.

Self-Concept and Self-Esteem

No review of personality would be complete without at least some mention of the self-concept. Over the years, many investigators have been more absorbed by the study of factors which affect the level or quality of self-esteem than by the effects of self-esteem on subsequent behavior. Perhaps those most attracted to such concepts tend to be less concerned with overt behavior and its prediction and more oriented toward feelings or cognitive states (Skinner 156). For example, Lefley (91) tested Seminole Indian children in their native language with Indian examiners and in English with Anglo examiners. The Anglo context seemed to lower certain aspects of self-esteem more than did an ethnic context. It would have been of interest to relate such changes to some external behavioral context.

On the other hand, several studies found self-esteem to be a mediator. Schneider & Turkat (145), combining need for approval with a self-esteem measure, conclude that defensive high self-esteem subjects present themselves more positively after failure than success, and they do this to a greater extent than so-called genuine high self-esteem subjects. In another study with defensive overtones, Shrauger & Lund (152) found that in high self-esteem subjects, credibility of an evaluator was dependent on the evaluator's favorability of comments. Low self-esteem subjects did not show any difference in their ratings of the credibility of the evaluator's comments when they were favorable as opposed to being unfavorable. In a study of romantic love, Dion & Dion (31) showed that low self-esteem subjects and females expressed greater affect and more trust toward their romantic partners, evaluated their partners more favorably, and showed less trait incongruency between ratings of self and partner.

CONCLUSION

This concludes our review of the 1975 personality literature. One of the major rewards for undertaking such a review is the expectation that after years of reading the literature in an unsystematic fashion, one finally will achieve a panoramic view of the field that will be followed by a sense of understanding and closure. So much for expectations.

Literature Cited

1. Aderman, D., Archer, R. L., Harris, J. L. 1975. Effect of emotional empathy on attribution of responsibility. *J. Pers.* 43:156–67
2. Alper, T. G. 1974. Achievement motivation in college women: A now-you-see-it-now-you-don't phenomenon. *Am. Psychol.* 29:194–203
3. Arkin, R. M., Duval, S. 1975. Focus of attention and causal attributions of actors and observers. *J. Exp. Soc. Psychol.* 11:427–38
4. Balch, P., Ross, A. W. 1975. Predicting success in weight reduction as a function of locus of control: A unidimensional and multidimensional approach. *J. Consult. Clin. Psychol.* 43:119
5. Bandura, A., Underwood, B., Fromson, M. E. 1975. Disinhibition of aggression through diffusion of responsibility and dehumanization of victims. *J. Res. Pers.* 9:253–69
6. Baron, R. A., Bell, P. A. 1975. Aggression and heat: Mediating effects of prior provocation and exposure to an aggressive model. *J. Pers. Soc. Psychol.* 31:825–32
7. Batson, C. D. 1975. Attribution as a mediator of bias in helping. *J. Pers. Soc. Psychol.* 32:455–66
8. Bem, S. L. 1974. The measurement of psychological androgeny. *J. Consult. Clin. Psychol.* 42:155–62
9. Bem, S. L. 1975. Sex role adaptability: One consequence of psychological androgeny. *J. Pers. Soc. Psychol.* 31:634–43
10. Bennett, D. H., Holmes, D. S. 1975. Influence of denial (situation redefinition) and projection on anxiety associated with threat to self-esteem. *J. Pers. Soc. Psychol.* 32:915–21
11. Bernstein, M. D., Russo, N. F. 1974. The history of psychology revisited: Or, up with our foremothers. *Am. Psychol.* 29:130–34
12. Bertilson, H. S., Dengerink, H. A. 1975. The effects of active choice, shock duration, shock experience, and probability on the choice between immediate and delayed shock. *J. Res. Pers.* 9:97–112
13. Bond, M. H., Dutton, D. G. 1975. The effect of interaction anticipation and experience as a victim on aggressive behavior. *J. Pers.* 43:515–27
14. Borden, R. J. 1975. Witnessed aggression: Influence of an observer's sex and values on aggressive responding. *J. Pers. Soc. Psychol.* 31:567–73

15. Boudewyns, P. A., Levis, D. J. 1975. Autonomic reactivity of high and low ego-strength subjects to repeated anxiety eliciting scenes. *J. Abnorm. Psychol.* 84:682–92
16. Brickman, P., Ryan, K., Wortman, C. B. 1975. Causal chains: Attribution of responsibility as a function of immediate and prior causes. *J. Pers. Soc. Psychol.* 32:1060–67
17. Brown, M., Jennings, J., Vanik, V. 1974. The motive to avoid success: A further examination. *J. Res. Pers.* 8:172–76
18. Byrne, D., Rasche, L., Kelley, K. 1974. When "I like you" indicates disagreement: An experimental differentiation of information and affect. *J. Res. Pers.* 8:207–17
19. Calder, B. J., Staw, B. M. 1975. Self-perception of intrinsic and extrinsic motivation. *J. Pers. Soc. Psychol.* 31:599–605
20. Cartwright, D. S. 1975. Trait and other sources of variance in the S-R inventory of anxiousness. *J. Pers. Soc. Psychol.* 32:408–14
21. Clark, R. D. 1975. The effects of reinforcement, punishment and dependency on helping behavior. *Pers. Soc. Psychol. Bull.* 1:596–99
22. Cravens, R. W. 1975. The need for approval and the private versus public disclosure of self. *J. Pers.* 43:503–14
23. Cronbach, L. J. 1975. Beyond the two disciplines of scientific psychology. *Am. Psychol.* 30:116–27
24. Curran, J. P., Lippold, S. 1975. The effects of physical attraction and attitude similarity on attraction in dating dyads. *J. Pers.* 43:528–39
25. Darley, J. M., Batson, C. D. 1973. "From Jerusalem to Jericho": A study of situational and dispositional variables in helping behavior. *J. Pers. Soc. Psychol.* 27:100–8
26. Deci, E. L., Cascio, W. F., Krusell, J. 1975. Cognitive evaluation theory and some comments on the Calder and Staw critique. *J. Pers. Soc. Psychol.* 31:81–85
27. Dengerink, H. A., Bertilson, H. S. 1974. The reduction of attack instigated aggression. *J. Res. Pers.* 8:254–62
28. Dengerink, H. A., O'Leary, M. R., Kasner, K. H. 1975. Individual differences in aggressive responses to attack: Internal-external locus of control and field dependence-independence. *J. Res. Pers.* 9:191–99

29. Dermer, M., Thiel, D. L. 1975. When beauty may fail. *J. Pers. Soc. Psychol.* 31:1168–76

30. Diener, E., Dineen, J., Endresen, K., Beaman, A. L., Fraser, S. C. 1975. Effects of altered responsibility, cognitive set, and modeling on physical aggression and deindividuation. *J. Pers. Soc. Psychol.* 31:328–37

31. Dion, K. K., Dion, K. L. 1975. Self-esteem and romantic love. *J. Pers.* 43:39–57

32. Dion, K. L. 1975. Women's reactions to discrimination from members of the same or opposite sex. *J. Res. Pers.* 9:294–306

33. Donnerstein, E., Donnerstein, M. 1975. The effect of attitudinal similarity on interracial aggression. *J. Pers.* 43:485–502

34. Donnerstein, E., Donnerstein, M., Evans, R. 1975. Erotic stimuli and aggression: Facilitation or inhibition. *J. Pers. Soc. Psychol.* 32:237–44

35. Dovidio, J. F., Morris, W. N. 1975. Effects of stress and commonality of fate on helping behavior. *J. Pers. Soc. Psychol.* 31:145–49

36. Dweck, C. S. 1975. The role of expectations and attributions in the alleviation of learned helplessness. *J. Pers. Soc. Psychol.* 31:674–85

37. Eaves, L., Eysenck, H. 1975. The nature of extraversion: A genetical analysis. *J. Pers. Soc. Psychol.* 32:102–12

38. Elms, A. C. 1975. The crisis of confidence in social psychology. *Am Psychol.* 30:967–76

39. Endler, N. S., Magnusson, D. 1975. *Interactional Psychology and Personality.* Washington DC: Hemisphere

40. Endler, N. S., Okada, M. 1975. A multidimensional measure of trait anxiety: The S-R Inventory of General Trait Anxiousness. *J. Consult. Clin. Psychol.* 43:319–29

41. Eysenck, M. W. 1975. Extraversion, arousal, and speed of retrieval from secondary storage. *J. Pers.* 43:390–401

42. Farr, J. L., Seaver, W. B. 1975. Stress and discomfort in psychological research. *Am. Psychol.* 30:770–73

43. Feather, N. T. 1975. Positive and negative reactions to male and female success and failure in relation to the perceived status and sex-typed appropriateness of occupations. *J. Pers. Soc. Psychol.* 31:536–48

44. Feather, N. T., Simon, J. G. 1975. Reactions to male and female success and failure in sex-linked occupations: Impressions of personality, causal attribu-tions, and perceived likelihood of different consequences. *J. Pers. Soc. Psychol.* 31:20–31

45. Finch, A. J. Jr., Kendall, P. C., Montgomery, L. E., Morris, T. 1975. Effects of two types of failure on anxiety. *J. Abnorm. Psychol.* 84:583–85

46. Fink, E. L., Rey, L. D., Johnson, K. W., Spenner, K. I., Morton, D. R., Flores, E. T. 1975. The effects of family occupational type, sex, and appeal style on helping behavior. *J. Exp. Soc. Psychol.* 11:43–52

47. Gadlin, H., Ingle, G. 1975. Through the one-way mirror. *Am. Psychol.* 30:1003–9

48. Garske, J. P. 1975. Interpersonal trust and construct complexity for positively and negatively evaluated persons. *Pers. Soc. Psychol. Bull.* 1:616–19

49. Gatchel, R. J., Paulus, P. B., Maples, C. W. 1975. Learned helplessness and self-reported affect. *J. Abnorm. Psychol.* 84:732–34

50. Geen, R. G. 1975. The meaning of observed violence: Real vs. fictional violence and consequent effects of aggression and emotional arousal. *J. Res. Pers.* 9:270–81

51. Geen, R. G., Stonner, D., Shope, G. L. 1975. The facilitation of aggression by aggression: Evidence against the catharsis hypothesis. *J. Pers. Soc. Psychol.* 31:721–26

52. Goldberg, P. A., Gottesdiener, M., Abramson, P. R. 1975. Another putdown of women?: Perceived attractiveness as a function of support for the feminist movement. *J. Pers. Soc. Psychol.* 32:113–15

53. Golding, S. L. 1975. Flies in the ointment: Methodological problems in the analysis of the percentage of variance due to persons and situations. *Psychol. Bull.* 82:278–88

54. Goldman, E. K. 1975. Need achievement as a motivational basis for the risky shift. *J. Pers.* 43:346–56

55. Goldstein, J. H., Davis, R. W., Herman, D. 1975. Escalation of aggression: Experimental studies. *J. Pers. Soc. Psychol.* 31:162–70

56. Green, R. A., Murray, E. J. 1975. Expression of feeling and cognitive reinterpretation in the reduction of hostile aggression. *J. Consult. Clin. Psychol.* 43:375–83

57. Greenwald, A. G. 1975. Does the Good Samaritan parable increase helping? A comment on Darley and Batson's no-effect conclusion. *J. Pers. Soc. Psychol.* 32:578–83

58. Grush, J. E., Clore, G. L., Costin, F. 1975. Dissimilarity and attraction: When difference makes a difference. *J. Pers. Soc. Psychol.* 32:783–89

59. Guilford, J. P. 1975. Factors and factors of personality. *Psychol. Bull.* 82:802–14

60. Gump, J. P. 1975. Comparative analysis of black women's and white women's sex-role attitudes. *J. Consult. Clin. Psychol.* 43:858–63

61. Gurwitz, S. B., Panciera, L. 1975. Attributions of freedom by actors and observers. *J. Pers. Soc. Psychol.* 32:531–39

62. Harkins, S., Geen, R. G. 1975. Discriminability and criterion differences between extraverts and introverts during vigilance. *J. Res. Pers.* 9:335–40

63. Harvey, J. H., Harris, B. 1975. Determinants of perceived choice and the relationship between perceived choice and expectancy about feelings of internal control. *J. Pers. Soc. Psychol.* 31:101–6

64. Heilbrun, A. B., Kleemeier, C. 1975. Male sex-gender identification: A source of achievement deficit in college females. *J. Pers.* 43:678–92

65. Hiroto, D. S., Seligman, M. E. P. 1975. Generality of learned helplessness in man. *J. Pers. Soc. Psychol.* 31:311–27

66. Hochreich, D. J. 1975. Defensive externality and blame projection following failure. *J. Pers. Soc. Psychol.* 32:540–46

67. Hochreich, D. J. 1975. Sex-role stereotypes for internal-external control and interpersonal trust. *J. Consult. Clin. Psychol.* 43:273

68. Hoffman, M. L. 1975. Sex differences in moral internalization and values. *J. Pers. Soc. Psychol.* 32:720–29

69. Holmes, D. S., Jackson, T. H. 1975. Influence of locus of control on interpersonal attraction and affective reactions in situations involving reward and punishment. *J. Pers. Soc. Psychol.* 31:132–36

70. Horner, M. 1968. *Sex differences in achievement motivation and performance in competitive and noncompetitive situations.* Unpublished PhD dissertation. Univ. Michigan, Ann Arbor, Mich.

71. Hornstein, H. A., LaKind, E., Frankel, G., Manne, S. 1975. Effects of knowledge about remote social events on prosocial behavior, social conception, and mood. *J. Pers. Soc. Psychol.* 32:1038–46

72. Johnson, D. W. 1975. Cooperativeness and social perspective taking. *J. Pers. Soc. Psychol.* 31:241–44

73. Johnson, J. H., Cerretto, M. C. 1975. Internal-external control and interpersonal attraction to a similar and dissimilar stranger. *Psychol. Rep.* 37:1122

74. Jones, E. E., Nisbett, R. E. 1971. *The Actor and the Observer: Divergent Perceptions of the Causes of Behavior.* Morristown, NJ: General Learning Press

75. Karaz, V., Perlman, D. 1975. Attribution at the wire: Consistency and outcome finish strong. *J. Exp. Soc. Psychol.* 11:470–77

76. Katz, I., Cohen, S., Glass, D. 1975. Some determinants of cross-racial helping. *J. Pers. Soc. Psychol.* 32:964–70

77. Kilmann, P. R., Albert, B. M., Sotile, W. M. 1975. Relationship between locus of control, structure of therapy, and outcome. *J. Consult. Clin. Psychol.* 43:588

78. Kleck, R. E., Rubenstein, C. 1975. Physical attractiveness, perceived attitude similarity, and interpersonal attraction in an opposite-sex encounter. *J. Pers. Soc. Psychol.* 31:107–14

79. Konečni, V. J. 1975. The mediation of aggressive behavior: Arousal level versus anger and cognitive labeling. *J. Pers. Soc. Psychol.* 32:706–12

80. Korte, C., Ypma, I., Toppen, A. 1975. Helpfulness in Dutch society as a function of urbanization and environmental input level. *J. Pers. Soc. Psychol.* 32:996–1003

81. Krebs, D. 1975. Empathy and altruism. *J. Pers. Soc. Psychol.* 32:1134–46

82. Krebs, D., Adinolfi, A. A. 1975. Physical attractiveness, social relations, and personality style. *J. Pers. Soc. Psychol.* 31:245–53

83. Kruglanski, A. W., Riter, A., Amitai, A., Margolin, B., Shabtai, L., Zaksh, D. 1975. Can money enhance intrinsic motivation? A test of the content-consequence hypothesis. *J. Pers. Soc. Psychol.* 31:744–50

84. Kruglanski, A. W., Riter, A., Arazi, D., Agassi, R., Monteqio, J., Peri, I., Peretz, M. 1975. Effects of task-intrinsic rewards upon extrinsic and intrinsic motivation. *J. Pers. Soc. Psychol.* 31:699–705

85. Kukla, A. 1974. Performance as a function of resultant achievement motivation (perceived ability) and perceived difficulty. *J. Res. Pers.* 7:374–83

86. Kukla, A. 1975. Preferences among impossibly difficult and trivially easy tasks:

A revision of Atkinson's theory of choice. *J. Pers. Soc. Psychol.* 32:338–45
87. Langer, E. J. 1975. The illusion of control. *J. Pers. Soc. Psychol.* 32:311–28
88. Langer, E. J., Roth, J. 1975. Heads I win, tails it's chance: The illusion of control as a function of the sequence of outcomes in a purely chance task. *J. Pers. Soc. Psychol.* 32:951–55
89. Lefcourt, H. M., Hogg, E., Sordoni, C. 1975. Locus of control, field dependence and the conditions arousing objective vs subjective self-awareness. *J. Res. Pers.* 9:21–36
90. Lefcourt, H. M., Hogg, E., Struthers, S., Holmes, C. 1975. Causal attributions as a function of locus of control, initial confidence, and performance outcomes. *J. Pers. Soc. Psychol.* 32:391–97
91. Lefley, H. P. 1975. Differential self-concept in American Indian children as a function of language and examiner. *J. Pers. Soc. Psychol.* 31:36–41
92. Leonard, R. L. Jr. 1975. Self-concept and attraction for similar and dissimilar others. *J. Pers. Soc. Psychol.* 31:926–29
93. Lepper, M. R., Greene, D. 1975. Turning play into work: Effects of adult surveillance and extrinsic rewards on children's intrinsic motivation. *J. Pers. Soc. Psychol.* 31:479–86
94. Lerner, M. J., Reavy, P. 1975. Locus of control, perceived responsibility for prior fate, and helping behavior. *J. Res. Pers.* 9:1–20
95. Levenson, H. 1974. Activism and powerful others: Distinctions within the concept of internal-external control. *J. Pers. Assess.* 38:377–83
96. Levy, J. M., McGee, R. K. 1975. Childbirth as crisis: A test of Janis's theory of communication and stress resolution. *J. Pers. Soc. Psychol.* 31:171–79
97. Leyens, J. P., Camino, L., Parke, R. D., Berkowitz, L. 1975. Effects of movie violence on aggression in a field setting as a function of group dominance and cohesion. *J. Pers. Soc. Psychol.* 32:346–60
98. Liem, G. R. 1975. Performance and satisfaction as affected by personal control over salient decisions. *J. Pers. Soc. Psychol.* 31:232–40
99. Loeb, R. C. 1975. Concomitants of boys' locus of control examined in parent-child interactions. *Dev. Psychol.* 11:353–58
100. Lombardo, J. P., Steigleder, M., Feinberg, R. 1975. Internality-externality: The perception of negatively valued personality characteristics and interper-

sonal attraction. *J. Rep. Res. Soc. Psychol.* 6:89–95
101. Long, G. T., Lerner, M. 1974. Deserving, the "personal contract," and altruistic behavior by children. *J. Pers. Soc. Psychol.* 29:551–56
102. Losco, J., Epstein, S. 1975. Humor preferences as a subtle measure of attitudes toward the same and the opposite sex. *J. Pers.* 43:321–34
103. Magnusson, D., Ekehammar, B. 1975. Perceptions of and reactions to stressful situations. *J. Pers. Soc. Psychol.* 31:1147–54
104. Manning, S. A., Taylor, D. A. 1975. Effects of viewed violence and aggression: Stimulation and catharsis. *J. Pers. Soc. Psychol.* 31:180–88
105. Martinez-Urrutia, A. 1975. Anxiety and pain in surgical patients. *J. Consult. Clin. Psychol.* 43:437–42
106. Mathews, K. E. Jr., Canon, L. K. 1975. Environmental noise level as a determinant of helping behavior. *J. Pers. Soc. Psychol.* 32:571–77
107. McAllister, A., Kiesler, D. J. 1975. Interviewee disclosure as a function of interpersonal trust, task modeling, and interviewer self-disclosure. *J. Consult. Clin. Psychol.* 43:428
108. McClelland, D. C. 1975. *Power: The Inner Experience.* New York: Irvington
109. McGee, M. G., Snyder, M. 1975. Attribution and behavior: Two field studies. *J. Pers. Soc. Psychol.* 32:185–90
110. McKillip, J., Posavac, E. J. 1975. Judgments of responsibility for an accident. *J. Pers.* 43:248–65
111. Mehryar, A. H., Khajavi, F., Hekmat, H. 1975. Comparison of Eysenck's PEN and Lanyon's Psychological Screening Inventory in a group of American students. *J. Consult. Clin. Psychol.* 43:9–12
112. Melamed, B. G., Siegel, L. J. 1975. Reduction of anxiety in children facing hospitalization and surgery by use of filmed modeling. *J. Consult. Clin. Psychol.* 43:511–21
113. Milgram, S., Shotland, R. L. 1973. *Television and Anti-Social Behavior: Field Experiments.* New York: Academic
114. Miller, A. G. 1975. Actor and observer perceptions of the learning of a task. *J. Exp. Soc. Psychol.* 11:95–111
115. Miller, D. T., Norman, S. A. 1975. Actor-observer differences in perceptions of effective control. *J. Pers. Soc. Psychol.* 31:503–15
116. Miller, D. T., Ross, M. 1975. Self-serving biases in the attribution of causality:

Fact or fiction? *Psychol. Bull.* 82: 213–25

117. Moser, A. J. 1975. Structured group interaction: A psychotherapeutic technique for modifying locus of control. *J. Contemp. Psychother.* 7:23–28

118. Naditch, M. P. 1975. Locus of control and drinking behavior in a sample of men in army basic training. *J. Consult. Clin. Psychol.* 43:96

119. Naditch, M. P., DeMaio, T. 1975. Locus of control and competence. *J. Pers.* 43:542–59

120. Naditch, M. P., Gargan, M. A., Michael, L. B. 1975. Denial, anxiety, locus of control, and the discrepancy between aspirations and achievements as components of depression. *J. Abnorm. Psychol.* 84:1–9

121. Newfeld, R. W. J. 1975. Effect of cognitive appraisal on d' and response bias to experimental stress. *J. Pers. Soc. Psychol.* 31:735–43

122. Notz, W. W. 1975. Work motivation and the negative effects of extrinsic rewards: A review with implications for theory and practice. *Am. Psychol.* 30:884–91

123. Nowicki, S. Jr., Blumberg, N. 1975. The role of locus of control of reinforcement in interpersonal attraction. *J. Res. Pers.* 9:48–56

124. O'Leary, V. E. 1974. Some attitudinal barriers to occupational aspirations in women. *Psychol. Bull.* 81:809–26

125. Page, M. M., Roy, R. E. 1975. Internal-external control and independence of judgment in course evaluations among college students. *Pers. Soc. Psychol. Bull.* 1:509–12

126. Phares, E. J. 1976. *Locus of Control in Personality.* Morristown, NJ: General Learning Press

127. Phares, E. J. 1976. Locus of control. In *Dimensions of Personality,* ed. H. London, J. Exner. New York: Wiley-Interscience

128. Phares, E. J., Lamiell, J. T. 1975. Internal-external control, interpersonal judgments of others in need, and attribution of responsibility. *J. Pers.* 43:23–38

129. Press, A. N., Crockett, W. H., Delia, J. G. 1975. Effects of cognitive complexity and of perceiver's set upon the organization of impressions. *J. Pers. Soc. Psychol.* 32:865–72

130. Prociuk, T. J., Breen, L. J. 1975. Defensive externality and its relation to academic performance. *J. Pers. Soc. Psychol.* 31:549–56

131. Prociuk, T. J., Lussier, R. J. 1975. Internal-external locus of control: An analysis and bibliography of two years of research (1973–1974). *Psychol. Rep.* 37:1323–37

132. Regan, D. T., Totten, J. 1975. Empathy and attribution: Turning observers into actors. *J. Pers. Soc. Psychol.* 32:850–56

133. Robbins, G. E. 1975. Dogmatism and information gathering in personality impression formation. *J. Res. Pers.* 9:74–84

134. Ross, M. 1975. Salience of reward and intrinsic motivation. *J. Pers. Soc. Psychol.* 32:245–54

135. Roth, S., Kubal, L. 1975. Effects of noncontingent reinforcement on tasks of differing importance: Facilitation and learned helplessness. *J. Pers. Soc. Psychol.* 32:680–91

136. Rotter, J. B. 1967. A new scale for the measurement of interpersonal trust. *J. Pers.* 35:651–55

137. Rotter, J. B. 1975. Some problems and misconceptions related to the construct of internal versus external control of reinforcement. *J. Consult. Clin. Psychol.* 43:56–67

138. Rotter, J. B., Hochreich, D. J. 1975. *Personality.* Glenview, Ill: Scott, Foresman

139. Rushton, J. P. 1975. Generosity in children: Immediate and long-term effects of modeling, preaching, and moral judgment. *J. Pers. Soc. Psychol.* 31: 459–66

140. Sachs, D. H. 1975. Belief similarity and attitude similarity as determinants of interpersonal attraction. *J. Res. Pers.* 9:57–65

141. Sanders, G. S., Baron, R. S. 1975. Pain cues and uncertainty as determinants of aggression in a situation involving repeated instigation. *J. Pers. Soc. Psychol.* 32:495–502

142. Sarason, I. G. 1975. Test anxiety and the self-disclosing coping model. *J. Consult. Clin. Psychol.* 43:148–53

143. Sarason, I. G., Smith, R. E., Diener, E. 1975. Personality research: Components of variance attributable to the person and situation. *J. Pers. Soc. Psychol.* 32:199–204

144. Sarason, I. G., Spielberger, C. D. 1975. *Stress and Anxiety.* Washington DC: Hemisphere

145. Schneider, D. J., Turkat, D. 1975. Self-presentation following success or failure: Defensive self-esteem models. *J. Pers.* 43:127–35

146. Schwartz, S. 1975. Individual differences in cognition: Some relationships between personality and memory. *J. Res. Pers.* 9:217–25

147. Seligman, M. E. P. 1975. *Helplessness: On Depression, Development, and Death.* San Francisco: Freeman

148. Shaver, K. G. 1975. *An Introduction to Attribution Processes.* Cambridge: Winthrop

149. Sherrod, D. R., Farber, J. 1975. The effect of previous actor/observer role experience on attribution of responsibility for failure. *J. Pers.* 43:231–47

150. Shields, S. A. 1975. Functionalism, Darwinism, and the psychology of women. *Am. Psychol.* 30:739–54

151. Shields, S. A. 1975. Ms. Pilgrim's progress: The contributions of Leta Stetter Hollingworth to the psychology of women. *Am. Psychol.* 30:852–57

152. Shrauger, J. S., Lund, A. K. 1975. Self-evaluation and reactions to evaluations from others. *J. Pers.* 43:94–108

153. Shweder, R. A. 1975. How relevant is an individual difference theory of personality? *J. Pers.* 43:455–84

154. Sigall, H., Ostrove, N. 1975. Beautiful but dangerous: Effects of offender attractiveness and nature of the crime on juridic judgment. *J. Pers. Soc. Psychol.* 31:410–14

155. Silvern, L. E. 1975. The effect of traditional vs. counter-culture attitudes on the relationship between the internal-external scale and political position. *J. Pers.* 43:58–73

156. Skinner, B. F. 1975. The steep and thorny way to a science of behavior. *Am Psychol.* 30:42–49

157. Snyder, M., Monson, T. C. 1975. Persons, situations, and the control of social behavior. *J. Pers. Soc. Psychol.* 32:637–44

158. Sorrentino, R. M., Short, J. 1974. Effects of fear of success on women's performance at masculine versus feminine tasks. *J. Res. Pers.* 8:277–90

159. Spence, J. T., Helmreich, R., Stapp, J. 1975. Ratings of self and peers on sex role attributes and their relation to self-esteem and conceptions of masculinity and femininity. *J. Pers. Soc. Psychol.* 32:29–39

160. Spielberger, C. D., Sarason, I. G. 1975. *Stress and Anxiety.* Washington DC: Hemisphere

161. Srull, T. K., Karabenick, S. A. 1975. Effects of personality-situation locus of control congruence. *J. Pers. Soc. Psychol.* 32:617–28

162. Stephan, W. G. 1975. Actor vs. observer: Attributions to behavior with positive or negative outcomes and empathy for the other role. *J. Exp. Soc. Psychol.* 11:205–14

163. Strahan, R. F. 1975. Remarks on Bem's measurement of psychological androgeny: Alternative methods and a supplementary analysis. *J. Consult. Clin. Psychol.* 43:568–71

164. Tannenbaum, P. H., Zillmann, D. 1975. Emotional arousal in the facilitation of aggression through communication. In *Advances in Experimental Social Psychology*, ed. L. Berkowitz. New York: Academic

165. Taub, S. I., Dollinger, S. J. 1975. Reward and purpose as incentives for children differing in locus of control expectancies. *J. Pers.* 43:179–95

166. Taylor, S. E., Fiske, S. T. 1975. Point of view and perceptions of causality. *J. Pers. Soc. Psychol.* 32:439–45

167. Taynor, J., Deaux, K. 1975. Equity and perceived sex differences: Role behavior as defined by the task, the mode, and the actor. *J. Pers. Soc. Psychol.* 32:381–90

168. Thornhill, M. A., Thornhill, G. J., Youngman, M. B. 1975. A computerized and categorized bibliography on locus of control. *Psychol. Rep.* 36:505–6

169. Touhey, J. C. 1975. Interpersonal congruency, attitude similarity, and interpersonal attraction. *J. Res. Pers.* 9:66–73

170. Trope, Y. 1975. Seeking information about one's own ability as a determinant of choice among tasks. *J. Pers. Soc. Psychol.* 32:1004–13

171. Trope, Y., Brickman, P. 1975. Difficulty and diagnosticity as determinants of choice among tasks. *J. Pers. Soc. Psychol.* 31:918–25

172. Turner, C. W., Layton, J. F., Simons, L. S. 1975. Naturalistic studies of aggressive behavior: Aggressive stimuli, victim visibility, and horn honking. *J. Pers. Soc. Psychol.* 31:1098–1107

173. Vogel, S. R., Rosenkratz, P. S. 1975. Sex-role self-concepts and life style plans of young women. *J. Consult. Clin. Psychol.* 43:427

174. Wagner, R. V. 1975. Complementary needs, role expectations, interpersonal attraction, and the stability of working relationships. *J. Pers. Soc. Psychol.* 32:116–24

175. Wegner, D. M., Crano, W. D. 1975. Racial factors in helping behavior: An unobtrusive field experiment. *J. Pers. Soc. Psychol.* 32:901–5

176. Weiner, B., Sierad, J. 1975. Misattribution for failure and enhancement of achievement strivings. *J. Pers. Soc. Psychol.* 31:415–21

177. Wilson, L., Rogers, R. W. 1975. The fire this time: Effects of race of target, insult, and potential retaliation on black aggression. *J. Pers. Soc. Psychol.* 32: 857–64

178. Wolk, S., Kurtz, J. 1975. Positive adjustment and involvement during aging and expectancy for internal control. *J. Consult. Clin. Psychol.* 43:173–78

179. Wolosin, R. J., Sherman, S. J., Mynatt, C. R. 1975. When self-interest and altruism conflict. *J. Pers. Soc. Psychol.* 32:752–60

180. Wortman, C. B. 1975. Some determinants of perceived control. *J. Pers. Soc. Psychol.* 31:282–94

181. Wortman, C. B., Brehm, J. W. 1975. Responses to uncontrollable outcomes: An integration of reactance theory and the learned helplessness model. In *Advances in Experimental Social Psychology,* ed. L. Berkowitz. New York: Academic

182. Wright, T. L., Maggied, P., Palmer, M. L. 1975. An unobstrusive study of interpersonal trust. *J. Pers. Soc. Psychol.* 32:446–48

183. Wright, T. L., Tedeschi, R. G. 1975. Factor analysis of the Interpersonal Trust Scale. *J. Consult. Clin. Psychol.* 43:470–77

184. Zillmann, D., Bryant, J., Cantor, J. R., Day, K. D. 1975. Irrelevance of mitigating circumstances in retaliatory behavior at high levels of excitation. *J. Res. Pers.* 9:282–93

185. Zimbardo, P. G. 1969. The human choice: Individuation, reason, and order versus deindividuation, impulse, and chaos. In *Nebraska Symposium on Motivation,* ed. W. J. Arnold, D. Levine. Lincoln: Univ. Nebraska Press

186. Zuckerman, M., Wheeler, L. 1975. To dispel fantasies about the fantasy-based measure of fear of success. *Psychol. Bull.* 82:932–46

Ann. Rev. Psychol. 1977. 28:141–73

EFFECTS OF MASS MEDIA   ❖270

Robert M. Liebert and Neala S. Schwartzberg

Department of Psychology, State University of New York, Stony Brook, NY 11794

INTRODUCTION

This review selectively covers the scientific literature on the nature and effects of mass media published between 1970 and 1975, with the occasional inclusion of earlier studies and a few that had not yet been published at the time of this writing. Four earlier reviews of mass communication research have appeared in the *Annual Review of Psychology:* by Schramm (232), Lumsdaine & May (168), Tannenbaum & Greenberg (249), and Weiss (267). Each of these earlier reviews tapped several different disciplines (e.g. communications, education, sociology), and we have also felt it important to adopt such an interdisciplinary approach. At the same time, we were struck with how few studies cited in previous reviews were concerned with the psychological effects of mass media, either in terms of attitudes or behavior. Thus, in contrast to those who have preceded us, we have given particular emphasis to psychological effects and to theory and research generated from a psychological vantage point. This decision is consistent with our mandate to write on the effects of mass media rather than on mass communication per se. Readers interested in an exhaustive annotated bibliography of studies on all aspects of the media will find a recent series of volumes by Comstock and his associates extremely useful (57–59), and several major papers on cable television, a topic excluded from this review, are also available (93, 101, 113, 137, 240).

Any review of the literature on media can easily become an organizational hodge-podge because the theories, constructs, approaches, and even substantive interests of each of the relevant disciplines are so diverse. Regardless of these differences, though, the effects of media seem necessarily to depend on patterns of audience use, the nature of the material to which the audience is exposed, the degree to which such exposure transmits information and cultivates beliefs, and finally, the extent to which media-cultivated information and beliefs influence the overt expression of social attitudes and behavior. The four major sections of this review correspond to each of these subareas within the literature.

Traditionally the mass media have been divided into those that are broadcast (i.e. radio and television) and those that reach their audience through printed copies (books, magazines, newspapers, and films), but with the advent of such practices as

141

broadcasting movies through television this division has lost much of its conceptual meaning except in the area of regulatory activity, where the print media enjoy greater freedom. Therefore, rather than relying on the print-broadcast distinction, we have treated each medium separately whenever there has been sufficient literature to warrant doing so. This organizational plan does not leave us with a symmetrical presentation, however, for there is a striking imbalance in the amount of attention each medium has received in the past decade. Television has been the medium which has attracted the most attention, both because of a major government inquiry into TV violence which occurred during the period (252) and because of the advent of "Sesame Street" (159). Films have been of interest principally because of their sexual content (216), and news presentations, broadcast and print, have been analyzed largely in terms of their political impact. Radio, books, and magazines have all received short shrift in the literature, and studies of the relative impact of the media on social behavior are almost nonexistent. What is more, there are many areas in which media portrayals have been studied exhaustively while their social effects have yet to be explored except at a very superficial level; sex and race-role presentations in the media are good examples. Necessarily, all these imbalances are reflected in our review.

Finally, readers should be warned that much of the literature we have examined is sadly deficient from a methodological point of view. Sampling procedures used for assessing the nature of media audiences or media portrayals are often too limited to make inferences to the relevant populations meaningful; in field studies, the well-established stricture that "correlation does not imply causation" is winked at all too often; and only recently have experimental studies begun to escape from the usual laboratory research models that sharply limit the external validity or generalizability of most findings. The only strong conclusions possible at this time are therefore those which have enjoyed successful replication across samples and investigators, and convincing patterns of this type are found in only a few of the areas covered below.

PATTERNS OF USE

The effects of mass media depend in large part on the frequency with which various audiences are exposed to them, as well as the informational needs and psychological gratifications to which media use is related.

Television

Reported hours of viewing per day has increased steadily since 1961 with the average adult now spending more than 3 hours a day watching television (226). However, the pattern of television use varies with age and race (26, 41, 67, 110, 169). Lyle & Hoffman (169) reported that nearly all the first graders in their California sample watched television every day, and most of them watched for at least 2–3 hours; well over one-third watched 4 hours or more. About 25% of the sixth and tenth graders had watched at least 5 1/2 hours of television on a given school day. The same investigators found that child viewership extends well beyond family viewing hours as usually defined; as many as 25% of sixth graders were still watching as late as 11:30 PM. The amount of viewing builds to a peak as the child approaches adolescence and then begins a slow decline (169); overall TV viewing drops throughout early adulthood, reaching a low in the 42–49 year old age bracket, then rises again dramatically in later life (41).

Blacks and whites show similar prime-time viewing patterns, although outside of prime-time blacks watch more than whites (26). Black children and adolescents view more than their white counterparts (67, 110). Among low income tenth and eleventh graders, Dominick & Greenberg (67) found blacks watched an average of 6.3 hours of TV on Sunday compared to white viewing of 4.6 hours. Middle-class whites watched even less: 3.7 hours. Low-income adults also watch considerably more entertainment television (an average of 5.2 hours of viewing per day) than the general population (109). Bogart (26) also found that income and education are negatively related to television use, although the pattern was more complex among blacks.

As Schramm, Lyle & Parker (233) had noted years before, Lyle & Hoffman (169) found that the brightest children were the heaviest television users. However, creativity, at least in high school students, appears to be negatively related to television viewing when IQ is partialled out (259).

Adult females generally watch more television than males, but reversal of these sex differences has been found among undergraduates; college males use television more than college females (207).

In contrast with general television viewing, television news viewing shows a different age trend among the general population, increasing into the late working years and then leveling off during the late 60s (41). It does not appear, however, that national news programs are well attended. Based on a national probability sample and television viewing diaries, Robinson (219) found that about 25% watched a national news program daily, but the majority did not see even one such program over a 2-week period.

PROGRAM PREFERENCES   Younger children, first through third graders, generally report a preference for cartoons and situation comedies (169, 197). Sixth graders like situation comedies and adventure programs; tenth graders like adventure and dramatic programs and music and variety shows (169). Females like violent characters less well than males (10, 74, 197), but even among males nonviolent characters are preferred to violent ones (197). Preference for television programs with violent heroes appears to be inversely related to intelligence (10).

Print

Overall newspaper reading and specific attention to public affairs and political topics in the print media generally follow similar paths: low in early adulthood, peaking after retirement, and dropping steeply in very old age (41). Black children and adults read newspapers less than their white counterparts, even when income and occupation are held constant (26, 110, 237); however, this difference disappeared when college graduates of both races were compared (26).

Determinants of Media Use

There has been a good deal of work on the topic of determinants of media use and preferences, beyond simple demographics. Media use has been related to life style variables (147) and to the structure of parent-child communication as a socializing influence (34, 39). Chaffee, McLeod & Atkin (39) found small but significant correlations between parents' media habits and those of their children on a host of measures including amount of TV watching in hours, frequency of watching news and interview shows, frequency of watching westerns, comedy or adventure shows, measures of newspaper and magazine reading, and interest in public affairs material. McLeod & O'Keefe (190) have suggested a "socialization perspective" to explain patterns of media use, emphasizing that the factors impinging on a person to determine uses and gratifications of the media vary systematically with chronological stages in the life cycle. Although Kline (147) suggests that higher education may suppress newspaper and television use through its association with organizational participation, Graney & Graney (104) found television viewing among female senior citizens was positively related to organizational participation. Thus the effect of life style variables may interact with age.

A major study of college undergraduates (207) suggests that there are substantial differences between media use patterns of undergraduates and other populations. Undergraduates appear to use less television and read slightly fewer newspapers and news magazines than older adults. Within the college population, TV entertainment and news viewing, as well as newspaper reading, increased steadily with age (207). The reasons for this unique pattern of media use by this subgroup are unclear, but the mere presence of such an atypical pattern limits the validity of media experimental studies which rely exclusively on college undergraduates as subjects.

INFORMATION-SEEKING AND CREDIBILITY   There is evidence from many sources to support the hypothesis that use of both media news and media entertainment is often guided by purposeful information-seeking on the part of viewers (6, 29, 44, 45, 67).

Roper (226), using a multiple choice technique and fairly general questions, found that since 1973 television has been the medium from which most Americans get most of their news, and, as in previous years, people find television news to be more believable than other media when they are in conflict. Other investigators, however, have found that news media believability depends on the specific topics considered (229). Clarke & Ruggels (46) found within the context of specific topics that broadcast media were preferred less than print. Edelstein (80), using a unique open-ended interview technique, found newspapers and television were mentioned about equally as informative about the Vietnam War. Roper's technique may have been too broad to discover these effects. The different media may be differentially suited to various aspects of news/political events and they may perform different functions. The topic of media credibility has been reviewed by Greenberg & Roloff (112).

GRATIFICATIONS   Recent work designed to identify the "gratifications" provided by various media has been reviewed by Katz, Blumler & Gurevitch (141), who see the audience as active and media use as goal directed. The most common approach to this area has been through factor analysis (37, 108, 180), although McGuire (184) provided a theoretical analysis of the possible psychological gratifications that may reinforce media use. Wiebe (270) offered an analysis explaining the high popularity of standard television over more meaningful drama based on a reluctance to cope even vicariously with difficult or complex situations. He suggests, among other things, that media advertising is effective precisely because it invites (through purchase) the audience member to participate directly in gratifying activities. A study done with British children suggested that the main factors influencing television viewing are those related to acquiring new information, feeding a television "habit," relaxation, arousal, distraction, and companionship (108). Using television to learn about life is related to perceived reality of television among children and adolescents (67, 110) and is related to the need for companionship among elderly persons (63). Several investigators have also pointed out that the media may not be the best way to satisfy the various needs generally mentioned as contributing to the use of the media (141, 142, 241).

A survey of children in Denmark revealed that most do not watch the news (even special "children's news") in order to gain information, but rather for entertainment or to avoid boredom (117). McLeod & Becker (187) have discussed factors implicated in the selection and avoidance of television programs featuring political candidates, and motivations for the use of media news have also been studied by Chaffee & Izcaray (37).

MEDIA CONTENT AND PORTRAYALS

Over the past decade there has been considerable interest in assessing tne nature of media portrayals which may have important social implications or social effects. One reason for this trend is certainly that many investigators have agreed with Gerbner's (99) thesis that all media carry a "hidden curriculum," in which views of life are presented and an explanation, however fictional, is provided of how things work. There has been less interest, however, in the decision-making processes and practices that determine the final content of mass media.

Violence, Crime, and Law Enforcement

Based on complete analyses of a week of prime-time and Saturday morning network broadcasts, Gerbner & Gross (100) report that violence—"the overt expression of physical force against others or self, or the compelling of action against one's will on pain of being hurt or killed" (98, p. 31)—has been a consistently emphasized theme in television entertainment through the 1969–1974 period. Gerbner (98) has established that prime-time television drama averages about eight acts of violence per program hour, and that on children's Saturday morning cartoons there is a violent act every 2 minutes. Slaby, Quarfoth & McConnachie (239), using a different sample, found that Saturday morning cartoons averaged 21.5 violent acts per hour, an impressively close replication. Inasmuch as most children watch at least 2 hours of entertainment television per day (169), it is generally agreed that children as well as adults are exposed to a great deal of television violence.

Dominick (65) analyzed the content of a week of prime-time drama and comedy. Over 60% of the shows portrayed at least one crime, and the motives for crime were generally either greed (32%) or to avoid detection (31%). The frequency of various crimes did not mirror their frequency in real life. On television, for example, murder and assault ranked as number one and number two crimes respectively; in real life, on the other hand, the two most frequent crimes are burglary and larceny. Dominick also found that most crimes on television are committed by whites (90%) and males (85%). While criminals are usually tracked down and caught, only 5% of the television criminals were ever shown during a trial or even had their trial mentioned during the drama. Thus justice, as a judicial process, appears to be almost never mentioned except in explicit courtroom dramas. Almost one-third of all law enforcers committed violence on entertainment television, and 92% of all enforcers who were violent had major theatrical roles.

It is striking that we found no analyses of the level of violence or treatment of crime and justice in the cinema, nor has recent attention been given to the portrayal of these themes in fictional print media.

Portrayal of Women

It is well documented that male and female roles are presented very differently through the mass media. In print, in television entertainment, and in commercials, females are numerically underrepresented and shown as more passive and deferent than males.

CHILDREN'S BOOKS   An examination of prize-winning children's books (268) showed that women were underrepresented in titles, central roles, and illustrations. Males predominated over females in a ratio of 11 to 1. And when females did appear in these stories, the presentations were stereotyped; males were more active, and females were prone to get into difficulties from which they were ultimately rescued by male heroes. In a study of 134 elementary school children's readers (271), boy-centered stories exceeded girl-centered stories in a ratio of 5 to 2; male biographies appeared six times more often than female biographies; even in folk and fantasy stories, males dominated 4 to 1. Male animal stories were more frequent than female animal stories in a ratio of 2 to 1.

MAGAZINE STORIES   Franzwa (88) examined fictional stories appearing in three major women's magazines between 1940 and 1970 and found that the majority of female characters had never worked; of those that had, most held only low-status jobs which they gave up on marrying. In another study of short stories in women's magazines (9), 9% of the female characters were found to have a career in 1957; this figure actually dropped 4% in 1967.

TELEVISION DRAMA   Tedesco (251) examined a 4-year sample of major characters in prime-time drama and found that 72% of the major characters were male; women, when shown, usually appeared in light or comic roles. Over half the females were married whereas less than one third of the men were. Violent characters were mostly males, but their victims were mostly female. Males were more powerful, smarter, more rational, and more stable; females were attractive, warm, happy, and youthful. Similarly, Seggar & Wheeler (235) found that roughly 20% of all afternoon and evening television portrayals (appearances of a character on screen performing some recognizable duty) were of women. McNeil (191) analyzed prime-time fictional series and found that males outnumbered females 3 to 1 in drama shows and 3 to 2 in comedies. Women tended to be shown as minor characters; the majority were unemployed and those who were employed were in occupations with lower power and prestige than those held by men. Donagher et al (70) found that women on prime-time television are shown as much less able to delay gratification and persist at tasks than men, but that they are shown as better able to resist temptation and as more altruistic. Even on educational television male characters predominate, and women tend to be shown in indoor, nonauthoritarian occupations and performing homemaking activities (32). Analyzing popular children's shows, Sternglanz & Serbin (246) found that males were portrayed as more aggressive and constructive than females, whereas females were shown as less effective, more deferent, and as being punished for high levels of activity. Women are victimized more than men on commercial entertainment television, and single women are victimized most of all (100).

It is most interesting that the foregoing pattern does not hold up for daytime serials, where the audience is predominantly female. Katzman (144) and Turow (256) found that women were on more equal footing in terms of power and giving and receiving orders on daytime serials than on prime time. Likewise, Downing (78) examined 300 episodes from 15 daytime serials and found that a serial housewife, in contrast to her prime-time counterpart, tends to be intelligent, self-reliant, and articulate. Professional women are treated sympathetically on daytime serials, rather than having to adjust to male activities and interests.

COMMERCIALS AND ADVERTISEMENTS   Women do not fare very well in TV commercials either. Here their occupational roles are much more limited than men's, and men are frequently shown as beneficiaries of women's efforts, particularly in the areas of cooking and cleaning (61). On prime-time commercials, both voice-over and on-camera salespersons are overwhelmingly male, while women are almost invariably shown indoors and most usually as housewives or mothers where they help to sell kitchen or bathroom products (69). Males are also more active than females on Saturday morning television commercials, and male voices dominate the audiotrack for these ads (258). Ads in the print media may be moving away from these traditional presentations, albeit in a limited way. Sexton & Haberman (236) examined magazine ads for 1950–51, 1960–61, and 1970–71 in a search for trends over time. In cigarette ads women are being shown increasingly in social rather than domestic situations, and in less traditional roles in ads for nonalcoholic beverages and appliances.

Blacks and Other Minorities

Greenberg & Mazingo (111) have reviewed and summarized recent studies and issues related to all facets of the portrayal of minorities. Blacks seem to be underrepresented in magazines, both in terms of their appearance in advertisements and in news stories (245), although there is a trend of increased exposure for blacks, particularly black children, in magazine ads (50).

Blacks and other minorities are also underrepresented on Saturday morning network television; interestingly, though, while blacks who do appear tend to be portrayed in a positive light, foreigners and other minority group members tend to be portrayed negatively (194). On prime-time television, black women are portrayed with somewhat higher occupational prestige than white women (235). They also receive a disproportionately large number of bit parts but are distinctly underrepresented in major roles (133). Apparently because of the availability of minor walk-on roles, blacks appear in some capacity in about half of regular network shows, but in only about 10% of commercials (217).

Blacks are shown as somewhat *less* likely than whites to initiate violence or engage in reprehensible acts (70, 133), but nonwhite minority group members are more likely to be victims of violence (100).

Portrayal of Drug Use

Hanneman & McEwen (118) content-analyzed drug abuse public service announcements and found that most presented no statistics or specific factual information. What is more, these announcements are usually embedded in fringe time programming. McEwen & Hanneman (182) content-analyzed 80 prime-time hours of television and found only one spot announcement with an antidrug message; in contrast, there were 127 persuasive appeals promoting licit drugs (alcohol, tobacco, and pharmaceuticals) during the same period. In the entertainment programming itself, alcohol was the drug most frequently depicted, generally shown in a positive context. Verbal references to drugs were most often negative, however, especially for illicit drugs.

Public Television

Public television programming has shown a general increase in number of stations and mean hours of broadcast per station relative to earlier years (145). The tendency has been to avoid political matters, however, and to emphasize children's programming. One mail survey of 133 public television stations disclosed that on the average they reported devoting only about 1.8% of their airtime to political broadcasting (193). In contrast, a 1972 content analysis of PBS programming revealed that 21.1% of all broadcast hours were devoted to productions of the Children's Television Workshop (145), and another study (225) showed that "Sesame Street" alone accounted for a whopping 60% of all children's broadcasting on public television.

Children's Television Commercials

Spurred in part by a powerful lobbying organization, Action for Children's Television (ACT), several studies have analyzed Saturday morning commercials. Barcus (16) reported that they were divided about equally among four categories: toys, cereals, candy, and other food snacks. He later found (17) a larger number and percentage of toy ads in November than in June, which may reflect a continuing seasonal pattern. Unsurprisingly, the sex of characters appearing in toy commercials could be predicted from the toys; boys were featured in ads for cars, planes, and other mechanical devices, whereas girls appeared in ads for dolls and other traditionally female products. Overall, all these ads appear to be generally dominated by males. Cereal commercials, much more than others, relied on premiums. In a later study, Doolittle & Pepper (76) content-analyzed Saturday morning commercials and found breakfast foods were the most heavily advertised, accounting for 40% of all ads; breakfast foods were followed by sweets, snacks, and a miscellany of toys and other products. All of the breakfast food ads mentioned premiums, contests, or other promotional appeals, whereas products in other categories were advertised on the basis of inherent product qualities and the implication of user satisfaction. Irrespective of product, there were more male than female characters, a finding replicated with a larger and more recent sample by Schuetz & Sprafkin (234).

Control of Content

The content of any mass medium may be influenced either by formal regulation (for example, through restrictions imposed by the FCC, FTC, or legislative bodies) or by the relatively informal decision-making procedures within the industry itself. By far the greatest amount of interest in formal control has focused on the broadcast media: television and radio. In addition to the FCC's ability to limit ownership of radio and television stations, reviewed in detail by Cherington, Hirsch & Brandwein (43), the agency may levy fines and revoke licenses for broadcasting material judged by the Commission to be "obscene, indecent or profane," regardless of whether criminal prosecution has been initiated. Although the FCC acts as a public censor of sexually related broadcast material (86), it has specifically taken the position that "programs containing criticism, ridicule or humor concerning the religious beliefs, race or national background of persons or groups [enjoy] the protection of the Constitutional guarantees of free speech" (86, p. 11). Likewise, the FCC's 1974 policy statement on children's television (85), though it emphasized the need for reduced commercialism and increased educational programming, demurred from regulatory action entirely and purposely avoided any detailed description of what would constitute reasonable practice in the area of children's television programming. The most significant and precedent-setting event regarding formal control in the past few years has been the banning of cigarette ads. Since January 1, 1971, it has been unlawful by act of Congress to advertise cigarettes on any electronic medium; since 1973 this ban has been extended to little cigars as well (86).

Informal control of broadcast media arises almost entirely within the industry, but is sensitive to government and public concerns especially with respect to sex and violence (11). A good example is the June 1975 revision of the Television Code of the National Association of Broadcasters, which created the "family viewing hour," the first hour of prime time, as a sanctuary from which "adult entertainment" is barred (203).

In the area of television news, control is almost entirely informal; this so-called "gatekeeping" function is exercised in various degrees at almost every level of the decision-making process. Warner (264) interviewed news vice presidents, executive producers, Washington bureau chiefs, and associate producers of major networks, as well as reporters and newscasters, and found that each had some rewrite power regarding TV news. Bailey & Lichty (8) provide a fascinating case history of the process, tracing the history of NBC's Tet execution film as the footage was gradually modified by reporters, editors, and producers before a final product was permitted to go on the air. Unsurprisingly, these decisions do influence the effects of news. Meyer (195) exposed viewers to the same film segment but with different reported descriptions and found that the descriptions significantly altered viewers' judgments as to whether the incident shown, the stabbing of a North Vietnamese prisoner of war, was justified. Even when news items have less complex political overtones, a discernible pattern of gatekeeping appears. A detailed analysis shows that stories of high impact, with an element of recent conflict among known principals or issues that lend themselves to video presentation, are the ones most likely to be aired on television news (30).

Perhaps because media gatekeepers share so many judgmental criteria, media news presentations are quite homogeneous. Anderson (4) compared radio and television owned by or with newspapers with those not affiliated with print media; in content and approach, the two groups were remarkably similar. Graber (103) analyzed the information presented by the press during the final 4 weeks of the 1968 U.S. presidential election by examining the contents of 20 newspapers selected to be a cross-section of the American press. An "astonishing" degree of similarity in campaign news was found across the country, but amount of information varied by area with the Northeast getting the largest amount of information and the South the smallest. Emphasis was heaviest on the personal qualities of the candidates, while professional qualifications received short shrift.

This is not to say, of course, that there are no systematic differences among or within the media regarding news coverage. TV news policy-makers seem to exercise stricter control over both reporters and what is reported than do their print media counterparts (264), and print reporters' personal opinions are consequently more influential in the stories they report than is the case with their broadcast counterparts. There is also some gatekeeping by print editors. Editors' authoritarianism, for example, influences coverage of political protest stories; more authoritarian editors are less willing to cover these stories at all (170).

Control of cinema content is entirely voluntary, except for allegedly obscene material. In fact, there is little actual control at all, but the Motion Picture Association of America has offered a voluntary rating service for films since 1968 (G, PG, R, and X); about two-thirds of adults with children report finding the service useful (257).

TRANSMISSION OF INFORMATION AND CULTIVATION OF BELIEFS

The concept of information transmission is intrinsic to the term "communication." Nonetheless the transmission of information will have no behavioral effects unless the information is comprehended, accepted, and absorbed by the message recipient (that is, the media user or communicatee) so as to influence his of her beliefs or attitudes (100, 162). The ability of the mass media to transmit information and cultivate beliefs is the central link between mass media content and use on the one hand, and behavioral and social effects on the other.

Working within this perspective, Gerbner & Gross (100) have reported a series of studies contrasting the world views of heavy and light television viewers. In one study done among both adolescents and adults, they have found that high viewing is associated with greater belief in the cultural and social stereotypes fostered by television. Adults who are heavy television viewers, for example, are much more likely than light viewers to overestimate the danger of violence to themselves in real life, a pattern consistent with television's unrealistically high murder and assault rate on crime shows. In a second study, these same investigators found that among black adolescents, those who are heavy television viewers are more likely than light viewers to perceive whites and males as "heroic" and to perceive black people more negatively than whites; very much the same pattern of effects on both black and white children has been shown by Graves (105) in an experimental study. Heavy child and adolescent viewers are also more likely than light viewers to hold stereotypic views of appropriate sex roles (92, 183), to have a restricted view of the range of real-life occupational choices that are in fact available to them (24), and to be generally more conventional in their views of life (265). Heavy viewers of crime shows express a stronger belief that criminals "usually get caught" than low viewers (66). Studies with children show that television entertainment is most likely to cultivate social beliefs in those areas where real-life information is least available (106, 123). The literature on these types of socializing effects has been reviewed by Leifer, Gordon & Graves (156) and by Liebert and his associates (164, 165).

Political Information and Socialization

During the past decade much attention has been given to the transmission of political information and the cultivation of political beliefs (i.e. political socialization) through the mass media. The overwhelming majority of studies in the former group concerned themselves with Watergate and those involved in it (36, 125, 158, 189, 206, 221, 224), while a minority were concerned with attitudes and information about the Vietnam War (80, 115, 134). Surveys indicate quite clearly that most persons were influenced by media treatment of these issues (81, 115, 134, 206), but the specific nature of the effects interacted with a host of factors (135, 189, 206, 221).

POLITICAL SOCIALIZATION   Recent studies related to media socialization have been quite diverse. The amount of political information an individual possesses is positively related to television availability (139), amount of media use (25), and newspaper exposure (37, 40). Other studies have shown how the media have been used purposefully as a form of political socialization in Cuba (130), Marxist China, and the USSR (215). Among sixth and seventh graders television appears to be an important information source about the President, Vice President, and Congress, but the print media are preferred for election information such as candidate and issue information (64). The general role of the media in political socialization has been reviewed by Becker, McCombs & McLeod (18), and by Kraus (150).

MEDIA EFFECTS ON VOTING   It appears that polls, endorsements, and issue/candidate information affect voting behavior but they also may interact with other variables.

Newspaper support of a presidential candidate appears to influence voting among readers of the paper but especially among those without strong party affiliation (220, 222). Media endorsements in senatorial races also appear to have an effect, but Roshwalb & Resnicoff (227) point out that the effect may be bidirectional, that is, endorsements dissuade some voters from a candidate even though they persuade others. In a unique school board trustee election where there were no incumbents and no party affiliations were shown on the ballot, newspaper endorsements had a significant effect (202).

Exposure to the results of pre-election polls also influences voting (5, 227), but only when the polls suggest a degree of support relatively stronger than the message recipient expected. Absolute figures do not appear to be important (5) and the effect of exposure to early returns on voters' later selections appears to have little effect (255).

Paid political advertisements have their greatest effect on late-deciders; as often as not, however, candidates were rejected after exposure to their ads rather than selected because of them (7). McClure & Patterson (175) examined the relationship between voter belief (where a candidate is perceived to stand on an issue) and exposure to political commercials and network news. They found strong correlations between voting intentions and beliefs about where the candidates stood on various issues, which is information typically gleaned from the media.

The effect of political ads also appears to depend on the type of election. With relatively minor elections, ads had a greater effect on voting intentions and less of an effect on attitude change than with major elections (228). Katz (140) contends that the media do more to reinforce voter intentions than to change them. There is some evidence that the entertainment value of a political message is related to its influence on voters (148) and that the quality of message content combines with audience characteristics (e.g. partisan interests) to determine attention and information gain (7). Unlike political ads, exposure to television network news had almost no effect among those with high political interest (175).

AGENDA SETTING   The agenda setting hypothesis states that the news media communicate to the public the relative importance of various political issues by extending differential coverage priorities to them. The most popular approach to testing the agenda setting hypothesis, although the most ambiguous, has been to search for positive correlations between media attention to various issues and survey data measuring perceived importance of these issues (28, 94, 95, 179). McCombs & Schulte (178), in their time-lagged correlational study, have shown a cumulative effect of media agenda setting upon the personal agendas of college sophmores. McCombs (177), using cross-lagged correlational analysis, also found support for the agenda setting effects of newspapers but not for television. McLeod, Becker & Byrnes (188) found that agenda setting through the newspapers seems to have its greatest effect on older voters and those who skim the medium. In a campaign situation, it is strongest among those least interested in the campaign. Agenda setting does not seem to occur when there is lack of consensus among the media on the issues and high stability in respondents' definition of the issues (254). It has been pointed out that investigators have used different methods of measuring personal agendas and, in particular, have failed to discriminate interpersonal importance (i.e. what one talks about with others) from importance as held privately by the individual (176).

Educational Television

There has been a great surge of interest in educational television, including applied tests and demonstrations of the effects of several broadcast series, most especially "Sesame Street" and "The Electric Company."

SESAME STREET   "Sesame Street" was developed on the basis of formative research designed to construct a show that would successfully attract a preschool audience and at the same time provide basic substantive knowledge and cognitive skills needed for elementary school (159); detailed reports of this formative research have not been published however, though Anderson & Levin (3) have reported some interesting findings regarding attention to the program. Summative evaluations of both the first and second years of "Sesame Street" were conducted and published by the Educational Television Service (12, 27). The ETS researchers concluded that "Sesame Street" did have significant educational effects, and also suggested that exposure to the series tended to narrow the achievement gap between advantaged and disadvantaged youngsters. Unfortunately, however, the research designs and analyses used by ETS were badly flawed. A close reanalysis (60) has disclosed that the actual effects of "Sesame Street" are much smaller than had been supposed, and that the achievement gap tends to be widened rather than narrowed when both middle and lower-class youngsters have access to the show. At least one other major investigation (199) failed to show any positive effects for "Sesame Street" on disadvantaged preschoolers, though more advantaged youngsters did seem to gain from the show.

OTHER SPECIALIZED EDUCATIONAL PROGRAMS   "The Electric Company," another product of the Children's Television Workshop and also built up from formative research, has received considerably less attention in research. The major summative evaluation was an experimental study by Ball & Bogatz (13) among first through fourth graders; in-school viewing of the show produced gains in various reading skills for children of all ages studied. The size of the effect was greater for first and second graders than for older children. Viewing with teacher instruction was more effective than teacher instruction alone. At-home viewing did not significantly improve reading skills.

A similar pattern of results was obtained by Olien, Tichenor & Donohue (209), who examined the effects of "Mulligan Stew," a series of six half-hour color TV films produced under the auspices of the U.S. Department of Agriculture. Consistent with the avowed aims of the show, the tendency to eat a balanced diet was directly related to the number of shows seen. In the absence of school support, however, the series was rarely seen and had no positive effect.

One of the most promising and thoughtful uses of educational television has been reported by Henderson and his associates (127–129). By carefully designing a set of instructional videotapes according to social learning principles, these investigators were able to teach preschool Papago Indian children a variety of cognitive skills such as conservation, seriation, and functionally effective techniques for answering questions.

AGE AS A MODERATOR VARIABLE   It is now abundantly documented that the age of the viewer is related to the amount and kind of information learned from exposure to the media.

Collins (51) found that learning of material central to a TV plot increases monotonically with the age of the child viewers; learning of peripheral content, on the other hand, shows an inverted U pattern with age. A similar pattern regarding peripheral material was reported earlier in a less definitive study by Hale and his associates (116) and by Hawkins (124) as well. A later study pertaining to central content (155) also found that children's ability to follow the continuity of a simple film story increases with age. The ability to comprehend the motives and infer logically necessary aspects of a story also increases with age among children (54, 55, 155).

Chandler, Greenspan & Barenboim (42) found some evidence that children respond to the intentions of characters in televised portrayals at a younger age than to characters in verbally presented stories. Most 7-year-olds responded to intentions when a moral dilemma was presented on TV, but to damage done when the same dilemma was part of a story read to them. This study, and an earlier one by Hebble (126) are consistent with the Piagetian view that there is a shift from damage done ("objective morality") to intentions ("subjective morality") as a basis for moral judgments during middle childhood.

Media Campaigns

There has been continued interest in media campaigns designed to transmit information and influence the beliefs of children, adolescents, and adults. Weiss et al (266) surveyed about 600 adolescents in two midwestern cities to determine the role of mass media and other potential sources (e.g. parents and schools) in providing teenagers with information about family planning. Mass media made the largest contribution by far to knowledge about family planning. Interpersonal communication with parents or peers had some influence, but the effects of school were minimal. Salcedo et al (230) found a multimedia campaign including radio and TV and newspaper announcements, together with direct mailings, substantially modified attitudes toward the safe use of pesticides in a midwestern city. Douglas, Westley & Chaffee (77) examined the effects of a multimedia campaign designed to provide information and improve attitudes toward the mentally retarded. In addition to finding that such a campaign resulted in significant attitude change, the investigators also found a moderately strong positive correlation between information gain and attitude change in the community experiencing the campaign; no such relationship was found in the control community. Finally, Marler (174) attempted an interesting field study of the relative effectiveness of reward-oriented, punishment-oriented, and neutral antilitter pamphlets as they affected both attitudes and actual littering behavior in three national park campsites. Demographic characteristics of subjects were, unfortunately, confounded with treatments, but the data suggested that the punishment-oriented messages were most effective.

Not all such campaigns are successful, of course. Hiett and his associates (131) found no significant effect for simple exposure to a series of print and television ads favoring gun control; the critical factors which did account for attitudes were owning a gun, size of hometown, and political leanings. Similarly, O'Keefe (208) surveyed almost 1000 persons to determine the effects of antismoking commercials on the attitudes of a cross section of the population. The great majority of smokers believed that smoking was bad for their health, but few were inclined to stop. Nonsmokers thought the campaign was more effective than smokers did. At the theoretical and methodological level there have been few new developments in this area, but one investigator (181) has developed a comprehensive set of measures for the assessment of receiver reactions to antidrug abuse messages, and another (192) has outlined some factors that seem to be important in designing an effective public information campaign.

CHILDREN'S TELEVISION COMMERCIALS Ward and his associates (261, 262) have established that understanding of television commercials increases with the age of the child and that increasing age in turn seems to bring increasing skepticism about the truthfulness of these messages. These findings have generally been replicated by Robertson & Rossiter (218), who interviewed first, third, and fifth grade children to determine their perception of commercials. Attribution of persuasive intent increased with age and was positively related to parental education, the ability to recognize the existence of a commercial sponsor, perceive the idea of an intended audience, and be able to cite examples where a product had not met their expectations based on a commercial message.

Nonetheless, the incredulity of older children may be limited to toys, cereal permiums, and "kiddie" products. Lewis & Lewis (160) found that 10 to 13 year old children generally accept as true the health-related messages found in product commercials for pain relievers, personal hygiene products, and the like. Older children are generally more likely than younger ones to rely on TV commercials as a source of product information (e.g. "How do you find out what new toys there are to buy?") (33, 263), and young adolescents specifically give "social utilitarian" responses, e.g. learning who buys what, for watching commercials (200).

MEDIA EFFECTS ON SOCIAL BEHAVIOR

The past 10 years have seen an enormous burgeoning of interest in the effects of the media on social behavior. A number of converging influences seem to account for the trend. One, certainly, is the publication of two major government reports dealing respectively with the effect of television violence on children and youth (252) and the other dealing with the effects of sexually explicit material or "pornography" (216). A second and equally important influence has been a change in the orientation of several subdisciplines within psychology, notably social and developmental psychology, toward the application of research in dealing with applied human concerns and in addressing questions which reflect immediate national needs (149).

Media Violence

Recent work on media violence can be divided up in many ways. The most important distinction involves the nature of the effects being explored. Following Bandura's famous "Bobo doll" studies in the early 1960s, many investigations have pursued the power of the media to instigate immediate and direct imitation of acts of aggression modeled in film or television formats. Increasingly, however, researchers have recognized that more generalized forms of disinhibition of aggressive behavior may occur as a result of exposure to media violence, and thus there has been a great interest in the disinhibition of whole classes of aggressive behavior. These latter investigations may in turn be divided in terms of whether they used a correlational or an experimental methodology and whether their focus was principally on demonstrating gross outcomes or on analyzing the underlying processes which may lead to those outcomes.

DIRECT IMITATION   Weiss (267) observed that studies of direct imitation of media aggression were limited to hostile displays against inanimate play objects. Since his review, a number of studies have indicated that young children will also imitate media acts of aggression directed against live human victims. In the first of these studies (120) 4- and 5-year-old boys from a Sunday school kindergarten served as subjects. Half the subjects observed a 2½ minute color sound film in which an adult model aggressed against a human clown, including a barrage of sharp and unprovoked verbal insults and beating the clown vigorously with a plastic mallet; the remaining children saw no film. The children were then permitted to play freely in a room containing various implements of aggression and either a human clown or an inanimate Bobo doll. In addition to replicating Bandura's basic finding that such a film increases aggression against toys, the investigators found that boys in the film group exhibited significant levels of physical aggression against the human clown. Among the children who had not seen the aggressive film, no physical assaults against the human clown occurred. In a second experiment (119), it was again found that a film of this type, without other provocation, would lead young children physically to assault a human victim. Moreover, such aggression was displayed by both boys and girls (only boys had participated in the first experiment) and for films in which both an 8-year-old boy and an adult served as models. This finding has been essentially replicated a third and a fourth time with somewhat older boys (121, 231), although in the Hanratty, O'Neal & Sulzer study (121) frustration did interact with film condition for these older and perhaps more inhibited observers.

In three somewhat more process-oriented studies with children, it has been shown that imitative aggression is more likely to occur if the modeled acts have been performed vigorously than if they have been performed less vigorously (213), that kindergarten children (but not fifth graders) will imitate filmed acts of aggression even when the model's acts are verbally criticized by an adult (114), and that imitation of televised aggression by preschool boys is enhanced if the test situation includes an aggressive peer relative to a nonaggressive one (205). One recent study has also shown that arousing conditions introduced 24 hours after exposure to film can instigate previously dormant imitation of the film's aggressive content (21), a finding which is in close accord with Bandura's (14) acquisition-performance analyses of imitative learning.

Direct imitation of media aggression by adults is less well established. Donnerstein & Donnerstein (73) found that seeing a film in which a white delivered high electric shock to a black victim stimulated imitative aggression against blacks by white viewers. Generally this effect was not diminished by having seen retaliation by the black victim within the film. On the other hand, Milgram & Shotland (198) performed a series of field experiments which showed that a single exposure to the antisocial behavior of one dispirited protagonist did not lead to imitation in adults. More seductive acts of antisocial behavior may nonetheless induce imitation in adults, as correlational studies on imitation of the criminal plots of such films as *The Doomsday Flight* seem to suggest (164).

DISINHIBITION OF AGGRESSION: CORRELATIONAL STUDIES   Five major correlational studies appear in the Surgeon General's report, and all of them found some association between TV violence viewing and aggressiveness. McIntyre & Teevan (185) found a significant relationship between the amount of violence in a youngster's favorite TV programs and the amount of aggressiveness he or she displayed on five scales of deviance (e.g. petty delinquency) and three measures of approval of violence among 2300 junior and senior high school boys and girls in a sample that was about 15% black and covered the gamut of SES backgrounds. Robinson & Bachman (223) found that adolescent boys high in TV violence viewing were more likely than low TV violence viewers to have gotten into a serious fight at school or work, hurt someone badly enough to need bandages, or to have participated in a gang fight. Studying almost 1000 fourth, fifth, and sixth grade boys and girls, Dominick & Greenberg (68) found that "the greater the level of exposure to television violence, the more the child was willing to use violence, to suggest it as a solution to conflict, and to perceive it as effective" (68, p. 329). McLeod, Atkin & Chaffee (186) found very much the same pattern for junior and senior high school boys and girls, even after partialing out the effects of SES and school performance. A virtually identical result has been reported more recently by Greenberg (107), who performed a study in London among 9, 12, and 15-year-old boys and girls, both middle and working class and drawn from both white and nonwhite populations. Positive correlations (.42–.62) between TV violence viewing and both perceived effectiveness of aggression and willingness to use it oneself were found. Greenberg also found a significant positive correlation between TV violence viewing and the expression of aggressive attitudes, even when exposure to nonviolent television was partialed out.

By far the most convincing of the correlational studies was done by Lefkowitz and associates (84, 153), who conducted a time-lagged correlational study over a 10 year span. They found that for boys the amount of TV violence viewed at age 9 was one of the best predictors of how aggressive the youngsters were at age 19, and their interpretation of the underlying process as a causal one (i.e. TV violence viewing cultivates aggressive attitudes and behavior) has been supported in several reanalyses (138, 146, 204).

DISINHIBITION OF AGGRESSION: EXPERIMENTAL STUDIES   True experiments, in which children are assigned randomly to treatment groups which vary in the amount of violence to which they are exposed, provide the firmest evidence that TV violence viewing can cause aggressive behavior. Experiments conducted for the Surgeon General's report by Leifer & Roberts (157), Liebert & Baron (163) and Stein & Friedrich (244) all showed that the process was operative. Experimental studies done independently of the Surgeon General's report reached substantially the same conclusion. Steuer, Applefield & Smith (247) and Ellis & Sekyra (83) showed that exposure to aggressive cartoons taken from standard Saturday morning fare significantly increased the interpersonal aggressive behavior of preschool and elementary school children respectively. Other experimental studies seem to show the generalization of the effects of exposure to TV violence, including lowered sensitivity to aggression (48, 79, 253) and decrements in cooperative behavior (122).

An apparently contradictory finding was reported by Feshbach & Singer (87), who found that mildly delinquent boys became more aggressive after exposure to a nonaggressive television diet than to an aggressive one. This study had several very serious methodological flaws, however, and several efforts at replication have failed to produce any confirmation for such cathartic effects (212, 269). In fact, these attempted replications showed that exposure to television and filmed violence increased interpersonal physical aggressive behavior among delinquent boys.

MODERATOR VARIABLES   Most of the experimental studies reported in the early 1970s had a "does it or doesn't it" flavor with respect to the effects of TV violence, and were methodologically superior to earlier studies principally because actual televised or filmed materials were used and aggression or aggressiveness was measured in an interpersonal context rather than in play against toy victims. Systematic efforts to delineate those situational and subject variables which make TV violence effects most and least likely to occur have only begun more recently. The number of studies which show that TV violence tends to have a greater effect on youngsters who are initially more aggressive is quite impressive (212, 244, 247, 269), although it should be emphasized that here we are talking about youngsters fully within the normal range (e.g. those above the median in initial aggression in a randomly chosen sample). A few studies also suggest that males are more influenced than females (153, 163), but interpretation of this finding is confounded with both the measures of aggression used and, more importantly, with the fact that the bulk of violent acts on television are perpetrated by males.

Collins and his associates (53, 56) have shown that elementary school age children become more aggressive after seeing an aggressive televised act performed by a villain with redeeming features than by a villain with uniformly bad motives. In a related study with college students, Meyer (196) has reported that those who see either real or fictional violence which is "justified," or fictional violence without explanation, are more aggressive than those who see unwarranted violence, unexplained real violence, or no violence.

There is also evidence to suggest that the absence or delay of undesirable consequences will increase the likelihood that an aggressive act will instigate aggression in viewers. In a study with elementary schoolers, Collins (52) found that aggressive attitudes are more likely to be induced when TV aggression has been separated in time from negative motives and undesirable consequences than when it is not. Zillman, Johnson & Hanrahan (276) found in an experimental study with adults that viewers of an aggressive film with a happy ending for the protagonist were less aggressive subsequently than those who saw the same film without such an ending. Inasmuch as a no-film control group was lacking, the absolute neutralizing effects of a happy ending (presumed by the investigators to release tension and induce relaxation) could not be assessed.

In addition to the foregoing specific explorations of process, two broad explanations, not necessarily mutually exclusive, have been suggested to explain the aggression-instigating effects of media violence on viewers.

The arousal-activation hypothesis   According to this view, media violence is emotionally arousing to viewers, an effect which in turn stimulates high magnitude responses. Support for the arousal hypothesis can be found in studies showing that exposure to aggressive material actually improves performance on certain simple tests (75), and that for college students the aggression-producing effects of a highly aggressive film clip dissipate quite rapidly over time. Physiological measures show directly that both children and adults do become aroused when exposed to aggressive material (75, 211). Finally, it is clear that exposure to erotic and humorous material can increase aggression under some circumstances (250, 273), a finding which is most plausibly interpreted in terms of heightened arousal which is then channeled in the direction of aggression by the immediate situation. In this context it is of interest that angered individuals show a higher preference for violent films than nonangered ones (89), suggesting the rather gloomy possibility that anger increases voluntary self-exposure to media violence, which in turn may arouse and activate aggressive responses.

A variant of the arousal hypothesis has been advanced by Berkowitz (21–23), who argues that media violence often presents stimulus cues previously associated in the viewer's experience with reinforced aggression; these cues, he feels, can intensify and evoke aggression in some situations. In an experimental study guided by this view, Geen & Stonner (97) found that college males who were "attacked" with electric shock became more aggressive than nonattacked subjects only if they had seen a revenge-oriented film clip.

The social learning hypothesis   By far the preponderance of theory and research on the effects of TV violence has been from a social learning perspective, which emphasizes the medium's ability to transmit both specific and novel ways of acting aggressively as well as attitudes, norms, and values which are conducive to aggressive behavior (15, 153, 156, 161, 243). Several short-term experiments have disclosed instigating effects for TV violence viewing even when arousal levels are controlled (163, 212), and the social learning hypothesis is also the one that seems best able to handle the time-lagged correlational data (35, 153). The fact that there is a patterned correlational relationship linking TV violence viewing to the acquisition of aggressive attitudes which are, in turn, associated with increases in aggressive behavior (38) further supports the social learning hypothesis.

DISTRACTING EFFECTS OF NONAGGRESSIVE FILMS   Donnerstein, Donnerstein & Barrett (71) have shown that angered college students exposed to a neutral (that is, nonaggressive) film were significantly less aggressive than a comparable group shown no film, even when elapsed time was controlled. Apparently, neutral entertainment material can have a distracting effect which reduces anger-motivated aggression. Also, individuals who saw an aggressive film and were then angered became more aggressive than those who were angered before they saw the aggressive film, a finding which further supports the distraction hypothesis. Zillman & Johnson (275) have also reported that exposure to a nonaggressive film after being severely angered seems to reduce subsequent aggression.

Pornography

A landmark study of attitudes toward and effects of sexual explicit media, most commonly referred to as "pornography" or "erotica," was reported in 1970 by the Commission on Obscenity and Pornography (216) and, along with 10 technical volumes of supporting research and documentation, constitutes the major (but not exclusive) source of new information in this area.

ATTITUDES TOWARD EROTICA   Abelson et al (1) conducted a national survey, employing a probability sample, to estimate the percentage of the population which had seen any film or photographic depiction of erotica. Seventy percent of adult females and 80% of adult males reported at least one such exposure during their lives, as did 80% of adolescent females and 87% of adolescent males. Adolescents were about as likely to have read erotic material as to have seen it, but adult reading of erotica was somewhat lower than their use of film material. Impressively, only 2% of the respondents spontaneously mentioned concern about erotica as a national problem, whereas 36% spontaneously mentioned racial conflict and civil rights and 20% mentioned a breakdown in law and order.

Higgins & Katzman (132) and Katzman (143) studied the characteristics of erotica which lead them to be judged obscene and found that materials depicting unattractive individuals or with low aesthetic appeal were likely to be so judged. Complete exposure of the pubic area was characteristic of almost all the material judged obscene.

AROUSAL   A majority of both sex educators (216) and the general public (1) believe that viewers may be sexually excited by exposure to sexually explicit material. This belief is well supported by research (171, 173, 201). Mosher (201) had male and female undergraduates view explicit erotic films and found that a clear majority of both sexes reported being aroused by them; about 80% of the males reported at least a partial erection and 85% of the females reported mild genital sensations.

Interestingly, two studies showed that less explicit portrayals may be more arousing than highly explicit ones (31, 248). One experimental study showed that among college-age males, the sexually arousing effect of erotica diminished with repeated exposure (136), a finding that jibes with several earlier and later reports (96, 172).

ALTERATION OF SEXUAL ATTITUDES   Exposure to erotica seems to increase conversation about sex in both young and middle-aged adults (62, 173, 201). Indeed, increased openness in discussing sex was claimed as a major benefit by an appreciable percentage of the married couples who participated in the study by Mann et al (173).

In a study of 194 single males and 183 single females (201), attitudes toward premarital sex became more liberal after viewing two erotic films, and respondents also became more likely to agree with the statement that "sexual intercourse is all right with a lesser degree of intimacy or affection." Both young and middle-aged married couples also express lowered inhibitions and increased willingness to experiment after exposure to erotic material (31, 173).

Howard et al (136) found that one major effect of exposure to erotica was to liberalize viewers' attitudes toward such material, but exposure to erotic materials may also temporarily stimulate feelings of guilt (1, 2, 20, 82).

STIMULATION OF SEXUAL BEHAVIOR   The experimental evidence from self-reports also seems to be fairly clear that exposure to erotica can stimulate interpersonal sexual activity, but that the effects diminish markedly within a day or two (152, 173). Masturbation also increases in frequency among a minority of both males and females (62, 173, 201), but only within the first 48 hours after exposure. The correlational evidence also seems to be fairly clear that experience with erotica is positively related to sexual activity and sexual satisfaction (1, 62, 272), but in the absence of time-lagged data, the direction of causality remains ambiguous.

Both Mosher (201) and Mann et al (173) reported no significant increases in such "low frequency" sexual behavior as cunnilingus, fellatio, and sado-masochistic activity as a result of exposure to erotica, but the limited sampling of erotica used in these studies and their exclusive reliance on self-report data sharply limit the generality of these "no-effect" findings.

DEVIANT AND ANTISOCIAL BEHAVIOR   The section on impact of the Report of the Commission on Obscenity and Pornography opens with the statement:

If a case is to be made against "pornography" in 1970, it will have to be made on grounds other than demonstrated effects of a damaging personal or social nature. Empirical research designed to clarify the question has found no reliable evidence to date that exposure to explicit sexual materials plays a significant role in the causation of delinquent or criminal sexual behavior among youth or adults (216, p. 139).

Today that statement would require some qualification. Its original basis seems to be that self-reports of sex offenders generally do not indicate greater exposure to or arousal by erotica than among nonoffenders (216). Pedophiles and homosexuals are somewhat less likely than those of traditional sexual orientation to report having seen photographic depictions of coitus as adolescents (102), and incarcerated rapists report having seen various sexual depictions somewhat *later* in their lives than nonoffenders (260). Another line of relevant evidence comes from the gross correlation of certain national statistics. Kupperstein & Wilson (151), for example, concluded that exposure to erotica does not lead to increases in juvenile sex crimes because, in the period 1960–1969, juvenile arrests for sex crimes actually decreased in the United States, although the availability of sexual materials increased substantially. On the other hand, forcible rape and arrests for forcible rape increased markedly during the 1960–1969 period (116% and 56%, respectively), along with increased availability of erotica (151). Here the Commission's assertion that "If the heightened availability of erotica were directly related to the incidence of sex offenses, one would have expected an increase of much greater magnitude than the available figures indicate" (216), p. 229) seems a bit of an obfuscation. In contrast, increased availability of erotica in Denmark was associated with a decrease in sexual offenses (19).

Several experimental studies have shown that under some circumstances exposure to erotic material can stimulate aggressive behavior (72, 250, 273, 274). For example, Zillman, Hoyt & Day (274) had an experimental confederate anger male undergraduates and then exposed them for 6 minutes to a neutral educational film, an aggressive prize fight, a violent shoot-out with many people killed by various weapons, or an erotic film of heterosexual foreplay and intercourse without aggressive overtones. Subjects were then given an opportunity to retaliate using obnoxious noise against their "tormentor." The subjects in the erotic conditions delivered significantly more intense noise than subjects in other conditions. Physiological measurements of systolic blood pressure and sympathetic activation indicated excitation after exposure to erotic film was consistently higher than in any other group. There is some reason to believe (72) that exposure to erotic material may have both an arousing effect which can stimulate aggression and a distracting effect which can reduce aggression; which of these influences will prevail depends on the immediate situation. Retrospectively, it is surprising that the Commission sponsored no studies of this type (no longitudinal studies were conducted either, because of time pressure), and Cline (47) has pointed out that limitations in the data base and analysis of the Commission's report leave various questions as to whether its conclusions might have been premature.

Prosocial Effects

The fact that media violence viewing can instigate aggressive behavior has led many investigators to hypothesize that appropriate media examples might also increase various forms of "prosocial" behavior such as cooperation, sharing, and helping. Studies in this area have been entirely limited to the effects of television, and with the exception of one investigation using a dubious methodology (167), they have all been done with children. We found no studies which examined the relative effects of a range of programming (although such studies are badly needed); instead most investigators have focused on the possible prosocial effects of a particular series.

"MISTER ROGERS NEIGHBORHOOD"   The pioneering study of prosocial media effects was conducted by Stein & Friedrich (90, 244), who found that among lower class preschoolers, exposure to the series "Mister Rogers Neighborhood" increased interpersonal prosocial behavior relative to those exposed to neutral or aggressive programming. The change was transitory, however, and was not found at all among children from higher socioeconomic backgrounds. In measures of self-control, children through the entire SES range showed improvement relative to control groups as a result of exposure to "Mister Rogers," but the effects were more pronounced for the higher IQ children. In a later study by the same investigators (91), exposure to "Mister Rogers" in the context of a Headstart program was examined, both by itself and along with special training by teachers. Mere exposure to the program had no more than slight effects, but when exposure was supplemented by teacher training and the children were provided with relevant play materials, considerable gains in both interpersonal prosocial behavior and such intrapersonal behaviors as imaginative play and role-playing fantasy were found. Singer & Singer (238) also found that preschoolers exposed to "Mister Rogers" showed greater imaginative play than those in a no-TV control group; in addition, children who watched the program with an adult who called their attention to its significant features and imitated some of its content were more influenced than those who watched without an adult.

"SESAME STREET"   In addition to its efforts to transmit cognitive and academic skills, discussed earlier, "Sesame Street" was designed with the secondary purpose of stimulating various forms of prosocial behavior among viewers, but results have been disappointing. Paulson (214) compared classrooms of 3- and 4-year-old children who viewed one hour of "Sesame Street" per day during the 1971–1972 season with classrooms of comparable children who did not receive this treatment on several measures of interpersonal cooperation. Those who had viewed "Sesame Street" showed significantly more cooperative behavior than controls in situations directly paralleling those portrayed in the program, but no evidence of generalization was found. Leifer (154) has also reported limited prosocial effects for "Sesame Street" on 4- to 6-year-olds, and likewise failed to find any generalization. A possible explanation of the relative superiority of "Mister Rogers" over "Sesame Street" in eliciting prosocial behavior is found in Coates & Pusser's (49) comparative content analysis of the two shows; they found that "Mister Rogers" contained more examples of positive reinforcement whereas "Sesame Street" contained more examples of punishment.

PROCESS STUDIES   Following the social learning hypothesis, a few investigators have begun to relate prosocial TV effects to the specific modeling cues embodied in television programs. Collins (53) found that among fourth, seventh, and tenth graders, exposure to coping TV models produced greater helpfulness and support for an unseen peer than exposure to aggressive TV models or to television programming in which no relevant models were present. More importantly, he also found that when conflict scenes involving positive coping models were arousing, the arousal appeared to energize constructive responses, thereby showing the joint operation of the social learning and arousal hypotheses. Sprafkin, Liebert & Poulos (242) used intact episodes from the series "Lassie" and showed that exposure to an episode containing a dramatic helping example increased elementary school children's own willingness to help in a similar situation. The same investigators also demonstrated that a television spot announcement designed specifically to provide modeling cues of interpersonal cooperative behavior effectively increased cooperation among elementary school viewers (166). Comstock (59), in an exhaustive survey, found that studies of prosocial behavior were seen as the number one priority for the future by media researchers, and so it seems likely that literature related to this topic will expand markedly in the next decade.

Literature Cited

1. Abelson, H., Cohen, R., Heaton, E., Suder, C. 1970. Public attitudes towards and experience with erotic materials. *Tech. Rep. Comm. Obscenity & Pornography* 6:1–137. Washington DC: GPO. 256 pp.
2. Amoroso, D. M., Brown, M., Preusse, M., Ware, E. E., Pilkey, D. W. 1970. An investigation of behavioral, psychological, and physiological reactions to pornographic stimuli. *Tech. Rep. Comm. Obscenity & Pornography* 8:1–40. Washington DC: GPO. 380 pp.
3. Anderson, D. R., Levin, S. R. 1976. Young children's attention to Sesame Street. *Child Dev.* In press
4. Anderson, J. A. 1971–72. The alliance of broadcast stations and newspapers: the problems of information control. *J. Broadcast.* 16:51–63
5. Atkin, C. K. 1969. The impact of political poll reports on candidate and issue preferences. *Journ. Q.* 46:515–21
6. Atkin, C. K. 1972. Anticipated communication and mass media information-seeking. *Public Opin. Q.* 36:188–99
7. Atkin, C. K., Bowen, L., Nayman, O. B., Sheinkopf, K. G. 1973. Quality versus quantity in televised political ads. *Public Opin. Q.* 37:209–24
8. Bailey, G. A., Lichty, L. W. 1972. Rough justice on a Saigon street: a gatekeeper study of NBC's tet execution film. *Journ. Q.* 49:221–29, 238
9. Bailey, M. 1969. The women's magazine short-story heroine in 1957 and 1967. *Journ. Q.* 46:364–66
10. Bailyn, L. 1959. Mass media and children. *Psychol. Monogr.* 73 (1):471

11. Baldwin, T. F., Lewis, C. 1972. Violence in television: the industry looks at itself. In *Television and Social Behavior, Vol. 1: Media Content and Control,* ed. G. A. Comstock, E. A. Rubinstein, pp. 290–373. Washington DC: GPO. 546 pp.
12. Ball, S., Bogatz, G. A. 1970. *The First Year of Sesame Street: An Evaluation.* Princeton, NJ: Educ. Test. Serv. 453 pp.
13. Ball, S., Bogatz, G. A. 1973. *Reading with Television: An Evaluation of the Electric Company.* Princeton, NJ: Educ. Test. Serv. 188 pp.
14. Bandura, A. 1965. Influence of model's reinforcement contingencies on the acquisition of imitative responses. *J. Pers. Soc. Psychol.* 1:589–95
15. Bandura, A. 1973. *Aggression: A Social Learning Analysis.* Englewood Cliffs, NJ: Prentice Hall. 390 pp.
16. Barcus, F. E. 1971. *Saturday Children's Television.* Newtonville, Mass: Action for Children's Television. 112 pp.
17. Barcus, F. E. 1972. *Network Programming and Advertising in the Saturday Children's Hours: A June and November Comparison.* Newtonville, Mass: Action for Children's Television. 32 pp.
18. Becker, L. B., McCombs, M. E., McLeod, J. M. 1975. The development of political cognitions. In *Political Communication,* ed. S. H. Chaffee, pp. 21–63. Beverly Hills: Sage
19. Ben-Veniste, R. 1970. Pornography and sex crime—the Danish experience. *Tech. Rep. Comm. Obscenity & Pornography,* 7:245–62. Washington DC: GPO. 340 pp.

20. Berger, A. S., Gagnon, J. H., Simon, W. 1970. Pornography: high school and college years. *Tech. Rep. Comm. Obscenity & Pornography* 9:165–208. Washington DC: GPO. 480 pp.

21. Berkowitz, L. 1970. The contagion of violence: an S-R mediational analysis of some effects of observed aggression. In *Nebraska Symp. Motiv.,* ed. W. Arnold, M. Page, pp. 95–135. Lincoln: Univ. Nebraska Press. 288 pp.

22. Berkowitz, L. 1973. Words and symbols as stimuli to aggressive responses. In *Control of Aggression: Implication from Basic Research,* ed. J. F. Knutson, pp. 113–142. Chicago: Aldine-Atherton. 310 pp.

23. Berkowitz, L. 1974. Some determinants of impulsive aggression: role of mediated association with reinforcements for aggression. *Psychol. Rev.* 81:165–76

24. Beuf, A. 1974. Doctor, lawyer, household drudge. *J. Commun.* 24:142–45

25. Bishop, M. 1973. Media use and democratic political orientation in Lima, Peru. *Journ. Q.* 50:60–67, 101

26. Bogart, L. 1972. Negro and white media exposure: new evidence. *Journ. Q.* 49:15–21

27. Bogatz, G. A., Ball, S. 1971. *The Second Year of Sesame Street: A Continuing Evaluation.* Princeton, NJ: Educ. Test. Serv. 429 pp.

28. Bowers, T. A. 1973. Newspaper political advertising and the agenda-setting function. *Journ. Q.* 50:552–56

29. Boyanowsky, E. O., Newtson, D., Walster, E. 1974. Film preferences following a murder. *Commun. Res.* 1:32–43

30. Buckalew, J. K. 1969–70. News elements and selection by television news editors. *J. Broadcast.* 14:47–54

31. Byrne, D., Lamberth, J. 1970. The effect of erotic stimuli on sex arousal, evaluative responses, and subsequent behavior. See Ref. 2, pp. 41–67

32. Cantor, M. G. 1975. Children's television: sex-role portrayals and employment discrimination. In *The Federal Role in Funding Children's Television Programming, Vol. 2: Commissioned Papers.* Bloomington, Ind: Inst. Commun. Res., Dep. Telecommunications, Indiana Univ.

33. Caron, A., Ward, S. 1975. Operation Santa Claus: a pilot study of decision-making by children and parents. *J. Advert. Res.* 15:15–20

34. Chaffee, S. H. 1972. The interpersonal context of mass communication. In *Current Perspectives in Mass Communi-cation,* ed. F. G. Kline, P. J. Tichenon, pp. 95–120. Beverly Hills: Sage. 320 pp.

35. Chaffee, S. H. 1972. Television and adolescent aggressiveness (overview). In *Television and Social Behavior, Vol. 3: Television and Adolescent Aggressiveness,* ed. G. A. Comstock, E. A. Rubinstein, pp. 1–34. Washington DC: GPO. 435 pp.

36. Chaffee, S. H., Becker, L. B. 1974. *Impact of Watergate on the Young Voter.* Presented at Central States Speech Assoc., Milwaukee, Wisc.

37. Chaffee, S. H., Izcaray, F. 1975. *Models of Mass Communication for a Media-Rich Developing Society.* Presented at World Assoc. Public Opin. Res. Congr., Montreux, Switzerland

38. Chaffee, S. H., McLeod, J. M. 1971. *Adolescents, Parents, and Television Violence.* Presented at Am. Psychol. Assoc., Washington DC

39. Chaffee, S. H., McLeod, J. M., Atkin, C. K. 1971. Parental influences on adolescent media use. In *Mass Communications and Youth: Some Current Perspectives,* ed. F. G. Kline, P. Clarke, pp. 21–38. Beverly Hills: Sage. 128 pp.

40. Chaffee, S. H., Ward, L. S., Tipton, L. P. 1970. Mass Communication and political socialization. *Journ. Q.* 47:647–59, 666

41. Chaffee, S. H., Wilson, D. 1975. *Adult Life Cycle Changes in Mass Media Use.* Presented at Assoc. Educ. Journ., Ottawa, Ontario

42. Chandler, M. J., Greenspan, S., Barenboim, C. 1973. Judgements of intentionality in response to videotaped and verbally presented moral dilemmas: the medium is the message. *Child Dev.* 44:315–20

43. Cherington, P. W., Hirsch, L. V., Brandwein, R. 1971. *Television Station Ownership: A Case Study of Federal Agency Regulation.* New York: Hasting House. 304 pp.

44. Clarke, P. 1971. Children's response to entertainment: effects of co-orientation on information-seeking. See Ref. 39, pp. 51–68

45. Clarke, P. 1972–73. Teenagers' co-orientation and information-seeking about pop music. *Am. Behav. Sci.* 16:551–66

46. Clarke, P., Ruggels, L. 1970. Preferences among news media for coverage of public affairs. *Journ. Q.* 47:464–71

47. Cline, V. B., ed. 1974. *Where Do You Draw the Line?* Utah: Brigham Young Univ. Press. 365 pp.

48. Cline, V. B., Croft, R. G., Courrier, S. 1973. Desensitization of children to television violence. *J. Pers. Soc. Psychol.* 27:360–65
49. Coates, B., Pusser, H. E. 1975. Positive reinforcement and punishment in "Sesame Street" and "Mister Rogers." *J. Broadcast.* 19:143–51
50. Colfax, J. D., Sternberg, S. F. 1972. The perpetuation of racial stereotypes: blacks in mass circulation magazine advertisements. *Public Opin. Q.* 36:8–18
51. Collins, W. A. 1970. Learning of media content: a developmental study. *Child Dev.* 41:1133–42
52. Collins, W. A. 1973. Effect of temporal separation between motivation, aggression and consequences: a developmental study. *Dev. Psychol.* 8:215–21
53. Collins, W. A. 1974. *Aspects of Television Content and Children's Social Behavior.* Univ. Minnesota: Inst. Child Dev.
54. Collins, W. A., Berndt, T., Hess, V. 1974. Observational learning of motives and consequences for television aggression: a developmental study. *Child Dev.* 45:799–802
55. Collins, W. A., Westby, S. D. 1975. *Children's Processing of Social Information from Televised Dramatic Programs.* Presented at Soc. Res. Child Dev., Denver, Colo.
56. Collins, W. A., Zimmerman, S. A. 1975. Convergent and divergent social cues: effects of televised aggression on children. *Commun. Res.* 2:331–46
57. Comstock, G. 1975. *Television and Human Behavior: The Key Studies.* Santa Monica: Rand Corp. 247 pp.
58. Comstock, G., Fisher, M. 1975. *Television and Human Behavior: A Guide to the Pertinent Scientific Literature.* Santa Monica: Rand Corp. 323 pp.
59. Comstock, G., Lindsey, G. 1975. *Television and Human Behavior: The Research Horizon, Future and Present.* Santa Monica: Rand Corp. 108 pp.
60. Cook, T. D., Appleton, H., Conner, R. F., Shaffer, A., Tomkin, G., Weber, S. J. 1975. *Sesame Street Revisited.* New York: Sage Found. 420 pp.
61. Courtney, A., Whipple, T. 1974. Women in TV commercials. *J. Commun.* 24:110–18
62. Davis, K. E., Braucht, G. N. 1970. Exposure to pornography, character and sexual deviance: A retrospective survey. See Ref. 19, pp. 173–244
63. Davis, R. H. 1971. Television and the older adult. *J. Broadcast.* 15:153–59

64. Dominick, J. R. 1972. Television and political socialization. *Educ. Broadcast. Rev.* 6:48–56
65. Dominick, J. R. 1973. Crime and law enforcement on prime-time television. *Public Opin. Q.* 37:241–50
66. Dominick, J. R. 1974. Children's viewing of crime shows and attitudes on law enforcement. *Journ. Q.* 51:5–12
67. Dominick, J. R., Greenberg, B. S. 1970. Mass media functions among low-income adolescents. In *Use of the Mass Media by Urban Poor,* ed. B. S. Greenberg, B. Dervin, pp. 31–50. New York: Praeger. 251 pp.
68. Dominick, J. R., Greenberg, B. S. 1972. Attitudes toward violence: the interaction of television exposure, family attitudes and social class. See Ref. 35, pp. 314–35
69. Dominick, J. R., Rauch, G. E. 1972. The image of women in network TV commercials. *J. Broadcast.* 16:259–65
70. Donagher, P. C., Poulos, R. W., Liebert, R. M., Davidson, E. S. 1975. Race, sex and social example: an analysis of character portrayals on inter-racial television entertainment. *Psychol. Rep.* 37:1023–34
71. Donnerstein, E., Donnerstein, M., Barrett, G. 1976. Where is the facilitation of media violence: the effects of nonexposure and placement of anger arousal. *J. Res. Pers.* In press
72. Donnerstein, E., Donnerstein, M., Evans, R. 1975. Erotic stimuli and aggression: facilitation or inhibition. *J. Pers. Soc. Psychol.* 32:237–44
73. Donnerstein, M., Donnerstein, E. 1976. Variables in interracial aggression: exposure to aggressive interracial interactions. *J. Soc. Psychol.* In press
74. Donohue, T. R. 1975. Black children's perceptions of favorite TV characters as models of antisocial behavior. *J. Broadcast.* 19:153–67
75. Doob, A. N., Kirshenbaum, H. M. 1973. The effects on arousal of frustration and aggressive films. *J. Exp. Soc. Psychol.* 9:57–64
76. Doolittle, J., Pepper, R. 1975. Children's TV ad content: 1974. *J. Broadcast.* 19:131–42
77. Douglas, D. F., Westley, B. H., Chaffee, S. H. 1970. An information campaign that changed community attitudes. *Journ. Q.* 47:479–87, 492
78. Downing, M., 1974. Heroine of the daytime serial. *J. Commun.* 24:130–37
79. Drabman, R. S., Thomas, M. H. 1974. Does media violence increase children's

toleration of real-life aggression? *Dev. Psychol.* 10:418-21
80. Edelstein, A. S. 1973. Decision-making and mass communication: a conceptual and methodological approach to public opinion. In *New Models for Communication Research,* ed. P. Clarke, pp. 81-118. Beverly Hills: Sage. 320 pp.
81. Edelstein, A. S., Tefft, D. P. 1974. Media credibility and respondent credibility with respect to Watergate. *Commun. Res.* 1:426-39
82. Elias, J. E. 1970. Exposure to erotic materials in adolescence. See Ref. 20, pp. 273-312
83. Ellis, G. T., Sekyra, F. 1972. The effect of aggressive cartoons on the behavior of first grade children. *J. Psychol.* 81:37-43
84. Eron, L. D., Huesmann, L. R., Lefkowitz, M. M., Walder, L. O. 1972. Does television violence cause aggression? *Am. Psychol.* 27:253-63
85. Federal Communications Commission 1974. Children's television programs. *Fed. Register* 39(#215):39395-424
86. Federal Communications Commission 1975. *The FCC and Broadcasting.* Washington DC: FCC Mimeo. #100-C&CDV. 15 pp.
87. Feshbach, S., Singer, R. D. 1971. *Television and Aggression: An Experimental Field Study.* San Francisco: Jossey-Bass
88. Franzwa, H. 1974. Working women in fact and fiction. *J. Commun.* 24:104-9
89. Friedman, J. S., Newtson, D. 1975. *The Effect of Anger on Preference for Filmed Violence.* Presented at Am. Psychol. Assoc., Chicago, Ill.
90. Friedrich, L. K., Stein, A. H. 1973. Aggressive and prosocial television programs and the natural behavior of preschool children. *Monogr. Soc. Res. Child Dev.* 38(4):151
91. Friedrich, L. K., Stein, A. H., Sussman, E. 1975. *The Effects of Prosocial Television and Environmental Conditions on Preschool Children.* Presented at Am. Psychol. Assoc., Chicago
92. Frueh, T., McGhee, P. 1975. Traditional sex-role development and amount of time spent watching television. *Dev. Psychol.* 11:109
93. Frutkin, A. 1974. *Direct/Community Broadcast Projects Using Space Satellites.* Presented at Reg. Conf. Dir. Broadcast Satellites and Space Law, Univ. Mississippi
94. Funkhouser, G. R. 1973. Trends in media coverage of the issues of the '60's. *Journ. Q.* 50:533-38
95. Funkhouser, G. R. 1973. The issues of the sixties: an exploratory study in the dynamics of public opinion. *Public Opin. Q.* 37:62-75
96. Gebhard, P. H., Gagnon, J. H., Pomeroy, W. B., Christenson, C. V. 1965. *Sex offenders: An Analysis of Types.* New York: Harper & Row. 923 pp.
97. Geen, R. G., Stonner, D. 1973. Context effects in observed violence. *J. Pers. Soc. Psychol.* 25:145-50
98. Gerbner, G. 1972. Violence in television drama: trends and symbolic functions. See Ref. 11, pp. 28-187
99. Gerbner, G. 1973. Teacher in mass culture. In *Communications Technology and Social Policy,* ed. G. Gerbner, L. Gross, W. Melody, 265-86. New York: Wiley. 573 pp.
100. Gerbner, G., Gross, L. 1974. *Violence Profile No. 6. Trends in Network Television Drama and Viewer Conceptions of Social Reality 1967-73.* Monogr. Annenberg Sch. Commun., Univ. Pennsylvania, Philadelphia
101. Gerbner, G., Gross, L., Melody, W., eds. 1973. *Communications, Technology, Social Policy.* New York: Wiley. 573 pp.
102. Goldstein, M. J., Kant, H. S., Judd, L. L., Rice, C. J., Green, R. 1970. Exposure to pornography and sexual behavior in deviant and normal groups. See Ref. 19, pp. 1-90
103. Graber, D. 1971. The press as opinion resource during the 1968 presidential campaign. *Public Opin. Q.* 35:168-82
104. Graney, M. J., Graney, E. 1974. Communications activity substitution in aging. *J. Commun.* 24:88-96
105. Graves, S. B. 1975. *How to Encourage Positive Racial Attitudes.* Presented at Soc. Res. Child Dev., Denver
106. Greenberg, B. S. 1972. Children's reactions to TV blacks. *Journ. Q.* 49:5-14
107. Greenberg, B. S. 1974. British children and televised violence. *Public Opin. Q.* 38:531-47
108. Greenberg, B. S. 1974. Gratifications of television viewing and their correlates for British Children. In *The Uses of Mass Communications: Current Perspectives on Gratifications Research,* ed. J. G. Blumler, E. Katz, pp. 71-92. Beverly Hills: Sage. 320 pp.
109. Greenberg, B. S., Dervin, B. 1970. The role of the mass media for urban poor adults. See Ref. 67, pp. 3-30
110. Greenberg, B. S., Dominick, J. R. 1970. Television behavior among disadvantaged children. See Ref. 67 pp. 51-72

111. Greenberg, B. S., Mazingo, S. L. 1975. Racial issues in mass media institutions. In *Towards the Elimination of Racism,* ed. P. Katz. New York: Pergamon
112. Greenberg, B. S., Roloff, M. E. 1974. *Mass Media Credibility: Research Results and Critical Issues.* News Res. Bull. No. 6. Washington DC: Am. Newspaper Publ. Assoc. 49 pp.
113. Grunig, J. E. 1973. *New Directions for Research in Communications and International Development: From the Study of Individuals to the Study of Formal Organizations.* Presented at Int. Commun. Assoc., Montreal
114. Grusec, J. E. 1973. Effects of co-observer evaluations on imitation: a developmental study. *Dev. Psychol.* 8:141
115. Haavelsrud, M. 1972. Learning resources in the formation of international orientation. *AV Commun. Rev.* 20:229–51
116. Hale, G. A., Miller, L. K., Stevenson, H. W. 1968. Incidental learning of film content: a developmental study. *Child Dev.* 39:69–77
117. Halloran, J. D., Eyre-Brook, E. 1969. *Children's News-Danish Project.* Cent. Mass Commun. Res., Univ. Leicester. 37 pp.
118. Hanneman, G. J., McEwen, W. J. 1973. Televised drug abuse appeals: a content analysis. *Journ. Q.* 50:329–33
119. Hanratty, M. A. 1969. *Imitation of film-mediated aggression against live and inanimate victims.* Unpublished MA thesis, Vanderbilt Univ., Nashville, Tenn.
120. Hanratty, M. A., Liebert, R. M., Morris, L. W., Fernandez, L. E. 1969. Imitation of film-mediated aggression against live and inanimate victims. *Proc. 77th Ann. Conv. APA,* pp. 457–58
121. Hanratty, M. A., O'Neal, E., Sulzer, J. L. 1972. Effect of frustration upon imitation of aggression. *J. Pers. Soc. Psychol.* 21:30–34
122. Hapkiewicz, W., Roden, A. 1971. The effect of aggressive cartoons on children's interpersonal play. *Child Dev.* 42:1583–85
123. Hartmann, P., Husband, C. 1970–71. The mass media and racial conflict. *Race* 12:267–82
124. Hawkins, R. P. 1973. Learning of peripheral content in films: a developmental study. *Child Dev.* 44:214–17
125. Hawkins, R. P., Pingree, S., Roberts, D. F. 1975. Watergate and political socialization. *Am. Polit. Q.* 3:406–22

126. Hebble, P. W. 1971. The development of elementary school children's judgment of intent. *Child Dev.* 42:1203–15
127. Henderson, R. W., Swanson, R., Zimmerman, B. J. 1975. Inquiry response induction in preschool children through televised modeling. *Dev. Psychol.* 11: 523–24
128. Henderson, R. W., Swanson, R., Zimmerman, B. J. 1975. Training seriation responses in young children through televised modeling of hierarchically sequenced rule components. *Am. Educ. Res. J.* 12:479–89
129. Henderson, R. W., Zimmerman, B. J., Swanson, R., Bergan, J. R. 1974. *Televised Cognitive Skill Instruction for Papago Native American Children.* Tucson: Arizona Cent. Educ. Res. Dev. 69 pp.
130. Hernandez, A. R. 1974. Film making and politics: The Cuban experience. *Am. Behav. Sci.* 17:360–92
131. Hiett, R., Youngren, H., Freund, D., Kennerly, J., Schanilec, W., Wong, H. T., Rucher, B. W. 1969. A study of the effectiveness of gun control advertising. *Journ. Q.* 46:592–94
132. Higgins, J. W., Katzman, M. B. 1969. Determinants in the judgment of obscenity. *Am. J. Psychiatry* 125 (12):147
133. Hinton, J. L., Seggar, J. F., Northcott, H. C., Fontes, B. F. 1974. Tokenism and improving imagery of blacks in TV drama and comedy: 1973. *J. Broadcast.* 18:423–32
134. Hollander, N. 1971. Adolescents and the war: the sources of socialization. *Journ. Q.* 48:472–79
135. Holm, J., Kraus, S., Bochner, A. P. 1974. Communication and opinion formation: issues generated by the Watergate hearings. *Commun. Res.* 1:368–90
136. Howard, J. L., Reifler, C. B., Liptzin, M. B. 1970. Effects of exposure to pornography. See Ref. 2, pp. 97–132
137. Hudson, H. E., Parker, E. D. 1975. Telecommunication planning for rural development. *IEEE Trans. Commun.* 23:1177–85
138. Huesmann, L. R., Eron, L. D., Lefkowitz, M. M., Walder, L. O. 1973. Television violence and aggression: the causal effect remains. *Am. Psychol.* 28:617–20
139. Johnson, N. 1973. Television and politicization: a test of competing models. *Journ. Q.* 50:448–55, 474
140. Katz, E. 1971. Platforms and windows: broadcasting's role in election campaigns. *Journ. Q.* 48:304–14

141. Katz, E., Blumler, J. P., Gurevitch, M. 1973. Uses and gratifications research. *Public Opin. Q.* 37:509–23

142. Katz, E., Gurevitch, M., Haas, H. 1973. On the use of the mass media for important things. *Am. Sociol. Rev.* 38:164–81

143. Katzman, M. 1970. Photograph characteristics influencing the judgement of obscenity. See Ref. 20, pp. 9–26

144. Katzman, N. 1972. Television soap operas: what's been going on anyway? *Public Opin. Q.* 36:200–12

145. Katzman, N. 1973. *One Week of Public Television, April 1972.* Washington DC: Corp. Public Broadcast. 85 pp.

146. Kenny, D. A. 1972. Threats to the internal validity of cross-lagged panel inference as related to "Television violence and child aggression": a follow-up study. See Ref. 35, pp. 136–40

147. Kline, F. G. 1971. Media time budgeting as a function of demographics and life style. *Journ. Q.* 48:211–21

148. Kline, F. G. 1972. *Mass Media and the General Election Process: Evidence and Speculation.* Presented at Syracuse Univ. Conf. Mass Media and Am. Politics, Syracuse, NY

149. Korten, F. F., Cook, S. W., Lacey, J. I., eds. 1971. *Psychology and the Problems of Society.* Washington DC: Am. Psychol. Assoc. 459 pp.

150. Kraus, S. 1973. Mass communication and political socialization: a re-assessment of two decades of research. *Q. J. Speech* 59:390–400

151. Kupperstein, L., Wilson, W. C. 1970. Erotica and anti-social behavior: An analysis of selected social indicator statistics. See Ref. 19, pp. 311–24

152. Kutchinsky, B. 1970. The effect of pornography—an experiment on perception, attitudes, and behavior. See Ref. 2, pp. 133–69

153. Lefkowitz, M. M., Eron, L. D., Walder, L. O., Huesmann, L. R. 1972. Television violence and child aggression: a follow-up study. See Ref. 35, pp. 35–135

154. Leifer, A. D. 1975. *How to Encourage Socially-Valued Behavior.* Presented at Soc. Res. Child Dev., Denver

155. Leifer, A. D., Collins, W. A., Gross, B. M., Taylor, P. H., Andrews, L., Blackmer, E. R. 1971. Developmental aspects of variables relevant to observational learning. *Child Dev.* 42:1509–16

156. Leifer, A. D., Gordon, N. J., Graves, S. B. 1974. Children's television: more than mere entertainment. *Harvard Educ. Rev.* 44:213–45

157. Leifer, A. D., Roberts, D. F. 1972. Children's responses to television violence. In *Television and Social Behavior, Vol. 2: Television and Social Learning,* ed. J. P. Murray, E. A. Rubinstein, G. A. Comstock, pp. 43–180. Washington DC: GPO

158. LeRoy, D. J., Wotring, C. E., Lyle, J. 1974. The public television viewer and the Watergate hearings. *Commun. Res.* 1:406–25

159. Lesser, G. S. 1974. *Children and Television: Lessons from Sesame Street.* New York: Random House

160. Lewis, C. E., Lewis, M. A. 1974. The impact of television commercials on health-related beliefs and behaviors of children. *Pediatrics* 53:431–35

161. Liebert, R. M., 1972. Television and Social Learning: Some Relationships Between Viewing Violence and Behaving Aggressively (Overview). See Ref. 157, pp. 1–42

162. Liebert, R. M. 1973. Observational learning: some social applications. In *Social Learning. Fourth Western Symposium on Learning,* ed. P. J. Elich, pp. 59–73. Bellingham: Western Washington State College. 124 pp.

163. Liebert, R. M., Baron, R. A. 1972. Some immediate effects of televised violence on children's behavior. *Dev. Psychol.* 2:469–75

164. Liebert, R. M., Neale, J. M., Davidson, E. S. 1973. *The Early Window: Effects of Television on Children and Youth.* Elmsford, NY: Pergamon. 186 pp.

165. Liebert, R. M., Poulos, R. W. 1975. Television and personality development: the socializing effects of an entertainment medium. In *Child Personality and Psychopathology: Current Topics,* ed. A. Davids, 2:61–97. New York: Wiley. 256 pp.

166. Liebert, R. M., Sprafkin, J. N., Poulos, R. W. 1975. Selling cooperation to children. In *20th Ann. Conf. Proc. Advertising Research Foundation,* ed. W. S. Hale pp. 54–57. New York: Advert. Res. Found. 65 pp.

167. Loye, D. 1975. *Mass. Entertainment and Human Survival: Television's Potential for Prosocial Effects on Adults.* Presented at Am. Psychol. Assoc., Chicago

168. Lumsdaine, A., May, M. 1965. Mass communication and educational media. *Ann. Rev. Psychol.* 16:475–534

169. Lyle, J., Hoffman, H. R. 1972. Children's use of television and other media. In *Television and Social Behavior, Vol.*

4, *Television in Day-to-Day Life: Patterns of Use*, ed. E. A. Rubinstein, G. A. Comstock, J. P. Murray, pp. 257–73. Washington DC: GPO 603 pp.

170. Madden, T. J. 1971. Editor authoritarianism and its effect on news display. *Journ. Q.* 48:660–66

171. Mann, J. 1970. The experimental induction of sexual arousal. *Tech. Rep. Comm. Obscenity and Pornography*, 1: 23–60. Washington DC: GPO. 195 pp.

172. Mann, J., Berkowitz, L., Sidman, J., Starr, S., West, S. 1974. Satiation of the transient stimulating effect of erotic films. *J. Pers. Soc. Psychol.* 30:729–35

173. Mann, J., Sidman, J., Starr, S. 1970. Effects of erotic films on sexual behaviors of married couples. See Ref. 2, pp. 170–254

174. Marler, L. 1971. A study of anti-litter messages. *J. Environ. Educ.* 3:52–53

175. McClure, R. D., Patterson, T. E. 1974. Television news and political advertising: the impact of exposure on voter beliefs. *Commun. Res.* 1:3–31

176. McCombs, M. E. 1974. *A Comparison of Intra-Personal and Inter-Personal Agendas of Public Issues*. Presented at Polit. Commun. Div. Int. Commun. Assoc., New Orleans

177. McCombs, M. E. 1975. *Mass Communication Effects Across Time*. Unpublished manuscript. Syracuse Univ., Syracuse, NY

178. McCombs, M. E., Schulte, H. F. 1975. *Expanding the Domain of the Agenda Setting Function of Mass Communication*. Presented at World Assoc. Public Opin. Res. Congr., Montreaux, Switzerland

179. McCombs, M. E., Shaw, D. L. 1972. The agenda setting function of mass media. *Public Opin. Q.* 36:176–87

180. McCroskey, J. C., Jenson, T. A. 1975. Image of mass media news sources. *J. Broadcast.* 19:169–80

181. McEwen, W. J. 1974. Evaluating media campaigns: using drug images to assess anti-drug abuse information. *Drug Forum* 3:283–93

182. McEwen, W. J., Hanneman, G. 1974. The depiction of drug use in televised programming. *J. Drug Educ.* 4:281–93

183. McGhee, P. E. 1975. *Television as a Source of Learning Sex Role Stereotypes*. Presented at Soc. Res. Child Dev., Denver

184. McGuire, W. J. 1974. Psychological motives and communication gratification. See Ref. 108, pp. 167–96

185. McIntyre, J. J., Teevan, J. J. Jr. 1972. Television violence and deviant behavior. See Ref. 35, pp. 383–435

186. McLeod, J. M., Atkin, C. K., Chaffee, S. H. 1972. Adolescents, parents and television use: self-report and other-report measures from the Wisconsin sample. See Ref. 35, pp. 239–313

187. McLeod, J. M., Becker, L. B. 1974. Testing the validity of gratification measures through political effects analysis. See Ref. 108, pp. 137–64

188. McLeod, J. M., Becker, L. B., Byrnes, J. E. 1974. Another look at the agenda-setting function of the press. *Commun. Res.* 1:131–66

189. McLeod, J. M., Brown, J. D., Becker, L. B. 1975. *Decline and Fall at the White House: A Longitudinal Analysis of Communication Effects*. Madison, Wis: Mass Commun. Res. Cent. 14 pp.

190. McLeod, J. M., O'Keefe, G. J. Jr. 1972. The socialization perspective and communication behavior. See Ref. 34, pp. 121–68

191. McNeil, J. C. 1975. Feminism, femininity and the television series: a content analysis. *J. Broadcast.* 19:259–71

192. Mendelsohn, H. 1973. Some reasons why information campaigns can succeed. *Public Opin. Q.* 37:50–61

193. Mendelsohn, H., Muchnik, M. M. 1970. Public television and political broadcasting: a matter of responsibility. *Educ. Broadcast. Rev.* 4:3–9

194. Mendelson, G., Young, M. 1972. *Network Children's Programming*. Washington DC: Black Efforts for Soul in Television. 10 pp.

195. Meyer, T. P. 1971. Some effects of real newsfilm violence on the behavior of viewers. *J. Broadcast.* 15:275–85

196. Meyer, T. P. 1972. Effects of viewing justified and unjustified real film violence on aggressive behavior. *J. Pers. Soc. Psychol.* 23:21–29

197. Meyer, T. P. 1973. Children's perceptions of favorite television characters as behavioral models. *Educ. Broadcast. Rev.* 7:25–33

198. Milgram, S., Shotland, R. 1973. *Television and Antisocial Behavior*. New York: Academic. 183 pp.

199. Minton, J. H. 1972. *The impact of Sesame Street on reading readiness of kindergarten children*. PhD thesis. Fordham Univ., New York, NY

200. Moore, R. L., Stephens, L. F. 1974. *Some Communication and Demographic Determinants of Consumer*

Learning Among Older and Younger Adolescents. Presented at Mass Commun. Div. Int. Commun. Assoc., New Orleans
201. Mosher, D. L. 1970. Psychological reactions to pornographic films. See Ref. 2, pp. 255–312
202. Mueller, J. E. 1970. Choosing among 133 candidates. Public Opin. Q. 34:395–402
203. National Association of Broadcasters 1975. The Television Code. Washington DC: NBC. 35 pp.
204. Neale, J. M. 1972. Comment on "Television Violence and Child aggression: a follow-up." See Ref. 35, pp. 141–48
205. O'Carroll, M., O'Neal, E., McDonald, P., Hori, R. 1976. Influence upon imitative aggression of a peer who also imitates. J. Soc. Psychol. In press
206. O'Keefe, G. J. Jr., Mendelsohn, H. 1974. Voter selectivity, partisanship, and the challenge of Watergate. Commun. Res. 1:345–67
207. O'Keefe, G. J. Jr., Spetnagel, H. T. 1973. Patterns of college undergraduates' use of selected news media. Journ. Q. 50:543–48
208. O'Keefe, M. T. 1971. The anti-smoking commercials: a study of television's impact on behavior. Public Opin. Q. 35:242–48
209. Olien, C. N., Tichenor, P. J., Donohue, G. A. 1975. A Systems Evaluation of a Purposive Message: The "Mulligan Stew" ETV Project. St. Paul: Agric. Ext. Serv., Inst. Agric., Forestry & Home Econ., Univ. Minnesota. 37 pp.
210. O'Neal, E., McDonald, P., Hori, R., McClinton, B. 1976. Arousal and imitation of aggression. Motivation and Emotion. In press
211. Osborn, D. K., Endsley, R. C. 1971. Emotional reactions of young children to TV violence. Child Dev. 42:321–31
212. Parke, R. D. 1974. A field experimental approach to children's aggression: some methodological problems and some future trends. In Determinants and Origins of Aggressive Behavior, ed. J. de Wit, W. W. Hartup, 499–508. The Hague: Mouton. 623 pp.
213. Parton, D., Geshuri, Y. 1971. Learning of aggression as a function of presence of a human model, response intensity and target of response. J. Exp. Child Psychol. 11:491–504
214. Paulson, F. L. 1974. Teaching cooperation on television. AV Commun. Rev. 22:229–46

215. Pool, I. de Sola 1974. Communication in totalitarian societies. In Handbook of Communication, ed. I. de Sola Pool, W. Schramm, pp. 462–511. Chicago: Rand McNally. 954 pp.
216. Report of the Commission on Obscenity and Pornography 1970. Washington DC: GPO 633 pp.
217. Roberts, C. 1970–71. The portrayal of blacks on network television. J. Broadcast. 15:45–53
218. Robertson, T. S., Rossiter, J. R. 1974. Children and commercial persuasion: an attribution theory analysis. J. Consum. Res. 1:13–20
219. Robinson, J. P. 1971. The audience for national TV news programs. Public Opin. Q. 35:403–5
220. Robinson, J. P. 1972. Perceived media bias and the 1968 vote: can the media affect behavior after all? Journ. Q. 49:239–46
221. Robinson, J. P. 1974. Public opinion during the Watergate crisis. Commun. Res. 1:391–405
222. Robinson, J. P. 1974. The press as king maker: what surveys from last five campaigns show. Journ. Q. 51:587–94, 606
223. Robinson, J. P., Bachman, J. G. 1972. Television viewing habits and aggression. See Ref. 35, pp. 372–82
224. Robinson, M. J. 1974. The impact of the televised Watergate hearings. J. Commun. 24:17–30
225. Rockman, S. 1971. One Week of Educational Television, #6. Bloomington, Ind: Natl. Instr. Telev. Cent. 57 pp.
226. Roper, B. W. 1975. Trends in Public Attitudes Toward Television and Other Mass Media, 1959–1974. New York: Telev. Inform. Off. 26 pp.
227. Roshwalb, I., Resnicoff, L. 1971. The impact of endorsements and published polls on the 1970 New York Senatorial election. Public Opin. Q. 35:410–14
228. Rothschild, M. L., Ray, M. L. 1974. Involvement and political advertising effect. Commun. Res. 1:264–85
229. Ryan, M. 1973. News content, geographical origin and perceived media credibility. Journ. Q. 50:312–18
230. Salcedo, R. N., Read, H., Evans, J. F., Kong, A. C. 1974. A successful information campaign on pesticides. Journ. Q. 51:91–95, 110
231. Savitsky, J. C., Rogers, R. W., Izard, C. E., Liebert, R. M. 1971. Role of frustration and anger in the imitation of filmed aggression against a human victim. Psychol. Rep. 29:807–10

232. Schramm, W. 1962. Mass communication. *Ann. Rev. Psychol.* 13:251–84
233. Schramm, W., Lyle, J., Parker, E. B. 1961. *Television in the Lives of Our Children.* Stanford Univ. Press. 324 pp.
234. Schuetz, S., Sprafkin, J. N. 1976. Spot messages appearing within Saturday morning television programs: a content analysis. In *Broadcast Advertising and Children: Hearings before the Subcommittee on Communications of the Committee on Interstate and Foreign Commerce,* pp. 327–35. Washington DC: GPO. 495 pp.
235. Seggar, J. F., Wheeler, P. 1973. World of work on TV: ethnic and sex representation in TV drama. *J. Broadcast.* 17:201–14
236. Sexton, D., Haberman, P. 1974. Women in magazine advertisements. *J. Advert. Res.* 14:41–46
237. Sharon, A. T. 1973. Racial differences in newspaper readership. *Public Opin. Q.* 37:611–17
238. Singer, J. L., Singer, D. G. 1974. *Fostering Imaginative Play in Preschool Children: Effects of Television Viewing and Direct Adult Modeling.* Presented at Am. Psychol. Assoc., New Orleans
239. Slaby, R. G., Quarfoth, G. R., McConnachie, G. A. 1976. Television violence and its sponsors. *J. Commun.* 26:88–96
240. Sloan Commission on Cable Communications 1971. *On The Cable.* New York: McGraw-Hill. 256 pp.
241. Smith, D. M. 1971–72. Some uses of mass media by 14 year olds. *J. Broadcast.* 16:37–49
242. Sprafkin, J. N., Liebert, R. M., Poulos, R. W. 1975. Effects of a prosocial televised example on children's helping. *J. Exp. Child Psychol.* 20:119–26
243. Stein, A. H. 1972. Mass media and young children's development. *Nat. Soc. Study Educ.* 71:181–202
244. Stein, A. H., Friedrich, L. K. 1972. Television content and young children's behavior. See Ref. 157, pp. 202–317
245. Stempel, G. H. III 1971. Visibility of blacks in news and news-picture magazines. *Journ. Q.* 48:337–39
246. Sternglanz, S., Serbin, L. 1974. Sex role stereotyping on children's television programs. *Dev. Psychol.* 10:710–15
247. Steuer, F. B., Applefield, J. M., Smith, R. 1971. Televised aggression and the interpersonal aggression of preschool children. *J. Exp. Child Psychol.* 11:442–47
248. Tannenbaum, P. H. 1970. Emotional arousal as a mediator of communication effects. See Ref. 2, pp. 326–56
249. Tannenbaum, P. H., Greenberg, B. S. 1968. Mass communication *Ann. Rev. Psychol.* 19:351–86
250. Tannenbaum, P. H., Zillman, D. 1975. Emotional arousal in the facilitation of aggression through communication. *Adv. Exp. Soc. Psychol.* 8:149–92
251. Tedesco, N. 1974. Patterns in primetime. *J. Commun.* 24:119–24
252. *Television and Growing Up: The Impact of Televised Violence.* 1972. Report to the Surgeon General, United States Public Health Service. Washington DC: GPO. 163 pp.
253. Thomas, M. H., Drabman, R. S. 1975. *Some New Faces of the One-Eyed Monster.* Presented at Soc. Res. Child Dev., Denver
254. Tipton, L., Haney, R. D., Baseheart, J. R. 1975. Media agenda-setting in the city and state election campaigns. *Journ. Q.* 52:15–22
255. Tuchman, S., Coffin, T. E. 1971. The influence of election night televised broadcasts in a close election. *Public Opin. Q.* 35:315–26
256. Turow, J. 1974. Advising and ordering: daytime, prime-time. *J. Commun.* 24:138–41
257. Valenti, J. 1975. *The Movie Rating System.* New York: Motion Picture Assoc. 11 pp.
258. Verna, M. E. 1975. The female image in children's TV commercials. *J. Broadcast.* 19:310–9
259. Wade, S. E. 1971. Adolescents, creativity, and media: an exploratory study. See Ref. 39, pp. 39–50
260. Walker, C. E. 1970. Erotic stimuli and the aggressive sexual offender. See Ref. 19, pp. 91–148
261. Ward, S., Reale, G., Levinson, D. 1972. Children's perceptions, explanations, and judgments of television advertising: a further exploration. See Ref. 169, pp. 468–90
262. Ward, S., Wackman, D. B. 1973. Children's information processing of television advertising. See Ref. 80, pp. 119–46
263. Ward, S., Wackman, D. B., Wartella, E. 1976. *Children Learning to Buy: The Development of Consumer Information Processing Skills.* Beverly Hills: Sage. In press
264. Warner, M. 1970. Decision-making in network television news. In *Media Sociology,* ed. J. Tunstall, pp. 158–67. Urbana: Univ. Illinois Press. 574 pp.

265. Weigel, R. H., Jessor, R. 1973. Television and adolescent conventionality: an exploratory study. *Public Opin. Q.* 37:76–90

266. Weiss, E., Kline, F. G., Rogers, E. M., Cohen, M. E., Dodge, J. A. 1974. *Communication and Population Socialization Among Youth.* Presented at Popul. Assoc. Am., New York

267. Weiss, W. 1971. Mass communication. *Ann. Rev. Psychol.* 22:309–36

268. Weitzman, L. J., Eifler, D., Hokada, E., Ross, C. 1971–72. Sex-role socialization in picture books for preschool children. *Am. J. Sociol.* 77:1125–50

269. Wells, W. D. 1972. Television and aggression: a replication of an experimental field study. Unpublished study cited in *Television and Growing Up: The Impact of Televised Violence.* Report to the Surgeon General, US Public Health Serv. Washington DC: GPO. 163 pp.

270. Wiebe, G. D. 1969–70. Two psychological factors in media audience behavior. *Public Opin. Q.* 33:523–36

271. Women on Words and Images 1972. *Dick and Jane as Victims.* Princeton, NJ. 51 pp.

272. Zetterberg, H. L. 1970. The consumers of pornography where it is easily available: the Swedish experience. See Ref. 20, pp. 453–68

273. Zillmann, D. 1971. Excitation transfer in communication-mediated aggressive behavior. *J. Exp. Soc. Psychol.* 7:419–34

274. Zillmann, D., Hoyt, J. L., Day, K. D. 1974. Strength and duration of the effect of aggressive violent and erotic communications on subsequent aggressive behavior. *Commun. Res.* 1:286–306

275. Zillmann, D., Johnson, R. C. 1973. Motivated aggressiveness perpetuated by exposure to nonaggressive films. *J. Res. Pers.* 7:261–76

276. Zillmann, D., Johnson, R. C., Hanrahan, J. 1973. Pacifying effect of happy ending of communications involving aggression *Psychol. Rep.* 32:967–70

Ann. Rev. Psychol. 1977. 28:175-96

PERSONNEL ATTITUDES ❖271
AND MOTIVATION

Abraham K. Korman[1]
Department of Psychology, Baruch College, CUNY, New York, NY 10010

Jeffrey H. Greenhaus
Department of Management Science, Stevens Institute of Technology, Hoboken, NJ 07030

Irwin J. Badin
Department of Psychology, Montclair State College, Upper Montclair, NJ 07043

In reviewing the research literature during 1974–1975, a number of distinct overall themes have emerged. First, a conceptual watershed seems to have been reached in that the theoretical schemas that have dominated the field of work motivation for the past decade are increasingly being described by their own proponents as being of limited usefulness and that much remains to be done in constructing more adequate theoretical frameworks.

Second, there is an increasing concern with some of the basic methatheoretical assumptions that have been utilized in the study of work motivation and satisfaction. Thus there is great interest in such topics as (a) the logic of contingency (or moderator) models and their potential fruitfulness; (b) the traditional dependent variables of the field (work achievement and job satisfaction), and the societal and personal implications of encouraging the maximization of each outcome.

A third theme concerns the vast cultural changes sweeping Western society concerning the meaning of work, the integration or acceleration of new groups into the workforce, the meaning of "success," the "fear of success" motive, and related topics. Tied in with these concerns is the continuing interest in the sociotechnical redesign of organizations and jobs as a mechanism for meeting these changes and for overcoming other problems that have plagued work organizations for years.

[1]We would like to thank Richard Barrett, John Bromer, J. Myron Johnson, Raymond Katzell, Richard Kopelman, and Gary Yukl for their helpful comments on an earlier draft of this manuscript.

175

Finally, there are the traditional concerns with such variables as leadership behavior as influences on motivation and work attitudes. These also have served as major areas of research and interest.

In this review we will concentrate the major portion of our discussion under these headings, bringing in other topics where they seem to be most relevant. Overall, at the risk of seeming unnecessarily sanguine, one of our major impressions is that the literature in general is increasingly that of a healthy field, one that is unafraid to take a look at some of its basic theories and revise them as they seem appropriate, and one that is looking to examine its basic conceptual assumptions and practical recommendations when this seems appropriate. Such willingness strikes us as doing much to assure the continued viability and usefulness of the field to individuals, organizations, and society in the years to come.

On the other hand, in a more negative vein, it is also our impression that some of the major contributions that we have reviewed come from individuals who are either primarily associated with fields of psychology other than those focusing on organizational behavior or who may not be psychologists at all. This is particularly true, we believe, in the area of cultural changes in work motivation and attitudes. We will expand on these points later.

THEORETICAL FRAMEWORKS

From the viewpoint of overall interest and popularity, the theoretical approach that has ranked first over the past decade has been the expectancy-value (EV) framework, originally popularized by Vroom (144) and since adopted and expanded by others. It is because of this popularity that Locke's (92) thorough and critical evaluation of the EV model has been long overdue, particularly since studies testing expectancy theory predictions have generated such inconsistent results.

For example, in a highly significant review of 31 studies testing the theory, House, Shapiro & Wahba (62) came to the following conclusions: (a) support for the theory is generally weak with the percent of criterion variance explained rather low; (b) it is unclear whether personal desires, perceived environmental incentives, or cognitive expectancies are the best predictors; and (c) the theory has boundary conditions, one of which may be the actual contingency of rewards on performance. Other research published since the House, Shapiro & Wahba paper continue to support these conclusions. Subsequent studies (8, 86, 115, 131), for example, have all found little support for the multiplicative relationships postulated by the theory.

Our position is not that the expectancy model is invalid but rather that the theory is like any other, i.e. useful under some conditions but not under others. What are these limiting conditions? One possibility, suggested by Locke (92), concerns the expectancy theory assumption that most people characteristically project the future consequences of their actions, consider many (as opposed to one) types of actions and consequences, and base their actions on a conscious calculation of expected pleasure and/or pain. It would seem that expectancy theory predictions should not hold for persons who do not act in such a rational manner. However, despite the reasonable nature of this suggested moderator of the EV model, the few studies relevant to this issue have not been consistent.

In one study, Turney (143) found that the behavior of employees classified as rational conformed more closely to the EV model than did employees classified as irrational. On the other hand, Korzeniowski (81) found that the EV model tended to predict self-rated effort better for emotional than for rational workers. Korzeniowski speculated that the organization was of a noncontingent nature, and therefore a rational person would not believe any connections between performance and rewards. If this explanation is sound, it would suggest that the boundary conditions for expectancy theory include not only the nature of the organization and the characteristics of the employees but some interaction between the two.

Also in this vein, Kopelman (75) proposed that the expectancy model would be moderated in its validity by such factors as (a) temporal considerations (it takes time for the cognitions to be translated into behavior); (b) the level of rewards involved (the higher the level of extrinsic need satisfaction, the greater the incentive value of intrinsic rewards); (c) levels of criterion behavior already attained; (d) organizational system responsiveness to performance; and (e) individual ability and task difficulty. Yet here, too, despite the logic of these proposals, there is already some negative evidence available (130, 131).

Highly relevant to expectancy theory is the research stemming from Deci's (23–26) hypothesis regarding the nonadditivity of incentives. Briefly, Deci claims that making pay contingent upon performance reduces the intrinsic motivation to perform a task. If this hypothesis continues to receive support (especially in an organizational setting), it would suggest that the force to perform at a high performance level may not simply be an additive function of the perceived connections between effective performance and valued outcomes. Notz (107) has reviewed this research and has found support for each of the following:

1. Under certain conditions, intrinsic and extrinsic rewards are nonadditive as incentives to behavior.
2. The arousal of extrinsic motivation may occur at the expense of intrinsic motivation.
3. The withdrawal of extrinsic motivation may increase intrinsic motivation.

Although there is some disagreement with Deci's interpretation of the data (120) and his assumptions (129), there is corroborating evidence as well. For example, it has been found (34, 35) that among both nationwide samples of potential Navy recruits and men already in the Navy, behavior is *not* a monotonically increasing function of incentives. Not only is "more" not necessarily "better," it may be worse. Perhaps the most cautious conclusion is that making a valued outcome contingent upon a given behavior may not automatically increase the probability of engaging in that behavior. What is needed, in our opinion, is more research on how people interpret behavior-contingent rewards. Does the locus of causality of the behavior shift? Are feelings of psychological reactance generated? If so, is the behavior consequently devalued? The answer to these questions may help clarify the inconsistent results expectancy theory has provided.

One further note concerns the method by which expectancy theory should be tested. It is clear that although the initial statements of expectancy theory (144) referred to a within-subject decision model, the vast majority of research studies has employed an across-subjects (normative) design (101). Although there are problems with an ipsative test of the model, both philosophical (77) and methodological (101), such studies may be necessary in future tests of the usefulness of the theory.

All in all, when we consider the inconsistent results to date, the problems we have mentioned, and other criticisms of the expectancy theory framework (27, 125), it would seem appropriate to expect and hope that future work with the EV model will involve more limited application with less sweeping claims and a greater recognition of the complexities involved.

Turning now to equity theory, studies continue to support the basic prediction that equitable outcomes are more satisfying than inequitable outcomes, particularly when they are expected (9). However, there are an increasing number of criticisms, such as those by Dunnette (29), that the Adams (3) equity model cannot be carried further until its very serious problems of operationalization and measurement have been resolved. One step in this direction has been taken by Goodman (44), who has published a significant paper on the referents people use in determining their input-outcome ratio.

Similarly, Korman (78, 79), while finding considerable support for the self-esteem consistency model he published some years ago, (45, 88, 147), has nevertheless proposed a revision (79) in order to eliminate the original theoretical prediction that invariably the "good get better" and the "poor get worse." Since it is clear that at times there are changes from effective to ineffective performance and vice versa, Korman suggests that increasing effectiveness over time, regardless of original performance level, is due to internal attribution of outcomes (success or failure) while decreasing effectiveness results from external attribution. Also concerned with longitudinal processes in an equity situation, Cook (20) suggests that those individuals who have been subject to overreward over time begin to increase their perception of their inputs (i.e. they believe they have greater ability than they thought). In addition, some of those in overreward situations may deal with it by attributing responsibility to others. We see such changes and revisions in equity theory as highly desirable. However, we think more are necessary, particularly with respect to the Adams model which has been so important for the past decade.

Another theoretical framework that obviously needs great revision is the need hierarchy proposed by Maslow (96, 97). Although of great societal popularity, need hierarchy as a theory continues to receive little empirical support. In a major review paper, Wahba & Bridwell (146) have come to the conclusion that there is little support for (a) the prediction that need structures are organized along the dimensions proposed by Maslow; (b) the prediction of a negative relationship between the level of need gratification and the activation of that need; and (c) the prediction of a positive relationship between the level of need gratification and the activation level of the next higher need.

We would make only one minor demurrer to this negative conclusion, and this concerns a possible shortcoming in much of the research testing Maslow's model. This has been the tendency to correlate the satisfaction of a given need with the *importance* of that need (negative correlation predicted) and the importance of the need at the next higher level (positive correlation predicted.) We wonder how closely the concept of need importance corresponds to Maslow's original concept of the absense or presence of an *active, dominant* need. The issue, it seems to us, is not whether the satisfaction of a need reduces the importance of that need or increases the importance of the next higher need, but rather whether it affects the motivating capacity or incentive value of the satisfied need or the next higher need. This aspect of Maslow's theory does not strike us as having been tested in an organizational setting. Despite this question, however, the available research should certainly generate a reluctance to accept unconditionally the implications of Maslow's hierarchy.

One theoretical approach which, although developed outside the field, we believe should find its way into the organizational behavior literature is Weiner's (153) merging of the traditional need-achievement model with an attribution-theory approach to the locus of causality for success and failure. One of his proposals is that affective reactions to success or failure (pride or shame) will depend on the extent to which individuals attribute their success or failure to internal factors such as ability or effort rather than to the external factors of task difficulty or luck. Weiner also predicts that the tendency to change goal expectations (raise after success, lower after failure) will be greater for persons who attribute their task performance to stable factors (task difficulty, ability) than for those who attribute performance to unstable factors (effort, luck).

Thus, if employees attribute their effective performance to luck, there is little likelihood that they will maintain or raise their performance expectancies as a result of their success. On the other hand, failure attributed to a temporary lack of effort should generate a higher future expectancy of successful behaviors than failure attributed to low ability. We may note also that since attribution theory has been used both here and in Korman's (79) revised model, it is useful to know that causal attributions can be experimentally changed (154).

It needs to be pointed out, however, that it is not necessary to use attribution theory in order to account for longitudinal effects on motivational processes. Dember (28) has discussed the possible role of ideology in motivational processes over time, while Raynor (114) has extended the traditional need achievement model by bringing in long-range cognitive structural variables such as the contingent and/or noncontingent implications of the choice to engage in achievement behavior. Thus, if a choice to achieve implies other outcomes with certain degrees of probability and incentive value, this will affect the likelihood of choice differently than if there are no contingencies or if they are of an "open" rather than closed nature. While we are not certain that this is not more than a clarification of the components of the traditional n Ach model, the clarification is desirable in and of itself since it is specifically oriented to the particular interests of the field of OB, i.e. career motivational choices with a long-range perspective. We also think it is desirable because of the continued support for the influence of achievement motivation on work behavior (1, 81).

One area of motivational research which is finally coming into its own, and which we applaud, is the concern with power motivation. What are the different kinds? What are the consequences of each? Under what conditions? One hypothesis is that the motivation to influence others toward goal achievement is a crucial organizational variable but that it becomes dysfunctional when the emphasis changes to people control rather than task orientation. But when does this change happen? Kipnis (74) suggests that it may occur simply as a function of one's level in a hierarchial organization (i.e. the higher the level, the greater the power motivation), a position consistent with the "corruption of power" hypothesis made popular by Watergate. On the other hand, research with the Miner role motivation theory suggests that some power motivation is necessary for effectiveness in hierarchical organizations (100). We would like to see more research devoted to these questions.

THEORETICAL ISSUES

Moderator Variables and the Contingency Approach

From the time of Lewin's famous programmatic equation that B=f(P, E), it has been a metatheoretical assumption of most psychologists that to understand behavior one must know the effects of the organismic variable, the environmental variable, and their interaction. Researchers in organizational behavior have certainly not been immune to this way of thinking; on the contrary, most researchers and practitioners have been hesitant to recommend any managerial or job design strategy without taking both employee and environmental characteristics into account.

The popularity of the moderator or contingency approach to work behavior (for this is what Lewin's argument is) has left us with rather mixed feelings. On the one hand, the moderator approach has stimulated a voluminous amount of interesting research and theory. In practically every area of organizational behavior, whether it be job design (17, 47, 116, 149), leadership (33, 72, 102, 119, 145), or pay (44, 53), the point has been made that a given organizational variable may not have identical effects under all situations. The problem is that the argument seems so reasonable that we lose sight of where such an approach might be taking us.

The issue, in our opinion, is not whether contingency effects exist in organizational settings; they clearly do, since every theory is eventually a contingency model. No theory accounts for everything. What is frequently not appreciated, however, is that the goal of identifying and acting on a systematic set of moderator effects is much more difficult than this recognition implies, a difficulty which we believe has implications for motivational theories and managerial practice.

This difficulty is discussed in a highly significant paper by Cronbach (21), who points out the inconsistency with which aptitude-treatment-interaction (i.e. moderator) effects have been obtained, even when all major variables are virtually identical. This inconsistency, he suggests, may be due to several factors. In the first place, second- or third-level interactions may cloud any simple moderator effect, or at least render it inconsistent from sample to sample. In addition, time (and its consequent socialization effects) may itself be a moderator that influences the magnitude and direction of other moderator effects. Thus relationships that hold in the 1970s may not be generalizable 10 years later.

These reservations lead Cronbach to propose: (*a*) moderate aspirations for theory-building, i.e. the mathematical precision of the moderator variable logic may be highly difficult to achieve; (b) a greater openness to experience in our research and a greater "clinical" understanding of the data at a local level; and (c) less concern with rigorous null-hypothesis testing models. Cronbach's article is just one of a whole series of papers during the time of this review which have questioned a blind obedience to the "scientific method" and which have called for a greater openness to subjective experience and for a recognition of the changing nature of "facts" over time. While some of these papers have focused on other areas of psychology and the behavioral sciences, their relevance to this field is clear (18, 30, 42, 80, 103, 122, 150).

What are the implications of these papers for research and practice in motivation and job attitudes?

One direction, suggested by Cronbach (21) and Warr (150), is fewer a priori hypothesis-testing, deductive studies and more research aimed at building relationships and associated contingencies through inductive, clinical-type observation. Here we are referring to the stance with which a researcher approaches an investigation. Are we going to concentrate our efforts on an a priori delineation of potential moderators, or will we try to understand a given independent variable (e.g. leader behavior, job design) with a clinical approach that demands an open-minded orientation? We suggest the latter may on occasion be more useful at this time and perhaps over the long run.

Second, we might hold off any statement of moderator effects until replications take place and conditions of replication are stated. Furthermore, even when moderator effects are replicated, we should be aware of their probable lack of precision. Here we may implement a suggestion by Cronbach that assignments to differential treatments (job designs, compensation schemes) on the basis of empirically determined moderator effects might take the form of an informed choice by the person(s) affected. For example, instead of automatically assigning employees with low "growth needs" to less enriched jobs, we might, in effect, present the data to the worker, note the imprecision of any prediction, and let the worker make the decision. Such an approach, which is consistent with Lawler's (85) plea for individualizing organizational life and with Argyris's (6) analysis of the dysfunctions of traditional scientific control and influence, has the virtue of attending to individual differences when they are clearly relevant without the illusion that the relationships established are immutable over time.

The Meaning of Achievement

It has been traditional to encourage task and work achievement as one of the major (if not the major) dependent variables of the field. However, under the pressure of societal and cultural changes, interest has begun to focus on different types of achievement and the behavioral effects of stressing an achievement orientation. In one significant paper, Maehr (94) has questioned some of the traditional definitions of achievement which psychologists use. He argues that we have been too tied to the type of achievement implied in the McClelland approach, i.e. a clearly defined task where some clear feedback of accomplishment is available. Maehr points out that other types of achievement (e.g. interaction effectiveness) are possible and are even the norm in other cultures. Maehr suggests that in addition to increasing our understanding of the values which people of different backgrounds bring to organizations (in terms of the goals they strive for), expanding our definition of success to include such behaviors as interaction or long-range planning effectiveness might also help us develop organizations which are better able to cope with the varied demands placed on them. As an illustration, developing our understanding of the factors associated with interaction effectiveness would be of great value in increasing managerial competence.

In a different direction, both Ogilvie & Porter (108) and Levinson (91) have analyzed some of the stresses of being a successful executive, while Slater (134) has continued his extensive questioning as to what acceptance of the traditional achievement ethic (i.e. vertical mobility) in a hierarchical organization implies. It is Slater's contention that such acceptance generates a lack of concern with one's emotional and interpersonal life because of the possible interference of the latter with one's desire for achievement. This ignoring of the emotional and interpersonal life generates severe social problems whose eventual outcome is disintegration of the social institution and perhaps also of the individual.

Thus research is increasing on the dysfunctional stress-inducing aspects of having a type A personality (19) and the so-called "male midlife crisis." Schultz (127) has found in a study of 1000 higher-level males that five of six went through some major midlife difficulty and that one of six never recovered. Also, in a somewhat similar vein, Argyris (6) has argued that trying to attain one's goals according to the rationally oriented, expected utility (EV) model of achievement behavior generates interpersonal and intergroup conflicts. This research and theory we see as examples of an increased questioning of our society of the traditional achievement ethic, questioning for which some indirect evidence exists. Because of the overriding importance of this question for individuals, organizations, and societies, we think it is crucial that explorations of this nature go forward and their implications explored.

The Meaning of Job Satisfaction

Despite the continued use of job satisfaction as a predictor and/or criterion in attitudinal and motivational research, we continue, as a result of this review, to perceive a certain lack of clarity surrounding the meaning of job satisfaction. Conceptually it seems to us that we may view job satisfaction as the overall level and direction of affect or emotional tone toward one's job and job situation. What may lead to a positive or negative level of affect, however, is not at all clear. Consistent with the general need for a longitudinal perspective which we have stressed earlier, an adequate theory of job satisfaction needs first of all to take into account people's changing conception of themselves and their needs (or values or expectations) over time. Assume for the moment that a person's job satisfaction results from a correspondence between the rewards an organization offers and an employee's expectation of receiving the rewards. At any given point in time, therefore, a person may be satisfied because he or she expects a moderate or large amount of rewards and obtains them or, alternatively, because the employee expects a small amount of rewards and obtains that amount. We submit that although satisfaction may result in either case, the meaning of the two situations may differ widely.

Thus, suppose a person enters the work force with moderate to high expectations of intrinsic need gratification but spends years working on a series of dull, repetitive, low-skill jobs. Will his or her expectations of potential satisfaction be dampened in order to meet this reality? Such a process would account for the replicated body of literature that lower expectations at the time of job entry lead to higher job satisfaction (63, 148). If this does happen, how many of these "lowered expectation" individuals comprise the 77% of the work force (67) who express satisfaction with their jobs? If so, how much of a psychological price (in terms of decrements in self-esteem) is paid for coming to terms with the environment in this manner. Will lower expectations as a result of work experience generalize to off-the-job pursuits? Will these lowered expectations of outcomes lead to lower levels of achievement motivation in general, a hypothesis which is consistent with much motivation theory?

We do not pretend to know the answers to these questions. But if one views job satisfaction as a process of coming to terms with organizational life, then we should determine how work, as a form of organized activity, affects *over time* what we value, expect, or think we deserve. Thus, while it has been found that job satisfaction is positively related to employee mental health (41), our line of reasoning would suggest a more complex relationship in which the direction of the relationship may depend on *how* the employees became satisfied. If we are talking about low-level, low-skill jobs, it may be that the greater the satisfaction, the lower the mental health, since satisfaction here may result from lowering expectations of need gratification. On the other hand, among high-level, high-skill jobs, we would predict a positive relationship between job satisfaction and mental health, even though the position may involve greater job tensions (110).

To the extent that this hypothesis is supported, i.e. that work does often operate to lower certain kinds of expectations, this would place the industrial-organizational psychologist in a dilemma. Should we not be encouraging greater self-esteem and value for the self, even if this might result in greater job demands and lower job satisfaction? Would not this be better for both the individual and the organization, or isn't life a matter of coming to grips with reality? How much do (or should) we compromise? Job satisfaction has long been valued as a positive outcome for individuals and organizations. We suggest that its value may depend on how the person becomes satisfied.

CULTURAL CHANGES IN THE WORLD OF WORK

Since women and minorities are increasingly becoming members of the contemporary work force (43), research on these "new groups" has also accelerated. Much of the research on women has concerned attitudinal bias in the treatment or evaluation of women at work. Thus some studies have found that the behavior of men and women may be evaluated by different standards corresponding to sex-role stereotypes (22, 32, 51, 65, 118). In addition, Rosen & Jerdee's (117) survey of

Harvard Business Review subscribers has documented the potential for differential treatment of men and women in such areas as selection, training, promotion, and career development while Acker & Van Houten (2) have argued that organizations tend to recruit and select women into more passive, compliant occupational roles and then develop control systems to reinforce these behavior patterns.

A particularly interesting experiment illustrating these mechanisms has been reported by Terborg & Ilgen (139). Using an in-basket simulation, they found that females were hired as frequently as identically qualified males, but were offered a lower starting salary and were offered second-year raises that increased the salary discrepancy between the sexes. We might note, however, that while discrimination against women in organizations will likely continue for a while at least, their problems outside their jobs may not be as great as some have feared. For example, Hoffman & Nye (58) and Weaver & Holmes (152) have found few differences in attitudes toward the self and the degree of personal satisfaction between full-time employed women and full-time housekeepers. Thus there may be little negative affect in going against cultural sex-role expectations. Similarly, in a comparison of female executives with female nonexecutives, Morrison & Sebald (105) found no difference with respect to early socialization, marital environment, or need for affiliation. However, female executives did have higher scores on the self-esteem component of n Ach, power motivation, and mental ability.

We applaud this trend toward studying the effects of organizational life on the newly emerging organizational woman, as well as her effects on the organization. Data on her levels and sources of satisfaction and the effects on her nonwork roles can be used to adjust organizational policies in order to make her entrance into and contributions to the organization more effective. In addition, findings from such studies can be used as guides for counseling women on the possible consequences of their new role. We were late in picking up on the organization's effects on the working man; we are pleased that this may not happen with respect to the working woman.

Research on performance assessment of women has been accompanied by a recognition of the importance of race in performance appraisal. In one study (51), subjects were asked to rate workers according to an objective criterion of effectiveness. Raters and workers were composed of both males and females and whites and blacks. The initial analysis revealed that high performers were rated as being more effective than low performers. However, the authors also found, among other things, that females were rated higher than males, (*b*) blacks rated blacks higher than whites, (*c*) whites rated whites higher than blacks, and (*d*) a greater distinction was made between high and low performing whites than between high and low performing blacks. Using a similar research design, Bigoness (15) found that raters tended to grant higher ratings to blacks than whites when performance was poor, yet rated high-performing whites and blacks similarly. Since this lack of differentiation between high- and low-performing blacks can result in committing more "errors" when hiring or promoting blacks than when making similar decisions with regard to whites, a negative consequence of this may be that it would validate already existing prejudicial attitudes toward blacks.

On the other hand, research on racial differences in reaction to work experiences (39, 68, 135) and work values (5, 7) has found few consistent results. Overall, there is a somewhat greater value for traditional concrete outcomes among disadvantaged groups, but differences in average levels of job satisfaction are not great (68) nor are the factorial structures different (135).

This concern for effective integration of women and minorities into organizations, as important as it is, has to be viewed against the background of more general societal change. Common in the popular media in recent years have been stories detailing presumed changes in the achievement (or so-called Protestant-work) ethic. There is considerable evidence in the research literature that we have reviewed to indicate that such changes may indeed have taken place. However, the changes are complex and not susceptible to glib interpretations.

One of the most important studies has been Yankelovich's (156) survey of job-related attitudes among American youth. In this study (based on nationwide samples of college and noncollege youth), strong preference was shown throughout the United States population (not just among those with high education levels) for careers involving self-control over one's job activities, an opportunity for interesting work, and great material rewards. This decreased difference in motivational characteristics between education-level groups, a finding which is also supported by Weaver (151), is, we believe, a highly significant cultural change that needs to be taken account of in the future.

In a second paper, Yankelovich (157) suggests, along with others (13), that emerging cultural trends have transformed the American work ethic into something very different from previous years. These trends include: (a) a changing definition of success to include self-realization and fulfillment; (b) lessening fears of economic insecurity; (c) a weakening of the rigid division of labor between the sexes; (d) a growing psychology of "entitlement" leading to new social and psychological rights; and (e) spreading doubts about the cult of efficiency. We think these trends will have a large impact on work organizations in the future.

Consistent with Yankelovich's research on cultural trends is the increasing evidence that the "fear of success" (FOS) motive is not as sex-linked as we have believed it to be. Rather, overall cultural influences which affect both males and females seem to be involved. Thus FOS seems to have become as common among college males as college females (57). In contrast to the earlier finding by Horner (60), Hoffman found FOS themes for 77% of the males, 65% of the females, and a general lower level of need achievement across the entire sample. Significantly, however, there was a sex difference in the reasons for FOS. Females cited possible affiliative loss while the males questioned the value of achievement itself. Additional support for this conclusion and the influence of cultural factors in general is emerging (4, 31, 89, 104, 142).

Also supporting a cultural explanation for FOS are Puryear & Mednick (113), who found that black female college students (traditionally lower in FOS than white female college students) involved with the black militant movement also have high FOS. This occurs, they suggest, because of the ideology of these movements supporting the significance of the black male. On the other hand, if the black female is romantically attached, the increased FOS with militancy does not occur. This result is consistent with the finding by Tomlinson-Keasey (141) that women with children show less FOS, regardless of age. Perhaps, at least in Western middle-class society, FOS occurs in women until they are "successful" as a woman, by marrying or having children; FOS then decreases. For males, on the other hand, perhaps the equivalent of FOS occurs because of doubts about achievement stemming from societal and cultural changes as well as personal experiences with increasing maturity. This interpretation is also implied by Sarason, Sarason & Cowden (123) in their analysis of age-related change in motivation and in the lack of opportunity for meaningful reform-oriented occupations in today's world.

One question that remains is whether FOS is a motive in the McClelland sense or whether it is a social expectation to which one responds in a given manner in order to be consistent with the expectation (16, 31, 142). The latter would suggest a consistency-motivational interpretation of FOS data. O'Leary (109), without taking a theoretical position, points out in a very interesting paper that the movement of women into more significant organizational positions will be hampered in great part by inappropriate role stereotypes which men and women have of each other and of themselves and by the tendency to act in a manner consistent with these stereotypes.

JOB ENRICHMENT

Of all the organizational interventions which are designed to have implications for work motivation, job enrichment seems to be in the forefront of discussion, research, and controversy. It has its advocates (56) and its skeptics (132). The critics argue, among other things, that an enriched job is not desired by most American workers, especially of blue-collar status. Indeed the research continues to show that a "quality" job (i.e. one that possesses variety, identity, significance, responsibility, and feedback) is not necessarily equally appropriate or satisfying to all workers (17, 116, 138, 149). On the other hand, the moderator effects in these studies are often not strong, and the research by Yankelovich (156, 157) suggests that differences between socioeconomic groups which might possibly have moderated reactions to job content in the past have been almost wiped out today. In addition, favorable overall results of job enrichment programs continue to be reported, both in terms of onging research and development (59) and critical evaluations of the research literature (69).

Promising, we believe, is the research program now being reported by Hackman and his colleagues (47, 48). Their approach has been to develop and validate an instrument, the Job Diagnostic Survey (JDS), which attempts to tap the "motivating potential" of a job, the current level of employee satisfaction and motivation, and the level of employee's "growth needs" or the readiness to perform on an enriched job.

In addition to the instrumentation involved, they have developed a sequential strategy for investigating the problems associated with negative work outcomes (poor quality, absenteeism, etc). What seems to underlie this strategy is the recognition that not all performance problems are due to low motivation and that not all cases of low motivation are due to the content of the job. This open-mindedness, and the willingness to consider alternatives to job enrichment if the data warrant them, constitutes a critical aspect of their methodology and one that job enrichment practitioners should adopt, although we do have doubts about their usage of Maslow's theory for the measurement of individual differences in need structure.

From the perspective of an overall evaluation of job enrichment, important summary papers have been published by O'Toole (110) and by Katzell and his co-workers (69). Not surprisingly, both take issue with the idea that job enrichment is a "quick, sure thing." O'Toole suggests that job enrichment is only a partial answer to problems of job satisfaction and that we need multidimensional approaches, including mid-career counseling, decreased discrimination, and increased participation in decision-making, while the emphasis of the Katzell group is on the need for overall sociotechnical system design.

Other points suggested by O'Toole which are worth noting are that (a) the enrichment of lower-level jobs can have significant effects; (b) we should not mistake lack of worker demand for changes up to now as indicators of the future; worker consciousness and expectancy of success have been low but this may be changing; (c) job enrichment may not be possible on the very poor jobs; perhaps all that can be done here is to increase pay, automate where possible, and rotate as much as possible so that no one is permanently sentenced to the poor job; (d) job characteristics need to be studied for their effects on physical and mental health since their significance in predicting coronary disorder, low self-esteem, and mid-life crisis are becoming more firmly established.

Several additional issues regarding job enrichment remain unresolved. For example, it is possible that as jobs become more enriched, they may also become more ambiguous. Role ambiguity, in turn, may generate tension and anxiety (52) and other dysfunctional outcomes on both an individual and organizational level (12). Yet this conclusion may not be true for all since Beehr (11) found that role ambiguity was less stressful for workers with high autonomy. This issue has implications for the meaning of job satisfaction since the same variable (role ambiguity) may generate dissatisfaction, organizational commitment (66), and tension at the same time.

Related somewhat to the notion of role stress is the emerging interest in mental health in industry, a trend we applaud. After several false starts, we are finally paying attention to the work experience as a social institution. Thus LeLemasters (87) has published an interesting series of participant-observer studies on the life-style of the blue-collar worker, and Gavin (38) has attempted both to develop a conceptual framework for mental health in organizational settings and also to isolate organizational correlates (37, 40) of employee mental health. There is much difficulty in this area in terms of conceptualization and research design (longitudinal studies are crucial) but the rewards are great. Furthermore, the public is demanding that we attend to these questions, judging by its reception to the work of Terkel (140), Garson (36), and Joseph Heller's (54) shattering novel about a "successful" executive.

Another important issue in job redesign involves the clarification of various types of interventions. Herzberg (56) continues to differentiate orthodox job enrichment from the more "socially" based strategies of participative management, sociotechnical systems, industrial democracy, and organization development. We agree that frequently there are major differences among the strategies, although there are certainly overlaps as well. We urge a more complete understanding of each strategy in terms of its intent, assumptions, expected consequences, and constraints, so that sound choices (including combinations of approaches) may be made. Scobel's (128) attempt to change the climate of a manufacturing organization represents, to us, a refreshingly flexible approach to organization change.

There is always the continuing question here of the salience of job activity in today's world. Shrank (132) has argued that what the blue-collar worker wants is not job enrichment but rather other benefits and amenities that have traditionally been the province of management (e.g. three-hour lunches). In other words, according to Shrank, the job context variables may be more important for some than the job content, and many employees want the freedom to do things on the job which are not job-related. This is a hypothesis which seems well worth investigating.

Another problem concerns continuing union opposition to job enrichment because of the fear that it will lead to speed-ups, fewer workers, harder jobs, and temporary job satisfaction with an eventual decrease in labor union protection and organization (160). We are in no position to evaluate these latter claims because organizational psychology as a field still has not recognized the fact that unions exist and have an influence on worker behavior. (We wonder how long this will continue.) We might note, however, that there is an indication that some unions have softened their opposition to job redesign, at least under certain conditions (121). The question is why and under what conditions.

Finally, it has been suggested (46) that the job enrichment movement may be at a critical point in its history. It is imperative that we learn from both our successes and failures. Hackman's analysis seems to suggest two major themes: the necessity for an accurate diagnosis of the work system (including the target job, surrounding jobs, current employees, and structural constraints), and a willingness by management to recognize, communicate, and act upon potential problems very early in the process. This second point suggests to us that job enrichment practitioners need to concentrate as much on the process of implementation (perhaps through such traditional OD techniques as team-building among managers, goal-setting, and conflict resolution) as on the specific changes in the content of the work.

MOTIVATION TECHNIQUES

MBO and Goal Setting

The usefulness of setting specific, difficult but attainable goals has continued to receive support in the literature (50, 73, 82, 83, 136, 137, 155). Latham & Yukl (84) have reviewed the literature on goal setting and have concluded that goal setting is effective in a variety of companies and over extended time periods. However, the effects of contingent rewards and of participative (vs assigned) goals are still not clear. Latham & Yukl also suggest that the effectiveness of a goal-setting program may be limited by such factors as: (a) the complexity of the job; (b) the interdependence of jobs; and (c) the support by top management (cf 64).

Organizational Behavior Modification

It is clear that the principles of operant conditioning are being applied in organizational settings at an accelerating rate. The publication of Luthans & Kreitner's (93) *Organizational Behavior Modification* reflects the growing attention to techniques formerly applied primarily to school and hospital settings.

In a sense, many of the techniques of OB Mod are hardly new to the organizational behavior literature. Tying valued outcomes to desired behavior is the cornerstone of expectancy theory. The use of reward as opposed to coercive power also has a rich history of research and theory, as does the importance of goal setting and the provision of clear feedback.

Where then lies the distinctiveness of the OB Mod approach? Its major characteristic may be the mental set with which the manager approaches a situation. OB Mod requires the manager to observe quantifiable behaviors, to establish base rates in order to determine the extent of the problem, to determine what reinforcers are supporting the undesirable behaviors, to estimate what stimulus will reinforce the desired behavior, and to chart the frequency of the desired behavior after the reinforcement intervention. It is this critical look at behaviors and contingencies that promises to provide a refreshing addition to the organizational behavior literature.

The published research, however, is far from conclusive. There is some evidence that work attendance can be boosted through the use of contingent reinforcers (111), but there is also a question about the durability of such changes (106). In addition, the presumed superiority of a variable-ratio reinforcement schedule is at present unclear (14, 158, 159). Much of the current research may be hampered, as Mawhinney (98) suggests, by unclear or incorrect usage of OB Mod techniques and concepts and by inappropriate research designs.

We suggest that there are also other important questions to consider. First, are all performance-related behaviors quantifiable and chartable? Can we, for example, quantify managerial or professional activities that we are frequently not in a position to witness? The same complexity and multidimensionality of a job that may hamper goal setting (84) may also render OB Mod less useful. Similarly, OB Mod's strong concern with quantifiable behavior may lead to the same narrowness of which MBO is frequently accused (90).

Finally, there is the question of whether OB Mod increases the dependence of a worker on his or her supervisor. When a supervisor dispenses reinforcers contingent upon specific behaviors, does this convey a hidden message to the employee that he or she is inevitably dependent on his or her supervisor? Some critics suggest that a reliance on contingent extrinsic rewards may reduce intrinsic motivation (25) or externalize attribution processes (79). Although there is nothing inherent in OB Mod that excludes intrinsic, self-reinforcement (93), it appears that many studies relevant to OB Mod deal with supervisory or organizationally mediated reinforcers (14, 106, 111, 155, 158, 159). The long-term consequences of using primarily externally mediated reinforcers need attention. For example, Meyer (99) has questioned the whole idea of merit pay as an incentive to behavior because such a policy generates resentment toward leadership, competitiveness and hostility toward others, takes away job interest, and decreases self-esteem (because of the dependency involved).

Leadership

In addition to MBO and OB Mod, leadership research has focused on understanding the dimensions of consideration and initiating structure. Kerr & Schriesheim (71) have reported an updated version of Korman's (76) earlier review of "consideration" (C) and "initiating structure" (IS), noting the resolution of some problems and the continuation of others.

One major activity seems to be a search for potential moderators of leader behavior. Although the consideration-satisfaction relationship still seems stable (10), some investigators (55, 70) have suggested situational moderators. The meaning and consequences of initiating structure, on the other hand, are undergoing considerable investigation. Schriesheim, House & Kerr (126) suggest that the item content of different IS scales may have been responsible for prior inconsistent results. In addition, contingency factors continue to be proposed (61, 72). Sometimes they are supported (133) and other times they are not (49).

In the meantime, research on leadership and sex status is beginning to emerge. Petty & Lee (112), for example, found that there was some tendency for male subordinates to be dissatisfied with female supervisors who were high on structure. Clearly this line of research assumes great importance as more women move into managerial and supervisory roles.

CONCLUSIONS

As we indicated in the introduction to our review, we have come away from our work with overall favorable affect. Highly significant questions are being asked about the meaning of work and achievement, about the nature of the work experience and how best to enhance it from the perspective of the individual, organization, and society. Most significantly, we are beginning to examine the sacred cow of "science" and, as maturing students, we are understanding how we can be scientists and still be able to develop methods appropriate to our field, rather than mindlessly copying inappropriate theory and technique.

All of this we applaud. We have much to contribute to society and, judging from the demand for our services, society has recognized our contributions. However, we will be derelict both to our fellow citizens and to ourselves if we allow this high opinion of our actual and potential contributions to detract us from dealing with some of the major problems still existing and, in some respects, becoming more serious. Thus, in addition to further examination of some of the issues we have raised above, the following problems strike us as being particularly fruitful for research endeavors:

1. The lack of interest in studying the impact of labor unions continues to astound us (even though we are as guilty as others). Is it because most of us seek out support from management for our research and consulting? We don't know, but we think it is time this situation needs to be changed and that OB people start to recognize the labor union and its contribution to organizational life, both good and bad.

2. There has been little interest that we can see in the seamier aspects of organizational life. Society has looked at and continues to examine the ethical behavior of executives, bribery of government officials, and employee thefts of all kinds. Where is our contribution to this examination? Why do people cheat, bribe, and steal in organizations? What kinds of organizational environments generate such behaviors? Why do we accept these behaviors?

3. We see little research on alcoholism, drug use, and other aberrant behaviors of a personal nature (see 95 for an exception). Much has been written in the popular press about these behaviors in organizational settings, but we, as a field, have done little. Where do these behaviors come from? Are they endemic to a competitive, achievement-oriented society, i.e. one that sees the "ideal" manager as a "traditional male" (124)? If not, what else is involved? Can effective change take place?

To conclude, we have much to be proud of, but there is even more left to do.

Literature Cited

1. Abramson, S. R. 1975. *Achievement motivation as a moderator of the relationship between expectancy times valence and effort.* PhD thesis. Stevens Inst. Technol. Hoboken, NJ
2. Acker, J., Van Houten, D. R. 1974. Differential recruitment and control: The sex structuring of organizations. *Admin. Sci. Q.* 19:152–63
3. Adams, J. S. 1963. Toward an understanding of inequity. *J. Abnorm. Soc. Psychol.* 67:422–36
4. Alper, T. G. 1974. Achievement motivation in college women: A now-you-see-it, now-you-don't phenomenon. *Am. Psychol.* 29:194–203
5. Alper, T. G. 1975. Racial differences in job and work environment priorities among newly hired college graduates. *J. Appl. Psychol.* 60:132–34
6. Argyris, C. 1975. Dangers in applying results from experimental social psychology. *Am. Psychol.* 30:469–85
7. Arvey, R. D., Mussio, S. J. 1974. Job expectations and valences of job rewards for culturally disadvantaged and advantaged clerical employees. *J. Appl. Psychol.* 59:230–32

8. Arvey, R. D., Neel, C. W. 1974. Testing expectancy theory predictions using behaviorally based measures of motivational effort for engineers. *J. Vocat. Behav.* 4:299–310
9. Austin, W., Walster, E. 1974. Reactions to confirmation and disconfirmation of equity and inequity. *J. Pers. Soc. Psychol.* 30:208–16
10. Badin, I. J. 1974. Some moderator influences on relationships between consideration, initiating structure, and organizational criteria. *J. Appl. Psychol.* 59:380–82
11. Beehr, T. A. 1976. Perceived situational moderators of the relationship between subjective role ambiguity and role strain. *J. Appl. Psychol.* 61:35–40
12. Beehr, T. A., Walsh, J. T., Taber, T. D. 1976. Relationship of stress to individually and organizationally valued states: Higher-order needs as a moderator. *J. Appl. Psychol.* 61:41–47
13. Bell, D. 1975. *The Cultural Contradictions of Capitalism.* New York: Basic Books
14. Berger, C. J., Cummings, L. L., Heneman, H. G. III. 1975. Expectancy the-

ory and operant conditioning predictions of performance under variable ratio and continuous schedules of reinforcement. *Organ. Behav. Hum. Perform.* 14:227–43

15. Bigoness, W. J. 1976. Effect of applicant's sex, race, and performance ratings: Some additional findings. *J. Appl. Psychol.* 61:80–84

16. Breedlove, C. J., Cicerelli, V. G. 1974. Women's fear of success in relation to personal characteristics and type of occupation. *J. Psychol.* 86:181–90

17. Brief, A. P., Aldag, R. J. 1975. Employee reactions to job characteristics: A constructive replication. *J. Appl. Psychol.* 60:182–86

18. Buss, A. R. 1975. The emerging field of the sociology of psychological knowledge. *Am. Psychol.* 30:988–1002

19. Caplan, R. D., Jones, K. W. 1975. Effects of work load, role ambiguity and type A personality on anxiety, depression and heart rate. *J. Appl. Psychol.* 60:713–19

20. Cook, K. S. 1975. Expectations, evaluations and equity. *Am. Sociol. Rev.* 40:372–88

21. Cronbach, L. J. 1975. Beyond the two disciplines of scientific psychology. *Am. Psychol.* 30:116–27

22. Deaux, K., Emswiller, T. 1974. Explanation of successful performance on sex-linked tasks: What is skill for the male is luck for the female. *J. Pers. Soc. Psychol.* 29:80–85

23. Deci, E. L. 1972. The effects of contingent and noncontingent rewards and controls on intrinsic motivation. *Organ. Behav. Hum. Perform.* 8:217–29

24. Deci, E. L. 1975. *Intrinsic Motivation.* New York: Plenum

25. Deci, E. L. 1976. Notes on the theory and metatheory of intrinsic motivation. *Organ. Behav. Hum. Perform.* 15:130–45

26. Deci, E. L., Benware, C., Landy, D. 1974. The attribution of motivation as a function of output and rewards. *J. Pers.* 42:652–67

27. Deleo, P. J., Pritchard, R. D. 1974. An examination of some methodological problems in testing expectancy—valence models with survey techniques. *Organ. Behav. Hum. Perform.* 12:143–48

28. Dember, W. N. 1974. Motivation and the cognitive revolution. *Am. Psychol.* 29:161–68

29. Dunnette, M. D. 1974. *Mishmash, mush, and milestones in organizational psychology.* Presented at ADA Conv. New Orleans

30. Elms, A. C. 1975. The crisis of confidence in social psychology. *Am. Psychol.* 30:967–76

31. Feather, N. T., Raphelson, A. C. 1974. Fear of success in Australian and American student groups: Motive or sex-role stereotype? *J. Pers.* 42:190–201

32. Feather, N. T., Simon, J. G. 1976. Reactions to male and female success in sex-linked occupations: Impressions of personality, causal attributions and perceived likelihood of different consequences. *J. Pers. Soc. Psychol.* 31:20–31

33. Fiedler, F. E., Chemers, M. M. 1974. *Leadership and Effective Management.* Glenview, Ill: Scott, Foresman

34. Frey, R. C. Jr., Glickman, A. S., Korman, A. K., Goodstadt, B. E., Romanczuk, A. P. 1974. A study of experimental incentives as an influence on enlistment intention: More is not better. *Am. Inst. Res. Tech. Rep. No. 3,* AIR-32201-6/74-TR-3

35. Frey, R. C. Jr., Goodstadt, B. E., Korman, A. K., Romanczuk, A. P., Glickman, A. S. 1974. Reinlistment incentives: More is not better in the fleet either. *Am. Inst. Res. Tech. Rep. No. 4,* AIR-32201-6/74-TR-4

36. Garson, B. 1975. *All the Livelong Day: The Meaning and Demeaning of Routine Work.* Garden City, NY: Doubleday

37. Gavin, J. F. 1975. Employee perceptions of the work environment and mental health: A suggestive study. *J. Vocat. Behav.* 6:217–34

38. Gavin, J. F. 1975. Mental health at work: An emergent concern. *Ind. Psychol. Assoc. Colorado Tech. Rep. No. 75-03*

39. Gavin, J. F., Ewen, R. 1974. Racial differences in job attitudes and performance: Some theoretical considerations and empirical findings. *Personnel Psychol.* 27:455–64

40. Gavin, J. F., Greenhaus, J. H. 1976. Organizational tenure, work environment perceptions, and employee mental health. *J. Vocat. Behav.* In press

41. Gechman, A. S., Wiener, Y. 1975. Job involvement and satisfaction as related to mental health and personal time devoted to work. *J. Appl. Psychol.* 60:521–23

42. Ghiselli, E. E. 1974. Some perspectives for industrial psychology. *Am. Psychol.* 29:80–87

43. Ginzberg, E. 1974. The changing American economy and labor force. In *The Worker and the Job*, ed. J. M. Rosow, pp. 49–71. Englewood Cliffs: Prentice-Hall

44. Goodman, P. S. 1974. An examination of referents used in the evaluation of pay. *Organ. Behav. Hum. Perform.* 12:170–95

45. Greenhaus, J. H., Badin, I. J. 1974. Self-esteem, performance, and satisfaction: Some tests of a theory. *J. Appl. Psychol.* 59:722–26

46. Hackman, J. R. 1975. Is job enrichment just a fad? *Harvard Bus. Rev.* 53:129–38

47. Hackman, J. R., Oldham, G. R. 1975. Development of the Job Diagnostic Survey. *J. Appl. Psychol.* 60:159–70

48. Hackman, J. R., Oldham, G. R., Janson, R., Purdy, K. 1975. A new strategy for job enrichment. *Calif. Manage. Rev.* 17:57–71

49. Hammer, T. H., Dachler, H. P. 1975. A test of some assumptions underlying the path goal model of supervision: Some suggested conceptual modifications. *Organ. Behav. Hum. Perform.* 14:60–75

50. Hamner, W. C., Harnett, D. L. 1974. Goal setting, performance and satisfaction in an interdependent task. *Organ. Behav. Hum. Perform.* 12:217–30

51. Hamner, W. C., Kim, J. S., Baird, L., Bigoness, W. J. 1974. Race and sex as determinants of ratings by potential employers in a simulated work-sampling task. *J. Appl. Psychol.* 59:705–11

52. Hamner, W. C., Tosi, H. 1974. Relationship of role conflict and role ambiguity to job involvement measures. *J. Appl. Psychol.* 59:497–99

53. Hechler, P. D., Wiener, Y. 1974. Chronic self-esteem as a moderator of performance consequences of expected pay. *Organ. Behav. Hum. Perform.* 11:97–105

54. Heller, J. 1975. *Something Happened.* New York: Ballantine

55. Herold, D. M. 1974. Interaction of subordinate and leader characteristics in moderating the consideration-satisfaction relationship. *J. Appl. Psychol.* 59:649–51

56. Herzberg, F. 1974. The wise old Turk. *Harvard Bus. Rev.* 52:70–80

57. Hoffman, L. W. 1974. Fear of success in males and females: 1965 and 1971. *J. Consult. Clin. Psychol.* 42:353–58

58. Hoffman, L. W., Nye, F. J. 1974. *Working Mothers.* San Francisco: Jossey-Bass

59. Horn, P. 1975. Worker involvement pays off. *Psychol. Today* 9:89

60. Horner, M. S. 1968. *Sex differences in achievement motivation and performance in competitive and noncompetitive situations.* PhD thesis. Univ. Michigan, Ann Arbor, Mich.

61. House, R. J., Dessler, G. 1973. *The path-goal theory of leadership: some post hoc and a priori tests.* Presented at 2nd Leadership Symp., Contingency Approaches to Leadership, Southern Illinois Univ., Carbondale, Ill.

62. House, R. J., Shapiro, H. J., Wahba, M. A. 1974. Expectancy theory as a predictor of work behavior and attitudes: A reevaluation of empirical evidence. *Decis. Sci.* 5:481–506

63. Ilgen, D. R., Seely, W. 1974. Realistic expectations as an aid in reducing voluntary resignations. *J. Appl. Psychol.* 59:452–55

64. Ivancevich, J. M. 1974. Changes in performance in a management by objectives program. *Admin. Sci. Q.* 19:563–74

65. Jacobson, M. B., Effertz, J. 1974. Sex roles and leadership: Perceptions of the leaders and the led. *Organ. Behav. Hum. Perform.* 12:383–96

66. Jamal, M. 1974. *Task specialization and organizational commitment: An examination among blue-collar workers.* Presented at Ann. Conv., Acad. Manage., Seattle, Wash.

67. Kahn, R. L., 1974. On the meaning of work. *J. Occup. Med.* 16:716–19

68. Katzell, R. A., Ewen, R., Korman, A. K. 1974. Job attitudes of black and white workers: Male blue-collar workers in six companies. *J. Vocat. Behav.* 4:365–76

69. Katzell, R. A., Yankelovich, D., Fein, M., Oornati, O. A., Nash, A. 1975. *Work, Productivity and Job Satisfaction.* New York: Psychol. Corp.

70. Kavanagh, M. J. 1975. Expected supervisory behavior, interpersonal trust and environmental preferences: Some relationships based on a dyadic model of leadership. *Organ. Behav. Hum. Perform.* 13:17–30

71. Kerr, S., Schriesheim, C. A. 1974. Consideration, initiating structure, and organizational criteria—An update of Korman's 1966 review. *Personnel Psychol.* 27:555–68

72. Kerr, S., Schriesheim, C. A., Murphy, C. J., Stogdill, R. M. 1974. Toward a contingency theory of leadership based upon the consideration and initiating

structure literature. *Organ. Behav. Hum. Perform.* 12:68–82

73. Kim, J. S., Hamner, W. C. 1976. Effect of performance feedback and goal setting on productivity and satisfaction in an organizational setting. *J. Appl. Psychol.* 61:48–57

74. Kipnis, D. 1974. The powerholder. In *Perspectives on Social Power,* ed. J. T. Tedeschi, pp. 82–123. Chicago: Aldine

75. Kopelman, R. E. 1974. *Factors complicating expectancy theory predictions of work motivation and job performance.* Presented at APA Conv., New Orleans, La.

76. Korman, A. K. 1966. Consideration, initiating structure, and organizational criteria—A review. *Personnel Psychol.* 19:349–61

77. Korman, A. K. 1974. *The Psychology of Motivation.* Englewood Cliffs: Prentice-Hall

78. Korman, A. K. 1974. Contingency approaches to leadership: An overview. In *Contingency Approaches to Leadership,* ed. J. G. Hunt, L. L. Larson, pp. 189–95. Carbondale, Ill: Southern Illinois Univ.

79. Korman, A. K. 1976. Hypothesis of work behavior revisited and an extension. *Acad. Manage. Rev.* 1:50–63

80. Korman, A. K., Tanofsky, R. 1975. Statistical problems of contingency models in organizational behavior. *Acad. Manage. J.* 18:393–97

81. Korzeniowski, M. H. 1975. *An empirical test of the generality of expectancy model predictions of job effort.* MS thesis. Stevens Inst. Technol., Hoboken, NJ

82. Latham, G. P., Baldes, J. J. 1975. The "practical significance" of Locke's theory of goal-setting. *J. Appl. Psychol.* 60:122–24

83. Latham, G. P., Kinne, S. B. 1974. Improving job performance through training in goal-setting. *J. Appl. Psychol.* 59:189–91

84. Latham, G. P., Yukl, G. A. 1975. A review of research on the application of goal setting in organizations. *Acad. Manage. J.* 18:824–45

85. Lawler, E. E. 1973. *Individualizing organizations: A needed emphasis in organizational psychology.* Presented at APA Conv., Montreal

86. Lawler, E. E., Kuleck, W. J., Rhode, J. G., Sorensen, J. E. 1975. Job choice and post decision dissonance. *Organ. Behav. Hum. Perform.* 13:133–45

87. LeLemasters, E. E. 1975. *Blue-collar Aristocrats: Life Styles of a Working Class Tavern.* Madison: Univ. Wisconsin Press

88. Leonard, R. L., Walsh, W. B., Osipow, S. H. 1973. Self-esteem, self-consistency, and second vocational choice. *J. Couns. Psychol.* 20:91–93

89. Levine, A., Crumrine, J. 1975. Women and the fear of success: A problem in replication. *Am. J. Sociol.* 80:964–73

90. Levinson, H. 1970. Management by whose objectives? *Harvard Bus. Rev.* 48:125–34

91. Levinson, H. 1975. On executive suicide. *Harvard Bus. Rev.* 53:118–22

92. Locke, E. A. 1975. Personnel attitudes and motivation. *Ann. Rev. Psychol.* 26:457–80

93. Luthans, F., Kreitner, R. 1975. *Organizational Behavior Modification.* Glenview, Ill: Scott, Foresman

94. Maehr, M. L. 1974. Culture and achievement motivation. *Am. Psychol.* 29:887–96

95. Mangione, T. W., Quinn, R. P. 1975. Job satisfaction, counterproductive behavior and drug use at work. *J. Appl. Psychol.* 60:114–16

96. Maslow, A. H. 1954. *Motivation and Personality.* New York: Harper & Row

97. Maslow, A. H. 1965. *Eupsychian Management.* Homewood, Ill: Irwin

98. Mawhinney, T. C. 1975. Operant terms and concepts in the description of individual work behavior: Some problems of interpretation, application, and evaluation. *J. Appl. Psychol.* 60:704–12

99. Meyer, H. H. 1975. The pay-for-performance dilemma. *Organ. Dyn.* 3:39–50

100. Miner, J. B., Rizzo, J. R., Harlow, D. N., Hill, J. W. 1974. Role motivation theory of managerial effectiveness in simulated organizations of varying degrees of structure. *J. Appl. Psychol.* 59:31–37

101. Mitchell, T. R. 1974. Expectancy models of job satisfaction, occupational preferences and effort: A theoretical, methodological and empirical appraisal. *Psychol. Bull.* 81:1053–77

102. Mitchell, T. R., Smyser, C. M., Weed, S. E. 1975. Locus of control: Supervision and work satisfaction. *Acad. Manage. J.* 18:623–31

103. Moberg, D. J., Koch, J. C. 1975. A critical appraisal of integrated treatments of contingency findings. *Acad. Manage. J.* 18:109–24

104. Monahan, L., Kuhn, D., Shaver, P. 1974. Intrapsychic versus cultural ex-

planations of the "fear of success" motive. *J. Pers. Soc. Psychol.* 29:60–64

105. Morrison, R. F., Sebald, M. C. 1974. Personal characteristics differentiating female executives from female nonexecutive personnel. *J. Appl. Psychol.* 59:656–59

106. Nord, W. R. 1970. Improving attendance through rewards. *Personnel Admin.* 33:37–41

107. Notz, W. W. 1975. Work motivation and the negative effects of extrinsic rewards: A review with implications for theory and practice. *Am. Psychol.* 30:884–92

108. Ogilvie, B. C., Porter, A. 1974. Business careers as treadmills to oblivion: The allure of cardio-vascular death. *Hum. Resource Manage.* 13:14–18

109. O'Leary, V. E. 1974. Some attitudinal barriers to occupational aspirations in women. *Psychol. Bull.* 81:809–26

110. O'Toole, J. 1974. Work in America and the great job satisfaction controversy. *J. Occup. Med.* 16:710–15

111. Pedalino, E., Gamboa, V. V. 1974. Behavior modification and absenteeism: Intervention in one industrial setting. *J. Appl. Psychol.* 59:694–98

112. Petty, M. M., Lee, G. K. 1975. Moderating effects of sex of supervisor and subordinate on relationships between supervisory behavior and subordinate satisfaction. *J. Appl. Psychol.* 60:624–28

113. Puryear, G. R., Mednick, M. S. 1974. Black militancy, affective attachment and the fear of success in black college women. *J. Consult. Clin. Psychol.* 42:263–66

114. Raynor, J. O. 1974. Future orientation in the study of achievement motivation. In *Motivation and Achievement*, ed. J. W. Atkinson and J. O. Raynor, pp. 121–54. Washington DC: Winston

115. Reinharth, L., Wahba, M. A. 1975. Expectancy theory as a predictor of work motivation, effort expenditure and job performance. *Acad. Manage. J.* 18: 520–37

116. Robey, D. 1974. Task design, work values, and worker response: An experimental test. *Organ. Behav. Hum. Perform.* 12:264–73

117. Rosen, B., Jerdee, T. H. 1974. Sex stereotyping in the executive suite. *Harvard Bus. Rev.* 52:45–58

118. Rosen, B., Jerdee, T. H. 1975. Effects of employee's sex and threatening vs. pleading appeals on managerial evaluation of grievances. *Harvard Bus. Rev.* 60:442–45

119. Runyon, K. E. 1973. Some interactions between personality variables and management styles. *J. Appl. Psychol.* 57:288–94

120. Salancik, G. R. 1975. Interaction effects of performance and money on self-perception of intrinsic motivation. *Organ. Behav. Hum. Perform.* 13:339–51

121. Salpukas, A. 1974. Unions: A new role? In *The Worker and the Job*, ed. J. M. Rosow, pp. 99–117. Englewood Cliffs: Prentice-Hall

122. Sarason, S. B. 1975. Psychology to the Finland station in the heavenly city of the Eighteenth Century philosophers. *Am. Psychol.* 30:1072–80

123. Sarason, S. B., Sarason, E. K., Cowden, P. 1975. Aging and the nature of the work. *Am. Psychol.* 30:584–92

124. Schein, V. E. 1975. Relationships between sex role stereotypes and requisite management characteristics among female managers. *J. Appl. Psychol.* 60:340–44

125. Schmidt, F. L. 1973. Implications of a measurement problem for expectancy theory research. *Organ. Behav. Hum. Perform.* 10:243–51

126. Schriesheim, C. A., House, R. J., Kerr, S. 1976. Leader initiating structure: A reconciliation of discrepant research results and some empirical tests. *Organ. Behav. Hum. Perform.* In press

127. Schultz, D. 1974. Managing the middle-aged manager. *Bus. Manage.* 7:8–17

128. Scobel, D. N. 1975. Doing away with the factory blues. *Harvard Bus. Rev.* 53:132–42

129. Scott, W. E. 1976. The effects of extrinsic rewards on "intrinsic motivation": A critique. *Organ. Behav. Hum. Perform.* 15:117–29

130. Sheridan, J. E., Downey, H. K., Slocum, J. W. 1975. *Dynamic correlational analysis of the expectancy model of motivation.* Presented at Midwest. Acad. Manage., Ann Arbor, Mich.

131. Sheridan, J. E., Slocum, J. W., Richards, M. D. 1974. Expectancy theory as a lead indicator of job behavior. *Decis. Sci.* 5:507–22

132. Shrank, R. 1974. Work in America: What do workers really want? *Ind. Relat.* 13:124–29

133. Sims, H. P., Szilagyi, A. O. 1975. Leader structure and subordinate satisfaction for two hospital administrative levels: A path analysis approach. *J. Appl. Psychol.* 60:194–97

134. Slater, P. 1974. *Earthwork.* Garden City, NY: Doubleday

135. Smith, P. C., Smith, O. W., Rollo, J. 1974. Factor structure for blacks and whites of the Job Descriptive Index and its discrimination of job satisfaction. *J. Appl. Psychol.* 59:99–100
136. Steers, R. M. 1975. Task-goal attributes, nAchievement, and supervisory performance. *Organ. Behav. Hum. Perform.* 13:392–403
137. Steers, R. M., Porter, L. W. 1974. The role of task-goal attributes in employee performance. *Psychol. Bull.* 81:434–52
138. Suzansky, J. W. 1974. *The effects of individual characteristics as moderating variables of the relation between job design quality and job satisfaction.* PhD thesis. Stevens Inst. Technol. Hoboken, NJ
139. Terborg, J. R., Ilgen, D. R. 1975. A theoretical approach to sex discrimination in traditional masculine occupations. *Organ. Behav. Hum. Perform.* 13:352–76
140. Terkel, S. 1972. *Working.* New York: Pantheon
141. Tomlinson-Keasey, C. 1974. Role variables: Their influence on female motivational constructs. *J. Couns. Psychol.* 21:323–27
142. Tresemer, D. 1974. Fear of success: Popular but unproven. *Psychol. Today* 7:82–84, 95
143. Turney, J. R. 1974. Activity outcome expectancies and intrinsic activity values as predictors of several motivation indexes for technical-professionals. *Organ. Behav. Hum. Perform.* 11:65–82
144. Vroom, V. H. 1964. *Work and Motivation.* New York: Wiley
145. Vroom, V. H., Yetton, P. W. 1973. *Leadership and Decision-making.* Univ. Pittsburgh Press
146. Wahba, M. A., Bridwell, L. G. 1976. Maslow reconsidered: A review of research on the need hierarchy theory. *Organ. Behav. Hum. Perform.* In press
147. Walsh, W. B., Lewis, R. O. 1972. Consistent, inconsistent, and undecided career preferences, and personality. *J. Vocat. Behav.* 2:309–16
148. Wanous, J. P. 1974. Effects of realistic job previews on job acceptance, job attitudes and job survival. *J. Appl. Psychol.* 58:327–32
149. Wanous, J. P. 1974. Individual differences and reactions to job characteristics. *J. Appl. Psychol.* 59:616–22
150. Warr, P. 1976. Theories of motivation. In *Personal Goals and Work Design,* ed. P. Warr. New York: Wiley. In press
151. Weaver, C. N. 1975. Job preferences of white collar and blue collar workers. *Acad. Manage. J.* 18:167–75
152. Weaver, C. N., Holmes, S. L. 1975. A comparative study of the work satisfaction of females with full-time employment and full-time housekeeping. *J. Appl. Psychol.* 60:117–18
153. Weiner, B. 1974. Achievement motivation as conceptualized by an attribution theorist. In *Achievement Motivation and Attribution Theory,* ed. B. Weiner, pp. 3–48. Morristown, NJ: General Learning Press
154. Weiner, B., Sierad, J. 1975. Misattribution for failure and enhancement of achievement strivings. *J. Pers. Soc. Psychol.* 31:415–21
155. Wexley, K. N., Nemeroff, W. F. 1975. Effectiveness of positive reinforcement and goal setting as methods of management development. *J. Appl. Psychol.* 60:446–50
156. Yankelovich, D. 1974. Turbulence in the working world: Angry workers, happy grads. *Psychol. Today* 8:80–89
157. Yankelovich, D. 1974. The meaning of work. In *The Worker and the Job,* ed. J. M. Rosow, pp. 19–47. Englewood Cliffs: Prentice-Hall.
158. Yukl, G. A., Latham, G. P. 1970. Consequences of reinforcement schedules and incentive magnitudes for employee performance: Problems encountered in an industrial setting. *J. Appl. Psychol.* 60:294–98
159. Yukl, G. A., Wexley, K. N., Seymour, J. D. 1972. Effectiveness of pay incentives under variable ratio and continuous reinforcement schedules. *J. Appl. Psychol.* 56:19–23
160. Zagoria, S. 1974. Policy implications and future agenda. In *The Worker and the Job,* ed. J. M. Rosow, pp. 177–201. Englewood Cliffs: Prentice-Hall

Ann. Rev. Psychol. 1977. 28:197–223
Copyright © 1977 by Annual Reviews Inc. All rights reserved

ORGANIZATION DEVELOPMENT

Clayton P. Alderfer[1]

School of Organization and Management, Yale University,
New Haven, Connecticut 06520

Organization development (OD) is at once a professional field of social action and an area of academic study. The practice of organization development is aimed toward improving the quality of life for members of human systems and increasing the institutional effectiveness of those systems. The scholarly investigation of organization development seeks to understand planned change processes, to assess the effects of efforts to promote social change, and to evolve better theories of change processes.

The 1974 volume of this series contained the first annual review of organization development, prepared by Friedlander and Brown. That chapter identified the origins of the field, presented the major conceptual distinctions in the area, reviewed the major empirical findings obtained to that date, and concluded by pointing out what those writers thought to be a major tension confronting the area. They predicted that research would either play an increasingly central role in the development of this field or become more irrelevant to it. The years since their review have served to confirm their prediction, in both parts. OD is today being practiced in a wider variety of institutions than several years ago, and in many of these new areas there is little, if any, systematic research being conducted. At the same time, the overall quality of research on OD is showing increasing signs of both rigor and vigor as more careful studies of OD processes and outcomes are being conducted and reported.

This chapter covers the literature on OD since the Friedlander & Brown (39) review. The first section examines the variety of value conflicts characteristic of the field today. The second portion reports the variety of new settings and new techniques that represent latest professional developments in OD. The third section critically reviews the most recent research on OD. Finally, the conclusion offers an

[1]The writer acknowledges the helpful comments of Richard Hackman and Mitchell McCorcle on an earlier version of this paper.

interpretation of the current status of OD in terms of the interdependencies among applied problems, technological developments, values, and research.

VALUES AND ORGANIZATION DEVELOPMENT

Human values have always played a key role in organization development. A strong force motivating the emergence of this field has been the desire to "humanize" organizations, that is, to enable organizations to be more responsive to the human concerns of members. Along with the pursuit of humane values, OD has also been advocated as a set of technologies for improving the effectiveness of organizations. In the earliest days of OD there was less reason to question whether these two classes of values conflicted with each other because the scope of OD applications was much narrower than it is today. Although there were variations among OD theoriests and practitioners in terms of relative emphasis on these two classes of values, most people in the field believed that they could pursue both with minimal conflict. As the field has grown, however, increasing numbers of questions have been raised about just how easy it is to pursue both kinds of values with approximately equal vigor. OD has always been a field that emphasized self-scrutiny by its members. Today there is a substantial and significant debate about the value implications of much of OD work among thinkers in the field. The literature on value implications has arisen from practitioners who question themselves in public and from systematic research efforts to determine how practitioners are thinking and acting.

Friedlander (38) attempted a philosophical inquiry into the underlying values of OD. He found that three philosophical systems—rationalism, pragmatism, and existentialism—each played a significant part in determining the basic values of OD. Rationalism stresses the importance of logic, consistency, and determinism. It calls for better empirical and conceptual research. In contrast, pragmatism presses for improvement in the immediate situation. Learning is accomplished by experiments which bring forth improved practice. While rationalism and pragmatism tended to have lengthy time perspectives, linking the past and future, existentialism emphasized the present. This position focused on the here-and-now and valued a person's own immediate, subjective experience. Friedlander (38) sees the contemporary value conflicts within OD as arising from the three philosophical positions.

Evidence for the value dilemmas confronting practitioners in the field arises from both existential and rational research traditions. Tichy (89, 91) reported personal interviews with Harrison and Pages. Both practitioner-researchers recounted severe value conflicts in their professional lives. Harrison said that he frequently found himself in conflict between the organization's need for more effective and efficient use of its resources and the individuals' needs for personal growth and development. Pages indicated that he had stopped working for organizations, preferring to help individuals destroy the organization forms in which they were imprisoned. Tichy (90) also reported the results of a survey comparing several types of change agents, including OD practitioners. Organization development change agents as a group were found to be incongruent with respect to their values and actions. In terms of values, they said that they wanted to promote individual freedom and power equalization in society, but in terms of behavior they said that they actually worked to improve productivity and problem-solving ability. In a later study Tichy (88) reported that the diagnostic orientation of OD practitioners was consistent with their value-practice discrepancies. OD practitioners were most likely to examine the culture and formal structure of the systems they worked with and to expect changes in problem-solving effectiveness to follow from changes in culture and formal structure.

While the basic work of OD consultants takes place inside social organizations, the systems themselves exist within turbulent external environments. It is becoming increasingly clear to many thoughtful observers that failure to take account of the value conflicts outside the system as well as inside can result in OD being used to dehumanize social processes rather than to humanize them. Singer & Wooton (83) drew some striking and disturbing parallels between the internally democratic and structurally imaginative organization strategies used by Albert Speer to build the Nazi war machinery and the approaches of many OD practitioners. Nord (71) severely criticized the OD field for failing to recognize the political and economic institutions in which modern organizations exist. He argued that OD has been largely unsuccessful in developing more humane organizations because the theory and values of the field have failed to take account of the potency of the larger political-economic institutions. Bennis (12, 13) made a complementary point arguing from a different perspective. As a major OD theorist who changed roles from academic-consultant to administrative practitioner, Bennis (13) initially raised questions about the relevance of OD methods for the needs of top level administrators in a public service bureaucracy when he changed roles. With so much time spent on external relationships, Bennis (12) felt he could not afford the luxury of team building with top level associates. A year later, however, he was reporting the benefits of OD intervention within his own group, despite the impact of external relations and the very large number of internal conflicting constituencies within the university (12).

At the crux of the value disputes within OD is the problem of power. OD professionals must struggle with whether their professional competence (power) is being used to advance humane values and with whether they can harness enough power to bring about desirable change in human organizations. Pettigrew (74) has confronted the issues directly, noting that for a long time the subject has been omitted from consideration by OD theorists. He argues that the internal consultant inevitably deals with political processes if change is to occur. The consultant's major choice is whether to be proactive or reactive in the use of power, and Pettigrew (74) clearly favors the proactive position. In his analysis of OD in transition, Burke (27) has noted that the growing amount of knowledge in the field has allowed and encouraged many practitioners to base more of their interventions on authoritative expertise as well as on the traditional nondirective methods.

Questions of values in the practice of organizational change have always been present. But one must say that as the field has grown and diversified the issues have become more complex. Vansina (94) has cautioned against the excessive simplicity of assuming that task accomplishment and other human values can be integrated easily by the adoption of a particular managerial style. Rather practitioners must be alert to the difficult choices between conflicting values, to the danger of their colluding with inhumane objectives, and to the inevitability of their participation in conflicts about the proper use of social power.

CURRENT TRENDS IN OD PRACTICE

There is little doubt that OD as a professional field is in transition (Burke 27). This section describes two major trends in the practice of OD: (a) expansion of the kinds of organizational settings in which traditional OD techniques are being used; and (b) elaboration of the kinds of techniques that are being developed by practitioners, regardless of the settings in which the practices are being employed. The first trend signals that OD's potential utility is not confined to the business and suburban education settings where it was originally begun, and the second thrust indicates that new technologies are being spawned in response to the challenges evoked by new kinds of problems which OD practitioners are asked or seek to solve.

New Settings

During the last several years the variety of settings where OD is practiced has increased enormously. This development undoubtedly reflects the crisis state of so many organizations and their willingness to seek help of the kind offered by OD. As this section shows, there are few, if any, types of organization where OD has not been attempted.

INTERNATIONAL RELATIONS   Vansina (95) analyzed the special problems and opportunities that OD methodology offers to the multinational industrial organization. He began by identifying a variety of conceptual misunderstandings common to those who attempt applications in the international arena. Multiple overlapping intergroup tensions determine the dynamics of any international system and strongly influence the experience of individual members of such systems. Vansina's (95) OD proposals aim at helping the organization become more of a multinational system. An international top management team, as a microcosm of the desired social system, is considered essential. Beyond that he described principles for temporary task forces (i.e. workshops) that were composed to allow members to identify personal, positional, cultural, and national influences on their perceptions and decision-making and which called upon them to work on a common real task that required their acceptance of a common subordinate goal.

Berlew & LeClere (14) described a project designed to facilitate economic and social development by providing motivation training to residents of Curacao, in the Netherlands Antilles. The program essentially had two parts: (a) training individuals in motivation and group decision making; (b) developing more effective and collaborative community organizations as outlets for the trained individuals. The descriptive report provides numerous accounts of significant new events that took place in the small Caribbean island in association with the behavioral science intervention. Hundreds of individuals were trained in the behavioral science technologies; the training skills were transferred to people in the country; and a community development workshop set new kinds of interinstitutional collaborative activities into motion. But the project lacked sustained followup or systematic evaluation of outcomes. It was an ambitious intervention whose full impact was not ascertained. It was also a project whose successes and failures were intimately linked to the power politics of the community in which the changes were attempted.

Perhaps the boldest and most turbulent of the attempts to use applied behavioral science methods for the resolution of interorganizational conflict was the Stirling Workshop directed to dealing with differences among the warring groups in Belfast, Northern Ireland. This intervention brought together 56 participants from various sectors of the Belfast community and 9 staff from the United States to examine group and intergroup dynamics as they might elucidate community dynamics (Alevy et al 6). The conference was a highly stressful event for staff and participants alike. Because of the intense workshop dynamics and the extreme tension surrounding the total enterprise, systematic data collection was not attempted. Results were reported showing considerable differences among various reporters as to what happened and with what consequences.

Application of OD methods to problems that involve international relations crosses the boundary between organizations and communities in which they are embedded. The reports by Vansina (95), Berlew & LeClere (14), and Alevy et al (6) each dealt with organizations and with the interaction between those organizations and their environments. The use of OD methods in public sector organizations within the United States faces similar dynamics from organization-environment interactions. Moreover, in public sector systems a very significant portion of the environment is explicitly political and may have strong norms against many of the values and practices associated with OD work (Eddy & Saunders 33).

DOMESTIC POLITICAL PROCESSES   Nonetheless, there are now a number of reports of OD efforts in an explicitly urban political context. Weisbord, Lamb & Drexler (101) provide a detailed case study of improving police department management through problem-solving task forces. From their work with a police department of 270 officers in a city of 80,000 people, they report significant changes in a variety of police management practices. Recognizing the political context in which police departments exist, both the consultant-reporters and police officials who participated in writing the case emphasize the importance of keeping OD task forces away from "external issues." As an example, efforts by police officers to influence court practices, an explicitly external issue, were blocked by the top administration of the department, while most recommendations for change on internal issues received strong support. Overall, the Weisbord et al (101) intervention showed many signs of constructive change, although their evaluation methods were somewhat limited by lack of systematic controls.

Golembiewski & Kiepper (43) applied standard team-building and intergroup problem-solving interventions to the start-up processes of the Metropolitan Atlanta Rapid Transit Authority (Marta). They employed team building with the top administrative group, and the board of directors. Intergroup problem solving was utilized to improve two separate sets of relationships: the senior staff with the board of directors and the third level department directors with the senior staff. While the senior staff were professional public managers, the board was a political body designed to represent various geographical units that would be influenced by the Marta project. Golembiewski & Kiepper (43) report positive reactions to their interventions, although they acknowledge that the events were more significant for the administrators than for the board members.

Brown (23) presented a detailed case history of organization development in Kansas City, Missouri. This program, with W. B. Eddy as the primary consultant, may be the most extensive effort to apply OD methods to a public sector system that has been undertaken to date. Within the city administration the program was heavily supported by the city manager. Team building, task force problem-solving, and data feedback were employed regularly over a 3 year period within the administration and between the city manager and the city council. Brown's (23) account is primarily historical and analytical, without efforts at systematic evaluation. Throughout the project political forces were operative. The account relies heavily on newspaper reports from Kansas City papers to document what was happening. Although contact between consultants and administrators began in the early 1960s, the program did not accelerate until a city manager committed to teamwork was joined by a mayor who espoused similar values. The program was substantially ended when a later mayor committed to adversary processes was influential in provoking the resignation of the city manager who had strongly supported the program.

The rise and fall of OD programs in public sector systems as a function of the values of politically appointed executives is further documented by Marrow's (64) report on developments in the U.S. State Department. Between 1964 and 1967 the State department underwent a wrenching attempt to modernize and humanize its management system. This process ended officially in early 1967 with the resignation of the chief internal agent of change. But the process started again in 1969, following a change in political administration. New tactics and new people were involved. Nonetheless, processes started several years earlier were resurrected by a new administration.

HEALTH CARE DELIVERY   Governmental settings bring OD practice into contact with political processes. Early experiments strongly suggest that OD's survival depends heavily on the intersection of political and administrative processes. Another institutional area in which OD work has recently begun is in health care delivery. This sector of society involves not only political and administrative considerations but also the presence of the powerful and technically sophisticated profession of medicine. Beckhard (11) has argued persuasively that OD practitioners should attempt to involve themselves in the health care field.

Rubin, Plovnick & Fry (79) analyzed the special problems of gaining entry into community health care organizations. They found sources of resistance to behavioral science application in the medical setting different from those in industry, and consequently these called for different behaviors on the part of the consultant.

Provision of comprehensive health care has become an inherently vague and ambiguous task confronted by severe pressures and transformed into immediate crisis management. The anxiety surrounding matters of life and death leads to a survival orientation and less willingness among clients to try anything that seems innovative or risky. Consultants become more directive and assertive than is their custom, especially as they are confronted with multiple sources of authority from the medical profession, the administrative hierarchy, and community boards. Their perceived value to a system may turn heavily on what they actually do in face-to-face encounters with clients working on real day-to-day problems.

Weisbord (100) examined the organization structure and role definitions of key administrators in a medical center from the perspective of Lawrence & Lorsch's (61) theory of differentiation and integration. He found that a major problem for most physician-executives was that they wore "multiple hats" resulting from their leadership roles in research, patient care, teaching, and administration. Caught among these multiple pulls, each with its conflicting values, the leaders tended to form committees whose major function seemed to be to prevent each other from converting their individual agendas into organization policy. The report describes a "mix model" for redesigning the medical center to differentiate functional departments (e.g. internal medicine) from programs (e.g. medical education) and summarizes the initial change activities undertaken to implement the new model.

In a study with more limited objectives and more precise measurement and evaluation, Bragg & Andrews (22a) report on the effects of introducing participative decision-making into a hospital laundry. They found that attitudes toward the program became increasingly positive as time passed, that absenteeism significantly decreased, and that productivity per employee significantly increased. The latter two measures were also compared with other groups in the hospital. This program had both administrative and union support and took place in a nonmedical sector of the hospital. When the success of the experiment was made known in the system and efforts were made to transfer the procedures to the nursing service, resistance from the medical staff hindered effective implementation.

Moos (67) employed a survey feedback technology to study and change the social environment of a psychiatric treatment ward and an adolescent residential center. In both settings the focus of data feedback was on different perceptions by the staff and residents of their respective settings. Following feedback, discussion, and action planning, efforts were made to implement desirable changes identified in the survey. Follow-up measures taken with the same instruments several months later showed indications that changes had taken place, but certainty about them was marred by lack of control observations.

SCHOOLS   Relatively early in the history of OD, both group training and survey feedback methods were applied in public schools (Schmuck & Miles 82a). Typically these projects were undertaken in suburban middle class settings where the stresses of a turbulent urban environment were not prominent and socioeconomic and ethnic differences between change agents and clients were not pronounced. More recently OD methods have been extended to urban schools and a private boarding school.

Among these programs there has been a great deal of variation in time invested, approaches to change, and rigor of research.

Langmeyer, Lansky & Reddy (60) described an intervention for professional staff in a public school system. Their efforts began at the top of the system with a workshop to examine the relations between the administrative staff and school principals. It was followed by analogous interventions designed for specific schools. A later workshop brought the principals and central administration back together again to improve communication and working relationships. This approach to school system change concentrated on hierarchical relations among administrative personnel and did not attempt to include parents or students.

An entire issue of *Education and Urban Society,* dedicated to OD in urban school systems (Derr & Demb 31), clearly emphasizes the insignificance of environmental turbulence on organizational change processes. Pointing out that the environment of urban public school tends not to be supportive of OD efforts and indeed tends to be threatening to the school itself, Derr & Demb (31) analyzed the special problems of entry in an urban school setting. Lack of competitive pressures from other schools, poor financing, crises generated by external groups, and limited interdependence among subsystems within schools make entry a significantly different process in urban schools than in industrial settings. Gabarro (40) examined OD processes in schools from the perspective of organization-environment fit. Particular attention was devoted to relations among units in the system required to meet environmental demands, relationships between the system and important groups in the environment, and the overall appropriateness of the administrative organization given these demands. As a special case of dealing with school and environmental relations, Schmuck (82) described the techniques developed at the Center for Educational Policy and Management at the University of Oregon for bringing parents and students into school management. Their technologies included interpersonal skill building, intergroup problem solving, and task force development. Blumberg, May & Perry (22) describe a case of an urban school that became more responsive to its external environmental relations after changing its internal decision-making processes to be more participative. After participative methods for decision-making were developed in the school, teachers took a more active role in managing their environmental relations. They were influential in having their views considered in the appointment of a new principal, who in turn was instrumental in increasing the involvement of parents in the management of the school.

Alderfer & Brown (3) reported a 4 year OD consultation and research project in a New England boarding school. Shielded from much of the turbulence found in urban educational environments, the boarding school showed many characteristics of being a total institution. Interventions, initiated by both internal and external consultants, focused primarily on internal issues and included activities with administration, faculty, and students—separately and together. Changes were observed in hazing practices, interpersonal behavior, involvement and satisfaction with the school, and social structure of the discipline system.

HIGHER EDUCATION   OD has also begun to be utilized in college and university settings. In fact, an entire issue of the *Journal of Higher Education* was devoted to organization development in higher education (Boyer & Crockett 21). There seem to be two basic goals to be realized in using OD in higher education. Group dynamics and other OD methods can be employed to change the content and process of teaching and learning processes. OD interventions can also be employed to change the behavior of subsystems and the university as a whole. Plovnick, Steele & Schein (75) described a workshop they conducted for architecture and urban planning students to help them understand system processes and apply those understandings to their own professional work. Boyer (20) reported a general program at the University of Cincinnati to help faculty members and students improve the quality of teaching and learning in the classroom. Staff at the University of Cincinnati have also used OD methods to intervene departmentally to help faculty groups function more effectively and university-wide to improve planning processes and the effectiveness of high level administrative teams (Bennis 13, Bolton & Boyer 16).

Applications of OD to higher education have illuminated some of the special properties of these systems. Boyer & Crockett (21) suggested that universities have more diverse goal structures, pluralistic subsystems, difficulty in measuring the quality of their products, and more dependence on the environment than industrial systems. Universities also tend to foster norms of individualism and autonomy in the conduct of research and teaching which tends to work against the cooperative norms encouraged by OD practice. Problems with power and conflict abound in universities. Greening (46) has presented a particularly thoughtful analysis of the covert power dynamics which he observed during his OD consultation with an experimental college.

CONCLUSION   There is no doubt that the range of settings to which OD methods are applied is expanding significantly. In addition to the sets of intervention efforts reviewed above, where several different projects can be reviewed for each setting, there were also reports of OD in a newspaper (Argyris 8), in religious communities (Barber & Rock 10), in a correctional system (Dubin 32), in an airport (Hutton & Connelly 54), and in the military (Mill 65). Partin (73) has compiled a series of first-person accounts by OD practitioners which also reveals the wide range of settings in which OD is being practiced.

New Techniques

The profession of OD is changing not only through the new settings where it is being employed but also as a result of new social technologies which are being developed by practitioners. New approaches to applying behavioral science to organizational settings involve modifications of well-known existing technologies and the invention of totally new methods of intervention. New technologies arise in part from the challenges posed by problems in more complex systems.

TEAM BUILDING   Team building is one of the most fundamental and basic of OD interventions (Fordyce & Weil 33a, French & Bell 36). Like so many OD techniques, it was originally developed for industrial settings where a unitary concept of authority generally prevails. The utilization of team building interventions in health care settings, where there are several sources of authority among interdisciplinary team members, therefore, called for modifications in design and implementation. Coordination among team members and establishing a shared consensus about task priorities are especially difficult activities for multidisciplinary groups. As a result, Rubin and co-workers (78) designed a new program for team development which placed highest priority on the setting of goals and priorities. This approach de-emphasizes the role of interpersonal issues among team members. After a team establishes a mission statement oriented to clarifying their goals and objectives, they analyze the way work is performed and examine how the team is managing its group processes. Only after these activities have been accomplished do they turn to interpersonal issues (Plovnick, Fry & Rubin 76). The authors report brief evaluation data from 13 community health care teams where their program has been implemented, and the results seem encouraging, though not systematic in character (Rubin et al 78). The program has also been tried in several industrial settings but there no evaluative results have been obtained (Plovnick et al 76). The bringing together of team development and objective setting has also been suggested by French & Holliman (37). They propose that traditional one-on-one management by objectives can be improved by making the process of objective setting among members of a management team collaborative among all members of the team rather than relying solely on dialogues between superiors and subordinates, a method which forces the superior to be sole coordinator of all objectives.

SURVEY FEEDBACK   New approaches to survey feedback have also been developed. Traditionally the unit for feedback has been the family group in which a superior and subordinates meet to review the results of questionnaires administered to their unit, to discuss the meaning of the results, and to determine where discrepancies between present conditions and ideal states imply changes should be attempted (Bowers & Franklin 17, 18). Developments in this basic technique involve the introduction of intergroup designs and the expansion of the type of data to be included in feedback.

Alderfer & Holbrook (4) propose the peer group-intergroup model for feeding back survey data when relations between superiors and subordinates are especially strained and when the data to be fed back heavily pertains to system-wide issues rather than to internal group dynamics. According to this model groups of peers who share common organizational fates first meet together to discuss how the data reflect their concerns and later join representatives from other groups, often hierarchically superior, to examine how both parties react to the survey information. Research on the processes of this approach to feedback showed that the time devoted to certain topics depended on peer group composition and that the interpersonal processes used to discuss various topics depended on the topic. Attitudes of senior managers toward the survey data changed toward increasing relevance and readiness to change as they worked through the peer-group intergroup design, and several structural changes in the system were made at the conclusion of the feedback.

Nadler, Mirvis & Cammann (69) describe an ongoing feedback system that included data on both performance and work attitudes. Rather than imposing an existing questionnaire on the system, the researchers worked with a task force of employees from the organization to design a questionnaire that met *their* needs for information rather than pre-existing ideas of the change agents. Consultants and clients together designed a system that brought feedback to the organization on a monthly basis. Observing the operation of the system over a year's period, the investigators noted that only about half of the experimental subsystems thoroughly invested themselves in the use of the feedback systems. While large changes in attitudes and performance were not observed over a year's period, there was evidence that the subsystems who used the system most extensively were more likely to benefit than either control subsystems, which did not employ feedback at all, or the low use subsystems, which only used feedback superficially.

STRUCTURAL APPROACHES   As OD practitioners have intervened with larger and larger units, they have been forced to find ways to deal with the more enduring properties of human organizations. Efforts to alter structural properties of organizations have become more prominent as a result. Dimensions of structure include territory, technology, and time (Miller 66). Recent developments in OD technology for changing structures have touched each of these dimensions.

Steele (85) analyzed the impact of the physical environment on changing organizational behavior. His most general principle proposes an interrelationship between the physical and social systems of organizations. He identifies six major functions of physical settings—security, social contact, symbolic identification, task instrumentality, pleasure, and growth—and shows how an analysis of these dimensions can aid organizational consultation. A setting may be diagnosed on each of these six dimensions by obtaining data from observations and interviews. Greater awareness of settings combined with competence in changing settings may then be used to provide better settings, use physical settings to support social system development, change physical settings to improve problem-solving, and employ OD processes to facilitate physical changes in the system.

Zand (104) proposed the concept of collateral organization as a means to increase the range of structural options available to managers to solve apparently intractable problems. The collateral organization is a supplemental organization coexisting with the usual, formal system and is particularly suited for solving ill-structured problems. It calls for new combinations of people, new channels of communication, and new ways of seeing old ideas. Outputs from the collateral organization are inputs to the formal organization. A manager is not restricted to his own subordinates in approaching people to solve problems. Zand (104) presented two cases illustrating the use of collateral organizations which show highly creative solutions to difficult organization problems.

Luke et al (63) describes a major structural change in the management of a retail food organization as a result of OD intervention. Their change significantly altered reporting relationships and role responsibilities in store management and thereby enabled several levels of management to gain more control over their jobs. The new structure provided an improved means for developing managerial personnel and reduced the degree of close supervision practiced in the system. And it was also associated with a number of performance improvements.

For a long time organizations assumed that the working hours of employees had to be precisely fixed and rigidly enforced. More recently, however, the concept of flexible working hours ("Flexi-time") has been proposed. According to one version of this approach, there is a core of five hour periods during which an employee must be at work each working day. In addition employees must be at work 35 hours each week. Within these work constraints and subject to restrictions of wage and hour laws when they apply, employees may select the hours when they work as long as their choices are congruent with the work requirements of their departments. Golembiewski, Hilles & Kagno (42) evaluated the effects of such a flexi-time program undertaken in an organization that had had extensive experience with OD values and practices. The program was explicitly called experimental; two experimental and one comparison groups were included in the analysis. Employees were informed that flexi-time would be discontinued if the study results did not show that it was useful. After 6 months of flexi-time, the attitudes of managers showed no change. At the end of a year the attitudes of both flexi-time employees and managers had become more positive than the comparison group. Evidence also showed a substantial decrease in absenteeism in the experimental groups while absenteeism increased in the comparison group over the same period of time. There was also no evidence of increased costs of support services to implement the flexi-time intervention. Overall, flexi-time proved to be a useful intervention in the setting where it was tried. Nonetheless, the authors conclude with a series of thoughtful cautions about the conditions under which flexi-time can be most effectively implemented and about the value conflicts that could arise in using the technique.

ENVIRONMENTAL INTERFACES   As OD practitioners have become more aware of the mutual influence of organizations and their environments they have attempted to construct interventions to deal with this interface more effectively. These approaches involve change agents working across organizational boundaries, an unfamiliar role for most OD practitioners. Targets for organization-environment intervention are limited only by the differentiation of the organization's environment. Actual examples include work with families of organization members, similar organizations who might share common problems, and the broader community in which the organization is embedded.

Culbert & Renshaw (30) report on the design and outcomes of a workshop designed to help husbands and wives cope more effectively with the stresses of travel brought on by job requirements. A two-day workshop away from home and organization was conducted by employing organization development technologies to improve the problem-solving effectiveness of the couples. A comparison group of husbands and wives from the same organization was studied over the same period as the intervention group. The workshop group showed statistically significant increases in problem-solving resources, capabilities to cope with travel stresses, and carry-over effects to their organizational lives. Participants seemed to develop more energy for dealing with work related issues.

Brown, Aram & Bachner (25) describe and evaluate an interorganizational intervention among seven schools of theology. Their attempt was to improve communication, coordination, conflict management, and goal definition among members of the consortium of schools. Evidence from a quasi-experimental evaluation of the intervention indicated that the intervention improved communication among the schools, but coordination did not improve. Instead participants increased their perception of the importance of coordination problems. Although the workshop design allowed for action planning, the problems of coordination were so severe within the workshop that this phase of the activities was never carried out. These results suggest that more attention to common goal definition in this system of multiple authorities might have had more beneficial effects.

Brown (24) reports on the results of a series of "dialogues" which brought together the social and economic elite of a city with activist representatives of "disadvantaged" communities to promote improved intergroup communication and long-term cooperation on social projects. In contrast to many other efforts to resolve intergroup tensions, the parties in this intervention were *not* closely interdependent. Without the dialogues they were essentially inaccessible to each other. The first of two dialogues resulted in intense communication between the parties but no agreement about joint projects to be carried out after the workshop ended. In redesigning the second dialogue the consultants spent more time in advance establishing rapport with both parties, arranged for a more heterogeneous mix of the elite, and provided more time for both groups to develop cohesion at the start of the meeting. At the outset of the second session the consultants said that the development of joint projects was one of two top priority goals. The second dialogue ended with enthusiastic agreement among the parties to develop several joint projects. Follow-up activities showed that several projects were launched and had obtained foundation support.

COGNITIVE DEVELOPMENTS   Among OD practitioners there has been a growing interest in using the intellect more fully and effectively (Alderfer 2). Practitioners have become more interested in theory and models. The cognitive work of clients has become a point of diagnosis and intervention.

Herman (53), for example, has taken principles from the theory and practice of Gestalt therapy and applied them to OD. His orientation in doing this has not been to change the culture of social systems, but rather to enable individuals to experience their own potency more fully and to cope more effectively with whatever organizational conditions they may face. Rather than withholding forcefulness out of "good human relations," Herman encourages clients to fully express their demands and thereby enhance the vitality of human interaction. Interdependence is not always a desired end state, nor is there an assumption that all decisions can be reached by participative methods. This Gestalt orientation supplies an antidote to excessive quests for power equalization and to submersion of individuality in the participative group. It also speaks to emerging issues of OD practice in systems of conflicting goals and objectives.

To a large extent, Herman's (53) orientation is a theory about actions and their consequences. OD theorists have also been concerned about how practitioners understand organizational events. Vaill (93), in particular, has emphasized the importance of the practitioner's frame of reference, i.e. his "practice theory" of OD. He has forcefully argued that characteristics of practice theories are significantly different than "scientific theories," and that too little attention has been paid to them by people who train practitioners.

Argyris & Schon (9) and Bolman (15), on the other hand, have made the diagnosis of theories of action a key point of social intervention. They want to help clients become better theorists and to increase the congruence between "espoused theories" (i.e. theories as explanations by clients for what they do) and "theories-in-use" (theories that predict what clients actually do). A key step in this process is for the consultant to work with the client to develop a "reconstructed theory" that makes explicit the goals, assumptions, and strategies used by the client. Analysis of the reconstructed theory then becomes the vehicle whereby espoused theories and theories-in-use can be brought into greater alignment and more effective theories-in-use can be developed.

Still another use of intellectual resources for planned change has been proposed by Lippitt (62). He has developed a set of heuristics for building models to facilitate organizational change. A major impetus in Lippitt's approach is to structure action for change in a logical way. In offering model building as a social technology, he in no way devalues intuitive and spontaneous processes for thinking and acting. His approach simply adds a wider range to the kinds of intellectual resources OD practitioners may employ.

CONCLUSION   There has been a wide variety of technological developments in OD during the last several years. No longer do OD consultants seem to be exclusively concerned with small group and interpersonal processes; a wider range of organization variables are now being influenced by OD interventions. OD technologies intervene with organization structures, environmental interfaces, and the cognitive work of clients and consultants.

ORGANIZATION DEVELOPMENT RESEARCH

Linked to both social science and social action, OD has a more complex relationship to the value of systematic social science than fields which are more strictly scientific or activist. If one examines OD practice only from the standpoint of scientific values, much can be found to criticize (Kahn 56). Comparatively few of the new techniques described in the preceding section were evaluated at all. Among those that were evaluated, an even smaller number were assessed by carefully controlled studies. The fact that only a small proportion of OD interventions are evaluated systematically, however, does not mean that scientific values are being driven from the field. In fact, there are indications that OD research is becoming more sophisticated along a number of dimensions. This section reviews studies which show the main developments in research design, measurement, and theory in OD. In addition there are indications that OD values and methods are having an impact on how more basic social research is being conducted.

Design Improvements

Coughlan & Cooke (29) report the results of a carefully studied collective decision-making intervention in elementary public schools. The collective decision-making structure was designed to complement the normal authority based decision-making found in schools and most other formal organizations. The purpose of the collective decision-making structure was to provide regular collaboration among teachers about teaching and learning, increase the overall participation of faculty in school affairs, and provide structural flexibility to the systems. Teachers used survey feedback data to identify issues that needed attention by the school. A modified four group design was used to evaluate the intervention. Twenty-four schools from five predominantly middle class school districts were randomly assigned to the four experimental and control conditions. Experimental schools showed a greater use of collective processes and more positive work attitude changes by teachers than control schools. This study is very possibly the most carefully controlled study of system-wide organization development reported to date.

Kimberly & Nielsen (57) evaluated the effects of extensive OD intervention in an automobile plant consisting of 2600 hourly and 200 salaried employees. During a period of 15 months all management personnel in the plant participated in skill building, data feedback, team building, and intergroup problem-solving. To measure the effects of the OD intervention on attitudes, only a pre-post analysis of questionnaire data was possible. But this study was unusual in having access to a 4 year time series of performance indicators. A wide variety of attitude changes referring both to organization climate and supervisory behavior were observed. In addition, production rates, which had been declining before the OD intervention, recovered to their pre-decline level, but were no higher after OD than before the decline. However, a further analysis showed that plant production rates were almost perfectly correlated with industry rates, suggesting that production rate was not directly under the control of plant management. There was a significant decrease in the variance of production from before to after the OD intervention, as well as increases in both quality of production and overall profit of the plant. The time series analysis of the several performance indicators makes a persuasive case for the effects of the OD intervention and for the need of such evaluations to be alert to the impact of external forces, such as market conditions, in accurately assessing which dependent variables should be expected to change as a function of intervention.

Hautaluoma & Gavin (52a) report the results of a thorough diagnosis and intervention effort with the employees and management of a small midwestern manufacturing company. They used a team of faculty members and graduate students to collect diagnostic data, feed it back to the system, and plan several interventions, which include team building for top management and supervisory skills training for first level management. A sample of blue collar employees participated in the supervisory skills workshop. Their assessment design was similar to the one employed by Kimberly & Nielson (57)—before and after measures of attitude changes and time series analysis of absenteeism. Results indicate markedly positive attitude changes for all employees, including blue collar workers. Turnover decreased significantly from before to after the intervention, and the time series analysis of absenteeism showed a significant decrease from before to after the intervention. Frank & Hackman (34) report the results of a job enrichment project that failed to produce the intended results. Using the Job Diagnostic Survey (Hackman & Oldham 50) to compare jobs before and after enrichment and to compare enriched with nonenriched positions, they found no evidence of changes in the expected directions. From interview and observational data collected during and after the attempted change, they were able to identify a number of factors that seemed crucial in determining the outcome. Technological difficulties related to the organization where the change was being undertaken became severe during the project. A key senior manager who was supporting the undertaking was called to a different assignment, and his replacement was not supportive of the change activity. A well-developed theory was not available to guide the efforts of the consultants. A full-fledged diagnosis of the target jobs and surrounding social system was not made, nor were those responsible for the change project prepared to identify and deal with anticipated problems as the intervention proceeded. The combination of quantitative and qualitive analysis of the job redesign experiment provided useful insights into the difficulties associated with the project.

Still another approach to evaluating OD interventions was employed by Alderfer & Brown (3) in a long-term boarding school study and intervention. Faced with conflict between themselves and a subgroup of the faculty in the school, the researcher-consultants proposed a joint approach to evaluate the effects of the project. A faculty committee was formed to evaluate the project and given full autonomy to collect information, provided they made some effort to collect data and evaluate their findings in relation to the original contract developed between the consultants and the school. Meanwhile the faculty committee also helped to readminister the original diagnostic instrument to see whether areas where intervention efforts had been directed showed signs of change. Both the faculty evaluation and the instrument readministration revealed signs of significant change in the school as well as areas that still needed improvement. As a result of their involvement with the evaluation, the faculty committee became more positive toward the project and enhanced its legitimacy within the school community. In this setting research evaluation and client evaluation served not only to determine the status of change activities but also to facilitate further change activities.

CONCLUSION   The various evaluation studies reported here show increasing sophistication on the part of OD researchers in achieving more rigorous research designs to evaluate intervention. Various forms of quasi-controls are used as the setting permits, and more valid inferences about the outcomes of interventions under some conditions are associated with certain kinds of constructive change. The increasing care with which some investigators are assessing their own and others' work provides reasons to be more confident about the results (positive or negative) of individual projects, but the diversity of dependent as well as independent variables prohits conclusions of a broad general nature.

In two settings where there have been long-term broadly supported OD programs, each with its own consistent intervention methodology, reviewers have recently attempted to examine their own set of projects to identify crucial variables in determining success and failure (Franklin 35, Runkel & Schmuck 80). Each group was able to identify a long list of variables, some determined statistically, which seemed to distinguish successful from unsuccessful interventions. In both programs, the number of such variables was very close to the number of projects reviewed, and for the purpose of making statistical inferences problems arise with respect to degrees of freedom. Moreover the evaluations reported in this section were done in types of settings—businesses and suburban schools—where OD has been practiced for the longest time and where environmental turbulence is significantly less than in many of the new settings where OD interventions are just beginning. Thus, while we may observe progress of a kind in terms of efforts to be more systematic in efforts to assess OD outcomes, these developments still significantly lag behind developments in technology.

Measurement Advances

Continuing advances in social technology have been followed by investigations aimed at improving the quality of measures employed to determine intervention effects. OD measurement research has been concerned with assessing the outcomes of specific projects, with the development of instruments which might be applied to a variety of interventions within a general class, and with determining whether interventions have differential effects on various groups within a system (Nadler & Pecorella 70). Measurement studies have focused on the validation of new instruments and on the discovery of measurement error and bias in existing instruments.

NEW INSTRUMENTS   Researchers at the U.S. Army Research Institute have been concerned with developing a series of measures that might be used to diagnose and evaluate OD intervention in the army (Cohen 28). Their primary instrument is the Work Environment Questionnaire (WEQ), which provides attitude measures of supervision and the work group, situational factors related to job performance, and the importance of the job as perceived by the respondent and his supervisors. WEQ measures have been validated against objective measures of job activity and self-perceived measures of effort. In addition the self-perceived measures of effort were validated with behavioral observations of job effort (Turney 92).

Moos (68) has undertaken an extensive effort to develop scales for assessing the organizational climate of a variety of correctional and rehabilitative settings. To date the scales have been used most extensively for diagnostic and research purposes, but as noted above, they have also been employed with survey feedback (Moos 67). The research program has evolved a large variety of specific scales, depending on the type of organization being studied. Organizing all scales are three basic conceptual dimensions: relationships, personal development, and system maintenance and change.

Hackman & Oldham (50) have developed the Job Diagnostic Survey (JDS) to diagnose target jobs prior to job enrichment interventions and to evaluate the effects of enriched jobs on the people who perform them. Central to the measurement of jobs by the JDS are five core dimensions—skill variety, task identity, task significance, autonomy, and feedback from the job itself. The instrument also contains measures of other job characteristics, critical psychological states, affective reactions to the job, and individual growth need strength. The conceptual model on which the instrument is based was developed by Hackman & Lawler (49) and generates a series of predictions which can be used to validate the instrument. Data presented by Hackman & Oldham (50) show that the instrument has satisfactory convergent and discriminant validity and that its variables relate in predictable ways to external criteria such as absenteeism and performance ratings.

Jenkins and associates (55) developed another method for measuring jobs by obtaining standardized observations. Their instrument contained 11 a priori task dimensions: variety, autonomy, task identity, task feedback, worker pace control, comfort, resource adequacy, certainty, required cooperation, external feedback, and required skills and abilities. Six of the observed dimensions showed both repeatability and homogeneity and were correlated with self-report measures of the same constructs obtained from interviews with job holders. Variety, skills, autonomy, and pace control showed satisfactory convergent validity, while certainty and cooperation did not. Autonomy and pace control failed to show satisfactory discriminant validity, while the other four variables did. There was also substantial evidence of common method variance among the observations, but, somewhat surprisingly, not among the interview measures.

MEASUREMENT ERROR   As OD researchers have become more systematic in their measurement efforts, they have also become more skeptical about the underlying constructs being tapped by various measures. To some degree these concerns simply reflect an increasing sophistication about psychometrics. But conceptual issues also arise because of the nature and dynamics of change processes.

Golembiewski & Munzenrider (44) question whether changes on Likert's System 4 scales might be partially explained by social desirability predispositions on the part of some respondents. They found, for example, that individuals who gave the highest System 4 ratings also tended to have the highest social desirability scores. Since the Likert items are very transparent and easily faked, high values on the System 4 scale might simply reflect a denial of organizational difficulties. Although the study cannot completely rule out statistical regression effects as an alternative explanation for observed change in Likert scale scores, the effect of approval-seeking by respondents in OD evaluations might produce misleading data in measuring the effects of interventions.

As social desirability may confound measures of the dependent variables in OD evaluation, so too may expectation effects determine the nature of the independent variables. King (58) found that variations in managerial expectations about the effects of a job enlargement intervention were associated with outcome differences subsequent to the change program. Managers who in advance were led to believe that job enrichment would lead to higher productivity found that their organizations did increase output after job enrichments, and managers who were told only to expect improvements in personnel relations did not find productivity improvements. From these results it appeared as though job enrichment per se did not cause changes in employee output, but rather management beliefs about the effects of job enrichment were responsible for the observed differences in output.

Moreover, the measurement of change is related to the conceptualization of change. Golembiewski, Billingsley & Yeager (41) distinguish among three types of "changes" which may occur as a function of OD intervention. *Alpha* change refers to movement along a scale reflecting relatively stable dimensions of reality. *Beta* change refers to a type of change that also involves recalibration of the scale intervals by which change is measured. *Gamma* change involves a redefinition of a conceptual domain so that the framework within which a phenomenon is viewed changes. All of these types of change apply to perceptual, self-report measures. To the extent that other than alpha changes occur, it becomes more difficult to interpret the meaning of pre-post differences. Potent OD interventions, insofar as they achieve their stated aims, may produce beta and gamma changes. The possibility of beta and gamma changes severely complicates any interpretations of change, or of no-change. Golembiewski, Billingsley & Yeager (41) suggest testing for differences in the factorial structure of measures across time as an operational way to determine whether gamma change takes place. Their analysis also points out the problems of relying exclusively on self-report measures to measure changes. Using behavioral indicators which are not subject to alterations in the cognitive structure of people could correct for many kinds of limitations associated with self-reports.

CONCLUSION   The design of OD research and the measurement of effects from interventions can be viewed as part of a broader activity called evaluation research. Today there is a large and rapidly growing body of scholarship in this field to which OD practitioners and researchers should devote more attention (Guttentag & Struening 47, Struening & Guttentag 87, Weiss 102, 103). Like OD itself, evaluation research is an activity born of multiple, sometimes conflicting, values (Angrist 7, Burgoyne & Cooper 26). Researchers may face trade-offs between the rigor of their designs and the perceived practical utility of the information generated. Results of the research, whether positive or negative, may be viewed quite differently by groups with differing vested interests in the outcome. There is at least one review suggesting that more rigorous designs are more likely to be employed by outsiders to the project being evaluated and that the more rigorous designs are less likely to show positive results (Gordon & Morse 45). This may explain why more high quality research is not done in connection with OD interventions.

Contributions to Social Science

The relationship between OD and more basic social science is not limited to the infusion research values and methods from the discipline-based fields to OD. There is also evidence that concepts from applied activities return to influence the nature of basic social science. This has happened through the development of new approaches to research methodology, the stimulation of concepts to be tested in more rigorous settings than field designs, and the formulation of new theoretical positions.

METHODS FOR RESEARCH   OD methods share similar properties with certain "clinical methodologies" developed by psychologists and anthropologists. As originally conceived, T-group methods were viewed as a means for helping people to learn greater awareness and competence in interpersonal and group behavior. Usually the role envisioned for T-group participants after training was leadership or membership. But Sandler (81) has recently recognized that the learning objectives of laboratory education are directly relevant to training for participant observation. She points out that laboratory education learnings typically include greater awareness of one's self, perception of self by others, sensitivity to covert dimensions in situations, and empathy. Increases in all of these skills should increase the research effectiveness of people in participant-observer roles.

Although the social psychology laboratory has been an important research tool for nearly 50 years, only recently have scholars begun to examine the organizational properties of the laboratory and its impact on research subjects (Argyris 8a, Kelman 56a, 56b). Frequently the social psychology laboratory calls for subjects to take on demeaning social roles which are often resented and resisted. To degrees that are often impossible to measure, data generated under these conditions are likely to be distorted. The social psychology laboratory as a human organization, therefore, may suffer similar problems as systems: poor quality of life for members and ineffectiveness in task performance (i.e. generation of valid data). Alderfer, Kaplan & Smith (5) describe a procedure by which they redesigned a social psychology laboratory to create more humane conditions for adult subjects and make it possible to obtain behavior and attitude measures heretofore unobtainable under true experimental conditions.

TOPICS FOR RESEARCH   OD may not only influence how a phenomenon is studied but also what is studied. Because of the great number of uncontrolled variables that exist in any field setting where OD is practiced, for scientific ends it might be desirable to transport phenomena from the field to the laboratory where greater experimental control is possible. Robey (77) was able to conduct a job enrichment experiment in the laboratory which showed an interaction between employee values and their behavioral and attitudinal responses to enriched jobs. Hand, Estafen & Sims (52) created an experiment to test the effects of survey feedback and team building on team performance in a complex management game. They found that the satisfaction of members receiving feedback compared to controls was greater, but no performance differences between conditions were observed.

IMPROVED THEORIES   A final contribution of OD to social science is influencing basic theory. Theory in this context refers to a series of interrelated abstract statements relating variables to one another and proposing to understand and predict social phenomena. Another product of research in OD can be stimulation of improved theories of social change processes. During the period since the last review of OD, writers have proposed a number of new theoretical positions which have grown directly out of OD activities.

Alderfer (1) provided a theory relating the choice of organizational diagnostic methods to the state of organizational boundaries in the system being studied.

Starting from a conceptual definition of organizational diagnosis, the theory identifies a series of organizational conditions which are hypothesized to affect the utility of certain diagnostic methods. The theory provides a set of constructs which enable a diagnostician to deduce which diagnostic methods should be used to increase efficient collection of valid information about a human system.

Bowers, Franklin & Pecorella (19) present a series of propositions for choosing interventions to change organizations. Their theory consists of three basic classes of variables. First, problematic behaviors are defined in terms of four categories of leadership behaviors: support, interaction facilitation, goal emphasis, and work facilitation. Second, conditions causing these behaviors are explained in terms of information, skill, situation, and values. Finally, the nature of interventions is viewed in terms of information, skills, and situation. The theory proposes matching interventions to problems and causes, starting change processes at key interfaces, and sequencing activities to solve simpler problems before more complex ones.

Alderfer & Brown (3, pp. 99–112) present six propositions to explain and predict long-term change processes in organizations. Their theory emphasizes the generation of valid information, the development of understanding of system consequences, and the alteration of undesirable structures and processes. Releasing and developmental interventions are employed to meet system needs for stability and to introduce planned evolutionary changes. In general, change is brought about by a series of interactive processes sustained over time.

Steele (86) used the development of innovative concepts as a way to identify gaps in existing theoretical statements about consulting. Emphasizing the client-consultant relationship as the focal point for learning from consultation, he analyzed the various actions consultants may or may not take which increase or decrease their own and clients' tendency to learn. For Steele (86) the major objective of consulting is learning—for client and consultant—and the major activity of the consultant is designing social psychological experiences which stimulate learning. His concepts provide a means for reflecting upon and improving these processes.

In the area of job enrichment, an approach for improving organizations that has been in existence for more than 20 years, there are developments which bring together social technology, theory, and measurement. Hackman et al (51) show how various "implementing strategies" for changing jobs based on the Walters (96) approach to job enrichment can be linked to the Hackman-Lawler (49) theory of job design. Oldham, Hackman & Pearce (72), in turn, using the Job Diagnostic Survey, demonstrate that both growth need strength and the work context moderate employee reactions to enriched jobs, thus elaborating the theory. Then Hackman (48), reasoning from both theory and empirical results, is able to suggest ways for improving the implementation of job enrichment. A related analysis concerning the tendency for successful work restructuring programs not to be diffused beyond the initial project was provided by Walton (97).

The expansion of OD to new settings, the efforts to redesign jobs, and the concern about quality of working life have brought OD into closer contact with organized labor. Recognizing that a broader and more differentiated view of OD is needed if it is to be useful and valued by all parties in labor-management relations, Kochan & Dyer (59) have presented a model of organizational change in the context of labor-management relations. More than any other approaches, their theory gives a central focus to goals, power, and conflict as key variables. It specifies the conditions under which an industrial relations system will be amenable to OD interventions. Particularly critical from both normative and descriptive perspectives is the extent to which the program is instrumental in attaining goals valued by each of the major interest groups involved.

CONCLUSION Thus, theoretical positions have arisen from efforts on the part of OD practitioners to understand and to predict planned change through applied behavioral science methods. As currently formulated these models are largely inductive; they are derived from experience with change projects. While some variables appear in several theories, there is no generally agreed-upon set of dimensions regularly found in a variety of theories. Interventions are not typically derived from theoretical propositions, nor are OD research projects usually concerned with testing hypotheses derived from systematic theoretical positions. Theoretical controversies comparing the merits of differing conceptual perspectives are almost unknown. In sum, theoretical work is taking place in OD but it is of a relatively primitive form.

CONCLUSION

One way to understand the variety of developments reviewed in the preceding pages is to think of OD as an interrelated professional system interacting with a most complex and turbulent environment. Like other systems, OD must first survive and then grow. Historically the field arose because it offered social technologies which were perceived as useful for solving various social problems arising within organizations and, more recently, between organizations and their environments. From its outset the field was based on a number of different values (e.g. self-realization for individuals, effectiveness for systems), but because of the types of systems where the original developments were undertaken, the potential value conflicts embedded in the field from the outset did not become as apparent as they are today. Relatively successful businesses, often without unions, and stable suburban school systems without urban unrest are not as likely to be influenced by severely conflicting interest groups as are many of the new types of systems where OD is being practiced today. The lack of conflicting values was supported when the practice of OD in its earliest days was confined to relatively homogeneous groups within the systems where it was being practiced.

But this pattern has changed radically. The value conflicts notable in OD today arise in part because of the greater diversity of settings in which OD is being attempted. To be effective at all in increasingly turbulent systems, OD must deal with the conflict inherent in those systems. Once touched by the differences in goals, power, and technologies found in urban schools, universities, political bureaucracies, labor-management relations, and health care systems, OD itself is forced to become clearer about the priorities among its own values. Professionals can no longer comfortably assume that there are no trade-offs between productivity and quality of life in organizations or that the interests of all groups in a system can be brought readily into alignment with each other.

The need to deal with these more conflictful and otherwise complex system problems has been a source of great stimulation for the field. New social technologies have arisen to contend with problems that did not readily lend themselves to straightforward application of existing methods. The nature of these new technologies reflects an attempt to respond to a greater variety of system complexities. Team building, for example, places greater emphasis on determining a common mission among members where once this technology might have assumed that team members shared common goals. Survey feedback models expand to provide methods for dealing with systemwide issues and alternative perceptions of system reality by different groups. There is an upsurge of interest in structural interventions including new developments in job design, interventions to alter reporting relationships, integration of physical and social considerations in the design of systems, and the modification of working hours. All this technological complexity has also motivated greater concern for conceptual development as an intervention strategy.

As OD has interacted with its external environment—particularly client systems and their problems—the nature of the field itself has changed to reflect these dynamics. New settings have called for new technologies, and broader views of traditional systems have necessitated more comprehensive approaches to system development. New technologies provide methods for containing value conflicts and in some cases for altering their outcomes.

As an applied behavioral science, OD has always experienced tension between practice and scientific goals. Today, as in earlier times, scientific achievements lag behind practical accomplishments (Burke 27, Weisbord 99). When a new social technology is first tried, it is unlikely to be systematically evaluated by a vigorous experimental or quasi-experimental design. There are a variety of reasons for this, arising from the training of many OD practitioners, the availability of funds for such research, and the social conditions surrounding many experiments with new social technologies. Many training programs for practitioners are not university based because universities do not recognize the kinds of contributions OD can make, and many OD practitioners resist the intellectual demands of universities. The value system of society at large provides relatively little money for OD research, and well-controlled field studies are usually quite expensive. When new OD approaches are first tried there is often so much energy required to make them work that reflection and evaluation activities only begin seriously after the intervention has been under way. Systematic research is much more difficult, if not impossible, under these circumstances.

Despite the tensions, however, there have been significant research developments in OD during the time covered by this review. More rigorous research designs have been employed to evaluate interventions; both positive and negative outcomes have been observed. There is clear evidence that better measuring instruments are being developed, and greater understanding of measurement errors is being obtained. As OD knowledge has become more sophisticated, its impact on social science methodology and theory building are being felt—however slightly.

Within OD, the scientific advances have a noticeable pattern. They are more likely to be undertaken by individuals with university affiliations working in less turbulent social systems over extended periods of time. The methods of social science are only gradually being adapted for work in more turbulent settings. Systems which defy understanding by practitioners for pragmatic ends tend to be no more accessible to social scientists using rigorous methods for scientific ends. Thus, if one may think of OD as having a stable core, where practice has been under way for the longest period of time and a dynamic perimeter where new developments are taking place, systematic research is more likely in the former than in the latter settings. Accordingly, research will tend to lag behind practice in OD as long as the system is organized as it currently is. Finally, returning full cycle to questions of values and ethics, writers in the field are beginning to explore these most difficult issues conceptually as well as pragmatically (Steele 84, Walton & Warwick 98).

In sum, OD at this point in history is dominated by practice values and led by new developments arising out of challenges to the field induced by real problems posed by clients. The tension between practice and science is alive and well and threatening to influence social science as well as social action.

Literature Cited

1. Alderfer, C. P. 1976. Boundary relations and organizational diagnosis. In *Humanizing Organizational Behavior,* ed. L. Meltzer, F. Wickert. Springfield, Ill: Thomas
2. Alderfer, C. P. 1974. The relevance of human intellect and organizational power for organization development. In *New Technologies in Organization Development,* ed. J. D. Adams, 2:119–38. LaJolla, Calif: Univ. Assoc.
3. Alderfer, C. P., Brown, L. D. 1975. *Learning from Changing: Organizational Diagnosis and Development.* Beverly Hills: Sage
4. Alderfer, C. P., Holbrook, J. 1973. A new design for survey feedback. *Educ. Urban Soc.* 5:437–64
5. Alderfer, C. P., Kaplan, R. E., Smith, K. K. 1974. The effect of variations in relatedness need satisfaction on relatedness desires. *Admin. Sci. Q.* 19:507–32
6. Alevy, D. I., Bunker, B. B., Doob, L. W., Foltz, W. J., French, N., Klein, E. B., Miller, J. C. 1974. Rationale, research, and role relations in the Stirling workshop. *J. Conflict Resolut.* 18: 276–84
7. Angrist, S. S. 1975. Evaluation research: possibilities and limitations. *J. Appl. Behav. Sci.* 11:75–91
8. Argyris, C. 1974. *Behind the Front Page.* San Francisco: Jossey-Bass
8a. Argyris, C. 1970. *Intervention Theory and Method.* Reading, Mass: Addison-Wesley
9. Argyris, C., Schon, D. 1974. *Theory in Practice: Increasing Professional Effectiveness.* San Francisco: Jossey-Bass. 224 pp.
10. Barber, W. H., Rock, L. P. 1975. Relationships and change in religious communities. *J. Relig. Health* 14:120–29
11. Beckhard, R. 1974. ABS in health care systems: Who needs it? *J. Appl. Behav. Sci.* 10:93–106
12. Bennis, W. 1974. Conversation with Warren Bennis. *Organ. Dyn.* Winter: 50–66
13. Bennis, W. 1973. An OD expert in the cat bird's seat. *J. Higher Educ.* 44:389–98
14. Berlew, D. E., LeClere, W. E. 1974. Social intervention in Curacao: a case study. *J. Appl. Behav. Sci.* 10:29–52
15. Bolman, L. 1974. The client as theorist: an approach to individual and organization development. See Ref. 2, pp. 269–85
16. Bolton, C. K., Boyer, R. K. 1973. Organization development for academic departments. *J. Higher Educ.* 44:352–69
17. Bowers, D. G., Franklin, J. L. 1974. Basic concepts of survey feedback. *The 1974 Annual Handbook for Group Facilitators*
18. Bowers, D. G., Franklin, J. L. 1972. Survey guided development: using human resources measurement in organizational change. *J. Contemp. Bus.* 1:43–55
19. Bowers, D. G., Franklin, J. L., Pecorella, P. A. 1975. Matching problems, precursors, and interventions in OD: a systemic approach. *J. Appl. Behav. Sci.* 11:391–410

20. Boyer, R. K. 1975. Organizational development approaches to improve teaching. Presented at 30th Natl. Conf. Am. Assoc. Higher Educ.
21. Boyer, R. K., Crockett, C. 1973. Organization development in higher education. J. Higher Educ. 44:339–51
22. Blumberg, A., May, J., Perry, R. 1974. An inner city school that changed—and continued to change. Educ. Urban Soc. 6:222–38
22a. Bragg, J. E., Andrews, I. R. 1973. Participative decision-making: an experimental study in a hospital. J. Appl. Behav. Sci. 9:727–36
23. Brown, F. G. 1974. Organization development in the city of Kansas City, Missouri. Unpublished PhD thesis. Univ. Pittsburgh, Pittsburgh, Pa.
24. Brown, L. D. 1976. Bridging the gap between "haves" and "have-nots": corporate presidents and street activists cooperate. Case Western Reserve Univ. Work. Pap.
25. Brown, L. D., Aram, J. D., Bachner, D. J. 1974. Interorganizational information sharing: a successful intervention that failed. J. Appl. Behav. Sci. 10: 533–54
26. Burgoyne, J. G., Cooper, C. L. 1975. J. Occup. Psychol. 48:53–62
27. Burke, W. W. 1976. Organization development in transition. J. Appl. Behav. Sci. 12:22–43
28. Cohen, S. L. 1975. Overview of the OD research program and its instrumentation. Arlington, Va: US Army Res. Inst.
29. Coughlan, R. J., Cooke, R. A. 1974. The structural development of educational organizations. Ann Arbor, Mich: Inst. Soc. Res.
30. Culbert, S. A., Renshaw, J. R. 1972. Coping with the stresses of travel as an opportunity for improving the quality of work and family life. Fam. Proc. 11:321–37
31. Derr, C. B., Demb, A. 1974. Entry and urban school systems: the context and culture of new markets. Educ. Urban Soc. 6:135–52
32. Dubin, H. N. 1975. Making training relevant: "hostage taking." Working paper from C.O.P.E., Elizabeth, NJ
33. Eddy, W. B., Saunders, R. J. 1972. Applied behavioral science in urban administrative/political systems. Public Admin. Rev. 32:11–16
33a. Fordyce, J. K., Weil, R. 1971. Managing with People. Reading, Mass: Addison-Wesley

34. Frank, L. L., Hackman, J. R. 1975. A failure of job enrichment: the case of change that wasn't. J. Appl. Behav. Sci. 11:413–36
35. Franklin, J. L. 1976. Characteristics of successful and unsuccessful organization development. Ann Arbor, Mich: Inst. Soc. Res.
36. French, W. L., Bell, C. H. 1973. Organization Development. Englewood Cliffs, NJ: Prentice-Hall
37. French, W. L., Holliman, R. W. 1975. Management by objectives: the team approach. Calif. Manage. Rev. 17:13–22
38. Friedlander, F. 1976. OD researches adolescence: an exploration of its underlying values. J. Appl. Behav. Sci. 12:7–21
39. Friedlander, F., Brown, L. D. 1974. Organization development. Ann. Rev. Psychol. 25:313–41
40. Gabarro, J. J. 1974. Diagnosing organization-environment "fit." Educ. Urban Soc. 6:153–78
41. Golembiewski, R. T., Billingsley, K., Yeager, S. 1975. Measuring change and persistence in human affairs: types of change generated by OD designs. J. Appl. Behav. Sci. 12:133–57
42. Golembiewski, R. T., Hilles, R., Kagno, M. S. 1974. A longitudinal study of flexi-time effects: some consequences of an OD structural intervention. J. Appl. Behav. Sci. 10:503–32
43. Golembiewski, R. T., Kiepper, A. 1976. MARTA: Toward an effective, open giant. Public Admin. Rev. In press
44. Golembiewski, R. T., Munzenrider, R. 1975. Social desirability as an intervening variable in interpreting OD effects. J. Appl. Behav. Sci. 11:317–32
45. Gordon, G., Morse, E. V. 1975. Evaluation research. Ann. Rev. Sociol. 1: 339–61
46. Greening, T. C. 1972. Power and decision-making in experimental colleges. In Toward a Community of Seekers, ed. W. E. Tubbs, pp. 66–83. Lincoln: Univ. Nebraska
47. Guttentag, M., Struening, E. L., eds. Handbook of Evaluation Research, Vol. 2. Beverly Hills: Sage
48. Hackman, J. R. 1975. On the coming demise of job enrichment. In Man and Work in Society, ed. E. L. Cass, F. G. Zimmer. New York: Van Nostrand
49. Hackman, J. R., Lawler, E. E. 1971. Employee reactions to job characteristics. J. Appl. Psychol. 55:259–86
50. Hackman, J. R., Oldham, G. R. 1975.

Development of the job diagnostic survey. *J. Appl. Psychol.* 60:159–70

51. Hackman, J. R., Oldham, G., Janson, R., Purdy, K. 1975. A new strategy for job enrichment. *Calif. Manage. Rev.* 17:57–71

52. Hand, H. H., Estafen, B. D., Sims, H. P. 1975. How effective is data survey and feedback as a technique of organization development? *J. Appl. Behav. Sci.* 11:333–47

52a. Hautaluoma, J. E., Gavin, J. F. 1975. Effects of organizational diagnosis and intervention on blue-collar blues. *J. Appl. Behav. Sci.* 11:475–96

53. Herman, S. M. 1972. A gestalt orientation to organization development. In *New Technologies in Organization Development*, Vol. 1, ed. W. Burke. LaJolla, Calif: Univ. Assoc.

54. Hutton, G., Connelly, R. 1972. *Managers and Their Airports.* Bristol, England: Univ. Bath School of Management

55. Jenkins, G. D., Nadler, D. A., Lawler, E. E., Cammann, C. 1975. Standardized observations: an approach to measuring the nature of jobs. *J. Appl. Psychol.* 60:171–81

56. Kahn, R. L. 1974. Organization development: some problems and proposals. *J. Appl. Behav. Sci.* 10:485–502

56a. Kelman, H. C. 1968. *A Time to Speak.* San Francisco: Jossey-Bass

56b. Kelman, H. C. 1972. The rights of the subject in social research. *Am. Psychol.* 27:989–1016

57. Kimberly, J. R., Nielsen, W. R. 1975. Organization development and change in organizational performance. *Admin. Sci. Q.* 20:191–206

58. King, A. S. 1974. Expectation effects in organizational change. *Admin. Sci. Q.* 19:221–30

59. Kochan, T. A., Dyer, L. 1976. A model of organizational change in the context of union-management relations. *J. Appl. Behav. Sci.* 12:59–78

60. Langmeyer, D., Lansky, L., Reddy, W. B. 1973. Organizational training in subsystems of a midwest school district. In *School Intervention*, ed. W. L. Claiborn, R. Cohen, pp. 191–205, New York: Behavioral Publ.

61. Lawrence, P. R., Lorsch, J. W. 1967. *Organization and Environment: Managing Differentiation and Integration.* Homewood, Ill: Irwin

62. Lippitt, G. L. 1974. Model building: an organization development technology. See Ref. 2, 37–70

63. Luke, R. A., Block, P., Davey, J. M., Averch, V. R. 1973. A structural approach to organizational change. *J. Appl. Behav. Sci.* 9:611–41

64. Marrow, A. J. 1974. *Making Waves in Foggy Bottom.* Washington DC: NTL Inst.

65. Mill, C. R. 1974. OD in a macrosystem—a three year progress report. See Ref. 2, 314–30

66. Miller, E. J. 1959. Technology, territory, and time: the internal differentiation of complex production systems. *Hum. Relat.* 12:243–72

67. Moos, R. H. 1973. Changing the social milieus of psychiatric treatment settings. *J. Appl. Behav. Sci.* 9:575–94

68. Moos, R. H. 1975. *Evaluating Correctional and Community Settings.* New York: Wiley

69. Nadler, D. A., Mirvis, P. H., Cammann, C. 1976. The ongoing feedback system: experimenting with a new managerial tool. *Organ. Dyn.* Spring: 63–80

70. Nadler, D. A., Pecorella, P. A. 1975. Differential effects of multiple interventions in an organization. *J. Appl. Behav. Sci.* 11:348–66

71. Nord, W. R. 1974. The failure of current applied behavioral science: a Marxian perspective. *J. Appl. Behav. Sci.* 10:557–78

72. Oldham, G. R., Hackman, J. R., Pearce, J. L. 1976. Conditions under which employees respond to enriched work. *J. Appl. Psychol.* 61:395–403

73. Partin, J. J. 1973. *Current Perspectives in Organization Development.* Reading, Mass: Addison-Wesley

74. Pettigrew, A. M. 1975. Towards a political theory of organizational intervention. *Hum. Relat.* 28:191–208

75. Plovnick, M. S., Steele, F., Schein, E. H. 1973. Expanding professional design education through workshops in the applied behavioral sciences. *J. Higher Educ.* 44:392–401

76. Plovnick, M., Fry, R., Rubin, I. 1975. New developments in OD technology. *Train. Dev. J.*, April

77. Robey, D. 1974. Task design, work values, and worker response: an experimental test. *Organ. Behav. Hum. Perform.* 12:264–73

78. Rubin, I., Fry, R., Plovnick, M., Stearns, N. 1976. *Improving the coordination of care: an educational program.* Cambridge, Mass: Sloan Sch. Manage. Work. Pap.

79. Rubin, I., Plovnick, M., Fry, R. 1974. Initiating planned change in health care

systems. *J. Appl. Behav. Sci.* 10:107–24
80. Runkel, P. J., Schmuck, R. A. 1974. Findings from research and development program on strategies of organizational change at CEPM-CASEA. Eugene: Univ. Oregon
81. Sandler, G. B. 1973. Improving participant observation: the T-group as an answer. *J. Appl. Behav. Sci.* 9:51–61
82. Schmuck, R. A. 1974. Bringing parents and students into school management. *Educ. Urban Soc* 6:205–21
82a. Schmuck, R., Miles, M. 1971. *Organization Development in Schools.* Palo Alto, Calif: Natl. Press
83. Singer, E. A., Wooton, L. M. 1976. The triumph and failure of Albert Speer's administrative genius. *J. Appl. Behav. Sci.* 12:79–103
84. Steele, F. I. 1975. *The Open Organization.* Reading, Mass: Addison-Wesley
85. Steele, F. I. 1973. *Physical Settings and Organization Development.* Reading, Mass: Addison-Wesley
86. Steele, F. I. 1975. *Consulting for Organizational Change.* Amherst, Mass: Univ. Massachusetts Press
87. Streuning, E. L., Guttentag, M., eds. *Handbook of Evaluation Research,* Vol. 1. Beverly Hills: Sage. 696 pp.
88. Tichy, N. 1975. How different types of change agents diagnose organizations. *Hum. Relat.* 28
89. Tichy, N. 1973. An interview with Roger Harrison. *J. Appl. Behav. Sci.* 9:701–29
90. Tichy, N. 1974. Agents of planned social change: congruence of values, cognitions, and actions. *Admin. Sci. Q.* 19:164–82
91. Tichy, N. 1974. An interview with Max Pages. *J. Appl. Behav. Sci.* 10:8–26

92. Turney, J. R. 1975. Utilization of behavior measures of effort in an OD program. Arlington, Va: US Army Res. Inst.
93. Vaill, P. B. 1974. Practice theories in organization development. See Ref. 2, pp. 71–84
94. Vansina, L. S. 1975. Beyond organizational development. In *Personal Goals and Work Design,* ed. P. T. Warr. New York: Wiley
95. Vansina, L. S. 1974. Improving international relations and effectiveness within multinational organizations. See Ref. 2, pp. 331–63
96. Walters, R. W. & Assoc. 1975. *Job Enrichment for Results.* Reading, Mass: Addison-Wesley
97. Walton, R. E. 1975. The diffusion of new work structures: explaining why success didn't take. *Organ. Dyn.* 3:3–22
98. Walton, R. E., Warwick, D. P. 1973. The ethics of organization development. *J. Appl. Behav. Sci.* 9:681–99
99. Weisbord, M. R. 1974. The gap between OD practice and theory—and publication. *J. Appl. Behav. Sci.* 10:476–84
100. Weisbord, M. R. 1974. A mixed model for medical centers: changing structure and behavior. See Ref. 2, pp. 211–254
101. Weisbord, M. R., Lamb, H., Drexler, A. 1974. *Improving Police Department Management Through Problem-Solving Task Forces.* Reading, Mass: Addison-Wesley
102. Weiss, C. H., 1972. *Evaluating Action Programs.* Boston: Allyn & Bacon
103. Weiss, C. H. 1972. *Evaluation Research.* Englewood Cliffs, N.J.: Prentice-Hall
104. Zand, D. E. 1974. Collateral organization: a new change strategy. *J. Appl. Behav. Sci.* 10:63–89

Ann. Rev. Psychol. 1977. 28:225–49

PSYCHOLOGICAL PERSPECTIVES ON DEATH

❖273

Robert Kastenbaum and Paul T. Costa, Jr.[1]

Department of Psychology, University of Massachusetts, Boston, Massachusetts 02125

INTRODUCTION

Although this is the first critical survey of the psychology of death between the covers of the *Annual Review of Psychology*, it is difficult to identify a more ancient topic. Death awareness already had a long history before Socrates attempted to calm his friends' agitation prior to quaffing the hemlock (127). The Gilgamesh Epic, known to the Sumerians of 3000 B.C. and probably of earlier origin, expressed both the intense desire to triumph over death and the doubt that magic, cunning, virtue, or strength could achieve this objective (64). Life prolongation and renewal were salient themes not only in *The Book of the Dead* (18), but throughout Egyptian culture (168). The prefix that we have made our own—*psyche*—often appeared in the Greek classical period within the context of reflections on death. The soul was that-which-departs, sometimes to return (as in dreams) and sometimes not. Dialogues on mortality and awareness of the complexities of phenomenological life began to flourish at the same time.

The faithful in biblical times knew a God of life. Death plunged one into a miserable subexistence more akin to the dank underworld imagined by ancient Mesopotamian civilizations than to a beatific immortality (16). Christianity's dramatic news of triumph over death came in for its share of astonishment and ridicule from Romans who believed in afterlife but could not credit the proposition that the dead would again put on flesh (25).

For centuries thereafter the death theme has played through both sacred and secular spheres. Gruman (60) documents the motivating force of the death-shall-be-overcome sentiment in the rise of alchemy and, eventually, modern science. Furthermore, Ponce de Leon's search for the fountain of youth was but one episode in a series of adventurings which contributed much to exploration and charting of planet Earth, even though the central purpose of outflanking aging and death was not achieved.

[1]The authors are grateful to Brian L. Mishara for his constructive suggestions in the preparation of this manuscript, and to Herman Feifel for his examination of a partial draft.

Pestilence, famine, and warfare during the Middle Ages maintained death as a familiar presence in society. The average lifespan had increased but little since antiquity, and the mortality rate in infancy, childhood, and childbirth was still catastrophic. The *ars moriendi* tradition flourished, producing sober tracts that were the best sellers of their day, crowned by Jeremy Taylor's *Art of Holy Dying* (151). New death-related themes were stimulated by the rise of technology and urbanization. Crowding on narrow city streets, for example, had its parallel in the metropolitan cemeteries of the eighteenth and early nineteenth centuries. The cemetery reform movement was one example of a new "do something" orientation. Another was the effort to resuscitate victims of drowning, lightening, and other traumatic events who customarily had been taken for dead (7). While Dr. Frankenstein's experiments were confined to the pages of a novel, real people were exploring the possibility of giving the apparently dead a second chance by galvanic stimulation (163). Thus the relationship between technology and death, sometimes thought to be a phenomenon unique to our own day, has been gathering momentum for years. *Resistance* to reforms, innovations, and experimental inquiries also has a tradition of its own.

Although psychology emerged from social and philosophical traditions in which the problem of death was prominent, the new science had other priorities for itself. Fechner inspired an experimental psychology that evinced no interest in his own *Little Book of Life After Death* (40), which sets forth a more-than-lifespan developmental psychology. William James admired this work and himself wrote on immortality (71), while G. Stanley Hall conducted an early empirical study of "thanataphobia" (61). Despite such contributions, however, the new and self-conscious discipline of psychology did not make a place for death. If a turn of the century psychologist did think of death, it was probably to sniff at reported communications with the dead, then a fashion both in the United States and Europe.

It appeared that death might become a major topic as modern sociology launched itself. Durkheim's *Suicide* (33) earned masterwork status, but was not followed by systematic exploration of death-related problems in general. The occasional sociologist who focused upon social dimensions of death would find himself a voice in the wilderness, e.g. Thomas D. Eliot's attention to bereavement and family structure (35). Anthropology, by contrast, produced death-related observations right from the start, and continues to do so. Notable among the pioneering contributions was Frazer's compendium of observations made in pretechnological societies around the world (47). It is difficult to imagine the field of anthropology without its detailed accounts of funeral practices, rituals of mourning, and other death-related cultural actions.

Among physicians, the name of Sir William Osler became almost synonymous with humane care of the dying patient. He also kindled an interest in "last words" (118). Yet neither Osler's work nor that of others who followed in his footsteps [e.g. Alfred Worcester (166)] made much impact upon the general medical orientation toward dying and death. Nevertheless, it was a Nobel prize-winning biomedical researcher, Ilya Illyich Mechnikov (108) who introduced the term "thanatology" that some have accepted as designation for the scientific field he envisioned around the turn of the century.

The voluminous output of psychiatric writings from the later years of the past century onward include a number of scattered references to death, but one could not say that it was considered a core problem either in theory or therapy.

With the exception of anthropology then, the new social and behavioral sciences had but fitful and peripheral contact with one of humankind's most ancient concerns. Socrates might have marveled at a psychology that could dispense with death as a relevant problem.

DEATH REDISCOVERED

Precisely why psychology and related fields began to see death as a relevant problem around the mid-1950s is open to conjecture, although disasters of war and a need to reconsider basic human values appear to have been influential (94). Today it is cliche (and increasingly less accurate) to speak of ours as a "death-denying" society. But taboos did in fact obstruct the inquiries of pioneering psychologists such as Herman Feifel. His persistence was rewarded, however, and Feifel made a discovery that many have since made for themselves: although physicians, family, and others may attempt to "protect" the dying person from awareness of his own situation, the patient himself often is grateful for the opportunity for dialogue. In addition to reporting his own research (e.g. 43), Feifel edited a book whose appearance in 1959 is considered by many as the first product of the new death awareness movement. *The Meaning of Death* (42) included contributions not only from C. G. Jung and Gardner Murphy, but also from representatives from philosophy, art history, and other fields. Much subsequent work on death-related problems has retained this multidisciplinary approach.

At about the same time, two other Southern California psychologists launched an innovative and vigorous attack on suicide. Norman Farberow and Edwin S. Shneidman developed new research strategies, concepts, and guidelines for suicide prevention (e.g. 39, 145). Among other activities, they established a prototypic crisis prevention center that has had national and international influence.

The next few years will be remembered by some as a time of self-instruction in death confrontations. The person who had dared to enter into psychotherapy with a dying person on Monday would be sought as an expert on Tuesday. Most researchers also had to begin at the beginning, lacking relevant theory, method, and bibliography. Tattered copies of Richard A. Kalish's annotated bibliography were prized. A mimeographed newsletter pieced together in the depths of a geriatric hospital became a sort of underground newspaper through which isolated "deathniks" could communicate with each other. Today, bibliographic resources include a periodically revised publication from a Center for Death Education and Research with almost 3000 entries in its latest version (51). The ragtag newsletter is now in its eighth year as *Omega, Journal of Death and Dying* (78), and another journal, *Suicide* (143), represents the interests of the American Association of Suicidology, itself a relatively young organization. Courses and workshops on psychological aspects of death can be found on many high school and college campuses and death is no longer a rare topic on programs of the American Psychological Association and other professional and scientific organizations.

Public interest in death was stimulated by Jessica Mitford's rollicking critique of *The American Way of Death* (112), which came down heavily on contemporary funeral practices. Psychiatrist Elizabeth Kubler-Ross aroused much concern for the plight of the dying person in her popular book, *On Death and Dying,* taken by some as the "bible" of the death awareness movement (85).

The first effort to evaluate and integrate scientific knowledge came forth in *The Psychology of Death* (79) in 1972. The individual's personal relationship to mortality was related to the culture's "death system." It was suggested that all cultures have a sociophysical network whose functions include predictions and warnings, attempts to prevent or inflict death, orientations toward the dying person, body disposal, social reconstruction after death, and efforts to explain or rationalize mortality. Death was regarded as, in a sense, both independent and dependent variable. While the first half of the book examined thoughts, feelings, attitudes, and actions *about* death, the second half examined death as a possible *outcome* of individual and social behavior. This general plan of organization will be used in the present review as well.

LIFESPAN DEVELOPMENT OF DEATH COGNITIONS AND ATTITUDES

Assumptions, Questions, and Methodologies

The new psychology of death has among its tasks the conversion of long-held assumptions into questions that can be answered through empirical observation. Several assumptions are of particular concern here. Freud's assertion (48, 49) that we cannot truly understand or accept our own mortality continues to be influential. Unfortunately, it has exercised a stifling effect upon inquiry. Since we "know" that we cannot know death, what would be the point of research? The context and basis for Freud's conclusion are seldom examined; his authority has served chiefly as a quick way to dismiss death as a nonproblem. This parallels the demotion of manifest concern over death to a neurotic quirk that is said to disguise a more primary underlying cause.

A triad of related assumptions focuses upon the child's relationship to death. Perhaps the most explicit of these is the assumption that children do not understand death. This is closely linked with the seldom-examined assumption that adults *do* comprehend death. Often these are associated with the further assumption that concern with death-related phenomena would be harmful to children. They *should not* think of death, even if they could. This triad preserves the image of childhood as a fantasyland into which harsh realities do not or should not intrude. The parent who excludes a child from the funeral and the circle of mourners and who steadfastly avoids death-related discussions often holds these assumptions (76). The child is presumed an innocent in both the realms of death and sexuality, and is to be kept in that blessed state as long as possible (59).

The general drift of all these assumptions is to minimize the significance of death as a force in the cognitive, personality, and social development of the child. Indeed, none of the brand name theories or text books in these areas have treated death as though it were a central concern or influence. The counter-assumption—that the child's relationship to death is of critical importance—has been implied by some philosophers (e.g. 11). It is also the challenge offered by many sociobehavioral scientists and clinicians who have become identified with the death awareness movement.

Some of the questions now being posed lend themselves to fairly straightforward descriptive research, e.g. what *does* the child know or understand about death at a particular time in its life? Other questions require more complex, varied, and converging lines of research. Representative questions of this type include (*a*) the relative influence of maturational and social-experiential factors in development of death cognitions; (*b*) relationship between development of death cognitions and such other concepts as reversibility, limits, futurity, object constancy, and deductive reasoning; (*c*) the extent to which orientation toward death is to be interpreted as a cognitive or an attitudinal-affective component of personality; (*d*) the range of individual differences in death cognitions and implications of same for subsequent development and adaptation.

The latter two problem areas deserve further comment here. Denial, fear, and ambivalence are among the most frequently advanced interpretations of individual and sociocultural orientations toward death. Each of these terms imply both perceptual-cognitive and affective components, but are seldom analyzed from that perspective. Furthermore, one observer may characterize a bit of verbal or nonverbal behavior as indicating an immature cognitive grasp of death, while another regards the same behavior as denial. Closer attention is necessary to the problem of distinguishing cognitive from attitudinal-affective components in death orientations, perhaps best accomplished within a lifespan developmental approach.

Most research on death orientations has made the usual developmental assumption that there is a single, universal "goal," "structure," or "achievement" to crown successful maturation. This assumption has been questioned recently (75). It appears as premature to conclude that there is a single "right" way to think of death as it is to assume that we cannot grasp or accept death at all. The advisability of avoiding premature allegiance to the traditional one-pathway model of development is underlined by the already noted failure to differentiate between cognition and attitude. What passes for the definitive, mature *cognitive* grasp of death might alternatively be interpreted as the culture's dominant *attitudinal* configuration.

Diverse methodologies have been applied to the study of death orientations. These include clinical case studies, questionnaires, interviews, naturalistic observations, expressive-projective behavior, and occasionally performance-type measures. Comparison of findings is difficult because of the diversity of techniques and samples employed, but this same diversity increases confidence in those results that appear with virtually any method of inquiry. Major gaps in methodology include the lack of longitudinal investigations, let alone any of the cross-sequential designs that permit evaluation of age change vs age differences. Experimental (variable-manipulating) research is poorly represented. There is little that could be called inventive in the developmental research to date, although the analysis of literature prepared for the eyes of children (140) has added a useful contextual dimension, and the analysis of children's games both historically and on the contemporary scene has turned up some fascinating material (117).

Infancy and Childhood

"When do children really understand about death?" is one of the questions most frequently raised both by the public and the research community. The answer most frequently given draws upon a 1948 study of Maria Nagy (114), in which she analyzed the words and drawings of 378 Hungarian children ranging in age from 3 to 10. Nagy found evidence for three stages of development. Stage 1, present until age 5, lacks appreciation of death as final and complete cessation. The dead are "less alive," and the condition might be reversed. *Separation* is the theme most clearly comprehended by the youngest children. Stage 2 children think of death as final. However, there continues to be a belief that death might be eluded; it is not inevitable. A strong tendency to *personify* was noted at this stage. One might outwit or outluck The Death Man. Stage 3, beginning at age 9 or 10, is marked by comprehension of death as both final and inevitable. The prospect of personal mortality seems to be accepted.

The attention given to the developmental achievement of comprehending death at about the tenth year of life has tended to obscure those aspects of Nagy's study indicative of earlier thoughts and attitudes. Even the youngest of the children she studied had ideas about death, typically built around realistic, concrete perceptions. This is consistent with the pioneering retrospective study in which Hall (61) found an abundance of perceptual detail on death in memories stretching back to early childhood.

Evidence that children often perceive death-related phenomena and are actively engaged in trying to understand them comes from a variety of sources. This was perhaps the most salient result of Sylvia Anthony's 1937–1939 studies in Great Britain, recently revised and reprinted (8). Both normal and disturbed children often thought of death, with separation and sorrow the dominant themes. Although flawed, Anthony's work remains valuable for its insights into the young child's attempts to integrate the concept of death into his life, and for its revelation of individual differences at all age levels. Rochlin's observations suggest that death-related themes frequently are expressed by children at play (133), while Opie & Opie (117) have documented the near-universal incorporation of such themes into the familiar games and songs of childhood.

Anecdotal reports suggest that the child's discovery of death begins much earlier than most cognitive theorists seem prepared to accept. Maurer (107) proposes that the 6-month-old's fascination for "peek-a-boo" and subsequent appearance-disappearance games involves the attempt to master the mysteries of being and nonbeing, darkness and light, separation and reunion. If attempts to understand and cope with separation are seen as part of the process that leads to fully realized death cognitions, then much of the material on infant and child behavior discussed by Bowlby would be relevant (15). Others have observed very young children who seem to have expressed spontaneous awareness of finitude, irreversibility, and life cessation. The most precocious example known to these writers from a dependable source features a 16-month-old boy who witnessed a fuzzy caterpillar being trampled upon (unwittingly) by an adult. The child had showed alarm as the big grown-up feet approached the caterpillar. After the event, he examined the residue and said in a resigned tone of voice, "No more!" (76). Obviously there are methodological reasons for hesitating to accept such anecdotal reports, as well as the danger of reading too much into them. But against the temptation to dismiss this kind of observation entirely must be set a basic respect for what is seen and heard in the naturalistic setting. It is possible that the truth may be discerned before solid documentation can be accomplished. Denial of the very young child's ability to tune in accurately to death-related phenomena fits in all too well with our culture's death system and with prevailing conceptions of cognitive development. An open-minded attitude appears wise at this time. Furthermore, glimmers supporting the very early development of "mature" death cognitions in at least some children have been observed in more controlled studies as well (e. g. 135).

Several post-Nagy studies have enriched our knowledge of death cognitions in childhood. Koocher (82) found that chronological age was not a reliable predictor of the child's level of death cognition, but that a Piagetian classification of mental operations did predict well. There was a clear difference between preoperational children on the one hand and those at a concrete or formal-operational level. Koocher's interpretation emphasizes *reciprocity:* only when the individual has acquired the ability to draw substantially from the experiences of others can he gain an understanding of what he personally has not encountered in his own life. Some of Koocher's side observations support those made by other researchers, namely, the matter-of-fact attitude toward death displayed by the younger children, the almost complete absence of personification responses (in contrast to the Nagy findings), and the wide range of sophistication to be discovered at a particular chronological age (as distinguished from developmental level).

Childs & Wimmer (24) discovered differential results for two components of death cognitions. A steady progression was noted with advancing age for mastery of the concept of death's *universality.* However, the concept of death as *final* was more difficult, with children as old as 10 still wavering in their views (although some 4-year-olds were decisive in declaring death to be nonreversible). This study indicates the value of a differentiated approach to death cognitions.

Studies by Safier (135), Gartley & Bernasconi (53), and Tallmer et al (150) all came up with an appreciation for the impact of television on children's orientations to death. There was the impression that children are less shielded from death than in previous generations, having a variety of real and make-believe fatalities regularly on display for them on the picture tube. Although these investigators all found evidence for maturational changes in death cognitions and attitudes, they also uncovered suggestions of cohort differences reflecting social change. The Swiss children studied by Piaget in the 1920s, for example, seem to have been more sheltered from death phenomena than contemporary American boys and girls (125). The Tallmer group found greater death awareness among lower class as compared with middle-class children, using both projective measures and interviews (150).

The Safier study is particularly interesting for its close examination of interrelationships between concepts of animate/inanimate and of death (135). The results in general supported her view that a common rationale binds concepts of life and death during each stage of development. Attempting to integrate the work of Piaget and Nagy, she sees a developmental progression from the idea of constant flux, through an externally engendered giving-or-taking of life, until the child attains the concept of both life and death as internal to the organism.

While there remains room for disagreement on a variety of questions, it does appear that the child's development of death cognitions is intimately related to its total construction or appreciation of the world, rather than standing outside the main developmental stream as a secondary or exotic process. Curiosity about impermanence and destinations seem as much a part of the child's intellectual orbit as the more frequently researched questions of permanence and origins. We believe that developmental psychology has overemphasized the processes through which the child comes to appreciate and acquire stability and equilibrium. Real children seem just as interested in disappearances, inconstancies, and disequilibriums. This perhaps is another way of saying that loss, endings, and death are core concerns from childhood onward.

Adolescence and Adulthood

The more purely cognitive aspects of the individual's relationship to death have hardly been touched in the years beyond childhood. This situation seems attributable, at least in part, to the assumption that mature cognitive modalities become established around adolescence and remain substantially unchanged thereafter. It is refreshing to see this view challenged by Riegel (132) and others. Most of the available studies focus on attitudes rather than clearly delineated cognitions of death. However, in adolescence and early adulthood there is a cluster of studies (e.g. 31, 69, 77) which emphasize key relationships between death concern and futurity. Time perspective investigations often do take cognitive factors into account, if not in the most familiar ways. How young people conceptualize futurity appears to provide important clues to their death orientations, e.g. the tendency of young men with relatively high manifest death anxiety to have a more limited future projection (165).

One of the surprises has been the finding that an appreciable number of adolescents and young adults expect to die within a few years, often by violent means (research reports on this topic are just starting to reach print, e.g. 62, 134). "Subjective life expectancy" (SLE) may become an increasingly significant dimension through which to understand the individual's general orientation to life at any chronological age level. Differences in SLE may be related to situational, personality, and demographic factors, e.g. low SLE among "hard core unemployed" whose statistical expectations for continued survival are, in fact, lower than the population in general (152). It might be informative to match individuals on the basis of SLE rather than chronological age (e.g. a 20-and an 80-year-old, both of whom expect to live 5 more years). Changes in one's expected and preferred life expectancies might serve as useful outcome measures for treatment programs.

From a cognitive standpoint, we still have much to learn about how the young person utilizes and integrates formal operational modes to create a personal framework in which death can be accommodated. From a psychodynamic standpoint, the relationship between maturing sexuality, role transition, identity formation and death cognitions remains to be probed more thoroughly. The influence of personal experiences with death upon thoughts and attitudes also is in need of clarification. Reversing the direction, it would be helpful to know more about the possible effect of death cognitions and experiences upon behaviors that influence survival, such as suicide and excessive risk-taking.

How do adults orient themselves to death? If we are to believe the ubiquitous critiques of our society as "death-denying" (e.g. 11, 41, 158), then the same attitude might reasonably be expected of the individual. There are data consistent with this view for physicians and nurses (e.g. 14, 16, 54, 55, 98), although one recent study (129) suggests important differences among these care-givers based upon area of specialization. In general, however, the contention that adults hold essentially a denying orientation has not been documented by direct research. Observers have instead supported this conclusion by references to treatment of death by the media, anecdotal reports, and behavior noted in special situations. The concept of death-denial itself needs more conceptual as well as empirical clarification.

In the absence of definitive research on death attitudes through the adult years it seems wise to recognize individual differences, (99, 160) and the likelihood that orientations are complex, multileveled, and subject to situational influence within the same individual (44, 79). Worth systematic research is the suggestion that in midlife one begins to think of his or her age more in terms of distance from death than from birth (92). The disengagement theory of aging (29) also proposes a shift in life-style with advancing adult age. The person is said to become more aware of the shortness of remaining time and the prospect of death, leading to both intra and interpersonal changes. While disengagement theory has engendered much research, this critical hypothesis rarely has been studied (23).

Most studies of death attitudes in old age indicate the ability of well integrated people to accommodate themselves to finitude (113). Distress at the prospect of death usually has been related to general agitation or to environmental stress or deprivation (160). There are indications that individual life-style is just as significant in old age as at other developmental periods for shaping the orientation toward death. It appears useful to distinguish also between healthy, independently functioning old men and women and those whose lives are in more immediate jeopardy (72, 73, 105, 148).

Death Fear and Anxiety

"Fear" and "anxiety" are among the terms most frequently used to characterize orientations toward death throughout the lifespan. Both the conceptual and methodological problems require careful consideration. Lester (89) opened the criticism of psychometric measures a decade ago. Even more fundamental perhaps is the careless interchange of "fear" and "anxiety," each of which implies different approaches to measurement. The psychoanalytic distinction between free-floating anxiety and fear of an object that is available to conscious awareness (79) is important here. Investigators typically assume that death universally elicits anxiety. Where manifest fear is not present, defensive denial often is inferred (58, 72, 131). Conscious fear of death is thought to occur only when there is a serious breakdown of the individual's defenses, as in extreme psychopathology. While perhaps true, this proposition is very difficult to translate into operational measures, and the evidence it its support is correspondingly weak.

In particular, it is highly questionable that direct self-report measures can be used as indicators of death anxiety. High scores on such a measure may indicate high fear of death, but this by definition is distinct from death anxiety, which is held to be unconscious. Occasionally, *low* scores on such a measure are taken as indices of anxiety, since they are presumed to derive from vigorous defense. Unless other types of data are available, this interpretation is gratuitous: low scoring subjects simply may not be much concerned with death.

Two general conclusions emerge from previous reviews of direct self-report measures (79, 89): (a) insufficient evidence of reliability and validity; (b) relatively rare expressions of high manifest death concern despite widespread acceptance among researchers of the belief that death anxiety is universal. These conclusions remain valid today, although researchers have addressed themselves more systematically to the behavior of their instruments. The relation between different measures of death concern has been examined in two recent studies. Durlak (34) found an average intercorrelation of .52 among four scales, using a sample of 94 undergraduates. Another study with 68 undergraduates yielded an average intercorrelation of .60 among four scales, giving some support to the convergent validity claims of these instruments (30). However, claims of discriminant validity are not warranted on the basis of these data.

Other studies have shown that various fear of death scales are correlated with measures of trait or general anxiety (30, 34, 63, 98). Correlations between various measures of trait anxiety are typically higher than correlations between trait anxiety and death anxiety scales, a phenomenon widely interpreted as evidence of discriminant validity (34, 98, 128, 153, 154). But an alternative view of these data would suggest that fear of death scales simply are poor measures of general (trait) anxiety. This view is supported by a single study which reports both general anxiety and fear of death correlations with a criterion measure (115).

It can also be argued that admitting to a fear of death is socially undesirable. The possibility that social desirability influences the observed relations between death fear and criterion measures cannot safely be ignored (28), although two studies produce inconsistent results on this question (30, 34). Future research in this area should routinely administer both trait anxiety and social desirability measures along with death concern scales, and control for their effects in evaluating results.

There are serious problems with the criteria that have been used to validate death concern scales. Religiosity, for example, often is assumed to indicate need for protection against death fear (88). Even if this were the case, it is not clear whether particularly religious persons would have a high fear of death (which would have intensified their religiosity) or a low fear (as a result of their faith). Given such conceptual unclarity, it is hardly surprising that no consistent relation between religion and manifest death concern emerges, (106). Handal & Rychlak (63), to cite another example, used death images in dream content as a criterion of death fear, although an orthodox Freudian approach would contend that anxiety-provoking material should be excluded from the manifest content of the dream. Throughout this area of research, the relationship between a concept and its measurement often has remained obscure.

Death concerns as measured by self-report have consistently shown no relation to age or demographic characteristics (88, 119). As already noted, only among groups characterized by general psychological disturbance has death anxiety been found to be a prominent concern (26, 156). Nevertheless, the assumption that death anxiety is universal (11) continues to be salvaged from such data through the interpretation that among healthy individuals, death anxiety is successfully defended against, while defenses have broken down among the psychiatrically disturbed. The more parsimonious interpretation that fear of death is an exceptional phenomenon limited to disturbed populations is rarely entertained. While defensive denial of death concerns may or may not characterize most individuals, denial of the evidence seems to characterize many researchers (e.g. 13, 17, 115).

Researchers who take seriously the premise of universal denial, or who are concerned with measuring covert aspects of death concern, often have turned to the use of *indirect* measures—of which an almost bewildering variety have already been explored. Unfortunately, many of the same problems of inappropriate criteria and lack of convergent and discriminant validity evidence are found here as well.

The GSR has been used in several studies since the pioneering work of Alexander, Colley & Adlerstein (3). These studies consistently show that death-related words elicit more autonomic arousal than neutral or basal words (1–3, 21, 44, 58, 101, 155, 164). But it has been more difficult to show differentiation between death-related and other affectively toned words. Autonomic arousal may or may not be accompanied by conscious awareness, and thus cannot be assumed to serve as a reliable index of unverbalized anxiety. Further, the nature of the emotion involved cannot be inferred directly; death may in fact be reacted to not as a source of anxiety, but as a sexually arousing stimulus (120). One study has found a low positive correlation between manifest anxiety and GSR reponse to death words in a psychiatric population (155), not sufficient evidence for confidence in the GSR as a measure of death anxiety, verbal or otherwise.

Other indirect approaches have included the use of latency measures from word association and tachistoscopic recognition tasks (58, 91, 99). The assumption that statistically significant latencies of 3/10 of a second represent defensive processes is a dubious one. While longer latency may indicate some differentiation between death related and neutral words, if it is a defense it is a poor one, affording only a fraction of a second's worth of protection. One study found no relation between a threshold recognition measure and a five-item death anxiety scale, although the predicted relation was found with a second indirect measure based on a semantic differential variance score (58).

At least three published studies have used the TAT (99, 131, 146). The first of these found that a neurotic MMPI profile was characteristic of high death anxiety respondents, who also showed higher somatic concern on the Cornell Medical

Index. A later study reported that only 15 out of 1008 TAT stories involved manifest death concerns (142).

Other indirect measures of unconscious death concern have made use of recalled dream content (63), self-ratings of mood after exposure to neutral, erotic, and death-related reading matter (120), semantic differential scores and sentence completion tasks (146), and word recognition tasks (26, 91, 109).

While the variety of methods introduced for the assessment of death anxiety is commendable and distinguishes this area from some in which a single method is relied upon exclusively, the lack of procedure replication casts some doubt on the validity of the findings. Research on death concerns would benefit from a systematic comparison and cross-validation of direct and indirect measures. Furthermore, it is possible that the focus on "anxiety" or "fear" has led to the neglect of other orientations toward death. The total human interpretation of death is too complex to be subsumed under the concepts most favored by research. Sorrow, curiosity, and even a sense of joyous expectancy are among the orientations that have been observed in nonresearch contexts (74). A broader approach to the meanings of death is indicated, as well as the more cohesive and systematic investigation of "anxiety" or "fear."

The problem of assessing unconscious material is hardly new to psychologists, but rarely has it been handled satisfactorily. Since the hypothesis that death is universally feared is so widely held, there is a temptation to infer "defense" in the absence of manifest fear. High priority should be given to resolving this question since it appears to be at the root of much research in this area.

Denial of death anxiety might be indicated by showing a high indirect demonstration of anxiety attributable to death concern in conjunction with low self reported death anxiety. This approach has not been widely used. Evidence for denial might be sought especially among groups for whom it would have practical significance (e.g. those who fail to make out wills, purchase life insurance, or have regular medical check-ups). Groups with specially relevant characteristics such as these might prove more informative than the college populations which continue to provide the "subject power" for most studies in this area.

An example of sophisticated research which might be taken as a model in the field of death concern is a study by Krieger, Epting & Leitner (83) which elicited 30 personal constructs (80) relevant to death from each respondent. Their measure of death threat was the discrepancy between the respondent's rating of "death" and of "self" on each of these 30 conceptual dimensions. Cognitive orientations proved to be intercorrelated when the Krieger et al "death threat index" was related to other measures of death concern, while affective components remained outside the network of substantial intercorrelations. The cognitive dimensions of death concern appear more amenable to present methodology and might provide a suitable entry point for researchers new to this field.

DEATH AS AN OUTCOME OF BEHAVIOR AND LIFE-STYLE

While all life-styles terminate in death, it is possible that when and how people die can be related to the psychosocial as well as the biomedical context. The spectrum of observations range from well-documented cases of suicide and homicide to subtle and ambiguous phenomena that resist controlled research. We will consider illustrative reports and interpretations from several points along this spectrum.

Deaths that Invite Psychological Explanation

Psychological factors typically receive attention in sudden, unexpected death or in circumstances in which the physical etiology is obscure. This introduces a bias, and also the possibility of fundamental confusion, namely, that there might be two types of death: the "purely physical," and the death with significant psychosocial causation. A more satisfactory alternative is that *all* deaths involve the interplay of psychological, social, and biological processes, just as all lives do (79, 144). However, this position runs counter to established attitudes and practices (e.g. official certification of "causes" of death) and requires more extensive documentation.

"Voodoo death" first received serious attention in the scientific literature when Walter B. Cannon, a distinguished biomedical researcher, collected and attempted to authenticate instances of sudden, apparently psychogenic deaths in Africa, New Zealand, Australia, and Central and South America (20). He noted some recurrent features in these diverse reports: the victims usually were men who died within 24 hours after being condemned, bewitched, or targeted by a "bone-pointing" rite. There were also instances in which counter-suggestions were said to have saved a hexed life. The critical response to such reports (e.g. 9) has questioned the precise mechanisms operative in the deaths, but not the beginning and end points: a psychosocial action followed shortly by death. Any explanation of so-called "voodoo deaths" probably should take into account the cultural belief system shared by hexer and hexed as well as the intervening or concurrent physiological mechanisms. Furthermore, the bidirectionality should not be ignored. If the power of the word, the ritual, the "will of the group" is thought sufficient in some instances to result in death, these influences are also relied upon to preserve life (as in faith healing and protective spells).

Rapid demise without obvious physical causation has been reported in concentration and prisoner of war camps, where a person characteristically seems to "turn his face to the wall, and die" (37). Hospital personnel also describe such phenomena in which a patient, not critically ill, dies soon after some disappointment or frustration has led him to "lose his will-to-live" (160). Although a loose and perhaps naive concept, will-to-live at least points to a process that warrants sophisticated investigation. Seligman's valuable research on the "learned helplessness" syndrome (141) may offer clues to sudden deaths of this type, and perhaps also to the phenomena subsumed under the exotic "voodoo" rubric. The fact that other people on the scene (fellow prisoners, nurses, patients, physicians) often take will-to-live dynamics seriously is itself worthy of attention, apart from whatever attitude one might take to the apparently psychogenic nature of the deaths themselves.

Sudden and unexpected death during psychological stress has also been reported many times in the midst of daily life, but has yet to be examined thoroughly. Engel's analysis of 170 anecdotal reports is a logical place to begin (36). While specifics of the stress differed appreciably, Engel characterized the stimuli as "impossible for the victims to ignore and to which their response is overwhelming excitation or giving up, or both." The trends in his admittedly incomplete data include apparent sex differences in the types of psychological stress most conducive to death, and are worth further examination.

Experienced clinicians believe they are able to distinguish between those who will and those who will not survive stressful treatment modalities on the basis of the patient's psychological state (12), a contention that has some support through controlled research (70, 157). This is an area in which incisive research would be welcomed by the allied health fields.

Statistical data based upon large population samples have raised still another possibility. Dips in the death rate have been found immediately before holidays and other days of particular significance, followed by a "catching up" soon after the important day has passed (46, 104, 124). These studies suggest that some people may have the ability to postpone imminent death for a matter of hours, days, or weeks. The investigators have been properly cautious in their interpretations, and the trends describe large group behavior rather than clearly predicting individual trajectories. Nevertheless, such studies represent another part of the total picture which converging lines of research eventually might put together. There is obviously a need for studies to bridge the gap between case histories and statistical analyses in large population samples.

Consider one more example of deaths that invite psychological explanation. The relocation of aged men and women from one environment to another has been associated with an increased mortality risk since the first studies in this area appeared in the early 1960s (e.g. 4, 27, 93). There is now a substantial research literature on this topic (57, 81, 93, 102, 169). Attention is given to specific influences both in the individual's life and in the environment—as well as the relocation process itself—in attempting to account for the differential mortality risk. The problem is one of much practical as well as theoretical significance, for relocations of the ill or frail aged are commonplace in this nation's present "system" for provision of extended care. The research activity in this field may be providing an alerting function, generating more concern for the well-being of the aged when relocation is in prospect. It seems likely, for example, that how well the relocation process is managed can make an appreciable difference in the risk to life (116), as can the individual's perception of the move as voluntary or involuntary (86). The complex interplay of biological, environmental, and psychosocial (including administrative decision-making) factors makes this an area of both theoretical and humanistic challenge.

Suicide

Self-murder is perhaps the clearest example of death as the outcome of behavior and life-style. And yet much remains unclear about the incidence as well as the dynamics of suicide. Specialists maintain that the true incidence is grossly underestimated by official statistics, a contention that now has some empirical support (45). There has been considerable reluctance to certify suicide as cause of death in some quarters (39). If there is uncertainty about the true incidence of completed suicide, questions of intent and attempt remain even more difficult to answer. It is usually assumed that more people contemplate than attempt suicide, and that more attempt than complete the act. Yet there is no convincing research on the ratios among thinking, attempting, and completing suicide (which may indeed differ among various populations). In this problem area, as in the lifespan development of death thoughts and attitudes, there is a serious lack of integrated longitudinal/cross-sectional research designs. On the basis of a pilot study with an undergraduate population, it is possible that systematic research would reveal a higher incidence of suicidal thoughts and actions than usually assumed (111).

Prediction of suicidal risk has been a major research aim, giving rise to a large and variable literature. Lester, himself a prolific researcher in this field, cast doubt upon the value of most of the available studies in a fairly recent compendium (90). Many studies were dismissed from serious consideration because of such basic flaws in research design as the absence of control groups and of appropriate statistical analyses. The present writers agree that one has to sift through many poorly designed and reported studies to locate those of merit (e.g. 10, 167). The typical "predictive" study often turns out to be a retrospective comparison of attempters and nonattempters within a psychiatric population. Generalizations sometimes are made about completed suicides when the data are limited to attempts. Unfortunately, there is still a tendency to claim that *Identifying Suicidal Potential* (6) is an established science while the research base remains all too modest.

One paradoxical fact makes it especially difficult either to predict suicide or to evaluate the effects of therapeutic interventions. Authorities agree there is "too much" suicide, and yet suicide is also a relatively uncommon event. It is difficult to winnow down the ratio of false positives when attempting to predict critical suicidality within a particular population, and it is also difficult to demonstrate from the incidence of completed suicides whether or not a particular program has made any impact. Certain populations are more at risk (e.g. alcoholics, depressives, the recently bereaved) than others. But clinical experience and expertise seems more useful than available research findings in helping to concentrate limited resources upon those most likely to kill themselves. Similarly, the relatively small number of reported suicides each year even in a major metropolitan area makes it difficult to evaluate the possible effect of a suicide prevention service or other modality of care. It is probable that the clinical art of identifying and reducing suicidality is more effective than can be demonstrated on the basis of existing statistical analytic models. However, the field is much in need of a breakthrough in research strategy. At present one is almost forced into relying either upon respect for case history evidence or skepticism based upon the weak and inconclusive research.

Better documentation of prediction and treatment efforts can be expected if satisfactory answers can be found to ethical and pragmatic problems associated with suicide prevention. Client confidentiality (and often total anonymity) is preserved by suicide intervention services, making follow-up evaluations difficult if not impossible. Studies requiring no-treatment groups also come up against the objection that some individuals might die because treatment has been withheld. Issues such as these are now being examined in depth by the American Association of Suicidology, which is also concerned about the adequacy of treatment services throughout the country. Fortunately, there have already been a few useful studies on the effects of specific treatment modalities with suicidal or self-injurious populations (97). However, studies comparing more than one method appear to be completely lacking. Professional bias against the care of suicide attempters, in the emergency room and elsewhere, has been documented by several studies (130, 162). Value judgments seem to invade the allied health professions' response to suicidal individuals. This is an area in which well-selected and trained volunteers from the community may have an advantage in relating to those in suicidal conflict.

But how is suicide to be *understood?* Apart from the significant questions of prediction and intervention or treatment, suicidal behavior challenges our basic comprehension of human motivation and action. Freud touched upon suicide throughout almost four decades of writing (96), but never integrated his observations into a consistent theory. In one of his better known formulations, Freud saw suicide as a failure to externalize aggressive impulses (50). Menninger (110) reinterpreted this explanation and characterized suicide as the translation of the aggressive wish to kill into a wish to be killed, and finally a wish to die. This view has been found useful by a number of clinicians and educators, although it has not been easy to translate into researchable terms.

More recently, Maurice Farber has offered a general theory in which suicide is characterized as a "disease of hope" (38). On the basis of his own cross-cultural research, Farber believes that "Suicides in the main are committed by psychologically damaged personalities confronted by a deprivational situation." His basic paradigm is written: $S = f (V, D)$. S, the probability of a completed suicide, is a function of the individual's vulnerability and deprivations. In Farber's detailed analysis particular attention is given to hope and hopelessness, concepts deriving from his previous work with Kurt Lewin. Farber's approach is welcome for its lucidity and scope. Unfortunately, the book has already lapsed from print although it was well received by suicidologists. Farber's theoretical orientation might serve as a useful guide for others who are interested in integrating individual and cultural factors in the study of suicide.

The current generation of suicide researchers is displaying a keen interest in the cultural forces that either encourage or inhibit self-destructive behavior (e.g. 32). Hendin has been a leading advocate of the position that each culture or subculture has its distinctive type of suicidality, therefore making it inadvisable to construct a general, culture-free theory (67). He offers vivid and insightful material to support his views, as in his discussions of "black suicide" (66), and a "growing up dead" syndrome he believes characteristic of college student suicidality today (65). However, the link between data and conclusion is tenuous and obscure in much of his work. Some of his conclusions have received uncritical acceptance in the media, but a more guarded reception in the research community.

A comprehensive understanding of suicide requires acquaintance with historical and philosophical traditions of the past (5) as well as a variety of ongoing trends in the area of occupational transitions (130), economics (68), religious belief (88), etc. Fundamentally, however, it just may not be very useful to concoct a general theory of suicide per se. Whatever else suicide might be, it is not an isolated human action. It may be naive to expect suicidal behavior to show much internal consistency when the people and their circumstances vary so extensively. Perhaps the more seminal, if less ambitious approach, is to take suicidal behavior more seriously within more limited realms of psychosocial phenomena, e.g. the meaning of suicide in adolescence and in old age, in role transition and in illness, in family dynamics and in economic adversity. Death by suicide, for all its impact and trauma, might more appropriately be the concern of all psychologists within their own specialty areas, rather than set apart entirely as a specialty area with theories and principles distinct from the field as a whole.

DYING

The plight of the terminally ill person has become the central focus of the current death awareness movement. Through the years a few psychologists have ventured into individual (87) and group (22) treatment of the terminally ill, and the work of pioneering researchers such as Feifel has already been noted. It is only recently, however, that a steady approach has been mounted by psychologists and their colleagues in related fields.

It has not taken long to discover that many of those who relate to the dying person are in distress themselves. Physicians and nurses, as the personnel most frequently in contact with the terminally ill, most frequently have been observed to engage in evasive and other self-protective maneuvers. Awkwardness and discomfort with the terminally ill has been demonstrated so consistently and with such a variety of research approaches that this general conclusion can scarcely be doubted (e.g. 54, 79, 98, 147, 159). For a fine-grained approach to the behavior patterns of staff members, the participant-observation work of Glaser & Strauss (54, 55) is particularly recommended. The Glaser-Strauss contributions include useful conceptualizations of "awareness contexts" and "dying trajectories," although the data themselves are reported in impressionistic terms.

When attention is given to the dying person himself, it is usually to discuss the "stages of dying" presented by Kubler-Ross (85). She states that the terminally ill person at first *denies* the seriousness of his condition. This is followed by *anger* ("Why me?"), with rage likely to be directed at anybody and everybody, including God. Next there is said to be a *bargaining* stage. The individual attempts to make some kind of deal or arrangement with fate. *Depression* follows as energy continues to be depleted by the illness process. There is a sense of great loss and the inevitable finality of one's condition. Finally—if the person passes through all the stages— comes *acceptance.* The struggle is over. Kubler-Ross also emphasizes the persistence of hope in various forms throughout all the stages.

The books and lectures of Kubler-Ross have awakened many to the emotional needs of the dying person. She has offered examples of problems that are likely to arise in relationships with the dying person at each stage, along with suggestions for coping with these problems. Her work has probably been more influential than any other person's in the encouragement of concern for the psychological needs of the terminally ill.

Unfortunately, however, much uncritical and simplistic application has been made of her contributions. The need for quick and reassuring answers to death-related distress seems to have resulted in the premature establishment of the "stages of dying" as the key to understanding and treatment. Psychologists have been reluctant to criticize a contribution that seems to be generating renewed concern for the dying person and to meet the care-giver's need for "something to go on." But critical evaluations are now beginning to appear (75, 139), and they indicate that fundamental problems exist at all levels, from data base through interpretation to practical application.

In brief, the "stages of dying" have been criticized as a very narrow and highly subjective interpretation in which observations and intuitions have been expanded into unwarranted generalizations. The "stages" are poorly defined; no evidence is presented that the same individual actually moves through all the stages; the significance of preterminal personality, developmental level, ethnic orientation and other life history factors is not considered, nor are such critical situational factors as the actual disease process, nature of the treatment, and the sociophysical environment in which the terminally ill person finds himself (74). The "stages" therefore are presented with exaggerated salience, isolated from the total context of the individual's previous life and current situation. This encourages an attitude in which, for example, staff or family can say, "He is just going through the anger stage" when there may, in fact, be specific, realistic factors that are arousing the patient's ire. While researchers are concerned about the weaknesses in description, analysis, and interpretation in stage theory, clinicians are more alarmed by the tendency to convert a questionable theory into a model of the perfect or desirable death.

A terminally ill person—like anybody else—may express denial, anger, a bargaining strategy, depression, or acceptance. But there is serious question that the depth and complexity of the dying person's situation can be understood by reliance upon this alleged sequence of responses.

There are many ways in which psychologists might contribute more to the care and understanding of the dying person and his family, e.g. as teachers of future nurses and physicians, providers of direct or consultative services, and evaluators of programmatic treatment efforts. This last point is worth elaboration. The health care community is showing signs of dissatisfaction with existing styles of care for the terminally ill person. Alternative models are being developed, among which the *hospice* has attracted special attention. The hospice (when fully actualized) is an integrated home-care and hospital-based program devoted entirely to people with advanced life-threatening illness (usually cancer). St. Christopher's Hospice in London is the most noted care system of this type currently in operation (136), while a system modeled along the same lines has recently been established in New Haven (84). Efforts such as these require exceptionally sensitive and sophisticated evaluation. Technical challenges to program evaluation and research are formidable. In addition, the evaluation and research dimensions must be integrated into the total functioning of the hospice without compromising the care-giving objectives. By bringing the best available psychological skills into innovative programs of this kind, it should be possible to influence future decisions that will be made regarding care of the terminally ill person. The lack of first-rate and relevant evaluation could seriously impair the development of an improved care system.

BEREAVEMENT, GRIEF, AND MOURNING

Death, for many people, is neither an abstract, generalized thought, nor concern for personal demise; rather, it is the actual or threatened loss of a significant person. Experiences with bereavement, grief, and mourning are more familiar to most people than are the phenomena of dying. This is reflected as well in the clinical and research literature. Technically, *bereavement* is simply a term indicative of survivorship status. It does not tell us anything about the survivor's actual response to the loss. *Grief* is the expression most often used to characterize the survivor's distressed state. The most vivid descriptions of grief have been made in circumstances of sudden, unexpected death, as in Lindemann's work in the aftermath of the Cocoanut Grove holocaust of 1942 (95). Acute grief often includes somatic as well as cognitive, affective, and behavioral disturbances. There is no gainsaying the pain of grief, although precisely what it "is" has not been firmly established. Switzer, who argues that what we call grief is essentially another term for anxiety, also offers a useful overview of other interpretations of this state (149). *Mourning* refers to the culturally patterned manner of expressing the response to death. Gorer (59) and others suggest that styles of mourning have been changing appreciably during the twentieth century and may still be in transition. Both grief and mourning usually are expected of the bereaved person, but one or both types of response may be either absent or attenuated.

Observations made with increasing frequency over the past few years suggest that bereavement and grief have much more impact than what is evident in the short-term period of acute suffering. Many clinicians have come to believe, for example, that bereavement leaves the individual in a state of heightened vulnerability to physical illness, even to death. There is a growing research literature (not limited to the United States) that gives circumstantial support to this impression (e.g. 19, 100, 122, 123, 149). Bereaved people generally do show more illness and mortality, as well as accidents, unemployment, and other indices of a damaged life. "More than who?", however, is a question asked by the cautious reasearcher. Some of the studies revealing the greatest impairments for the bereaved person employed comparison groups whose relative freedom from illness and mortality could be attributed to factors other than nonbereavement. When a widowed adult is compared with one who is still married, for example, it is not just bereavement that differs but marital status: single adults have a higher mortality rate than the married, even when they have not been bereaved. Nevertheless, the balance of research leads to tentative acceptance of the proposition that bereaved adults are at greater risk than the nonbereaved. Two recent contributions (56, 121) provide sophisticated (although rather brief) overviews as well as new data emphasizing the impact of bereavement on physical and mental health.

We see a particular need at this point for research to clarify the specific ways in which bereaved status and the grief response heighten vulnerability. There are probably a variety of pathways leading from bereavement to illness or death. Is there a breakdown in the body's defense system against cancer at the same time the individual is too depressed to eat, sleep, and take proper care of himself? Do accidents and subintentioned suicides increase because of a desire to be reunited with the deceased as well as reduced competence in operating automobiles and other machinery? Under what conditions does the lack of interpersonal support for the survivor contribute materially to illness and misadventure? These are but a few of the questions that might be raised and which await appropriate investigation.

Two of the most poignant forms of bereavement may also have some of the most powerful effects upon the survivor: the parent who loses a child; the child who loses a parent (52). Rupture of the parent-child relationship can be expected to have important consequences whatever the cause. As a matter of fact, it is only when research takes marital separation and divorce into account as parallel phenomena that the effects of bereavement as such can be fully evaluated. There do seem to be consequences relatively specific to parental bereavement (103), but some otherwise persuasive studies have neglected the relevant comparison groups. Clinicians in general and child development specialists in particular now have some useful contributions available on the dynamics of bereavement for both the individual and the family (e.g. 19, 126).

Two other dimensions of the problem deserve mention even in this very brief review. There has been increasing recognition of a phenomenon known as *anticipatory grief* (137, 138). At times this constellation of thought, feeling, and behavior can be distinguished from the grief of the survivor only by the fact that it is expressed prior to the death. Grief in the anticipation of death perhaps occurs more frequently today because of the shift in mortality from relatively swift causes to the "lingering trajectories" (54) of people with chronic and often multiple disorders. More needs to be learned about the implications of anticipatory grief for the mental and physical health of the survivor-to-be, and for the adjustment to the death when it finally does happen.

There has also been increasing recognition of the parallels between bereavement and other types of significant loss. The dynamics of marital separation, for example, (161) echo some of the phenomena that are salient in the response to death, and perhaps to dying as well. Whatever psychologists have learned about loss and vulnerability in general is likely to be relevant to the understanding of bereavement, grief, and mourning.

A CONCLUDING NOTE

It is unreasonable to expect psychology—either independently or in consort with other fields—to provide quick and sure solutions to the problems associated with death. Nevertheless, there is considerable pressure on mental health specialists and social scientists to explain (or explain away) the death-related phenomena that have become more prominent in our culture's awareness. For years to come we will have the challenge not only of confronting the intellectual and emotional problems in this area, but of maintaining a balance between what is expected or promised and what can be delivered. Yet it is hard to identify a topic more significant to individual and society—or more mind-stretching for those who take up the challenge.

Literature Cited

1. Alexander, I. E., Adlerstein, A. M. 1959. Death and religion. In *The Meaning of Death*, ed. H. Feifel, pp. 271–83. New York: McGraw-Hill
2. Alexander, I. E., Adlerstein, A. M. 1958. Affective responses to the concept of death in a population of children and early adolescents. *J. Genet. Psychol.* 93:167–77
3. Alexander, I. E., Colley, R. S., Adlerstein, A. M. 1957. Is death a matter of indifference? *J. Psychol.* 43:277–83
4. Aldrich, C., Mendkoff, E. 1963. Relocation of the aged and disabled: a mortality study. *J. Am. Geriatr. Soc.* 11:185–94
5. Alvarez, A. 1972. *The Savage God: A Study of Suicide.* New York: Random House
6. Anderson, D. B., McClean, L. J. 1971. *Identifying Suicide Potential.* New York: Behav. Publ.
7. Anonymous 1820. *Annual Report of the Royal Humane Society.* London
8. Anthony, S. 1972. *The Discovery of Death in Childhood and After.* New York: Basic Books
9. Barber, T. X. 1961. Death by suggestion. *Psychosom. Med.* 23:153–55
10. Beck, A. T., Resnick, H. L. P., Lettieri, D. J. 1974. *The Prediction of Suicide.* Bowie, Md: Charles Press
11. Becker, E. 1974. *The Denial of Death.* New York: Free Press
12. Beigler, J. S. 1957. Anxiety as an aid in the prognostication of impending death. *A.M.A. Arch. Neurol. Psychol.* 77: 171–77
13. Bluestone, H., McGahee, C. L. 1962. Reaction to extreme stress: impending death by execution. *Am. J. Psychiatry* 119:393–96
14. Bowers, M. K., Jackson, E., Knight, J., LeShan, L. 1964. *Counselling the Dying.* New York: Nelson
15. Bowlby, J. 1974. *Separation.* New York: Basic Books
16. Brandon, S. G. F. 1967. *The Judgment of the Dead: The Idea of Life After Death in the Major Religions.* New York: Scribner's
17. Brown, D. J. 1972. The fear of death

and the Western-Protestant ethic personality identity. *Diss. Abstr.* 32:7302
18. Budge, E. A. T. W. 1960. *The Book of the Dead.* New Hyde Park, NY: Univ. Books
19. Cain, A. C., ed. 1972. *Survivors of Suicide.* Springfield, Ill: Thomas
20. Cannon, W. B. 1942. "Voodoo" death. *Am. Anthropol.* 44:169–81
21. Carson, W. J. 1974. Modes of coping with death concern. *Diss. Abstr.* 35:815
22. Chandler, K. A. 1965. Three processes of dying and their behavioral effects. *J. Consult. Psychol.* 29:292–301
23. Chellam, G. 1965. The disengagement theory: awareness of death and self-engagement. *Diss. Abstr.* 25:6806
24. Childs, P., Wimmer, M. 1971. The concept of death in early childhood. *Child Dev.* 43:705–15
25. Choron, J. 1963. *Death and Western Thought.* New York: Collier
26. Christ, A. E. 1961. Attitudes toward death among a group of acute geriatric psychiatric patients. *J. Gerontol.* 16: 56–59
27. Costello, J. P., Tanaka, G. M. 1961. Mortality and morbidity in long-term institutional care of the aged. *J. Am. Geriatr. Soc.* 9:959–63
28. Crown, B., O'Donovan, D., Thompson, T. G. 1967. Attitudes toward attitudes toward death. *Psychol. Rep.* 20:1181–82
29. Cumming, E., Henry, W. E. 1961. *Growing Old.* New York: Basic Books
30. Dickstein, L. S. 1976. Attitudes toward death, anxiety, and social desirability. *Omega.* In press
31. Dickstein, L. S., Blatt, S. 1966. Death concern, futurity, and anticipation. *J. Consult. Psychol.* 30:11–17
32. Douglas, J. D. 1967. *The Social Meanings of Suicide.* Princeton, NJ: Princeton Univ. Press
33. Durkheim, E. 1951. *Suicide.* Glencoe, Ill: Free Press
34. Durlak, J. A. 1972. Relationship between various measures of death concern and fear of death. *J. Consult. Clin. Psychol.* 41:162
35. Eliot, T. D. 1930. The adjustive behavior of bereaved families: a new field for research. *Soc. Forces* 8:543–49

36. Engel, G. L. 1971. Sudden and rapid death during psychological stress: folklore or folk wisdom? *Ann. Intern. Med.* 74:771-82
37. Engel, G. L., Schmale, A. H. 1967. Psychoanalytic theory of somatic disorders. *J. Am. Psychoanal. Assoc.* 15:344-65
38. Farber, M. L. 1968. *Theory of Suicide.* New York: Funk & Wagnalls
39. Farberow, N. L., Shneidman, E. S., eds. 1965. *The Cry for Help.* New York: McGraw-Hill
40. Fechner, G. T. 1904. *The Little Book of Life after Death (1836).* Boston: Little, Brown
41. Feifel, H. 1963. The taboo on death. *Am. Behav. Sci.* 6:66-67
42. Feifel, H., ed. 1959. *The Meaning of Death.* New York: McGraw-Hill
43. Feifel, H. 1956. Older persons look at death. *Geriatrics* 11:127-30
44. Feifel, H., Branscomb, A. B. 1973. Who's afraid of death? *J. Abnorm. Psychol.* 81:282-88
45. Ferrence, R. A., Johnson, F. G. 1974. Factors affecting reported rates of self-injury. *Life Threatening Behav.* 4:54-66
46. Fischer, H. K., Dlin, B. M. 1972. Psychogenetic determination of time of illness or death by anniversary reactions and emotional deadlines. *Psychosomatics* 13:170-73
47. Frazer, J. G. 1933. *The Fear of the Dead in Primitive Religions.* London: Macmillan
48. Freud, S. 1959. "Mourning and Melancholia" (1917). *Collected Papers,* Vol. 4. New York: Basic Books
49. Freud, S. 1956. "Our Attitude Toward Death" (1915). *Collected Papers,* Vol. 4. London: Hogarth
50. Freud, S. 1918. *Reflections on War and Death.* New York: Moffat, Yard
51. Fulton, R. J. 1973. *A Bibliography on Death, Grief and Bereavement, 1845-1973.* Center for Death Educ. Res., Univ. Minnesota. 3rd rev. ed.
52. Furman, E. 1974. *A Child's Parent Dies.* New Haven: Yale Univ. Press
53. Gartley, W., Bernasconi, M. 1967. The concept of death in children. *J. Genet. Psychol.* 110:71-85
54. Glaser, B. G., Strauss, A. L. 1968. *Time for Dying.* Chicago: Aldine
55. Glaser, B. G., Strauss, A. L. 1965. *Awareness of Dying.* Chicago: Aldine
56. Glick, I., Weiss, R. S., Parkes, C. M. 1974. *The First Year of Bereavement.* New York: Wiley-Interscience
57. Goldfarb, A. I., Shahinian, S. P., Burr, H. T. 1972. Death rates of relocated nursing home residents. In *Research Planning, and Action for the Elderly,* ed. D. Kent, R. Kastenbaum, S. Sherwood, pp. 525-35. New York: Behav. Publ.
58. Golding, S. L., Atwood, G. E., Goodman, R. A. 1966. Anxiety and two cognitive forms of resistance to the idea of death. *Psychol. Rep.* 18:359-64
59. Gorer, G. 1965. *Death, Grief, and Mourning.* New York: Doubleday
60. Gruman, G. J. 1966. *A History of the Ideas About the Prolongation of Life.* Philadelphia: Am. Philos. Soc.
61. Hall, G. S. 1915. Thanatophobia and immortality. *Am. J. Psychol.* 26:550-613
62. Handal, P. J. 1969. The relationship between subjective life expectancy, death anxiety, and general anxiety. *J. Clin. Psychol.* 25:39-42
63. Handal, P. J., Rychlak, J. F. 1971. Curvilinearity between dream content and death anxiety and the relationship of death anxiety to repression-sensitization. *J. Abnorm. Psychol.* 77:11-16
64. Heibel, A. 1970. *The Gilgamesh Epic and Old Testament Parallels.* Univ. Chicago Press
65. Hendin, H. 1975. Growing up dead: student suicide. *Am. J. Psychother.* 29:327-38
66. Hendin, H. 1969. *Black Suicide.* New York: Basic Books
67. Hendin, H. 1964. *Suicide and Scandinavia.* New York: Grune & Stratton
68. Henry, A. F., Short, J. F. 1954. *Suicide and Homicide.* New York: Free Press
69. Hooper, T., Spilka, B. 1970. Some meanings and correlates of future time and death among college students. *Omega:* 1:49-56
70. Janis, I. L. 1958. *Psychological Stress: Psychoanalytic and Behavioral Studies of Surgical Patients.* New York: Wiley
71. James, W. 1910. *The Varieties of Religious Experience.* Boston: Longmans, Green
72. Jeffers, F. C., Nichols, C. R., Eisdorfer, C. 1961. Attitudes of older persons toward death: a preliminary study. *J. Gerontol.* 16:53-56
73. Jeffers, F. C., Verwoerdt, A. 1969. How the old face death. In *Behavior and Adaptation in Late Life,* ed. E. W. Busse, E. R. Pfeiffer, pp. 163-82. Boston: Little, Brown
74. Kastenbaum, R. 1977. *Death, Society, and Human Behavior.* St. Louis: Mosby
75. Kastenbaum, R. 1975. Is death a life crisis? In *Life-Span Developmental Psy-*

chology: Normative Life Crises, ed. N. Datan, L. Ginsberg, pp. 19–50. New York: Academic

76. Kastenbaum, R. 1974. Childhood: the kingdom where creatures die. *J. Clin. Child Psychol.* 3:11–14

77. Kastenbaum, R. 1959. Time and death in adolescence. In *The Meaning of Death,* ed. H. Feifel, pp. 99–113. New York: McGraw-Hill

78. Kastenbaum, R., ed. 1970. *Omega: Journal of Death and Dying.* Farmingdale. NY: Baywood Publ.

79. Kastenbaum, R., Aisenberg, R. 1972. *The Psychology of Death.* New York: Springer

80. Kelly, G. A. 1955. *The Psychology of Personal Constructs,* Vol. 1. New York: Norton

81. Killian, E. C. 1970. Effects of geriatric transfer on mortality rates. *Soc. Work* 15:19–26

82. Koocher, G. 1973. Childhood, death and cognitive development. *Dev. Psychol.* 9:369–75

83. Krieger, S. R., Epting, F. R., Leitner, L. M. 1974. Personal constructs, threat, and attitudes toward death. *Omega* 5:299–310

84. Kron, J. 1976. Designing a better place to die. *New York Mag.* 1:43–49

85. Kubler-Ross, E. 1969. *On Death and Dying.* New York: Macmillan

86. Lawton, M. P., Yaffee, S. 1970. Mortality, morbidity, and voluntary change of residence by older people. *J. Am. Geriatr. Soc.* 18:823–31

87. LeShan, L., LeShan, E. 1961. Psychotherapy and the patient with a limited life span. *Psychiatry* 24:318–23

88. Lester, D. 1972. Religious behaviors and attitudes toward death. In *Death and Presence: Studies in the Psychology of Religion,* ed. A. Godin, pp. 107–24. Brussels, Belgium: Lumen Vitae

89. Lester, D. 1967. Experimental and correlational studies of the fear of death. *Psychol. Bull.* 67:27–36

90. Lester, D. 1972. *Why Do People Kill Themselves?* Springfield, Ill: Thomas

91. Lester, G., Lester, D. 1970. The fear of death, the fear of dying, and threshold differences for death words and neutral words. *Omega* 1:175–79

92. Lieberman, M. A., Caplan, A. S. 1970. Distance from death as a variable in the study of aging. *Dev. Psychol.* 2:71–84

93. Lieberman, M. A. 1961. Relationship of mortality rates to entrance to a home for the aged. *Geriatrics* 16:515–19

94. Lifton, R. J. 1975. On death and the continuity of life: a psychohistorical perspective. *Omega* 6:143–60

95. Lindemann, E. 1944. Symptomatology and management of acute grief. *Am. J. Psychiatry* 101:141–48

96. Litman, R. E. 1966. Sigmund Freud on suicide. *Psychoanal. Forum* 1:206–20

97. Litman, R. E. 1971. Suicide prevention: evaluating effectiveness. *Life Threatening Behav.* 1:155–62

98. Livingston, P. B., Zimet, C. N. 1965. Death anxiety, authoritarianism and choice of specialty in medical students. *J. Nerv. Ment. Dis.* 140:222–30

99. Lowry, R. J. 1966. Male-female differences in attitudes toward death. *Diss. Abstr.* 27:1607–8

100. Maddison, D., Viola, A. 1968. The health of widows in the year following bereavement. *J. Psychosom. Res.* 12:297–306

101. Magni, K. G. 1972. The fear of death. In *Death and Presence: Studies in the Psychology of Religion,* ed. A. Godin, pp. 25–38. Brussels, Belgium: Lumen Vitae

102. Marcus, E., Blenkner, M., Blum, M., Downs, T. 1972. Some factors and their association with post relocation mortality among institutionalized aged persons. *J. Gerontol.* 27:376–82

103. Markusen, E., Fulton, R. 1971. Childhood bereavement and behavioral disorders: a critical review. *Omega* 2:107–17

104. Marriot, C., Harshbarger, D. 1973. The hollow holiday: Christmas, a time of death in Appalachia. *Omega* 4:259–66

105. Marshall, V. W. 1973. Game-analyzable dilemmas in a retirement village: a case study. *Aging Hum. Dev.* 4:285–92

106. Martin, D., Wrightsman, L. S. 1965. The relationship between religious behavior and concern about death. *J. Soc. Psychol.* 65:317–23

107. Maurer, A. 1961. The child's knowledge of non-existence. *J. Existent. Psychiatry* 2:193–212

108. Mechnikov, I. I. 1901. *The Prolongation of Life.* London: Heinemann

109. Meisner, W. W. 1958. Affective responses to psychoanalytic death symbols. *J. Abnorm. Soc. Psychol.* 56:295–99

110. Menninger, K. A. 1938. *Man Against Himself.* New York: Harcourt Brace

111. Mishara, B. L., Baker, A. H., Mishara, T. 1976. The frequency of suicide attempts: a retrospective approach ap-

plied to college students. *Am. J. Psychiatry.* In press

112. Mitford, J. 1963. *The American Way of Death.* New York: Simon & Schuster

113. Munnichs, J. M. A. 1966. *Old Age and Finitude.* New York: Karger

114. Nagy, M. H. 1948. The child's theories concerning death. *J. Genet. Psychol.* 73:3–27

115. Nogas, C., Schweitzer, K., Grumet, J. 1974. An investigation of death anxiety, sense of competence, and need for achievement. *Omega* 5:245–55

116. Novick, L. J. 1967. Easing the stress of moving day. *Hospitals* 41:64–74

117. Opie, I., Opie, P. 1969. *Childrens' Games in Street and Playground.* London: Oxford Univ. Press

118. Osler, W. 1904. *Science and Immortality: the Ingersoll Lecture, 1904.* Boston, New York: Houghton Mifflin

119. Pandey, R. E., Templer, D. I. 1972. Use of the death anxiety scale in an interracial setting. *Omega* 3:127–30

120. Paris, J., Goodstein, L. D. 1966. Responses to death and sex stimulus materials as a function of repression-sensitization. *Psychol. Rep.* 19:1283–91

121. Parkes, C. M. 1972. *Bereavement.* New York: Int. Univ. Press

122. Parkes, C. M. 1964. Recent bereavement as a cause of mental illness. *Br. J. Psychiatry* 110:198–204

123. Parkes, C. M. 1964. Effects of bereavement on physical and mental health—a study of the medical records of widows. *Br. Med. J.* 2:274–79

124. Phillips, D. P. 1972. Deathday and birthday: an unexpected connection. In *Statistics: A Guide to the Unknown,* ed. J. N. Tannur. San Francisco: Holden-Doug

125. Piaget, J. 1929. *The Child's Conception of the World.* London: Kegan Paul

126. Pincus, L. 1974. *Death and the Family.* New York: Pantheon

127. Plato 1875. Phaedrus. In *The Dialogues of Plato,* transl. B. Jowett, 2:75–160. London: Macmillan

128. Ray, J. J., Najman, J. 1974. Death anxiety and death acceptance: a preliminary approach. *Omega* 5:311–15

129. Rea, M. P., Greenspoon, S., Spilka, B. 1976. Physicians and the terminally ill patient: some selected attitudes and beliefs. *Omega.* In press

130. Resnick, H. L. P., ed. 1968. *Suicidal Behavior: Diagnosis and Management.* Boston: Little, Brown

131. Rhudick, P. J., Dibner, A. S. 1961. Age, personality and health correlates of death concerns in normal aged individuals. *J. Gerontol.* 16:44–49

132. Riegel, K. 1973. Dialectic operations: The final period of cognitive development. *Hum. Dev.* 16:346–70

133. Rochlin, G. 1965. *Griefs and Discontents: The Focus of Change.* Boston: Little, Brown

134. Sabatini, P., Kastenbaum, R. 1973. The do-it-yourself death certificate as a research technique. *Life Threatening Behav.* 3:20–32

135. Safier, G. 1964. A study in relationships between life-death concepts in children. *J. Genet. Psychol.* 105:238–95

136. Saunders, C. 1976. *Annual Report.* London: St. Christopher's Hospice

137. Schoenberg, R., Carr, A. C., Kutscher, A. H., Peretz, D., Goldberg, I., eds. 1974. *Anticipatory Grief.* NY: Columbia Univ. Press

138. Schoenberg, B. B., Carr, A. C., Peretz, D., Kutscher, A. H., eds. 1970. *Loss and Grief.* New York: Columbia Univ. Press

139. Schulz, R., Aderman, D. 1974. Clinical research and the stages of dying. *Omega* 5:137–43

140. Schur, T. J. 1971. What man has told children about death. *Omega* 2:84–90

141. Seligman, M. 1975. *Helplessness.* San Francisco: Freeman

142. Selvey, C. L. 1973. Concerns about death in relation to sex, dependency, guilt about hostility and feelings of powerlessness. *Omega* 4:209–19

143. Shneidman, E., ed. *Suicide* (journal). Morningside Heights, NY: Behav. Publ.

144. Shneidman, E. 1973. *The Deaths of Man.* New York: Quadrangle

145. Shneidman, E., Farberow, N. L. 1965. The Los Angeles Suicide Prevention Center: a demonstration of public health feasibilities. *Am. J. Public Health* 55:21

146. Shrut, S. D. 1958. Attitudes toward old age and death. *Ment. Hyg.* 42:259–66

147. Sudnow, D. 1967. *Passing on: The Social Organization of Dying.* Englewood Cliffs, NJ: Prentice-Hall

148. Swenson, W. M. 1961. Attitudes toward death in an aged population. *J. Gerontol.* 16:49–52

149. Switzer, D. K. 1970. *Dynamics of Grief: Its Sources, Pain and Healing.* Nashville: Abingdon

150. Tallmer, M., Formanek, R., Tallmer, J. 1974. Factors influencing children's concepts of death. *J. Clin. Child Psychol.* 3:17–19

151. Taylor, J. (1651), 1819. *Art of Holy Dying*. London: Longman, Hurst, Reese, Orme & Brown. (op) Reprinted by Arno Press, NY. In press

152. Teahan, J., Kastenbaum, R. 1970. Subjective life expectancy and future time perspective as predictors of job success in the "Hard Core Unemployed". *Omega* 1:189–200

153. Templer, D. I. 1970. The construction and validation of a Death Anxiety Scale. *J. Genet. Psychol.* 82:165–77

154. Templer, D. I. 1970. Religious correlates of death anxiety. *Psychol. Rep.* 26:895–97

155. Templer, D. I. 1971. The relationship between verbalized and nonverbalized death anxiety. *J. Genet. Psychol.* 119:211–14

156. Templer, D. I., Ruff, C. F. 1971. Death anxiety scale means, standard deviation, and embedding. *Psychol. Rep.* 29:174

157. Titchener, J., Zwirling, I., Gottschalk, L. A., Levine, M. 1958. Psychological reactions of the aged in surgery: the reactions of renewal and depletion. *A.M.A. Arch. Neurol. Psychol.* 79:63–73

158. Toynbee, A. 1968. *Man's Concern with Death*. New York: McGraw-Hill

159. Weisman, A. D. 1972. *On Dying and Denying*. New York: Behav. Publ.

160. Weisman, A. D., Kastenbaum, R. 1968. *The Psychological Autopsy: A Study of the Terminal Phase of Life*. New York: Behav. Publ.

161. Weiss, R. 1975. *Marital Separation*. New York: Basic Books

162. Welu, T. C. 1972. Psychological reactions of emergency room staff to suicide attempters. *Omega* 3:103–10

163. Whiter, W. 1819. *The Disorder of Death*. London: Deighton

164. Williams, R. L., Cole, S. 1968. Religiosity, generalized anxiety, and apprehension concerning death. *J. Soc. Psychol.* 75:111–17

165. Wohlford, P. 1966. Extension of personal time, affective states, and expectation of personal death. *J. Pers. Soc. Psychol.* 3:559–66

166. Worcester, A. 1961. *The Care of the Aged, the Dying and the Dead*. Springfield, Ill: Thomas

167. Worden, J. W., Sterling-Smith, R. S. 1973. Lethality patterns in multiple suicide attempters. *Life Threatening Behav.* 3:95–104

168. Zandee, J. 1960. *Death as an Enemy According to Ancient Egyptian Conceptions*. Leiden, Netherlands: Brill

169. Zweig, J. P., Csank, J. Z. 1975. Effects of relocation on chronically ill geriatric patients in a medical unit: mortality rates. *J. Am. Geriatr. Soc.* 23:123–32

Ann. Rev. Psychol. 1977. 28:251–93

HUMAN INFANCY

❖274

Marshall M. Haith and Joseph J. Campos[1]

Department of Psychology, University of Denver, Denver, Colorado 80210

INTRODUCTION AND OVERVIEW

The allocation of a whole chapter in the *Annual Review of Psychology* to "Infancy" is only one of many indications that the field has come into its own. The last half decade hosted a wide variety of books, collections of readings, monographs, and chapters solely dedicated to the infant, a sure sign that there is indeed a field to talk about. Not that it suddenly emerged from nowhere. The 1970 chapter on infancy in Mussen's revision of *Carmichael's Manual* (171) logged in excess of 2000 references, but the recent appearance of large programmatic reports contrasts sharply with the pre-1970s. We pick up here with work published in 1971 and continue through September 1975, with the exception of a number of "in press" manuscripts we had on hand. We were forced by limitation of space and/or knowledge to give partial or no review to several topics—abnormal development, longitudinal, intervention and individual differences studies, language acquisition, orienting, EEG studies, and general methodology. Sex differences were also not considered.

Although our *Annual Review* odyssey has been replete with the traditional agonies (over selection and oversight), resentment (about space limitation), and questioning (of how we got ourselves into this), a half-decade's perspective of the field did emerge. Like Kagan's (159) characterization of development over the first 2 years,[2] we found several themes of change and continuity. One theme concerns the role of theory. In the 1960s, theory in the dominant fields of learning, orienting, and habituation was adult-oriented, "tests" consisting of downward extensions of established principles. By contrast, there are now several examples of conceptions which belong to infancy alone—Piaget's on sensorimotor intelligence, neurophysiological

[1] We thank Bennett Bertenthal, Rosemary Campos, Robert Emde, Kurt Fischer, Susan Harter, Kathy Lochridge, Brian MacWhinney, Morton Mendelson, Bruce Platt, Doug Ramsay, and Phil Salapatek for comments and suggestions on earlier drafts. Betty Richardson typed the manuscript and Kelly Sullivan organized the references. Portions of the work reported here and release time were made possible by grants MH23412 to M. Haith and MH23556 to J. Campos. The co-authors contributed equally to the preparation of this chapter.

[2] For brevity and clarity the ages of infants reported in this chapter are approximate.

approaches to the ontogeny of visual perception, and ethological approaches to mother-infant signaling systems, to name a few.

Change and continuity are also seen in the evolving view of the infant's "competence." No longer does that term quite reflect the aura of wonderment which so many reports had in the 1960s. ("Look what Baby can do!") In many respects it has been replaced by an emphasis on the infant's *limitations,* his subsequent acquisition of competence, and the process of transition between the two. Predictably, this has led to a sharp increase in the number of longitudinal studies of developmental shifts. Nevertheless, competence in a more limited sense still applies to the infant; he is seen as a determiner of his experience as well as considerably more than a "blank tablet" at birth.

A third theme is a shift away from methodological toward more conceptual concerns. The 1960s hosted several impressive technological advances in such physiological measures as EKG, EOG, VER, EEG, in behavior measures such as eye movements and sucking, and in paradigms to study learning, attention, and discrimination. These methods almost defined "experimental child psychology," in contrast to the older and less rigorous field of "developmental psychology." We now see the two fields merging; the methodological product of the last decade is being used to answer classic developmental questions such as those on the origins of intelligence and emotions.

There has been a noticeable loss of self-consciousness about what constitutes "Science." Infancy research in the 1950s and the 1960s often bore the mark of a field seeking acceptance by the world of experimental psychology. Design and procedural elegance often took precedence over considerations about the baby. One example was the concern about selection bias in newborn studies which was handled by random assignment regardless of state; as a result, startle-producing stimuli were required to assure responsiveness from babies who might be sleeping or crying. More recent investigations reflect increasing confidence and common sense. Subjects may be selected only if they are in a particular state (172), stimulus trials may be varied in duration or number depending on the individual subject's behavior (152), and stiff performance criteria may be set for inclusion of a baby's data (118); limits on generalizability are simply acknowledged. In short, the field has developed its own procedural and design personality.

A fifth theme, seen in publications of books, chapters, and monographs, is movement away from single-shot studies toward more programmatic efforts. These do not consist of series of tedious parametric investigations; rather the "parametry" is more conceptual than dimensional. Investigators are striving for prototheories which utilize internal constructs and seem less preoccupied with stimulus-oriented accounts of behavior.

A final theme concerns the emphasis on early infancy, which continues an earlier trend. But no longer does the neonate hold a monopoly, and there seem to be two modal ages of study: 1–4 months and 9–12 months. An age-associated content emphasis still exists; research in the early part of infancy tends to be on the topics of learning, perception, sensation, and memory. Studies of emotional development and cognition concentrate on older subjects.

Our chapter begins with a review of research on sensory functions, followed by perception, attention, habituation, learning, and memory. These sections are concerned almost exclusively with infants in the first one-half year of life. By contrast the following sections, dealing with the areas of cognition and affect, generally concern development between 6 months and 2 years. A word about ground rules. We limited severely our mentioning of authors' names which will produce some inconvenience for the reader. The choice was unavoidable given the span of years and topics covered in the space we were allocated.

Sensory Functions

Research on sensory functions yields to no overarching conceptual theme; investigations typically reflect straightforward attempts to determine the age at which basic skills are attained. Vision maintained its dominant position in this report period as the most studied sense, followed not very closely by audition, with the minor senses lagging well behind.

VISION   The application of established psychophysical and neurophysiological techniques to infant vision increased dramatically. These techniques have been used to study the active and adjustive components of vision as well as the receptive aspects.

Accommodation and binocular vision   One of the most frequently cited and replicated (333) facts of infant vision is that variable accommodation does not occur until about 2 months of age. It was puzzling how the notion of fixed accommodation could fit an early report of similar acuity estimates for newborns over a wide range of target distances (110). A possible resolution was suggested in three recent reports which indicated that 2-month-olds do not respond to spatial frequencies greater than about 3 cycles/degree (13,265–267). (Adults respond up to 30–40 cycles/degree.) Salapatek and his co-workers suggested that the mature accommodation system may utilize high spatial-frequency information for focusing which the immature system may not detect; if so, poor accommodation may reflect limits on sensitivity rather than adaptability. An implication of these findings is that object distance is not as crucial in visual studies as has been supposed. Whatever the case, 1- to 3-month-olds suck appropriately to clear up a fuzzy movie they are watching and look less when it goes out of focus (161).

Information about the developmental course of binocular vision is limited. Somewhat contradictory data have been reported from studies employing corneal reflection techniques to estimate degree of convergence (286). This technique requires exact knowledge about the relation between the optical and geometric axes of the infant eye for precise specification of fixation point; unfortunately, this knowledge does not exist (204, 268, 286, 287). Since even a minute amount of deconvergence between the two eyes prevents stereopsis (less than 10' of visual angle for the adult), this technique may never be precise enough for the task. Most estimates put the achievement of binocular vision before 5 months and some even in the first days (288). A retrospective report (15) indicates that there may be a critical period for attainment of stereopsis. Subjects with surgically corrected congenital esotropia were more likely to achieve stereopsis if the operation was done prior to 2 years of age.

Peripheral vision   The human retina is not uniformly sensitive across its surface as greater receptor density in the central foveal area than in the peripheral areas permits greater resolution. Considerable interest has centered on the functional division of effort that exists between the foveal and peripheral areas. The fovea is believed to be crucial for form discrimination and identification whereas the peripheral retina is highly sensitive to movement, spatial location, and gross shape of forms (49). Little is known about the functional capacities of peripheral vision in infants, but even newborns make directionally appropriate eye movements to peripheral stimuli whether they are scanning an edge (172) or responding to onset of light (142). However, the range over which they respond appears to increase over the first few months, and location saccades become faster (12, 142, 316). Although we can conclude that peripheral vision is functional quite early, we have no information about how peripheral and foveal functioning are integrated at various ages— whether, in fact, a division of processing effort exists at an early age.

Color vision   The most frequent question asked the psychologist of infant vision is "Can a newborn see?"; a confident yes is rapidly followed by "When do babies see color?". The answer to the question has been of interest for over 100 years. We still do not know for sure, but a bevy of studies indicates at least by 2 to 4 months. These studies serve as a marvelous example of conceptual convergence and procedural diversity. The additional convergence of time (all were published or presented in 1974 and 1975) suggests a true *zeitgeist* in color vision. A major difficulty in testing color vision in any organism is the deconfounding of intensity and wavelength differences. Color scales equated for intensity for the human adult are available, but variation exists for particular individuals, and there is no assurance that the intensity-color functions hold for infants. There is special reason for questioning adult-infant similarity in the short-wavelength region because the lens yellows with age, selectively filtering these colors. Brighter stimuli are usually preferred by infants (e.g. 276), and at least by 2 months they respond to bar-ground intensity differences as slight as 0.08 log units (241). Some of the technicalities involved can be quickly appreciated by reading a recent exchange (105, 337).

The intensity-wavelength confound dampened color vision research until the recent burst of investigations. One approach estimated the intensity-wavelength function for the infant and varied the intensity relation between two colors so broadly that the intensity relations must have reversed at some point (241, 276). Since color discrimination persisted across the full band of intensity relations, hue must have been the critical dimension. Another study (232) used 3 X 3 matrices of squares, eight of which were achromatic and varied in brightness from black to white; the ninth was either a color patch or still another achromatic patch. Clear preference for the "color" matrices was found. Other approaches finessed or ignored the brightness problem. Checkerboards comprised of two hues became more attractive as the wavelength differences between the hues increased (105). Still a different approach (32) compared adult and infant color preferences. A close match was obtained with maximum preferences close to the center of primary color categories and minimum preferences near category boundaries. After habituation to a standard hue, infant looking recovered less to a second hue which remained within an adult-defined color category than to a hue which crossed the intercategory boundary despite the fact that both dishabituation cues were an equal number of wavelengths from the standard (33). The most parsimonious interpretation of all these findings is that infant color vision is similar to that of the adult at least by 4 months.

Movement   Although movement has historically occupied an important role in theories of visual perception, few infant studies have been carried out. Stable individual differences in visual tracking exist at birth (18), some aspects of which correlate with tracking and attention at later ages (19). A moving edge is a high attention-getter for newborns (132), and movement enhances attractiveness of real faces (24, 61) for older infants.

AUDITION   It seems as though researchers in audition have an advantage over those in vision, at least in stimulus presentation, but one finds the usual number of technical and interpretive problems here. What can be purer than a pure tone sine-wave stimulus? Yet investigators disagree not only about whether young infants discriminate sine-wave frequencies, but also about whether pure tones are even heard. For example, Turkewitz, Birch & Cooper (318) found no sensitivity by newborns to a wide frequency range of fairly loud (90 dB) brief pure tones whereas more "complex" wide-band white noise was effective. On the basis of these findings pure tones were deemed as probably "totally ineffective." These findings supported earlier work, and in turn were supported by a report of no discrimination between widely varying tones in infants as old as 4 months (314). However, the conclusion was probably premature. Studies which have exerted more precise control over state and used stimulus durations longer than 1 sec have obtained pure-tone responding in newborns which is as strong as the response to white-noise bands (165); further, pure-tone discrimination has been demonstrated as early as 1 month (289, 336). When one ventures ever so slightly from the pure sine-wave tone to square-wave pulses, for example, the methodological complexity increases dramatically (11, 23, 155). Because of speaker characteristics, square-wave electrical pulses generate broadband acoustic frequencies; the lower the square-wave frequency, the broader the band. Since frequency sensitivity and bandwidth sensitivity are confounded, it is difficult to interpret either positive or negative findings of a frequency discrimination study using square-wave stimuli. [The situation is complicated by a bewildering array of other factors which the reader can appreciate by a small set of articles (11, 23, 155).]

Hutt (155) proposed that most data on frequency sensitivity suggest that the greater the proportion of the basilar membrane stimulated, the greater the response. More faithful transmission of low-to-middle frequency stimuli by the relatively flaccid eardrum and ossicle of the newborn makes him more sensitive to these frequencies. This consideration raises an interesting question which parallels the extended difficulty researchers have confronted in attempts to demonstrate color vision. That is, if varying frequencies are not transmitted equally faithfully to the basilar membrane, how does one know that differential responding to frequency is not dependent on intensity differences? For some reason this consideration has not been extensively treated, but interested workers may want to take a page from the history of research on color vision; the applicability of paradigms and techniques to sound-frequency discrimination seems obvious.

TASTE, SMELL, AND TOUCH   Only a handful of studies on the "minor" senses appeared, all with newborns. Sucking rate was used to index a preference of sucrose over glucose (100). An earlier report of olfactory sensitivity to asafoetida, lavender, and valerian was supported (280), and surprisingly subtle discrimination was demonstrated between aliphatic alcohols equated for subjective intensity and differing only in the length of the carbon chain (261). Finally, newborns were reported to be more sensitive on the right than left side to tactile stimuli in the perioral region (136).

Our review of infant sensory research reveals a heavy emphasis on vision which in part simply reflects the general interest of psychologists in man's "primary sense." However, progress in vision also reflects clever adaptation of established psychophysical techniques to infant paradigms. We hope the message is heard by researchers interested in the other senses. Work in audition especially could be on the threshold of significant progress.

Perception

Early perception continues to intrigue researchers with form and face perception as dominant subareas. But new forays into space and depth perception, the interaction between visual and auditory perception, and the development of information-acquisition strategies have also appeared. Compared to the frankly empirical work on sensory function, research in perception is often undertaken with one eye on implications for cognitive development and another on implications for brain maturation with changes around 2 months of age attracting special interest.

VISUAL PERCEPTION   Several comprehensive reviews and conceptual contributions in early pattern and form perception appeared (31, 108, 135, 148, 164, 265).

Pattern and form perception   There is general consensus that before approximately 1½ months the infant processes elements of form but is insensitive to visual organization or configuration (31, 108, 135, 265). Sensitivity to contour has been documented at birth both by measures of visual preference and detailed scanning (135, 172). Bond (31), Fantz, Fagan & Miranda (108), and Salapatek (265) have suggested that patterns which have a high potential for triggering visual cortical cells (in area 17) are given priority, and Haith (135) has argued that newborn visual scanning obeys a principle of maximizing neural firing (to an asymptote). This interpretation accommodates a wide variety of findings: scanning of newborns in darkness and in patternless fields; fixation and crossing of contour; early preference for contour density and high contrast stimuli; and later development of accommodation and binocular fixation (135).

The demonstrated power of contour density to control early visual behavior fits a cortical firing hypothesis, but the majority of evidence is based on studies using checkerboard patterns. An often cited and replicated finding of early preference of an acute angle over a straight edge seemingly challenges the idea that contour density alone controls early visual behavior. However, because two edges lie in close proximity for an acute angle, the angle may actually comprise more contour density than the edge; in fact, the preference does not hold for right angles (135). Studies using other types of stimuli demonstrated that factors other than contour density are operative early. Fantz & Fagan (107) deconfounded the changes in element size and number which accompany manipulation of density with checkerboard stimuli. Size of element was most important before 1 month and then decreased while the importance of number of elements increased. A recent report of newborn preference for curved contour (109) is also not easily accommodated by a contour density hypothesis.

Most accounts of visual behavior have considered only the parameters of the stimulus. It is also important to consider the relation between patterns and the young infant's scanning capabilities. For example, because newborns scan primarily along the horizontal axis, the particular location of vertical edges in the field is relatively uncritical, but a horizontal edge as much as 18° off center is not scanned (172). The problem is not insensitivity or lack of preference for horizontal contour, because a centered horizontal edge does engage scanning (135). Thus "contour" is more or less effective depending on its match to the baby's scanning ability. A methodological caution is worth mentioning: preference for some patterns over others may reflect differences in the location of critical elements with respect to a narrow vertical scanning window (as eyes in upright vs inverted faces) rather than differences in perceptual appeal.

Intriguing changes in form responsiveness have been reported around 2 months of age. Before this time infants neither scan internal features of a form nor appear to detect a change in an internal feature (108, 214, 264). Whereas 1-month-olds principally scan external features of an adult's face, such as the chin-garment or hair-skin border, 1½- to 2-month-olds scan the internal features, mostly the eyes (24, 205); further, they scan internal form features and detect both internal and external change (108, 214, 264). A second transition, probably related to the first, is that infants become more sensitive to organization or configuration of form as shown by differentiation of such pattern characteristics as linearity-curvilinearity, regularity-irregularity, concentricity, number of line directions, and orientation of elements (75, 108, 263). Whether sensitivity to configuration per se is at issue is difficult to say as infants near the same age do not seem to pick out aspects of patterns that would be predicted on the basis of whole-pattern sensitivity. An odd element in a matrix (say a line or triangle in a matrix of squares) immediately attracts the adult's attention as well as that of 2½- and 3½-year-olds. Yet extensive efforts to demonstrate similar attraction in 2- to 3-month-olds have not proved successful (265).

Research on infant form and pattern perception has made significant strides in this review period. However, the absence of a satisfactory metric of form continues to hamper researchers. Clarity has not been achieved on exactly what constitutes a "configuration" for the baby in the gestalt sense. Often, evidence for "configurational" responding can as easily be attributed to sensitivity to local interactions between elements of patterns. Finally, more work is needed on the role of three dimensionality in form perception as well as on perception of real objects. The role that meaning plays in object perception has also been ignored.

Space perception Objects in the real world occupy locations with respect to a multitude of other objects. The "visual frame" has characteristics of upness, downness, rightness, leftness, and farness, properties typically considered under the rubric of "space." Although most studies in infant perception ignore these facts, infant space perception is a venerable topic having its roots in the nativist-empiricist controversies. Helmholtz argued long ago that newborn babies had no sense of direction or location, locating the mother's breast or a candle only through trial-and-error head and eye movements. Helmholtz was probably wrong. Newborns make directionally appropriate, if sluggish, eye movements to stimuli presented peripherally (142), an ability which becomes reasonably smooth and efficient by 1 month of age (12).

Depth perception has been studied both in terms of infant sensitivity to distance and object solidity. Even nonmobile infants show cardiac responding to the deep side of a visual cliff (57), and babies as young as 1½ months show declining visual preference for objects as distance extends beyond 30 cm (212). Either real solid objects or photographic representations of solid objects are discriminated from flat objects at 2 months of age (108). Findings also indicate sensitivity to solidity before then; when depth cues are added to a complexity series, newborns' preferences are shifted from that shown for a two-dimensional set (158). Also, a bar stimulus in depth is looked at more than one flat against its background by 1-month-olds and scanned differently by 2-month-olds (245). Finally, after 2-month-old infants were habituated on a 2D projection of a stimulus, a stereoscopic version produced dishabituation (9).

Although less heavily researched, orientation and movement are also related to space perception. By 2 months, infants learned a vertical-horizontal discrimination (211), and by 6 months they responded to or ignored a new orientation of an object depending on whether they had seen it in varying orientations or not (209). Finally, 2-month-olds found movement of an object with respect to its ground more attractive than movement of both together, suggesting sensitivity to object-field relations (141).

Somewhat more complicated is the question of intercoordination of spatial information from different modes. The traditional English, Russian, and Piagetian positions hold that such cross-modal integration occurs only through experience. However, the newborn moves his eyes in the direction of a laterally displaced voice and will scan a spatially congruent visual stimulus (213); as the voice continues to change but the visual stimulus remains constant, the newborn eventually looks elsewhere, possibly for a changing stimulus. Perhaps a congenital bias exists to respond to sound in a spatially appropriate visual manner, but flexibility is also present to learn about auditory-visual relations which may not be spatially consonant. In a related study (10), presentation of mother-face combinations which were directionally congruent or noncongruent produced more distress (tonguing) in the noncongruent condition in 1- to 2-month-olds. However, correction of several methodological errors eliminated the interesting findings (210). Lyons-Ruth (201) found that 4-month-olds who were first presented sound-object combinations were later surprised when one or the other elements occurred alone.

The topics considered in this section form a loose set even when rationalized as components of space perception. Our impression is that studies have often not been guided by a general theory of spatial perception in infancy. The problem is that few are clear on what the topic should include, which is probably no surprise since the physical sciences have also found easy definition elusive. Yonas & Pick (338) have written a much needed discussion of the conceptual and methodological issues involved in understanding this topic as well as a review of recent literature. There is need for more conceptual discussion of what this topic implies. A rereading of Gibson's (126) elegant description of the visual world with which the infant must learn to cope gives one the impression that past attempts have been much too confined. Hopefully, the importance of this topic will be matched by future increments in research activity and conceptualization.

Face perception   Although the meaningless stimuli used in most experiments satisfy the need for rigorous stimulus control, they often lack environmental validity. The logic that competencies, such as configurational responding, might emerge earlier for naturally occurring events than for artificial ones has no doubt motivated much of the interest in facial responsiveness. In some cases the ecologically-valid real face has been augmented by natural movement (61) and by an equally valid real voice (24). As mentioned earlier, babies under 7 weeks scan the external hair-skin and chin-garment borders (high contrast areas) of the real face, whereas older infants principally scan the eye area (24, 205). Contrary to expectation, when the adult speaks (increasing lip movement and lip-tooth contrast) mouth looking does not increase but intensification of scanning in the eye area sometimes does (24), suggesting that eye attraction may not be based on physical parameters alone and that scanning routines are affected by acoustic input. A similar study combined a photograph of a face or a highly stylized face-like picture with tones or a voice and replicated some of these findings but found few voice-tone differences (86). Final opinion concerning whether or not the voice enjoys special status should be reserved until this study is repeated with real faces. A similar reservation could be raised for an extensive study of response to graphically represented facial features. Here evidence was obtained in 4- to 5-month-olds that the shape of the head is more salient than internal features and that the mouth area approaches the level of salience of the eye area only at about 5 months (59). A methodological advance by

Papoušek & Papoušek (234) permits investigation of how infants respond to their own face when contingent movement and eye-contact are varied and should generate even more interest in how babies respond to natural stimuli.

Two visual systems   Recent attention has been given to the neurophysiological components of vision in attempts to explain the changes that occur in form and depth perception in the second month (49, 88). A distinction has been made between two major visual pathways: the retinal-geniculate striate-cortex path serving the primary visual system and the phylogenetically older retinal-colliculus path (with projections via the pulvinar to the prestriate and temporal cortex) which serves the second visual system. It has been argued (49, 88) that the second, subcortical visual system, which is concerned with spatial location, has principal control over activity until the second month, and that the primary system, concerned with form and detail, is virtually nonfunctional before that time. One implication of this argument is that the newborn has a blind macula and hence, "doughnut vision." This interpretation is presumably supported by records of repeated fixations by newborns which cross edges, a consequence of their attempt to place edges on a blind fovea. Space does not permit an adequate treatment of this thesis, but we caution against uncritical acceptance of such a dichotomy to "explain" age shifts and offer these observations: (*a*) Weiskrantz (329) recently criticized the two visual system idea as too simplistic; recent neuroanatomical work has revealed a far more complicated set of structures and interconnections than originally believed; (*b*) neuroanatomical data on the retina used to support the argument have been called into question (135); (*c*) it appears that the newborn primary visual system is functional from visual evoked response data; (*d*) newborns are less likely and slower to locate a peripherally appearing stimulus if a central one remains than if the central one disappears (142), also suggesting that foveal vision is functional; (*e*) the newborn's peripheral-location ability, presumably mediated by the second visual system, is not impressive; whereas adult response time to a peripheral light is on the order of 200 msec, newborns took up to 5 sec to make an initial response to a peripheral stimulus (142); (*f*) it is unreasonable to assume that the newborn would be wired to relocate contours repetitively on a blind fovea or not to use pathways known to be functional. The two visual system argument rightly calls attention to the neural substrate of visual behavior, but reintroduces an old subcortical-cortical dichotomy to distinguish the newborn and older infant. It may be more fruitful to recognize that all neural systems in early infancy are immature (Parmelee, personal communication). The task is to describe how those immature systems are orchestrated.

SPEECH DISCRIMINATION   Exciting developments have occurred in the area of speech discrimination. Sophisticated electronic sound-generating gear has been coupled with sensitive measurement techniques to examine infant discrimination between speech sounds that differ in only one definable aspect. The evidence indicates that infants are sensitive to phonemic contrasts at a very early age, which poses a serious threat to theories that claim that such discrimination is learned only by imitation or selective reinforcement (221). Consider two synthetic speech sounds, "bah" and "gah," both of which last 250 msec and are produced by identical first (F1) and third (F3) formants. The difference is produced in the second (F2) formant over the first 55 msec; for "bah" the frequency rises gently then plateaus, whereas for "gah" the frequency drops sharply and then plateaus. Infants 5 to 6 months old were first habituated to one of these sounds. When the second sound was presented, dishabituation occurred as measured by cardiac deceleration (221). A more sensitive procedure has been successful in uncovering even more dramatic auditory competence. The experimenter first measures the range of amplitudes with which the infant sucks a pacifier. Then a criterion level is set and only above-criterion sucks control presentation of a syllable. Infants typically increase high-amplitude sucking (HAS) for a while and then decrease, presumably as the reinforcing value of the first syllable declines. After above-criterion sucking declines below some preset level, a sound-contrast is presented; if HAS rate increases reliably, it is inferred that the new sound was discriminated from the old. The HAS procedure has revealed sensitivity to consonant contrasts of [ba] - [ga], [pa] - [pi], and [ta] - [ti] as early as 1 month of age (228, 315), as well as to the intonational contrast of [ba-] - [ba+], the first reflecting a falling voice and the second a rising voice (228). The vowel sounds [a] - [i] and [i] - [u] are also discriminated (314). These discriminations seem truly remarkable in light of earlier theory. Findings do not appear to be a function of some artifact associated with "machine sounds," as natural sound contrasts similar to those used in synthetic-sound studies have produced comparable results (315).

Do these findings mean that babies "hear" phonemes as such as early as 1 month, or is it possible that these findings only reflect discrimination along a sound continuum? Apparently there is something more going on than simple discrimination along a continuum. Take two sounds [pa] - [ba] which differ only in the timing of F1. For [pa] the onset of F1 lags behind the onset of F2 and F3 by about 100 msec; for [ba] the lag is only 10 msec. These particular sounds have categorical features; that is, adults hear the same syllable even though the F1 onset times vary as long as the critical boundary of about 20 msec is not crossed. Thus one can ask what will happen if an infant is habituated to one sound, say [pa], and the F1 onset time is either decreased so as to cross the critical boundary or increased an equal amount, thereby remaining within the subjective adult category. One- to 5-month-olds respond more dramatically to the cross-boundary shift (92), indicating that in some respects babies respond to these sounds like adults. However, these dramatic findings may not imply that humans are specially wired to hear speech. Since similar findings have been uncovered with chinchillas (185), they may only say that speech sounds were developed to accommodate constraints of the acoustic system. Eisenberg (93), in a comprehensive treatment of auditory competence in early infancy, noted that the phonemic competence demonstrated so far can be accounted for by five acoustic variables to which many species are sensitive. One can expect interesting comparative-developmental work in this area in the next several years.

Hemispheric specialization   A related topic concerns the ontogeny of function of the cerebral hemispheres, which in adult man are differentially specialized to process verbal and spatial information (84). Controversy has arisen over whether specialization is present at birth (101, 222, 223) or emerges with the development of language and maturation of the brain (193).

Recent evidence favoring innate or preverbal lateralization has come from findings of anatomical differences in the planum temporale of neonates, part of the brain involved in language reception in adults (311, 324, 335). Behavioral evidence for early cerebral specialization has been provided by an adaptation of a dichotic listening task for use with infants (101), and by auditory evoked potentials recorded from neonates and older infants (222, 223). Other evidence comes from results on photic driving (78) and head orientation bias in neonates (319). Lesion studies, taken by some to suggest development of lateralization, are now more often being interpreted as reflecting a decrease in compensatory potential by other areas of the brain with increasing age, rather than an increase in lateralization (146, 174, 175).

However, the behavioral studies should not yet be taken as conclusive on the issue of early or innate cerebral specialization. After an initial flurry of positive results with adults in the early 1970s, many recent studies have failed to link evoked potentials to lateralization (121, 123, 309, 310). Other reports have noted that dichotic listening tasks can confound very different levels of linguistic processing (246). The use of a simple converging operation such as the direction of eye movements following stimulation (173, 277) may prove fruitful in answering questions regarding the ontogeny of hemispheric specialization. No infant studies we know of have yet tried this approach.

Attention

Since Fantz's introduction of the preference looking paradigm, psychologists have expended a tremendous amount of effort toward understanding infant attention. In the early 1960s interest shifted from what stimuli the baby *could* respond to, to what stimuli he chose to respond to. Optimism was high that it would only be a matter of time before the attractiveness hierarchy of visual dimensions would be known as well as how it changed with age. This information was expected to be crucial to a theory of the development of perceptual and cognitive organization through infancy. Investigators quickly turned away from the lowest-level physical parameters as major organizers of infant attention and focused on constructs which considered the baby's experience. Three major "theories" guided work—novelty theory, discrepancy theory, and complexity theory.

NOVELTY   Prior to this review period, stimulus novelty had been shown to govern infant attention beyond 2 months of age. Findings from more recent work agreed (73, 262, 331) and demonstrated that novelty effects increase over the first months of life (137, 330, 332). Some new research trends also emerged. Hunt (153) had proposed that the act of recognition might itself be reinforcing in early infancy whereas novelty might become reinforcing in later infancy as recognition becomes commonplace. The prediction of a shift in attention from the familiar to the novel around 2 months received some support from Cohen's laboratories (330, 332). However, Milewski & Siqueland (215), using a reinforcement paradigm (the HAS procedure), reported that 1-month-olds found a changed, novel stimulus more reinforcing than a familiar one. These studies differed along many dimensions, but a critical factor may have been the more extensive familiarization of infants in the latter. Perhaps the criterion for rejection of familiarity simply declines with age. A second trend was toward expansion of the age range into the second year of life and, consequently, into the realm of locomotion, play, and responsiveness to novel humans. Ten-month-olds smiled more at a novel adult than to a familiarized one (91), and 12-month-olds left their mothers to explore novel rooms and toys even in a strange laboratory after only 5 min of familiarization (258, 260); approach to strange toys was even faster in a novel than a familiar environment (239). Finally, toys that offered more variety both acoustically and physically were preferred play objects for 7½- to 11½-month-olds (206).

DISCREPANCY   The discrepancy theory of attention asserts that the infant forms schemas of objects and events through experience (159). Attention is governed by the degree of discrepancy from an established schema because it reflects the infant's effort to assimilate the discrepant event to the schema. If the stimulus is close to the established schema, little time is required for assimilation. If it is too discrepant, the infant will soon give up because a fit can not be accomplished. Maximal attention should occur to a stimulus with an intermediate, optimal level of discrepancy, at least after 6 to 8 weeks of age. Before this time physical parameters of stimuli are held to predominate.

Discrepancy and novelty theories agree that the relation between the particular stimulus and the infant's representation of similar stimuli is crucial. However, discrepancy theory differs from novelty theory in predicting a curvilinear relation between the degree of difference and attention; additionally, discrepancy theory places emphasis on the categorical relation between schema and discrepant stimuli whereas novelty theory does not. These differences are noteworthy inasmuch as the term "discrepancy" has become increasingly broad and fuzzy, at times meaning no more than novelty or change (151, 331).

Two studies were carried out to test the discrepancy position. Four-month-olds who were exposed to a mobile for 3 weeks at home yielded an inverted-U looking curve to a standard stimulus as a function of its discrepancy from the home mobile (308). In the second study (341), the looking time of 7½-month-olds increased as the shape of comparison objects varied systematically from a standard, but declined to an extreme comparison which differed multidimensionally from the standard. Unfortunately, both of these studies were flawed, the former providing no compelling a priori definition of discrepancy, the latter providing no separate evaluation of the attractiveness of the extreme variation. In a less vulnerable study (208) 3- to 4½-month-olds were first habituated to either a set of arrows pointing up and down or left and right. Independent groups were then shown 30°, 60°, or 90° rotations of the arrow. Clearly, "discrepancy" was tied to a convincing dimension. Unfortunately, the findings were ambiguous. Fast habituators yielded the predicted inverted-U curve as a function of angle of rotation, but slow habituators produced a monotonically increasing response with increasing rotation.

COMPLEXITY AND CONTOUR DENSITY   Complexity theory, introduced by Dember & Earl (82), portrays the baby and the stimulus world in terms of points along a complexity continuum. "Pacer" stimuli which are optimally beyond the baby's complexity point are processed, whereas those too close are ignored because they are boring and those too distant because they cannot be processed. Because the processing of a pacer stimulus moves the baby forward on the complexity continuum, the theory predicts attention shifts toward increasingly more complex stimuli with age. Complexity theory shares with discrepancy theory the notion of an optimal point on a dimension and the consequent prediction of an inverted-U relation between attention and the dimension. However, complexity theory is not concerned with the infant's representation of past experience or the relation between stimulus and schema. Rather, the relation between the infant's current "set point" for information flow and the amount of information provided by the stimulus are of primary concern. Earlier findings of preference for intermediate-complexity checkerboards by young infants (1½ months) and for high complexity checkerboards by older infants were confirmed (71, 131). Before this review period, several investigators suggested that complexity manipulations had confounded variation in number of checks with variation in amount of contour. Karmel, in particular, argued that complexity data could be handled by assuming that babies respond to contour density (the total length of black-white contour in the stimulus), preferring increasing density with age (e.g. 162). This more parsimonious explanation was supported by evidence that randomization of location of the checks in a checkerboard stimulus, a factor substantially increasing complexity, had no effect on preference that could not be predicted from variation in contour density. Karmel organized results of several studies by plotting preference as a function of contour density for several age groups. These plots revealed that preference was a curvilinear function of the square root of contour density and that peak preference occurred at greater densities with increasing age after 1½ months. Contour density predicted less well for infants under 1½ months (164).

Unfortunately, complexity has rarely been manipulated with stimulus sets other than checkerboards. Greenberg & O'Donnell (131) did vary complexity of three different stimulus patterns—checkerboards, stripes, and dots—with 6- and 11-week-olds. Generally, the usual checkerboard functions were replicated with the two other sets. However, pattern effects and pattern-complexity interactions were obtained; since each complexity level had been equated for amount of contour across patterns, they argued that the effects could not be handled exclusively by a contour density interpretation. (Incidentally, this finding was just as damaging to an exclusive complexity interpretation.) Karmel (162) pointed out that their calculation of contour density had not included the black-white border of the stimulus panels; his recalculation presumably accommodated their data to his family of age curves. However, careful examination of the fit of their data to Karmel's theoretical function reveals substantial discrepancy with several ordinal reversals. Examination of the original data suggests strongly different pattern-density functions at least for 11-week-olds, so it appears that type of pattern as well as complexity and amount of contour affect looking in this age range.

Stronger evidence for complexity as an important dimension might be obtained by interpreting it in its information-theory sense as uncertainty. But contrary to prediction, when the spatial and temporal predictability of a flashing light sequence were varied, suppression of limb-movement (an index of attention) was greatest for the most predictable and most unpredictable levels (74). The authors stressed the importance of analyzing the baby's attempts to process the episodes rather than the question of which stimulus dimension was operative. Specifically, it appeared that the intermediate uncertainty level engaged subjects in attempts to anticipate the light flashes; the nonsuppression of movement may have reflected frustration from erroneous anticipations.

To sum up, there is some evidence in favor of all the theories proposed to date —novelty, discrepancy, complexity, and a new offshoot, contour density. The suggestion that all factors control attention should not strain credibility, but we have yet to uncover serious treatment of such a possibility. Although each position has supporting evidence, there are aspects of each which do not make sense or are troublesome. The contour-density position predicts poorly before 1½ months, but well between 1½ and 6 months. We would expect just the opposite because the definition of density—amount of contour—makes no provision for *arrangement* of contour and thus cannot handle the increasing responsivity to pattern organization after 1½ months or the special appeal of faces around 4 months of age. Perhaps contour density predicts performance for infants beyond 1½ months only when other attractive options are not available. Haith (135) argued that a definition of contour density which considers limits on scanning ability might accommodate the findings on infants younger than 1½ months.

Novelty and discrepancy theories share the problem of definition. Typically, an internal "standard" is established by presenting one stimulus followed by comparison stimuli. However, the internal comparison may not be what the experimenter supposes. The infant may compare against any of a number of other internal standards especially when an extreme novel or discrepant variant is presented. Discrepancy theory has provided no rules by which new schemas are invented since stimuli which do not fit a present schema are presumably ignored. The problem of defining discrepancy is even more difficult than defining novelty. Attempts to use adult judgments may prove useful (341), and Thomas's introduction of Coomb's unfolding theory (312) to scale the infant's dimensions may provide a wedge into this problem.

Theoretical disagreements notwithstanding, Cohen has argued for better articulation of the behavioral components of attention (70) through a two-process model which includes attention-getting and attention-holding components. The first aspect refers to the power of a stimulus to attract fixation by peripheral vision through such factors as size and movement. The second refers to the power of a stimulus to maintain fixation through such factors as novelty and complexity. Cohen and his co-workers have found that these components respond differently to experience, e.g. the maintenance aspect habituates easily whereas the attraction component does not (73).

COMMENT ON ATTENTION STUDIES   It is legitimate to question both the explicit and implicit goals of these theories. All characterize the baby as a preference organism, and the explicit goal is to explain his preference behavior. The implicit goal, however, is to specify the factors that govern his attentional behavior and how he gathers information about the world. It is in this latter aspect that we feel the approaches are wanting. No visual system of any organism operates in a whole-stimulus discrete-selection fashion, but rather it is a sampling system which is constantly active. If theories are concerned with visual information-seeking activity, they should strive to explain what a baby is actually doing while he is "attending" to a preferred stimulus, what he is doing while attending to a nonpreferred stimulus (reliable preferred-nonpreferred differences have been as slight as 3–4%), what he is doing when attending to neither (about 50% of the time) and, in fact, what happens when no "preferred" stimulus is available. Clearly, the system does not shut down in the latter case.

This basic question of what the baby is up to when he shows a preference for something can be posed for all duration-of-looking data. One might predict, for example, that if looking at a pattern reflects "enjoyment" (as implied by novelty, complexity, and contour density notions) or attempts to match a schema (discrepancy theory), then that pattern should be reinforcing. However, when 3½-month-old infants are given the opportunity to control (by sucking) the onset of a 24 × 24 checkerboard which they prefer to a 2 × 2 checkerboard, they do *not* suck more to turn on the former than the latter (117).

Karmel and his co-workers (163) have suggested that preference for particular levels of contour density is a function of their effect on cortical firing rate. Impressive evidence for their view includes the finding that after 1½ months, like looking, the amplitude of the visual evoked potential (a gross indication of pooled cortical activity) varied as an inverted-U function of contour density. The peak amplitude occurred at increasing contour densities with age and at approximately the contour density levels eliciting peak preference.

There is a puzzle here still. If neural activity is the common denominator of "preference," why are not all "high firing" stimuli reinforcing? Moreover, why should the absolute level of neural activity not account for looking before 1½ months but account for it later when factors such as meaningfulness and stimulus organization come into play (factors that probably depend on the pattern rather than absolute *rate* of cortical firing)? Haith (135) argued that instead of thinking of a stimulus as lying on a "preference" dimension, one can think of each stimulus array as engaging a particular fixation and scan routine. This approach accommodates the notion that the infant is constantly active and is capable of processing any stimulus, preferred or nonpreferred. There is no reason for one stimulus to be more reinforcing than another; duration of looking is simply a summary measure of detailed processing activity. Space does not permit a full description, but it is argued that findings for infants under 1½ months were presumably less predictable because definitions of contour density did not take into account the limitations on the young infant's scanning ability. In brief, we would argue that the idea of "preference" or choice becomes as limited in significance for the infant as it would be for an adult, useful for talking about the relation between two stimuli but of little value in describing information acquisition.

Visual behavior in an adult serves at least two functions: to inventory the general contents of the visual field and to collect task-relevant information. It may be fruitful to view the infant from this perspective. If visual activity were described in a way that captures its continuous dynamic character and its sensitivity to organism intent as well as environmental control, more might be learned about his "agenda." Perhaps the dimensions of control specified so far—discrepancy, novelty, complexity, contour density—may some day be seen as factors which at times control task-specific scan routines but also may at other times only momentarily seduce the infant from his natural ongoing pattern of activity.

Habituation

The study of habituation was of considerable interest to investigators during this period, and an examination of the research and theory in this field tells an interesting story. A major review of research just prior to this review period (171) pointed out a variety of problems in prior work and concluded that although no definitive study had been done to demonstrate habituation in the infant, the weight of evidence indicated its presence. Several excellent reviews of the literature have appeared since this time (66, 72, 157, 231). No longer can the presence of habituation be questioned, as studies employing counterbalanced habituating and dishabituating stimuli have produced definitive results (76, 188, 208, 330–332).

The great interest in habituation has reflected both methodological and theoretical concerns. Because a response already available is studied, the habituation paradigm offers a convenient methodology to study discrimination. Of greater interest was Sokolov's suggestion (290) that the decline of attention to a stimulus occurs through an internal model-building process. When the model is completed the organism no longer responds to the stimulus. If Sokolov were correct, the study of habituation could be used to study individual and age differences in cognitive functioning. Presumably, much of the work on infants under 2 months of age was motivated by this concern. In a review of this research, Jeffrey & Cohen (157) commented "It would appear . . . that infants under 2 months of age do not habituate to visual stimulation." The exciting speculation based on such findings was that under 2 months of age infants cannot create internal models. Since the 2 month period is also a time at which other major changes occur—i.e. some reflexes drop out, smiling occurs, conditioning becomes easier, babies sleep through the night, more regular EEG rhythms appear (96)—it seemed as though more might be learned about brain functioning by demonstrating the truth of this proposition. Unfortunately, recent research has disabused us of yet another age-related dichotomy. Several adequately designed studies have now demonstrated habituation in infants under 2 months to visual stimuli (118–120, 215) when individually tailored criteria of habituation or long exposures are used. In one case habituation was found more readily in 1- to 1½-month-olds than in 3- to 3½-month-olds (233, 279). We find ourselves in substantial agreement with Horowitz, who concludes ". . . whether response decrement is obtained to repeated stimulation is a function of the particular set of stimuli rather than the age of the infant, per se" (152, p. 108).

Such a conclusion takes a great deal of gloss off the phenomenon, but one can ask, now that the ability to habituate has been pushed back to the newborn period, what more is known about brain functioning at this age? Very little, despite one study (43) which noted slower, possibly absent, habituation in an anencephalic infant. Since the original preparation for establishing the habituation model was the decerebrate cat, little more should have been expected (285, 313). Habituation, like learning and adaptation, is such a pervasive characteristic of living material that it should be surprising when it cannot be demonstrated. No single central mechanism mediates such processes.

Nevertheless, it is still true that the habituation *paradigm* has proved useful for studying other phenomena of interest, such as discriminative abilities (9, 79, 80, 189, 219, 331) and intermodal interaction (42, 79, 233, 279). But it should also be recognized that several concepts have now run the course from an initial status as explanatory constructs of key aspects of development to paradigms for studying something else. The best examples are learning, attention, and habituation. Clearly, researchers have been aiming for an inappropriate level of explanation; it is time the historical cycle was stopped.

Infant Learning

From the forefront of research in the field in the mid-1960s, the study of infant learning has dwindled to a minor role. Cairns (56) argued that the very factors which are of importance to developmentalists today are among those which traditional learning theories have ignored or held constant in their studies. In particular, the role of maturational and biological factors must be considered in the learning process, and experience must be seen as involved not only in the reinforcement and acquisition of responses, but also in initiating and maintaining developmental changes [Zelazo's (340, 343) study on the effects of exercising the walking reflex presumably would be an example of the latter].

Consistent with Cairn's analysis, a recent review of classical conditioning in infancy found more evidence for *constraints* on learning than on universal applicability of learning principles in early infancy (113). Among the constraints noted were: maturational levels, individual differences in orienting, the neurological system being conditioned (skeletal or autonomic), and biobehavioral state. Sameroff (269, 270) has also argued that cognitive levels constitute a constraint on learning in neonates. He felt that neonates could not be classically conditioned because the association of CS and UCS requires intercoordination of sensorimotor schemes, which Piagetian theory holds is not present until a later age (242). However, two subsequent studies have not supported this view: CS-UCS association across different modalities has been obtained (64, 298).

At a later age, cognitive level has been shown to be a constraint on infant learning (217, 218). When the manipulandum was in one place, and the feedback source in a very different place (displaced 60°), 9-month-olds learned, but 6-month-olds did not. Since 6-month-olds were able to learn when the feedback and the manipulation were *not* spatially separated, a deficiency in integration of spatial information at that age seems a plausible inference.

Almost all the rest of the studies reviewed dealt with straightforward parametric investigations of the effects of state and response requirements (65, 67), reinforcers (14, 17, 85, 143, 250, 251, 334), and delay of reinforcement (216).

Surprisingly, except for studies by Bruner (53, 54, 181) to be discussed later, there was no evidence of interest in complex learning processes such as learning set, detour behavior, transfer of training, reversal learning, delayed reactions, and observational learning. Complex learning has not only been studied fruitfully in infrahuman primates, but it is also likely to bring the study of learning closer to the current interest in cognition.

Memory

A distinct new trend to appear in this review period concerns infantile memory. Of course, it can be argued that memory has been implied through the demonstration of a number of other more traditional processes of interest to researchers (72)—imitation, learning, attachment, habituation, object permanence, and novelty preference. However, investigations were not directly concerned with memory and contributed little to an empirical base or consistent conceptual approach. The research discussed here concerns direct questions about the temporal, interference, and stimulus parameters affecting the memory engram. In one study (103) 5-month-olds were presented three pattern problems in series and then tested for recognition of the familiar pattern for each problem 1, 4, or 7 min after initial exposure. Infants recognized the familiar stimulus under all time exposures even in the face of possible proactive and retroactive interference. The conclusion seems appropriate: "[The] infant appears capable of acquiring, storing, and, at various points in time, retrieving the perceptual traces of a number of visual targets, even when the stimuli to be processed are presented in relatively close temporal succession and the possibilities of both proactive and retroactive interference exist" (103, p. 24).

An important paper by Fagan (104) described five experiments on interesting aspects of memory in 5-month-olds. For all experiments the infant was first familiarized with one stimulus of a 3-stimulus set for 2 min and then tested for memory by the pairing of the familiar stimulus with each of the other two stimuli for 10 sec both immediately and at a later time. The first study demonstrated stable differentiation of abstract patterns over both 24 and 48 hours, supporting an earlier finding (307). Remarkably, Study 2 demonstrated memory for achromatic face photographs of a man, a woman, and a baby for 2 weeks with only a slight indication of a decline over time. The possibility that babies this age may not forget at all was dispelled by Study 3. Here, lifelike 3D face masks were used; although immediate memory for the familiarized mask was demonstrated, no evidence for memory was obtained after 3 hr. Inasmuch as face masks were the only stimuli used to this point for which likenesses occur in the real world, it seemed likely that retroactive interference by real faces occurred in the 3-hr interval. The role of retroactive interference was tested in Studies 4 and 5, using achromatic face photos. After the infant was familiarized to one photo, one of three "interfering" photos was presented after zero delay or just before the 3-hr test for memory. Interference was produced only by the immediate interference and only by an inversion of the familiarized photo; a highly similar or very different photo had no effect.

Collectively these studies reveal striking storage capacities in young infants and the operation of such factors as interference and consolidation which are highly familiar to memory researchers. It is also interesting to note that memory for static visual displays does not support Piagetian motor schematic theory or Bruner's enactive-representation systems in early infancy. Although these positions can appeal to eye-movement activity as the motor-enactive scheme, they hardly seem as straightforward as Kagan's (159) notions of schemas as skeleton featural representations. It would be useful to know if the relation between visual scanning patterns during original exposure and the delayed test are more similar for recognized than for unrecognized pictures.

The potential for a breakthrough in our understanding of infant memory seems quite clear. Fagan (106) has demonstrated effects of stimulus familiarization lasting for as little as 5 sec, suggesting the paired-comparison procedure is very amenable for work with young infants. Additionally, the time/familiarity functions assumed a different meaningful form for different sets of stimuli; i.e. for a given level of novel-familiar differentiation, simple patterns required the least amount of time, followed by pattern arrangement, face photos, and line drawings of faces, respectively. Thus the rate of acquisition and decay of the memory engram for different stimulus sets might be tapped. The further implication for a study of individual differences and of age seems obvious. Perhaps soon we will know more fully what the ". . . dramatic change in memory ability between two and three months of age," concluded by Cohen & Gelber (72, p. 45), is telling us.

Sensorimotor Intelligence

The in-depth investigation of Piaget's notions of the development of sensorimotor intelligence has been one of the most important research thrusts that has taken place in recent years. American research in this area actually began in the early 1960s, with the construction by Uzgiris and Hunt of their scales of sensorimotor development based on Piagetian theory. That work has now reached fruition with the publication of the book describing the scales (322), and some of the research to date with them (154, 320, 321, 323). A second phase of research on sensorimotor intelligence came about when laboratory studies first began to test selected predictions from Piagetian theory. Almost all of this research has involved object permanence, probably because it is the easiest sensorimotor development to understand, and certainly the most readily operationalized. At this writing, a third phase seems to be emerging and involves studying other sensorimotor developments than object permanence.

The field has been favored with excellent recent reviews on selected topics, which will be supplemented rather than duplicated here. Uzgiris (321) reviewed the psychometric research on scales of sensorimotor intelligence, including those devised by others. Her discussion of the issue of stage sequence and stage congruence is particularly clear and important. The laboratory research was reviewed by several researchers who have made important contributions to the field (36, 37, 128, 140).

REPRESENTATION   The emergence of deferred imitation, symbolic play, insightful problem solving, following of invisible displacements, and the reconstruction of causes on the basis only of their effects were among the many converging operations which Piaget brought to bear on his conclusion that representation (making present mentally something not present physically) is achieved in the sixth stage of sensorimotor intelligence. Nevertheless, there have been attempts to prove Piaget wrong. One paradigm involves the study of surprise reactions to the *failure of reappearance* of an occluded object or the *reappearance of a different object* than the one hidden. Bower (35) studied the former, measuring "heart rate change" (direction of change unspecified), and concluded that even 1-month-olds noted the failure of reappearance if the occlusion interval was brief enough, while 3-month-olds reacted even at the longest occlusion interval tested (15 sec). LeCompte & Gratch (190) used the latter paradigm with 9-, 12-, and 18-month-old infants, who showed surprise to a toy switch. Infants at all ages continued to search on the toy switch trials.

Unfortunately, important problems beset both studies. Bower's work needs confirmation with better specification of how heart rate responses were quantified, especially in view of reports that heart rate may not be sensitive to surprise conditions in infancy (34, 252; Kagan, personal communication). The LeCompte & Gratch study had a different problem: because they presented infants with a new toy after hiding, their experimental operations were appropriate to infer *recognition* of the toy after reappearance, but not necessarily the *recall* of the toy during hiding. It is the issue of recall, of course, that bears on the problem of representation. Furthermore, their finding of continued search after a toy switch need not unequivocally indicate recall, if one assumes that infants, like adults, sometimes search without knowing what they are searching for (252).

A second research strategy tried to show that "out of sight" is not "out of mind" in 5-month-olds. Infants were reported to reach out and grasp an object when it was placed out of sight, not by occlusion, but by plunging the entire room into darkness (40). Unfortunately, the positive results reported are uninterpretable for two reasons: (*a*) the infants may have been in the act of reaching when the lights went out, in which case successful capture in darkness would be an instance of the "extension of the movements of accommodation," which Piaget considers a Stage 3 accomplishment; and (*b*) some tactile groping to retrieve a perceptual experience may occur even in Stage 3 (see Observation 17 in 243).

A third strategy taken as evidence for representation was a demonstration of apparently accurate interpolation of an invisible trajectory with eye movements, well before a demonstration of manual search (Mundy-Castle & Anglin, cited in 36). Unfortunately, important details of this unpublished study[3] were lacking, making it impossible to rule out the competing hypothesis that the eye movements reflected the extension of movements of accommodation. However, because the paradigm is conceptually promising, replication and confirmation of this study seems called for. Meanwhile, it cannot be taken as evidence for early representation.

Related to the notion of representation in infancy is what has come to be called the AB error. In stage 4, infants who have shown successful search in place A for a hidden object will continue to search in A even when the object is now hidden in place B. This surprising behavior by infants was taken by Piaget as evidence that the Stage 4 infant's notion of objects is still not entirely freed from action. A number of investigations focused on this theoretically important and counterintuitive error (55, 102, 129, 138, 139). In one of these studies, a corollary to Piaget's theory was added by the discovery that the AB error was made even when a new toy was hidden at B (102). In another, the error was prevented in 9-month-olds if the delay between hiding and the infant's search was very brief (less than 1 sec), or if the infant persisted in gazing and attending at B after hiding (129). This led to the suggestion that proactive interference accounts for the error (138), a suggestion subsequently withdrawn when it was found that the error occurred even when 12-month-olds could clearly see the object hidden behind an occluding but transparent screen (139, 140). Although the AB error is now well-documented, its occurrence as late as 12 months is theoretically puzzling in view of other findings that infants can be in early Stage 6 by 10 months (235) or shortly thereafter (21, 51).

IDENTITY   Sensorimotor development need not be conceptualized only in terms of object permanence or representational development. Piaget (243) pointed out that it also involves the construction of the "sensorimotor group," a cognitive structure characterized by four criteria: identity, reversibility, associativity, and combinativity [see (244) for definitions]. Piaget argued that all these criteria are met at the level of perception in Stage 5 and at the level of representation in Stage 6.

The criterion of identity has come in for considerable study, particularly by Bower & Moore (36, 38, 39, 225). In early research, Bower implied that size and shape constancy (and therefore some degree of identity) was present in infants by 2 months of age (summarized in 36). However, in more recent research, Bower (36) claimed to find conditions in the first 5 months of life when the infant's notion of identity seemed very crude. In one particularly striking study, so long as an object's trajectory was kept constant, all its other perceptual features could be changed without eliciting surprise in the infant. On the other hand, any detectable change of trajectory (such as by more rapid emergence of an object from behind an occluder than possible, given its trajectory and speed) produced surprise at the same age. By 5 months of age, however, both features and trajectory were said to define the identity

---

[3]It is not clear that the study cited by Bower is the same as one reprinted in *The Competent Infant* (229).

of an object for infants—i.e. infants showed surprise at impossible changes in either of these variables.

OTHER GROUP CHARACTERISTICS   Bruner is one of the few to study the development of detour behavior (related by Piaget to associativity). Infants of 8, 12, and 16 months showed increasing ability with age to "detour-reach" around a transparent barrier with the target object placed increasingly beyond the leading edge of the barrier. The younger infants, as would be expected from Piaget's theory, persisted longer in trying to reach the target by what Bruner called straight-line reaching. Older subjects were more likely to attempt a detour reach even without initially attempting to go around the barrier (53). Another report described the strategies used by infants to obtain a desired toy which was beyond reach but obtainable by manipulation of a lazy-susan-like apparatus (181). Two general developments were noted: problem solving proceeded by involving (a) "successive levels of organization of components," and (b) by the infant's "concentrating on individual components one at a time to the exclusion of the rest."

SELF-RECOGNITION   Piaget predicted that as objects are progressively freed from action in sensorimotor development, the self is increasingly localized as one among many objects in space (243). Recently the use of mirrors provided a paradigm to study the emergence of self-recognition, a phenomenon which Piaget never explicitly studied. Amsterdam (5) reported an apparent progression with age in infant reactions to mirrors, from treating the mirror image as a "sociable playmate" or an interesting spectacle at 3 to 8 months of age, to using the mirror to guide the hand to touch a dot of rouge on the nose, or to naming himself in the mirror, at 18 to 24 months of age. Brooks-Gunn & Lewis (50) also demonstrated an increase with age in rouge-mark-directed behavior, but felt that a stage theory could not account for their data. However, Bertenthal & Fischer (26), in the most thorough self-recognition study yet reported, demonstrated by scalogram analyses strong evidence for stage progression from 6 to 24 months in five tasks: Task 1—no special mirror behavior other than touching and reaching toward it; Task 2—correct localization of an object in space, but only if the object's movement and self movement were closely correlated; Task 3—correct localization of an object in space when object movements and self movement were dissociated; Task 4—rouge task implying representation of facial features of self; Task 5—correct naming of self in mirror.

DECALAGE   Piagetians have begun to deal increasingly with the problem of horizontal decalage, a term referring to time lags in development across cognitive domains, and to the lack of agreement across indicators of stage attainment. Piaget (242, 243) predicted a number of sensorimotor decalages, but the one most studied concerns the notion that search for absent persons (person permanence) develops prior to search for absent toys (object permanence). Although a number of studies reported apparent confirmation of such a decalage (21, 51, 127, 235; St. Pierre cited in 81), it is not at all clear that person permanence precedes object permanence because (a) those studies confounded what was being searched for (persons vs objects), with the task demands (e.g. searching under small screens for toys, vs behind large furniture for persons), and (*b*) the scoring criteria for search for persons may have been less demanding than for toys. A recent study overcame these problems and reported little evidence for decalage between persons and objects when task demands were constant, but a very large decalage was obtained when task requirements differed in a fashion analogous to the requirements confounded in the previous work on person permanence (Jackson, Campos & Fischer, submitted). The role of task requirements in decalage has also been reported by others (180).

EMERGING TRENDS IN STUDIES OF SENSORIMOTOR INTELLIGENCE   As mentioned earlier, recent indications point to a spread of interest to many of the other areas of sensorimotor development described by Piaget besides object permanence. For example, the infant's notion of causality has begun to be studied (167), as have symbolic play (112, 327) and sensorimotor imitation (125, 207, 226). The infant's notion of space is an important area of investigation (199), and is reviewed elsewhere in this chapter. The relation between sensorimotor development and language development is likely to move rapidly from its present speculative phase (20, 30) toward empirical testing. Only the infant's sensorimotor constructions of time and dreams have failed to arouse interest.

Emotional Development

Although often ignored today in other branches of psychology, emotional development has probably been the single most studied topic in infancy. There are several reasons for this: the striking emergence of new behaviors such as fear, laughter, and attachment; the importance of this area for historic and contemporary theories of child development; the linkage of infant emotion to later personality development; and most recently, the need for basic information on reactions to parents and unfamiliar persons as a result of the increasing importance of day care.

STRANGER DISTRESS   The most studied affective development has been reactions to strangers. Whether because fear of strangers was believed to index the beginning of signal anxiety (294), the termination of a sensitive period in the formation of attachments (149), or the disruption of phase sequences or expectancies (47, 48, 144), the emphasis has been on the onset of *negative* reactions to strangers in the second half-year of life. Positive reactions to strangers at this age were taken to indicate abnormal or delayed attachment, such as can occur with institutionalized infants.

It is now generally agreed that the emphasis on negative reactions was a gross oversimplification. Rheingold & Eckerman (255) have been most emphatic on this point. Their empirical work had revealed little or no evidence for such distress (77, 90, 91, 255, 259), and they severely criticized previous research for serious inadequacies in the operational definition of fear, in the attribution of cause of the distress to the stranger, and in failure to unconfound separation and stranger distress. They also noted two facts inconsistent with stranger fear as a developmental milestone:

the low percentage of infants showing fear at any one age, and the large variability in age of onset. They wondered whether there was such a phenomenon as fear of strangers left to account for.

Subsequent studies, however, confirmed the existence of a developmental shift with much more appropriate methods. Longitudinal studies continued to show decreased positive responding and increased negative reactions to strangers in nearly all infants tested (116, 122). The sight of a stranger was reported to be punishing for bar pressing at 9 months, but not at 6, whereas the sight of the mother was positively reinforcing at both ages (114; see 16 for a related study). While younger infants showed cardiac orienting responses to strangers, older ones showed defensive accelerations, as well as wary facial expressions (58, 247, 326). Stranger distress has also been found, though in much attenuated form, even in the absence of maternal separation (58, 96, 256, 296). Finally, when mother and stranger behaved in the same graduated, naturalistic style, negative reactions were still greater to strangers (178).

Nevertheless, stranger distress is neither as predictable nor universal at any one age as once thought. For example, it is not consistently manifested upon repeated testing even only a few days apart (283, 291). Furthermore, because laboratory studies generally involve stilted approaches not paced in relation to the infant's reaction to the stranger (282, 284, 292), there is now some question whether the source of the fear observed in the lab is due to the strange *person* (as predicted by various theories), or to the person's strange *behavior*. A significant study by Rafman (248) supports the latter view: training unfamiliar adults to behave like the mother prevented the expression of some of the negative reactions to strangers.

Such complex findings as these are leading investigators to treat emotional reactions as the outcome of multiple processes, the balance of which determines the observed response (46). Systems approaches, already proposed by some (28, 41), are likely to become much more prevalent in the field.

Explanations of age shifts in stranger reactions   Attempts to explain negative reactions to strangers have generally centered on the "incongruity hypothesis," which predicts fear to be elicited by the novel or unfamiliar (47). As for the parallel case of infant attention, this hypothesis suffers from the absence of a metric for determining the degree of discrepancy (197, 254, 255). In addition, there is ambiguity about whether discrepancy (however measured) produces *fear,* as Hebb's 1946 paper (144) implied, and as others believe (41, 47), or only produces *excitement,* as Hebb later argued in his 1949 book (145), where he proposed that specific emotions are produced by other factors in interaction with discrepancy.

Hebb's second position seems closer to the truth. Persons who are reasonably equivalent in terms of incongruity or discrepancy produce very different affective reactions: unfamiliar adults elicit *negative* reactions (197), an unfamiliar child elicits *interest* or smiles (130, 194, 197), and a midget elicits prolonged staring (196). Furthermore, the same discrepant stimulus (e.g. a mask) elicits wariness in one context and laughter in another (296). Finally, infants can be shown to detect novelty and discrepancy long before they become wary of such (239, 272–275).

Attempting to defend incongruity theory, Bronson (48) argued that nearly half his sample showed wariness by 4 months of age, when, on the basis of previous reports, he had expected infants to be able to discriminate mother from stranger. However, that discrimination has recently been pushed back in three separate studies (60, 116, 220) to as early as 2 to 3 weeks of age, when fear of strangers clearly does not occur. Furthermore, Bronson's own study failed to find the expected evidence for distress elicited by incongruous toys.

Dissatisfaction with incongruity theory has led to even more complex formulations of the development of fear of strangers—for instance, failure to assimilate (160), discrepancy of the perception of the stranger from a self-image (197), and evaluation of the context (296). Testing these complex formulations is likely to prove very difficult, although studies such as those on Down's Syndrome infants may prove helpful in detecting cognitive influences on emotional development (63, 95, 281).

The most prevalent alternative theory links Piagetian sensorimotor assessments (especially object permanence) to onset of fear of strangers and of separation from the mother. The assumption is that Stage 4 of sensorimotor intelligence is necessary for these developments to take place because it involves the beginnings of cognitive reactions to absent objects, as well as the development of understanding of the identity of persons and objects in the environment (81, 244, 272). However, the empirical evidence so far is poor. Neither Scarr & Salapatek (271) nor Emde (96) were able to link sensorimotor scales to onset of stranger distress. Similar negative findings were reported for scales of person permanence (51) and causality (127). The positive findings which have occasionally been reported (e.g. 195, 235) are irrelevant to understanding the onset of the phenomena, because the studies tested infants beyond the appropriate age. Finally, Piagetian approaches must take into account (but have not thus far) the frequent reports of early wariness of strangers in the first 6 months of life (48, 58, 227), i. e. before Stage 4 is reached.

One last theoretical development bears special mention. Social learning approaches appear to be making a comeback in this area. Lewis & Brooks (197) suggested that infants may react negatively toward unfamiliar adults but not toward unfamiliar children because only the former serve as discriminative stimuli for maternal separation. Bronson (submitted manuscript) was more explicit: in a change of theoretical stance, he argued that individual differences in reactions to strangers in the second 6 months of life reflect differences in previous encounters with strangers.

POSITIVE EMOTIONS   Most emotions studied in infancy have been negative ones, reflecting the importance of such emotions for later personality. But a change is in the wind. Smiling and laughter show developmental shifts that are every bit as dramatic as fear, and both have come in for important empirical and theoretical study. A major developmental shift from the endogenous to exogenous control of smiling has been recently documented, and some neurophysiological substrates of smiling proposed (97). Smiling has also been related to cognitive mastery and recognition (339, 342). After years of neglect as a topic of investigation, laughter and the developmental changes in its elicitation have been studied. At its onset at 4 months, vigorous physical stimulation most readily elicits a laugh; subsequently, it occurs to more subtle and more cognitive stimulation (297). A model to explain the occurrence of laughter and its close relation to fear links both to tension fluctuations, but laughter expresses sudden tension release, while fear reflects a continuation of tension buildup (295). Both laughter and fear are related to the infant's evaluation of the situation. Attempts to test the model with Down's Syndrome infants, who show little tension buildup (63), and with physiological measures of tension arousal (295) have just begun.

ATTACHMENT TO MOTHER   Without doubt, the most programmatic and potentially significant work on attachment has been that of Ainsworth and her colleagues (1–4, 21, 22, 299–301). They have undertaken a three-faceted approach to the study of attachment: 1. a year-long longitudinal study of infants in their homes; 2. the development of a 20-min laboratory test (the "strange situation") designed to highlight individual differences in quality of attachment; 3. the assessment of maternal determinants of quality of infant attachment.

There are a number of unique features to this research program. One is its emphasis on qualitative differences in attachment, rather than on "strength of attachment" as assessed by one or more dependent variables (2). (The latter is the strategy employed by most other researchers.) Another is a strong opposition to using distress vocalizations upon separation as the indicator of attachment (300). Furthermore, they depart from the customary insistence on objective measurements by assessing qualitative differences in attachment through the use of rating scales of proximity-seeking, contact-maintaining, proximity-avoidance, and contact-resistance (3). Finally, they feel that it is not separation, but the reunion following separation, which best highlights the quality of an infant's attachment (3).

Three generic types of attachment quality have been identified in strange situation behavior: "secure attachment," characterized by happy greeting of mother, proximity-seeking and nonavoidance; "ambivalent attachment," reflected in a curious pattern of high scores on contact-resistance, proximity-seeking, and contact-maintaining; and "avoidant attachment," characterized by low scores on proximity-seeking and high on proximity-avoidance. This classification has been reported to reflect similar behaviors at home and to stem from important individual differences in maternal behavior (3).

Rating maternal-infant interaction on scales of sensitivity, cooperation, accessibility to and acceptance of their infant, they found that mothers who rated high on these scales had infants who were securely attached (3), more compliant to verbal commands (301), and searched at higher levels for persons than objects (21). Furthermore, contrary to their expectations from learning theory, Bell & Ainsworth (22) found that mothers who promptly responded to an infant's cry had infants who cried *less* on subsequent observations. On the other hand, mothers who rejected and ignored their infants had avoidantly attached (203) infants; insensitive, interfering, or ignoring mothers had ambivalently attached infants (Blehar & others, submitted).

This impressive set of findings is not without its problems. Although many studies now use the strange situation, a number have not found the reunion episodes to be as useful as expected (111, 202). To what extent this results from other investigators not using the four proximity and contact ratings is not clear. Furthermore, the strange situation has been criticized for lacking a control condition in which a familiarized adult is compared with the mother (68, 111). In addition, the Ainsworth group's emphasis on direction of effects from mother to infant is often argued very unpersuasively, and the level of analysis used to assess mother-infant interaction may be too gross to be useful. Two studies (124, 303) have now shown that when the mother appears upon global observation to be influencing her infant, her behavior can actually be under the infant's control! Finally, although the coders in these studies are blind as to the nature of the hypotheses, it is not clear that the same is true of the observers in the home, or that attempts have been made to prevent contamination of observations between sessions.

ATTACHMENT TO FATHER   One area of research generally ignored by Ainsworth and almost all researchers prior to 1972 concerns attachment to the father. Both by their presence (200) and by their absence (27), fathers have been shown to play a significant role in subsequent personality and intellectual development. As role divisions in the family change, the father's role in infancy looms larger. Consequently, the father has increasingly become a focus of study at all ages.

All of the reports dealing with attachment behaviors in older infants agree in finding that the father elicits attachment responses that are more similar to the mother's than to an unfamiliar adult's (69, 111, 168, 182, 183, 186, 187, 195, 257). This is true for both American (182, 183) and Guatemalan (195) infants. The earliest age reported so far for attachment behaviors directed to the father has been 8 months (186, 187). Interestingly, there are hints of qualitative differences in attachment behaviors directed at the two parents: maternal separation elicits more distress (168), and mothers attract more attachment behaviors than fathers in the presumbly more stressful setting of a lab (187). On the other hand, the reverse is true at home (186), and more positive responses are directed at the father when he is present than are directed at the mother (168).

Few studies have yet to go beyond *whether* the father is an attachment object to determine *how* he becomes an attachment object. One speculation is that the father's role in the family is more that of a playful companion, whereas the mother's is more that of caretaker and disciplinarian (187). Others stress the father's role as a source of stimulation for the infant (240). Consistent with this notion, and in contrast to an early report of minimal interaction between fathers and infants (253), fathers were reported to play a major stimulating role even with neonates (236–238). Future research will need to document more completely the specific manner in which father attachment originates.

SUBSTITUTE CAREGIVING   The negative implications of the early work on maternal deprivation on infants, and the increasing importance of careers for many mothers, created an interest in the effects of day care or maternal employment in infancy. Three recent reviews dealt with this topic (134, 150, 230), as have a few empirical studies. The latter have been thoroughly inconsistent so far, some noting deleterious effects (29, 278), others not (87, 166, 249, 256). The reasons for the inconsistencies are clear. Investigators must begin to partial out the effects of variables such as age of entry into and duration of stay in day care, reason for maternal employment, type of attachment behavior recorded, and how these are elicited, to name but a few.

MATERNAL ATTACHMENT TO INFANT   What has been called the "reverse side of the human attachment situation"—the attachment of mother toward her infant —has aroused recent interest (169, 170, 176, 177, 191, 192). Because mother-infant separation in animals such as goats, sheep, and cows often leads to failure of the mother to care for her young upon reunion, some investigators have felt that separation of human mother and neonate after birth may similarly affect mother-to-infant attachment.

In one study, mothers given extended contact with their newborns during the first 3 days, when compared to controls, responded more favorably about their infants in an interview, and showed more *"en face"* behavior, and more interest and concern for the infant in a physical examination 1 month later (176). After 1 year, these mothers stated that they missed their babies more when they had to leave them and were more likely to spend time soothing the baby when it cried (169). Even on 2 year follow-up, differences persisted between extended contact and control mothers: extended contact mothers were reported to use more words, more questions, and fewer commands than controls (170).

Although the random assignment of subjects to conditions, the blind scoring of filmed observations and interviews, and the long-term follow-up were admirable features of this research, it has been met with skepticism. It does not seem likely that one or a series of experiences immediately after birth would be sufficient to produce such long-term effects (191). Another study dealing with temporary separation of a human mother from her infant in the immediate postpartum period found minimal effects on attachment behaviors, although there was a trend for higher incidence of divorce and relinquishing of infants in the separated group (192). Furthermore, the differences that initially had been obtained proved evanescent upon an 11-month follow-up (191). Some are now arguing that the early postpartum period, rather than being a sensitive period for formation of attachment of mother to infant, might rather be a time when relationships between mother and baby are buffered against difficulties in adjustment (89). Needless to say, further research is warranted.

SIGNAL SYSTEMS   Recent ethology (e.g. 44) has stressed how behavioral messages such as gestures, vocalizations, and facial expressions can affect another individual's behavior no less than do speech or physical stimuli. Although conceptual, methodological, and statistical problems in the field are considerable (198), this is an exciting and novel area of research. It offers the hope of providing a better level of analysis for understanding the precise mechanisms of adult-infant social interaction which was lacking in much of the previous attachment research, and which proved fruitful in understanding why infants react negatively to some strangers and not others (248). Furthermore, it may lead to the identification of potentially clinically significant individual differences in both the *signal transmission* and *signal reception* characteristics of either the adult caregiver, the infant, or both. Finally, no single area of research more clearly points out the futility of linear models of research. Signal systems simply force a transactional model of causation on the infant psychologist.

One research strategy has studied whether and at what age *infants* detect adult behavioral messages. For example, infants 4 to 10 months of age were shown the facial and vocal expressions of angry, sad, happy, and neutral feeling states acted by an adult and discriminated the negative states first, reacting to the anger and sadness by 6 months (62, 184). Although Browne (52) studied a similar problem using the habituation-dishabituation paradigm, and reported that 4-month-olds could discriminate happy from surprised facial expressions, the interpretation of that study is not clear. The dishabituation paradigm cannot specify the source of a discrimination when multiple dimensions of perceptual displays are manipulated (9).

Another strategy has involved studying the *adult's* detection of the infant's behavioral messages. The reactions of adults to blind infants who, in Fraiberg's words, lack a "vocabulary of signs and signals," have been implicitly contrasted with reactions to normal infants (115). Adults generally feel that blind infants are disinterested in them and their activities, and find it difficult to "tell what these infants want." Fraiberg has also made the significant observation that blind infants possess a hand language, rich in affective information, which the adult caregivers fail to note without special training.

Studying normal *patterns* of interactions, Stern and his collaborators (156, 303–305) have shown how gaze behavior of a dyad can conform to a Markov chain model, and speculated about how such interactive patterns can both reflect and regulate the arousal level of the infant (304).

Finally, the *disruption* of the normal nonverbal communication pattern has been studied by Brazelton et al (45), who have pointed out how a blind mother, necessarily unresponsive to her infant's facial language, produces unusual nonverbal behavior in her infant (conspicuous gaze aversion). They have also shown how similar findings can be produced by sighted mothers if they happen to be "still-faced" and unresponsive to their infants, i.e. when mothers transmit the normal conversational cut-off cue to the child (317).

SLEEP AND STRESS   There have been important methodological and conceptual developments in recent infant sleep research. Not only have infant sleep scoring criteria been standardized (8), and computer programs for automated data analysis been made available (6, 325), but nonintrusive observational methods for study of sleep states have been developed and found to correlate satisfactorily with polygraphic assessments (25, 179, 293).

Conceptually, two major developments stand out, both related to stress. Stress has been shown to affect infant sleep, and infant sleep, in turn, is suspected of generating life-threatening stresses in predisposed infants. The first development is clearly evident in studies comparing naturalistic observations of sleep states in home or nursery with polygraphic assessment in the lab. The laboratory situation and placement of electrodes in the infant disturbs sleep states, leading to a reduction in REM percentage, faster latencies to NREM sleep onset, and disturbance of the pattern of sleep in infants of various ages (25, 293). Conclusions based on laboratory studies of infant sleep must henceforth take this factor into account. Other work has shown how circumcision affects sleep and wakefulness: with the persistent pain and progressive necrosis from Plastibel circumcisions, a sharp increase in NREM sleep, interpreted as an adaptive withdrawal to a lower arousal state, was found (98). With the more acutely painful but less chronic procedure of the Gomco technique, sleep onset was delayed, but REM and NREM percentages were not altered (7).

It is well known in the adult literature that sleep states, particularly REM, can inflict physical stress on the body (328). Exaggeration of some of the physiological changes during sleep (in particular, sleep apneas) now are suspected of involvement in sudden infant death syndrome (SIDS) (302). Research involves careful study of physiological changes in infants at high risk for SIDS either because of a previous "near miss" or because of familial predisposition. At present there is disagreement whether REM (302) or NREM (83, 133) states produce the greatest incidence of the suspected sleep apneas. Regardless, an important precaution has emerged from this work. As a result of identification of different patterns of sleep apnea, the use of apnea monitors which measure only chest or diaphragm movements is not recommended. These monitors are insensitive to upper airway obstructions which block air exchange in the presence of continued diaphragm movements—i.e. precisely to the type of apnea believed by some to be involved in SIDS (133).

Future directions in the field are likely to include a continuation of the predominant physiological concerns which now dominate it. However, we look for this field, as well as EEG work in general, to branch into important psychological directions. Already we note a trend toward use of CNS parameters in prediction of subsequent behavior (94, 147, 224). Certainly the recent work on physical stressors makes the field ripe for a natural transition to study psychological factors that may affect infant sleep. Furthermore, circadian and ultradian rhythms are likely to be related to important effects on infant behavior (99, 306).

PERSPECTIVE

As we have read the products of this report period, we have experienced the manic and depressive states anyone feels in reviewing his field. Certainly one need randomly sample only a few *Annual Review* chapters to get the feeling that the reviewer probably abandoned his field after the experience. Of course, we have collected the usual number of examples of poor research for our methods and infancy courses, yet our general mood is positive. The thought that gives cause for optimism is certainly not the current state-of-the-art but the rate of progress which can be appreciated through answering this question: Could this chapter have been written 10 or even 5 years ago? We think not. The "infant" field of infancy has moved quickly through the early stages—the tooling-up sensorimotor period of the 1960s —as well as through part of the preconceptual stage. Currently the field seems to be in about a concrete-operational, pretheoretical stage. Although we would hope for formal-operational accomplishments, it is probably early to expect so much. Aside from the question of relative sophistication of the field, there is also the special status that work in early human infancy continues to enjoy; it is still good fun to learn new things about babies.

Literature Cited

1. Ainsworth, M. D. S. 1972. Attachment and dependency: A comparison. In *Attachment and Dependency,* ed. J. L. Gewirtz, 97–137. Washington DC: Winston. 251 pp.

2. Ainsworth, M. D. S. 1973. Anxious attachment and defensive reactions in a strange situation and their relationship to behavior at home. Presented at *Meet. Soc. Res. Child Dev.,* Philadelphia

3. Ainsworth, M. D. S., Bell, S. M. V., Stayton, D. J. 1971. Individual differences in strange-situation behavior of one year olds. In *The Origins of Human Social Relations,* ed. H. R. Schaffer, 17-52. New York: Academic

4. Ainsworth, M. D. S., Bell, S. M. V., Stayton, D. J. 1972. Individual differences in the development of some attachment behaviors. *Merrill-Palmer Q.* 18:123–43

5. Amsterdam, B. 1972. Mirror self-image reactions before age two. *Dev. Psychobiol.* 5:297–305

6. Anders, T. 1976. The infant sleep profile. *Neuropaediatrie.* In press

7. Anders, T., Chalemian, R. 1974. The effects of circumcision on sleep-wake states in human neonates. *Psychosom. Med.* 36:174–79

8. Anders, T., Emde, R., Parmelee, A., eds. 1971. *A Manual of Standardized Terminology, Techniques, and Criteria for the Scoring of States of Sleep and Wakefulness in the Newborn Infant.* Brain Inform. Serv., Univ. California, Los Angeles

9. Appel, M., Campos, J. 1976. Binocular disparity as a discriminable stimulus parameter in early infancy. *J. Exp. Child Psychol.* In press

10. Aronson, E., Rosenbloom, S. 1971. Space perception in early infancy: Perception within a common auditory-visual space. *Science* 172:1161–63

11. Ashton, R. 1973. Reply to Bench. *J. Exp. Child Psychol.* 16:528–29

12. Aslin, R. N., Salapatek, P. 1973. Saccadic localization of visual targets by the very young human infant. Presented at *Meet. Psychon. Sci.,* St. Louis

13. Atkinson, J., Braddick, O., Braddick, F. 1974. Acuity and contrast sensitivity of infant vision. *Nature* 247:403–4

14. Banikiotes, F., Montgomery, A., Banikiotes, P. 1972. Male and female auditory reinforcement of infant vocalizations. *Dev. Psychol.* 6:476–81

15. Banks, M. S., Aslin, R. N., Letson, R. D. 1975. Critical period for the development of human binocular vision. *Science* 190:675–77

16. Barrera, M., Ramey, C. 1974. Conditions influencing the preference for mothers and strangers. Presented at *Meet. Southeast. Psychol. Assoc.,* Hollywood, Fla.

17. Barrett-Goldfarb, M., Whitehurst, G. 1973. Infant vocalizations as a function of parental voice selection. *Dev. Psychol.* 8:273–76

18. Barten, S., Birns, B., Ronch, J. 1971. Individual differences in the visual pursuit behavior of neonates. *Child Dev.* 42:313–19

19. Barten, S., Ronch, J. 1971. Continuity in the development of visual behavior in young infants. *Child Dev.* 42:1566–71

20. Bates, E., Benigni, L., Bretherton, I., Camaioni, L., Volterra, V. 1976. From gesture to first word: On cognitive and social prerequisites. In *Origins of Behavior: Communication and Language,* ed. M. Lewis, L. Rosenblum. New York: Wiley. In press

21. Bell, S. 1970. The development of the concept of the object and its relation-

ship to infant-mother attachment. *Child Dev.* 41:291–312

22. Bell, S., Ainsworth, M. 1972. Infant crying and maternal responsiveness. *Child Dev.* 43:1171–90

23. Bench, J. 1973. "Square-wave stimuli" and neonatal behavior: Some comments on Ashton (1971), Hutt et al (1968) and Lenard et al (1969). *J. Exp. Child Psychol.* 16:521–27

24. Bergman, T., Haith, M. M., Mann, L. 1971. Development of eye contact and facial scanning in infants. Presented at *Meet. Soc. Res. Child Dev.,* Minneapolis

25. Bernstein, P., Emde, R., Campos, J. 1973. REM sleep in four-month infants under home and laboratory conditions. *Psychosom. Med.* 35:322–29

26. Bertenthal, B., Fischer, K. 1976. The development of self-recognition in the child. Presented at *Meet. East. Psychol. Assoc.,* New York City

27. Biller, H. 1970. Father absence and personality development of the male child. *Dev. Psychol.* 2:181–201

28. Bischof, N. 1975. A systems approach toward the functional connections of attachment and fear. *Child Dev.* 46:801–17

29. Blehar, M. 1974. Anxious attachment and defensive reactions associated with day care. *Child Dev.* 45:683–92

30. Bloom, L. 1975. Language development. In *Review of Child Development Research,* ed. F. Horowitz, E. Hetherington, S. Scarr-Salapatek, G. Siegel, 4:245–303. Univ. Chicago Press

31. Bond, E. K. 1972. Perception of form by the human infant. *Psychol. Bull.* 77(4):225–45

32. Bornstein, M. H. 1975. Qualities of color vision in infancy. *J. Exp. Child Psychol.* 19:401–19

33. Bornstein, M. H., Kessen, W., Weiskopf, S. 1975. Color vision and hue categorization in young human infants. *Science* 191:201–2

34. Bower, T. 1967. The development of object-permanence: Some studies of existence constancy. *Percept. Psychophys.* 2:411–18

35. Bower, T. 1971. The object in the world of the infant. *Sci. Am.* 225(4):30–38

36. Bower, T. 1974. *Development in Infancy.* San Francisco: Freeman

37. Bower, T. 1975. Infant perception of the third dimension and object concept development. In *Infant Perception: From Sensation to Cognition,* ed. L. B. Cohen, P. Salapatek, 2:33–50. New York: Academic. 245 pp.

38. Bower, T., Broughton, J., Moore, K. M. 1971. The development of the object concept as manifested by changes in the tracking behavior of infants. *J. Exp. Child Psychol.* 12:182–93

39. Bower, T., Paterson, J. 1973. The separation of place, movement, and object in the world of the infant. *J. Exp. Child Psychol.* 15:161–68

40. Bower, T., Wishart, J. 1972. The effects of motor skill on object permanence. *Cognition* 1:165–71

41. Bowlby, J. 1969. *Attachment and Loss,* Vol. 1:*Attachment.* New York: Basic Books

42. Boyd, E. F. 1975. Visual fixation and voice discrimination in 2-month-old infants. In *Monogr. Soc. Res. Child Dev.,* ed. F. Horowitz, 39(5–6, Serial No. 158):63–77. 140 pp.

43. Brackbill, Y. 1971. The role of the cortex in orienting: Orienting reflex in an anencephalic human infant. *Dev. Psychol.* 5(2):195–201

44. Brannigan, C., Humphries, D. 1972. Human non-verbal behaviour, a means of communication. In *Ethological Studies of Child Behaviour,* ed. N. Blurton-Jones, 37–64. Cambridge, England: Cambridge Univ. Press. 400 pp.

45. Brazelton, T., Tronick, E., Adamson, L., Als, H., Wise, S. 1975. Early mother-infant reciprocity. In *Parent-Infant Interaction.* New York: Elsevier/Excerpta Med./North-Holland

46. Bretherton, I., Ainsworth, M. 1974. Responses of one-year-olds to a stranger in a strange situation. In *The Origins of Fear,* ed. M. Lewis, L. Rosenblum, pp. 131–64. New York: Wiley. 284 pp.

47. Bronson, G. 1968. The fear of novelty. *Psychol. Bull.* 69:350–58

48. Bronson, G. 1972. Infants' reactions to unfamiliar persons and novel objects. *Monogr. Soc. Res. Child Dev.* 37(3, Serial No. 148)

49. Bronson, G. 1974. The postnatal growth of visual capacity. *Child Dev.* 45:873–90

50. Brooks-Gunn, J., Lewis, M. 1975. Mirror-image stimulation and self-recognition in infancy. Presented at *Meet. Soc. Res. Child Dev.,* Denver

51. Brossard, M. D. 1974. The infant's conception of object permanence and his reactions to strangers. See Ref. 81, pp. 97–116

52. Browne, G. Y. 1975. Discrimination of normative facial expressions by 12 week old infants. Presented at *Meet. Soc. Res. Child Dev.,* Denver

53. Bruner, J. 1970. The growth and structure of skill. In *Mechanisms of Motor Skill Development*, ed. K. Connelly, pp. 63–92. New York: Academic
54. Bruner, J. 1973. Organization of early skilled action. *Child Dev.* 44:1–11
55. Butterworth, G. 1975. Object identity in infancy: The interaction of spatial location codes in determining search errors. *Child Dev.* 46:866–70
56. Cairns, R. 1972. Attachment and dependency: A psychobiological and social learning synthesis. See Ref. 1, pp. 29–80
57. Campos, J. 1976. Heart rate: A sensitive tool for the study of emotional development. In *Developmental Psychobiology: The Significance of Infancy*, ed. L. Lipsitt. Hillsdale, NJ:Erlbaum.
58. Campos, J., Emde, R., Gaensbauer, T., Henderson, C. 1975. Cardiac and behavioral interrelationships in the reactions of infants to strangers. *Dev. Psychol.* 11:589–601
59. Caron, A. J., Caron, R. F., Caldwell, R. C., Weiss, S. J. 1973. Infant perception of the structural properties of the face. *Dev. Psychol.* 9(3):385–99
60. Carpenter, G. C. 1973. Mother-stranger discrimination in early weeks of life. Presented at *Meet. Soc. Res. Child Dev.*, Philadelphia
61. Carpenter, G. C. 1974. Visual regard of moving and stationary faces in early infancy. *Merrill-Palmer Q.* 20:181–94
62. Charlesworth, W., Kreutzer, M. 1973. Facial expressions of infants and children. In *Darwin and Facial Expression*, ed. P. Ekman, pp. 91–168. New York: Academic
63. Cicchetti, D., Sroufe, L. 1975. The relationship between affective and cognitive development in Down's Syndrome infants. Presented at *Meet. Soc. Res. Child Dev.*, Denver
64. Clifton, R. K. 1974. Heart rate conditioning in the newborn infant. *J. Exp. Child Psychol.* 18:9–21
65. Clifton, R. K., Meyers, W., Solomons, G. 1972. Methodological problems in conditioning the head turning response of newborn infants. *J. Exp. Child Psychol.* 13:29–42
66. Clifton, R. K., Nelson, M. N. 1976. Developmental study of habituation in infants: The importance of paradigm, response system and state. In *Habituation: Perspectives from Child Development, Animal Behavior, and Neurophysiology*, ed. T. J. Tighe, R. N. Leaton. Hillsdale, NJ: Erlbaum. In press

67. Clifton, R. K., Siqueland, E., Lipsitt, L. 1972. Conditioned head turning in human newborns as a function of conditioned response requirements and states of wakefulness. *J. Exp. Child Psychol.* 13:43–57
68. Cohen, L. 1974. The operational definition of human attachment. *Psychol. Bull.* 81:207–17
69. Cohen, L., Campos, J. 1974. Father, mother and stranger as elicitors of attachment behaviors in infancy. *Dev. Psychol.* 10:146–54
70. Cohen, L. B. 1972. Attention-getting and attention-holding processes of infant visual preferences. *Child Dev.* 43:869–79
71. Cohen, L. B., DeLoache, J. S., Rissman, M. N. 1975. The effect of stimulus complexity on infant visual attention and habituation. *Child Dev.* 46:611–17
72. Cohen, L. B., Gelber, E. R. 1975. Infant visual memory. See Ref. 37, 1:347–403
73. Cohen, L. B., Gelber, E. R., Lazar, M. A. 1971. Infant habituation and generalization to differing degrees of stimulus novelty. *J. Exp. Child Psychol.* 11: 379–89
74. Collins, D., Kessen, W., Haith, M. M. 1972. Note on an attempt to replicate a relation between stimulus unpredictability and infant attention. *J. Exp. Child Psychol.* 13:1–8
75. Cornell, E. H. 1975. Infants' visual attention to pattern arrangement and orientation. *Child Dev.* 46:229–32
76. Cornell, E. H., Strauss, M. S. 1973. Infants' responsiveness to compounds of habituated visual stimuli. *Dev. Psychol.* 9(1):73–78
77. Corter, C. 1973. A comparison of the mother's and stranger's control over the behavior of infants. *Child Dev.* 44: 705–13
78. Crowell, D., Jones, R., Kapuniai, L., Nakagawa, J. 1973. Unilateral cortical activity in newborn humans: An early index of cerebral dominance? *Science* 180:205–7
79. Culp, R. E. 1975. The use of the mother's voice to control infant attending behavior. See Ref. 42, pp. 42–51
80. Culp, R. E., Boyd, E. F. 1975. Visual fixation and the effect of voice quality and content differences in 2-month-old infants. See Ref. 42, pp. 78–91
81. Décarie, T. G. 1974. *The Infant's Reaction to Strangers.* New York: Int. Univ. Press
82. Dember, W. N., Earl, R. W. 1957. Analysis of exploratory, manipulatory,

and curiosity behaviors. *Psychol. Rev.* 64:91–96

83. Deuel, R. 1973. Polygraphic monitoring of apneic spells. *Arch. Neurol.* 28:71–76

84. Dimond, S., Beaumont, J. 1974. *Hemisphere Function in the Human Brain.* New York: Wiley

85. Dodd, B. 1972. Effects of social and vocal stimulation on infant babbling. *Dev. Psychol.* 7:80–83

86. Donnee, L. 1972. *The development of infants' scanning patterns to face and face-like stimuli under various auditory conditions.* PhD thesis. Harvard Univ., Cambridge, Mass.

87. Doyle, A. 1975. Infant development in day care. *Dev. Psychol.* 11:655–56

88. duPreez, P. 1974. The development of conscious visual perception. *Bull. Br. Psychol. Soc.* 27:15–18

89. Dunn, J. 1975. Consistency and change in styles of mothering. See Ref. 45, pp. 155–76

90. Eckerman, C. O., Rheingold, H. 1974. Infants' exploratory responses to toys and people. *Dev. Psychol.* 10:255–59

91. Eckerman, C. O., Whatley, J. L. 1975. Infants' reactions to unfamiliar adults varying in novelty. *Dev. Psychol.* 11:562–66

92. Eimas, P. D., Siqueland, E. R., Jusczyk, P., Vigorito, J. 1971. Speech perception in infants. *Science* 171:303–6

93. Eisenberg, R. B. 1976. *Auditory Competence in Early Life: The Roots of Communicative Behavior.* Baltimore: Univ. Park Press

94. Ellingson, R., Dutch, S., McIntire, M. 1974. EEG's of prematures: 3-8 year follow-up study. *Dev. Psychobiol.* 7: 529–38

95. Emde, R. 1976. Social-affective development in infancy. NIMH Prog. Rep., Grant #MH-22803. 75 pp.

96. Emde, R., Gaensbauer, T., Harmon, R. 1976. Emotional expression in infancy: A biobehavioral study. *Psychol. Issues* 10: Monogr. 37. New York: Int. Univ. Press

97. Emde, R., Harmon, R. 1972. Endogenous and exogenous smiling systems in early infancy. *J. Am. Acad. Child Psychiatry* 11:77–100

98. Emde, R., Harmon, R., Metcalf, D., Koenig, K., Wagonfeld, S. 1971. Stress and neonatal sleep. *Psychosom. Med.* 33:491–97

99. Emde, R., Swedberg, J., Suzuki, B. 1975. Human wakefulness and biological rhythms after birth. *Arch. Gen. Psychiatry* 32:780–89

100. Engen, T., Lipsitt, L., Peck, M. B. 1974. Ability of newborn infants to discriminate sapid substances. *Dev. Psychol.* 10:741–44

101. Entus, A. K. 1975. Hemispheric asymmetry in processing of dichotically presented speech and nonspeech stimuli by infants. Presented at *Meet. Soc. Res. Child. Dev.,* Denver

102. Evans, W., Gratch, G. 1972. The Stage IV error in Piaget's theory of object concept development: Difficulties in object conceptualization or spatial localization? *Child Dev.* 43:682–88

103. Fagan, J. F. III. 1971. Infants' recognition memory for a series of visual stimuli. *J. Exp. Child Psychol.* 11: 244–50

104. Fagan, J. F. III. 1973. Infants' delayed recognition memory and forgetting. *J. Exp. Child Psychol.* 16(3):424–50

105. Fagan, J. F. III. 1974. Infant color perception. *Science* 183:973–75

106. Fagan, J. F. III. 1974. Infant recognition memory: The effects of length of familiarization and type of discrimination task. *Child Dev.* 45:351–56

107. Fantz, R. L., Fagan, J. F. III. 1975. Visual attention to size and number of pattern details by term and preterm infants during the first six months. *Child Dev.* 46:3–18

108. Fantz, R. L., Fagan, J. F. III, Miranda, S. B. 1975. Early visual selectivity. See Ref. 37, 1:249–345

109. Fantz, R. L., Miranda, S. B. 1975. Newborn infant attention to form of contour. *Child Dev.* 46:224–28

110. Fantz, R. L., Ordy, J. M., Udelf, M. S. 1962. Maturation of pattern vision in infants during the first six months. *J. Comp. Physiol. Psychol.* 55:907–17

111. Feldman, S., Ingham, M. 1975. Attachment behavior: A validation study in two age groups. *Child Dev.* 46:319–30

112. Fenson, L., Kagan, J., Kearsley, R., Zelazo, P. 1976. The developmental progression of manipulative play in the first two years. *Child Dev.* 47:232–36

113. Fitzgerald, H., Brackbill, Y. 1976. Classical conditioning in infancy: Development and constraints. *Psychol. Bull.* 83:353–76

114. Fouts, G., Atlas, P. 1974. Attachment and stranger anxiety: Mother and stranger as reinforcers. Presented at *Meet. Am. Psychol. Assoc.,* New Orleans

115. Fraiberg, S. 1974. Blind infants and their mothers: An examination of the

sign system. In *The Effect of the Infant on the Caregiver*, ed. M. Lewis, L. Rosenblum, pp. 215–32. New York: Wiley. 264 pp.

116. Fraiberg, S. 1975. The development of human attachments in infants blind from birth. *Merrill-Palmer Q.* 21: 315–34

117. Franks, A., Berg, W. K. 1975. Effects of visual complexity and sex of infant in the conjugate reinforcement paradigm. *Dev. Psychol.* 11:388–89

118. Friedman, S. 1972. Habituation and recovery of visual response in the alert human newborn. *J. Exp. Child Psychol.* 13:339–49

119. Friedman, S., Bruno, L. A., Vietze, P. 1974. Newborn habituation to visual stimuli: A sex difference in novelty detection. *J. Exp. Child Psychol.* 18: 242–51

120. Friedman, S., Carpenter, G. C. 1971. Visual response decrement as a function of age of human newborn. *Child Dev.* 42:1967–73

121. Friedman, D., Simson, R., Ritter, W., Rapin, I. 1975. Cortical evoked potentials elicited by real speech worlds and human sounds *Electroencephalogr. Clin. Neurophysiol.* 38:13–19

122. Gaensbauer, T., Emde, R., Campos, J. 1976. "Stranger" distress: Confirmation of a developmental shift in a longitudinal sample. *Percept. Mot. Skills* 43:99–106

123. Galambos, R., Benson, P., Smith, T., Shulman-Galambos, C., Osier, H. 1975. On hemispheric differences in evoked potentials to speech stimuli. *Electroencephalogr. Clin. Neurophysiol.* 39: 279–83

124. Gewirtz, J. L., Boyd, E. F. 1976. Experiments on mother-infant interaction underlying mutual attachment acquisition: The infant conditions the mother. In *Attachment Behavior. Advances in the Study of Communication and Affect*, Vol. 3, ed. T. Alloway, L. Krames, P. Pliner. New York: Plenum. In press

125. Giblin, P. 1971. Development of imitation in Piaget's sensory-motor period of infant development (Stages III-VI). *Proc. APA Conv.* 6:137–38

126. Gibson, J. J. 1966. *The Senses Considered as Perceptual Systems.* New York: Houghton-Mifflin

127. Goulet, J. 1974. The infant's conception of causality and his reactions to strangers. See Ref. 81, pp. 59–96

128. Gratch, G. 1975. Recent studies based on Piaget's view of object concept development. See Ref. 37, 2:51–99

129. Gratch, G., Appel, K., Evans, W., LeCompte, G., Wright, N. 1974. Piaget's Stage IV object concept error: Evidence of forgetting or object conception? *Child Dev.* 45:71–77

130. Greenberg, D., Hillman, D., Grice, D. 1973. Infant and stranger variables related to stranger anxiety in the first year of life. *Dev. Psychol.* 9:207–12

131. Greenberg, D. J., O'Donnell, W. J. 1972. Infancy and the optimal level of stimulation. *Child Dev.* 43:639–45

132. Gregg, C., Clifton, R. K., Haith, M. M. 1976. A possible explanation for the frequent failure to find cardiac orienting in the newborn infant. *Dev. Psychol.* 12: 75–76

133. Guilleminault, C., Peraita, R., Souquet, M., Dement, W. 1975. Apneas during sleep in infants: Possible relationship with sudden infant death syndrome. *Science* 190:677–79

134. Haith, M. M. 1972. *Day Care and Intervention Programs for Infants.* Atlanta, Ga: Atavar

135. Haith, M. M. 1976. Visual competence in early infancy. In *Handbook of Sensory Physiology*, Vol. 8, ed. R. Held, H. Leibowitz, H. L. Teuber. Berlin: Springer-Verlag. In press

136. Hammer, M., Turkewitz, G. 1974. A sensory basis for the lateral difference in the newborn infant's response to somesthetic stimulation. *J. Exp. Child Psychol.* 18:304–12

137. Harris, P. 1973. Eye movements between adjacent stimuli: An age change in infancy. *Br. J. Psychol.* 64:215–18

138. Harris, P. 1973. Perseverative errors in search by young infants. *Child Dev.* 44:28–33

139. Harris, P. 1974. Perseverative search at a visibly empty place by young infants. *J. Exp. Child Psychol.* 18:535–42

140. Harris, P. 1975. Development of search and object permanence during infancy. *Psychol. Bull.* 82:332–44

141. Harris, P., Cassel, T. Z., Bamborough, P. 1974. Tracking by young infants. *Br. J. Psychol.* 65:345–49

142. Harris, P., MacFarlane, A. 1974. The growth of the effective visual field from birth to seven weeks. *J. Exp. Child Psychol.* 18:340–48

143. Haugan, G., McIntire, R. 1972. Comparisons of vocal imitation, tactile stimulation, and food as reinforcers for infant vocalizations. *Dev. Psychol.* 6: 201–9

144. Hebb, D. 1946. On the nature of fear. *Psychol. Rev.* 53:259–76
145. Hebb, D. 1949. *The Organization of Behavior.* New York: Wiley
146. Hecaen, H. 1976. Acquired aphasia in children and the ontogenesis of hemispheric functional specialization. *Brain Lang.* 3:114–34
147. Henderson, N., Engel, R. 1974. Neonatal visual evoked potentials as predictors of psychoeducational tests at age seven. *Dev. Psychol.* 10:269–76
148. Hershenson, M. 1971. The development of visual perceptual systems. In *The Ontogeny of Vertebrate Behavior,* ed. H. Moltz. New York: Academic
149. Hess, E. 1970. Ethology and developmental psychology. In *Carmichael's Manual of Child Psychology,* ed. P. Mussen, pp. 1–38. New York: Wiley. 3rd ed.
150. Hoffman, L. 1974. Effects of maternal employment of the child—a review of the research. *Dev. Psychol.* 10:204–28
151. Horowitz, A. B. 1972. Habituation and memory: Infant cardiac responses to familiar and discrepant auditory stimuli. *Child Dev.* 43:43–53
152. Horowitz, F., ed. 1975. Visual attention, auditory stimulation, and language discrimination in young infants. See Ref. 42 (abstr.)
153. Hunt, J. McV. 1963. Piaget's observations as a source of hypotheses concerning motivation. *Merrill-Palmer Q.* 9:263–75
154. Hunt, J. McV. 1976. The utility of ordinal scales inspired by Piaget's observations. *Merrill-Palmer Q.* 22(1):31–45
155. Hutt, S. J. 1973. Square-wave stimuli and neonatal auditory behavior: Reply to Bench. *J. Exp. Child Psychol.* 16:530–33
156. Jaffe, J., Stern, D., Peery, J. 1973. "Conversational" coupling of gaze behavior in prelinguistic human development. *J. Psycholing. Res.* 2:321–29
157. Jeffrey, W. E., Cohen, L. B. 1971. Habituation in the human infant. In *Advances in Child Development and Behavior,* ed. H. Reese, 6:63–97. New York: Academic
158. Jones-Molfese, V. J. 1972. Individual differences in neonatal preferences for planometric and stereometric visual patterns. *Child Dev.* 43:1289–96
159. Kagan, J. 1971. *Change and Continuity in Infancy.* New York: Wiley
160. Kagan, J. 1974. Discrepancy, temperament, and infant distress. See Ref. 46, pp. 229–48

161. Kalnins, I. V., Bruner, J. S. 1973. The coordination of visual observation and instrumental behavior in early infancy. *Perception* 2:307–14
162. Karmel, B. Z. 1974. Contour effects and pattern preferences in infants: A reply to Greenberg and O'Donnell (1972). *Child Dev.* 45:196–99
163. Karmel, B. Z., Hoffman, R. F., Fegy, M. J. 1974. Processing of contour information by human infants evidenced by pattern-dependent evoked potentials. *Child Dev.* 45:39–48
164. Karmel, B. Z., Maisel, E. B. 1975. A neuronal activity model for infant visual attention. See Ref. 37, 1:78–131
165. Kearsley, R. 1973. The newborn's response to auditory stimulation: A demonstration of orienting and reflexive behavior. *Child Dev.* 44:582–90
166. Kearsley, R., Zelazo, P., Kagan, J., Hartmann, R. 1975. Separation protest in day-care and home-reared infants. *Pediatrics* 55:171–75
167. Keil, P. F. 1975. The development of the young child's ability to anticipate the outcome of simple causal events. Presented at *Meet. Soc. Res. Child Dev.,* Denver
168. Keller, H., Montgomery, B., Moss, J., Sharp, J., Wheeler, J. 1975. Differential parental effects among one-year-old infants in a stranger and separation situation. Presented at *Meet. Soc. Res. Child Dev.,* Denver
169. Kennell, J., Jerauld, R., Wolfe, H., Chesler, D., Kreger, N., McAlpine, W., Steffa, M., Klaus, M. 1974. Maternal behavior one year after early and extended post-partum contact. *Dev. Med. Child Neurol.* 16:172–79
170. Kennell, J., Trause, M., Klaus, M. 1975. Evidence for a sensitive period in the human mother. See Ref. 45, pp. 87–101
171. Kessen, W., Haith, M. M., Salapatek, P. 1970. Human infancy: A bibliography and guide. See Ref. 149, pp. 287–445
172. Kessen, W., Salapatek, P., Haith, M. M. 1972. The visual response of the human newborn to linear contour. *J. Exp. Child Psychol.* 13:9–20
173. Kinsbourne, M. 1972. Eye and head turning indicates cerebral dominance. *Science* 176:539–41
174. Kinsbourne, M. 1974. Mechanisms of hemispheric interaction in man. In *Hemispheric Disconnection and Cerebral Function,* ed. M. Kinsbourne, W. Smith. Springfield, Ill: Thomas

175. Kinsbourne, M. 1975. The ontogeny of cerebral dominance. Presented at *Symp. NY Acad. Sci.,* New York City
176. Klaus, M., Jerauld, R., Kreger, N., McAlpine, W., Steffa, M., Kennell, J. 1972. Maternal attachment: Importance of the first post-partum days. *N. Engl. J. Med.* 286:460–63
177. Klaus, M., Trause, M., Kennell, J. 1975. Does human maternal behaviour after delivery show a characteristic pattern? See Ref. 45, pp. 69–95
178. Klein, R., Durfee, J. 1976. Infants' reactions to unfamiliar adults versus mothers. *Child Dev.* In press
179. Kligman, D., Smyrl, R., Emde, R. 1975. A "nonintrusive" longitudinal study of infant sleep. *Psychosom. Med.* 37:448–53
180. Kopp, C., O'Connor, M., Finger, I. 1975. Task characteristics and a Stage 6 sensorimotor problem. *Child Dev.* 46:569–73
181. Koslowski, B., Bruner, J. 1972. Learning to use a lever. *Child Dev.* 43:790–99
182. Kotelchuk, M. 1973. The nature of the infant's tie to his father. Presented at *Soc. Res. Child Dev.,* Philadelphia
183. Kotelchuk, M., Zelazo, P., Kagan, J., Spelke, E. 1975. Infant reaction to parental separation when left with familiar and unfamiliar adults. *J. Gen. Psychol.* 126:255–62
184. Kreutzer, M., Charlesworth, W. 1973. Infants' reactions to different expressions of emotions. Presented at *Meet. Soc. Res. Child Dev.,* Philadelphia
185. Kuhl, P., Miller, J. 1975. Speech perception by the chinchilla: Voiced-voiceless distinction in alveolar plosive consonants. *Science* 190:69–72
186. Lamb, M. 1975. Infant attachment to mothers and fathers. Presented at *Meet. Soc. Res. Child Dev.,* Denver
187. Lamb, M. 1975. Infants, fathers, and mothers: Interaction at 8 months of age in the home and in the laboratory. Presented at *Meet. East. Psychol. Assoc.,* New York
188. Laub, K. W., Bhana, K. 1975. Infant control, response decrement, and recovery as an index of visual discrimination in young infants. See Ref. 42, pp. 52–62
189. Laub, K. W., McCluskey, K. A. 1975. Visual discrimination of social stimuli with and without auditory cues. See Ref. 42, pp. 92–104
190. LeCompte, G., Gratch, G. 1972. Violation of a rule as a method of diagnosing infants' level of object concept. *Child Dev.* 43:385–96

191. Leiderman, P., Seashore, M. 1975. Mother-infant neonatal separation: Some delayed consequences. See Ref. 45, pp. 213–39
192. Leifer, A., Leiderman, P., Barnett, C., Williams, J. 1972. Effects of mother-infant separation on maternal attachment behavior. *Child Dev.* 43:1203–18
193. Lenneberg, E. 1966. Speech development: Its anatomical and physiological concomitants. In *Brain Function III: Speech Language and Communication,* ed. E. Carterette. Berkeley: Univ. California Press
194. Lenssen, B. 1975. Infant's reactions to peer strangers. Presented at *Meet. Soc. Res. Child Dev.,* Denver
195. Lester, B., Kotelchuk, M., Spelke, E., Sellers, M., Klein, R. 1974. Separation protest in Guatemalan infants: Cross-cultural and cognitive findings. *Dev. Psychol.* 10:79–85
196. Lewis, M. 1975. The meaning of fear. Presented at *Meet. Soc. Res. Child Dev.,* Denver
197. Lewis, M., Brooks, J. 1974. Self, other and fear: Infants' reactions to people. See Ref. 46, pp. 195–227
198. Lewis, M., Lee-Painter, S. 1974. An interactional approach to the mother-infant dyad. See Ref. 115, pp. 21–48
199. Lucas, T. C., Uzgiris, I. C. 1975. Spatial factors in the development of the object concept. Presented at *Meet. Am. Psychol. Assoc.,* Chicago
200. Lynn, D. 1974. *The Father: His Role in Child Development.* Monterey, Calif: Brooks/Cole
201. Lyons-Ruth, K. 1974. *Integration of auditory and visual information during early infancy: The perception of sound as a spatially correlated property of the object.* PhD thesis. Harvard Univ., Cambridge, Mass.
202. Maccoby, E., Feldman, S. 1972. Mother-attachment and stranger reactions in the third year of life. See Ref. 48, pp. 1–85
203. Main, M. 1975. Mother-avoiding babies. Presented at *Meet. Soc. Res. Child Dev.,* Denver
204. Maurer, D. 1975. Infant visual perception: Methods of study. See Ref. 37, pp. 1–65
205. Maurer, D., Salapatek, P. 1976. Developmental changes in the scanning of faces by infants. *Child Dev.* 47:523–27
206. McCall, R. B. 1974. Exploratory manipulation and play in the human infant. In *Monogr. Soc. Res. Child Dev.* 39(Whole No. 2).

207. McCall, R. B. 1975. Imitation in infancy. Presented at *Meet. Soc. Res. Child Dev.*, Denver
208. McCall, R. B., Hogarty, P. S., Hamilton, J. S., Vincent, J. H. 1973. Habituation rate and the infant's response to visual discrepancies. *Child Dev.* 44: 280–87
209. McGurk, H. 1972. Infant discrimination of orientation. *J. Exp. Child Psychol.* 14:151–64
210. McGurk, H., Lewis, M. 1974. Space perception in early infancy: Perception within a common auditory-visual space? *Science* 186:649–50
211. McKenzie, B., Day, R. H. 1971. Orientation discrimination in infants: A comparison of visual fixation and operant training. *J. Exp. Psychol.* 11:366–75
212. McKenzie, B. E., Day, R. H. 1972. Object distance as a determinant of visual fixation in early infancy. *Science* 178:1108–10
213. Mendelson, M. J., Haith, M. M. 1976. The relation between audition and vision in the human newborn. *Monogr. Soc. Res. Child Dev.* In press
214. Milewski, A. 1976. Infant's discrimination of internal and external pattern elements. *J. Exp. Psychol.* In press
215. Milewski, A., Siqueland, E. R. 1975. Discrimination of color and pattern novelty in one month human infants. *J. Exp. Child Psychol.* 19:122–36
216. Millar, W. S. 1972. A study of operant conditioning under delayed reinforcement in early infancy. *Monogr. Soc. Res. Child Dev.* (Serial No. 147)
217. Millar, W. S. 1974. The role of visual-holding cues and the simultanizing strategy in infant operant learning. *Br. J. Psychol.* 65:505–18
218. Millar, W. S., Schaffer, H. R. 1973. Visual-manipulative response strategies in infant operant conditioning with spatially displaced feedback. *Br. J. Psychol.* 64:545–52
219. Miller, D. J. 1972. Visual habituation in the human infant. *Child Dev.* 43:481–93
220. Mills, M., Melhuish, E. 1974. Recognition of mother's voice in early infancy. *Nature* 252:123–24
221. Moffitt, A. R. 1971. Consonant cue perception by twenty- to twenty-four-week-old infants. *Child Dev.* 42:717–31
222. Molfese, D. 1975. The ontogeny of brain lateralization for speech and non-speech stimuli. *Brain Lang.* 2:356–68
223. Molfese, D., Nunez, V., Seibert, S., Ramanaiah, N. 1976. Cerebral asymmetry: Changes in factors affecting its development. *Ann. NY Acad. Sci.* In press
224. Monod, N., Pajot, N., Guidasci, S. 1972. The neonatal EEG: Statistical studies and prognostic value in full-term and pre-term babies. *Electroencephalogr. Clin. Neurophysiol.* 32: 529–44
225. Moore, M. 1975. Object permanence and object identity: A stage-developmental model. Presented at *Meet. Soc. Res. Child Dev.*, Denver
226. Moore, M., Meltzosf, A. 1975. Neonate imitation: A test of existence and mechanism. Presented at *Meet. Soc. Res. Child Dev.*, Denver
227. Morgan, G. 1973. Determinants of infants' reactions to strangers: Effects of age, and situational differences. Presented at *Meet. Soc. Res. Child Dev.*, Philadelphia
228. Morse, P. H. 1972. The discrimination of speech and nonspeech stimuli in early infancy. *J. Exp. Child Psychol.* 14: 477–92
229. Mundy-Castle, A., Anglin, J. 1973. Looking strategies in infants. In *The Competent Infant: Research and Commentary*, ed. L. Stone, H. Smith, L. Murphy. New York: Basic Books
230. Murray, A. 1975. Maternal employment reconsidered: Effects on infants. *Am. J. Orthopsychiatry* 45:773–90
231. Olson, G. M. 1976. An information processing analysis of visual memory and habituation in infants. See Ref. 66
232. Oster, H. S. 1975. Color perception in ten-week-old infants. Presented at *Meet. Soc. Res. Child Dev.*, Denver
233. Paden, L. Y. 1975. The effects of variations of auditory stimulation (music) and interspersed stimulus procedures on visual attending behavior in infants. See Ref. 42, pp. 29–41
234. Papoušek, H., Papoušek, M. 1974. Mirror image and self-recognition in young human infants: I. A new method of experimental analysis. *Dev. Psychobiol.* 7:149–57
235. Paradise, E., Curcio, F. 1974. Relationship of cognitive and affective behaviors to fear of strangers in male infants. *Dev. Psychol.* 10:476–83
236. Parke, R. 1973. Family interaction in the newborn period: Some findings, some observations and some unresolved issues. Presented at *Meet. Int. Soc. Study Behav. Dev.*, Ann Arbor
237. Parke, R., O'Leary, S. 1976. Father-mother-infant interaction in the newborn period: Some findings, some obser-

vations and some unresolved issues. In *The Developing Individual in a Changing World* Vol. 2, *Social and Environmental Issues*, ed. K. Riegel, J. Meacham. The Hague: Mouton. In press

238. Parke, R., O'Leary, S., West, S. 1972. Mother-father-newborn interaction: Effects of maternal medication, labor and sex of infant. *Proc. 80th Ann. Conv. Am. Psychol. Assoc.*

239. Parry, M. H. 1972. Infants' responses to novelty in familiar and unfamiliar settings. *Child Dev.* 43:233–37

240. Pedersen, F., Rubenstein, J., Yarrow, L. 1973. Father absence in infancy. Presented at *Meet. Soc. Res. Child Dev.*, Philadelphia

241. Peeples, D. R., Teller, D. Y. 1975. Color vision and brightness discrimination in two-month-old infants. *Science* 189:1102–3

242. Piaget, J. 1951. *The Origins of Intelligence in Children.* New York: Norton

243. Piaget, J. 1954. *The Construction of Reality in the Child.* New York: Basic Books

244. Piaget, J. 1960. *Psychology of Intelligence.* Paterson, NJ: Littlefield, Adams

245. Pipp, S. L. 1975. Infant visual scanning patterns to depth and contrast. Presented at *Meet. Soc. Res. Child Dev.*, Denver

246. Porter, R., Berlin, C. 1975. On interpreting developmental changes in the dichotic right-ear advantage. *Brain Lang.* 2:186–200

247. Provost, M., Décarie, T. G. 1974. Modifications du rhythme cardiaque chez des enfants de 9–12 mois au cours de la rencontre avec la personne étrangère. *Can. J. Behav. Sci.* 6:154–68

248. Rafman, S. 1974. The infant's reaction to imitation of the mother's behavior by the stranger. See Ref. 81, pp. 117–48

249. Ragozin, A. 1975. Attachment in day care children: Field and laboratory findings. Presented at *Meet. Soc. Res. Child Dev.*, Denver

250. Ramey, C., Hieger, L., Klisz, D. 1972. Synchronous reinforcement of vocal responses in failure-to-thrive infants. *Child Dev.* 43:1449–55

251. Ramey, C., Watson, J. 1972. Nonsocial reinforcement of infants' vocalizations. *Dev. Psychol.* 6:538

252. Ramsay, D., Campos, J. 1975. Memory by the infant in an object notion task. *Dev. Psychol.* 11:411–12

253. Rebelsky, F., Hanks, C. 1971. Fathers' verbal interaction with infants in the first three months of life. *Child Dev.* 42:63–68

254. Rheingold, H. 1974. General issues in the study of fear. See Ref. 46, pp. 249–53

255. Rheingold, H., Eckerman, C. 1973. Fear of the stranger: A critical examination. *Adv. Child Dev. Behav.*, Vol. 8

256. Ricciuti, H. 1974. Fear and the development of social attachments in the first year of life. See Ref. 46, pp. 73–106

257. Ross, G., Kagan, J., Zelazo, P., Kotelchuk, M. 1975. Separation protest in infants in home and laboratory. *Dev. Psychol.* 11:256–57

258. Ross, H. S. 1974. The influence of novelty and complexity on exploratory behavior in 12-month-old infants. *J. Exp. Child Psychol.* 17:436–51

259. Ross, H. S. 1975. The effects of increasing familiarity on infants' reactions to adult strangers. *J. Exp. Child Psychol.* 20:226–39

260. Ross, H. S., Rheingold, H. L., Eckerman, C. O. 1972. Approach and exploration of a novel alternative by 12-month-old infants. *J. Exp. Child Psychol.* 13:85–93

261. Rovee, C. K. 1972. Olfactory cross-adaptation and facilitation in human neonates. *J. Exp. Child Psychol.* 13:368–81

262. Rubinstein, J. 1974. A concordance of visual and manipulative responsiveness to novel and familiar stimuli in six-month-old infants. *Child Dev.* 45:194–95

263. Ruff, H. A., Birch, H. G. 1974. Infant visual fixation: The effects of concentricity, curvilinearity, and number of directions. *J. Exp. Child Psychol.* 17:460–73

264. Salapatek, P. 1973. Visual investigation of geometric pattern by the human infant. Presented at *Meet. Soc. Res. Child Dev.*, Philadelphia

265. Salapatek, P. 1975. Pattern perception in early infancy. See Ref. 37, 1:133–248

266. Salapatek, P., Banks, M. S., Aslin, R. N. 1974. Pattern perception in very young human infants: I. Visual acuity and accommodation. II. A critical period for the development of binocular vision. Presented at *Symp. Dev. Ocular Abnorm.*, Temple Univ.

267. Salapatek, P., Bechtold, A. G., Bushnell, E. N. 1975. Infant accommodation and acuity threshold as a function of viewing distance. Presented at *Meet. Soc. Res. Child Dev.*, Denver

268. Salapatek, P., Haith, M. M., Maurer, D., Kessen, W. 1972. Error in the corneal-reflection technique: A note on Slater and Findlay. *J. Exp. Child Psychol.* 14:493–97

269. Sameroff, A. 1971. Can conditioned responses be established in the newborn infant: 1971? *Dev. Psychol.* 5:1–12

270. Sameroff, A. 1972. Learning and adaptation in infancy: A comparison of models. *Adv. Child Dev. Behav.* 7:170–214

271. Scarr, S., Salapatek, P. 1970. Patterns of fear development during infancy. *Merrill-Palmer Q.* 16:53–90

272. Schaffer, H. R. 1974. Cognitive components of the infant's response to strangeness. See Ref. 46, pp. 11–24

273. Schaffer, H. R. 1975. Concordance of visual and manipulative responses to novel and familiar stimuli: A reply to Rubinstein (1974). *Child Dev.* 46: 290–91

274. Schaffer, H. R., Greenwood, A., Parry, M. 1972. The onset of wariness. *Child Dev.* 43:165–76

275. Schaffer, H. R., Parry, M. 1972. Effects of stimulus movement on infants' wariness of unfamiliar objects. *Dev. Psychol.* 7:81

276. Schaller, M. J. 1975. Chromatic vision in human infants: Conditioned operant fixation to "hues" of varying intensity. *Bull. Psychon. Sci.* 6:39–42

277. Schwartz, G., Davidson, R., Maer, F. 1975. Right hemisphere lateralization for emotion in the human brain: Interactions with cognition. *Science* 190:286–88

278. Schwarz, J., Strickland, R., Krolick, G. 1974. Infant day care: Behavioral effects at preschool age. *Dev. Psychol.* 10: 502–6

279. Self, P. A. 1975. Control of infant visual attending by auditory and interspersed stimulation. See Ref. 42, pp. 16–28

280. Self, P. A., Horowitz, F. D., Paden, L. Y. Olfaction in newborn infants. *Dev. Psychol.* 7:349–63

281. Serafica, F., Cicchetti, D. 1976. Down's syndrome children in a strange situation: Attachment and exploration behaviors. *Merrill-Palmer Q.* 22:137–50

282. Shaffran, R. 1974. Modes of approach and the infant's reaction to the stranger. See Ref. 81, pp. 149–97

283. Shaffran, R., Décarie, T. G. 1973. Short term stability of infants' responses to strangers. Presented at *Meet. Soc. Res. Child Dev.,* Philadelphia

284. Shaffran, R., Décarie, T. G. 1973. Have strangers frightened infants in trying to find out if infants were frightened of strangers? Presented at *Meet. Can. Psychol. Assoc.* Victoria, B.C.

285. Sharpless, A., Jasper, H. 1956. Habituation of the arousal reaction. *Brain* 79:655–80

286. Slater, A. M., Findlay, J. M. 1972. The measurement of fixation position in the newborn baby. *J. Exp. Child Psychol.* 14:349–64

287. Slater, A. M., Findlay, J. M. 1975. The corneal reflection technique and the visual preference method: Sources of error. *J. Exp. Child Psychol.* 20:240–47

288. Slater, A. M., Findlay, J. M. 1975. Binocular fixation in the newborn baby. *J. Exp. Child Psychol.* 20:248–73

289. Soderquist, D. R., Hoenigmann, N. 1973. Infant responsivity to pure tone stimulation. *J. Aud. Res.* 13:321–27

290. Sokolov, E. N. 1960. *Perception and the Conditioned Reflex.* New York: MacMillan

291. Solomon, R., Décarie, T. G. 1976. Fear of strangers: A developmental milestone or an overstudied phenomenon? *Can. J. Behav. Sci.* In press

292. Solomon-Shaffran, R., Décarie, T. G. 1976. A more natural approach for use in the evaluation of infants' stranger reactions. *Can. J. Behav. Sci.* 8:98–101

293. Sostek, A., Anders, T. 1975. Effects of varying laboratory conditions on behavioral-state organization in two- and eight-week-old infants. *Child Dev.* 46:871–78

294. Spitz, R. 1950. Anxiety in infancy: A study of its manifestations in the first year of life. *Int. J. Psychoanal.* 31: 138–43

295. Sroufe, L., Waters, E. 1976. The ontogenesis of smiling and laughter: A perspective on the organization of development in infancy. *Psychol. Rev.* 83: 173–89

296. Sroufe, L. A., Waters, E., Matas, L. 1974. Contextual determinants of infant affective response. See Ref. 46, pp. 49–72

297. Sroufe, L., Wunsch, J. 1972. The development of laughter in the first year of life. *Child Dev.* 43:1326–44

298. Stamps, L., Porges, S. 1975. Heart rate conditioning in newborn infants: Relationships among conditionability, heart rate variability and sex. *Dev. Psychol.* 11:424–31

299. Stayton, D., Ainsworth, M. D. S. 1973. Individual differences in infant responses to brief, everyday separations as

related to other infant and maternal behaviors. *Dev. Psychol.* 9:226–35

300. Stayton, D., Ainsworth, M. D. S., Main, M. 1973. Development of separation behavior in the first year of life: Protest, following and greeting. *Dev. Psychol.* 9:213–25

301. Stayton, D., Hogan, R., Ainsworth, M. D. S. 1971. Infant obedience and maternal behavior: The origins of socialization reconsidered. *Child Dev.* 42: 1057–69

302. Steinschneider, A. 1975. Implications of the sudden infant death syndrome for the study of sleep in infancy. *Minn. Symp. Child Psychol.* 9:106–34

303. Stern, D. 1971. A micro-analysis of mother-infant interaction: Behavior regulating social contact between a mother and her 3½-month-old twins. *J. Am. Acad. Child Psychiatry* 10:501–17

304. Stern, D. 1974. Mother and infant at play: The dyadic interaction involving facial, vocal and gaze behaviors. See Ref. 115, pp. 187–213

305. Stern, D., Jaffe, J., Beebe, B., Bennett, S. 1975. Vocalizing in unison and in alternation: Two modes of communication within the mother-infant dyad. *Ann. NY Acad. Sci.* 263:89–100

306. Stern, E., Parmelee, A., Harris, M. 1973. Sleep state periodicity in premature and young infants. *Dev. Psychobiol.* 6:357–65

307. Super, C. M. 1972. *Long-term memory in early infancy.* PhD thesis. Harvard Univ., Cambridge, Mass.

308. Super, C. M., Kagan, J., Morrison, F. J., Haith, M. M., Weiffenbach, J. 1972. Discrepancy and attention in the five-month infant. *Gen. Psychol. Monogr.* 85:305–31

309. Tanguay, P., Taub, J., Doubleday, C., Clarkson, D. 1976. An inter-hemispheric comparison of auditory evoked responses to consonant-vowel stimuli. *Physiol. Psychol.* In press

310. Taub, J., Tanguay, P., Doubleday, C., Clarkson, D., Remington, R. 1976. Hemisphere- and ear-asymmetry in the auditory evoked response to musical chord stimuli. *Physiol. Psychol.* 4:11–17

311. Teszner, D., Tzavaras, A., Bruner, J., Hecaen, H. 1972. L'asymetrie droite-gauche du Planum temporale. A propos de l'etude anatomique de 100 cerveaux. *Rev. Neurol.* 126:444–49

312. Thomas, H. 1973. Unfolding the baby's mind: The infant's selection of visual stimuli. *Psychol. Rev.* 80:468–88

313. Thompson, R. F., Spencer, W. A. 1966. Habituation: A model phenomenon for the study of neuronal substrates of behavior. *Psychol. Rev.* 73:16–43

314. Trehub, S. E. 1973. Infants' sensitivity to vowel and tonal contrasts. *Dev. Psychol.* 9:91–96

315. Trehub, S. E., Rabinovitch, M. S. 1972. Auditory-linguistic sensitivity in early infancy. *Dev. Psychol.* 6:74–77

316. Tronick, E. 1972. Stimulus control and the growth of the infant's effective visual field. *Percept. Psychophys.* 11: 373–76

317. Tronick, E., Adamson, L., Wise, S., Als, H., Brazelton, T. 1975. The infant's response to entrapment between contradictory messages in face-to-face interaction. Presented at *Meet. Soc. Res. Child Dev.,* Denver

318. Turkewitz, G., Birch, H. G., Cooper, K. K. 1972. Responsiveness to simple and complex auditory stimuli in the human newborn. *Dev. Psychobiol.* 5:7–19

319. Turkewitz, G., Creighton, S. 1975. Changes in lateral differentiation of head posture in the human neonate. *Dev. Psychobiol.* 8:85–89

320. Uzgiris, I. C. 1976. Infant development from a Piagetian approach: Introduction to a symposium. *Merrill-Palmer Q.* 22:3–10

321. Uzgiris, I. C. 1976. Organization of sensorimotor intelligence. In *The Origins of Intelligence,* ed. M. Lewis. New York: Plenum

322. Uzgiris, I. C., Hunt, J. 1975. *Assessment in Infancy: Ordinal Scales of Psychological Development.* Urbana: Univ. Illinois Press

323. Wachs, T. D. 1976. Utilization of a Piagetian approach in the investigation of early experience effects: A research strategy and some illustrative data. *Merrill-Palmer Q.* 22:11–30

324. Wada, J., Clark, R., Hamm, A. 1975. Cerebral hemispheric asymmetry in humans. *Arch. Neurol.* 32:239–46

325. Walker, S., Emde, R. 1975. CRISP: Sleep state scoring in human infants. *Behav. Res. Methods Instrum.* 7(4):379

326. Waters, E., Matas, L., Sroufe, L. 1975. Infants' reactions to an approaching stranger: Description, validation and functional significance of wariness. *Child Dev.* 46:348–56

327. Watson, M. W., Fischer, K. 1976. The relationship of pretend play to role-playing: A developmental sequence in late infancy. Presented at *Symp. South-*

west. Psychol. Assoc. Ann. Meet., Albuquerque

328. Webb, W. 1975. *Sleep.* Englewood Cliffs, NJ: Prentice Hall. 180 pp.

329. Weiskrantz, L. 1974. The interaction between occipital and temporal cortex in vision: An overview. In *The Neurosciences Third Study Program,* ed. F. O. Schmitt, F. G. Worden, 189–204. Cambridge, Mass: MIT Press

330. Weizmann, F., Cohen, L. B., Pratt, R. J. 1971. Novelty, familiarity and the development of infant attention. *Dev. Psychol.* 4(2):149–54

331. Welch, M. J. 1974. Infants' visual attention to varying degrees of novelty. *Child Dev.* 45:344–50

332. Wetherford, M. J., Cohen, L. B. 1973. Developmental changes in infant visual preferences for novelty and familiarity. *Child Dev.* 44:416–24

333. White, B. L. 1971. *Human Infants.* Englewood Cliffs, NJ: Prentice-Hall

334. Wiegerink, R., Harris, C., Simeonsson, R., Pearson, M. 1974. Social stimulation of vocalizations in delayed infants: Familiar and novel agent. *Child Dev.* 45:866–72

335. Witelson, S., Pallie, W. 1973. Left hemisphere specialization for language in the newborn. *Brain* 96:641–46

336. Womuth, S. J., Pankhurst, D., Moffitt, A. R. 1975. Frequency discrimination by young infants. *Child Dev.* 46:272–75

337. Wooten, B. R. 1975. Infant color vision? *Science* 187:275–77

338. Yonas, A., Pick, H. L. Jr. 1975. An approach to the study of infant perception. See Ref. 37, 2:1–31

339. Zelazo, P. R. 1972. Smiling and vocalizing: A cognitive emphasis. *Merrill-Palmer Q.* 18:349–65

340. Zelazo, P. R. 1976. From reflexive to instrumental behavior. See Ref. 57

341. Zelazo, P. R., Hopkins, J. R., Jacobson, S., Kagan J. 1974. Psychological reactivity to discrepant events. *Int. J. Cogn. Psychol.* 2:385–93

342. Zelazo, P. R., Komer, M. 1971. Infant smiling to non-social stimuli and the recognition hypothesis. *Child Dev.* 42:1327–39

343. Zelazo, P. R., Zelazo, N., Kolb, S. 1972. "Walking" in the newborn. *Science* 176:314–15

Ann. Rev. Psychol. 1977. 28:295–321
Copyright © 1977 by Annual Reviews Inc. All rights reserved

PERSONALITY AND SOCIAL DEVELOPMENT

❖275

Martin L. Hoffman
Department of Psychology, University of Michigan, Ann Arbor, Michigan 48109

Since this is the first chapter in the *Annual Review of Psychology* to be devoted exclusively to personality and social development, a brief historical note seems appropriate. The general topic has long interested psychologists, although little progress was made in the early years due to its being dominated by grand theorists such as Freud, and the early social interactionists like Cooley and Mead, whose views had appeal because they encompassed so much but which did not lend themselves very well to research. By the early 1950s the need for testable hypotheses of modest scope was recognized, and the stage appeared set for new advances to be made. However, owing perhaps to the national concern about the need for scientific talent which was heightened by Sputnik, the attention to developmental psychology was preempted by the cognitive domain. The interest in cognitive development was additionally reinforced by the War on Poverty and the inauguration of Head Start, and cognitive development continues to be a major focus of research effort.

The past few years, however, have seen a rebirth of interest in social development, and here, too, societal rather than purely scientific concerns seem to have provided the major impetus. It is probably more than coincidence that the student activism of the 1960s, the rising crime rate, and such heavily publicized events as Watergate and the street murder of Kitty Genovese have their parallels in the intensification of research on internalization of moral norms, a topic of long-standing interest, and in the emergence of new areas of study such as empathy, role-taking, altruism, and the impact of television violence on children. The women's movement has, no doubt, contributed to the renewal of interest in sex role development. And the very recent research on equity and other forms of distributional justice may in part reflect a sensitivity to the rising demands of poor people and poor nations for a greater share of the earth's resources.

Each of the above topics is now the object of intensive research that is more or less interrelated and cumulative and guided by theoretical models that are constantly being revised on the basis of the findings. Consequently there is reason to hope that some gaps in our knowledge of these important aspects of human development will soon be filled. I have therefore tried to fulfill my assignment—to do a selective review that points up the current state of the field—by making these topics the central focus of the chapter.

Research on personality dimensions lacking the obvious social connotations of the above mentioned topics has not shown as dramatic an increase. And the studies that have been done tend to be scattered, giving one little feeling of a cumulative body of knowledge. Some of this research does seem to have potential value, however, and the work done in two rather narrowly defined areas is illustrative. One pertains to the processes involved in the child's ability to delay gratification, which is the only ego skill to be studied intensively. The other pertains to the child's spontaneous, intrinsic motivation to engage in certain activities and how this motivation may be undermined by external factors. Both these bodies of research will be presented here in the hope of stimulating research in the larger, neglected areas of motivation and ego development.

We begin with role-taking and empathy because these concepts are pertinent to later discussions. We then take up moral internalization, prosocial behavior, sex-role development, delay of gratification, and intrinsic motivation. The impact of the mass media and social development in infancy are treated elsewhere in this volume.

DEVELOPMENT OF ROLE-TAKING SKILLS

Role-taking has long been a central concept in social and psychological theory, although empirical research is only recent. A decade ago cognitive developmentalists shifted from exclusive concern with problem solving in the physical world to an equal interest in children's development of the understanding of thoughts, feelings, and intentions of other people. Piaget's influence is apparent here as in the earlier, more purely cognitive research. Comprehensive reviews have recently appeared on role-taking by Shantz (110) and on communication of messages to others, which implies some role-taking ability, by Glucksberg, Krauss & Higgins (35).

Spatial Role-Taking

Research on taking another's spatial or perceptual viewpoint when it differs from one's own derives from Piaget's famous three-mountain landscape task, on which children below 6 years of age typically made the egocentric error of attributing their own viewpoint to a doll situated in various locations around the landscape. The research has since shown that certain aspects of Piaget's original task (e.g. size and complexity of the objects displayed, their asymmetrical placement, requiring a verbal response) may have served to mask the role-taking competence of younger subjects. Three-year-olds, for example, make very few errors when the display contains discrete, easily differentiated objects (small toys) and a verbal response is not required; that is, the subject indicates the other's point of view by manipulating an exact duplicate of the display (12). Two-year-olds will turn a picture toward another person who asks to see it; and even one-year-olds rarely orient the picture so that only they can see it (67).

Affective Role-Taking

Affective role-taking, the cognitive awareness of another's feelings, is usually assessed as follows: The child is told a brief story about a simple situation illustrating a particular emotion (e.g. attending a birthday party, losing a pet, being lost), while looking at a picture or a series of slides illustrating the events in the story (e.g. 11). He is then asked to indicate how the story character feels—either verbally or by selecting from several pictured faces the one expressing the correct emotion. The general findings are that simple, familiar situations involving happiness are recognized by three- and four-year-olds; and accuracy increases for fear, sadness, and anger until about age 7. It is unclear whether facial or situational cues are predominantly used.

This method is plagued with the problem that similarity between subject and story character facilitates high scores. Affective role-taking ability is thus confounded with actual similarity, and young children can perform well by simply attributing their own past or probable response to the story character. This may account for the frequent finding that dissimilarity (as to sex, age, race) or use of unfamiliar situations results in decreased accuracy scores especially in younger children. Only at 9–12 years of age do children consistently recognize emotions of people dissimilar to themselves, who are in unfamiliar situations (110). In several studies in which the story character's facial expressions and the situation are incongruous (e.g. he frowns at his birthday party), the results suggest that preschool children typically recognize the emotion in the face or in the situation, whichever is salient, without taking the incongruity into account (e.g. 61, 118).

Cognitive Role-Taking

Cognitive role-taking, inferring what another person knows or is thinking, is assessed in a variety of ways. These include playing games which require making inferences about another person's strategy and realizing that he is doing the same; selecting appropriate gifts for males and females of different ages; communicating messages to people whose perspective is lacking (e.g. they are blindfolded, very young, or enter the situation late and consequently lack certain necessary information); retelling a story from the point of view of each character in it. Several descriptive developmental stage theories (e.g. 109) have been advanced, which Shantz (110) has put together with the research findings, to arrive at the following generalizations: (a) By about age 6 the child can infer that another person may have thoughts or knowledge independent of his own; (b) by about age 8 he knows that his behavior can be the object of the other person's inferences; (c) by about age 10 he can infer what the other is thinking with considerable accuracy while at the same time realizing that the other may do the same with respect to him; (d) inferential accuracy and recognition of the nature of recursive thinking (thinking about thinking, etc) continue to develop at least into late adolescence.

Recent research suggests, as with spatial role-taking, that with simple tasks cognitive role-taking competence appears much earlier than previously thought. For decades following Piaget's landmark study of moral judgment, for example, it was widely assumed that children do not take the actor's intentions into account until

8 or 9 years of age. Recent research has clarified the ambiguities in Piaget's original stories (e.g. whether the child reaching for the jam really had bad intentions) and shown that even 5-year-olds can infer whether another's actions are intentional or accidental. Furthermore, children that age weigh intentions heavily when making moral judgments if the consequences of the intended act are as harmful as the consequences of the accidental act, rather than less harmful, as in Piaget's original stories (56, 102).

Research is also accumulating that indicates even 4-year-olds can take the perspective of others under certain conditions. For example, children this age who watched two short videotaped action sequences, accompanied by an explanatory audio portion, showed awareness that someone else (their mothers) would not understand the story when the sound was turned off (89). Four-year-olds also chose appropriate birthday gifts for their mothers, rather than toys attractive to themselves (76). This age group has also been found to take the listener's perspective into account in verbal communication tasks. They used simpler and more attention-getting language, for example, when talking to children much younger than themselves than when talking to peers or adults (111); they were more explicit verbally when giving instructions to someone who apparently could not see than to someone who could (75); they modified their language appropriately when discussing an experience they had a week earlier, depending on whether the listener had shared that experience or knew nothing about it (78). And finally, contrary to Piaget's assertion that discourse between children under 5 is merely a "collective mono-logue," it now appears that even 2-year-olds show the rudiments of focused dyadic interaction (attending to each other; taking turns speaking) when necessary for exchanging information or resolving disputes (26).

The foregoing indicates that very young children may demonstrate awareness of other perspectives in tasks that are simpler, closer to real life, involve more familiar people, and perhaps arouse more motivation than the tasks used in previous research. This, together with the fact that Piaget's view about egocentrism in childhood was based on spatial role-taking performance, which we now know bears little relation to other types of role-taking (110), indicates a clear need to reexamine the concept of egocentrism. The emerging evidence suggests, for example, that children may be aware of the independent existence of other people's inner states shortly after becoming aware of others as distinct physical entities (49). Egocentrism may thus be a far more transitory phenomenon than previously assumed. And the seemingly egocentric errors that children make may often reflect not a self-other fusion but a tendency, sometimes evident even in adults, to make inferences about other people's inner states on the basis of one's own perspective when unaware of other more relevant cues. The errors may thus be cognitive but not egocentric, and they may be expected to diminish with age. There is evidence that they may also diminish to the extent that the child is provided with labels for other people's covert responses to his behavior and given opportunities to enact various roles (110).

I have suggested elsewhere that role-taking is one of four broad phases in the development of a cognitive sense of the other (49): (*a*) for most of the first year, a fusion between self and other; (*b*) at about 11–12 months, "person permanence" or awareness of others as distinct physical entities (5); (c) shortly thereafter, a rudimentary sense of others as having independent inner states—the first step in role-taking which continues to develop over the years into the more complex forms noted above; (d) by middle or late childhood (the research is unclear which), awareness of others as having personal identities and life experiences that extend beyond the immediate situation.

EMPATHY

Empathy has been defined both as the awareness of and the vicarious affective response to another person's feelings. I have treated the first as affective role-taking since it is a cognitive response. The second concept has for centuries intrigued philosophers and more recently psychologists who see it as a necessary basis for social life, morality, and altruism (40). Research on empathy is still primitive, however, as indicated in the following summary.

The ideal measure of an empathic response would include evidence that (a) affect has been aroused in the observer and (b) the quality and direction of the affect correspond to that experienced by the other person. Physiological indices, which have been used with adults and at first appear ideal, fall down on the second criterion unless supplemented with other data indicating the nature of the affect aroused in the observer. The most often used child measure, based on verbalized affective responses to slide sequences showing other children in various affect-eliciting situations, yielded these results with 4- to 7-year-old children: empathy did not increase with age nor did it relate to aggression in girls. In boys, it did increase with age and it also related positively to aggression in the younger group, negatively in the older group (29).

Another index of empathy, which has the advantage of being both spontaneous and nonverbal, involves assessing whether the child's facial expression corresponds to the emotions depicted in a film. Using this index, most of the facial expressions of preschoolers, second, and fifth graders have been found to correspond to the expressions of the models in happy and sad films; and the younger children did as well as older ones (39). In an unusual design, preschoolers watched a series of emotionally loaded color slides (15). Their mothers and a group of undergraduates were asked to judge from the child's facial expressions alone (they could not see the slides) whether the child was watching a pleasant or an unpleasant slide. The child's "sending ability" was positively related to teacher ratings of outgoing characteristics (e.g. activity level, aggressiveness, impulsiveness, bossiness, sociality) and negatively to shyness, cooperation, emotional inhibition and control.

One- and 2-day-old infants have been found to cry in response to the sound of another infant's cry (104, 112). This reactive cry is not merely a response to a noxious stimulus or a simple imitative or conditioned verbal response lacking an affective component. Rather, it is vigorous, intense, in all respects resembles a spontaneous cry, and it occurs far less in response to equally loud nonhuman sounds. Though obviously not a full-fledged empathic response, it must therefore be considered as a possibly constitutionally based, early precursor of empathy.

A theory of empathy as unfolding through a series of developmental stages has recently been presented by Hoffman (40). Empathy is seen as having an affective component that is given increasingly complex meaning as the child progresses through the four phases in the development of a cognitive sense of the other, summarized earlier. Thus the infant's empathic response to another's distress includes no awareness of who is actually in distress. With "person permanence," this awareness exists but the other's inner states are unknown and assumed to be the same as one's own. With role-taking development, empathy becomes an increasingly veridical response to the other's inner states in the situation. By late childhood the final empathic stage is achieved wherein the affective response is synthesized with a mental representation of the other person's general life experiences. These empathic levels are assumed to form the basis of a motive to help others in distress.

MORAL INTERNALIZATION

Psychologists have long been intrigued with moral internalization probably because it epitomizes the age-old problem of how individuals come to manage the inevitable conflict between personal needs and social obligations. The legacy of Freud and Durkheim is the agreement among social scientists that most people do not go through life viewing society's norms as external, coercively imposed pressures to which they must submit. Though the norms are initially external to the individual and often in conflict with his desires, they eventually become part of his motive system and guide his behavior even in the absence of external authority. Theoretical disagreement revolves around which socialization experiences are most likely to foster this internalization process.

Parental Discipline

The general rationale for assuming discipline to be important is that moral internalization implies the motivation to weigh one's desires against the moral requirements of the situation; and one's earliest experience of doing this occurs in response to parental discipline, although in that case the moral requirements are of course external (47).

The research, done mainly in the 1950s and 1960s, shows a fairly consistent positive relation between moral internalization and the parent's frequent use of inductive discipline, techniques which point up the harmful consequences of the child's behavior for others. A morality based on fear of punishment is associated with power assertive discipline, e.g. physical punishment, deprivation of privileges, or the threat of these (45). There is also evidence for two morally internalized types: a humanistic, flexible type which is related to parental discipline that varies with the situation and includes occasional use of power assertion when the child is openly and unreasonably defiant; and a conventional, rigid type which is characterized by the parent's frequent use of love-withdrawal (46). Recent research suggests that humanistic children may be somewhat less dependent on the environment as a source of evaluation of their actions and thus more internalized than conventional children (20).

This research has been challenged because it is correlational, and since children have an impact on parents (e.g. 40), it may seem as plausible to infer that the child's moral orientation affects the parent's discipline as the reverse (4). While agreeing in general, I recently argued for making a causal inference in this particular case (47). The main point is this: In early infancy the child has the greatest impact on parents, who are aware of his helplessness and need for care. There is evidence, however, that before the child is 2, parents shift from primarily caretakers to disciplinarians who put considerable pressure on the child to change his behavior. From then on, the child not only has little control over the parent but is frequently compelled to comply (e.g. 73, 82, 119). Furthermore, the inner states aroused in the child by different discipline techniques (e.g. self-blame, fear) are remarkably similar to the inner states aroused by the moral encounter in internalized and noninternalized persons (guilt, fear). Since early discipline encounters predate internal moral development, it follows that parental discipline is more likely to be an antecedent than a consequent of moral internalization. Final resolution of this issue awaits research employing appropriate (e.g. cross-lagged) designs.

The most recent theoretical account of how induction fosters internalization (52a) may be summarized as follows: (a) Most techniques have some power-assertive, love-withdrawing, and inductive properties. (b) The first two comprise the motive arousal component which is necessary to get the child to stop what he is doing and attend. (c) Having attended, the child will often be influenced cognitively and affectively (through empathy arousal) by the information contained in the inductive component and thus experience a reduced sense of opposition between his desires and external demands. (d) Too little arousal and the child may ignore the parent; too much and the resulting fear or resentment may prevent effective processing of the inductive content, thus perpetuating the felt opposition between desires and demands. Inductions ordinarily achieve the best balance and are therefore most effective in the discipline encounter. Furthermore, in keeping with recent developmental research on memory (117a), the child may be expected over time to remember the ideas communicated in inductions but to forget that they originated with the parent. With no external agent to whom to attribute these ideas, he may then be expected to attribute them to himself.

Experimental Research on Discipline

The experimental research began in the mid-1960s and has now virtually replaced the correlational approach to the study of discipline and moral internalization. In the most frequently used paradigm the child is first trained or "socialized" by presenting him with several toys of varying degrees of attractiveness. When he handles a particular toy (e.g. the most attractive one) he is "punished" by an unpleasant noise, the timing and intensity of which may be varied. The child is then left alone with the toys and observed through a one-way mirror. Resistance-to-temptation scores are based on whether or not, how soon after the experimenter left, and for how long the child plays with the prohibited toy. Recently a verbal component has been added to the training session (e.g. 16, 17, 63–66). This may be a simple instruction [e.g. "Don't touch the green toy" (16)] or a complex reason resembling induction. In general, these studies have found that (a) without a verbal component, variations in timing and intensity of punishment have effects similar to those observed with lower animals: the child is less apt to perform a deviant act when the training consists of intense punishment or punishment that was applied at the onset of that act; (*b*) these effects of timing and intensity of punishment are reduced when a verbal component is added; (*c*) the verbal component is more effective with mild than with severe punishment, and with older than with younger children.

A second, less frequently used paradigm deals not with inhibition of an overt act but with creating a self-critical verbal response following a deviant act. The usual procedure is to give the subject a task to perform such as guessing which direction a doll is facing, or knocking toy soldiers down so as to move a toy nurse to safety. The subject has no control over the task nor can he see the actual results of his actions. There are a number of training trials, on some of which, according to a predetermined schedule, the subject receives punishment (e.g. the experimenter takes candy from a supply that was given the subject earlier, or frowns and expresses disappointment). The experimenter verbalizes the word designated as the critical label (e.g. careless, rough, bumper, blue) when the punishment is administered. In the test trial the child is not punished but a cue is provided indicating that he has transgressed (e.g. the toy nurse is made to appear to break, or a buzzer sounds). The subject's self-criticism score depends on whether or not he then applies the self-critical label to his act. The relevance of the earlier studies of this type to moral internalization is questionable since an adult was present throughout the experiment. In the most recent study (37) this and other deficiencies were corrected. The findings were that the self-criticism scores were not affected by two types of discipline manipulations, "withdrawal of love-induction" and "withdrawal of material reward," but they were increased by direct reinforcement of the label.

The experimental research has recently been criticized on several grounds (52b). First, the quality and intensity of the parent-child relation, which may be assumed to influence the child's response to discipline, is lost. Second, though the simulated discipline techniques fit certain theoretical categories of the investigator, they often bear little resemblance to what parents actually do [e.g. "It is wrong for you to want to play with that toy or to think about playing with that toy" (65)]. Third, and more fundamentally, the socialization process is so drastically telescoped as to lose some of its essential features, notably the distinction between a moral act and the child's immediate response to a discipline technique. This is most apparent in designs involving a single adult-child interaction, wherein a particular "discipline technique" is administered and the child's immediate response serves as the moral index. A fourth, related problem is that the act designated as deviant is not a spontaneous transgression by the child but one that is actually induced by the experimenter's instructions (e.g. to play with the toys), arbitrarily defined as deviant and punished; or the child is given a task and is punished for doing something that he cannot prevent because he cannot see what he is doing (37). In such unusual, ambiguous circumstances, the child's only clue to appropriate action comes from the experimenter; and learning may therefore simply reflect blind compliance. Finally, we must be skeptical about using compliance to an arbitrary request as a moral index, in view of Milgram's well-known finding that compliance may also result in highly antimoral action.

For these reasons, the experiments have questionable relevance to moral internalization. They may tell us a great deal, however, about the processes in the child's immediate reactions to discipline. Consider the research by Cheyne (16, 17). The forbidden-toy design was used in which children were exposed to these conditions: severe punishment (a) with and (b) without a verbal rule; mild punishment (c) with and (d) without a rule. Telemetered heart-rate data were obtained throughout. The major result was that only condition c resulted in the apparently ideal combination of both resistance to temptation and heart-rate deceleration, which is generally associated with attention and cognitive processing. Condition d produced little resistance to temptation and heart-rate change. And, although some subjects in b resisted temptation, this was generally accompanied by heart-rate acceleration which has been found to be associated with emotional stress. These findings fit the model of optimal arousal in the discipline encounter discussed in the previous section. The rule used was too simple to qualify as an induction, but it would appear that with certain modifications this type of experiment may be uniquely well suited for investigating the processes involved in the child's immediate reactions to discipline, knowledge about which may be necessary for full understanding of the role of discipline in moral internalization.

Models

The 1960s saw numerous experimental studies of the effect of models on behavior. Those investigating the effects of adult models on resistance to temptation are especially pertinent here because of their possible bearing on the parent's role as model in the child's moral development.[1] The overall results of the early research are as follows (45): Observing models who yield to temptation and perform in a manner prohibited by the experimenter consistently produces similar behavior in the child, as though such models serve to legitimize the deviant behavior and undermine the subject's prior socialization against deviance. Observing models who resist the temptation to behave deviantly however, does not result in a reduction of deviant behavior by the child. Recent research raises the possibility that this generalization may reflect the predominantly middle class background of the subjects in those earlier studies. Rosenkoetter (100) studied lower class, mostly white third graders in a Luthern parochial school, half of whom were from broken homes. The subjects were assigned a dull task, to be carried out while an exciting animated cartoon was being shown nearby. The results, as in the previous research, were that the effects of prior observation of an adult model who yielded to temptation and left the assigned task to see the film far exceeded the effects of observing a model who resisted temptation and stayed with the task. The resisting model in this study, however, did have a statistically borderline effect. Fry (32) studied 8- and 9-year-old

[1]The many experiments on the effects of observing models who are punished for deviant behavior are not discussed because their relevance to the actual influence of models is questionable. The subject very likely perceives the punishment to the model as an indication of what to expect if he deviates, and he acts accordingly. Any effects found may thus not be due to imitation of the model but to the message from the experimenter, the model merely serving as the medium for that message.

Indian children and American middle class children living in India, using the forbidden-toy paradigm. For the Americans, the yielding model was effective but not the resisting model, which fits the previous research. With Indian children, however, the resisting and yielding models were both effective, though marginally. Fry's suggestion that adult models who resist temptation may be effective in cultures which stress the importance of obedience may also apply to Rosenkoetter's findings.

Cognitive Disequilibrium

Piaget suggested 50 years ago that cognitive development and role-taking experiences that among other things produce cognitive disequilibrium are major contributors to moral internalization. These views continue to stimulate research. Most recently, the level of moral judgment was found to relate positively to the cognitive level displayed in solving mathematics and physics problems by 4- to 8-year-olds and to the role-taking ability of children at various ages (1, 19, 86, 108).

In experimental attempts to alter moral judgments, children who tend to make judgments on the basis of the consequences of action are exposed to an adult model who employs the presumably more mature criterion of intentions. The findings in general indicate that the children not only shift their verbal responses toward the model, but they actually increase their understanding of the principle that intentions should be taken into account when making moral evaluations of behavior (e.g. 23, 34, 116).[2] Furthermore, the effects appear to last up to a year, though not beyond (116). That mere exposure to models can produce such shifts has been interpreted as evidence against the cognitive developmental view that advances in moral level require cognitive disequilibrium (62). Another interpretation (52), however, is that the children were not merely imitating the model. Rather, they knew that acts may or may not be intentional but before observing the model they gave intentions less weight than consequences, perhaps because the stories used, like Piaget's, portrayed more harmful consequences for accidental than for intended acts. This fits the evidence cited earlier that children even younger than the subjects in these modeling studies usually weigh intentions heavily when the consequences of accidental and intended acts are equally harmful. Repeated exposure to an adult model who consistently assigns greater weight to intentions despite the disparity in consequences might then have produced cognitive disequilibrium, which the subjects reduced by reexamining and changing their views. This interpretation is consonant with cognitive developmental theory, but it does not make the cognitive developmental assumption that movement is always progressive, since a model who espouses "consequences," the less mature response, might also be expected to produce cognitive disequilibrium.

Kohlberg's stage theory, which has contributed much to current ferment in the field, has recently come under heavy attack. Kurtines & Greif (62) point up the many psychometric deficiencies in Kohlberg's measures. They also note that in

[2]For perspective on the intentions-consequences dichotomy, it is worth noting that in making judgments about competence, consequences (i.e. performance) rather than intentions (i.e. effort) appear to become more important with age (118a).

Kohlberg's longitudinal study there were actually few significant changes in moral judgment over time, stage 4 being predominant at all ages (16, 20, and 24 years); there was no evidence that the subjects passed through the stages in a fixed order; and college students often obtained lower scores than they did when in high school. Kohlberg interpreted the last as a measurement problem, but the fact remains that the longitudinal results do not support the postulated developmental sequence. A 3-year longitudinal study by Holstein (54) also provides evidence against the expected stepwise progression, since stages were skipped and some backsliding occurred. Kurtines & Greif also point up some anomalies in the research relating Kohlberg's stages to overt behavior, e.g. stage 3 characterized delinquents in one study (31) and social conformists in another (105). And finally, they note certain flaws in Turiel's experiment, in which subjects are exposed to levels of moral reasoning differing in varying degrees from their own level, and which is often cited as basic support for the assumption that moral growth is stimulated by exposure to optimally higher levels.

In a recent study using an improved version of Turiel's design (117), seventh grade children who initially scored at Kohlberg's lowest two moral stages (but not the higher-stage subjects) were influenced in the expected manner, that is, they shifted more in the direction of higher than lower levels of moral judgment. These same lower-stage subjects, however, also obtained high scores on a social desirability measure and furthermore, within this group social desirability was found to relate positively to the amount of shift. Since these subjects had an external moral orientation to begin with (the lowest two stages are external), these findings suggest that direct social influence processes may account for their shift in judgment rather than the disequilibrium and "structural match" postulated in cognitive-developmental theory.

The studies of comprehension and preference for higher moral levels, which also follow Turiel's format (e.g. 95) appear to have other problems (52). The findings were that comprehension was high up to the subject's own predominant stage, and then fell off rapidly; the highest stage comprehended was the most preferred of those comprehended. Stage 6 statements, however, were the most preferred of all, which means that the subject's predominant stage did not predict his preference. It is also possible that high-stage statements may have been inadvertently phrased more attractively than low-stage statements, which would introduce a spurious element into the subjects' choices.

From the few studies reporting moral judgment scores in different situations, there is evidence against Kohlberg's assumption that the stages are homogeneous. Not one subject in a sample of 75 college students obtained the same stage score in five Kohlberg dilemmas (30). The scores obtained by adolescent boys and also by their mothers showed considerable "scatter" (55). And two-thirds of a large college sample used different stages in Kohlberg's dilemmas than in evaluating a social protest movement (38). To explain this much variation in terms of Piaget's concept of "decalage" might raise questions about that concept's usefullness.

In response to the criticisms, Kohlberg suggests that the problem may lie in his coding procedures and that future research with his new codes may provide support for the theory (59). The theory, however, has also been attacked: (*a*) for neglecting motivation, which may be needed for translating abstract moral concepts into moral action (91); (*b*) for claiming universality though it is actually based on Western modes of thought and social organization (e.g. stage 5 makes sense only in a constitutional democracy and stage 6 may require a level of abstract thought that disqualifies most of the world's population (113); and (*c*) on various philosophical grounds (e.g. 2, 91).

More definitive tests of Kohlberg's theory need to be made. For one thing, it has provided the guidelines for major new efforts in moral education. And, despite the lack of empirical support to date, certain of the concepts in the theory continue to have appeal. Cognitive disequilibrium and structural match, for example, may help account for the developmental progression from a rudimentary moral sense, that perhaps originates in the discipline encounter as discussed earlier, to the complex moral concepts often held by adults.

PROSOCIAL BEHAVIOR

Research on prosocial behavior, especially altruism and certain concepts pertaining to distributional justice, has recently burgeoned.

Altruism

Half a dozen research reviews on altruism have appeared since 1970. In the most recent, Bryan (14) surveyed about a hundred mostly experimental studies done in the past decade. Problems of definition abound, revolving mainly around whether an act, to be called altruistic, must be devoid of any expectation of personal gain by the actor. Operationally, two types of altruistic behavior have been studied: exerting effort to help another person in need; and giving up something one wants, to help another. The sacrifice is typically made privately and toward a stranger.

The most frequently studied determiner of altruistic behavior in children is exposure to models. Altruistic models do produce altruistic behavior and the effect varies depending on such model characteristics as warmth, power, and hypocrisy. Altruism then joins an ever-growing list of behaviors that are influenced by live or televised models. Perhaps any act involving little cost to the observer is amenable to such influence. This suggests that these studies may reflect nothing more than the effect of demand characteristics of the experiment, which are communicated by the model's actions. In a recent study, the effect of altruistic models lasted two months (103), but since the initial and posttest situations were similar, an explanation in terms of demand characteristics may still apply.

The results of recent correlational research (48) suggest that the parent may serve as an effective model for altruism, but it is difficult to separate these effects from those of two other aspects of the parent's role—disciplinarian and giver of affection. Altruistic behavior in fifth-grade, first-born children was assessed by peer ratings. Parental data were obtained in separate interviews with each parent. The altruistic children were found to have at least one parent who communicated altruistic values and thus may have served as a model, and one who frequently used inductive discipline techniques; affection was an influential factor only in the mother-son dyad. In another recent study, using a combined correlational and experimental approach, an inductive appeal to fifth and eighth graders for contributions to UNICEF was more effective than a power oriented appeal, but only with children who reported that their parents used inductive discipline (22).

There is considerable research on the effects of a person's well-being on his helping behavior. Children who are successful, popular, emotionally secure, or self-confident —or who have positive moods and feelings of success aroused in them experimentally—are more likely to help others (e.g. 3, 99, 120). A possible explanation is that fulfillment of the child's egoistic needs may reduce preoccupation with his own concerns and leave him open and responsive to the needs of others.

Both sharing with and helping a younger child have been found to relate positively to cognitive role-taking in 7-year-olds (101). This is consistent with an experimental study in which kindergarteners trained in role-taking skills were more likely to aid a younger child, an effect which persisted for a week (115). These findings are not surprising since a person should be more likely to help another if he can take the other's perspective. We must, however, not lose sight of the fact that role-taking is very likely a neutral skill and may therefore be expected to serve egoistic motives in situations presenting others as competitors (as indeed it does in some role-taking measures) rather than as people in need.

As noted earlier, empathy has long been viewed as significant in altruism, and a stage theory of empathy has been advanced as the basis for altruistic motive development. The pertinent research is scanty and confined mainly to adults. In general, adults have been found to respond to others in distress with an affective, presumably empathic response, as well as an overt attempt to help; the intensity of the affect and the speed of the overt response increase with the number and intensity of distress cues from the victim; and the observer's affect tends to subside when he helps (49). Something like the last was obtained in Murphy's classic nursery school study (90). When children helped others, their affective response diminished; when they did not help, the affect continued. The younger children were also found to react to another's distress with a worried, anxious look but do nothing, whereas older children typically looked concerned but also tried to help. There is also anecdotal evidence that 2-year-olds may both show concern and try to help, though their efforts are often inappropriate (49). These findings all suggest that (a) empathy may be an early, primitive response; (b) it motivates helpful action insofar as one is capable of such action; and (c) like other motives, its intensity is reduced by relevant action. More direct systematic developmental research on the relation between empathy and altruism is needed before such conceptions can be evaluated.

Cooperation

Cook & Stingle (18) recently reviewed the literature on cooperation and competition in young children. Most of the research was done years ago and was concerned with age, sex, and cultural differences. Generally, cooperation and competition increase with age, competition appearing at about age 4 and cooperation a year later. The recent research is sparse but useful because it seeks connections between these behaviors and empathy and role-taking. Thus cooperative behavior has been found to correlate positively with affective, but not with spatial, role-taking competence in fourth and fifth graders (57, 58). Murphy's report of a positive relationship between empathy and cooperation in preschoolers, however, was not replicated in a recent study of 4-year-olds (71), perhaps because the experimental procedures used for assessing empathy and cooperation put different constraints on the child's behavior than did Murphy's naturalistic observations. The rules of the cooperation game, for example, were more salient to the subject than his partner's emotional state, which suggests that his empathic capability may not have been engaged during the game. Whether the same would be true of older children remains to be seen.

Distributional Justice

A newly emerging body of experimental research derives from social concerns about distributional justice, defined as the process for allocating valued goods according to a principle of deservingness. Lerner (69) suggests that three such principles underlie major economic theories: parity (equal division of resources), need (to each according to his needs), equity (to each according to his contribution); and he describes three experiments with children. In one, kindergarteners who worked together with others as a team closely followed the rule of parity in distributing rewards. In another, first graders exhibited parity when defined as a team and equity when defined as independent co-workers. In both studies children showed little evidence of self-interest (maximizing own reward), which may be due to demand characteristics and the presence of the experimenter, although in a supplementary study little selfishness was displayed in the experimenter's absence.

Equity has also been found in preschoolers and second graders, who allocated more rewards to children who performed more competently on a task than to less competent performers (70). In a study of moral judgment, Brickman & Bryan (13) had fifth-grade girls observe a model who surreptitiously modified the distribution of rewards in a four-person group such that the model (a) either augmented or reduced her own reward (theft or charity), and (b) in so doing made the entire distribution of rewards either more or less equal. The model's charitable action was viewed more favorably if it resulted in parity than if it produced a less equal distribution. This pattern was not obtained with theft. Equity was not an issue since the allocation of rewards was unrelated to the recipients' performance.

In a recent developmental study reported by Sampson (106), children 3–12 years old were presented with two doll-play situations. In one, the dolls did an equal amount of work; in the other, the work done was unequal. The results indicated that with increasing age the boys tended to allocate rewards equitably when the work investment differed, and equally when the work investment was equal. Girls of all ages tended to allocate in a similar manner whether the work investment was equal or not. This suggests that males tend to become more sensitive to an equity principle with age, while females do not, which is consistent with the fact that males receive more socialization toward instrumental competence than females.

The possible relationship between equity and altruism was studied by Long & Lerner (72). Fourth graders who were overpaid for a task were more likely to donate some of their earnings to poor orphans than fourth graders who were properly paid. Furthermore, this pattern was most pronounced in children who obtained high scores on an independent test of willingness to delay gratification, which was assumed to reflect belief in the principle of equity (if a person gives up something now, he deserves to receive more in the future). The principle of equity may, of course, at times be incompatible with altruism; for example, 4- and 5-year-olds rarely made donations after receiving what appeared to be less than their fair share of a reward (77).

SEX-ROLE DEVELOPMENT

Past research on sex-role development derived mainly from the concept of identification. Psychoanalytic writers stressed the child's anxiety over physical punishment or loss of parental love; to avoid anxiety, the child strives desperately to be the parent and thus acquires, among other things, an appropriate sex-role identity. Social learning theorists view the child as emulating the parent to acquire the parent's power, mastery, and other resources. The research, done mainly in the 1960s, provides scattered support for the view that culturally approved sex-role preference (regarding toys, games, occupations) is associated in boys with paternal affection and power.

There is considerable evidence that, other things being equal, children imitate same-sexed models (74). Theorists as different as Mischel and Kohlberg assume this is because of the similarity to the self, although Kohlberg views the child as not just imitating but cognitively processing the information from the model. Slaby & Frey (114), following Kohlberg, predicted that as children progress toward a stable gender identity (knowledge of one's gender as an identifiable, stable, consistent human attribute) they tend increasingly to emulate same-sexed models. The expected positive relation between level of gender identity and time spent watching same-sexed models was found in 2- to 5-year-olds, though significantly only in boys. The low relationship in girls fits past research in which both sexes show culturally approved sex-typed preferences and identification with same-sexed parents, but females cross over more than males.

Sex-role differentiation theory, which stresses role interaction rather than parent identification and views fathers as being as important for females as for males, has only recently begun to stimulate research. Hetherington, for example, has shown the importance of fathers for sex-role development in girls and also presents evidence that the effects of having no father vary depending on whether the absence is due to divorce or death (41, 42).

Achievement and Fear of Success

According to cultural stereotypes and various sex-role theories, males are more motivated to achieve than are females. The research to date suggests there is no sex difference (74). The achievement measures (e.g. preference for difficult tasks, achievement themes in response to school-related projective stimuli, level of aspiration), however, do not require the subject to choose between achievement and other values. In a recent study (50), children and adults rated the importance of 18 personal attributes which included "trying your best in everything you do" and "doing well in school (work)." In five large, independent samples (one fifth grade, two seventh grade, two adult) the males chose these two achievement items more often than the females, who preferred items pertaining to consideration for others. Thus males do appear to place greater value on achievement, although the previous research indicates females are as likely as males to have achievement motives aroused in situations that call for achievement and do not conflict with their other values.

Horner's work suggesting a fear of success in women spawned a large body of research that was recently reviewed by Zuckerman & Wheeler (121). They conclude that Horner's projective measure is deficient because it does not yield consistent age or sex differences, it may tap a stereotype rather than a motive, and it does not relate to career choice, achievement motivation, and impaired performance in competitive situations. Two recent studies not included in that review are discussed here because of their developmental and validity implications.

Romer (96) gave a slightly modified Horner measure to children in the fifth through eleventh grades and also had them perform several tasks under competitive and noncompetitive conditions. No sex differences or age trends in fear-of-success imagery were found. However, at the two older grade levels the fear-of-success girls performed more poorly in the competitive condition; those without fear of success did not. Romer suggests that although fear-of-success imagery exists earlier, "it may not become established in a female's motivational network until well into adolescence . . ." and may thus "be considered a developmental phenomenon affected by puberty, the onset of heterosexual dating, clearer sex role expectations, etc."

In the only long-term follow-up study to date, Hoffman (44) readministered the fear-of-success measure to Horner's original subjects and also asked questions about their lives during the intervening years. There were some interesting findings. (a) Fear-of-success scores of female subjects dropped significantly over the 9-year period. The drop probably reflects the shift from academic to marriage-and-motherhood concerns rather than milieu effects (changing sex-role norms), since in a 1972 replication of Horner's study the female students' scores were virtually the same as Horner's subjects' (43). (b) If fear-of-success reflects a conflict in which success signifies affiliative loss and failure as a woman, women with this fear in 1966 might be expected to marry and have children sooner. They did both. (c) Hoffman theorized further that marriages often require the male to be more successful than the female, and any change in the established balance becomes a threat, especially for women who fear success. An ideal way out is to become pregnant because it removes the woman from the achievement area, confirms her femininity, and reestablishes her affiliative relation to her husband. The respondents who had had a pregnancy were asked about the events preceding it, and the responses were coded blind for anything suggesting change in the husband-wife success balance (e.g. she is to start work, get a better job, or enter graduate school; he has a career or academic setback). The results supported the hypothesis that women with fear-of-success in college more often become pregnant when faced with success relative to their husbands.

The results for males in both studies fit no apparent pattern, and the authors conclude that the measure may be invalid for males. They also note, as do others (e.g. 88), that while female fear-of-success themes involve rejection or loss of femininity, male responses more often are bizarre or reflect cynicism about success.

Sex Differences

Maccoby & Jacklin's volume (74) is now the major reference point for assessing sex differences in all categories of behavior. The only clear sex differences to emerge from their review are that males are more aggressive, defined in terms of intent to harm another, and, starting in early adolescence, they become more competent in visual spatial ability and mathematical skills and less competent in verbal ability. It also appears, on the basis of cross-cultural and hormonal research, that these differences may have a genetic component. The sexes do not differ in most other aspects of behavior (e.g. self-esteem, suggestibility, dependency, empathy, role learning, analytical ability, achievement motivation). Maccoby & Jacklin also report that except for a few narrowly defined sex-typed behaviors, there was "a remarkable degree of uniformity in the socialization of the two sexes" (74, p. 348). For example, there were no differences in verbal stimulation, protectiveness, and encouragement of aggression.

In an enterprise of such broad scope as Maccoby & Jacklin's it is inevitable that deficiencies will be uncovered as specialists examine the conclusions against actual findings and bring to bear the results of new research. Block (7), in a highly detailed, probing critique has pointed out a number of methodological shortcomings, both in the research literature itself (e.g. poor design, undependable measures, poor sampling) and in the evaluative framework used by Maccoby & Jacklin to organize it (e.g. limitations of the classifying rubrics and the box-score approach used, insufficiencies and omissions in the research summarized, discrepancies between the evidence presented and the conclusions reached). And more specifically with regard to sex role socialization, Block (8) suggests that the importance of the "narrowly defined" sex-typed differences reported by Maccoby & Jacklin (which, as they note, includes shaping children in sex-appropriate ways through differences in clothes and toys, handling and playing with boys more roughly than girls, and punishing boys more than girls for sex-inappropriate behavior) should not be underplayed, since they probably contribute importantly to the child's conception of himself in relation to gender and sex roles.

Block's main point, however, is that the way Maccoby & Jacklin organized the data increased the likelihood of false acceptance of the null hypothesis; that is, (a) heterogeneous, conceptually distinct behaviors are often classified into one category; and (b) studies differing widely in statistical power and psychometric quality are aggregated and given equal weight. The result is that the research summaries tend to suggest inconsistencies or to level differences that would otherwise be seen. Sex differences would less likely be obscured if the findings were grouped according to more highly specified areas of socialization and sorted as to age of child and sex of parent. Block notes, for example, that when the few studies of children over 5 are examined, excluding those with very small samples, clear trends in differential socialization of the sexes do appear; and when the findings for fathers are examined separately, it becomes clear that cognitive achievement, especially of sons, is more salient for them. In this connection, a recent study by Block, Block & Harrington (9) is especially interesting. Mothers and fathers separately taught their preschool children four cognitive tasks. Observers, using a Q-sort technique, found no sex differences in actual teaching strategies, but they did find that fathers applied more pressure to achieve, especially to boys. Whereas the fathers emphasized the cognitive aspects of the teaching situation with sons, they exhibited less concern with their daughter's performance and more with the interpersonal aspects of the situation (e.g. they were more protective and tried to make the situation more fun).

Maccoby & Jacklin's conclusion that there is no clear tendency for females to be more empathic has also been questioned. As noted by Hoffman (51), this appears to be a premature interpretation resulting from grouping together such highly diverse measures as perceiving alternative solutions to interpersonal problems, communicative role-taking vs egocentrism, the effect of another's affective tone on one's performance of a task, and vicarious affective response to another's expressions of affect. Only the last corresponds to what is most commonly thought of as a true empathic response. Six of the comparisons summarized by Maccoby & Jacklin employed this type of measure and in all six the females obtained higher scores. Hoffman adds ten more such comparisons from recent research and in all of these, too, the females obtained higher scores. Though few differences were significant, it is unlikely that all 16 would be in the same direction by chance. Thus females do appear to be more empathic than males. They were not more competent in affective and cognitive role-taking, however, and there was a trend favoring males in spatial role-taking, which fits Maccoby & Jacklin's conclusions.

In the same paper Hoffman reviewed research which suggests that another person's giving or withholding affection has no more effect on the task performance of girls than that of boys, hence that female empathy is not part of a larger sensitivity that includes a heightened reaction to other people's feelings toward the self. This generalization may only be true of young children, however, since the subjects were in the 4 to 8 year range. In a national sample of children ranging upwards from 8 years, Rosenberg & Simmons (98) found that females 15 years and older described themselves on a personality inventory as more self-conscious and concerned about others' attitudes toward the self than did males. The 8–11 year old group did not differ. This type of sensitivity may thus begin to differentiate the sexes in adolescence.

As for the behavior of males, in one empathy study 4-year-old boys gave more active, coping responses when asked how they felt after viewing the Feshbach-and-Roe slide sequences (53) than did girls. This is consistent with theories that characterize males as more instrumental or "agentic," and with the recent finding that 4-year-old boys suggested more alternative solutions to physical-barrier problems than did girls (10). Giving an instrumental response to a request for feeling may thus reflect a general tendency for boys to consider ameliorative action alternatives rather than to empathize in interpersonal situations. Whether it also reflects a difficulty in responding affectively, perhaps a type of resistance or defensive misinterpretation of the experimenter's request for feeling, is a matter for future research.

In Freud's view, owing to anatomical differences, girls are not compelled to resolve the Oedipus complex quickly and dramatically and thus do not identify with the parent as fully as boys do. Consequently, girls have less internalized moral structures. Freud's followers differed in details but drew the same conclusion. In the Hoffman study cited earlier (50), projective story-completion items were used in which a protagonist who is portrayed sympathetically commits a moral transgression. The story completions were coded for internal guilt feelings and fear of detection and punishment. The results in all child and adult samples indicate that moral transgressions are more likely to be associated with guilt in females and fear in males. This difference may be due in part to differences in child-rearing practices: more induction and affection for girls and power assertion for boys (50, 122). There was also evidence that males' achievement values may reflect an egoistic rather than an internal moral orientation. Extrapolating from sex-role differentiation theory, the results for adults as well as children might best be explained by differences in sex-role socialization and increasing pressures on males over the life cycle to achieve and succeed, which may often conflict with moral concerns. In any case, since guilt and empathy are the two major known prosocial affects, females appear to have a greater prosocial affective base than males.

Sex-Role Preference and Personal Adjustment

There is increasing evidence that traditional sex-role socialization may not be conducive to adjustment. In a direct test of this proposition, Bem (6) found that college males with strong masculine preferences showed an impaired capacity for tenderness (in interacting with a kitten) and females with strong feminine preferences found it difficult to resist irrational social pressures to conform. Androgenous subjects of either sex showed both types of competence. Indirect evidence comes from a recent study by Rosenfeld (97), who presented four masculine and feminine sex-typed toys, controlled on relevant variables such as cost, to children in grades one to three and asked them to "think of the strangest, most exciting, and most interesting way you can for changing this toy so that boys and girls will have more fun playing with it." Both boys and girls responded with far more varied approaches for improving the masculine toys. If feminine toys thus lack inventive potential, they may elicit little creative competence, and parents who encourage girls to play with them may do them a disservice. There is evidence from parental reports and home observations of 18–24 month old infants (27, 28), and observations of adults interacting with a 3-month-old infant introduced as a male or female (107), that parents still do encourage girls to play with feminine toys, although they also sometimes offer them masculine toys (28).

Applying life-cycle criteria is another way of illuminating deficiences of traditional sex-role socialization. As Emmerich (25) and Pleck (92) have observed, later role requirements may contradict socialization goals of earlier periods. Pleck, noting that same-sex interests and traits peak in adolescence, reminds us of data from the Berkeley Growth Study showing that boys rated highly masculine in adolescence also scored high on adjustment but lost ground later in life when masculine attributes became less important. Apparently, due to the high status associated with masculinity, they found it less necessary to develop interpersonal and intellectual skills and were consequently disadvantaged as adults. Such discontinuities have always existed but current changes in sex roles may intensify the effects. Douvan (24) argues that the trend toward de-differentiation of sex roles poses more problems for males than females. The new challenge for girls to develop and sustain individual achievement goals does not introduce a radically new motive for most of them, nor does it require them to deny previously developed motives, since their early schooling trained them to achieve, compete, and use their individual competencies. Besides, in the emerging postindustrial era, the emphasis is shifting from production and technical skills to manipulation of words and ideas and interacting with people —skills similar to those involved in traditional female socialization. The challenge is greater for males because they are increasingly expected to contribute their share to the more "expressive" side of family and social life. This implies the expression of motives and interests that may well have been forcefully socialized out of them in childhood. Traditional masculine socialization may thus be a particular handicap for boys growing up during this period of cultural transition.

Androgenous socialization then may best equip people to handle changing role demands throughout the life cycle. And the roles themselves may also become less stereotyped as they are increasingly fulfilled by androgenous individuals.

DELAY OF GRATIFICATION

The voluntary postponement of immediate gratification for future gain has long held a central place in Western social theory. It is viewed as essential to the Protestant Ethic, to saving and investing, and therefore as an individually adaptive and societally functional response in capitalist society. The ability to tolerate delay of gratification has also been viewed since Freud as basic to the transition from primary to secondary processes, and therefore as a significant aspect of ego development. As already noted, it is the one ego function extensively researched with children. In the usual method, the subject chooses between an item available now and a more desirable one available in the future.

The early research focused mainly on socialization patterns, ethnic and social class differences, and personality correlates of choosing immediate or delayed rewards. The recent focus is not on choice but on the cognitive and motivational processes that enhance or detract from the child's ability to delay. Experiments on preschool children by Mischel and his colleagues suggest that the physical presence or imagined representation of a deferred reward operates against the ability to delay because it increases the associated frustration. Consequently, if given the opportunity, the subjects will terminate the delay and accept the less preferred item. Encouraging the child to engage in pleasant, distracting thoughts, on the other hand, facilitates delay (e.g. 84, 85).

These findings at first seem to contradict the Freudian hypothesis that generating a mental image of the delayed goal object enables the child to "bind the time" until the object becomes available, hence to tolerate delay. To account for this apparent discrepancy, Miller & Karniol (79, 80) noted that Mischel's paradigm involves a voluntary, self-imposed delay, whereas Freud was concerned with externally imposed delay situations (the mother leaves and the infant tolerates her absence by generating images of her breasts). Miller & Karniol found that in a voluntary delay condition like Mischel's, third-grade children exhibited more frustration and engaged in more reward-irrelevant, presumably distracting behavior when the reward was salient. Using a modified design in which delay was externally imposed, however, the opposite pattern was found. Also, increasing the delay time resulted in decreased attention to a reward-relevant cue (a clock) under self-imposed but not under externally imposed delay. These findings seem to suggest two types of delay dynamics: when delay is externally imposed and compulsory, salience of the desired object helps the child anticipate having it and thus reduces frustration. When delay is voluntary, salience of the object increases temptation which the child tries to reduce by diverting his attention and doing other things.

Subsequent research by Mischel using the voluntary delay paradigm seems to blur this distinction a bit (83). Showing preschool children a picture of the absent, desired object facilitated delay and did so more effectively than distraction. Mischel suggests the picture operates as a cue or reminder of what the child will get, but is not motive arousing and therefore does not interfere with delay. Following the same line of thought, he also predicted, and found, that instructing the child to think of the absent object in a nonconsummatory manner (e.g. "think of the marshmallow as a cloud or a powder puff") would facilitate delay, whereas instructing him to think of it in a comsummatory fashion (e.g. "think of how soft and chewy it is") would impede delay. Finally, when Mischel's subjects were allowed to choose what happens during the waiting period (by pushing buttons they could determine whether the object, a picture of it, or nothing at all would remain in front of them) they typically chose the object, which is least functional from the standpoint of enabling them to tolerate delay. This raises questions about the ecological validity of all these studies. Perhaps they do not demonstrate the processes underlying the child's delay of gratification in real life but the cognitive delay-facilitating activities that he can utilize under external prodding. These capabilities may of course be a preview of what he does spontaneously at a later age, although this has not yet been demonstrated.

There is recent evidence that the child's affective state may have an impact on voluntary delay behavior. Preschool children who were asked to think about and verbally describe things that made them "happy" tended to choose delayed rewards; children asked to think about "sad" things chose immediate rewards (87). This suggests that feeling unhappy or sad may make one more vulnerable to immediate temptation, perhaps to offset the unpleasantness. When feeling good, one may experience less pressure for immediate gratification and therefore be better able to give up present pleasures for future gain.

INTRINSIC MOTIVATION AND EXTERNAL CONDITIONS

A newly emerging body of research, mainly by Lepper and his associates, may bear on the view, long held by progressive educators, that the schooling process often fails to capitalize on the spontaneous interest in learning and exploration that the child initially seems to possess, and indeed may often undermine this interest. In several recent studies, for example, preschoolers and 6–7 year olds have been found to lose some of their initial spontaneous interest in a play activity (drawing, listening to a story) after being promised a reward for engaging in that activity (36, 68, 93, 94). The usual explanation, based on attribution theory, is that if a person engages in a preferred activity in order to obtain a reward, he will subsequently see himself as engaging in that activity only to obtain rewards rather than because he likes it. An alternative explanation is that the promised reward in these studies led to reduced interest in the activity because the reward served as a novel, distracting, and competing stimulus (93, 94). Support for this view is the finding that there was no reduction in intrinsic interest in 5-year-olds when the reward did not compete with the activity (93). Furthermore, although rewards that are logically unrelated to the activity may decrease intrinsic interest, there may actually be an increase in instrinsic interest when the rewards are an inherent part of the activity, e.g. winning money in a "stock market" game (60).

Whatever the explanation, it appears that offering rewards may often reduce intrinsic motivation. Rewards may also have an adverse effect on performance. Sixth graders who liked to help younger children were found to be more demanding and critical, less patient, and less effective (their pupils did more poorly) in teaching a sorting game to first graders, if promised movie tickets for successful performance than if no reward was promised (33). Finally, another external factor, adult surveillance, also appears capable of diminishing intrinsic motivation. Preschool children lost interest in an activity after engaging in it while being monitored by a television camera (68).

If external reward reduces intrinsic motivation, the question may be asked, how does one create intrinsic motivation in the first place? Lepper suggests that external rewards may contribute to intrinsic interest under certain conditions, for example, by involving the child in activities that may later become intrinsically attractive once he has attained some minimal level of mastery. This seems to suggest that there may be an optimal balance between external incentive and the child's initial level of interest.

A recent study by Miller, Brickman & Bolen (81) suggests that the simple expedient of attributing intrinsic motivation to the child may actually help create it. The attempt was to teach fifth-grade classes not to litter and to clean up after others. An attribution group was told once a day for eight days that they were neat and tidy people. A persuasion group was told, with the same frequency, that they should be neat and tidy and were given reasons for doing so. Attribution proved considerably more effective in modifying littering behavior, as measured both on the tenth day and two weeks later. The investigators suggest that attribution may have worked because it implies something positive about the child and thus provides a positive link to the self system, whereas persuasion implies something negative. They also suggest that attribution may have had the advantage of disguising persuasive intent. Older, more sophisticated subjects, however, might be expected to see through the subterfuge and to attribute manipulative intent. Further research is needed to give perspective on the effectiveness of this technique.

CONCLUDING REMARKS

There are endless studies that theoretically could be done, and many that have been done, relating one or another type of social influence to some personality dimension at a particular age. For this review the scattered, isolated studies were omitted and certain clusters of research were the focus. This seemed the best way to represent the current state of the field. As for the future, we can only expect that some of the research presented here will continue to be seminal, some will fall by the wayside, and some totally new, important topics will emerge. One of the more significant though recently neglected areas that I anticipate will see a rekindling of interest is the development of motives. Motivation is of course implicit or explicit in most of the concepts dealt with in this review, but what is needed is a far more systematic study of the full gamut of human motives and how they develop. The recent excitement about ethology, evolution, and the possible biological contribution to social behavior may provide the spark for such study. In any case, the serious study of motive development will very likely, in turn, require theoretical models for integrating cognitive and affective processes. A few such examples were cited in this review. Perhaps it is time for the cognitive and affective parts of the person, long separated for purposes of analysis and research, to be put back together again—not in the global, holistic manner of old, but in a manner that utilizes the knowledge and methodological sophistication acquired over the years.

A selective overview of the literature such as this is bound to reflect the author's biases. I can only hope that, together with future reviews by different people, my effort will in the end contribute to a balanced perspective and help provide definition for this as yet amorphous field.

Literature Cited

1. Ambron, S. R., Irwin, D. M. 1975. Role-taking and moral judgment in five- and seven-year-olds. *Dev. Psychol.* 11:102
2. Baier, K. 1974. Moral development. *Monist* 58:601–15
3. Barnett, M. A., Bryan, J. H. 1974. Effects of competition with outcome feedback on children's helping behavior. *Dev. Psychol.* 10:838–42
4. Bell, R. Q. 1968. A reinterpretation of the direction of effects in studies of socialization. *Psychol. Rev.* 75:81–95
5. Bell, S. M. 1970. The development of the concept of the object as related to infant-mother attachment. *Child Dev.* 41:291–311
6. Bem, S. L. 1975. Sex role adaptability: One consequence of psychological androgyny. *J. Pers. Soc. Psychol.* 31:634–43
7. Block, J. H. 1976. Assessing sex differences: Issues, problems, and pitfalls. *Merrill-Palmer Q.* 22:283–308
8. Block, J. H. 1976. Another look at sex differentiation in the socialization behaviors of mothers and fathers. In *Psychology of women: Future directions of research.* In press
9. Block, J. H., Block, J., Harrington, D. M. 1974. *The relationships of parental teaching strategies to ego resiliency in preschool children.* Presented at Western Psychol. Assoc., San Francisco
10. Block, J. H., Block, J., Harrington, D. M. 1975. *Sex-role typing and instrumental behavior: A developmental study.* Presented at Soc. Res. Child Dev., Denver
11. Borke, H. 1973. The development of empathy in Chinese and American children between three and six years of age. *Dev. Psychol.* 9:102–8

12. Borke, H. 1975. Piaget's mountains revisited: Changes in the egocentric landscape. *Dev. Psychol.* 11:240–43
13. Brickman, P., Bryan, J. H. 1975. Moral judgment of theft, charity, and third party transfers that increase or decrease equality. *J. Pers. Soc. Psychol.* 31:156–61
14. Bryan, J. H. 1975. Children's cooperation and helping behaviors. In *Review of Child Development Research,* ed. E. M. Hetherington, 5:127–81. Univ. Chicago Press
15. Buck, R. W. 1975. Nonverbal communication of affect in children. *J. Pers. Soc. Psychol.* 31:644–53
16. Cheyne, J. A., Goyeche, J. R. M., Walters, R. H. 1969. Attention, anxiety, and rules in resistance-to-deviation in children. *J. Exp. Child Psychol.* 8:127–39
17. Cheyne, J. A., Walters, R. H. 1969. Itensity of punishment, timing of punishment, and cognitive structure as determinants of response inhibition. *J. Exp. Child Psychol.* 7:231–44
18. Cook, H., Stingle, S. 1974. Cooperative behavior in children. *Psychol. Bull.* 81:918–33
19. Damon, W. V. 1975. Early conceptions of positive justice as related to the development of logical operations. *Child Dev.* 46:301–12
20. DePalma, D. J. 1974. Effects of social class, moral orientation, and severity of punishment on boys' moral responses to transgression and generosity. *Dev. Psychol.* 10:890–900
21. Deutsch, F. 1974. Female preschooler's perceptions of affective responses and interpersonal behavior in video-taped episodes. *Dev. Psychol.* 10:733–40
22. Dlugokinski, E. L., Firestone, I. J. 1974. Other centeredness and susceptibility to charitable appeals: Effects of perceived discipline. *Dev. Psychol.* 10:21–28
23. Dorr, D. A., Fay, S. 1974. Relative power of symbolic adult and peer models in the modification of children's moral choice behavior. *J. Pers. Soc. Psychol.* 29:335–41
24. Douvan, E. 1975. Sex differences in opportunities, demands, and development of youth. In *NSSE Yearbook,* ed. R. J. Havighurst, P. H. Dreyer, Part 1, pp. 27–45
25. Emmerich, W. 1973. Socialization and sex role development. In *Life-Span Developmental Psychology,* ed. P. B. Baltes, K. W. Schaie, pp. 124–44. New York: Academic

26. Ervin-Tripp, S. 1976. *Turn-taking in children.* Presented at Univ. Michigan
27. Fagot, B. I. 1974. Sex differences in toddler's behavior and parental reaction. *Dev. Psychol.* 10:554–58
28. Fein, G., Johnson, D., Kosson, N., Stork, L., Wasserman, L. M. 1975. Sex stereotypes and preferences in the toy choices of 20-month-old boys and girls. *Dev. Psychol.* 11:527–28
29. Feshbach, N. D., Feshbach, S. 1969. The relationship between empathy and aggression in two age groups. *Dev. Psychol.* 1:102–7
30. ·Fishkin, J., Keniston, K., MacKinnon, C. 1973. Moral reasoning and political ideology. *J. Pers. Soc. Psychol.* 27:109–19
31. Fodor, E. M. 1972. Delinquency and susceptibility to social influence among adolescents as a function of moral development. *J. Soc. Psychol.* 257–60
32. Fry, P. S. 1975. The resistance of temptation: Inhibitory and disinhibitory effects of models in children from India and the United States. *J. Cross-Cult. Psychol.* 6:189–202
33. Garbarino, J. 1975. The impact of anticipated reward upon cross-age tutoring. *J. Pers. Soc. Psychol.* 32:421–28
34. Glassco, J., Milgram, N. A., Youniss, J. 1970. The stability of training effects on intentionality of moral judgment in children. *J. Pers. Soc. Psychol.* 14:360–65
35. Glucksberg, S., Krauss, R., Higgins, E. T. 1975. The development of referential communication skills. In *Review of Child Development Research,* ed. F. D. Herowitz, 4:305–45. Univ. Chicago Press
36. Greene, D. M., Lepper, M. R. 1974. Effects of extrinsic rewards on children's subsequent intrinsic interest. *Child Dev.* 45:1141–45
37. Grusec, J. E., Ezrin, S. A. 1972. Techniques of punishment and the development of self-criticism. *Child Dev.* 43:1273–88
38. Haan, N. 1975. Hypothetical and actual moral reasoning in a situation of civil disobedience. *J. Pers. Soc. Psychol.* 32:255–70
39. Hamilton, M. L. 1973. Imitative behavior and expression of emotion. *Dev. Psychol.* 8:138 (and personal communication)
40. Harper, L. V. 1975. The scope of offspring effects: From caregiver to culture. *Psychol. Bull.* 82:784–801

41. Hetherington, E. M. 1972. Effects of father absence on personality development in adolescent daughters. *Dev. Psychol.* 7:313–26
42. Hetherington, E. M., Cox, M., Cox, R. 1975. *Beyond father absence: Conceptualization of effects of divorce.* Presented at Soc. Res. Child Dev., Denver
43. Hoffman, L. W. 1974. Fear of success in males and females: 1965 and 1972. *J. Consult. Clin. Psychol.* 42:353–58
44. Hoffman, L. W. 1976. Fear of success in 1965 and 1974: A follow-up study. *J. Consult. Clin. Psychol.* In press
45. Hoffman, M. L. 1970. Moral development. In *Carmichael's Handbook of Child Psychology,* ed. P. H. Mussen. New York: Wiley
46. Hoffman, M. L. 1970. Conscience, personality, and socialization techniques. *Hum. Dev.* 13:90–126
47. Hoffman, M. L. 1975. Moral internalization, parental power, and the nature of parent-child interaction. *Dev. Psychol.* 11(2):228–39
48. Hoffman, M. L. 1975. Altruistic behavior and the parent-child relationship. *J. Pers. Soc. Psychol.* 31:937–43
49. Hoffman, M. L. 1975. Developmental synthesis of affect and cognition and its implications for altruistic motivation. *Dev. Psychol.* 11:607–22
50. Hoffman, M. L. 1975. Sex differences in moral internalization and values. *J. Pers. Soc. Psychol.* 32:720–29
51. Hoffman, M. L. 1977. Sex differences in empathy and related behaviors. *Psychol. Bull.* In press
52. Hoffman, M. L. 1977. Moral internalization and behavior. *Adv. Exp. Soc. Psychol.* In press
52a. Hoffman, M. L. 1976. Parental discipline and moral internalization: A theoretical analysis. *Dev. Rep. No. 85.* Univ. Michigan
52b. Hoffman, M. L. 1976. A critique of experimental research on discipline and moral behavior. *Dev. Rep. No. 86.* Univ. Michigan
53. Hoffman, M. L., Levine, L. E. 1976. Early sex differences in empathy. *Dev. Psychol.* In press
54. Holstein, C. B. 1976. Irreversible, stepwise sequence in the development of moral judgment: A longitudinal study of males and females. *Child Dev.* 47:51–61
55. Hudgins, W., Prentice, N. 1973. Moral judgment in delinquent and nondelinquent adolescents and their mothers. *J. Abnorm. Psychol.* 82:145–52

56. Imamoglu, E. O. 1975. Children's awareness and usage of intention cues. *Child Dev.* 46:39–45
57. Johnson, D. W. 1975. Affective perspective taking and cooperative predisposition. *Dev. Psychol.* 11:869–70
58. Johnson, D. W. 1975. Cooperativeness and social perspective taking. *J. Pers. Soc. Psychol.* 31:241–44
59. Kohlberg, L. 1976. Moral stages and moralization. In *Moral Development: Current Theory and Research,* ed. T. Likona. New York: Holt, Rinehart, & Winston
60. Kruglanski, A. W., Riter, A., Amitai, A., Margolin, B., Shabtai, L., Zaksh, D. 1975. Can money enhance intrinsic motivation? A test of the content-consequence hypothesis. *J. Pers. Soc. Psychol.* 31:744–50
61. Kurdek, L. A., Rodgon, M. M. 1975. Perceptual, cognitive, and affective perspective taking in kindergarten through sixth-grade children. *Dev. Psychol.* 11: 643–50
62. Kurtines, W., Greif, E. B. 1974. The development of moral thought: Review and evaluation of Kohlberg's approach. *Psychol. Bull.* 81:453–70
63. LaVoie, J. C. 1973. Punishment and adolescent self-control. *Dev. Psychol.* 8:16–24
64. LaVoie, J. C. 1974. Type of punishment as a determinant of resistance to deviation. *Dev. Psychol.* 10:181–89
65. LaVoie, J. C. 1974. Cognitive determinants of resistance to deviation in seven-, nine-, and eleven-year-old children of low and high maturity of moral judgment. *Dev. Psychol.* 10:393–403
66. Leizer, J. I., Rogers, R. W. 1974. Effects of method of discipline, timing of punishment, and timing of test on resistance to temptation. *Child Dev.* 45:790–93
67. Lempers, J. D., Flavell, E. R., Flavell, J. H. The development in very young children of tacit knowledge concerning visual perception. Unpublished
68. Lepper, M. R., Greene, D. M. 1975. Turning play into work: Effects of adult surveillance and extrinsic rewards on children's intrinsic motivation. *J. Pers. Soc. Psychol.* 31:479–86
69. Lerner, M. J. 1974. The justice motive: "Equity" and "parity" among children. *J. Pers. Soc. Psychol.* 29:539–50
70. Leventhal, G. S., Popp, A. L. 1973. Equity or equality in children's allocation of reward to other persons. *Child Dev.* 44:753–76

71. Levine, L. E., Hoffman, M. L. 1975. Empathy and cooperation in 4-year-olds. *Dev. Psychol.* 11:533
72. Long, G. T., Lerner, M. J. 1974. Deserving the "personal contract" and altruistic behavior by children. *J. Pers. Soc. Psychol.* 29:551–56
73. Lytton, H., Zwirner, W. 1975. Compliance and its controlling stimuli in a national setting. *Dev. Psychol.* 11:769–79
74. Maccoby, E. E., Jacklin, C. N. 1974. *Psychology of Sex Differences.* California: Stanford Univ. Press
75. Maratsos, M. P. 1973. Nonegocentric communication abilities in preschool children. *Child Dev.* 44:697–700
76. Marvin, R. S. 1974. Aspects of the preschool child's changing conception of his mother. Unpublished
77. Masters, J. C. 1971. Effects of social comparison upon children's self-reinforcement and altruism toward competitors and friends. *Dev. Psychol.* 5:67–72
78. Menig-Peterson, C. L. 1975. The modification of communicative behavior in pre-school-aged children as a function of the listener's perspective. *Child Dev.* 46:1015–18
79. Miller, D. T., Karniol, R. Coping strategies and attentional mechanisms in self-imposed and externally imposed delay situations. *J. Pers. Soc. Psychol.* In press
80. Miller, D. T., Karniol, R. The role of rewards in externally and self-imposed delay of gratification. *J. Pers. Soc. Psychol.* In press
81. Miller, R. L., Brickman, P., Bolen, D. 1975. Attribution versus persuasion as a means for modifying behavior. *J. Pers. Soc. Psychol.* 31:430–41
82. Minton, C., Kagan, J., Levine, J. 1971. Maternal control and obedience in the two-year-old. *Child Dev.* 42:1873–94
83. Mischel, W. 1976. Cognition and the delay of gratification. Presented at Univ. Michigan Psychol. Dep. Colloq.
84. Mischel, W., Baker, N. 1975. Cognitive appraisals and transformation in delay behavior. *J. Pers. Soc. Psychol.* 31:254–61
85. Mischel, W., Moore, B. S. 1973. Effects of attention to symbolically presented rewards on self control. *J. Pers. Soc. Psychol.* 28:172–79
86. Moir, D. J. 1974. Egocentrism and the emergence of conventional morality in preadolescent girls. *Child Dev.* 45:299–304
87. Moore, B. S., Clyburn, A., Underwood, B. 1976. The role of affect in delay of gratification. *Child Dev.* 47:273–76
88. Morgan, S. W., Mausner, B. 1973. Behavioral and fantasied indicators of avoidance of success in men and women. *J. Pers.* 41:457–69
89. Mossler, D. G., Marvin, R. S., Greenberg, M. T. 1976. Conceptual perspective taking in 2- to 6-year-old children. *Dev. Psychol.* 12:85–86
90. Murphy, L. B. 1937. Social behavior and child personality. New York: Columbia Univ. Press
91. Peters, R. S. 1971. Moral development: A plea for pluralism. See Ref. 1, pp. 237–67
92. Pleck, J. H. 1975. Masculinity-femininity: Current and alternative paradigms. *Sex Roles* 1:161–78
93. Reiss, S., Sushinsky, L. W. 1975. Overjustification, competing responses, and the acquisition of intrinsic interest. *J. Pers. Soc. Psychol.* 31:116–25
94. Reiss, S., Sushinsky, L. W. 1976. The competing response hypothesis of decreased play effects: A reply to Lepper and Greene. *J. Pers. Soc. Psychol.* 33:233–44
95. Rest, J. R. 1973. The hierarchical nature of moral judgment: A study of patterns of comprehension preference of moral stages. *J. Pers.* 41:86–109
96. Romer, N. 1975. The motivation to avoid success and its effects on performance in school-age males and females. *Dev. Psychol.* 11:689–99
97. Rosenfeld, E. F. 1975. *The relationship of sex-typed toys to the development of competency and sex-role identification in children.* Presented at Soc. Res. Child Dev., Denver
98. Rosenberg, F. R., Simmons, R. G. 1975. Sex differences in self-concept in adolescence. *Sex Roles* 1:147–60
99. Rosenhan, D. L., Underwood, B., Moore, B. 1974. Affect moderates self-gratification and altruism. *J. Pers. Soc. Psychol.* 30:546–52
100. Rosenkoetter, L. I. 1973. Resistance to temptation: Inhibitory and disinhibitory effects of models. *Dev. Psychol.* 8:80–84
101. Rubin, H. K., Schneider, F. W. 1973. The relationship between moral judgment, egocentrism, and altruistic behavior. *Child Dev.* 44:661–65
102. Rule, B. G., Nesdale, A. R., McAra, M. J. 1974. Children's reactions to information about the intentions underlying an aggressive act. *Child Dev.* 45:794–98

103. Rushton, J. P. 1975. Generosity in children: Immediate and long-term effects of modeling, preaching, and moral judgment. *J. Pers. Soc. Psychol.* 31: 459–66

104. Sagi, A., Hoffman, M. L. 1976. Empathic distress in newborns. *Dev. Psychol.* 12:175–76

105. Saltzstein, H. D., Diamond, R. M., Belenky, M. 1972. Moral judgment level and conformity behavior. *Dev. Psychol.* 7:327–36

106. Sampson, E. E. 1975. On justice as equality. *J. Soc. Issues* 31(3): 21–43

107. Seavy, C. A., Katz, P. A., Zalk, S. R. 1975. Baby X: The effect of gender labels on adult responses to infants. *Sex Roles* 1:103–10

108. Selman, R. 1971. The relation of role taking to the development of moral judgments in children. *Child Dev.* 42:79–91

109. Selman, R. L., Byrne, D. F. 1974. A structural developmental analysis of levels of role-taking in middle childhood. *Child Dev.* 45:803–6

110. Shantz, C. U. 1975. The development of social cognition. See Ref. 14, pp. 257–323

111. Shatz, M., Gelman, R. 1973. The development of communication skills: Modification in the speech of young children as a function of listener. *Monogr. Soc. Res. Child Dev.* 38: (No. 5, Serial No. 152)

112. Simner, M. L. 1971. Newborn's response to the cry of another infant. *Dev. Psychol.* 5:136–50

113. Simpson, E. L. 1974. Moral development research: A case study of scientific cultural bias. *Hum. Dev.* 17:81–106

114. Slaby, R. G., Frey, K. S. 1975. Development of gender constancy and selective attention to same-sex models. *Child Dev.* 46:849–56

115. Staub, E. 1974. Helping a distressed person. *Adv. Exp. Soc. Psychol.* 7:294–341

116. Sternlieb, J. L., Youniss, J. 1975. Moral judgments one year after intentional or consequence modeling. *J. Pers. Soc. Psychol.* 31:895–97

117. Tracy, J. J., Cross, H. J. 1973. Antecedents of shift in moral judgment. *J. Pers. Soc. Psychol.* 26:238–44

117a. Tulving, E. 1972. Episodic and semantic memory. In *Organization of Memory*, ed. E. Tulving, W. Donaldson. New York: Academic

118. Watson, M. S. 1975. *A developmental study of empathy-egocentrism to sociocentrism or simple reasoning to complex reasoning?* Presented at Soc. Res. Child Dev., Denver

118a. Weiner, B., Peter, N. 1973. A cognitive-developmental analysis of achievement and moral judgment. *Dev. Psychol.* 4:290–309

119. Wright, H. F. 1967. *Recording and Analyzing Child Behavior.* New York: Harper & Row

120. Yarrow, M. R., Scott, P. M., Waxler, C. Z. 1973. Learning concern for others. *Dev. Psychol.* 8:240–60

121. Zuckerman, M., Wheeler, L. 1975. To dispel fantasies about the fantasy-based measure of fear of success. *Psychol. Bull.* 82:932–46

122. Zussman, J. U. 1975. *Demographic factors influencing parental discipline techniques.* Presented at Am. Psychol. Assoc., Chicago

Ann. Rev. Psychol. 1977. 28:323–61

SOCIAL AND COMMUNITY INTERVENTIONS[1]

♦276

James G. Kelly[2]

School of Community Service and Public Affairs and Department of Psychology,
University of Oregon, Eugene, Oregon 97403

Lonnie R. Snowden

Department of Psychology, University of Oregon, Eugene, Oregon 97403

Ricardo F. Muñoz

Department of Psychology, University of Oregon, Eugene, Oregon 97403

SOCIAL AND COMMUNITY INTERVENTION METHODS

Planned and unplanned influences on the life of a small group, organization, or community by benefactors and strangers go on every day. Professionals and citizens will continue to develop new helping services and social programs so that those who are in need of personal, economic, or political assistance can receive it. There is nothing really new about individual and collective efforts organized for social justice

---

[1] The initials SCI in the text refer to "Social and Community Interventions."

[2] The preparation and completion of this review could not have been done without the enthusiasm, good humor, and continuous and competent secretarial leadership of Jeanne Mandvill. The authors acknowledge her contribution with thanks, appreciation, and respect. The work also benefitted from the help of Virginia Lickey of the University of Oregon Library, who got us started using the Lockheed Information Service. Ted Fay searched for salient content in nonpsychological literature, and Brian Dobbs assisted with the retrieval and organization of material. Al Junge, MLS, and the late Terry Clingan were major librarian resources for the retrieval and abstracting of literature, as well as the preparation of the bibliography and the *Appendix*.

Colleagues gave us good feedback and helped us touch up the manuscript. Our particular appreciation is expressed to Jerry Bass, Bernie Bloom, Emory Cowen, Barbara Dohrenwend, George Fairweather, Bart Hirsch, Ben Gottlieb, Ed Lichtenstein, Rudy Moos, John Monahan, Laurel Ramsay, and Milt Shore for helping by being candid.

and a social good. What is new about these deeds is the extensive involvement of psychologists' time and effort.

Since World War II, but particularly since the 1960s, psychology as a profession has been giving increasing attention to the design and evaluation of community-based programs to prevent or reduce social and personal disorganization and to promote community well-being. This chapter builds upon the initial analysis of this topic in Volume 24 of the *Annual Review of Psychology* (73). Our search has focused on books and articles, as well as unpublished material, from January 1972 through January 1976.

We have scanned widely to locate material because of the authors' belief that useful community work is done by a variety of professions. We have been alert to cite ideas and methods that suggest new social processes for the design of social and community interventions.

The review includes eight major topics. The first topic includes material related to *Patterns of Service Delivery*. The remaining topics include services for *Diverse Cultures;* studies and concepts related to *Primary Prevention* and the learning of *Competences;* material related to the *Social Environment* and its impact upon the design of community programs; essays and research focusing upon *Social Change and Public Policy;* the status of *Theory* about social and community interventions; *Methods* for community research; examples of *Education and Training* for community service, including the education of citizens; and a *Finale.* We end each of the eight sections with conclusions derived from the literature and, in italics, our reflections stimulated by doing this review.

Work on social and community interventions is in a period of creative thrust, reflected by the publication of two texts (242, 384); the allotment of a major segment of a text on clinical psychology to community psychology (192); a handbook (132); a third text in press (285); the arrival of two journals, the *Journal of Community Psychology* and the *American Journal of Community Psychology;* and a review, the *Community Mental Health Review.* In spite of diverse disciplinary heritages and assorted vocabularies, facts and generalizations are emerging. We hope that this review reflects the range of available and useful facts.

PATTERNS OF SERVICE DELIVERY

Many persons both inside and outside of psychology identify social and community interventions with innovative, indivdual, small group, or organizationally focused services. By service delivery the present authors refer to implementing new services in new settings and adapting existing services to make them more palatable and accessible to formerly unreached persons.

Consultation

In mental health consultation, a consulting specialist enhances consultee skill at optimizing the mental health consequences of his or her usual work. The primary advantages of mental health consultation are its radiation of positive effects through the consultee to a greatly expanded population, and its potential applicability in the diverse settings where police, ministers, and other informal caregivers field mental health problems.

Mannino, McLennan & Shore's *The Practice of Mental Health Consultation* (215) is an exhaustive, perhaps definitive, work on mental health consultation. The book's text discusses definition and scope, training, and practice. The volume includes an updated version of a useful, well-organized reference guide to the consultation literature.

Three issues emerge from the theoretical literature on consultation; ideological and political issues for the consultant, consultation styles, and contexts for doing consultation. Articles of the first type remind us that consultation is not always the proper intervention (62, 140) and that inevitably the consultant takes an implicit stand on what ought to be changed in whom (245, 268). Consultants are advised to think through the political and value implications of consulting in a particular environment. As might be expected, process and behavioral consultants operate quite differently (379). Four distinct approaches (consultee-centered, group process, social action, and ecological) have been identified (99). None of these is always right; circumstances dictate which is preferable. A model should not become a mask; consumers detect inflexibility and pedantry (103).

Because it is a portable intervention, consultation concerns will vary with the setting where it is applied. The literature suggests unique issues raised by consulting in schools (46), community action programs (109), rural communities (148), and prisons(243). Consultation should accommodate to the sensitivities, constraints, and opportunities of its context and clientele.

The characteristics of the consultant are equally important. Consultants who are not psychiatrists or psychologists particularly are being cautioned concerning problems of resistance (319) and role ambiguity (79). Nontraditional consultants do perform effectively.

Although theorizing still predominates, articles reporting data are increasingly common. Mannino & Shore comprehensively and critically review consultation research of all kinds in one publication (216) while focusing on outcome studies in another (217). The failure to integrate findings into a conceptual framework hinders comparisons across studies, discourages replication, and gives to the research the character of an accumulation of fragments. Mannino & Shore report that 69% of outcome studies can be characterized as showing beneficial change in consultee, client, system, or some combination of the targets (217). This encouraging success rate cannot be accepted uncritically as methodological shortcomings leave many studies vulnerable to alternative interpretations. Besides the usual exhortation to greater rigor, which is certainly in order, attempts to detect change at multiple system levels should be increased.

Much of the recent research presents frequency counts and evaluations of consultation behaviors and processes (84, 197, 203, 254). Such studies are useful for explicating what happens in consultation and for providing normative data. However, the field will really advance on the shoulders of studies which objectively assess changes in consultee, client, and system. One such study by Keutzer et al (186) points the way.

Paraprofessionals

An early strategy to increase helping resources was to invest in training paraprofessionals. The paraprofessional movement is becoming institutionalized, as evidenced by increased paraprofessional concern with traditional preoccupations such as career advancement and working conditions (122).

By a wide margin the paraprofessional activity receiving the greatest attention has been psychotherapy. The latest full-scale review (175), in harmony with its predecessors, concludes that paraprofessional effectiveness with impatient psychotic adults has been established and is probable with outpatient adults. The present authors would add children (79, 80) and even infants (169) as probable beneficiaries.

The Group Assessment of Interpersonal Traits (GAIT) technique originated by Goodman (138) has stimulated well-controlled research on selection and training of paraprofessional therapeutic talent. The technique involves having individuals assume the roles of both discloser and facilitative listener in a small group context. These performances are rated on several therapy-relevant parameters. GAIT scores have been found acceptably reliable (91). Validity evidence comes from demonstrations that GAIT behaviors generalize to therapy-like conditions, and have expected consequences on group cohesiveness (85, 86). When applied to an actual selection problem, several subscales of the GAIT proved to be statistically significant in forecasting a counseling readiness criterion (91a). Selection studies which tabulate "hits" and errors and evaluate efficiency in selecting therapeutic talent would confirm the technique's worth.

The crisis telephone movement has spawned commentary and data on issues in paraprofessional selection and training for therapeutic-like roles. France (117) sorts expected performances of crisis telephone workers into three roles: helpers, referral agents, and technique-equipped behavior changers. He concludes that the first function is probably performed adequately, but effective performance in the other two areas is doubtful. Efforts to increase telephone counselor effectiveness should benefit from the development of a selection instrument (87, 237) and of a scale which measures volunteer technical effectiveness (116).

The literature is relatively uninformative as to how paraprofessionals function as outreachers, advocates, consultants, managers, community developers, or any other equally valuable helping role. These are important areas for future thought and study.

Crisis Intervention

Crisis intervention involves taking extra time to make services available during initial, acute phases of distress. Classical crisis theory holds that how a crisis is resolved has important consequences for future development. Constructive resolution can mark a turning point toward mastery and healthy development; unsuccessful resolution can crystalize destructive processes.

Several volumes exhaustively define and analyze the tasks involved in establishing, operating, and evaluating crisis intervention services (43, 87, 222, 328). These volumes give detailed consideration to case management strategies, counseling techniques, and programmatic concerns such as selection and training of volunteers, policy, and funding. Process and evaluation research have increased. One research group identified and cross-validated the process variable of client responsiveness to referral during the telephone contact against a criterion of appearing for a scheduled appointment (324, 357). Two studies evaluated hot line performance without violating caller anonymity. One surveyed the population of potential consumers (325) to identify users who rated the service positively. Another (37) had students role-play distressed callers to four hot lines after prior permission had been obtained.

There is evidence that suicide prevention centers fail to affect suicide rates (144, 201, 202, 238). This is not to diminish their distress relieving value; drawing a distinction between suicide and other crisis services appears less and less tenable.

The potential of hospital emergency rooms as a setting for crisis service has been recognized and developed. Two studies followed up crisis clients seen in emergency room based programs. Improvements in depression and self-esteem (218) and satisfaction with services (126) were among the findings. However, a third study (141) raises the possibility of spontaneous remission. By arranging a nontreatment control group, it was discovered that improvement in hope, personal organization, and other parameters of adjustment occurs in the absence of intervention.

Several writers point up the need for more innovative styles of service, including elimination of deleterious forces in the client's social framework (187, 376). Brook (45) describes one evaluated service which intervenes in the client's social environment. One new direction is a program which invited lonely, isolated people to register for regular calls by volunteers (264).

Police

An increasingly common community intervention aims at enhancing the interpersonal awareness and skillfulness of police. Psychologists have increased police effectiveness as conflict managers (97, 208) and helped reduce friction in police-citizen contacts (271). A program with additional features (214) arranged conferences between police and mental health agencies besides performing consultation and training. Zacker & Bard (382) convincingly demonstrated that conflict management training improves police effectiveness and safety in handling criminal matters.

Learning to communicate skillfully is no panacea. For instance, as a result of attempting to train for improved dialogue between black and white officers, one program (339) produced negative attitude shifts among the white officers. In addition, R. M. Kelly (184) concludes that citizen involvement and control are superior to human relations training when the goal is improving police-community relations.

One innovative approach to institutional reform had violence-prone policemen design and test strategies for nonviolent handling of volatile situations (344). In a second project phase, these former "problem officers" led groups of violence-prone policement who in turn devised department programs for violence reduction.

These well-designed, executed, and evaluated programs increase the positive mental health consequences of normal police functions. The future holds challenges such as controlling or preventing violence by identifying violence-eliciting situations (231).

Community Mental Health Centers

Community mental health services are a sizable share of the current mental health effort. The concepts guiding community mental health are evolving into a new "human service" ideology which views human needs as an interrelated whole requiring comprehensive, coordinated, accessible services (11, 316).

A systems perspective on mental health networks promises to increase service efficiency and effectiveness. Events outside of a service organization can significantly affect staff and client behavior, whether or not they are acknowledged (310). A volume edited by Harshbarger & Maley (147) examines relationships between funding sources and agencies, interagency relations, and agency-consumer relations in discussing factors which help or hinder service delivery.

The federal community mental health centers program was expected to usher in a new era of high quality, broadly reaching, community based care. Chu & Trotter (66) provide an illuminating critique of how political and professional group interests conspire with economic realities to blunt and deflect the program's thrust. A more recent review (372) summarized a NIMH evaluation of seven process goals such as accessibility, responsiveness, and continuity of care. Though cautious, the authors find encouraging accomplishments in developing evaluation methods, and evidence of goal attainment in at least the service responsiveness area. The possibility that program goals are unattainable, as Chu & Trotter suggest, remains an open question.

The functioning of individual centers has in some cases provided valuable learning experiences. There is evidence of considerable variability in citizen awareness of center existence and services (151), and greater emphasis on accounting for these differences would be useful. Goldberg & Kane (134) describe an ingenious alternative to fee for services. Clients are allowed to contribute services ranging from baby-sitting to co-therapy, which reinforce client competency, self-esteem, and independence.

Technical developments, applicable in any service delivery setting, should improve integration and continuity of care. New methods include a technique for measuring continuity of care (19, 20) and a method for monitoring and evaluating referral resources (343).

Historically an important goal has been provision of a community-based alternative to psychiatric hospitalization. One well-designed study reports that community-based treatment costs more and achieves neither improved patient social competence nor a lower incidence of rehospitalization (326). However, the bulk of the evidence suggests improved community adaptation as a consequence of community-based treatment (111, 293, 364). While a definite conclusion cannot be drawn, the evidence to date is largely encouraging.

The volume of literature on consultation, crisis intervention, paraprofessional treatment, and community mental health services remains quite large. Psychotherapy by paraprofessionals, training police to be crisis and conflict managers, and mental health consultation in particular seem to work. Increased and explicit attention is being directed to the role of organizational, social, and political factors in facilitating or obstructing attainment of SCI goals.

Community services will evolve into SCI as they integrate persons into their sociocultural milieu. This requires comprehensive SCI which: teach personal and social competences, improve opportunities for economic well-being, and increase the supportiveness of social structures.

DIVERSE CULTURES

One of the most important characteristics of social-community interventions is that they take into account and work with diverse societal groups. The YAVIS client— young, attractive, verbal, intelligent, and successful (315)—is no longer our sole preoccupation. Active efforts to work with people who are old, of low status, working class, uneducated, and poor have begun. Much of the force behind this emphasis has come from these people themselves, such as women and presently politically weak minorities.

The first order of business has been to assess whether existing services are of use to these intranational groups. Though very recent data show some improvement (38), the general picture has been one of underutilization of services: blacks tend to drop out of treatment at a high rate after initial contact (335), members of La Raza have generally been underrepresented in their use of mental health facilities (259, 347), Asian Americans use psychiatric services less than would be expected by their numbers (334), although they do overutilize college counseling centers (332).

One of the reasons cited for this state of affairs is the mental health system's inability to adapt its services to what are, in fact, diverse cultures. Lack of knowledge about these clients' values, customs, and language is a barrier to effective work. Stereotyping is not limited to nonwhite clients, however. Less liberal counselors attribute significantly greater pathology to left politically active females than to left politically active males (2). The possible deleterious effects of old age stereotyping by professionals on the aged have also been pointed out (51). And low income patients' attrition rates and program outcome may be a function of therapists' attitudes toward treating such clients (209).

A number of books attempting to present available information on these cultural subgroups have been making their appearance. Padilla has co-authored two extremely helpful sources on Latino mental health literature (257, 258). The relationship between the black experience and mental health has been explored (170, 371), as have psychological perspectives of Asian American (336), women (63), and the aged (104). Statistical information about native Americans (204) and many U.S. minorites (205) has also appeared recently. At a more direct service-oriented level, workers are beginning to devise innovative programs defined with specific groups in mind, such as the poor (137), Spanish-speaking minorities (1, 69, 176), blacks (22, 272), and the elderly (145). The use of indigenous paraprofessionals is becoming a preferred practice in such instances (22, 333).

The need to provide responsive traditional mental health services that are specifically tuned to diverse groups has necessitated a large investment of time and energy. This accounts for the slow development of more progressive, preventive, and social change-oriented programs directed at these same groups. Nevertheless, some community mental health centers actively espouse social action (272). Efforts to promote ethnic awareness, identity, and pride are encouraged on the grounds that such interventions may be conducive to the prevention of psychological problems (281, 340). And there is evidence that the promotion of people as natural resources is finally being put into practice; skilled indigenous people have been assisted in setting up services desired by their community (286).

At a more speculative level, there are those who are demanding that social science study the powerful and their influence on social ills, rather than studying the victim and making the results available only to the elite (124). In a similar attempt to redirect the focus of intervention, it has been suggested, after a review of the research literature on racial attitudes, that "reforms designed to guarantee jobs and a base income to America's poor show the greatest promise for reducing racial inequality" (302).

Economic factors are repeatedly implicated in findings of greater psychological distress in certain national subgroups. Barbara Dohrenwend (89) has found evidence that major life changes—both avoidable and unavoidable ones—occur more frequently among women and the poor. [Later studies yield mixed results (see 220, 224).] A recent major epidemiological study carried out in the southeastern United States found low socioeconomic status to be the most powerful predictor of poor mental health scores (360). In none of these studies was race alone a significant risk factor, though certain groups, such as blacks and members of La Raza, were disproportionately represented in the lowest socioeconomic levels. An examination of the evidence from child psychiatry and developmental theory for identifying children at risk concludes that "the only high risk population that is defined by actuarial criteria refers to children reared in severe and chronic poverty" (107). Thus it may be that it is not discrimination due to race, sex, or age which is the significant factor in the psychological well-being of diverse groups. Economic independence may be the key.

Women, the aged, and members of other groups presently at the bottom of the economic ladder do not have general access to mental health services which work for them. The few examples designed with them in mind, however, do show promise of therapeutic and preventive effectiveness.

A combined benefit to these groups and the mental health field will result from their active participation in both planning and implenting services, recognizing and promoting their own positive qualities, and strengthening their economic position.

PRIMARY PREVENTION AND COMPETENCES

The most ambitious of social and community interventions continues to be primary prevention. The review of this area in Volume 26 of the *Annual Review of Psychology* emphasized the wide, often confusing range of opinion and theory that has been included within the words "primary prevention" (185). Based on our present review, the authors advocate editorial policies which allow this term to be used only when the author specifies (*a*) how today's program has impact for tomorrow, and (*b*) how this impact can be assessed. A tighter use of the term will help to underline the importance of the concept it represents.

Major issues and realities in the quest for prevention have been clearly enumerated: the empirical evidence for the efficacy of preventive work has been found wanting (356), the impact of over- and underprevention has been logically analyzed (323), and the assumptions behind major preventive strategies have been clearly described (295).

The role of the economy on psychological well-being is becoming a serious research topic (41). Suggestions are being made to use economic data as early warning indicators to set up preventive programs (92). From another perspective, economic arguments for a more rational distribution of mental health resources have been made (146). They suggest allocating a greater share of revenue to primary prevention than it is now receiving.

Many perspectives have been used to deal with questions of application: shifting the role of the school counselor from corrective to preventive work (16); considering ecological factors (365); using learning techniques to innoculate against specific debilitating conditions (273); using peer reinforcement to increase school attendance (253); diffusion of mental health knowledge through community resources, such as "natural neighbors," that is, individuals who have ongoing contact with many families (71); and preventive activities by private mental health groups (355).

Wolkon & Moriwaki (378) have reported on the preventive possibilities of ombudsman programs. They cite the work of a radio station's community complaint department, which had a high rate of success in solving citizen problems. This early problem-solving approach was seen as having wide salutary impact as a stress reducer.

Three preventive efforts, the St. Louis County Project, the Milwaukee Project, and the Stanford Heart Disease Prevention Program, are exemplary because they designed their studies with reasonable control groups and planned for enough follow-up time to be able to ascertain whether the treated sample was performing better than the untreated sample on the target variables. Newly published data from the St. Louis County school mental health program (129) indicate that parents who participated in parent discussions led by lay persons at a school where there was a consultation program reported fewer new child behavior symptoms, such as nervousness and eating trouble, over a 30-month period than parents who did not receive these services; these results were observed for boys but not for girls.

Preliminary reports from the Milwaukee Project (149) appear promising. Women with low IQs were chosen because earlier data showed that they have high probability of bearing children who would be later identified as retarded. A massive intervention, including cognitive and social training of their children from age 3 months, and occupational and home-care training for the mothers, was begun. By age 5½, the treated group was 30 IQ points ahead of the untreated group. Though sharp criticisms have been leveled against the experimental validity of this study (260, 342), judgment must be held in abeyance until more complete data are published. In addition, the importance of these findings requires independent replication. Of value in themselves are Throne's (342) arguments for the superiority of a multiple baseline design (as opposed to a control group strategy) in field experiments such as this.

The Stanford Heart Disease Prevention Program exemplifies what can be done to produce behavioral change at the individual level by means of community-wide intervention. Matched towns received either a mass media campaign plus face-to-face instruction or the media campaign alone; a matched control town received no intervention. The intervention achieved a decline in heart disease risk (11, 212).

The lean diet of studies which satisfy the requirements for primary prevention has led Cowen (74) to suggest that SCI focus on building support systems and competences.

There is good reason to believe that effective social support reduces vulnerability to disorder (58, 174). Although just beginning, systematic empirical studies of social support systems seem most promising (345). This work includes tapping sociological and anthropological sources for concepts and methods such as network mapping. This anthropological and sociological literature (81, 368) is potentially rich in facts, ideas, and techniques for understanding support systems. While the therapeutic use of social networks has been developed (327), preventive social network interventions are in their infancy. One of the few examples published shows how mental health knowledge can be disseminated through the social networks of "natural neighbors," who are persons with many ongoing community relationships (71).

Competence-building is an area that shows great promise for integrating social and community work, clinical psychology, and education. The latter field is already involved in skill training—though at present the skills taught in school are predominantly academic in nature. Clinical psychologists are in a particularly good stiuation to observe which competences are lacking in most of their clients. They could probably ascertain which ways of thinking and behaving are most helpful in dealing effectively with daily life. These skills could be taught to people before they are in dire need of them (240). A rich source of basic adult skills needed to get along in this society is being compiled and investigated nationwide by the adult performance level project at the University of Texas (255).

"Personality assets" found to be related to "positive mental health" in the Stirling County Study in Nova Scotia include a number of teachable competences such as planning ability, interpersonal skills, and adaptability (27, 28).

The life cycle provides a good framework for organizing this intervention approach (241, 250, 251). Useful background material can be found in the West Virginia Conference on Life-Span Development Psychology (15, 247), in Chess & Thomas' *Annual Progress in Child Psychiatry and Child Development* (64), and in the life history research literature (292).

Social and cognitive skills can be promoted starting as early as 3 months of age (149). School children can be encouraged to learn to ask questions (36) and to problem solve (199, 329). Problem solving has been found to be positively related to adjustment (321).

Later examples of competency-training include: teaching better childrearing (32), parenting skills for parents of delinquents (155), training parents as teacher's aides (31), training volunteers to work with maladjusted school children at early levels of disturbance (76, 80), and marital enrichment programs (24,311). Skills such as assertion training (121) and meditation are being used widely by nonclinical populations.

The social learning armamentarium has a number of skill training methods which could be used preventively (101, 171, 213, 225, 262, 263, 296, 363). This approach, which emphasizes the use of specific techniques to learn or relearn coping skills, lends itself readily to early intervention.

In studying competency learning, it is important to remember that environmental factors may directly affect the development of competences. Cohen, Glass & Singer (70) found that reading ability in children was correlated to the distance they lived from traffic noise. In testing tenants of a 32-story building situated directly over an expressway, they found that lower-floor children showed greater impairment of auditory discrimination and reading achievement than children living in higher-floor apartment, and thus farther away from the noise. In this case, reading competence was directly related to an everyday physical environmental factor.

Differences in cognitive styles resulting from diverse cultural backgrounds must also be taken into account. Ramirez & Castaneda (284) are a good source for ideas and techniques which respect the value of culturally democratic educational practices.

What is needed now is a major effort to conduct competency training and concurrent longitudinal evaluation. We need to determine empirically which skills, if learned, will lead to healthier lives. Examples of genuinely preventive programs are appearing. Factors common to effective programs are (a) a focus on clearly specifiable personal skills, and (b) working with the social milieu so that it encourages the changes being made.

There are glimmers in the literature that the elusive goal of primary prevention can be realized if long-term impact is an intrinsic element in the work, if systemic factors for personal and social development are the focus, and if people's integration with their community is fostered. In the final analysis, primary prevention requires a radically different kind of psychology, that is, one which commits itself to long-term intervention in people's natural habitat.

SOCIAL ENVIRONMENT

The design of social and community interventions illuminates the latent relationships between community psychology and the fields of social organizational, and environmental psychology (127,163, 164, 168, 232, 236). The variety of theory, research, and practice from these fields can be of value to SCI (18, 52, 96, 143, 173, 189, 206, 278, 348, 349, 369). Professionals are increasingly seeking help to design and preserve community-oriented research so that it has impact in the face of vested political interests and resistances to change (29, 226).

A detailed analysis of the OEO-HEW funded neighborhood health centers provides helpful insights as to the inevitable intrusion of political factors when comprehensive, preventive services are generated in local communities by federal demonstration funds (160).

The lessons for future demonstration projects are clear: Invest heavily early on—from day one—in evaluation systems that will generate information in time to wage a more effective fight for survival a few years later. Sit hard on the coattails of colleagues eager to preach the myriad virtues of the new approach and to promise quick rewards from the requested public investments. Build in incentives for efficiency. Watch out for faint-hearted friends. Know the opposition (160, p. 11).

Whether we professionals like it or not, it seems unrealistic to expect that the design of social and community interventions can ever be politically neutral or value-free. More time and thought is needed on this nagging question.

Particularly provocative for the design of social and community interventions are examples of research and observations on such topics as the effect of environmental factors such as crowding and noise on health (69a), housing design for urban residents (283), the physical environment of the child (375), and how urban recreational spaces affect social participation (47). The research of Holahan & Saegert (158) is illustrative of efforts to identify relationships between the physical environment and the social environment. Repainting a dayroom of a hospital ward, along with the addition of new furniture, increased the frequency of social participation of patients. In addition to more socializing among patients significantly less isolated, passive behaviors were expressed on the altered ward in contrast to the control ward. Outdoor recreational behavior (157) and university dormitories (156) present additional opportunities for defining the relationship between physical environment and the social environment. Proshansky (280, 280a) and independently Catalano & Monahan (61) have raised important philosophical and methodological questions about how and why psychologists should focus on the physical and social environment. One compelling point made by Proshansky is for our methods to evolve out of the phenomena we study (280).

The efforts of Moos and colleagues to create evaluation methods for the social climate of therapeutic wards in psychiatric facilities, halfway houses, university dormitories, high school classrooms, and other settings have been a hallmark (232a, 233, 234). Moos has developed scales for three types of environmental variables— *relationship variables, personal growth variables,* and *system maintenance and system change variables.* He has also gone beyond just the assessment of the social environment by using feedback of the research results as an intervention and then evaluating the impact of the feedback (232). In an invited address at the 1975 Annual Meeting of the American Psychological Association, he raised an important topic for our attention: how persons can *resist* environmental pressure (235).

The social environment as an independent variable has been very much influenced by the work of Fairweather and co-workers (111). Several doctoral dissertations, completed at Michigan State University under Fairweather's direction, show how topics such as delinquency of youth can be understood and prevented by the operation of a community-based, peer-operated, automotive repair business (367), and how the development of autonomous, task-oriented, problem-solving, cohesive groups can contribute to increased participation in community health planning by citizens (23). It is now apparent that effective social programs can be designed if the social environment is included as an independent variable. Fairweather's research has significantly contributed to the fact that community-based programs can work when the social environment of the client is included as an essential part of the total design (299).

Methods and techniques for assessing social environments and social settings are in use. These methods are not only helping to improve psychological knowledge about social organizations, but they suggest how to measure the impact of social settings upon individuals.

The dynamic relationship between the social context and the person is emerging as a priority topic for the design of SCI. In fact, there is evidence that the social environment is a key influence for long-lasting SCI impact.

SOCIAL CHANGE AND PUBLIC POLICY

One of the basic assumptions of social and community oriented professionals is that the environment—social and physical—has great influence on the well-being of its inhabitants. Therefore, it is their goal to monitor and, if need be, change the direction of social processes so as to insure health-enhancing milieus. Social scientists work with social change in three ways: they describe it, measure it, and try to implement it.

Sociological and anthropological sources are particularly adept at describing social change. Among valuable examples are literature recounting the development of a community change organization on the west side of Chicago (312), and presenting first person reports by organizers and planners for social change (102). Leighton & Stone (200) capitalized on an unexpected opportunity to observe social change. As a result of new jobs in a bordering community, residents in the area under study experienced improved economic circumstances and a rise in mental health. The hypotheses of a general relationship between economic conditions and the need for mental health services have been supported elsewhere (41).

The literature regarding measurement of social change is slowly expanding from traditional economic indicators to social areas such as health, public safety, and education (350). One of the most significant ways of viewing these data is considering how human beings interpret and react to social change. Campbell & Converse (56) compiled discussions of how indices of leisure, work, family, and satisfaction are affected by social change. Other literature considers perceived well-being in detail (55). The pitfalls and limitations of social indicators have also been noted. For example, focusing attention on a particular indicator can make the entire measurement process reactive (57).

It is rare to find the research base for social interventions summarized and wedded with practical guidelines for implementation. Jack Rothman (303) has performed an invaluable service by reviewing literature from 30 major journals, distilling generalizations, rating their empirical support, and advancing "intervention principles."

The availability of effective behavior change techniques has stimulated thinking about their applicability to social change. There are a number of studies applying the operant approach to enhancing ecological and conservation practices. Operant programs have increased deposit of trash in receptacles (190), litter removal from campgrounds (274), use of returnable beverage containers (125), and energy conservation (374). Winett (373) develops fully the case for using behavior modification principles to produce planned social change under citizen control.

Implementing social change is difficult even under the best of conditions. Even when programs are well funded, have community acceptance, and the need is apparent, the everyday foibles of people and organizations obstruct change (275, 276).

Fairweather (110) and Fairweather, Sanders & Tornatzky (111) ingeniously apply research methods to the study of implementation. Taking their validated lodge program for ex-mental patients as a starting point, they experimentally tested the importance of several factors in attempting to persuade 255 state hospitals to adopt the program. This concern for, and systematic study of, nationwide organizational innovation is exemplary.

It is the business of government to initiate, encourage, or obstruct much social change. The policy domain is an important, perhaps unavoidable, arena for persons working on social change. Indeed, policy decisions affect social change in the social sciences, as exemplified by the reapportionment of funds which shifted emphasis from basic to applied research (12).

One model of social science involvement in public policy, embracing unblushingly the professional-technical policy role, is the social experimentation movement. In several cogent publications (211, 290, 299a), a group of social scientists have mounted the case for applying experimental methodology to learn about the effects of policy. A related approach calls for wide-scale application of validated technological solutions to social problems as a shortcut to social change (108).

Reasoned, qualified positions can enlighten policy debate. An example is the work of a task force on the classification and labeling of exceptional children. Their recommendations followed a thorough analysis of labeling practices and their consequences (279). It is also important to correct policy practices which assume nonexistent knowledge. It has been demonstrated that involuntary institutionalization and detention policies rest on the invalid premise that whether an individual will commit harmful acts can be accurately forecasted (228, 229). Katkin, Bullington & Levine (177) present an excellent discussion of considerations and criteria to judge whether knowledge is sufficiently trustworthy to justify policy recommendations.

Although the policy evaluator role has received the greatest attention, other possibilities, including having experts perform time limited administration of policy programs and studying the formation of policy decisions, should not be overlooked (230). The potential shortcomings of having policy evaluation define the boundaries of psychologist involvement have not gone unnoticed. Limiting our work merely to measuring policy effects may blind our capacity for envisioning a fundamentally altered society (142, 330).

An important, rarely scrutinized process preceding policy formation and evaluation is problem definition. Working exclusively to evaluate existing policies holds the real danger of perpetuating the dogmatic attribution of problem causes to people instead of situations (60) and ignoring the fact that proposed solutions by experts often view people without power with faulty and incomplete ideas (139). What policy impact does social science currently have? One study (59) identified a surprisingly large incidence of social science knowledge utilization in federal policy decisions. However, the major determinant of use was the political implications of a research finding.

It is important for social scientists to avoid putting services entirely at the disposal of others. The risk of being used to serve narrow interests is considerable. The Congressional Information Service (CIS) is a computer retrieval system for keeping abreast of legislative activities which are forums for policy debate. Prior discussion has emphasized two or three perspectives on policy change enumerated by Crowfoot & Chesler (82): professional-technical and political. The counter-cultural perspective presents alternatives to existing societal processes. Kanter (172) presents a thoughtful appraisal of communal counter-cultural experiments. Other sources of challenging perspectives include the works of Callenbach (53, 54), Lappe (198), Roszak (300, 301), and economists Heilbroner (150) and Schumacher (317). A unique catalog of the counter-cultural literature is published periodically by the American Library Association (7). Those of us in the academic enterprise are taught to devalue such "unscientific' proposals; therefore, these sources of ideas need to be sought after through more conscious effort. The redefinition of social values that one can find in counter-cultural literature is an integral part of social change efforts and cannot be ignored.

Recent techniques have been developed and tested which seem suitable to producing changes in social practices at the community level. Implementation of social innovations has been subjected to controlled experimentation. Existing social science research is now used for policy making whether or not it was intended for that purpose. There are examples of effective use of social science skills for the expressed purpose of both proposing and evaluating public policy.

Working on social change penetrates many social, political, and economic institutions and requires a multidisciplinary perspective. A critical attitude and a commitment to engage in the formation of public policy are needed to both influence public policy and contribute to social change.

THEORY

At present, the field of SCI has no broad, integrative theories. However, it does have a number of research traditions and perspectives. Preston (277) enumerates several of these traditions such as the ecological approach, the social system perspective, and the cultural-ethnographic approach. In addition to these conceptual schemes, there is an array of hypotheses that has prompted much social science research. Rothman (303) has compiled and evaluated the vast amount of empirical evidence regarding these hypotheses. His work serves as a model for the integration of findings and distilling of guidelines for effective action. The applicability of these catalogued principles begs to be tested in the field. A newly published manual by Rothman and colleagues will provide direction in accomplishing this task (304). Effort is now being spent in defining the field. The historical context of community psychology has been analyzed[3] (154, 308). So has its realtionships to other SCI endeavors: Community clinical psychology is seen as the straight application of clinical techniques at a community-wide level (306); Community mental health includes prevention and consultation, but with the view of adapting individuals to social circumstances; Community psychology, Rappaport proposes, has the broader aim of adapting society to individual and group needs (285).

Whatever meaning the word "community" has for a psychologist will influence the kind of program that he or she will implement. For example, some community mental health clinics gear their services to vocal minorities, others to people within a geographical area, others to society-at-large. These differing conceptual frameworks will result in different staff characteristics, awareness of needs, and effects on the target population (288).

Newbrough (248) has made a formal attempt to specify the ideological framework of community psychology and organizes this ideology into 13 major components. He calls attention to topics which are often unrecognized or taken for granted, such as the generic complexity of community processes. In addition, he makes explicit four facets implicit in the definition of community psychology: the philosophy behind it, its work approach, its methods of inquiry, and its professional characteristics.

A major characteristic of the field is its emphasis on a contextual understanding of human functioning. This is reflected in the popularity of the ecological analogy (159, 183), and in the conceptualization of the community as a context which can itself be competent or dysfunctional (165). Glidewell, building on the concepts of organizational change and small group research, has developed a theoretical statement for social change by focusing upon the topics of personal commitment, access to other social systems, and creative mastery of organizational tensions (128).

Foreshadowings of future theorizing are found in the constructive criticisms of Seymour Sarason. In two major books (307, 308), he accuses the field of not grappling directly with the psychological sense of community. He creatively sets the stage for future work by presenting the concept of community in its two aspects— as an objective human creation and as a subjective human experience. In addition, he suggests that by actively engaging in community interventions, social and community workers will increase their chances of learning to deal with this elusive but vital topic.

In a somewhat similar vein, Starr (330) reminds us that the aims of social science and not its methods are what provide its distinctiveness and importance. Theory construction, therefore, ought not to shirk from morals and values, nor be shaped merely by the availability of objective techniques.

[3]S.R. Roen 1968 "Historical and Conceptual Development of Community Psychology." Unpublished manuscript.

A final important area of thought has to do with how the field conceptualizes its own growth. The great increase in human service personnel throughout our society has been a cause for concern to many. In 1900, 38% of employed U.S. workers were in agriculture, 38% in industry, and 24% in services. In 1970, 4% were in agriculture, 35% in industry, and 61% in services (123). Is the emphasis on human services hurting productivity or eroding the vitality of our society? No, say Gartner & Riessman (123). They develop a novel concept—the consumer as producer—and then suggest concretely how human services could be better reflected in Gross National Product figures. They draw implications of their analysis which predict that as the service ethic becomes more prevalent, it may have positive repercussions on the quality of life. This conceptualization could provide a rationale for the continued growth of SCI. But its implications deserve careful study before it is used in this manner.

At this time, SCI stand in the void between the individual focus of psychology and the conglomerate focus of other behavioral sciences. Though firmly anchored at both ends, the conceptual bridge over the void between disciplines elicits uncertainty. As more and more ideas strengthen this bridge, a unique foundation is laid for researchable social and community theories.

Practical problem solving is receiving much more attention than theoretical issues at present. Frameworks and analogies from varied sources are being used to help conceptualize SCI.

Precise SCI theory construction requires a particularly close coordination with ongoing social and community processes. The complexity of naturally occurring events is best captured by both adapted and new perspectives.

METHODS

The problems and promise of empirical research in natural settings go back at least to Kurt Lewin and "action research" (17). If community research's promise is rich, its problems are formidable. Cowen, Lorion & Dorr characterize the community researcher's fate as that of a trespasser in a changing social system which values "doing" more than "studying" (77). They encourage investigators to share their struggles in hopes that documented lessons will accumulate. One essay in this vein showed how the structure and values of a host organization dictated specific methodological accommodations (114).

Community researchers must grapple with another challenge besides inconvenience. Social community interventions are obliged ultimately to explain community forces and not simply sidestep them as research obstacles. The methodological problem is capturing the holism of natural processes without sacrificing precision and the possibility of sorting out cause and effect. Such challenges probably contribute to the high ratio of anecdote and theory to research (73, 291).

SCI problems increasingly attract the attention of expert methodologists. Evaluation research, a specialty generating solutions appropriate for all field research, has gained enormously in sophistication and prestige. Major approaches are organized and surveyed in a chapter appearing in Volume 27 of the *Annual Review of Psychology* (270). The *Handbook of Evaluation Research* (331) is an excellent reference to evaluation methods which includes a wide variety of applications.

Like the community intervener, the community researcher must be broadly knowledgeable, flexible, and inventive. Researchers in the Rochester, New York, Primary Mental Health Project have devised instrumentation and experimental designs to secure informative data from a natural setting. They have developed teacher referral and screening instruments (67, 75), a technique for classifying students according to problem type (210), and applied factor analysis to the study of nonprofessional therapist characteristics (95).

The plan of another flexible research program has appeared (194, 318). This program uses multiple techniques to obtain and analyze data on paraprofessionals, clients, and the social system where they interact. Isolating predictors of therapist effectiveness, for example, employed a variety of multivariate procedures, and necessitated inventing a new procedure for analyzing multitrait, multimethod matrices (136). In community work, particularly where community priorities guide problem selection, doing good work means selecting or inventing methods to suit the problem rather than focusing on problems which fit familiar methods.

One possibility to expand the empirical base of social and community interventions is to use existing information such as social indicators. Quasi-experimental methods allow existing data on social phenomena to approximate "natural experiments" (14, 298, 314). In one example (196), displaying frequency of reported sex crimes in time series demonstrated the positive effects of liberalizing pornography laws. The study tested and did not find support to alternative hypotheses (e.g. changes in attitudes toward reporting sex crimes) for the observed decline. Similarly, psychiatric case registers are existing data sources with potential for answering important research questions. Case registers have been applied to studying social and family aspects of mental disorders (34) and for follow-up comparisons in evaluating community-based interventions (78).

There are several techniques which, though rarely reported, are naturalistic, unobtrusive, and comprehensive. One well-established technique, participant observation, has been recommended to program evaluators (13, 120) and seems appropriate for many social community purposes. Intensive multivariate study of the single case is well suited to the study of social processes over time (21). Given information about client referrals and client pathways through the human service network, the methods of network analysis (49, 50) and systems analysis (246) have much to contribute. These procedures quantify transactions among interdependent social units. All of the above methods make it possible to work with large-scale, complex phenomena without abandoning an empirical orientation.

Many social and community theories have variables represented in forms not controllable by an experimenter. However, we need not abandon hope of establishing causation. Williams (370) describes a process for building empirically based theory about social conflict which has general application to social and to community theory building. He sketches a sequence in which field observations suggest hypotheses that are tested in the laboratory and then retested for validity under natural conditions in controlled field studies. Construction of quantitative causal models is another approach to theory testing. Frequently we are forced to rely on only correlational data. An existing procedure, path analysis (35) provides rules for making causal inferences from networks of correlations. Maris (219) illustrates the application of path analysis in testing a theory of suicide attempts. Nonetheless, causal inferences from path analysis can be equivocal. The classical randomized experiment which nails down causality is feasible under naturalistic conditions and has an important role in SCI methodology (112, 290).

Epidemiology is most closely identified with the body of knowledge on occurrence and distribution of disorders (88). Epidemiological methods are well suited for data gathering to tackle several social and community problems (152, 291). One novel application of epidemiology is counting incidence and prevalence of disorder to keep abreast of community needs. King, Morgan & Smith (188) describe how monthly tabulating of the incidence of problems reported by callers to a telephone crisis center provides an index of problem trends. These data served as a community-wide assessment which gives a basis for rational allocation of helping resources. Newbrough (249) relates how establishing the frequency of presumably stressful events can point the way for primary prevention.

Epidemiological indices can also serve as criterion variables. Bloom (38) measured the impact of reorganizing mental health services community wide by comparing epidemiological data collected before and after the change. As the field matures, epidemiology should supply the "acid test" of interventions purportedly delivering effective mental health services on a truly community scale.

Multiple foci and consequences of intervention require simultaneous use of many methods for studying the problem at hand. The field of program evaluation is an active source of rigorous methodology. Innovative uses of epidemiological methods and already existing data, such as social indicators and psychiatric case registers, seem promising.

Seeking out methods of data collection and analysis which conform to situational constraints is a weighty challenge. The character of social community problems demands methodological resourcefulness and flexibility.

EDUCATION AND TRAINING

There is a large literature on training professionals, nonprofessionals, and citizens for roles in community mental health and community service. Primary sources for this literature are: 10, 98, 122, 135, 207, 269, 322, 380, 381. The examination of professional roles as they relate to community work includes articles on nursing (383), the clergy (100), biostatistics (44), social work (362), and the psychiatric aide (72). At long last, one of the most important persons in the mental health enterprise has been cited and applauded: the secretary (256). These publications examine the similarities and differences between doing community work and doing clinical work, describe community-oriented training programs, and point out how mental health professionals can learn skills for doing community work. A framework for satisfying extended community service needs through the use of cost-effective ancillary resources has been suggested.[4]

The PhD Psychologist

Attention to the psychologists' role in social and community interventions has continued following the commentary on training by Iscoe & Spielberger in 1970 (166). These reflections focus primarily upon either the delineation of clinical-community vs community psychology roles (39, 161, 162, 306) or offer new preferred roles for the community psychologist (3, 4, 8, 30, 165, 180, 182, 248, 297, 318, 353).

A contribution for understanding the developmental histories of community psychologists is a collection of essays by five community psychologists—J. Chinsky, I. Iscoe, J.R. Newbrough, G. Rosenblum, and E. Trickett. They openly discuss their careers, their worries, and the work that makes them feel good (130). The report of the conference on levels and patterns of professional training held in Vail, Colorado, in 1973 includes recommendations for the training of community psychologists (193). The report of the National Conference on Training in Community Psychology, held at Austin, Texas, in the spring of 1975 evaluates the first decade of the field and presents new conceptual frameworks for the future (167).

In addition to program descriptions emphasizing graduate education for careers in community work within departments of psychology, published reports are available about training in autonomous professional schools (93, 118) and multidisciplinary programs (33, 40, 346, 351, 352, 354). These discussions highlight the glow arising from achieving new insights along with the role strain produced by working in new and different settings. Both the Vail and Austin conferences encourage psychology to venture out and develop a variety of settings for education. Pluralistic approaches to education have been advocated; the task now is to act on these ideas.

Renner (289) has raised the question of whether community psychology and community psychologists have become, perhaps unwittingly, servants of national, state, or local political goals. The awareness of this unspoken yet basic issue for the future education of community psychologists was eloquently articulated by Seymour Sarason in an invited address to the American Psychological Association in 1975 (309). The topic of community psychologists' relationship to public policy is expected to be seen more often in print including the searching of souls about past cooptations.

Community Service by Persons Trained at the A.A. and B.A. Levels

A.A. and B.A. level persons are as important as doctoral level workers in the development of effective mental health services. During the period of this review,

---

[4]Christensen, A., Miller, W.R., Muñoz, R.F. "Paraprofessionals, Partners, Peers, Paraphernalia, and Print: A Model for the Use of Therapeutic Adjuncts in Prevention, Treatment, and Maintenance." Submitted for publication, 1976.

a number of useful handbooks, guidelines, and procedures have become available (87, 115, 119, 239) as well as a directory of degree-granting programs in the human services (282).

The B.A. Level and Nondegree Worker

The role of the undergraduate student as an active participant in community programs as tutor, companion, and behavioral therapist has increased (9, 131, 133, 169, 179, 181, 221, 287, 313, 320, 337, 358). A very provocative and comprehensive report of the role of the undergraduate in community work is a published report of a Master's thesis at the University of Illinois (5). College volunteers working with first grade and kindergarten children from poverty level families instituted two intervention programs: structured reading and companionship. The structured reading program was found to be more effective with both first grade and kindergarten children. Comparing treatments in this way is essential in illuminating valid service roles.

A number of articles present frank accounts of attempts to design service roles for citizens with or without A.A. or B.A. level degrees or specific training. The articles as a group express the "do's and don'ts" when training "indigenous" persons (6, 48, 68, 106, 153, 195, 341, 361, 385).

The level of education, B.A. or A.A. degree, is not the only variable for effecting the performance of human service roles. The University of Rochester program (94, 95) is providing a framework for predicting the performance of effective nonprofessionals, both in terms of job performance and personality attributes. An incisive and coherent source for thinking about the education of the paraprofessional is the writings of Pearl (265–267). He persuasively advocates that the nonprofessionals must have a workable theory of social change, personal and professional competences, active social support, and political savvy to create new professional roles for themselves.

The Citizen as Influential Volunteer

There is estimated to be 50 million Americans involved in five million voluntary groups (83). The reader can choose from illustrative examples describing the effectiveness of volunteers in community service programs (25, 26, 105, 178, 252, 305, 324, 338, 359, 366). The general pattern of the evaluations is that citizens who carry out helping roles do perform very well and increase their own sense of self-worth when doing so. Volunteering for community work is good for the community and for the volunteer.

Citizens serving on governing boards of community service agencies can breathe easier. The published work of Briscoe et al (42), Meyers et al (223, 224), Beck (23), and the excellent reviews of the literature prepared by Paschall (261) and Mogulof (227) all point to these facts: citizens can be trained to be better problem solvers as board members (42); citizen board accomplishment can be predicted (223, 224); for citizen participation to work, both professionals and citizens will need training (227, 261). A manual for CMHC board members offers explicit and helpful guidelines for citizen participation (377).

Koleda (191), in reflecting upon our society and our education, suggests that the common goal for all training and education is a "guaranteed lifelong usefulness." He advocates continuing education, job upgrading opportunities, and career switching options as a matter of course at all levels of education and for all ages. Now that is a good notion for a community psychology!

The mental health professions are sorting out the similarities and differences between clinical and community service. Debates over role boundaries and preferences for professional practice are expected to continue.

SCI skills are beginning to be identified as important topics in their own right. There is an optimistic mood in the literature that competences for SCI work will be defined and realized.

It is established that persons with A.A. and B.A. degrees as well as citizens, either as volunteers or as paid staff, provide quality community service. As yet they are not recognized in terms of salary, occupational mobility, or professional status for their contributions.

As new roles for SCI develop, the variety and availability of A.A. and B.A. professionals, and citizens, can provide new resources. The delivery of SCI can accommodate to the competences of the person doing the work, rather than relying upon the formal level of achieved education as the sole criterion for professional worth.

FINALE

The conclusions presented at the close of each section of the chapter summarize the trends expressed in the literature. We have focused upon the data, the theoretical ideas, and the examples of service delivery that are observable issues for the years 1972–76. We have intended to reflect and communicate the major themes, to denote them, and to clearly set them before you.

The literature that has accummulated during the past 4 years expresses a maturity and a sense of confidence when coping with doing community work. There is a tangible, positive mood and an explicit movement away from doing work derived solely from the traditional orientations of the psychologist. Psychologists are adapting traditional methods and concepts, and coming up with new SCI that go to the heart of applied problems to meet the needs and hopes of citizens.

There is an obvious and compelling complexity in trying to understand the work of SCI. We expect that the creation of methods and theories developed by the psychologist can continue to expand so that new SCI can affect public policy and produce useful community and preventive programs. We have the belief that a definite part of SCI is intuitive and personal, not shared, and not yet in print. We urge the field to provide opportunities for those who are doing community work but not publishing it to share with us what they know. We urge the creation of oral history programs to document the intricacies and subtleties of doing community work. We believe that the field needs supplements to material published in the journals and books, particularly related to the process of the hows and whys of doing community work. Biographical and autobiographical accounts are needed to go beyond the abstract, technical, and often truncated presentations of substantive findings.

We have been impressed and gratified to see others besides psychologists work, worry out loud, and write about the scientific and value issues facing the community-oriented psychologist. In this regard, the psychologist devoted to SCI can benefit and be encouraged by the material published in the journals of other professions. There are an increasing number of social and behavioral scientists, planners, journalists, and citizens, who are interested and are working hard on the same or related topics. Yet the psychologists' contributions are still unique. Looking for and relating to the writings of nonpsychologists not only educate us, but help clarify for us what it is in SCI that is uniquely psychological. Our identity is clarified by seeing how we fit. These are the latent directions. What about the future?

We present the following options to ourselves and to the reader for propelling the evolution of SCI. In the future SCI can:

1. Design new means of communication and new social settings for those of us doing, evaluating, and thinking about SCI, so that our results are widely seen, articulated, digested, and considered.

2. Become more directly involved with the evaluation of public policy in the governmental, political, and community settings where policy is made.

3. Instill within our education and training programs a tradition of devoting a proportion of SCI resources expressly for working on citizen-selected problems.

4. Increase the commitment of psychologists to work with other professions and citizens on SCI. We can know our place in the world of SCI by working with others unlike ourselves.

5. Clarify, sort out, and make explicit the boundaries and the roles for citizens and professionals in service delivery, program evaluation, program development, and public policy. Can we psychologists in SCI do anything better than anyone else can do?

6. Place more intellectual and financial resources and attention on the design and evaluation of community based social experiments. We should not shy away from investing in planned trial and error.

7. Pay attention to the economic properties of social and community interventions. Social and community interventions carried out without a commitment to improve economic resources of the community or the economic well-being of citizens will be pale and inconsequential.

8. Increase efforts to understand the personal qualities and abilities involved in designing and carrying out community work. Can we select, educate, and train for community work? Does the performance of SCI involve the same or different qualities as carrying out other professional roles? So far we have only vague hunches.

9. Spend more time, energy, and creativity to understand natural support systems, social networks, and social support. Understanding these social processes will help us understand what is valuable in the social organization of communities. If we can increase our insight about the workings of social structures, we can know better why and where we should intervene.

10. Pay more attention to theories and philosophies of social change. SCI are often derived from implicit premises about how social organizations work that don't always fit natural conditions. We also need to know more about the motivations

and aspirations in ourselves for doing SCI. If we aren't sure why we are doing what we are doing, how can we cope well with the resistances to our work?

11. Learn as much as possible about the management of conflict. SCI involves, whether we anticipate it or expect it, the management of personal, organizational, and community conflict. When a SCI is set in motion, we are raising the level of conflict. Can we anticipate the positive and negative forces we set in motion?

12. Direct more efforts to the teaching of personal and social competences, and give more conscious attention to the creation of supportive environments. These acts may give substance to the concept of primary prevention.

These are some ideas that stand out. They make sense to us for the next phase of SCI.

APPENDIX

Information on social and community interventions is available through a variety of sources including automated information retrieval systems, abstracting and indexing services, government publications, informal reports of research projects, proceedings, dissertations, pamphlets, and specialized publications. A brief list of information sources is cited below:

Search Systems

Automated search and retrieval systems represent the quickest and most efficient method of bibliographic control. Christian (65) lists selected publishers of machine-readable data bases. The search systems include:

1. PsychINFO — American Psychological Association, 1200 17th Street, N.W., Washington, D.C. 20036, the automated data base version of *Psychological Abstracts.*
2. COMPUTER INFORMATION SERVICES OF THE NATIONAL CLEAR-INGHOUSE FOR MENTAL HEALTH INFORMATION (NCMHI) — Alcohol, Drug Abuse, and Mental Health Administration, 5600 Fishers Lane, Rockville, Md. 20852. Reader generated bibliographies are available without charge to anyone within the mental health professions.
3. DATA BANK OF PROGRAM EVALUATION (DOPE) — School of Public Health, U.C.L.A., 10833 LeConte Avenue, Los Angeles, Calif. 90024. A computerized field of brief reports of evaluations in the mental health field appearing in over 100 journals and unpublished sources since 1969.
4. NATIONAL TECHNICAL INFORMATION SERVICE (NTIS) — 5285 Port Royal Rd., Springfield, Va. 22151. A semi-monthly, computer-printed, bibliographic data base by the U.S. Department of Commerce for information generated under federally funded research. NTIS also issues *Behavior & Society,* a weekly news service.
5. LOCKHEED INFORMATION SOURCES — 3251 Hanover Street, Palo Alto, Calif. 94304. A commercial data base including *Psychological Abstracts, ERIC,* and *NTIS.*

Indexing and Abstracting Services

In addition to *Psychological Abstracts* and the *Catalog of Selected Documents in Psychology,* published by the American Psychological Association, five other helpful indexing and abstracting services for the topic of social and community interventions are:

1. SOCIAL SCIENCES CITATION INDEX — Institute for Scientific Information, 325 Chestnut Street, Philadelphia, Pa. 19106. Issued three times a year. Access to information is also available through a Permuterm (subject) index, corporate index, and source index.
2. BULLETIN OF THE PUBLIC AFFAIRS INFORMATION SERVICE (PAID) — Public Affairs Information Service, Inc., 11 West 40th Street, New York, NY 10018. A selective list of latest books, pamphlets, government publications, reports of public and private agencies, periodical articles relating to economic and social conditions, public administration and international relations published in English throughout the world. Issued weekly except for the last two weeks of each quarter.
3. SUBJECT GUIDE TO FORTHCOMING BOOKS — R.R. Bowker Company, 1180 Avenue of the Americas, New York, N.Y. 10036. A list of books expected to be published in the United States during the next five months. Issued bi-monthly.
4. JOURNAL OF HUMAN SERVICES/ABSTRACTS — Project Share, P.O. Box 2309, Rockville, Md. 20852. January 1976 was the first issue of this quarterly journal of documents. Project Share makes available a broad range of documentation of subjects of concern to those responsible for the planning, management, and delivery of human services.
5. EDUCATIONAL RESOURCES INFORMATION CENTER (ERIC) — National Institute of Education, Washington, D.C. 20208. Indexes and abstracts documents processed through clearinghouses in the ERIC system. Contains author, subject, and institution indexes. Issued monthly.

Federal Sources

The following federal government sources are recommended for the topic of social and community interventions:

1. MONTHLY CATALOG OF UNITED STATES GOVERNMENT PUBLICATIONS — Superintendent of Documents, U.S. Government Printing Office, Washington, D.C. 20402.
2. INDEX TO U.S. GOVERNMENT PERIODICALS — Infordata International, Inc., Suite 4602, 175 E. Delaware Place, Chicago, Ill, 60611. Published in May, August, November, and March.
3. CIS/INDEX TO PUBLICATIONS OF THE U.S. CONGRESS and AMERICAN STATISTICS INDEX — Published by the Congressional Information Service, Inc., 7101 Wisconsin Avenue, Washington, D.C. 20014. A comprehensive guide and index to the statistical publications of the U.S. government. These

two sources will yield valuable data concerning hearings, witnesses, proposals, legislation, and other vital information including corresponding statistical data related to federal government activities in the mental health field.

Specialized Sources

1. InterDOK — A directory of published proceedings, InterDOK Corporation, P.O. Box 326, Harrison, NY 10528, is a bibliographic directory of preprints and published proceedings of congresses, conferences, symposia, meetings, seminars, and summer schools. Issued monthly 10 times a year, September to June.
2. RESEARCH GRANTS INDEX — U.S. National Institutes of Health, Division of Research Grants, Bethesda, Md. 20014. This annual publication provides information on health research currently being conducted by non-Federal institutions and supported by the health agencies of the Department of Health, Education, and Welfare.
3. PUBLIC AFFAIRS PAMPHLETS — 381 Park Avenue, S., New York, NY 10016, issues interesting and easy-to-read pamphlets addressing problems in mental health, family relations, social problems, etc.
4. ALTERNATIVES IN PRINT: CATALOG OF SOCIAL CHANGE PUBLICATIONS, 1975–76 (7) — A specialized guide to publications available from nonprofit, antiprofit, counterculture, Third World movement groups and the free press.

The personal and informal exchange of information among us still remains the most important and most valuable information source.

Literature Cited

1. Abad, V., Ramos, J., Boyce, E. 1974. A model for delivery of mental health services to Spanish-speaking minorities. *Am. J. Orthopsychiatry* 44:584–95
2. Abramowitz, S. I., Abramowitz, C. V., Jackson, C., Gomes, B. 1973. The politics of clinical judgement: What nonliberal examiners infer about women who do not stifle themselves. *J. Consult. Clin. Psychol.* 41:385–91
3. Adelson, D. 1974. Community psychology as man's encounter with history: Or self and social reconstruction as two aspects of the same process: A point of view. *J. Community Psychol.* 2:402–5
4. Albee, G. W. 1975. *Human services: Innovative roles for psychologists.* Presented at AAAS meeting, New York City
5. Alden, L., Rappaport, J., Seidman, E. 1975. College students as interventionists for primary-grade children. *Am. J. Community Psychol.* 3:261–71
6. Alley, S., Blanton, J. 1976. A study of paraprofessionals in mental health. *Community Ment. Health J.* In press
7. American Library Association 1975–76. Social responsibilities. Round table. Task Force on Alternatives in Print. *Alternatives in Print: Catalog of Social Change Publications.* San Francisco: Glide. 346 pp.
8. Aponte, J. F. 1974. In search of an educational model for community psychology. *J. Community Psychol.* 2:301–5
9. Arthur, G. L., Donnan, H. H., Lair, C. V. 1973. Companionship therapy with nursing home aged. *Gerontologist* 13:167–70
10. Baker, E. J. 1972. The mental health associate: A new approach in mental health. *Community Ment. Health J.* 8:281–91
11. Baker, F. 1974. From community mental health to human service ideology. *Am. J. Public Health* 64:576–81
12. Baker, K. 1975. A new grantsmanship. *Am. Sociol.* 10:206–19

13. Balaban, R. M. 1973. The contribution of participant observation to the study of process in program evaluation. *Int. J. Ment. Health* 2:59–70

14. Baldus, D. C. 1973. Welfare as loan: The recovery of public assistance in the United States. *Stanford Univ. Law Rev.* 25:123–250

15. Baltes, P. B., Schaie, K. W., eds. 1973. *Life-Span Developmental Psychology: Personality and Socialization.* New York: Academic

16. Banikiotes, P. G. 1973. A preventive approach to mental health in the schools. *Couns. Values* 17:112–17

17. Bard, M. 1972. A model for action research. In *Man as the Measure: The Crossroads*, ed. D. Adelson, 17–28. New York: Behavioral. 146 pp.

18. Barker, R. G., Schoggen, P. 1973. *Qualities of Community Life.* San Francisco: Jossey-Bass. 562 pp.

19. Bass, R. D., Windle, C. 1972. Continuity of care: An approach to measurement. *Am. J. Psychiatry* 129:196–201

20. Bass, R. D., Windle, C. 1973. A preliminary attempt to measure continuity of care in a community mental health center. *Community Ment. Health J.* 9:53–62

21. Bath, K. 1974. The use of intensive individual designs in community research. *Community Ment. Health J.* 10:418–25

22. Bauman, G., Grunes, R. 1974. *Psychiatric Rehabilitation in the Ghetto: An Educational Approach.* Lexington, Mass: Heath. 177 pp.

23. Beck, A. A. 1973. *The application of small group techniques to training in community participation: A field experiment.* PhD thesis. Michigan State Univ., East Lansing, Mich. 145 pp.

24. Beck, D. F. 1975. Research findings on the outcomes of marital counseling. *Soc. Casework* 56:153–81

25. Beckman, L. 1972. Locus of control and attitudes toward mental illness among mental health volunteers. *J. Consult. Clin. Psychol.* 38:84–89

26. Beier, E. G., Robinson, P., Micheletti, G. 1971. Susanville: A community helps itself in mobilization of community resources for self-help in mental health. *J. Consult. Clin. Psychol.* 36:142–50

27. Beiser, M. 1971. A study of personality assets in a rural community. *Arch. Gen. Psychiatry* 24:244–54

28. Beiser, M., Feldman, J. J., Egelhoff, C. J. 1972. Assets and affects. *Arch. Gen. Psychiatry* 27:545–49

29. Beisser, A. R. 1972. Organizational models and strategies of intervention. *Smith Coll. Stud. Soc. Work* 42:125–45

30. Bender, M. P. 1972. The role of a community psychologist. *Bull. Br. Psychol. Soc.* 25:211–18

31. Berlin, R., Berlin, I. N. 1975. Parents' advocate role in education as primary prevention. In *Advocacy for Child Mental Health*, ed. I. N. Berlin, 145–57. New York: Brunner/Mazel. 338 pp.

32. Bernal, M. E. 1971. Training parents in child management. In *Behavior Modification of Learning Disabilities*, ed. R. H. Bradfield, pp. 41–67. San Rafael, Calif: Academic Therapy. 172 pp.

33. Binder, A. 1972. A new context for psychology: Social ecology. *Am. Psychol.* 27:903–8

34. Birtchnell, J. 1973. The use of a psychiatric case register to study social and familial aspects of mental illness. *Soc. Sci. Med.* 7:145–53

35. Blalock, H. M., ed. 1971. *Causal Models in the Social Sciences.* Chicago: Aldine, 515 pp.

36. Blank, S. S., Covington, M. 1965. Inducing children to ask questions in solving problems. *J. Educ. Res.* 59:21–27

37. Bleach, G., Claiborn, W. L. 1974. Initial evaluation of hot-line telephone crisis centers. *Community Ment. Health J.* 10:387–94

38. Bloom, B. 1975. *Changing Patterns of Psychiatric Care.* New York: Behavioral. 360 pp.

39. Bloom, B. L. 1973. The domain of community psychology. *Am. J. Community Psychol.* 1:8–11

40. Brayfield, A. H. 1976. How to create a new profession: Issues and answers. *Am. Psychol.* 31:200–5

41. Brenner, M. H. 1973. *Mental Illness and the Economy.* Cambridge: Harvard. 287 pp.

42. Briscoe, R. V., Hoffman, D. B., Bailey, J. S. 1975. Behavioral community psychology: Training a community board to problem solve. *J. Appl. Behav. Anal.* 8:157–68

43. Brockopp, G. W., Lester, D., eds. 1973. *Crisis Intervention and Counseling by Telephone.* Springfield, Ill: Thomas. 322 pp.

44. Brogan, D. R., Greenberg, B. G. 1973. An educational program in mental health statistics. *Community Ment. Health J.* 9:68–78

45. Brook, B. D. 1973. Crisis hostel: An alternative to psychiatric hospitaliza-

tion for emergency patients. *Hosp. Community Psychiatry* 24:621–24
46. Broskowski, A. 1973. Concepts of teacher-centered consultation. *Prof. Psychol.* 4:50–58
47. Brower, S. N., Williamson, P. 1974. Outdoor recreation as a function of the urban housing environment. *Environ. Behav.* 6:295–345
48. Brown, W. F. 1974. Effectiveness of paraprofessionals: The evidence. *Personnel Guid. J.* 53:257–63
49. Burgess, J. H. 1974. Mental health service systems: Approaches to evaluation. *Am. J. Community Psychol.* 2:87–93
50. Burgess, J., Nelson, R. H., Wallhaus, R. 1974. Network analysis as a method for the evaluation of service delivery systems. *Community Ment. Health J.* 10:337–44
51. Butler, R. N., Lewis, M. I. 1973. *Aging and Mental Health: Positive Psycho-Social Approaches.* St. Louis: Mosby. 306 pp.
52. Buttimer, A. 1972. Social space and the planning of residential areas. *Environ. Behav.* 4:279–318
53. Callenbach, E. 1975. *Ecotopia.* Berkeley: Banyan Tree. 168 pp.
54. Callenbach, E. 1972. *Living Poor with Style.* New York: Bantam. 600 pp.
55. Campbell, A. 1976. Subjective measures of well-being. *Am. Psychol.* 31:117–24
56. Campbell, A., Converse, P. E., eds. 1972. *The Human Meaning of Social Change.* New York: Sage. 547 pp.
57. Campbell, D. T. 1975. Assessing the impact of planned social change. See Ref. 211, pp. 3–45
58. Caplan, G. 1974. *Support Systems and Community Mental Health.* New York: Behavioral
59. Caplan, N., Morrison, A., Stambaugh, R. J. 1975. *The Use of Social Science Knowledge in Policy Decisions at the National Level.* Ann Arbor: Univ. Mich. 63 pp.
60. Caplan, N., Nelson, S. D. 1973. On being useful: The nature and consequences of psychological research on social problems. *Am. Psychol.* 28:199–211
61. Catalano, R., Monahan, J. 1975. The community psychologist as a social planner: Designing optimal environments. *Am. J. Community Psychol.* 3:327–34
62. Cherniss, C. 1976. Pre-entry issues in consultation. *Am. J. Community Psychol.* In press

63. Chesler, P. 1972. *Women and Madness.* New York: Avon. 359 pp.
64. Chess, S., Thomas, A. 1975. *Ann. Prog. Child Psychiatry Child Dev.* 541 pp.
65. Christian, R. W. 1975. *The Electronic Library: Bibliographic Data Bases 1975–76.* White Plains, NY: Knowledge Ind. Publ. 118 pp.
66. Chu, F. D., Trotter, S. 1974. *The Madness Establishment: Ralph Nader's Study Group Report on the National Institute of Mental Health.* New York: Grossman. 232 pp.
67. Clarfield, S. 1974. The development of a teacher referral form for identifying early school maladaptation. *Am. J. Community Psychol.* 2:199–210
68. Clarfield, S., McMillan, R. 1973. Tuned-out secondary school students as mental health aides in the elementary school. *Am. J. Community Psychol.* 1:212–18
69. Cohen, R. E. 1972. Principles of preventive mental health programs for ethnic minority populations: The acculturation of Puerto Ricans to the United States. *Am. J. Psychiatry* 128:1529–33
69a. Cohen, S., Glass, D. C., Phillips, S. 1977. Environmental factors in health. In *Handbook of Medical Sociology,* ed. H. E. Freeman, S. Levine, L. G. Reeder. Englewood Cliffs, NJ: Prentice-Hall. In press
70. Cohen, S., Glass, D. C., Singer, J. E. 1973. Apartment noise, auditory discrimination, and reading ability in children. *J. Exp. Soc. Psychol.* 9:407–22
71. Collins, A. H. 1973. Natural delivery systems: Accessible sources of power for mental health. *Am. J. Orthopsychiatry* 43:46–52
72. Cook, D. W., Kunce, J. T., Sleater, S. M. 1974. Vicarious behavior induction and training psychiatric aides. *J. Community Psychol.* 2:293–97
73. Cowen, E. L. 1973. Social and community interventions. *Ann. Rev. Psychol.* 24:423–72
74. Cowen, E. L. 1976. Demystifying primary prevention in mental health. *Social Policy.* In press
75. Cowen, E. L., Dorr, D., Clarfield, S., Kreling, B., McWilliams, S. A., Pokracki, F., Pratt, D. M., Terrell, D., Wilson, A. 1973. The AML: A quick-screening device for early identification of school maladaptation. *Am. J. Community Psychol.* 1:12–35
76. Cowen, E. L., Dorr, D. A., Trost, M. A., Izzo, L. D. 1972. Follow-up study of maladapting school children seen by

nonprofessionals. *J. Consult. Clin. Psychol.* 39:235–38
77. Cowen, E. L., Lorion R. P., Dorr, D. 1974. Research in the community cauldron: A case history. *Can. Psychol.* 15:313–25
78. Cowen, E. L., Pederson, A., Babigian, H., Izzo, L. D., Trost, M. A. 1973. Long-term follow-up of early detected vulnerable children. *J. Consult. Clin. Psychol.* 41:438–46
79. Cowen, E. L., Trost, M. A., Izzo, L. D. 1973. Nonprofessional human-service personnel in consulting roles. *Community Ment. Health J.* 9:335–41
80. Cowen, E. L., Trost, M. A., Lorion, R. P., Dorr, D., Izzo, L. D., Isaacson, R. V. 1975. *New Ways in School Mental Health: Early Detection and Prevention of School Maladaptation.* New York: Human Sciences. 396 pp.
81. Craven, P., Wellman, B. 1973. The network city. *Soc. Inq.* 43:57–88
82. Crowfoot, J. E., Chesler, M. A. 1974. Contemporary perspectives on planned social change: A comparison. *J. Appl. Behav. Sci.* 10:278–303
83. Cull, J. G., Hardy, R. E. 1974. *Volunteerism: An Emerging Profession.* Springfield, Ill: Thomas. 199 pp.
84. Daggett, D. R., Jones, M. E., Feider, L., Clarke, R. 1974. Mental health consultation improves care of the aged in community facilities. *Hosp. Community Psychiatry* 25:170–72
85. D'Augelli, A. R. 1973. Group composition using interpersonal skills: An analogue study on the efforts of members' interpersonal skills on peer ratings and group cohesiveness. *J. Couns. Psychol.* 20:531–43
86. D'Augelli, A. R., Chinsky, J. M. 1974. Interpersonal skills and pretraining: Implications for the use of group procedures for interpersonal learning and for the selection of non-professional mental health workers. *J. Consult. Clin. Psychol.* 42:65–72
87. Delworth, U., Rudow, E. H., Taub, J. 1972. *Crisis Center Hotline: A Guidebook to Beginning and Operating.* Springfield, Ill: Thomas. 144 pp.
88. Dohrenwend, B. P., Dohrenwend, B. S. 1974. Social and cultural influences on psychopathology. *Ann. Rev. Psychol.* 25:417–52
89. Dohrenwend, B. S. 1973. Social status and stressful life events. *J. Pers. Soc. Psychol.* 28:225–35
90. Dohrenwend, B. S., Dohrenwend, B. P., eds. 1974. *Stressful Life Events: Their Nature and Effects.* New York: Wiley, 340 pp.
91. Dooley, D. 1975. Assessing nonprofessional mental health workers with the GAIT: An evaluation of peer ratings. *Am. J. Community Psychol.* 3:99–110
91a. Dooley, D. 1975. Selecting non-professional counselor trainees with the Group Assessment of Interpersonal Traits (GAIT). *Am. J. Community Psychol.* 3:371–83
92. Dooley, D., Catalano, R. 1976. Money and mental disorders: Toward behavioral cost accounting for primary prevention. *Am. J. Community Psychol.* In press
93. Dorken, H. 1975. Private professional sector innovation in higher education: The California school of professional psychology. *J. Community Psychol.* 3:15–21
94. Dorr, D., Cowen, E. L., Kraus, R. 1973. Mental health professionals view nonprofessional mental health workers. *Am. J. Community Psychol.* 1:258–65
95. Dorr, D., Cowen, E. L., Sandler, I., Pratt, D. M. 1973. Dimensionality of a test battery for nonprofessional mental health workers. *J. Consult. Clin. Psychol.* 41:181–85
96. Doyle, M., Brown, A. A. 1975. Community transaction analysis as a community-oriented research tool. *J. Community Psychol.* 3:358–64
97. Driscoll, J. M., Meyer, R. G., Schanie, C. F. 1973. Training police in family crisis intervention. *J. Appl. Behav. Sci.* 9:62–82
98. Dugger, J. G. 1975. *The New Professional: Introduction for the Human Services Mental Health Worker.* Monterey, Calif: Brooks/Cole. 191 pp.
99. Dworkin, A. L., Dworkin, E. P. 1975. A conceptual overview of selected consultation models. *Am. J. Community Psychol.* 3:151–59
100. Dworkin, E. P. 1974. Implementation and evaluation of a clergy inservice training program in personal counseling. *J. Community Psychol.* 2:232–37
101. D'Zurrilla, J. J., Goldfried, M. R. 1971. Problem solving and behavior modification. *J. Abnorm. Psychol.* 78:107–29
102. Ecklein, J. L., Lauffer, A. A. 1972. *Community Organizers and Social Planners.* New York: Wiley. 378 pp.
103. Eisdorfer, C., Batton, L. 1972. The mental health consultant as seen by his consultees. *Community Ment. Health J.* 8:171–77

104. Eisdorfer, C., Lawton, M. P., eds. 1973. *The Psychology of Adult Development and Aging.* Washington DC: Am. Psychol. Assoc. 718 pp.

105. Engs, R. C., Kirk, R. H. 1974. The characteristics of volunteers in crisis intervention centers. *Public Health Rep.* 89:459–64

106. Epstein, Y. M. 1973. Work-study programs: Do they work? *Am. J. Community Psychol.* 1:159–72

107. Escalona, S. K. 1974. Intervention programs for children at psychiatric risk: The contribution of child psychiatry and development theory. In *The Child in His Family: Children at Psychiatric Risk,* ed. E. J. Anthony, C. Koupernik, 3:33–46. New York: Wiley. 547 pp.

108. Etzioni, A., Remp, R. 1973. *Technological Shortcuts to Social Change.* New York: Sage. 235 pp.

109. Evans, D. A. 1973. Problems and challenges for the mental health professional consulting to a community action organization. *Community Ment. Health J.* 9:46–52

110. Fairweather, G. W. 1972. *Social Change: The Challenge to Survival.* Morristown, NJ: General Learning. 43 pp.

111. Fairweather, G. W., Sanders, D. H., Tornatzky, L. G. 1974. *Creating Change in Mental Health Organizations.* New York: Pergamon. 219 pp.

112. Fairweather, G. W., Tornatzky, L. 1976. *Experimental Methods for Social Policy Research.* Elmsford, NY: Pergamon. In press

113. Farquhar, J. W. 1975. *Interdisciplinary approaches to heart disease prevention: Results of a community-based risk reduction campaign using mass media.* Presented at Am. Assoc. Adv. Sci. Meet., New York

114. Feldman, R. A., Wodarski, J. J. 1974. Bureaucratic constraints and methodological adaptations in community-based research. *Am. J. Community Psychol.* 2:211–24

115. Felton, G. S., Wallach, H. F., Gallo, C. L. 1974. New roles for new professional mental health workers: Training the patient advocate, the integrator, and the therapist. *Community Ment. Health J.* 10:52–65

116. Fowler, D. E., McGee, R. K. 1973. Assessing the performance of telephone crisis workers: The development of technical effectiveness scale. See Ref. 43, pp. 287–97

117. France, K. 1975. Evaluation of lay volunteer crisis telephone workers. *Am. J. Community Psychol.* 3:197–220

118. Freedman, M. B. 1976. The premise and problems of an independent graduate school. *Am. Psychol.* 31:182–88

119. Freudenberger, H. J. 1974. Crisis intervention, individual and group counseling, and the psychology of the counseling staff in a free clinic. *J. Soc. Issues* 30:77–86

120. Fry, L. J. 1973. Participant observation and program evaluation. *J. Health Soc. Behav.* 14:274–78

121. Galassi, J. P., Kostka, M. P., Galassi, M. D. 1975. Assertive training: A one year follow-up. *J. Couns. Psychol.* 22:451–52

122. Gartner, A., Riessman, F. 1974. The paraprofessional movement in perspective. *Personnel Guid. J.* 53:253–56

123. Gartner, A., Riessman, F. 1974. *The Service Society and the Consumer Vanguard.* New York: Harper & Row. 266 pp.

124. Gedicks, A. 1973. Guerrilla research: Reversing the machinery. *J. Appl. Behav. Sci.* 9:645–63

125. Geller, E. S., Farris, J. C., Post, D. S. 1973. Prompting a consumer behavior for pollution control. *J. Appl. Behav. Anal.* 6:367–76

126. Getz, W. L., Fujita, B. N., Allen, D. 1975. The use of paraprofessionals in crisis intervention: Evaluation of an innovative program. *Am. J. Community Psychol.* 3:135–44

127. Glidewell, J. C. 1972. A social psychology of mental health. See Ref. 132, pp. 211–46

128. Glidewell, J. C. 1976. A theory of induced social change. *Am. J. Community Psychol.* In press

129. Glidewell, J. C., Gildea, M. C. L., Kaufman, M. K. 1973. The preventive and therapeutic effects of two school mental health programs. *Am. J. Community Psychol.* 1:295–329

130. Golann, S. E., Baker, J., eds. 1975. *Current and Future Trends in Community Psychology.* New York: Human Sciences. 235 pp.

131. Golann, S. E., Baker, J., Frydman, A. 1973. Demands and coping in the undergraduate therapeutic-companion experience. *Am. J. Community Psychol.* 1:228–37

132. Golann, S. E., Eisdorfer, C., eds. 1972. *Handbook of Community Mental Health.* New York: Appleton-Century-Crofts. 982 pp.

133. Golann, S. E., Pomerantz, J. M., Baker, J. 1974. *The Bethlehem Diaries.* San Francisco: Canfield. 229 pp.
134. Goldberg, C., Kane, J. 1974. Services-in-kind: A form of compensation for mental health services. *Hosp. Community Psychiatry* 25:161–64
135. Goldenberg, I. I., ed. 1973. *The Helping Professions in the World of Action.* Lexington, Mass: Heath. 273 pp.
136. Golding, S. L., Seidman, E. 1974. Analysis of multitrait-multimethod matrices: A two-step principle components procedure. *Multivar. Behav. Res.* 9:479–96
137. Goldstein, A. P. 1973. *Structured Learning Therapy: Toward A Psychotherapy for the Poor.* New York: Academic. 421 pp.
138. Goodman, G. 1972. *Companionship Therapy: Studies in Structured Intimacy.* San Francisco: Jossey-Bass. 298 pp.
139. Goodwin, L. 1973. Bridging the gap between social research and public policy: Welfare, a case in point. *J. Appl. Behav. Sci.* 9:85–114
140. Gottlieb, B. H. 1974. Re-examining the preventive potential of mental health consultation. *Can. Ment. Health* 22:4–6
141. Gottschalk, L. A., Fox, R. A., Bates, D. E. 1973. A study of prediction and outcome in a mental health crisis clinic. *Am. J. Psychiatry* 130:1107–11
142. Gottschalk, S. S. 1973. The community-based welfare system: An alternative to public welfare. *J. Appl. Behav. Sci.* 9:233–42
143. Graham, J. R., Friedman, I., Lilly, R. S., Thiesen, J. W., Hinko, E. N. 1975. The home environment perception scales. *J. Community Psychol.* 3:40–49
144. Greaves, G., Ghent, L. 1972. Comparison of accomplished suicides with persons contacting a crisis intervention clinic. *Psychol. Rep.* 31:290
145. Hall, G. H., Mathiasen, G., eds. 1973. *Guide to Development of Protective Services for Older People.* Springfield, Ill: Thomas. 141 pp.
146. Harper, R., Balch, P. 1975. Some economic arguments in favor of primary prevention. *Prof. Psychol.* 6:17–25
147. Harshbarger, D., Maley, R. F., eds. 1974. *Behavior Analysis and Systems Analysis: An integrative Approach to Mental Health Programs.* Kalamazoo, Mich: Behaviordelia. 403 pp.
148. Hartung, J. G., Kershaw, R. W., Anderson, J. B., Reeve, W. A., Reeve, S. 1972. Consulting in rural community

organization. *Proc. Ann. Meet. Am. Psychol. Assoc., 80th,* 7:803–4
149. Heber, R., Garber, H., Harrington, S., Hoffman, C., Falender, C. 1972. *Rehabilitation of Families at Risk for Mental Retardation.* Madison: Univ. Wisconsin
150. Heilbroner, R. L. 1975. *Inquiry into the Human Prospect.* New York: Norton. 180 pp.
151. Heinemann, S. H., Perlmutter, F., Yudin, L. W. 1974. The community mental health center and community awareness. *Community Ment. Health J.* 10: 221–27
152. Heller, K., Monahan, J. 1976. Methodologies of special relevance to the community. In *Community Psychology: Perspectives in Social Intervention.* Homewood, Ill: Dorsey. In press
153. Herbert, G. K., Chevalier, M. C., Meyers, C. L. 1974. Factors contributing to the successful use of indigenous mental health workers. *Hosp. Community Psychiatry* 25:308-10
154. Hersch, C. 1972. Social history, mental health, and community control. *Am. Psychol.* 27:749–54
155. Higgins, T. 1975. Juvenile delinquency: Seeking effective prevention. *Public Affairs Rep.* 16:1–7
156. Holahan, C. J. 1974. *Human ecology: A new role for the university counseling center.* Presented at Ann. Meet. Am. Psychol. Assoc., 82nd, New Orleans
157. Holahan, C. J. 1976. Environmental effects on outdoor social behavior in a low-income urban neighborhood: A naturalistic investigation. *J. Appl. Soc. Psychol.* In press
158. Holahan, C. J., Saegert, S. 1973. Behavioral and attitudinal effects of large scale variation in the physical environment of psychiatric wards. *J. Abnorm. Psychol.* 82:454–62
159. Holahan, C. J., Wilcox, B. L. 1976. Ecological strategies in community psychology: A case study. *Am. J. Community Psychol.* In press
160. Hollister, R. M., Kramer, B. M., Bellin, S. S., eds. 1974. *Neighborhood Health Centers.* Lexington, Mass.: Heath. 349 pp.
161. Holroyd, J. 1972. Squeezing community psychologists into the scientist-professional model. *Prof. Psychol.* 3:138–42
162. Howe, H. F. 1974. An empirical description of a community-clinical training program. *Prof. Psychol.* 5:277–85

163. Insel, P. M., Moos, R. H., eds. 1974. *Health and the Social Environment.* Lexington, Mass: Heath. 460 pp.
164. Insel, P. M., Moos, R. H. 1974. Psychological environments: Expanding the scope of human ecology. *Am. Psychol.* 29:179–88
165. Iscoe, I. 1974. Community psychology and the competent community. *Am. Psychol.* 29:607–13
166. Iscoe, I., Spielberger, C. D., eds. 1970. *Community Psychology: Perspectives in Training and Research.* New York: Appleton-Century-Crofts. 285 pp.
167. Iscoe, I., Spielberger, C. D., Bloom, B., eds. 1976. *Community Psychology in the 70's.* Washington DC: Hemisphere. In press
168. Ittelson, W. H., ed. 1973. *Environment and Cognition.* New York: Seminar. 187 pp.
169. Jason, L., Clarfield, S., Cowen, E. L. 1973. Preventive intervention with young disadvantaged children. *Am. J. Community Psychol.* 1:50–61
170. Jones, R. L., ed. 1972. *Black Psychology.* New York: Harper & Row. 432 pp.
171. Kanfer, F. H., Goldstein, A. P. 1975. *Helping People Change.* New York: Pergamon. 536 pp.
172. Kanter, R. M. 1972. *Commitment and Community: Communes and Utopias in Sociological Perspective.* Cambridge, Mass: Harvard Univ. Press. 302 pp.
173. Kaplan, B., ed. 1971. *Psychiatric Disorder and the Urban Environment.* New York: Behavioral. 310 pp.
174. Kaplan, B. H., Cassel, J. C., Gore, S. 1973. *Social support and health.* Presented at Am. Public Health Assoc. Meet., San Francisco
175. Karlsruher, A. E. 1974. The nonprofessional as a psychotherapeutic agent: A review of the empirical evidence pertaining to his effectiveness. *Am. J. Community Psychol.* 2:61–77
176. Karno, M., Morales, A. 1971. A community mental health service for Mexican-Americans in metropolis. In *Chicanos: Social and Psychological Perspectives,* ed. N. N. Wagner, M. J. Haug, pp. 281–85. St. Louis: Mosby. 303 pp.
177. Katkin, D., Bullington, B., Levine, M. 1974. Above and beyond the best interests of the child: An inquiry into the relationship between social science and social action. *Law & Soc. Rev.: J. Law. Soc. Assoc.* pp. 669–87
178. Keating, G. W., Brown, W. A., Standley, K. 1973. The volunteer rescue

squad: The impact of a group on the psychological adaptation of its members. *Am. J. Psychiatry* 130:278–82
179. Keeley, S. M., Shemberg, K. M., Ferger, H. 1973. The training and use of undergraduates as behavior analysts in the consultative process. *Prof. Psychol.* 4:59–63
180. Kelly, J. G. 1971. Qualities for the community psychologists. *Am. Psychol.* 26:897–903
181. Kelly, J. G. 1973. *Careers in community service and public affairs at the B. A. level: The University of Oregon experience.* Presented at Ann. Meet. Am. Psychol. Assoc., 81st, Montreal
182. Kelly, J. G. 1975. Community psychology: Some priorities for the immediate future. *J. Community Psychol.* 3:205–9
183. Kelly, J. G. 1975. *The ecological analogy and community work.* Presented at Int. Soc. Behav. Dev. Meet., Univ. Surrey, Guildford, England
184. Kelly, R. M. 1975. Generalizations from an OEO experiment in Washington, D.C. *J. Soc. Issues* 31:57–86
185. Kessler, M., Albee, G. W. 1975. Primary prevention. *Ann. Rev. Psychol.* 26:557–91
186. Keutzer, C. S., Fosmire, F. R., Diller, R., Smith, M. D. 1971. Laboratory training in a new social system: Evaluation of a consulting relationship with a high school faculty. *J. Appl. Behav. Sci.* 1:493–501
187. Kiev, A. 1974. Prognostic factors in attempted suicide. *Am. J. Psychiatry* 131:987–90
188. King, G. D., Morgan, J. P., Smith, B. 1974. The telephone counseling center as a community mental health assessment tool. *Am. J. Community Psychol.* 2:53–60
189. Klausner, S. Z. 1971. *On Man in His Environment: Social Scientific Foundation for Research and Policy.* San Francisco: Jossey-Bass. 224 pp.
190. Kohlenberg, R., Phillips, T. 1973. Reinforcement and rate of litter depositing. *J. Appl. Behav. Anal.* 6:391–96
191. Koleda, M. S. 1972. Guaranteed lifelong usefulness. *Am. Psychol.* 27:482–85
192. Korchin, S. J. 1976. *Modern Clinical Psychology: Principles of Intervention in the Clinic and Community.* New York: Basic. 672 pp.
193. Korman, M., ed. 1976. *Levels and Patterns of Professional Training in Psy-*

chology. Washington DC: Am. Psychol. Assoc. 163 pp.

194. Kramer, J. A., Rappaport, J., Seidman, E. 1974. *The college student interventionist: Selection, training and outcome research*. Presented at Ann. Meet. Am. Psychol. Assoc., 82nd, New Orleans

195. Kroll, J. 1974. The career ladder and the mental health generalist at the state hospital. *Psychol. Q.* 48:184–92

196. Kutchinsky, B. 1973. The effect of easy availability of pornography on the incidence of sex crimes: The Danish experience. *J. Soc. Issues* 29:163–81

197. Lambert, N. M., Sandoval, J., Corder, R. 1975. Teacher perceptions of school-based consultants. *Prof. Psychol.* 6:204–16

198. Lappe, F. M. 1975. *Diet for a Small Planet*. New York: Ballantine. 301 pp.

199. Larsen, S. W., Selinger, H. V., Lochman, J. E., Chinsky, J. M., Allen, G. J. 1974. *Implementation and evaluation of a multilevel preventive mental health program in a school system*. Presented at Ann. Meet. Am. Psychol. Assoc., 82nd, New Orleans

200. Leighton, D. C., Stone, I. T. 1974. Community development as a therapeutic force: A case study with measurements. In *Sociological Perspectives on Community Mental Health*, ed. P. M. Roman, H. M. Trice, pp. 209–32. Philadelphia: Davis. 253 pp.

201. Lester, D. 1972. The myth of suicide prevention. *Compr. Psychiatry* 13:555–60

202. Lester, D. 1974. Effects of suicide prevention centers on suicide rates in the United States. *Health Serv. Rep.* 89:37–39

203. Levine, M., Brocking, M. 1974. Mental health consultation with senior nursing students. *Am. J. Community Psychol.* 2:229–42

204. Levitan, S. A., Johnston, W. B. 1975. *Indian Giving: Federal Programs for Native Americans*. Baltimore: Johns Hopkins. 82 pp.

205. Levitan, S. A., Johnston, W. B., Taggart, R. 1975. *Minorities in the United States: Problems, Progress, and Prospects*. Washington DC: Public Affairs. 106 pp.

206. Levy, L., Rowitz, L. 1973. *The Ecology of Mental Disorder*. New York: Behavioral. 209 pp.

207. Lieberman, E. J., ed. 1975. *Mental Health: The Public Health Challenge*. Washington DC: Am. Public Health Assoc. 293 pp.

208. Liebman, D. A., Schwartz, J. A. 1973. Police programs in domestic crisis intervention: A review. In *The Urban Policeman in Transition: A Psychological and Sociological Review*, ed. J. R. Snibbe, H. M. Snibbe, pp. 421–72. Springfield, Ill: Thomas. 610 pp.

209. Lorion, R. P. 1974. Patient and therapist variables in the treatment of low-income patients. *Psychol. Bull.* 81:344–54

210. Lorion, R. P., Cowen, E. L., Caldwell, R. A. 1974. Problem types of children referred to a school-based mental health program: Identification and outcome. *J. Consult. Clin. Psychol.* 42:491–96

211. Lyons, G. M., ed. 1975. *Social Research and Public Policies: The Dartmouth/OECD Conference*. Hanover, NH: Univ. Press of New England. 205 pp.

212. Maccoby, N. 1975. *Achieving behavior change via mass media and interpersonal communication*. Presented at Am. Assoc. Adv. Sci. Meet., New York City

213. Mahoney, M. J., Thoreson, C. E. 1974. *Self-Control: Power to the Person*. Monterey, Calif: Brooks-Cole. 368 pp.

214. Mann, P. A. 1973. Student consultants: Evaluation by consultees. *Am. J. Community Psychol.* 1:182–93

215. Mannino, F. V., MacLennan, B. W., Shore, M. F. 1975. *The Practice of Mental Health Consultation*. New York: Gardner. 255 pp.

216. Mannino, F. V., Shore, M. F. 1972. Research in mental health consultation. See Ref. 132, pp. 755–77

217. Mannino, F. V., Shore, M. F. 1975. The effects of consultation: A review of empirical studies. *Am. J. Community Psychol.* 3:1–21

218. Maris, R. W., Connor, H. E. 1973. Do crisis services work? A follow-up of a psychiatric outpatient sample. *J. Health Soc. Behav.* 14:311–22

219. Maris, R. W. 1971. Deviance as therapy: The paradox of the self-destructive female. *J. Health Soc. Behav.* 12:113–24

220. Markush, R. E., Favero, R. V. 1974. Epidemiologic assessment of stressful life events, depressed mood, and psychophysiological symptoms: A preliminary report. See Ref. 90, pp. 171–90

221. McGee, J. P., Pope, B. 1975. Baccalaureate program for mental health workers. *Prof. Psychol.* 6:80–87

222. McGee, R. K. 1974. *Crisis Intervention in the Community*. Baltimore: University Park. 307 pp.

223. Meyers, W. R., Dorwart, R. A., Hutcheson, B. R., Decker, D. 1974. Organizational and attitudinal correlates of citizen board accomplishment in mental health and retardation. *Community Ment. Health J.* 10:192–97

224. Meyers, W. R., Grisell, J., Gollin, A., Papernow, P., Hutcheson, B. R., Serlin, E. 1972. Methods of measuring citizen board accomplishment in mental health retardation. *Community Ment. Health J.* 8:313–20

225. Miller, W. R., Muñoz, R. F. 1976. *How to Control Your Drinking.* Englewood Cliffs, NJ: Prentice-Hall. In press

226. Miran, M., Lehrer, P. M., Koehler, R., Miran, E. 1974. What happens when deviant behavior begins to change? The relevance of a social systems approach for behavioral programs with adolescents. *J. Community Psychol.* 2:370–75

227. Mogulof, M. B. 1974. Advocates for themselves: Citizen participation in federally-supported community organizations. *Community Ment. Health J.* 10: 66–76

228. Monahan, J. 1975. The prediction of violence. In *Violence and Criminal Justice,* ed. D. Chappell, J. Monahan, pp. 15–32. Lexington, Mass: Heath. 176 pp.

229. Monahan, J. 1975. Social policy implications of the inability to predict violence. *J. Soc. Issues* 31:153–64

230. Monahan, J. 1976. Community psychology and public policy: The promise and the pitfalls. In *Psychology and the Legal Process,* ed. B. Sales. New York: Spectrum. In press

231. Monahan, J. 1976. The prevention of violence. In *Community Mental Health and the Criminal Justice System,* ed. J. Monahan, pp. 13–34. Elmsford, NY: Pergamon. 350 pp. In press

232. Moos, R. H. 1973. Changing the social milieus of psychiatric treatment settings. *J. Appl. Behav. Sci.* 9:575–93

232a. Moos, R. H. 1973. Conceptualizations of human environments. *Am. Psychol.* 28:652–65

233. Moos, R. H. 1974. *Evaluating Treatment Environments.* New York: Wiley. 388 pp.

234. Moos, R. H. 1975. *Evaluating Correctional and Community Settings.* New York: Wiley. 377 pp.

235. Moos, R. H. 1976. Evaluating and changing community settings. *Am. J. Community Psychol.* In press

236. Moos, R. H., Insel, P. M., eds. 1974. *Issues in Social Ecology: Human Mi-*

237. Morgan, J. P., King, G. D. 1975. The selection and evaluation of the volunteer paraprofessional telephone counselor: A validity study. *Am. J. Community Psychol.* 3:237–49

238. Motto, J. A. 1971. Evaluation of a suicide prevention center by sampling the population at risk. *Life-Threatening Behav.* 1:18–22

239. Mullin, M. L., Blakeney, R. N., Bell, E. C. 1974. Training paraprofessionals as community mental health counselors through consultation: A case history. *J. Community Psychol.* 2:251–53

240. Muñoz, R. F. 1976. The prevention of problem drinking. See Ref. 225.

241. Muñoz, R. F., Kelly, J. G. 1975. *The Prevention of Mental Disorders.* Homewood, Ill: Learning Systems. 50 pp.

242. Murrell, S. A. 1973. *Community Psychology and Social Systems: A Conceptual Framework and Intervention Guide.* New York: Behavioral. 287 pp.

243. Musante, G., Gallemore, J. L. 1973. Utilization of a staff development group in prison consultation. *Community Ment. Health J.* 9:224–32

244. Myers, J. K., Lindenthal, J. J., Pepper, M. P. 1974. Social class, life events, and psychiatric symptoms: A longitudinal study. See Ref. 90, pp. 191–205

245. Nagler, S., Cook, P. E. 1973. Some ideological considerations underlying a mental health consultation program to the public schools. *Community Ment. Health J.* 9:244–52

246. Nelson, R. H., Burgess, J. H. 1973. An open adaptive systems analysis of community mental health services. *Soc. Psychiatry* 8:192–97

247. Nesselroade, J. R., Reese, H. W., eds. 1973. *Life-Span Developmental Psychology: Methodological Issues.* New York: Academic

248. Newbrough, J. R. 1973. Community psychology: A new holism. *Am. J. Community Psychol.* 1:201–11

249. Newbrough, J. R. 1974. *Needs assessment for preventive programming from a social indicators system.* Presented at Ann. Meet. Am. Psychol. Assoc., 82nd, New Orleans

250. Newman, B. M., Newman, P. R. 1975. *Development Through Life: A Psychosocial Approach.* Homewood, Ill: Dorsey. 399 pp.

251. Newman, B. M., Newman, P. R., eds. 1976. *Development Through Life: A*

Case Study Approach. Homewood, Ill: Dorsey. 335 pp.
252. Nicoletti, J., Flater, L. 1975. A community-oriented program for training and using volunteers. *Community Ment. Health J.* 11:58–63
253. Noonan, J. R., Thibeault, R. 1974. Primary prevention in Appalachian Kentucky: Peer reinforcement of classroom attendance. *J. Community Psychol.* 2:260–64
254. Norman, E. C., Forti, T. J. 1972. A study of the process and the outcome of mental health consultation. *Community Ment. Health J.* 8:261–70
255. Northcutt, N., Selz, N., Shelton, E., Nyer, L., Hickok, D., Humble, M. 1975. *Adult Functional Competency: A Summary.* Austin: Univ. Texas, Adult Performance Level Project
256. Nyman, G. W., Watson, D., Schmidt, D., James, S. E. 1975. Training the secretary in community mental health: A second model for integrating secretaries into the therapeutic team in community mental health. *Community Ment. Health J.* 11:163–69
257. Padilla, A. M., Aranda, P. 1974. *Latino Mental Health: Bibliography and Abstracts.* Washington DC: GPO. 288 pp.
258. Padilla, A. M., Ruiz, R. A. 1973. *Latino Mental Health: A Review of Literature.* Washington DC: GPO. 189 pp.
259. Padilla, A. M., Ruiz, R. A., Alvarez, R. 1975. Community mental health services for the Spanish-speaking-surnamed population. *Am. Psychol.* 30:892–905
260. Page, E. B. 1972. Miracle in Milwaukee: Raising the I.Q. *Educ. Res.* 1:8–16
261. Paschall, N. C. 1974. *Citizen participation in mental health: A review of the literature.* Report to NIMH, Contract No. ADM-42-74-85(MH)
262. Patterson, G. R. 1971. *Families: Applications of Social Learning to Family Life.* Champaign, Ill: Research Press. 143 pp.
263. Patterson, G. R. 1974. Interventions for boys with conduct problems: Multiple settings, treatments, and criteria. *J. Consult. Clin. Psychol.* 42:471–81
264. Paull, H. 1972. RX for loneliness: A plan for establishing a social network of individualized caring through care-ring. *Crisis Intervention* 4:63–83
265. Pearl, A. 1972. *The Atrocity of Education.* New York: Dutton. 365 pp.
266. Pearl, A. 1973. *Landslide: The How and Why of Nixon's Victory.* Secaucus, NJ: Citadel. 240 pp.

267. Pearl, A. 1974. Paraprofessionals and social change. *Personnel Guid. J.* 53:264–68
268. Pearl, A. 1974. The psychological consultant as change agent. *Prof. Psychol.* 5:292–98
269. Perlman, R. 1975. *Consumers and Social Services.* New York: Wiley. 126 pp.
270. Perloff, R., Perloff, E., Sussna, E. 1976. Program evaluation. *Ann. Rev. Psychol.* 27:569–94
271. Pfister, G. 1975. Outcomes of laboratory training for police officers. *J. Soc. Issues* 31:115–21
272. Pierce, W. D. 1972. The comprehensive community mental health program and the black community. See Ref. 170, pp. 398–405
273. Poser, E. G. 1970. Toward a theory of "behavioral prophylaxis." *J. Behav. Ther. Exp. Psychiatry* 1:39–43
274. Powers, R. B., Osborne, J. G., Anderson, E. G. 1973. Positive reinforcement of litter removal in the natural environment. *J. Appl. Behav. Anal.* 6:579–86
275. Pressman, J. 1975. *Federal Programs and City Politics: The Dynamics of the Aid Process in Oakland.* Berkeley: Univ. California. 162 pp.
276. Pressman, J. L., Wildavsky, A. 1973. *Implementation.* Berkeley: Univ. California. 182 pp.
277. Preston, J. D. 1974. The meaning of "community" in community psychiatry. See Ref. 294, pp. 51–67
278. Price, R. H., Blashfield, R. K. 1975. Explorations in the taxonomy of behavior settings: Analysis of dimensions and classification of settings. *Am. J. Community Psychol.* 3:335–51
279. Project on Classification of Exceptional Children 1974. *The Futures of Children: Categories, Labels, and Their Consequences.* Nashville: Vanderbilt Univ. 309 pp.
280. Proshansky, H. M. 1972. Methodology in environmental psychology: Problems and issues. *Hum. Factors* 14:451–60
280a. Proshansky, H. M. 1973. The environmental crisis in human dignity. *J. Soc. Issues* 29:1–20
281. Pugh, R. W. 1972. Psychological aspects of the black revolution. See Ref. 170, pp. 344–55
282. Queens College, Flushing, NY New Human Services Institute 1975. *College Programs for Paraprofessionals.* New York: Human Sciences. 135 pp.
283. Rainwater, L. 1973. Fear and the house as haven in the lower class. In *Urbanman: The Psychology of Urban Survival,*

ed. J. Helmer, N. A. Eddington, pp. 92–106. New York: Free Press. 274 pp.

284. Ramirez, M. III, Castañeda, A. 1974. *Cultural Democracy, Bicognitive Development and Education.* New York: Academic. 189 pp.

285. Rappaport, J. 1977. *Community Psychology: Values, Research, and Action.* New York: Holt, Rinehart & Winston. In press

286. Rappaport, J., Davidson, W. S., Wilson, M. N., Mitchell, A. 1975. Alternatives to blaming the victim or the environment: Our places to stand have not moved the earth. *Am. Psychol.* 30: 525–28

287. Rappaport, J., Gross, T., Lepper, C. 1973. Modeling, sensitivity training, and instruction: Implications for the training of college student volunteers and for outcome research. *J. Consult. Clin. Psychol.* 40:99–107

288. Regester, D. C. 1974. Community mental health—For whose community? *Am. J. Public Health* 64:886–93

289. Renner, K. E. 1974. Some issues surrounding the academic sheltering of community psychology. *Am. J. Community Psychol.* 2:95–105

290. Riecken, H. W., Boruch, R. F., eds. 1974. *Social Experimentation: A Method for Planning and Evaluating Social Intervention.* New York: Academic. 339 pp.

291. Roen, S. R. 1971. Evaluative research and community mental health. In *Handbook of Psychotheraphy and Behavior Change,* ed. A. E. Bergin, S. L. Garfield, pp. 776–811. New York: Wiley. 957 pp.

292. Roff, M., Robins, L. N., Pollack, M., eds. 1972. *Life History Research in Psychopathology.* Minneapolis: Univ. Minnesota Press. 291 pp.

293. Rog, D. J., Raush, H. L. 1975. The psychiatric halfway house: How is it measuring up? *Community Ment. Health J.* 11:155–62

294. Roman, P. M., Trice, H. M., eds. 1974. *Sociological Perspectives on Community Mental Health.* Philadelphia: Davis. 253 pp..

295. Roman, P. M., Trice, H. M. 1974. Strategies of preventive psychiatry and social reality: The case of alcoholism. See Ref. 294, pp. 95–111

296. Rosen, G. 1976. *Don't Be Afraid: A Self-Help Program for Overcoming Your Fears and Phobias.* Englewood Cliffs, NJ: Prentice-Hall. In press

297. Rosenblum, G. 1973. Advanced training in community psychology: The role of training in community systems. *Community Ment. Health J.* 9:63–67

298. Ross, H. L. 1973. Law, science, and accidents: The British road safety act of 1967. *J. Legal Stud.* 2:1–75

299. Rossi, J. J., Filstead, W. J. 1973. *The Therapeutic Community: A Source Book of Readings.* New York: Behavioral. 344 pp.

299a. Rossi, P. H., Williams, W., eds. 1972. *Evaluating Social Programs: Theory, Practice, and Politics.* New York: Seminar. 326 pp.

300. Roszak, T. 1972. *Where the Wasteland Ends: Politics and Transcendence in Post-Industrial Society.* New York: Anchor. 451 pp.

301. Roszak, T. 1975. *The Unfinished Animal.* New York: Harper & Row. 271 pp.

302. Rothbart, M. 1975. Achieving racial equality: An analysis of resistance to social reform. In *Toward the Elimination of Racism,* ed. P. Katz. New York: Pergamon

303. Rothman, J. 1974. *Planning and Organizing for Social Change: Action Principles from Social Science Research.* New York: Columbia Univ. 628 pp.

304. Rothman, J., Erlich, J. L., Teresa, J. G. 1976. *Promoting Innovation and Change in Organizations and Communities: A Planning Manual.* New York: Wiley. 309 pp.

305. Sakowitz, M. L., Hirschman, R. 1975. Self-ideal congruency and therapeutic skill development in nonpaid paraprofessionals. *J. Community Psychol.* 3:275–80

306. Sarason, I. G. 1973. The evolution of community psychology. *Am. J. Community Psychol.* 1:91–97

307. Sarason, S. B. 1972. *The Creation of Settings and the Future Societies.* San Francisco: Jossey-Bass. 295 pp.

308. Sarason, S. B. 1974. *The Psychological Sense of Community: Prospects for a Community Psychology.* San Francisco: Jossey-Bass. 290 pp.

309. Sarason, S. B. 1976. Community psychology and the anarchist insight. *Am. J. Community Psychol.* In press

310. Sarata, B. P. V., Reppucci, N. D. 1975. The problem is outside: Staff and client behavior as a function of external events. *Community Ment. Health J.* 11:91–100

311. Sauber, S. R. 1974. Primary prevention

and the marital enrichment group. *J. Fam. Couns.* 2:39–44

312. Schensul, S. L. 1974. Commentary: Skills needed in action anthropology: Lessons from El Centro de la Causa. *Hum. Organ.* 33:203–9

313. Schnelle, J. F., McNees, P., Huff, T. M., Marshall, R. S., Hannah, J. T. 1975. Behavior intervention teams: The utilization of paraprofessionals in a community mental health center. *J. Community Psychol.* 3:258–65

314. Schnelle, J. F., Weathers, M. T., Hannah, J. T., McNees, M. P. 1975. Community social evaluation: A multiple baseline analysis of the effect of a legalized liquor law in four middle Tennessee counties. *J. Community Psychol.* 3:224–31

315. Schofield, W. 1964. *Psychotherapy: The Purchase of Friendship.* Englewood Cliffs, NJ: Prenctice-Hall. 186 pp.

316. Schulberg, H. C. 1972. Challenge of human service programs for psychologists. *Am. Psychol.* 27:566–73

317. Schumacher, E. F. 1973. *Small is Beautiful: Economics As If People Mattered.* New York: Harper & Row. 305 pp.

318. Seidman, E., Rappaport, J. 1974. The educational pyramid: A paradigm for training, research, and manpower utilization in community psychology. *Am. J. Community Psychol.* 2:119–30

319. Severin, N. K., Becker, R. E. 1974. Nurses as psychiatric consultants in a general hospital emergency room. *Community Ment. Health J.* 10:261–67

320. Shulman, A. D., James, S. A. 1973. Undergraduate community psychology work-study programs: Effects on self-actualization and vocational plans. *Am. J. Community Psychol.* 1:173–81

321. Shure, M. B., Spivack, G. 1972. Means-ends thinking, adjustment, and social class among elementary-school-aged children. *J. Consult. Clin. Psychol.* 38:348–53

322. Simon, R., Silverstein, S., Shriver, B. M., eds. 1975. *Explorations in Mental Health Training: Project Summaries.* Washington DC: Natl. Inst. Ment. Health. 244 pp.

323. Simon, W. B. 1972. Some issues in the logic of prevention. *Soc. Sci. Med.* 6:95–107

324. Slaikeu, K. A., Tulkin, S. R., Speer, D.C. 1975. Process and outcome in the evaluation of telephone counseling referrals. *J. Consult. Clin. Psychol.* 43:700–7

325. Slem, C. M., Cotler, S. 1973. Crisis phone services: Evaluation of a hotline program. *Am. J. Community Psychol.* 1:219–27

326. Smith, W. G. 1975. Evaluation of the clinical services of a regional mental health center. *Community Ment. Health J.* 11:47–57

327. Speck, R. V., Attneave, C. L. 1973. *Family Networks.* New York: Pantheon. 160 pp.

328. Specter, G. A., Claiborn, W. L., eds. 1973. *Crisis Intervention.* New York: Behavioral. 210 pp.

329. Spivack, G., Shure, M. B. 1974. *Social Adjustment of Young Children.* San Francisco: Jossey-Bass. 212 pp.

330. Starr, P. 1974. The edge of social science. *Harvard Educ. Rev.* 44:393–415

331. Struening, E. L., Guttentag, M., eds. 1975. *Handbook of Evaluation Research,* Vols. 1, 2. Beverly Hills: Sage. 696 pp., 736 pp.

332. Sue, D. W., Kirk, B. A. 1975. Asian-Americans: Use of counseling and psychiatric services on a college campus. *J. Couns. Psychol.* 22:84–86

333. Sue, S. 1973. Training of "third world" students to function as counselors. *J. Couns. Psychol.* 20:73–78

334. Sue, S., McKinney, H. 1975. Asian Americans in the community mental health care system. *Am. J. Orthopsychiatry* 45:111–18

335. Sue, S., McKinney, H., Allen, D., Hall, J. 1974. Delivery of community mental health services to black and white clients. *J. Consult. Clin. Psychol.* 42:794–801

336. Sue, S., Wagner, N. N. 1973. *Asian-Americans: Psychological Perspectives.* Ben Lomond, Calif: Science & Behavior. 298 pp.

337. Suinn, R. M. 1974. Traits for selection of paraprofessionals for behavior-modification consultation training. *Community Ment. Health J.* 10:441–49

338. Tapp, J. T., Spanier, D. 1973. Personal characteristics of volunteer phone counselors. *J. Consult. Clin. Psychol.* 41:245–50

339. Teahan, J. E. 1975. Role playing and group experience to facilitate attitude and value changes among black and white police officers. *J. Soc. Issues* 31:35–45

340. Thomas, C. W. 1974. The significance of the E(thnocentrism) factor in mental health. *J. Non-White Concerns in Personnel Guid.* 2:60–69

341. Thomas, L. E., Yates, R. I. 1974. Paraprofessionals in minority programs. *Personnel Guid. J.* 53:285–88

342. Throne, J. M. 1975. The replicability fetish and the Milwaukee project. *Ment. Retard.* 13:14–17

343. Tippett, J., Owens, R., Frome, F. 1974. Indirect services and referral system for community mental health centers: Implementation and methods of measurement. *Community Ment. Health J.* 10:450–65

344. Toch, H., Grant, J. D., Galvin, R. T. 1975. *Agents of Change: A Study in Police Reform.* New York: Wiley. 437 pp.

345. Todd, D. M. 1975. *Support and coping: Concepts, research, and applications for community psychology.* Presented at Am. Psychol. Assoc. Ann. Meet., 83rd, Chicago

346. Tornatzky, L. G. 1976. How a Ph.D. program aimed at survival issues survived. *Am. Psychol.* 31:189–92

347. Torrey, E. F. 1972. *The Mind Game: Witchdoctors and Psychiatrists.* New York: Bantam Books. 270 pp.

348. Turk, H. 1973. Comparative urban structure from an interorganizational perspective. *Admin. Sci. Q.* 18:37–55

349. U.S. Department of Justice, LEAA, National Institute of Law Enforcement and Criminal Justice 1975. *New Research Directions in Environmental Design.* 4 pp.

350. U.S. Office of Management and Budget. Statistical Policy Division 1973. Introduction. In *Social Indicators,* pp. xiii–xiv. Washington DC: GPO. 258 pp.

351. University of California, Berkeley 1975. *Announcement: The Experimental Program in Health and Medical Sciences.* Berkeley: Univ. California. 6 pp.

352. Vallance, T. R. 1972. Processes, problems, and prospects for innovating within the university: Lessons from 45 experiences. *J. Higher Educ.* 43:720–36

353. Vallance, T. R. 1975. Uses and abuses of metaphors in community psychology: Or community psychology is dead. *J. Community Psychol.* 3:405–9

354. Vallance, T. R. 1976. The professional non-psychology graduate program for psychologists. *Am. Psychol.* 31:193–99

355. Vaughan, W. T., Huntington, D. S., Samuels, T. E., Bilmes, M., Shapiro, M. I. 1975. Family mental health maintenance: A new approach to primary prevention. *Hosp. Community Psychiatry* 26:503–9

356. Wagenfeld, M. O. 1972. The primary prevention of mental illness: A sociological perspective. *J. Health Soc. Behav.* 13:195–203

357. Walfish, S., Tapp, J. T., Tulkin, S. R., Slaikeu, K. A., Russell, M. 1975. The prediction of "shows" and "no-shows" to a crisis center: A replication. *Am. J. Community Psychol.* 3:367–70

358. Wallace School of Community Service and Public Affairs 1975. *Undergraduate education for professional careers: An Oregon story.* Presented at the Ann. Meet. Am. Psychol. Assoc., 83rd, Chicago

359. Walsh, J. A. 1975. Volunteers in mental health: A program model. *J. Community Psychol.* 3:380–83

360. Warheit, G. J., Holzer, C. E., Arey, S. A. 1975. Race and mental illness: An epidemiological update. *J. Health Soc. Behav.* 16:243–56

361. Wasserman, C. W., Messersmith, C. E., Ferree, E. H. 1975. Professional therapists, paraprofessional helpers, and graduate students: An uneasy alliance. *Prof. Psychol.* 6:337–43

362. Watkins, T. R. 1975. The comprehensive community mental health center as a field placement for graduate social work students. *Community Ment. Health J.* 11:27–32

363. Watson, D. L., Tharp, R. G. 1972. *Self-Directed Behavior: Self-Modification for Personal Adjustment.* Monterey, Calif: Brooks-Cole. 264 pp.

364. Weinman, B., Kleiner, R., Yu, J. H., Tillson, V. A. 1974. Social treatment of the chronic psychotic patient in the community. *J. Community Psychol.* 2:358–65

365. Weinstein, M., Frankel, M. 1974. Ecological and psychological approaches to community psychology. *Am. J. Community Psychol.* 2:43–52

366. White Bird Socio-Medical Aid Station 1974. The counselor training program at White Bird Socio-Medical Aid Station, Inc. *J. Soc. Issues* 30:105–11

367. Whitney, W. M. 1974. *An evaluation of a community-based delinquency prevention program on the basis of group and individual employment.* PhD thesis. Michigan State Univ., East Lansing, Mich. 140 pp.

368. Whitten, N. E., Wolfe, A. W. 1969. Network analysis. In *The Handbook of Social and Cultural Anthropology,* ed. J. Honigmann, pp. 717–46. Chicago: Rand McNally

369. Wilkinson, L., Reppucci, N. D. 1973. Perceptions of social climate among participants in token economy and non-

token economy cottages in a juvenile correctional institution. *Am J. Community Psychol.* 1:36–43

370. Williams, R. M. 1972. Conflict and social order: A research strategy for complex propositions. *J. Soc. Issues* 28: 11–26

371. Willie, C. V., Kramer, B. M., Brown, B. S., eds. 1973. *Racism and Mental Health: Essays.* Univ. Pittsburgh Press. 604 pp.

372. Windle, C., Bass, R. D., Taube, C. A. 1974. PR aside: Initial results from NIMH's service program evaluation studies. *Am. J. Community Psychol.* 2: 311–27

373. Winett, R. 1974. Behavior modification and social change. *Prof. Psychol.* 5:244–50

374. Winett, R., Neitzel, M. 1975. Behavioral ecology: Contingency management of consumer energy use. *Am. J. Community Psychol.* 3:123–33

375. Wohlwill, J. R., Heft, H. 1976. Environments fit for the developing child. In *Ecological Factors in Human Development,* ed. H. McGurk. Amsterdam: North-Holland. In press

376. Wold, C. I., Litman, R. E. 1973. Suicide after contact with a suicide prevention center. *Arch. Gen. Psychiatry* 28:735–39

377. Wolfgang S. Price Associates 1975. *Manual on Governance and Policy Planning for CMHC Board Members.* Silver Springs, Md: Price Associates. 234 pp.

378. Wolkon, G. H., Moriwaki, S. 1973. The ombudsman programme: A primary prevention of psychological disorders. *Int. J. Soc. Psychol.* 19:220–25

379. Woody, R. H. 1975. Process and behavioral consultation. *Am. J. Community Psychol.* 3:277–86

380. Young, C. E., True, J. E., Packard, M. E. 1974. A national survey of associate degree mental health programs. *Community Ment. Health J.* 10:466–74

381. Young, C. E., True, J. E., Packard, M. E. 1976. A national study of associate degree mental health and human services workers. *J. Community Psychol.* 4:89–95

382. Zacker, J., Bard, M. 1973. Effects of conflict management training on police performance. *J. Appl. Psychol.* 58:202–8

383. Zahourek, R., Morrison, K. 1974. Help with problem patients: Mental health nurses as consultants to staff nurses. *Am. J. Nurs.* 74:2034–36

384. Zax, M., Specter, G. A. 1974. *An Introduction to Community Psychology.* New York: Wiley. 496 pp.

385. Zimmerman, T. F. 1974. Is professionalization the answer to improving health care? *Am. J. Occup. Ther.* 28:465–68

Ann. Rev. Psychol. 1977. 28:363–92

TWENTY YEARS OF EXPERIMENTAL GAMING: CRITIQUE, SYNTHESIS, AND SUGGESTIONS FOR THE FUTURE[1]

❖277

Dean G. Pruitt and Melvin J. Kimmel[2]

Department of Psychology, State University of New York, Buffalo, New York 14226

The purpose of this chapter is not to summarize past research on experimental gaming but to examine and diagnose this 20-year tradition. Gaming research has a peculiar status. On the one hand, it has been immensely popular, with over 1000 published studies (36, 105, 138). But on the other hand, the results of these studies have been largely ignored by the broader field. Our diagnosis of this situation stresses an undesirable method bound approach, lacking in theory and with little concern for external validity. Our prescription involves theory building, and we offer a possible synthesis in the domain of the prisoner's dilemma game. This takes the form of a "goal/expectation theory," which will be described and the evidence for which will be presented in the latter half of this paper. We find the patient in uncertain health but with strengths that can be exploited if there is a change in life style.

WHAT ARE EXPERIMENTAL GAMES?

An experimental game can be described as a laboratory task used to study how people behave in an interdependent situation, where (*a*) each individual must make one or more decisions that affect his own and the other's welfare; (*b*) the outcomes of these decisions are expressed in numerical form; and (*c*) the numbers that express these outcomes are chosen beforehand by the experimenter. Most of the research

[1]Preparation of this manuscript was supported by NSF Grants BNS7610963 and SOC-74–08917 and by National Institutes of Health Fellowship IF 22 MH 02624–02.

[2]The authors would like to thank Thomas Bonoma, Scott Britton, Pamela Engram, Harold Kelley, S. S. Komorita, Steven Lewis, John Magenau, Robert Rice, Jeffrey Rubin, W. E. Vinacke, and James Wall for their constructive comments on an earlier draft of this chapter.

has focused on so-called "mixed-motive" games, in which the interests of the parties partially coincide and partially conflict.

Four main classes of experimental games can be distinguished:

Matrix Games

Here the subjects are given an abstract reward structure in the form of a matrix. The 2 X 2 matrix shown in Figure 1 is an example of the well-known prisoner's dilemma game (PDG), the most widely used of this class. Each party must choose one of two options, with Party I controlling the rows and Party II the columns. The outcomes of a joint decision are given by the intersection between the row and column chosen. The first number in each cell refers to the outcome for Party I, the second to the outcome for Party II. Most studies employ a series of trials with subjects responding either simultaneously or sequentially. Although the 2 X 2 version is the most common, multiparty and multioption matrices have also been used. Many summaries of research on matrix games have appeared (2, 4, 6, 17, 21, 30c, 40, 79, 82, 84, 98, 102, 105, 124, 131, 138).

Negotiation Games

These games entail a simulation of formal negotiation. A variety of possible agreements is available. The two parties exchange offers until (a) an agreement is reached, (b) one party withdraws from negotiation, or (c) an experimenter-imposed deadline is reached. At this point, numerical outcomes are awarded. An example would be a task in which the subjects play the roles of buyer and seller in a hypothetical used car market (64). They exchange notes until they have agreed on a price for a particular vehicle. The seller's outcome is the difference between this price and the $2500 he has allegedly paid for the car. The buyer's outcome is the difference between this price and the $3500 for which he can purportedly sell the car. Many variations are found. For example, subjects sometimes can talk freely to one another rather than exchanging notes. Also, they may or may not have information about one another's potential outcomes. Several articles have been published summarizing the experimental research on negotiation (16, 17, 25, 26, 37, 49, 93, 105).

Coalition Games

Most of this research has employed a three-party task developed by Vinacke & Arkoff (132). Each subject moves his counter around a 67-space Parchesi board,

Figure 1   Example of a 2 X 2 game matrix—The prisoner's dilemma game.

beginning at "start" and ending at "home." Each counter is assigned a particular weight which when multiplied by a die toss indicates the number of spaces that may be moved. The object is to reach "home" first, with the winner or winners receiving a prize in points or money. The subjects are told that they can work individually or form coalitions to pool their separate weights. If a coalition is formed, its members must decide how to divide the prize should they win. The major interest in this research has centered around which (if any) coalitions are formed as a function of the power structure (as defined by the weights), individual differences, etc. More than three parties can be used in the game. Research on coalition formation has been reviewed in several places (32, 34, 118, 131).

Locomotion Games

Several games have been inspired by the Deutsch & Krauss (22) "trucking game." In this task, each of two subjects plays the role of a truck driver trying to move as fast as possible to his destination. Each has two possible routes, one considerably shorter than the other. Choosing between these routes poses a dilemma, because the shorter includes a stretch of one-lane road over which both parties must pass to reach their destinations. A collaborative approach is available, involving alternating use of the one-lane road. In some versions, one or both subjects control "gates" that can be used to block the progress of the other. Several summaries of research on locomotion games can be found (21, 46, 105).

HISTORY OF EXPERIMENTAL GAMING RESEARCH

The origin of experimental gaming probably can be traced to conceptual developments in two fields of study: social conflict and interpersonal relations. Earlier thinking in each field ignored the impact of incentives on social behavior and hence failed to acknowledge the importance of the way in which parties are interdependent. New concepts and theories were developed to remedy these defects. These led to a need for new research tools, and hence to development of the experimental game.

Two concepts dominated early psychological thinking about conflict: "attitude," as in the early studies of racial and international prejudice (1, 57, 114), and "aggression," which was more or less openly conceptualized as a behavioral manifestation of anger (23). But this theoretical framework was too narrow, ignoring perceived differences of interest which clearly play a major part in generating most conflicts. When labor and management confront each other at the picket line, for example, negative attitudes and aggressive tendencies are often not the major cause, though they may play some part. Usually there is a genuine difference of opinion about the way in which profits should be spent, resulting from basic contradictions in perceived interest.

A shift in psychological thinking became apparent in the late 1940s and early 1950s. Some scholars (18, 111) began to see differences of interest as antecedent to the more virulent forms of conflict and consonance of interest as a road to conflict resolution. Hence attention began to focus on the ways in which conflicting parties are interdependent.

As with the social conflict tradition, the earliest theoretical approaches to inter-personal relations stressed the importance of attitudes, perceptions, and feelings (15, 41). A major departure from this emphasis came in the late 1950s with the development of social exchange theories (43, 128). These stressed the impact on behavior of incentives (rewards and penalties) that are under the control of other people. Hence they also focussed on the nature of interpersonal interdependence.

Thibaut & Kelley's version of exchange theory (128) was very much influenced by the theory of games (66, 134), a branch of economics and mathematics. Game theorists seek to devise formal models of "rational" behavior in situations where people are dependent on one another for their outcomes They assume that people understand the reward structures of these settings (by "reward structure" is meant the way in which the outcome values are associated with the various possible combinations of options), and they try to prescribe rules for making decisions that will achieve maximal value. Game theory has not been the source of many testable hypotheses about human behavior; but it has contributed concepts, notation, and many of the building blocks for constructing experimental games.

Experimental games appear to be an operational outgrowth of the theoretical developments that had taken place in the prior decade. These games facilitate a precise definition of the reward structure encountered by the subjects and hence of the way they are dependent on one another. Of the experimental games described earlier, the matrix game (Figure 1) is most clearly influenced by game theory. This is nothing other than the mathematicians' "game in normal form" translated for use in the laboratory. The earliest negotiation game (112), which has served as a partial model for all of the others, was specifically designed to test an hypothesis drawn directly from game theory. Although the influence of game theory cannot be seen so easily in the early coalition and locomotion games, these games also involve an interest in human reactions to reward structures and hence are clearly associated with the same world view.

There are other reasons for the popularity of these methods besides the ease of specifying interdependence: (a) They yield behavioral, as opposed to questionnaire, measures and hence appeal to the desire for objective observations shared by most experimental psychologists. (b) They permit precise measurement of such elusive variables as "extent of cooperation" and "coalition composition." (c) They are usually easy to employ and economical. (d) Many sources of variance found in more naturalistic settings are absent to experimental games, enhancing the power of tests of significance. (e) Heavy competitive or hostile behavior can be manifested without injury to people or their relationships—one might say that these games permit conflict without tears.

This last reason appears to have been especially important at first. Experimental gaming was developed at a time of heavy East/West tensions. Many of its early users were alarmed about these tensions and hoped to find ways of resolving them through laboratory experimentation. The experimental gaming and peace research movements were closely related at this time, as can be seen in the fact that the *Journal of Conflict Resolution: A Quarterly for the Study of War and Peace* had a special section for articles based on experimental gaming. Hence there was an initial aura of urgency and even sacredness about the research, which probably contributed to its rapid proliferation. This initial enthusiasm has largely dissipated today, and the methods have taken their place alongside others with more mundane beginnings.

CURRENT STATUS AND CRITIQUE

While the crest may have passed in the number of gaming studies published per year, the field is by no means dying. Studies continue to appear regularly in major journals, and there has been an increase in the number of summary articles within the past few years (17). The only real change has been a shift of interest away from matrix games and toward negotiation games.

Though the gaming tradition is clearly alive, its health has begun to be doubted. Questions have been raised about its relevance to real-life settings (2, 78, 79) and to other parts of the field of social psychology (42). It has emerged as something of a social isolate, as evidenced by its position in standard social psychological reference sources. For example, the *Handbook of Social Psychology* devotes only a few scattered pages to gaming results, most of them written by a sociologist interested in international behavior (29). Also, with the exception of an excellent summary by Davis et al (17), chapters on small group research in the *Annual Review of Psychology* send their readers to other sources. The tradition has found its way into some social psychology textbooks; but the writers seem unable to integrate the findings with those from other parts of the field and simply report them in a separate section, as one might add a boxcar to a freight train.

Clearly external validity is one of the biggest problems of this tradition. Why should this be?

The most immediate source of this problem would appear to be twofold: (*a*) most researchers who use games simply report their results with no attempt to speculate about the real-life implications and (*b*) the concepts used to report these results often lack clear external referents, being either too specialized (e.g. "D–D lock in"[3]) or too vague (e.g. "cooperation-competition"). But these are only symptoms. There are at least two more basic difficulties.

One difficulty is that some researchers are not interested in generalizing beyond the laboratory. This philosophy is most clearly articulated by Rapoport (97), who has had a major influence on the field by virtue of his many gaming experiments and his position (until recently) as gaming editor of the *Journal of Conflict Resolution*. His research strategy is exclusively one of developing laws about how subjects handle the PDG in the laboratory. He is unwilling to extrapolate from the laboratory to real life because "the same laws [do not] govern both the events in the laboratory and those of the cosmos" (97, p. 40). Rather, he feels that laboratory results are mainly valuable for the perspectives they suggest and the questions they raise. We find this position hard to accept, believing as do some other authors (21, 54) that there is continuity between between the laboratory and the real world.

---

[3]In the PDG, subjects are said to experience a D–D lock in when they both choose D over a series of trials.

The other basic difficulty lies in confusion about how to generalize. Real-life phenomena can be found that both illustrate and refute almost any laboratory result. For example, Deutsch & Kraus (22) found that bilateral threat capacity reduces the liklihood of coordination in the trucking game. Real-life examples of this effect can be cited, but so can counterexamples. In the face of such contradictions, many researchers prefer to "stand on the facts" generated in their laboratories rather than engage in dubious and perhaps misleading extrapolations. We believe it is preferable for researchers to try to generalize their findings, because an analysis of limitations to plausible generalization can stimulate hypothesis building and the development of new research tasks. But it is necessary to understand the sources of this difficulty.

A relationship between an independent and dependent variable can usually not be generalized to all settings, but only to those that share certain "background conditions" with the setting in which the relationship was established (54). These background conditions are particular levels on moderator variables that interact with the independent variable. Hence to discover the settings to which an experimental result can be generalized, we must know what variables interact with the ones we are manipulating. Yet investigators in this field pay little attention to interactions and hence to the background conditions that govern how the variables interrelate.

Nemeth (78) had the issues of generalizing and background conditions in mind when she speculated that cooperation is seldom reciprocated in the PDG because the parties rarely have the opportunity to communicate and hence lack clarity about motives underlying cooperative behavior. Her comments suggest the need for a factorial design, involving several levels of confederate cooperation and several types of communication about the intentions underlying that cooperation. Six years after her article, this design has not yet been implemented; and we continue to face difficulty generalizing the laboratory results on reciprocity in the PDG. Likewise, in an insightful set of speculations about threats, Kelley (46) suggested a number of conditions under which the Deutsch/Krauss results should and should not be found. But again, years later, these insights have not been subjected to experimental test. As will be seen below, more studies are now being performed involving the systematic exploration of interactions. But lack of attention to background conditions is still a major difficulty.

Another problem is the lack of theory in much of this research.[4] Hypotheses, where they are employed at all, are usually based on hunches rather than systematic derivations; and results are often reported without theoretical interpretation. Hence very little of this research is cumulative. Summary articles ordinarily classify results

[4]There are a few largely isolated exceptions to this general trend: Research on coalition formation (32, 34, 118) has often been guided by theory; Tedeschi and his associates (123) have a theoretically based program on the effect of threats and promises in the PDG; Rubin & Brown (105) take a theoretical stance in several chapters of their recent book on bargaining and negotiation; Kelley (48, 49) has tested two minitheories of concession making in negotiation; and Bonacich (12) has performed theory-based research on the conditions under which norms and norm enforcement will develop in the multiparty PD.

by superficial characteristics of the variables manipulated, rather than categories that have some relationship to one another. Theory would provide a basis for developing hypotheses and summarizing experimental results. It would also help solve the problem of external validity by clarifying just what is being manipulated and measured and by pointing to background conditions that may limit generality.

In its lack of theory, gaming research is in the distinguished company of many other social psychological traditions (116). But we must still ask, Why so little theory? One answer to this question is that the "theoretical advances" that established the need for gaming research were weak in predictive power. Take, for example, exchange theory. In the crucible of the late 1950s, it provided a new set of concepts and helped to forge a new methodology. But, outside the realm of equity phenomena (9, 63), it has not proven very useful for generating new hypotheses. The same is true of modern conflict theory (21, 111), which is strong in the realm of intra- and intergroup processes but weak in the realm of strategic choice. Surprisingly there is not much empirical research in the areas where this theory is the strongest, leading to the strange phenomenon of books that contain separate and largely unrelated chapters on theory and research (21, 96).

Furthermore, we are again faced with the influential Rapoport tradition. Rapoport (97) currently endorses theory but only of a "behavioral" sort, i.e. a summary of empirical observations. He seems to abjure hypothetical constructs of the type used by psychologists. We suspect that he is tying his hands behind his back in taking this stance, because psychological constructs are frequently successful in the prediction of human behavior.

One might think that, in the absence of theory, researchers would engage in a good deal of process analysis so as to generate theoretical leads. But such analyses are seldom found, despite evidence that subjects can often supply plausible explanations for their behavior (55, 71, 91) and that interesting leads can be derived from (a) content analysis of free communications between subjects (12, 94); (b) subject ratings on post-questionnaires (50); and (c) the contingencies exhibited in sequences of responses (10, 100, 108, 121). Instead the input-output model of experimental design is still very much in evidence.

Another problem of this field is that it is rather method bound. Researchers often seem to start with the experimental game and ask questions secondarily about what to study. Variables are frequently chosen for their ease of manipulation or because they are suggested by the experimental setting. A case in point is the sex variable, which has been used in at least 68 PDG studies. Rubin & Brown explain the popularity of this variable as follows: "The answer, we believe, has to do with the relative economy of the sex variable; the fact that it can be easily and efficiently varied; the fact that college populations tend to be coed in composition; the fact that it is therefore easier to complete a bargaining study" (105, p. 169).

We suspect that this method boundedness has its origins in the lack of theory and inadequate concern for external validity discussed earlier. With a more vigorous theoretical tradition, hypotheses would come first and questions about how to test them second. Likewise the naturalistic observations that would result from efforts to bridge the gap between laboratory and real life could serve as an independent source of hypotheses and encourage methodological innovation in the form of efforts to simulate realistic phenomena. Interestingly, the branch of gaming research that is most concerned about real-life applications, the study of negotiation, is also the most innovative methodologically.

PRESCRIPTION FOR THE FIELD

We have described a research tradition that is both loved and hated. Its supporters generate myriads of studies, while its detractors see only people playing games. What is the prescription? We think it is theory building in the context of concern about real-life applications. We are with McGuire (73) in asserting that there should be less emphasis on hypothesis testing and more on creative hypothesis building.

The question in our minds is not whether to develop theory, but how. Can we build on the data already collected or must we start anew? Our inclination is toward the former. We are attracted by the metaphysical assumptions of the gaming paradigm—that behavior should be viewed as a set of decisions aimed at achieving valued outcomes. If these assumptions are valid, then we can view past research as rough "outcroppings" or surface phenomena that can guide us to the underlying veins of theoretical ore.

In order to synthesize existing results, we must first examine some special features of the gaming setting that determine how the variables interrelate. We believe that experimental games usually place people in an *unfamiliar strategic environment* and that the findings reflect the limitations of such a setting. The unfamiliarity of this environment means that well-rehearsed habits of analysis and behavior are not readily available, and subjects must innovate. Hence we may be on soundest ground by building a theory about how individuals devise strategies and how groups develop social norms.[5]

A "strategic environment" is one in which people are trying to be as rational as possible in pursuit of certain ends. They engage in cool calculation and view their opponent in impersonal terms, making attributions only to qualities that directly relate to attaining their goals. In such a setting, conventional social norms, attitudes, sentiments, and most social motives have relatively little impact on behavior because they seem irrelevant to the task at hand. Rather, behavior is likely to be mainly a function of the nature of the surroundings, as interpreted in the context of the salient goals.

We offer the following evidence for the assertion that experimental games typically involve a strategic environment. On the one hand, the most consistent findings result from manipulating situational variables—the opponent's strategy, matrix values, instructional set, etc. While on the other hand, the vast majority of studies that have manipulated personality and attitudinal variables find little or no relationship to game behavior (4, 105, 124). Another indication of a strategic environment is that reciprocity is uncommon in gaming settings (78). Reciprocity is to be ex-

---

[5]Games have been explicitly used for studying the development of strategies by Kelley (47) and the development of norms by Bonacich (12) and Thibaut and his colleagues (126, 127).

pected where people are trying to follow conventional norms but is often absent where they are devising strategies in a search for individual gain.

Further evidence that the standard gaming setting places people in an impersonal, strategic frame of mind is provided by studies which ask subjects for their feelings about the other person following game play. Most investigators find these sentiments to be unrelated to the subject's or to the other party's prior behavior (12, 14a, 28, 30a, 45, 56, 65, 65a, 75, 108, 135a). There are some exceptions to this general trend (5, 30b, 44, 56a, 67, 130a). But in each instance, the interpersonal nature of the situation was highlighted by the experimenter, presumably counteracting the normally impersonal quality of a gaming setting. These exceptions suggest that not all gaming environments produce an equally strategic outlook. If the environment is sufficiently enriched in terms of interpersonal contact, social-motivational forces may have some impact. Evidence for this assertion can be seen in several studies of the PDG where greater intimacy has been found to produce somewhat more cooperative behavior (26a, 28a, 31, 71, 135). However, it appears that the usual gaming setting does not entail a particularly intimate environment (79).

The common finding that perceived similarity and friendship enhance cooperation (1, 7, 60, 72, 74, 77, 83, 103, 109, 119, 120, 130) might be seen as contrary to the assumption of a strategic environment. However, for reasons given below we believe that perceived similarity and friendship affect expectations about how the other party will behave, and hence have a place in efforts to make rational decisions about strategy.

The theory to be presented concerns behavior in situations that involve a prisoner's dilemma reward structure. We distinguish this theoretical concept (which will be called "PD") from the concrete prisoner's dilemma game as used in the laboratory (which we have been calling "PDG"). One reason for making this distinction is that the evidence synthesized by our theory is drawn from research on negotiation games as well as on PDG. In limiting our theory to a single reward structure, we are in sympathy with the views of Rapoport (98)—in contrast to those of Rubin & Brown (105), who try to generalize gaming results to all settings involving interpersonal dependence. We observe this limit because there is evidence that situational variables interact with type of reward structure (82).

WHAT IS THE PRISONER'S DILEMMA AND WHAT DOES IT MODEL?

Before presenting our theory, we shall define the PD and describe the various forms it takes. Examples will be given of each form so that the reader will have some guidance about how to extend the theory to reality. Like many other authors (e.g. 99), we believe that this reward structure is characteristic of a large number of socially significant real-life settings.

The PD is best known in its 2 X 2 matrix version, which is shown schematically in Figure 2. For this to be PD, as opposed to one of 77 other 2 X 2 games distinguished by Rapoport & Guyer (101), it is necessary that $T > R > P > S$. Some authors add the further requirement that $2R > T + S$.

Party II

C   D

Party I

C | R, R | S, T
D | T, S | P, P

Figure 2   Schematic 2 X 2 game matrix.

The letters C and D ordinarily stand for the words "cooperation" and "defection" respectively. After much soul searching, we have decided to retain the label "cooperation," with the explicit understanding that it refers to an individual response rather than joint behavior. When both parties behave cooperatively at the same time, we speak of "mutual cooperation," not "cooperation." However, we have decided not to use the term "defection" because it implies the prior existence of an agreement to cooperate with the other party which clearly does not exist in most studies. The term "competition" is also used at times to refer to the D option. We have rejected this term as well, because it implies that one party is trying to outdo the other, which is often not true. Instead, we have opted for the more neutral term "noncooperation" as a label for the D option.

The reward structure of the PD is such that each party is motivated not to cooperate and yet, paradoxically, both prefer mutual cooperation to mutual noncooperation. In other words, individual rationality leads to collective irrationality. A real-life example would be that of two barbers in the same vicinity trying to decide whether to open their shops on Monday, a traditional day of tonsorial rest in many cities. Each will attract more customers by opening (choosing D) regardless of what the other does. Yet, making the reasonable assumption that most of Monday's customers will be available on Tuesday, both will achieve a net savings (in time and other resources) if both stay closed (CC) than if both open (DD). Likewise, in a controversy between two adjacent nations, it may seem rational for each to mass its troops on the border (D) in an effort to advance or defend its interests. Yet if both do so (DD), both will be worse off than if neither does so (CC) (113).

To describe a game fully, it is necessary to specify several psychologically important dimensions in addition to its reward structure. We must also indicate the number of times it is played (once vs repeatedly), order of plays (e.g. parties move simultaneously vs successively), timing of outcomes (e.g. outcomes occur after every pair of moves vs whenever both parties are satisfied with their moves), mode of display (whether in standard or decomposed form), number of options (two-choice vs expanded version), and number of parties (two-party vs multiparty version). The last three dimensions deserve special attention.

A standard PD and three decompositions based on it are shown in Figure 3. In a decomposition each party receives the same matrix and, like the standard PD, both must choose between alternatives C and D. Unlike the standard PD, however, the decomposed version specifies, for each alternative, a payment to oneself and a

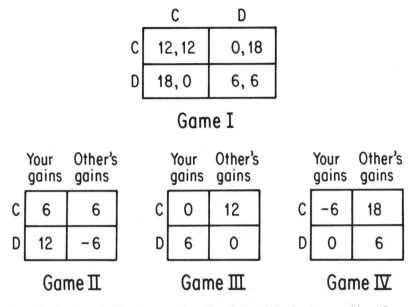

Figure 3   A prisoner's dilemma game (Game 1) and three derivative decompositions (Games II, III, and IV).

payment to the other party. In calculating one's own final outcome, one must consider how much he has given himself *and* how much the other party has given him. Though the reward structure looks quite different, it can be seen that the outcomes in all decompositions of Figure 3 are mathematically identical to those in the standard PD matrix of Game I. This can be demonstrated by calculating the final outcomes in Game III when both parties choose C. Both gain 0 as a result of their own decision and gain 12 as a result of the other's choice. The final outcome is 12 for each, which is identical to the CC outcome in Game I.

Although algebraically the outcomes are the same, behavior toward a decomposition often differs from that toward its parent standard version. In addition, all decompositions of a given game are not handled similarly (89, 91). Decomposition III in Figure 3 models many reality situations where two parties face the choice between generous and stingy behavior. For example, consider two neighbors who must occasionally choose between lending (C) and not lending (D) the other a tool, bottle of milk, etc. Each is tempted not to lend because of the inconvenience to himself. Yet both are better off if both engage in lending.

When there are more than two options, we speak of an expanded prisoner's dilemma. For example, suppose that in each time period two nations must decide whether to add or destroy one missile. The reward structure might well resemble that shown in Figure 4A, with the outcomes representing units of security. This is a PD because every block of 4 cells, whether adjacent or not, forms a traditional 2 X 2 PD matrix. As in the 2 X 2 version, each party is tempted to behave

Number of missiles Party II
has after move

Number of Missiles Party I has after move	0	1	2	3	4
0	6,6	4,7	2,8	0,9	-2,10
1	7,4	5,5	3,6	1,7	-1,8
2	8,2	6,3	4,4	2,5	0,6
3	9,0	7,1	5,2	3,3	1,4
4	10,-2	8,-1	6,0	4,1	2,2

(a.)

Option advocated by Party II

Option advocated by Party I	A_2	B_2	C_2	D_2	E_2
E_1					-7,15
D_1				-2,8	-4,11
C_1			2,2	-1,5	-3,6
B_1		8,-2	5,-1	1,1	-2,3
A_1	15,-7	11,-4	6,-3	3,-2	0,0

(b.)

Figure 4 Expanded prisoner's dilemma game. Game (a) is an armament/disarmament game adapted from Pilisuk & Skolnick (87). Game (b) models a negotiation situation.

noncooperatively (i.e. to add missiles), yet both are better off if they behave cooperatively (i.e. destroy missiles).

The expanded PD shown in Figure 4B is a model of concession making in negotiation.[6] At any point in time, each party must choose between advocating options A, B, C, D, or E. If both advocate the same option (e.g. C_1C_2) the negotiation ends. Otherwise it continues. Option A is preferred by Party I and option E by Party II. Hence, they start bargaining at A_1E_2. The outcomes are ordered such that each party is happier the closer he and/or the other party are to his preferred option. There are no outcomes above the diagonal, because it seldom happens that both parties advocate an option more preferred by the other. We can speak of a "concession dilemma" (92) in this situation, because each party is motivated not to concede, yet both are better off if both concede. For example, suppose that they are deadlocked at A_1E_2. Both would be better off if they could reach agreement at C_1C_2. Yet neither is individually motivated to make the first move toward C.

By no means do all PDs involve only two parties. Indeed, in an unpublished paper, Komorita has argued that the N-party PD is more important for society than the 2-party version. In the former, all parties are better off if all cooperate, but each is tempted by selfish advantage to defect from the coalition of the whole. Examples would include dues paying (80), escape from a burning theater (110), and in earlier days the use of a town's common grazing lands (38).

[6]Sawyer & Guetzkow (106) first proposed the view of concession making as a move in the PD. Other authors (e.g. 113) have argued that it is a move in a game of "chicken," which differs from the PD in that $T > R > S > P$. This perspective accounts for the occasional success of the tactic of positional commitment. In our view, negotiation is ordinarily PD but becomes "chicken" as a deadline (e.g. a strike deadline) approaches or if one party can articulate a credible commitment.

A THEORY OF BEHAVIOR IN THE MULTIPLAY PRISONER'S DILEMMA

Our theory concerns the behavior of two people who are engaged in repeated interaction with one another and are trying to devise strategies for maximizing their own benefits. The theory can be easily extended to the multiparty case but is more simply described for the 2-party case.

How the parties behave at any given point depends on whether they take a short-range or long-range perspective—whether they are only concerned with options and outcomes in the current situation or are trying to achieve some future goals.

In our view, short-range thinking ordinarily leads to noncooperation in the PD. Such behavior seems rational regardless of what the other is about to do. If the other is about to cooperate, the largest profits are made by trying to "exploit" him (choosing D while he chooses C). If he is unlikely to cooperate, it seems important to defend oneself—to fail to cooperate so as to avoid being exploited.

Cooperative behavior usually results from long-range thinking. It is designed to achieve the *goal of establishing and/or maintaining continued mutual cooperation.* Three perceptions contribute to the development of this goal: (*a*) perceived dependence on the other, i.e. a recognition of the importance of the other's cooperation; (*b*) pessimism about the likelihood that the other can be exploited (i.e. that he will cooperate unilaterally for any period of time); and (*c*) insight into the necessity of cooperating with the other in order to achieve his cooperation. The latter two perceptions amount to a recognition that the dyad must choose between mutual cooperation and mutual noncooperation and that the former is preferable to the latter. We are aware that cooperative behavior may also be adopted with the ultimate purpose of exploiting the other when his guard is down (i.e. choosing D at a later stage when he has begun to choose C). But we view this motive as unlikely to persist because it is frequently quite unproductive in the long run.

While usually necessary, the goal of achieving mutual cooperation is insufficient to elicit cooperative behavior. It must be accompanied by an *expectation that the other will cooperate* either immediately or in response to the actor's cooperation. Otherwise the actor would be simply laying himself open to exploitation. If the other does not seem ready to cooperate, short-range defensive considerations ordinarily take precedence over long-range cooperative aims, and the actor also fails to cooperate. The expectation of cooperation is sometimes called "trust" (19, 21). However, this term usually has broader connotations, referring also to aspects of the actor's attitudes and personality traits or his perception of the other's attitudes and personality traits (56, 104). Because we are limiting our theory to behavior in strategic situations, we prefer to be more precise and speak of "expectations."

Logically speaking, either the mutual cooperation goal or the expectation of cooperation can exist in the absence of the other. However, we suspect that in reality the goal often comes first, because it necessarily raises the question of whether the other party can be relied on to cooperate.

We have just articulated a goal/expectation theory of individual cooperation in the PD. This theory is useful, but it is incomplete in that both parties must cooperate at the same time for either to continue cooperating. To be a theory of continued cooperation, it must be reformulated to account for *simultaneous cooperation* by both parties. This is easily done. Simultaneous cooperation is assumed to arise if and when both parties have a goal of mutual cooperation and an expectation that the other is ready to cooperate. Scheff (107), to whom we are most indebted for the goal/expectation formulation, adds the further requirement that each party must perceive that the other expects him to cooperate. We acknowledge that this may contribute to cooperation in some instances, but we do not deem it an essential element.

The goal-expectation theory deals with psychological forces that shape people's behavior when they are trying to be strategic. We recognize that *non*strategic forces such as attitudes, feelings, and norms also influence social behavior, including behavior in settings that have a PD reward structure. However, our theory does not deal with such forces because they have little influence on behavior in strategic environments such as the gaming laboratory.

We limit our theory further to people whose basic aims are "individualistic"— who are trying to maximize their own benefits. We recognize that some subjects in experimental games are being strategic about other aims, such as achieving a competitive advantage or improving the collective welfare (61, 71). But we stress the individualistic for three reasons: (*a*) Subjects are ordinarily instructed to pursue this aim. (*b*) Research evidence suggests that this aim is adopted by most subjects, either overtly or underlying an easily ruptured veneer of concern about the collective welfare (61). (*c*) Situational variables, which are involved in most of the replicable findings in this field, have their greatest impact on people who have this aim (19).

In the next few pages, we shall present a series of laboratory findings that can be interpreted plausibly within the the framework of our goal/expectation theory. Most of these findings entail measures of level of cooperation rather than of goals or expectations. Hence our interpretations are mainly speculative, though we feel that they are based on reasonable assumptions about the antecedents of goals and expectations. These assumptions are also elements of our theory, which in its fullest form is a complex set of hypotheses about the conditions that affect goals and expectations and thus influence behavior in the PD.

Conditions that Primarily Produce the Goal of Mutual Cooperation

Research by Rapoport & Chammah (100) shows that cooperation in the multiplay PDG is a U-shaped function of *time elapsed*. Percent cooperation initially declines. But then, between trials 30 and 60, it begins to ascend; and many dyads that were initially "locked into" mutual noncooperation (DD) switch to consistent mutual cooperation (CC).

We interpret these results as reflecting a shift from short-range to long-range thinking. At first, most subjects concentrate their attention on the trial at hand. Some choose D in order to try to exploit the other or defend themselves from his anticipated efforts at exploitation. Others choose C out of confusion or because of concern for the collective welfare and then shift to D as a reaction to other's D playing. This leads to a period of mutual noncooperation and poor outcomes that encourage thought about the situation. At this point, the three perceptions described in out theory develop: (a) each party begins to see himself as dependent on the other, (b) exploiting the other (achieving DC) begins to seem hopeless, and (c) the basic choice becomes one between mutual cooperation (CC) and mutual noncooperation (DD). The result is a longer range perspective focusing on the goal of achieving mutual cooperation.

At this point, cooperation will ensue to the extent that each expects the other to cooperate. We assume that the subject who first "breaks the ice" and chooses C does not expect the other to play C on the same trial but to imitate him on future trials. (Such an expectation may result from a perception that the other is similar to oneself and hence likely to have the same goals, confidence is one's capacity to influence other people, etc.). This initial cooperative choice presumably strengthens the other's expectation of cooperation, making him also more likely to venture reciprocal cooperation. The result is mutual cooperation.

A quote from one of Terhune's subjects nicely summarizes most of the postulated processes: "In the beginning I was trying to earn more and soon realized that we were both losing in the process. I then decided upon a small gain rather than a big loss and tried to get the other person to mark C's as I was doing" (125, p. 671).

The research just cited suggests that a *two-stage process* develops naturally in the PD. The initial stage, which involves defensive and/or exploitative motives, is often followed by a stage involving the goal of mutual cooperation. As we see it, the critical element of the first stage that ushers in the second is the *experience of mutual noncooperation*. Evidence favoring this interpretation can be seen in two lines of research.

One is research on the effect of the "reformed sinner" strategy in which a confederate fails to cooperate for awhile and then begins to cooperate. Evidence from several PDG studies (11, 39, 136) shows that the subject is initially noncooperative and then becomes unusually cooperative when the confederate changes his approach. An analogous phenomenon is also seen in research on negotiation, where a strategy of starting with high demands and gradually conceding has been found to elicit more return concessions than a strategy of consistently high or consistently low demands (8). We assume that the initial phase of this kind of strategy produces an experience of mutual noncooperation which leads to insight into the value of mutual cooperation as a result of the three perceptions mentioned earlier. The goal of mutual cooperation then motivates reciprocation of the other's cooperative behavior, because the latter produces an expectation of further cooperation from the other.

Deutsch (21) has found that the reformed sinner effect is less evident when there are stronger incentives favoring exploitative behavior. This fits our interpretation if we assume that such incentives enhance the likelihood of maintaining an exploitative goal and hence reduce the likelihood of adopting the goal of mutual cooperation.

The second line of evidence comes from a study of the behavior of people who have observed PD play (14). Subjects were found to be more cooperative when they had observed two other people engage in a noncooperative exchange than when the people being watched had been mutually cooperative or one had succeeded in exploiting the other. This result and those on the reformed sinner suggest that any experience with mutual noncooperation, whether direct or vicarious, can produce the goal of mutual cooperation.

We are postulating that a process of insight underlies development of the goal of mutual cooperation. This suggests that people who have experience with the PD should develop such a goal more readily if they have *time to think* or are otherwise stimulated into examining their experiences. Such an hypothesis is supported by the finding that cooperation increases after a 2 minute break in PDG play (85), after within-team discussions where the parties are groups rather than individual (85), and when the subject gets a chance to try out a sequence of moves before making a binding decision (86).

The strength of the mutual cooperation goal is also apparently affected by *mode of display.* Several lines of evidence (30, 89) indicate that people are unusually cooperative in decompositions where each party's best outcomes result from the other's cooperation, e.g. in Games III and IV as opposed to Game II in Figure 3. Subjects who cooperate in the games explain their behavior in terms of the mutual cooperation goal (91). Perhaps this kind of display emphasizes one's dependence on the other party's willingness to cooperate and thus facilitates development of the mutual cooperation goal.

Other evidence (91, 129) suggests that, in decompositions inducing cooperative behavior, people are especially quick to reciprocate the other's cooperation and especially slow to react defensively to his noncooperation. Conceivably this is the characteristic mode of response when one is seized with the goal of achieving mutual cooperation. Unfortunately, few authors have reported the kind of trial-by-trial data needed to detect this pattern.

It is also reasonable to assume that the strength of the goal of achieving mutual cooperation will be a function of the *incentives* attached to this and other outcomes. This goal should be a positive function of the profits associated with mutual cooperation and, in line with our theory, an inverse function of those associated with exploitation and mutual noncooperation. Assuming that amount of cooperation is a good measure of the strength of the mutual cooperation goal, all of these predictions have been supported (12, 33, 100, 115).

Research shows that cooperation is less likely to the extent that it benefits one party more than the other (70, 122) and to the extent that the two parties start with unequal assets (3). These findings suggest the importance of *equity* considerations. We postulate that the goal of mutual cooperation is less attractive to the extent that it yields an inequitable outcome or fails to remedy existing inequities.

There is also evidence of especially high cooperation under conditions of *reversibility,* where decision are not final until both parties are satisfied with their outcomes (19). Far from being due to an artifact, as suggested by Rubin & Brown (105), this finding can be easily explained within the framework of our theory. During the course of experimenting with various options, both parties presumably learn that it is impossible to exploit the other for very long because he will always shift to D.

Hence they develop a goal of mutual cooperation. The expectation that the other will cooperate is probably not necessary in this case, because cooperation is totally without risk in that one can withdraw from cooperation without penalty if the other does not follow suit. In other words, reversibility provides a kind of substitute for trust that makes cooperation entirely dependent on development of the mutual cooperation goal—itself a highly probable outcome under reversibility.

Conditions that Encourage an Expectation that the Other Will Cooperate

Expectations about another person's cooperative intentions in the PDG have been measured directly by Kelley & Stahelski (51, 52). Their judges were either the other player or a third party, and the only source of evidence was the behavior of the person being judged. Not surprisingly, consistently cooperative or noncooperative behavior had more effect on expectations than inconsistent behavior. In the inconsistent case, recent behavior seemed to be more heavily weighted than earlier behavior. People with noncooperative intentions tended to be judged accurately. However, those with cooperative intentions were often misjudged when paired with noncooperators, probably because they shifted to noncooperative behavior for defensive reasons and were judged by this later behavior. One interesting implication of this finding is that noncooperators often misinterpret defensive reactions to their own behavior as evidence that the other also has noncooperative intentions (53). The result is the familiar self-fulfilling prophecy, which often underlies persistent mutual noncooperation.

Indirect evidence about the determinants of expectations can be derived from studies that measure amount of cooperation in the PDG. Cooperation is enhanced by certain situational factors which can be interpreted reasonably as producing an expectation of cooperation from the other. Among these are knowledge that the other has cooperated in his past dealings with a third party (14), receipt of a message indicating cooperative intent (19), sending a message indicating that cooperation is expected (19), knowledge that the other's incentives encourage cooperation (13), knowledge that he has been instructed to be cooperative (13), and knowledge that he is dependent on oneself (19).

It might seem reasonable to suppose that perceived characteristics of the other would influence behavior by affecting expectations about his future cooperation. However, results are not consistent on this issue, with some finding a positive relationship between perceived attributes and behavior (5, 69), while others report no such effect (2, 56, 137). As noted earlier, we suggest that character traits are a useful basis for predicting the other's behavior only to the extent that the traits are seen as relevant to accomplishing strategic goals. In general, we would expect dispositional qualities to have little impact in an impersonal setting as represented by most gaming environments.

Conditions Affecting Both Goals and Expectations

The variables cited so far are presumed to exert their major influence either on attainment of a mutual cooperation goal or on expectations about the other's behavior. However, there are some factors that can be interpreted most reasonably as affecting both elements of our theory. Two such factors are strategies employed by one of the parties and communication.

In studies of strategy, the subject (whom we shall call the "actor") believes that he is interacting with another person but is actually dealing with a programmed strategy or confederate (whom we shall call the "strategist"). Of the strategies studied to date, the tit-for-tat strategy and its variations seem to be the most effective for eliciting cooperative behavior from the actor (21, 61, 82). This involves matching the actor's recent behavior— cooperating when he cooperates and failing to cooperate when he fails to cooperate. We hypothesize that this strategy is so effective because it encourages two reactions from the actor: (a) a realization that the strategist will not tolerate being exploited, which should lead to an effort to achieve the next best outcome, mutual cooperation, and (b) an expectation that the strategist will cooperate if the other does so.

For individualistically oriented subjects, the tit-for-tat strategy induces considerably more cooperation than the consistently cooperative (100% C) strategy (21, 61, 82). Indeed the latter is rather ineffective in this regard (21, 61, 98), despite the reasonable assumption that it produces a high expectation of cooperation. Clearly such an expectation is not sufficient to induce high cooperation, despite early theoretical formulations that placed exclusive emphasis on trust (19). The defect in the strategy of consistent cooperation is presumably that it encourages adoption of exploitative motives and hence militates against development of the goal of mutual cooperation.

Similar effects of strategy have been observed in a study of negotiation (58) in which the actor conceded more when the strategist matched his concessions (tit-for-tat) than when the strategist conceded on every trial. The latter strategy was, in turn, more effective than never making a concession. Chertkoff & Esser (16) argue that the matching strategy was effective in this study because it induced a perception of the strategist as both "strong" and "fair." This interpretation is similar to our own. A perception that the other is strong presumably leads one to abandon the goal of exploiting him, and a perception that the other is fair is tantamount to an expectation that he will cooperate. The fact that research on concession making yields similar results to that on the PD strengthens our conviction that the former phenomenon entails a PD reward structure.

A common finding (19, 133, 135) is that verbal communication enhances the likelihood of cooperation in the PDG. Unfortunately, the black-box nature of most of this research makes it hard to know the reasons for this effect. We can guess that it permits the parties to share insights about the dynamics of the PD, to assure one another of any intentions to cooperate and to warn one another to expect noncooperation in return for noncooperation (19). These are likely to affect both goals and expectations. Another important function of communication is to help the parties coordinate the development of their goals and expectations, so that both begin cooperating simultaneously. As mentioned earlier, simultaneous cooperation is the key to continued cooperation.

Interactions Between the Determinants of Goal and Expectation

The most distinctive prediction from our theory is an interaction between the determinants of goal and expectation, such that cooperation will be unusually high when both are present. This is illustrated in Figure 5, where we predict low cooperation in cells B, C, and D and high cooperation in cell A. A number of studies involving the PDG and the negotiation game report data that seem to fit this prediction.

Some PDG findings suggest the existence of an interaction between time elapsed and determinants of the expectation that the other will cooperate, such that expectations have a larger effect as time goes on. This fits our theory if we can assume, as postulated earlier, that the goal of achieving mutual cooperation strengthens over time. One such finding (95) is an increasing correlation between cooperation and measured expectation of cooperation from the other. In addition, there is evidence that communications about what one intends to do and what one expects from the other have a greater impact in later stages of game playing (133). Such communications can be reasonably presumed to strengthen expectations of cooperation in the minds of the receiver and sender respectively.

Interactions with time have also been found in some studies that manipulated similarity of (2, 130), and friendship with (72, 120), the other party. In these studies, the manipulated variable had no initial effect on game play but was positively related to level of cooperation at later stages. These results have sometimes been interpreted as reflecting the impact of positive feelings on cooperation. But this seems unreasonable since it would logically predict an *immediate* effect of these variables. We suspect that experience with mutual noncooperation during the early trials of these studies led to development of a mutual cooperation goal. Once this goal developed, a subject had to ask whether the other had also developed the goal. If the other was seen as similar to himself, either by virtue of friendship or of information provided by the experimenter, he reasoned that the other must also have developed the same goal. Hence he came to expect cooperation from the other and was willing to risk a cooperative choice.

Expectation of Cooperation from the Other

		Present	Absent
Goal of Achieving Mutual Cooperation	Present	A	B
	Absent	C	D

Figure 5   Schematic version of the experimental design used in studies showing an interaction between the determinants of goal and expectation.

Another interaction involving perceived similarity can be interpreted in a comparable fashion. McNeel & Reid (74) found an especially high level of cooperation when the other was seen as similar and his initial response was *non*cooperative. Our interpretation assumes that the initial noncooperative response had the same effect as the first part of the reformed-sinner strategy, discouraging the subject from believing he could exploit the other and thus encouraging him to adopt the mutual cooperation goal. Perceived similarity then led him to suspect that the other had the same goal, producing cooperative behavior. A comparable interpretation can be given to the Swingle & Gillis (120) finding of a reformed-sinner effect only when the other was a friend and hence presumably similar to oneself.

Several PDG and negotiation studies (59, 65, 76, 128a) have shown an interaction between relative threat capacity and the other's degree of cooperation. By far the greatest cooperation was exhibited by subjects who were weak in comparison to the other but experienced cooperative behavior from him. In other words, relative weakness produced a tendency to *reciprocate* the other's cooperative behavior. Our interpretation is that low power encourages a belief that one cannot force the other to cooperate and hence leads to development of a mutual cooperation goal. The other's initial cooperation encourages an expectation of further cooperation, which, in combination with this goal, results in cooperative behavior.

While unequal power may encourage the low-power party to reciprocate the other's cooperation, it is not likely to encourage *bilateral* cooperation, because the party with higher power is unlikely to adopt this goal. Rather, our theory predicts the highest level of bilateral cooperation when both parties perceive that the two of them have equal power, and hence neither thinks he can force the other to cooperate. This prediction is amply supported by the research literature (105, 126).

The predicted interaction can also be seen in the results of a PDG study by Bixenstine & Gaebelein (10). This study compared several tit-for-tat strategies involving various combinations of quick (Q) and slow (S) reciprocation of the other's behavior. A quick cooperative response was defined as one in which the strategist cooperated 100% of the time after the other cooperated. A slow cooperative response was one in which he cooperated 60% of the time after the other's first cooperative response, 80% after the second sequential cooperative response, and 100% only after the other had cooperated three times in a row. Comparable definitions were given to quick and slow noncooperative responses. A 2 X 2 design was employed, with the following cells: QQ, QS, SQ, and SS (the first letter referring to the response to cooperation and the second to the response to noncooperation). An interaction was found such that other was most cooperative when the strategist employed SS. The traditional QQ tit-for-tat strategy was a poor second. In other words, the most effective strategy involved slow retaliation, such that the other was often given a second chance to cooperate before one defended himself, *but also* slow forgiveness, such that the other often had to cooperate several times before one abandoned a previously adopted defensive stance.

We interpret these results as follows: A quick cooperative response may encourage the other's exploitative behavior. Again and again he can take advantage of the strategist and then quickly get back into the latter's good graces. But this is much less possible with a slow cooperative response, which therefore encourages develop-ment of the goal of mutual cooperation. (An analysis provided by Bixenstine & Gaebelein of the frequency of various response sequences supports these points.) In line with Kelley & Stahelski's (51) finding that noncooperators misinterpret inten-tions, we assume that a quick noncooperative response discourages faith in the strategist's cooperation intentions because many people do not perceive him as reacting to their own behavior, but rather as intentionally failing to cooperate. Only when the strategist is slow to retaliate will a substantial number of people *blame themselves* and hence continue to expect the strategist to cooperate if they cooperate. In short, the SS strategy is so effective because it produces both a goal of mutual cooperation and an expectation of cooperation from the other.

Our theory may also help illuminate the results of two studies in which the anticipation of informal future contact with the other party interacted with evidence concerning the other's fairness and likelihood of cooperating (35, 69). In both studies, subjects who believed that they would meet the other at the end of the experimental session were more prone to imitate the other's level of expected cooper-ation than those who did not hold such a belief. We assume that anticipation of future contact leads to a sense of dependence on the other's good will (perception *a* in our theory) and hence to a goal of achieving mutual cooperation in the present. Given this goal, our theory predicts behavior that matches the other's expected level of cooperation.

The results of a recent study of integrative bargaining (68) can also be interpreted in terms of perceived dependence on the other party. An interaction was found such that subjects were especially likely to exhibit cooperative behavior (i.e. reveal infor-mation about their preferences) when they had high aspirations and knew that the other had been instructed to cooperate. We assume that the high aspirations en-hanced perceived dependence on the other because his cooperation was viewed as necessary for goal achievement. This, in turn, encouraged development of the goal of mutual cooperation. Knowledge that the other had been instructed to cooperate produced the necessary expectation, and the result was cooperative behavior.

In many of the studies just reported (2, 10, 35, 59, 65, 68, 69, 72, 74, 130, 133), cooperation was *lowest* in the cell labeled "B" in Figure 5. This is the condition where the goal of mutual cooperation was presumably strongest and the other was seen as actually or potentially *non*cooperative. This result is not predicted by our theory but does not contradict it. One possible explanation is that the other's noncooperation is particularly frustrating when one has a goal of mutual cooper-ation. Hence one is especially punitive if the other fails to cooperate.

Not all studies have found the interaction postulated in our theory. For example, our theory predicts more reciprocation of the other's cooperation behavior under decompositions like III and IV in Figure 3. But a study of this matter (91) found only nonsignificant trends in the predicted direction. While not supporting the theory, these results certainly do not contradict it. In another study (90), the tendency to reciprocate the other's cooperative behavior was not affected by the other's future capacity to provide reward, as might be expected from the theory. Perhaps the problem here was that each subject made only a single decision sandwiched between two confederate decisions. Hence the concept of mutual cooperation in the future, and therefore the goal of achieving this state, may have had little meaning.

Summary of the Factors Affecting Goal and Expectation

As mentioned earlier, the interpretations of research findings which we have outlined above are an integral part of our theory. These interpretations can be summarized as follows: The goal of achieving mutual cooperation is more likely to the extent that: (a) one has had experience with the situation over time, especially if this experience has involved mutual noncooperation; (b) one has had time to think or has otherwise been stimulated into examining his experience; (c) the PD is decomposed such that one must look to the other for his best outcomes; (d) high outcomes are associated with mutual cooperation; (e) low outcomes are associated with exploitation and mutual noncooperation; (f) mutual cooperation yields equitable outcomes; (g) decisions can be reversed so long as either party is dissatisfied with his outcomes; (h) the other party employs a tit-for-tat strategy, especially if it involves slow reciprocation of newly cooperative behavior; (i) the parties communicate with one another; (j) one sees oneself as weaker than the other party; (k) one anticipates continued interaction with the other; and (l) one's aspirations are so high that the other's cooperation is apparently needed to achieve them. The expectation of future cooperation from the other is stronger to the extent that (a) the other has recently cooperated with oneself or another party; (b) the other has consistently cooperated; (c) one has sent a message requesting cooperation or received one assuring cooperation; (d) one knows that the other's incentives or instructions favor cooperation; (e) the other is seen as dependent on oneself; (f) the other employs a tit-for-tat strategy involving slow retaliation when one fails to cooperate; and, assuming that one has adopted a goal of mutual cooperation, (g) the other is seen as similar to oneself or as a friend. There is considerable evidence of an interaction between variables that affect goals and expectations, such that maximal cooperation is found when both goal and expectation are present. One manifestation of this interaction is a tendency for people who have adopted the mutual cooperation goal to reciprocate the other party's cooperation.

IMPLICATIONS OF THE GOAL/EXPECTATION THEORY

The value of a theory can be gauged by whether it contributes new research problems and hypotheses, suggests new experimental methods, and helps to see real-life implications of research results. We believe that our theory has potential value in all three directions.

Among the researchable questions suggested are: (a) How much independent impact does each of the three perceptions that precede establishment of a mutual cooperation goal (i.e. that one is dependent on the other, that prolonged exploitation is hopeless, and that one must cooperate if he is to expect the other to do likewise) have on goal formation? (b) Is Scheff (107) right in asserting that cooperation is encouraged when the other is seen as believing that one is about to cooperate? (c) What sort of person is most likely to be the first to break the ice and cooperate at the bottom of the U-shaped curve? Possible new hypotheses include: (d) People who have watched third parties engage in mutual cooperation will reciprocate the other's cooperation more readily than those who have not. (e) Development of a goal of mutual cooperation leads to efforts to ascertain the other's willingness to cooperate. (f) People who have such a goal are more likely to employ a QS or an SS strategy than those who do not.

One of our major hopes is that the goal/expectation theory will stimulate development of new research techniques and thus help overcome this field's excessive reliance on a few methods. For example, our theory suggests that measures of goals and expectations should be routinely introduced into gaming studies. Also, hypothesis e above suggests the need to develop methods for studying how people gather information about one another's willingness to cooperate. Moreover, by pointing out that experimental games encourage subjects to adopt a narrow strategic perspective, we hope to stimulate the development of new mixed-motive tasks which foster nonstrategic approaches. For example, we suspect that attitudes, personality traits, and attributions about the other party's characteristics would have an impact on behavior if the feedback about outcomes were non-numerical. In short, the study of behavior in mixed-motive settings should not be limited to gaming methodology.

A particularly interesting feature of our theory is the perspective it can provide on real-life phenomena. We present now some parallels between certain realistic events and certain laboratory results, as interpreted by our theory. We hope that these examples will encourage further efforts to extend gaming results beyond the laboratory by providing some possible "shared exemplars," as the term is used by Kuhn (62).

Deutsch (20) has argued that gaming research can contribute to Man's understanding of international relations. This seems reasonable from our perspective in that both settings involve a strategic environment and hence share crucial background conditions. A possible case in point would be the convergence between the U-shaped curve that relates time to percent cooperation in the PDG (100) and the time course of friendship between the United States and the Soviet Union since World War II. Interestingly, the most dramatic upturn in East-West relations came in 1963 on the heels of the most frightening postwar incident, the Cuban Missile Crisis. Our theory can account for this element of timing, in that we trace the development of a goal of mutual cooperation to a discouraging experience with mutual noncooperation. The Cuban Missile Crisis may well have produced such an experience and hence encouraged this goal to develop on both sides.

In a move-by-move analysis of the upturn of 1963, Etzioni (29a) has noted that the United States first made a series of unilateral tension-reducing moves, which were then reciprocated by the Soviet Union. At first blush, this description would seem to contradict many gaming findings, inasmuch as persistent unilateral cooperation is so often exploited rather than reciprocated in laboratory environments (78, 82). But our theory predicts just such reciprocation if we assume that the Soviets had adopted a goal of mutual cooperation at this time. The American initiatives would, in that case, have fostered the belief that the United States was also ready for mutual cooperation and thus encouraged return cooperation.

Osgood (81) has suggested that, in order to elicit cooperation from an adversary, a nation should adopt a strategy of making a series of tension reducing moves similar to that described by Etzioni (29a). An effort to verify this hypothesis in the laboratory (87) met with limited success. However, this study was probably not a good test of the hypothesis in that the subjects had not experienced a *period of mutual noncooperation* prior to the introduction of the strategy (17), a background condition that was specified by Osgood and seems important from the perspective of our theory. Probably the closest anyone has come in the laboratory to successfully testing Osgood's hypothesis is the group of studies indicating that the reformed sinner strategy of noncooperation followed by persistent cooperation induces reciprocation during the cooperative phase (21, 61, 82).

The U-shaped curve can be thought of as reflecting a two-stage process: the first stage involving competitive jousting, and the second involving collaboration in an effort to achieve mutual cooperation. Similar stages have been observed in successful labor-management (24, 117) and international bargaining (113). Pruitt (92) has postulated a PD analysis of such bargaining sequences, which is related to elements of our theory. In the first stage, both bargainers try to persuade the other to concede while they themselves hold firm. At first such efforts may look promising or seem successful; but after awhile one and eventually both parties come to recognize the existence of a deadlock. Continued competitive behavior now seems costly and futile, and a goal develops of collaborating with the other party to achieve a settlement. If the other is seen as having a similar goal, concessions are made in anticipation of reciprocity. If not, such concessions are likely to be viewed as risking "image loss," in the sense of encouraging the other to continue his efforts to gain a competitive advantage. "Indirect communication" is often employed at this point in an effort to test the other's perceptions or communicate one's own viewpoint.

PROGNOSIS FOR THE FIELD

Our goal/expectation theory is not a finished product. It is undoubtedly overgeneralized and faulty in some respects and will require future modification, if not outright rejection. However, we agree with Bacon that, "Truth emerges more easily from error than from confusion" (62), and feel strongly that some sort of theory is needed at this stage—even if it only succeeds in stimulating efforts to build a better one.

Even if our theory proves useful, it cannot hope to account for all phenomena found in gaming research and certainly not for all behavior in mixed-motive settings, since much of this behavior is nonstrategic in origin. Some authors (2, 79, 88) have commented adversely on the limited scope of both theory and research in this tradition. We agree that broader horizons are needed, but are with Elms (27) in noting that global theories have not proven very heuristic in social psychology. We are advocates of theoretical pluralism and urge the development of coordinate theories to account for the impact of phenomena such as attitudes and personality traits which are not salient in strategic environments but are nevertheless important in many mixed-motive settings.

At several points in this chapter, we have advocated efforts to extrapolate from gaming findings to real-life settings. We suspect that important implications have been missed because such efforts have usually not been made and believe that such efforts will stimulate hypothesis formation. However, at the same time, one must be aware of the dangers of overgeneralizing as a result of ignoring critical background conditions that differ between the laboratory and the target setting. For instance, the strategic nature of the gaming environment is characteristic of only certain settings and frames of mind in the outside world. The process of abstraction from reality that takes place when one designs any laboratory task is sure to produce other background conditions that limit the generality of laboratory findings.

While it may be possible to identify critical background conditions theoretically, the ultimate proof or any extrapolation must be empirical. Hence we recommend that generality studies be performed to assess how far each research finding can be pushed in explaining other social behavior. If we have done our theoretical homework, we should be able to predict both convergences and divergences—successful and unsuccessful extensions of any finding. Such generality studies should take us well beyond the gaming laboratory into field studies, simulations, and statistical analyses of historical data.

What we have been suggesting in this chapter is that gaming research must break out of the narrow method-bound course it has pursued to date. More time should be put into theory building—as illustrated by our goal/expectation theory—and less into seat-of-the-pants empiricism. Furthermore, the barriers that gaming researchers have set up between themselves and the rest of social science should come down. Such barriers may have the virtue of permitting development of a critical mass of studies upon which theory can be erected. But at this point, they seem to be more harmful than helpful.

Literature Cited

1. Allport, G. W. 1954. *The Nature of Prejudice.* Cambridge, Mass: Addison-Wesley. 537 pp.
2. Apfelbaum, E. 1974. On conflicts and bargaining. *Adv. Exp. Soc. Psychol.* 7:103–56
3. Aranoff, D., Tedeschi, J. T. 1968. Original stakes and behavior in the prisoner's dilemma game. *Psychon. Sci.* 12:79–80
4. Baxter, G. W. Jr. 1972. Personality and attitudinal characteristics in two-person games. See Ref. 138, 97–103
5. Baxter, G. W. Jr. 1973. Prejudiced liberals? Race and information effects in a two-person game. *J. Confl. Resolut.* 17:131–61
6. Becker, G. M., McClintock, C. G. 1967.

Value: Behavioral decision theory. *Ann. Rev. Psychol.* 18:239–86
7. Benton, A. A. 1971. Productivity, distributive justice, and bargaining among children. *J. Pers. Soc. Psychol.* 18:68–78
8. Benton, A. A., Kelley, H. H., Liebling, B. 1972. Effects of extremity of offers and concession rate on the outcomes of bargaining. *J. Pers. Soc. Psychol.* 24:73–83
9. Berkowitz, L., Walster, E., eds. 1976. *Equity Theory: Toward a General Theory of Social Interaction.* New York: Academic. 263 pp.
10. Bixenstine, V. E., Gaebelein, J. W. 1971. Strategies of "real" opponents in eliciting cooperative choice in a pris-

oner's dilemma game. *J. Confl. Resolut.* 15:157–66

11. Bixenstine, V. E., Wilson, K. V. 1963. Effects of level of cooperative choice by the other player on choices in a prisoner's dilemma game. Part II. *J. Abnorm. Soc. Psychol.* 67:139–47

12. Bonacich, P. 1972. Norms and cohesion as adaptive responses to potential conflict: An experimental study. *Sociometry* 35:357–75

13. Braver, S. L., Barnett, B. 1974. Perception of opponent's motives and cooperation in a mixed-motive game. *J. Confl. Resolut.* 18:686–99

14. Braver, S. L., Barnett, B. 1976. Effects of modeling on cooperation in a prisoner's dilemma game. *J. Pers. Soc. Psychol.* 33:161–69

14a. Brown, R., Smith, R. B., Tedeschi, J. T. 1971. Impressions of a promiser after social deprivation or satiation. *Psychon. Sci.* 23:135–36

15. Cartwright, D., ed. 1951. *Field Theory in Social Sciences: Selected Theoretical Papers by Kurt Lewin.* New York: Harper. 346 pp.

16. Chertkoff, J. M., Esser, J. K. 1976. A review of experiments in explicit bargaining. *J. Exp. Soc. Psychol.* In press

17. Davis, J. H., Laughlin, P. R., Komorita, S. S. 1976. The social psychology of small groups. *Ann. Rev. Psychol.* 27:501–42

18. Deutsch, M. 1949. A theory of cooperation and competition. *Hum. Relat.* 2:129–51

19. Deutsch, M. 1958. Trust and suspicion. *J. Confl. Resolut.* 2:265–79

20. Deutsch, M. 1969. Socially relevant science: Reflections on some studies of conflict. *Am. Psychol.* 24:1076–92

21. Deutsch, M. 1973. *The Resolution of Conflict: Constructive and Destructive Processes.* New Haven: Yale. 420 pp.

22. Deutsch, M., Krauss, R. M. 1960. The effect of threat upon interpersonal bargaining. *J. Abnorm. Soc. Psychol.* 61:181–89

23. Dollard, J., Doob, L. W., Miller, N. E., Mowrer, O. H., Sears, R. 1939. *Frustration and Aggression.* New Haven: Yale. 150 pp.

24. Douglas, A. 1962. *Industrial Peacemaking.* New York: Columbia Univ. 675 pp.

25. Druckman, D. 1973. *Human Factors in International Negotiations: Social-Psychological Aspects of International Conflict.* Beverly Hills: Sage. 95 pp.

26. Druckman, D., ed. 1976. *Negotiations: A Social Psychological Perspective.* New York: Sage-Halsted. In press

26a. Durkin, J. E. 1972. Moment-of-truth encounters in prisoner's dilemma. See Ref. 138, pp. 192–96

27. Elms, A. C. 1975. The crisis of confidence in social psychology. *Am. Psychol.* 30:967–76

28. Enzle, M. E., Hansen, R. D., Lowe, C. A. 1975. Causal attribution in mixed-motive games: Effects of facilitory and inhibitory environmental forces. *J. Pers. Soc. Psychol.* 31:50–54

28a. Enzle, M. E., Hansen, R. D., Lowe, C. A. 1975. Humanizing the mixed-motive paradigm: Methodological innovations from attribution theory. *Simulation and Games* 6:151–65

29. Etzioni, A. 1968. Social-psychological aspects of international relations. In *The Handbook of Social Psychology,* ed. G. Lindzey, E. Aronson, 5:538–601. Reading, Mass: Addison-Wesley. 786 pp. 2nd ed.

29a. Etzioni, A. 1967. The Kennedy experiment. *West. Polit. Q.* 20:361–80

30. Evans, G., Crumbaugh, C. M. 1966. Effects of prisoner's dilemma format on cooperative behavior. *J. Pers. Soc. Psychol.* 3:486–88

30a. Faley, T., Tedeschi, J. T. 1971. Status and reactions to threat. *J. Pers. Soc. Psychol.* 17:192–99

30b. Gallo, P. S. 1969. Personality impression formation in a maximizing difference game. *J. Confl. Resolut.* 13:118–22

30c. Gallo, P. S., Jr., McClintock, C. G. 1965. Cooperative and competitive behavior in mixed-motive games. *J. Confl. Resolut.* 9:68–78

31. Gardin, H., Kaplan, K. J., Firestone, I. J., Cowan, G. A. 1973. Proxemic effects on cooperation, attitudes, and approach-avoidance in a prisoner's dilemma game. *J. Pers. Soc. Psychol.* 27:13–18

32. Gamson, W. A. 1964. Experimental studies of coalition formation. *Adv. Exp. Soc. Psychol.* 1:82–110

33. Goehring, D. J., Kahan, J. P. 1976. The uniform n-person prisoner's dilemma game: Construction and test of an index of cooperation. *J. Confl. Resolut.* 20:111–28

34. Groennings, S., Kelley, E. W., Leiserson, M., eds. 1970. *The Study of Coalition Behaviors.* New York: Holt, Rinehart & Winston. 489 pp.

35. Gruder, C. L. 1971. Relationships with opponent and partner in mixed-motive

bargaining. *J. Confl. Resolut.* 15: 403–16
36. Guyer, M., Perkel, B. 1972. Experimental games: A bibliography 1945–1971. *Commun. No. 293.* Ann Arbor, Mich.: Ment. Health Res. Inst.
37. Hamner, W. C. 1977. The influence of structural, individual and strategic differences on bargaining outcomes: A review. In *Bargaining Behavior and Personality,* ed. D. L. Harnett, L. L. Cummings. Bloomington: Univ. Indiana Press. In press
38. Hardin, G. 1968. The tragedy of the commons. *Science* 162:1243–48
39. Harford, T., Solomon, L. 1967. "Reformed sinner" and "lapsed saint" strategies in the prisoner's dilemma game. *J. Confl. Resolut.* 11:104–9
40. Harris, R. J. 1971. Experimental games as a tool for personality research. In *Advances in Psychological Assessment,* ed. P. McReynolds, 2:236–59. Palo Alto: Science & Behavior Books. 327 pp.
41. Heider, F. 1958. *The Psychology of Interpersonal Relations.* New York: Wiley. 322 pp.
42. Helmreich, R., Bakeman, R., Scherwitz, L. 1973. The study of small groups. *Ann. Rev. Psychol.* 24:337–54
43. Homans, G. C. 1961. *Social Behavior: Its Elementary Forms.* New York: Harcourt, Brace, World. 404 pp.
44. Jones, S. C., Panitch, D. 1971. The self-fulfilling prophecy and interpersonal attraction. *J. Exp. Soc. Psychol.* 7:356–66
45. Kahn, A., Hottes, J., Davis, W. L. 1971. Cooperation and optimal responding in the PDG: Effects of sex and physical attractiveness. *J. Pers. Soc. Psychol.* 17:267–79
46. Kelley, H. H. 1965. Experimental studies of threats in interpersonal negotiations. *J. Confl. Resolut.* 9:79–105
47. Kelley, H. H. 1966. A classroom study of the dilemmas in interpersonal negotiations. In *Strategic Interaction and Conflict,* ed. K. Archibald, pp. 49–73. Berkeley: Univ. California. 227 pp.
48. Kelley, H. H., Beckman, L. L., Fischer, C. S. 1967. Negotiating the division of a reward under incomplete information. *J. Exp. Soc. Psychol.* 3:361–98
49. Kelley, H. H., Schenitzki, D. P. 1972. Bargaining. In *Experimental Social Psychology,* ed. C. G. McClintock, pp. 298–337. New York: Holt, Rinehart & Winston. 585 pp.
50. Kelley, H. H., Shure, G. H., Deutsch, M., Faucheux, C., Lanzetta, J. T., Moscovici, S., Nuttin, J. M. Jr., Rabbie, J.

M., Thibaut, J. W. 1970. A comparative experimental study of negotiation behavior. *J. Pers. Soc. Psychol.* 16:411–38
51. Kelley, H. H., Stahelski, A. J. 1970. Errors in perception of intentions in a mixed-motive game. *J. Exp. Soc. Psychol.* 6:379–400
52. Kelley, H. H., Stahelski, A. J. 1970. The inference of intentions from moves in the prisoner's dilemma game. *J. Exp. Soc. Psychol.* 6:401–19
53. Kelley, H. H., Stahelski, A. J. 1970. Social interaction basis of cooperators' and competitors' beliefs about others. *J. Pers. Soc. Psychol.* 16:66–91
54. Kelman, H. C. 1968. *A Time to Speak: On Human Values and Social Research.* San Francisco: Jossey-Bass. 349 pp.
55. Kimmel, M. J. 1974. *On distinguishing interpersonal trust from cooperative responding in the prisoner's dilemma game.* PhD thesis. Wayne State Univ., Detroit. 128 pp.
56. Kimmel, M. J. 1975. *Distinguishing Trusting Orientation From Game Behavior in the Prisoner's Dilemma.* Presented at Ann. Meet. Am. Psychol. Assoc., 83rd, Chicago
56a. Kleinke, C. L., Pohlen, P. D. 1971. Affective and emotional response as a function of other person's gaze and cooperativeness in a two-person game. *J. Pers. Soc. Psychol.* 17:308–13
57. Klineberg, O. 1950. *Tensions Affecting International Understanding.* New York: Soc. Sci. Res. Counc. 227 pp.
58. Komorita, S. S., Esser, J. K. 1975. Frequency of reciprocated concessions in bargaining. *J. Pers. Soc. Psychol.* 32:699–705
59. Komorita, S. S., Sheposh, J. P., Braver, S. L. 1968. Power, the use of power, and cooperative choice in a two-person game. *J. Pers. Soc. Psychol.* 8:134–42
60. Krauss, R. M. 1966. Structural and attitudinal factors in interpersonal bargaining. *J. Exp. Soc. Psychol.* 2:42–55
61. Kuhlman, D. M., Marshello, A. F. J. 1975. Individual differences in game motivation as moderators of preprogrammed strategy effects in prisoner's dilemma. *J. Pers. Soc. Psychol.* 32: 922–31
62. Kuhn, T. S. 1970. *The Structure of Scientific Revolutions.* Univ. Chicago Press. 210 pp. 2nd ed.
63. Leventhal, G. S. 1976. *Fairness in Social Relationships.* Morristown, NJ: Gen. Learn. Press
64. Liebert, R. M., Smith, W. P., Keiffer, M., Hill, J. H. 1968. The efforts of infor-

mation and magnitude of initial offer on interpersonal negotiation. *J. Exp. Soc. Psychol.* 4:431–41
65. Lindskold, S., Bennett, R. 1973. Attributing trust and conciliatory intent from coercive power capability. *J. Pers. Soc. Psychol.* 28:180–86
65a. Lindskold, S., Bonoma, T., Tedeschi, J. T. 1969. Relative costs and reactions to threats. *Psychon. Sci.* 15:205–7
66. Luce, R. D., Raiffa, H. 1957. *Games and Decisions.* New York: Wiley. 509 pp.
67. Mack, D., Knight, G. P. 1974. Identification of other players' characteristics in the reiterated prisoner's dilemma. *Psychol. Rec.* 24:93–100
68. Magenau, J., Pruitt, D. G., Konar, E., Kimmel, M. J. 1976. *The Impact of Trust on Information Exchange in Bargaining.* Presented at Ann. Meet. East. Psychol. Assoc., New York
69. Marlowe, D., Gergen, K. J., Doob, A. N. 1966. Opponents' personality, expectation of social interaction, and interpersonal bargaining. *J. Pers. Soc. Psychol.* 3:206–13
70. Marwell, G., Schmitt, D. R. 1975. *Cooperation: An Experimental Analysis.* New York: Academic. 209 pp.
71. McClintock, C. G. 1972. Game behavior and social motivation in interpersonal settings. In *Experimental Social Psychology,* ed. C. G. McClintock, pp. 271–97. New York: Holt, Rinehart & Winston. 585 pp.
72. McClintock, C. G., Nuttin, J. M. Jr., McNeel, S. P. 1970. Sociometric choice, visual presence, and game playing behavior. *Behav. Sci.* 15:124–31
73. McGuire, W. J. 1973. The yin and yang of progress in social psychology: Seven koan. *J. Pers. Soc. Psychol.* 26:446–56
74. McNeel, S. P., Reid, E. C. 1975. Attitude similarity, social goals, and cooperation. *J. Confl. Resolut.* 19:665–81
75. Michelini, R. L. 1971. Effects of prior interaction, contact, strategy and expectation of meeting on game behavior and sentiment. *J. Confl. Resolut.* 15:97–103
76. Michener, H. A., Vaske, J. J., Schleifer, S. L., Plazewski, J. G., Chapman, L. J. 1975. Factors affecting concession rate and threat usage in bilateral conflict. *Sociometry* 38:62–80
77. Morgan, W. R., Sawyer, J. 1967. Bargaining, expectations, and the preference for equality over equity. *J. Pers. Soc. Psychol.* 6:173–80
78. Nemeth, C. 1970. Bargaining and reciprocity. *Psychol. Bull.* 74:297–308

79. Nemeth, C. 1972. A critical analysis of research utilizing the prisoner's dilemma paradigm for the study of bargaining. *Adv. Exp. Soc. Psychol.* 6:203–34
80. Olson, M. 1965. *The Logic of Collective Action.* Cambridge, Mass: Harvard Univ. Press. 176 pp.
81. Osgood, C. E. 1962. *An Alternative to War or Surrender.* Urbana: Univ. Illinois Press. 183 pp.
82. Oskamp, S. 1971. Effects of programmed strategies on cooperation in the prisoner's dilemma and other mixed-motive games. *J. Confl. Resolut.* 15:225–59
83. Oskamp, S., Perlman, D. 1966. Effects of friendship and disliking on cooperation in a mixed-motive game. *J. Confl. Resolut.* 10:221–26
84. Patchen, M. 1970. Models of cooperation and conflict: A critical review. *J. Confl. Resolut.* 14:389–408
85. Pilisuk, M., Kiritz, S., Clampitt, S. 1971. Undoing deadlocks of distrust: Hip Berkeley students and the ROTC. *J. Confl. Resolut.* 15:81–95
86. Pilisuk, M., Potter, P., Rapoport, A., Winter, J. A. 1965. War hawks and peace doves: Alternative resolutions of experimental conflicts. *J. Confl. Resolut.* 9:491–508
87. Pilisuk, M., Skolnick, P. 1968. Inducing trust: A test of the Osgood proposal. *J. Pers. Soc. Psychol.* 8:121–33
88. Plon, M. 1974. On the meaning of the notion of conflict and its study in social psychology. *Eur. J. Psychol.* 4:389–436
89. Pruitt, D. G. 1967. Reward structure and cooperation: The decomposed prisoner's dilemma game. *J. Pers. Soc. Psychol.* 7:21–27
90. Pruitt, D. G. 1968. Reciprocity and credit building in a laboratory dyad. *J. Pers. Soc. Psychol.* 8:143–47
91. Pruitt, D. G. 1970. Motivational processes in the decomposed prisoner's dilemma game. *J. Pers. Soc. Psychol.* 14:227–38
92. Pruitt, D. G. 1971. Indirect communication and the search for agreement in negotiation. *J. Appl. Soc. Psychol.* 1:205–39
93. Pruitt, D. G. 1976. Power and bargaining. In *Social Psychology: An Introduction,* ed. B. Seidenberg, A. Snadowsky, pp. 343–75. New York: Free Press. 561 pp.
94. Pruitt, D. G., Lewis, S. A. 1975. Development of integrative solutions in bilat-

eral negotiation. *J. Pers. Soc. Psychol.* 31:621–33
95. Pylyshyn, Z., Agnew, N., Illingworth, J. 1966. Comparison of individuals and pairs as participants in a mixed-motive game. *J. Confl. Resolut.* 10:211–20
96. Rapoport, A. 1964. *Strategy and Conscience.* New York: Harper. 323 pp.
97. Rapoport, A. 1970. Conflict resolution in the light of game theory and beyond. In *The Structure of Conflict,* ed. P. Swingle, pp. 1–42. New York: Academic. 305 pp.
98. Rapoport, A. 1973. *Experimental Games and Their Uses in Psychology.* Morristown, NJ: Gen. Learn. Press. 40 pp.
99. Rapoport, A. 1974. Prisoner's Dilemma: Recollections and observations. In *Game Theory as a Theory of Conflict Resolution,* ed. A. Rapoport, pp. 17–34. Dordrect, Holland: Reidel. 283 pp.
100. Rapoport, A., Chammah, A. M. 1965. *Prisoner's Dilemma: A Study in Conflict and Cooperation.* Ann Arbor: Univ. Michigan Press. 258 pp.
101. Rapoport, A., Guyer, M. 1966. A taxonomy of 2 × 2 games. *Gen. Syst.* 11:203–14
102. Rapoport, A., Orwant, C. 1962. Experimental games: A review. *Behav. Sci.* 7:1–37
103. Riker, W. H., Niemi, R. G. 1964. Anonymity and rationality in the essential three-person game. *Hum. Relat.* 17:131–41
104. Rotter, J. B. 1971. Generalized expectancies for interpersonal trust. *Am. Psychol.* 26:443–51
105. Rubin, J. Z., Brown, B. R. 1975. *The Social Psychology of Bargaining and Negotiation.* New York: Academic. 359 pp.
106. Sawyer, J., Guetzkow, H. 1965. Bargaining and negotiation in international relations. In *International Behavior: A Social-Psychological Analysis,* ed. H. Kelman, pp. 466–520. New York: Holt, Rinehart & Winston. 626 pp.
107. Scheff, T. J. 1967. A theory of social coordination applicable to mixed-motive games. *Sociometry* 30:215–34
108. Schlenker, B. R., Helm, B., Tedeschi, J. T. 1973. The effects of personality and situational variables on behavioral trust. *J. Pers. Soc. Psychol.* 25:419–27
109. Schlenker, B. R., Tedeschi, J. T. 1972. Interpersonal attraction and the exercise of coercive and reward power. *Hum. Relat.* 25:427–39

110. Schultz, D. P. 1964. *Panic Behavior.* New York: Random House. 146 pp.
111. Sherif, M., Sherif, C. W. 1953. *Groups in Harmony and Tension.* New York: Harper. 316 pp.
112. Siegel, S., Fouraker, L. E. 1960. *Bargaining and Group Decision Making: Experiments in Bilateral Monopoly.* New York: McGraw-Hill. 132 pp.
113. Snyder, G. H., Diesing, P. 1977. *Bargains, Systems, Decisions: A Theory of International Crisis Behavior.* Princeton, NJ: Princeton Univ. Press. In press
114. Stagner, R. 1942. Some factors related to attitude toward war, 1938. *J. Soc. Psychol.* 16:131–42
115. Steele, M. W., Tedeschi, J. T. 1967. Matrix indices and strategy choices in mixed-motive games. *J. Confl. Resolut.* 11:198–205
116. Steiner, I. D. 1974. Whatever happened to the group in social psychology? *J. Exp. Soc. Psychol.* 10:93–108
117. Stevens, C. M. 1963. *Strategy and Collective Bargaining Negotiation.* New York: McGraw-Hill. 192 pp.
118. Stryker, S. 1972. Coalition behavior. See Ref. 49, pp. 338–80
119. Swingle, P. G. 1966. Effects of the emotional relationship between protagonists in a two person game. *J. Pers. Soc. Psychol.* 4:270–79
120. Swingle, P. G., Gillis, J. S. 1968. Effects of emotional relationship between protagonists in the prisoner's dilemma. *J. Pers. Soc. Psychol.* 8:160–65
121. Tedeschi, J. T., Hiester, D. S., Gahagan, J. P. 1968. Trust and the prisoner's dilemma game. *J. Soc. Psychol.* 75:199–207
122. Tedeschi, J. T., Lindskold, S., Horai, J., Gahagan, J. P. 1969. Social power and the credibility of promises. *J. Pers. Soc. Psychol.* 13:253–61
123. Tedeschi, J. T., Schlenker, B. R., Bonoma, T. V. 1973. *Conflict, Power, and Games.* Chicago: Aldine. 270 pp.
124. Terhune, K. W. 1970. The effects of personality in cooperation and conflict. See Ref. 97, pp. 193–234
125. Terhune, K. W. 1974. "Wash-in," "wash-out," and systematic effects in extended prisoner's dilemma. *J. Confl. Resolut.* 18:656–85
126. Thibaut, J. W., Faucheux, C. 1965. The development of contractual norms in a bargaining situation under two types of stress. *J. Exp. Soc. Psychol.* 1:89–102
127. Thibaut, J., Friedland, N., Walker, L. 1974. Compliance with rules: Some so-

cial determinants. *J. Pers. Soc. Psychol.* 30:792–801

128. Thibaut, J. W., Kelley, H. H. 1959. *The Social Psychology of Groups.* New York: Wiley. 313 pp.

128a. Tjosveld, D., Okun, M. A. 1976. *Corrupting Effects of Unequal Power: Cognitive Perspective-Taking and Cooperation.* Presented at Ann. Meet. Am. Psychol. Assoc., 84th, Washington DC

129. Tognoli, J. 1975. Reciprocation of generosity and knowledge of game termination in the decomposed prisoner's dilemma game. *Eur. J. Soc. Psychol.* 5:297–312

130. Tornatzky, L., Geiwitz, P. J. 1968. The effects of threat and attraction on interpersonal bargaining. *Psychon. Sci.* 13:125–26

130a. Uejio, C. K., Wrightsman, L. S. 1967. Ethnic-group differences in the relationship of trusting attitudes to cooperative behavior. *Psychol. Rep.* 20:563–71

131. Vinacke, W. E. 1969. Variables in experimental games: Toward a field theory. *Psychol. Bull.* 71:293–317

132. Vinacke, W. E., Arkoff, A. 1957. An experimental study of coalitions in the triad. *Am. Sociol. Rev.* 22:406–14

133. Voissem, N. H., Sistrunk, F. 1971. Communication schedules and cooperative game behavior. *J. Pers. Soc. Psychol.* 19:160–67

134. Von Neumann, J., Morganstern, O. 1947. *Theory of Games and Economic Behavior.* Princeton, NJ: Princeton Univ. Press. 641 pp.

135. Wichman, H. 1972. Effects of isolation and communication on cooperation in a two-person game. See Ref. 138, pp. 197–205

135a. Wilson, W. 1969. Cooperation and cooperativeness of the other player. *J. Confl. Resolut.* 13:110–17

136. Wilson, W. 1971. Reciprocation and other techniques for inducing cooperation in the Prisoner's Dilemma game. *J. Confl. Resolut.* 15:167–96

137. Wrightsman, L. S. Jr., Baxter, G. W., Bilsky, L., Nelson, L. N. 1969. *Effects of Information About Other Player and Other Player's Game Behavior Upon Cooperation in a Mixed-Motive Game.* Presented at Ann. Meet. West. Psychol. Assoc., Vancouver, BC

138. Wrightsman, L. S. Jr., O'Connor, J., Baker, N. J., eds. 1972. *Cooperation and Competition: Readings in Mixed-Motive Games.* Belmont, Calif: Brooks/Cole. 348 pp.

Ann. Rev. Psychol. 1977. 28:393–415

VERBAL LEARNING
AND MEMORY

♦278

Lloyd R. Peterson

Department of Psychology, Indiana University, Bloomington, Indiana 47401

INTRODUCTION

The objective of this chapter is to review selectively the literature dealing with aspects of verbal memory for which there is a fair amount of current research interest. One constraint is that, according to the tradition established in previous volumes, the topics related to memory which are reviewed separately in the series will not be touched to any extent: psycholinguistics, mathematical models of learning, thinking and concept attainment, and cognitive development.

It will be assumed that the reader has at least a limited acquaintance with the topics to be discussed. The previous review by Postman (84) provides background for current developments. Very few references to the literature prior to 1974 are cited here.

One notable recent event was the appearance of a bestseller on memorizing written by Lorayne & Lucas (65). In it the authors describe a number of mnemonic systems which can be used to organize various types of information. Rather than being an object of scorn for the academician—merely another how-to-do-it book— it is a source of information on what two memory experts have found effective in the way of subjective organization. They say, in essence, "Look at what we can do; if you don't believe it works, try it yourself." This challenge is not too different from that of authors in our prestigious experimental journals. "This is what we found; see if you can replicate it."

If one asks what relevance the book has for psychologists, at the least it would seem that no general theory of memory can be adequate without being able to account in principle for the efficiency of mnemonic systems. In addition, the set of interlocking systems described in the book hints at a solution to the problem of whether memory should be conceived as unitary, or whether it involves multiple structural stores. There seems to be a current trend for psychologists to view memory as incorporating a number of functional stores not unlike the interacting systems of professional mnemonists. Once a mnemonic system has been acquired, it can be used over and over again to store new information. Each system is a

393

specialized store which functions with a specific class of information. Even though one drew a diagram to display their interrelationships, no one would mistake the boxes in the diagram for representations of discrete physiological structures. They refer to functional systems, and there is no set limit on their number. In a given situation, one or two or more may interact to furnish a basis for efficient performance. No one is *the* short-term store; whichever systems are currently active support retention of recent events.

COMPONENTS OF MEMORY

The proliferation of models that was deplored by Postman (84) has slowed somewhat, but no consensus has developed for any of the extant models. The present writer is inclined to be favorably disposed to efforts to provide provisional organizations of the various aspects of memory involved in the processing and storage of information. The precedent of the classical learning theorists in providing visual aids to communicate their views of the important relationships among their constructs might be cited. Flow charts of stages of processing have been found useful by computer programmers in the organization of their thinking on difficult, complex problems. It is not surprising that their use has spread to assist psychologists in their organization of equally difficult problems. Apart from their role in communicating and thinking, models and their accompanying spatial diagrams are useful mnemonic devices.

Models

The Atkinson-Shiffrin three-store model (5), the one most frequently passed on to classes of beginning students through introductory texts, has been modified by one of its authors and changed more radically by the other. On the one hand, Atkinson (4) remains fairly close to the 1968 formulation, but he acquiesces in the view that the stores need not be considered discrete neurological systems, rather "the different components of the system may simply represent different phases of activation of a single neurological system" (4, p. 103). In addition, the long-term store is now partitioned into a conceptual store and an event-knowledge store, apparently in correspondence with Tulving's (101) distinction between semantic and episodic memory.

Shiffrin (96), on the other hand, has integrated the three stores to a greater degree, and the former terminology has to be reinterpreted. The short-term store has become the temporarily active portion of the long-term store. Studies of attention lead him to believe that information from sensory receptors activates long-term structures directly, and that the concept of attention refers to continuation of that activity rather than a filtering of information prior to entrance into the short-term store. What then is the meaning of transfer to the long-term store? The phrase refers to establishment of associations between elements already in the long-term store.

Perhaps the differences among current models of memory are not as great as might appear on the surface. They all attempt to put the major experimental findings of recent years into perspective, and so they are limited as to how much they can differ. There is fair agreement on some of the main components of short-term remembering that can be isolated by experimental manipulations, so we mention recent studies related to these components rather than attempting to evaluate current models.

Auditory Memory

The evidence for inferences about echoic memory, storage of auditory information in an uncategorized form, has been reviewed by Crowder (25). The stimulus-suffix paradigm, in which the sequence of items given in a test of memory span ends with an extra redundant item, has been suggestive. Echoic memory is inferred from disruption of recall when the suffix is in the same modality as the preceding items, together with data showing that the advantage of auditory over visual presentations is eliminated by an auditory suffix in the auditory sequence. However, not all investigators obtain the elimination of the modality effect (31). There is a possibility that the suffix effect can be explained as attentional rather than as due to uncategorized auditory memory. Hitch (44) showed that a visual suffix effect can be eliminated by training subjects to ignore the suffix. The auditory suffix effect could not be eliminated in this manner, so there remains evidence for precategorical acoustic storage.

Evidence from experiments on speech perception provide more compelling reasons for attributing importance to echoic memory (19, 27, 83). Differences between consonants and vowels appear in various studies, related to retention characteristics of each. There is a suffix effect with vowels, but not with initial stop consonants. The manipulations of small intervals between two speech sounds in recognition tests produce differences in performance with vowels and consonants. Vowels with their greater acoustic energy provide auditory cues for a time, while stop consonants must be categorized immediately or memory for them is lost.

Visual Memory

The persistence of uncategorized visual storage for any longer than an extremely brief interval is a matter for debate (17, 20, 40, 46). Kroll (58) summarizes evidence for storage of visual information in some form over extended periods of time. Retention of a visual letter after a retention interval filled with shadowing of auditory material is superior to that of a letter presented aurally. While this suggests that the visual letter had not been coded into a phonemic format, it is unlikely that uncategorized visual memory endures for this length of time. There seems to be visual rehearsal involved, and this might well require categorization of some form, as well as the participation of control processes (59).

There is some question as to whether visual rehearsal of moderately complex visual stimuli occurs, even during an unfilled interval between presentations. Shaffer & Shiffrin (95) did not find that lengthening the intervals between presentations improved memory for pictures. However, their intervals were randomly varied for a given subject, and occurrences of very short intervals may have discouraged subjects from using longer intervals for rehearsal. Weaver (112) varied duration of intervals separating photos between subjects, and he found that recognition was directly related to length of the interval. Tversky & Sherman (104) used blocks of tests with the same length of interval and obtained similar results. There is no doubt that visual rehearsal can occur, but the degree of detail that can be preserved during this rehearsal is undoubtedly limited. The most recent evidence suggests that more detail can be rehearsed than was formerly considered possible.

Phonemic Memory

Phonemic confusions arise not only after auditory presentations but also in recall of visual presentations. The effects of phonemic similarity can be eliminated by engaging the subjects in concurrent vocalization of an irrelevant kind. The findings suggest speech production mechanisms are involved, and that rehearsal after visual presentations includes phonemic coding unless subvocal articulation is experimentally suppressed. A phonemic buffer related to speech production is important in maintaining memory for serial order (32). Recent evidence for a phonemic buffer comes from findings that length of the span of immediate memory is inversely related to the length of the words presented (9). This relationship between memory span and word length can be eliminated by having the subject articulate irrelevant sounds during visual presentations, although the relationship is still found with auditory presentations during vocalic suppression. Apparently phenomic coding can occur through either of two sources, an auditory input or articulation.

Interactions

Semantic coding is assumed to offer support for memory over long intervals. This does not preclude the relevance of semantic coding for short intervals, but no single component can be said to account for short-term retention by itself, and multiple components are assumed to work together whenever conditions are appropriate. Levy & Craik (61) found additive effects from combining several sources in the free recall of unrelated words. Two kinds of instructions were given to induce semantic versus nonsemantic coding; the subjects were either told to relate word meanings in sentences, stories, or images, or they were told to repeat the words to themselves. This variable was combined with mode of presentation, either visual plus auditory, or visual alone. Retention was found to be higher when both auditory and semantic coding were induced than with either alone.

The claim that phonemic coding underlies the recency effect in free recall of unrelated words is disputed by Baddeley & Hitch (8), who note that a recency effect occurs after visual presentation with suppression of articulatory coding by irrelevant vocalization. Although recall in their experiment was reduced for both early and late positions in the list, a recency effect remained. Reduced recall for early and late positions is also found when the concurrent task does not require vocal or verbal responses. Anderson & Craik (1) presented a choice reaction with lights or tones as stimuli during concurrent presentation of a list of words. With visual presentation of the list and auditory stimuli in the other task, number of stimulus alternatives was inversely related to recall throughout the list. This indicates that attention is important for retention over short as well as long intervals. On the other hand, with auditory presentation of the list and visual stimuli in the concurrent task, the number of stimuli in the concurrent task did not affect terminal positions in the list. The implication is that echoic memory counterbalanced attentional deficits when presentations were aural.

Watkins compared several methods of measuring the recency effect in free recall in the context of a discussion of primary memory (109). Different methods were applied to the same set of data, and the minimal degree of variability for the measures was found with a technique introduced by Tulving & Colotla (102). A word was attributed to primary memory if no more than seven presentations and/or recalls of other words separated presentation and recall of the word being classified. The only assumption underlying the method was that displacement from primary memory was due to interference from either input or output events. It is a useful empirical method, and its availability need not be limited to those who hold to a two-store interpretation of memory. One could call what it measures by some neutral term such as active memory, referring to multiple components taken collectively.

LEVELS OF PROCESSING

The paper by Craik & Lockhart (23) on levels of processing was the most influential single force leading to loosening of the rigid conceptions of multiple-store theories. In it they suggested that memory was better conceived as a by-product of perceptual processing, with duration of memory dependent on the depth of processing carried out on the stimulus material. Incidental learning studies have provided a substantial amount of data to support this interpretation. Subjects are not informed that they are to memorize verbal items presented to them; instead an orienting task of some kind exposes them to the material, and they perform the orienting task under the impression that the experimenter is interested in that task for its own sake.

A series of ten experiments described by Craik & Tulving (24) are illustrative of the class of experiments being reported in large numbers as support for the general approach, but the paper also introduces some modifications in the details of the concept. A word was exposed in a tachistoscope briefly, and memory was tested after a series of such exposures. Each word was preceded by a question which the subject answered by pressing one of two keys immediately after the exposure; this constituted the orienting task. The memory test at the end furnished a measure of the incidental learning retained at the end of the session. The type of question was the variable of interest, since that determined the depth to which the word was processed. A question about the word in terms of superficial appearance, whether it was in upper or lower case type, resulted in poorer retention than a question as to whether it rhymed with another word. The rhyming question in turn produced less effective coding than asking whether the word fit a sentence frame included in the question. The general finding was that processing a word in terms of visual characteristics was very ineffective, while semantic coding was highly effective. The differential effects were large and robust, and they endured in spite of changes in procedure. They appeared whether learning was incidental or intentional. They showed up in recall as well as recognition tests. They persisted in spite of rewards offered to motivate performance on the superficial orienting task. Even when more time was required for a superficial orienting task, the semantic orientation resulted in better retention.

Spread of Processing

One aspect of their work led Craik and Tulving to modify the concept of levels of processing. Schulman (94) earlier noted in some classification studies based on questions that when a word was congruous with its context it was better recalled than a word that was incongruous. Subjects were more likely to remember the noun in "Is a twinge sudden?" than to remember the noun in "Is spinach ecstatic?" In both cases semantic analysis was required, so that processing was carried to the semantic level, but there were differences in quality of processing at that level.

The Craik & Tulving studies found differences in retention depending on whether the correct answer to a question was yes or no. In both cases the word had to be processed to the semantic level, but in one case, that requiring a "yes" answer, the target word fit the context of the question. In the other case, that of a question calling for a "no" answer, the target word was inappropriate. Plainly, differential processing could occur within a given level and produce differential retention. The concept of spread of processing was introduced to describe this second dimension of processing which was added to depth of processing. Additional evidence for the concept of spread of processing was found in a study relating retention to length and complexity of the question. Short questions were not as effective as long questions even though both were semantic.

The Role of Attention

Several studies challenge the assumption that superficial characteristics of presentation are forgotten rapidly. Under some circumstances nonsemantic details can influence performance for long periods of time. Words are recognized better when spoken by the same voice even after 2 minutes have elapsed (22). A more spectacular demonstration has been described by Kolers & Ostry (56) in which information about characteristics of typography had an effect on recognition memory for 32 days. The reading of 60 sentences, half printed normally and half inverted, was described to subjects as a study of reading, and there was no mention of any memory test. A test reading occurred after some interval between 3 minutes and 32 days, when new sentences were mixed in with the old. Each sentence was classified as (a) old and in the same orientation, (b) old but in a new orientation, or (c) new. Sentences presented in the same orientation were better recognized than those changed, and sentences inverted on the first presentation were better recognized than those in normal orientation.

Kolers & Ostry (56) suggest that the operations performed in reading formed a part of the representation that was stored. The perceptual operations were reactivated at the second reading and participated in the recognition. This interpretation ties retention to perception in an intimate way, but the levels of processing view of hierarchical levels from sensory to semantic being rigidly correlated with duration of retention is denied. A further study (55) found memory for inverted text to be poor after long practice in reading such text. As perceptual processing reaches the automatic level of a highly practiced skill, subjects attend less to the details of the processing and hence they are not encoded as well as in the initial stage of learning.

The failures of Craik and Tulving to boost retention in their low-level orienting task are hard to reconcile with other findings of memory for nonsemantic detail. Other studies show (48, 49, 62) that instructions can bias a nonsemantic encoding. Other evidence suggests that the relationship between type of orienting task and type of retention task may be important (38), with imagery orientation resulting in superior performance on a recognition test, while categorization produces superior recall. Perhaps the questions that Craik and Tulving used in their low-level task were too uniform to provide cues that could become effective. The questions as to appearance seem to have been simpler than those related to semantic judgments. Even though there is ample support or the general efficiency of semantic processing as compared with nonsemantic processing (35, 100), there can be additional processing even within the lower levels that will enhance retention. Such considerations have led Craik & Jacoby (21) to de-emphasize the rigidly determined series of stages, and place more emphasis on the previously described concept of spread of encoding.

Rehearsal

The levels of processing approach distinguished between maintenance rehearsal and elaborative rehearsal, the former simply maintaining information at a given level, and the latter transferring information to a higher level. Several studies have added support for the interpretation that rote rehearsal does not tend to support encoding for the long intervals tested in a final free recall test, even though rote rehearsal provides good immediate free recall. Mazuryk & Lockhart (70) compared four processing activities during presentation of five-item lists: silent rehearsal, overt rehearsal, rhyme generation, or verbal associates generation. The two rehearsal conditions were superior in immediate recall to the association conditions, but in final free recall the relationship was reversed. The authors conclude that negative recency in final free recall is the result of strategies which maximize recall of recent items. A trade-off of a similar kind is found in other studies (12, 15). When elaborative coding is induced, a positive recency effect in final free recall can be observed.

It is another question whether rote rehearsal is of no lasting benefit at all. The original levels of processing approach implied it was not. Woodward, Bjork & Jongeward (117) found final free recall to be independent of number of maintenance rehearsals, but at the same time final tests of recognition showed improvement with such rehearsal. More recently, Darley & Glass (26) found free recall to be related to amount of maintenance rehearsal during search of lists for a target word. A number of 40-word lists were searched, each for a different target. The target word on a given list had to be stored until it was found in the list. The amount of maintenance rehearsal was varied by having the target placed in different parts of the list. Final free recall of target words was a direct function of how far into the list the target word had been placed. The authors suggest that this kind of rehearsal involved attention of a sort not necessary for rote repetition, although it would seem to fit any reasonable definition of maintenance rehearsal.

ENCODING SPECIFICITY

Tulving (101) coined the phrase "episodic memory" as a contrast to the term semantic memory. Episodic memory referred to information about temporally dated events in a particular place, and it included the memory tested with subjects in a typical laboratory list-learning task. The subject already knows the words given him to memorize; he stores the information that he heard this list in the lab at a particular time. The principle of encoding specificity relates to this episodic memory, and it states that a stored representation is determined by its perceptual encoding, and the representation in turn determines what retrieval cues will provide access to it.

New Cues at Recall

An obvious test of encoding specificity is to present cues at recall that were not present at the time of encoding. Of course, in order to be sure that such retrieval cues were not part of the subject's own idiosyncratic encoding, it is necessary to provide some other cue in the encoding stage. The critical test pairs the word during presentation with a weak associate (by word association norms); then a strong associate is provided as a cue on the occasion of the retention test. The principle of encoding specificity makes the counterintuitive prediction that this strong cue at test will not aid in recall of its associate. And indeed, evidence has been presented that not only is the strong associate no help in recall, in some circumstances it may be worse than no cue at all (103). Thus the assumption of the principle of encoding specificity that the previously established association is a part of semantic memory, and hence will not be helpful for episodic tests, is supported.

A number of experimenters have varied the circumstances surrounding the switch from weak cue to strong cue, in an attempt to determine the limits within which the described result can be obtained. Santa & Lamwers (92) found that informing their subjects of the relationship between strong cue and its associate made the strong cue effective in recall. Reder, Anderson & Bjork (89) found that decrements with the shift were lessened when frequency of occurrence in general usage of the target words was low rather than high. This is interpreted as supporting the idea that change in context in this paradigm results in a change in meaning for the target word. The low frequency words should have fewer meanings, while the high frequency words should have more. The magnitude of recall decrement due to changing cues would therefore depend on frequency of usage.

Postman (85) sought to minimize any set by the subject to regard the task as paired associates, a set which might make him reluctant to give an old response to a new cue in the test phase. Half the words were presented singly and half with a context word; similarly in recall half the responses were cued and the others were not. The associative strength of cues at input and at recall was varied factorially. The results showed strong cues at recall were more effective than weak cues whether or not they had been presented at input. The only support for encoding specificity lay in the finding that recall tended to be higher when cues remained the same. However, encoding specificity could not explain the finding that a shift from weak to strong produced better recall than a shift from strong to weak. This latter finding had been true of an earlier study (99) in which the comparison was acknowledged to be inexplicable by the principle of encoding specificity.

Recall after Recognition Failure

A second type of experiment that has been cited as supporting the principle of encoding specificity also pits strong associates against weak associates. However, in this case following the initial stage in which a cue is paired with a weak associate, the subject generates multiple associates to strong cues for the target words of the first phase. Inevitably some of the word associations are target words, and in the third stage the subject is tested for recognition of the target words from among his associations. Performance is far from perfect, and in fact when the weak cues are given in a fourth stage many words are recalled which were not recognized earlier. Recall after recognition failure was found by Watkins & Tulving (110) under a variety of conditions different from the original experiment. Some of these changes included recognition tests prepared by the experimenter rather than subject-generated tests, use of three-alternative forced choice tests, omission of any verbal task between study trial and the recognition test, and omission of practice lists prior to the study trial. Recall after recognition is said to be inexplicable by traditional two-process theories of recall which postulate generation of a response followed by recognition of the response. In this analysis recognition tests by this theory require only the second of the two processes, since the generation phase occurs automatically in recognition tests. There should not be any recall after recognition failure. On the other hand, Watkins & Tulving hold that words are not identical from one situation to another; rather they are encoded uniquely in episodic memory along with other cues present at encoding.

A number of individuals have objected to the interpretation involving recognition failure of recallable words. Martin (68) argues that the graphemes may have been the same in the recognition and recall tests, but the meanings were different, so that the word senses that were not recognized were not the same senses that were recalled. Other criticisms have been summarized by Light, Kimble & Pellegrino (63), among them the point that conditions were not the same for the recognition test as for the recall test. Watkins & Tulving (111) reply that their critics have missed the point, and that it is exactly those conditions under which recognition exceeds recall that are of interest.

In an experimental test of the generality of recall following recognition failure, Postman (85) introduced some changes in procedure aimed at reducing intrasession transfer and providing control conditions. Recall was not superior to recognition, although some words were recalled that had not been recognized. Postman concludes that a strong interpretation of the principle of encoding specificity does not seem warranted, since the predictions from the principle did not survive modifications in the experimental arrangements.

There is no doubt that changing context from study to test of retention reduces performance. However, as Pellegrino & Salzberg (79) point out, there are multiple considerations influencing the subject's performance when context is varied. The subject may become more cautious on discovering a novel cue. The amount of overlap of context conceived in terms of number of common semantic features can range from 0 to 100%. The total number of potential semantic features may vary from word to word, as in differences between high and low frequency words (89). In view of these multiple factors it is not surprising that there are differences in the magnitude of effects produced by shifting cues in both recognition and recall tests.

Experiments showing the effect of context changes on recognition memory have led several theorists to modify their views. Kintsch (56) has incorporated the principle of encoding specificity into his most recent model of memory. Anderson & Bower (2) have modified their propositional theory of recognition memory by dropping the assumption that words presented for recognition automatically access their meanings. Currently they hold that such an assumption is still justified when words are not presented in special semantic contexts. But going from a sense to a word in recall and from a word to a sense in recognition, cannot be considered automatic in the general case.

In the light of the many experimental tests of the principle of encoding specificity, the original distinction between episodic and semantic memory may need reassessment. Clearly there are task differences that emphasize discrimination of features that are related to time and space, but does this necessitate two memory stores even in a functional sense? Semantic cues appear to interact with contextual cues in both short- and long-term retention tests. Furthermore, it seems obvious that the knowledge of the world which is now regarded as context-free was acquired in a specific context. Two plus two equals four, that is semantic information. One may or may not remember the specific occasions that were the learning trials for this information. In most cases one cannot remember much of such context due to occurrence of other contexts which interfere. With an item of knowledge obtained on a recent trial, one may be more successful in describing the context in which information was obtained. One might speculate that context-free semantic memories emerge through the interfering effects of occurrence in a variety of contexts.

ABSTRACTION OF IDEAS

The passage from specific details to general structure goes by various names. Considerations of differences in retention as a function of level of encoding leads into the discussion of the integration of simple ideas into complex wholes. Franks & Bransford (33) write of linguistic integration in connection with the development of a unified structure through presentation of individual sentences.

Loss of Detail

Franks & Bransford reported that individual sentences lost their identity for subjects who integrated them into wholes, and that recognition judgments were based on the number of components from the complex idea that the test sentence contained. Thus confidence in their judgments as well as percent of yes responses were directly related to the number of simple ideas in a test sentence that corresponded to the complex whole. Katz, Atkeson & Lee (51) suggest that this linear effect is an artifact of the presentation procedure. When they present only sentences containing a single idea rather than a variety of sentences, ratings for single ideas are markedly higher than in the comparison case. This finding does not seem surprising since subjects would be expected to learn to discriminate the simple sentences from more complex ones under these circumstances. Of course, this is evidence that all memory for detail is not lost when complex structures are developed. Katz & Gruenewald (52) find a significant linear relationship between number of components and confidence ratings when meaningless sentences are presented. They suggest that a guessing strategy is the basis for the linear effect. Small (97) obtains similar results using arbitrarily chosen sets of words instead of sentences. Small groups of new words were given lower recognition ratings than large groups of new words.

Development of a complex representation from information presented in pictures has been studied by Baggett (10). In this case subjects could accurately identify pictures not seen but whose meaning fit the story for as long as 3 days.

Moeser (71) found that concreteness of words, as well as instructions to use imagery, both affected the degree of integration of sentences, in that imagery instructions and concrete words led to better rejection of sentences that contained components of more than one complex idea. This investigator departed from previous procedures to introduce overlap among simple ideas from one whole to another.

Linear Orderings

Problems dealing with linear orderings constitute another experimental approach to the integration of information. A series of sentences is presented, each sentence describing an order relationship between two terms; for instance, Bill is taller than Jim. The whole which the sentences collectively describe can be represented as $A > B > C > D > E$ . . . Scholz & Potts (93) describe six-term problems in which only adjacent pairs were presented in sentences and all combinations were tested for truth value. The finding of interest was that accuracy was greatest for nonadjacent pairs; these were not originally presented. This could be due to the subject imagining a scale on which the terms are ordered, and from which discriminations can be made which depend on distance between terms. The greater the distance, the easier the discrimination.

An endpoint effect is also possible, in that if subjects know what the ends of the scale are, they can respond most easily if an endpoint is part of a comparison. In the earlier studies using four terms, the end-term effect could not be distinguished from a distance effect, since nonadjacent pairs would inevitably involve an end term. The use of six terms permits unconfounding of the two effects by testing remote pairs that do not include an end term. These latter pairs were found to be judged more accurately than adjacent pairs which had actually been presented, hence a distance effect was inferred. In addition there was evidence for an end-term effect, so both effects were necessary to account for the data. Potts (87) reported similar findings using latency as a response measure. The findings are evidence that subjects construct an integrated scale and make inferential judgments from it rather than storing individual sentences. Presumably visual imagery is involved in the integrated structure, since if it were necessary to process items serially, it should take longer to judge a remote pair involving more than two items than to process an adjacent pair with just two items.

Humphreys (47) notes that the presentation phase of a linear ordering task resembles a verbal discrimination task, and he suggests that frequency discrimination may be the basis for both the end-term effect and the remote comparison effect. If one assumes that subjects rehearse the greater member of a pair on presentation, and that all possible pairings are so rehearsed, then the subjective frequencies that accrue to individual terms will be rank ordered appropriately. A linear ordering experiment was reported using verbal discrimination instructions. Analogous results to those of linear ordering tasks were obtained, and Humphreys suggests that frequency could be the basis of the two effects reported by Scholz & Potts. Of course, the latter did not present all possible combinations, so it would have to be assumed that in reading the paragraph subjects themselves generated the other remote pairings in the process of studying the problem.

Barclay & Reid (11) report a study of inferred relationships from linear arrays of a slightly more complex kind than those of the previous paragraphs. They used multiple trials to establish verbatim memory of a subset from the set of all combinations of terms in the array. On Trial 1 recalls were distributed randomly over the acquisition sentences and five types of inferred sentences (errors). With additional learning trials on the same set of acquisition sentences, verbatim recall improved and the five inference types declined uniformly.

IMAGERY

Instructions to imagine are found in connection with many types of tasks, and the justification for treating it separately may lie in the ambiguous relationship that exists between imaginal and verbal tasks. Experiments which go beyond simply showing an advantageous effect from instructions to imagine offer the possibility of clarifying the nature of imagery and its role in memory.

Spatial Information

One approach is to test subjects for storage of spatial information by a method which makes it seem implausible that the information was stored in verbal form. An intriguing effort of this type was initiated by Moyer (72), who suggested that comparing the size of objects on the basis of memory involves an internal psychophysics. He found that the time required to decide which of two names refers to the larger animal is an inverse function of the estimated difference in size between the two animals. The larger the difference in size, the shorter the latency, which is what would be expected if a direct perceptual comparison were being tested.

Paivio (77) confirmed Moyer's results and added some variations on the theme with pictures. When the size of remembered objects was incongruous with the relative size of their pictures, the judgments were significantly slower than when the two were congruent. When distance was judged rather than size, the congruency effect was reversed, as would be predicted on the basis of visual experiments on distance in relation to size. Although size comparisons from memory were faster with pictures than with words, the relationship was reversed when pronounceability of names of pictures and the printed names was judged. Paivio attempted to rule out the use of labels as the basis for the size comparisons, as for example the individual having stored in memory the label "large" for elephant, "small" for mouse, and "medium" for dog. He scaled the names of objects for estimated size and had subjects make size judgments between names of objects from limited regions of the extended scale. The relationship between size difference and latency was found to hold for regions near the ends of the scale as well as in the middle. Therefore, the judgments were assumed to be made on some basis other than a list of discrete attributes associated with each name in semantic memory. Paivio concludes that an imaginal system was responsible for the size judgments, and a verbal system was responsible for pronounceability judgments. In contrast, he considered the data difficult to explain by theories that assume an abstract propositional basis for memory.

An alternative view which might accommodate Paivio's data has been put forward by Kosslyn (57). He interprets imagery in terms of a computer graphics metaphor. A visual image is considered to be analogous to a display on a cathode ray tube in a computer installation. The underlying structure is abstract in both cases—a computer program in the one case and an analogous structure in memory in the other. The image, like the display, is limited in size, but objects can be made to shrink or expand within the limited capacity available. The conception was tested by attempting to vary size of subjects' images through indirect instruction. The subject was told to imagine a pair of animals, and it was assumed that a rabbit imagined standing next to an elephant would have a smaller image than one imagined standing next to a fly. The subject was then asked to judge whether the rabbit had some specified property. It required longer to make the judgment when the subjective image was small than when it was large. The image was considered analogous to a percept, and a processor of some kind was postulated to analyze it along dimensions relevant to perceptual processing. In this way spatial judgments could be made even though the underlying structure was abstract.

Other experimenters have also studied similarities between visual perception and imagery. Recall of letters in various cells of a four by four matrix was found best for corner cells whether the matrices were seen or imagined, while a verbal control condition did not show the effect (81). In another experiment, a probe of imaginary words indicated parallel processing of limited numbers of letters, a type of processing also found in visual perception (113).

Selective Interference

Another kind of evidence providing inferences about imagery involves selective interference either at the same time as the imagining or during the retention interval that follows. Baddeley et al (7) describe a series of three studies in which visual pursuit tracking was a concurrent activity during other tasks. In the first a decrement was found in the pursuit tracking when subjects imagined counting corners in an imaginary letter, but no significant decrement occurred when the other task was verbal. In a second study, memory for spatial positions in an imaginary matrix suffered when visual tracking was carried on currently, while a nonspatial task did not suffer. In a third study, subjects learned pairs of concrete or abstract words with or without concurrent visual tracking. The visual tracking was not found to have any greater effect on the concrete words than on the abstract. The usual superiority for concrete words was found, and a slight decrease in amount recalled was found with both kinds of words, but there was no differential effect on the easily imaginable words as compared to the abstract words. Apparently the superiority of the concrete words was due to something more than a stimulus for imagining. The authors distinguish between concreteness as a semantic feature and imagery conceived as a control process. The former presumably is independent of the visual system, while the latter requires part of the visual processing system.

Some support for this interpretation comes from Powell, Hamon & Young (88), who had subjects learn paired-associates under either imagery or verbal-mediation instructions. Inserted between pairs of concrete nouns was either a shape selection task or a name-of-shape selection task. When the pairs of associates were tested after the single study trial, shapes interfered most with study under imagery instructions, while the naming task interfered most with learning under the verbal-mediation instructions. The learning task was the same in both cases; only the instructions were different. Interference acted selectively upon the strategy employed.

Several investigators (7) have mentioned difficulty in replicating Atwood's (6) study of selective interference. Atwood found a selective effect, but he confounded type of instruction with the concrete-abstract dimension. The studies just cited appear to account for both Atwood's original finding and the difficulties in replicating it. A visual task interferes with imagining as induced by instructions, but it does not have a differential effect on concrete as compared with abstract words. What this implies for the effect of concreteness on learning is another matter.

Pellegrino, Siegel & Dhawan (80) reported that combined visual and auditory distraction during a short retention interval produced more forgetting with pictures than with words, leading them to affirm a dual coding interpretation, visual and verbal encoding of pictures, while words are encoded verbally. Gardiner, Thompson & Maskarinec (36) found that with auditory presentations counting backward during a 30 sec delay interval resulted in negative recency in free recall, while copying digits during the interval resulted in positive recency. These are encouraging indications that application of selective interference techniques to standard paradigms may throw new light on the encoding process.

PROACTIVE INTERFERENCE

The use of distractor activity during a short interval after presentation of three words does not ordinarily reduce recall of the words unless two or more tests have been given consecutively without long rest intervals separating them. The task is of interest for its use as a tool in exploring dimensions of encoding, as well as a paradigm for investigating proactive interference.

Encoding Dimensions

When three or four short-term retention tests have reduced recall for three-word messages, switching to a new class of items on the next test results in markedly improved recall depending on the basis for the classification. Wickens (114) views this release from proactive interference as a technique for delineating the attributes of coding, for if release occurs after a change of some attribute, the subject must have been encoding on that attribute. Multiple dimensions can be encoded on the same presentation, for instance, acoustic and semantic dimensions (115). Since many kinds of shifts bring relief from proactive interference, it follows that coding occurs simultaneously on many characteristics of the words.

Underwood (105) has argued that such an approach overestimates the amount of coding that occurs when a single word is presented by itself. Priming occurs in the release paradigm as subjects process many words from the same category, so that a dimension of encoding may become critical through repetition of examples of the same category. Evidence for such priming was found by Bennett & Bennett (14) in that the amount of release from proactive interference increased with the number of tests in the same category prior to a change to a new category. Cermak (16) has obtained similar evidence for priming when the class change involved antonyms on the release test.

Mechanisms of Interference

Historically, proactive interference has been attributed to competition at recall, rather than a change in encoding characteristics with successive tests. Current evidence supporting this is the finding that in a recognition test the difficulty of the choice is a function of how far back the distractor item occurred originally (13). Discrimination of recency rather than forgetting of previous test items is involved. Strengthening by repetition of preceding items does not increase forgetting of a test item (116). Furthermore, the more dissimilar the intervening activity the better able the subject will be to differentiate the current item from previous items from the same class (37). Finally, final free recall is not related to position in the test sequence even though position had been correlated with substantial differences in initial recall (64).

On the other hand, a case can be made for proactive interference to result from failure to generate the test item. Dillon & Thomas (29) find that subjects can usually distinguish previous items from the current message, so if encouraged to guess, they produce many intrusions without substantially improving recall. If required to recall both the current message and the preceding one, they are able to both recall and identify may items though there remain some that cannot be recalled.

Increasing inadequacy of encoding with repeated tests could be a source of proactive decrement. Provision of a category cue can stimulate response generation (28), and in general the category name can be considered a common cue to all words in the category whether named by the experimenter or not. The situation is not unlike the A–D, A–B paradigm in paired-associate list learning, wherein stimulus members of the first list are paired with new responses in the second list. In such a paradigm, Postman, Stark & Burns (86) report evidence that proactive interference in later recall of the second list may result from inadequate second-list learning. A plausible hypothesis is that when the subject has to find a new mediator for the second response to a stimulus, the second mediator may be less effective than the one that was used for the first response. Better learning of the second list when the first was learned incidentally is indirect evidence for this, since no mediator would be expected to be used in incidental learning. More direct evidence was found by Hasher & Johnson (40) when they asked subjects for mediators which they had used in the A–B, A–D paradigm. When the mediators were given to new subjects to use in learning a single list, mediators from first-list learning were found to be more effective than those reported from second-list learning.

The most reasonable interpretation of proactive interference suggests a multiple-factor analysis. Forgetting can be the result of both increasingly inadequate encoding and difficulty in discriminating among competing items at recall. Boundary conditions can be changed to emphasize either of these sources.

Decay

Reitman (90) now considers that her earlier results showing no forgetting of words during a 15 sec interval of signal detection have to be reinterpreted. Using more sensitive techniques to assess rehearsal during the retention interval, she eliminated data from assumed rehearsers from the analysis. Contrary to previous reports, when there is no reason to suspect rehearsal during an interval awaiting a signal, there is forgetting during the interval. Reitman attributed this forgetting to decay, and surprisingly made no mention of the possibility of proactive interference as the source of the forgetting. Five nouns were used in each message, a number which would be predicted to result in heavier interference than in the usual three-word message (34). Time between tests was not long enough to expect dissipation of proactive interference over a rest interval.

LIST DIFFERENTIATION

The identification of list membership has been interpreted in terms of item-specific associative interference by Anderson & Bower (3). A context marker was assumed to be stored with each item in a series of partially overlapping lists. A signal detection analysis corrected for interlist generalization, and the indices of discrimination showed substantial proactive effects and somewhat weaker retroactive interference. Appearance of an item in several lists interfered with identification of the list(s) in which it had appeared.

Sternberg & Bower (98) interpret the negative transfer found with part-whole lists in free recall to be a matter of failure of list differentiation. Tests of list membership showed the locus of negative transfer to be difficulty in assigning List-2 markers to words that appeared in both lists. A list differentiation account is incomplete, according to Petrich, Pellegrino & Dhawan (82), because it fails to account for facilitation of learning of new items when subjects are informed of the list relationship. They suggest that negative transfer may arise due to a priority strategy for new items. Informing subjects of the list overlap may stimulate this strategy, leading to interference with old items. They accept list differentiation as a partial explanation, however. Okada & Carey (75) provide data compatible with a list-discrimination explanation of whole-part transfer, in that when whole-list retention is tested after whole-part learning, there is strong retention. Thus subjective reorganization of the first list presumably did not occur during second-list learning, rather list-discrimination was learned.

ORGANIZATION

Subjective organization has undergone disruptive arrangements by several experimenters. Murdock, Anderson & Ho (74) report failure to disrupt organization through manipulation of presentation order. They conclude that organization into clusters is well shielded from the influences of list order. Similarly, Mandler, Worden & Graesser (66) find that replacing alternate words from a recall trial with new words does not reduce recall to the level of a group receiving all new words. The authors suggest that higher-order organization is not disrupted by such maneuvers, and that pairwise dependencies do not furnish an adequate measure of subjective organization. Pelligrino & Battig (78) present a technique for measuring higher-order organization which examines data for organized units of any size. From their analysis they infer several different organizational strategies depending on type of task and stage of practice. Subjects tend to begin with a dominant strategy to recall in order of presentation, then adopt recency and priority-for-new-words strategies, and eventually develop higher-order subjective units.

Meanwhile, subjective organization has been observed in individual protocols of subjects in serial learning tasks. Martin & Noreen (69) gave a free recall test and one trial of backward serial anticipation to subjects who had reached a low criterion of learning on a serial list. Organized subsequences were identified in the response patterns of individuals on the original learning, and these carried over into free recall and backward anticipation. When serial learning was carried to a higher criterion, subjective organization could be recognized in free recall under speed stress. Martin (67) regards serial learning as a multilevel process including learning within subsequences and learning the orders of subsequences.

Multilevel organization of serial learning has also been investigated with hierarchically structured lists of words. Underwood, Reichardt & Malmi (108) provided three levels of hierarchical structure in learning a list in which positions were cues for words in a hybrid serial and paired-associate task. In a constant order condition, subjects soon inferred that the list consisted of blocks of instances of several concepts, thus restricting alternatives after the first instance of a concept. The second-level concepts facilitated the learning of order of the blocks, and little of the facilitation by structure seemed due to the highest level concepts.

A hierarchical organization has been contrasted with a linear organization in serial pattern learning of digits. Jones & Zamostny (50) devised patterns that related to one or the other, and found that the first halves of linear patterns were easier than the corresponding hierarchical patterns, but the relationship was reversed for the second halves. With a hierarchical pattern the second half could be generated on the basis of knowledge of the first half plus recall of one rule. The generality of the findings beyond the patterns used is unknown.

An extensive analysis of serial-position curves has led Harcum (39) to emphasize strategies and organization tendencies of the subject in standard serial learning tasks. These are "paralearning" factors in his analysis. An adequate review of his book is beyond the scope of this paper.

SPACING OF PRESENTATIONS

The interval separating successive presentations has been found to affect memory in a wide range of tasks. Hintzman (41) has reviewed explanations of the phenomenon without arriving at any strong conclusion. Contemporary theorists favor the view that it is not the interval itself that underlies the effect, as in consolidation or rehearsal theories, but the effect the interval has on processing at the end of the interval. Elmes & Bjork (30) tested the hypothesis that inadequate coding of the second presentation occurs with short spacing. By requiring rote rehearsal of the second presentation at long intervals and elaborative rehearsal at short intervals, the effect of spacing should be eliminated. Unfortunately, their findings do not support the hypothesis. Hintzman et al (43) tested the hypothesis that there is inadequate attention paid to the second presentation when it immediately follows the previous presentation, also with negative results. Hintzman, Summers & Block (42) found largely negative evidence for a recovery from habituation theory, an involuntary attention explanation.

Theories postulating something happening during the interval have not died out completely. Landauer (60) has offered experimental evidence for consolidation after a single presentation of a paired associate. The pairing was followed by others and finally tested. The critical variable was the number of dissimilar pairs that followed the target pair before a block of similar pairs was presented. There was a trend for recall after 20 min to be better the longer the interval filled with dissimilar pairs preceding the presentations of similar pairs. Consolidation presumably continues during presentation of dissimilar pairs as in the spacing interval between two presentations, and the longer the interval the more the consolidation of the first study trial. Of course, if the interval is unfilled and subjects are instructed to rehearse, it is not surprising that retention improves (91). Hintzman (41) considers the finding that there is a spacing effect with pictures as critical evidence against a rehearsal explanation (76). However, the recent experiments mentioned earlier indicate that visual rehearsal during a blank interval is feasible. Evidence for a rehearsal explanation has come from a study by Ciccone & Brelsford (18) using a continuous recognition task. When a variable rehearsal strategy was suggested to subjects, and overt rehearsals were monitored, rehearsal was found to be correlated with recognition accuracy. The nonmonotonic relationship between performance and length of the spacing interval was similar to that found in a number of previous studies.

As with other verbal phenomena, it is quite possible that more than one factor underlies the spacing effect. At the moment no one can say with assurance what explanation is best.

VERBAL DISCRIMINATION LEARNING

Frequency continues to dominate explanations of the ability to remember which of two words was originally designated as correct. Frequency theory assumes that rehearsals as well as presentations are represented in memory so that the correct member of a pair has a higher subjective frequency than the incorrect member. Underwood (106) has extended the frequency interpretation to judgments on pairs of words, and he obtains evidence that frequency information on the pair as a unit can provide the basis for verbal discrimination. Performance is poorer when pairings are broken up than when a pairing is preserved, even though the repairing combines two correct words. Curiously, pre-experimental associations do not seem to influence recognition. Frequency information is assumed to be stored with respect to three classes of events, each of the two individual words plus the pair as a unit.

Kausler, Pavur & Yadrick (53) reinterpret frequency theory by assigning frequency tags to individual features of words. Verbal discrimination learning is considered to be a subclass of recognition memory testing, and is renamed multiple-item recognition learning in contrast to that subclass in which recognition for single words is tested. When the two are compared by having a single-item test follow a verbal discrimination study, prior items designated right had higher hit rates on the recognition test than prior wrong items.

A double-function list in which the same word is right in one pairing and wrong in another is learned very slowly. Frequency theory offers no reason why it should be learned at all, and contingency associations do not seem to be the answer unless heroic efforts are made by the experimenter to elicit them (107). Single image instructions have not helped, nor have compound image instructions been effective. The instruction to make a sentence using both words, the right word always being the subject of the sentence, has been found effective (73).

Even though a single mechanism such as frequency discrimination is the dominant basis for a task, it can be muted in contrived situations, whereupon the subject will find another way. Perhaps more important than such manipulations would be the discovery of how frequency is represented in memory. Are we taxing credulity by suggesting that features of words, the words themselves, and pairs of words all have frequency counters which are incremented at each presentation or rehearsal? Or is a relative frequency determination made at time of testing on samples of recent events? A direct attack on the nature of frequency discrimination should assist in understanding verbal discrimination learning as well as being of interest for its own sake.

FINAL REMARKS

Experimental tasks have a life of their own once a critical momentum has developed, but eventually their vitality weakens as new techniques replace them. In contrast to 20 years ago, there is now little interest in studying lists of nonsense syllables. The trend is to study organization in sets of words, sentences, and paragraphs. For the immediate future there will be a continuation of the current interest in coding techniques and strategies. Research on nonverbal systems and their interaction with verbal systems will further expand. Eventually, one speculates, this will lead to a greater emphasis on the studying of learning and memory in young children. The young adult is too complex to exhibit the beginnings of organized systems. In order to learn how an organized verbal subsystem develops, basing itself on a nonverbal foundation, the most direct way is to study the child. This is arduous labor, however, and most of us will continue to search for intriguing results from more disciplined subjects. We must look to energetic young people to plan and execute the more difficult research.

Literature Cited

1. Anderson, C. M. B., Craik, F. I. M. 1974. The effect of a concurrent task on recall from primary memory. *J. Verb. Learn. Verb. Behav.* 13:107–13
2. Anderson, J. R., Bower, G. H. 1974. A propositional theory of recognition memory. *Mem. Cognit.* 2:406–12
3. Anderson, J. R., Bower, G. H. 1974. Interference in memory for multiple contexts. *Mem. Cognit.* 2:509–14
4. Atkinson, R. C., Herrmann, S. J., Wescourt, K. T. 1974. Search processes in recognition memory. In *Theories in Cognitive Psychology: The Loyola Symposium*, ed. R. L. Solso, pp. 101–46. Potomac, Md: Erlbaum
5. Atkinson, R. C., Shiffrin, R. M. 1968. Human memory: A proposed system and its control processes. In *The Psychology of Learning and Motivation*, ed. K. W. Spence, J. T. Spence, 2:89–195. New York: Academic
6. Atwood, G. 1971. An experimental study of visual imagination and memory. *Cognit. Psychol.* 2:290–99
7. Baddeley, A. D., Grant, S., Wight, E., Thomson, N. 1975. Imagery and visual working memory. In *Attention and Performance*, ed. P. M. A. Rabbitt, S. Dornic, 5:205–17. New York: Academic
8. Baddeley, A. D., Hitch, G. 1974. Working memory. In *The Psychology of Learning and Motivation*, ed. G. H. Bower, 8:47–89
9. Baddeley, A. D., Thomson, N., Buchanan, M. 1975. Word length and the structure of short-term memory. *J. Verb. Learn. Verb. Behav.* 14:575–89
10. Baggett, P. 1975. Memory for explicit and implicit information in picture stories. *J. Verb. Learn. Verb. Behav.* 14:538–48
11. Barclay, J. R., Reid, M. 1974. Characteristics of memory representations of sentence sets describing linear arrays. *J. Verb. Learn. Verb. Behav.* 13:133–37

12. Bellezza, F. S., Walker, R. J. 1974. Storage-coding trade-off in short-term store. *J. Exp. Psychol.* 102:629–33
13. Bennett, R. W. 1975. Proactive interference in short-term memory: Fundamental forgetting processes. *J. Verb. Learn. Verb. Behav.* 14:123–44
14. Bennett, R. W., Bennett, I. F. 1974. PI release as a function of the number of prerelease trials. *J. Verb. Learn. Verb. Behav.* 13:573–84
15. Bjork, R. A. 1975. Short-term storage: The ordered output of a central processor. In *Cognitive Theory*, ed. F. R. Restle, R. M. Shiffrin, N. J. Castellan, H. R. Lindman, D. B. Pisoni, 1:151–71. Hillsdale, NJ: Erlbaum
16. Cermak, L. S. 1974. Recall of antonyms from short-term memory. *J. Exp. Psychol.* 102:740–42
17. Chow, S. L., Murdock, B. B. Jr. 1975. The effect of a subsidiary task on iconic memory. *Mem. Cognit.* 3:678–88
18. Ciccone, D. S., Brelsford, J. W. 1974. Interpresentation lag and rehearsal mode in recognition memory. *J. Exp. Psychol.* 103:900–6
19. Cole, R. A., Sales, B. D., Haber, R. N. 1974. Mechanisms of aural encoding: VII. Differences in consonant-vowel recall in a Peterson and Peterson short-term memory paradigm. *Mem. Cognit.* 2:211–14
20. Coltheart, M. 1975. Iconic memory: A reply to Professor Holding. *Mem. Cognit.* 3:42–48
21. Craik, F. I. M., Jacoby, L. L. 1975. A process view of short-term retention. See Ref. 15, pp. 173–92
22. Craik, F. I. M., Kirsner, K. 1974. The effect of speaker's voice on word recognition. *Q. J. Exp. Psychol.* 26:274–84
23. Craik, F. I. M., Lockhart, R. S. 1972. Levels of processing: A framework for memory research. *J. Verb. Learn. Verb. Behav.* 12:599–607
24. Craik, F. I. M., Tulving, E. 1975. Depth

of processing and the retention of words in episodic memory. *J. Exp. Psychol. Gen.* 104:268–94

25. Crowder, R. G. 1975. Inferential problems in echoic memory. See Ref. 7, pp. 218–29

26. Darley, C. F., Glass, A. L. 1975. Effects of rehearsal and serial list position on recall. *J. Exp. Psychol. Hum. Learn. Mem.* 1:453–58

27. Darwin, C. J., Baddeley, A. D. 1974. Acoustic memory and the perception of speech. *Cognit. Psychol.* 6:41–60

28. Dillon, R. F., Bittner, L. A. 1975. Analysis of retrieval cues and release from proactive inhibition. *J. Verb. Learn. Verb. Behav.* 14:616–22

29. Dillon, R. F., Thomas, H. 1975. The role of response confusion in proactive interference. *J. Verb. Learn. Verb. Behav.* 14:603–15

30. Elmes, D. G., Bjork, R. A. 1975. The interaction of encoding and rehearsal processes in the recall of repeated and nonrepeated items. *J. Verb. Learn. Verb. Behav.* 14:30–42

31. Engle, R. W. 1974. The modality effect: Is precategorical acoustic storage responsible? *J. Exp. Psychol.* 102:824–29

32. Estes, W. K. 1973. Phonemic coding and rehearsal in short-term memory. *J. Verb. Learn. Verb. Behav.* 12:360–72

33. Franks, J. J., Bransford, J. D. 1974. A brief note on linguistic integration. *J. Verb. Learn. Verb. Behav.* 13:217–19

34. Fuchs, A. H., Melton, A. W. 1974. Effects of frequency of presentation and stimulus length on retention in the Brown-Peterson paradigm. *J. Exp. Psychol.* 103:629–37

35. Gardiner, J. M. 1974. Levels of processing in word recognition and subsequent free recall. *J. Exp. Psychol.* 102:101–5

36. Gardiner, J. M., Thompson, C. P., Maskarinec, A. S. 1974. Negative recency in initial free recall. *J. Exp. Psychol.* 103:71–78

37. Goggin, J., Riley, D. A. 1974. Maintenance of interference in short-term memory. *J. Exp. Psychol.* 102:1027–34

38. Griffith, D. 1975. Comparison of control processes for recognition and recall. *J. Exp. Psychol. Hum. Learn. Mem.* 1:223–28

39. Harcum, E. R. 1975. *Serial Learning and Paralearning.* New York: Wiley. 448 pp.

40. Hasher, L., Johnson, M. K. 1975. Interpretive factors in forgetting. *J. Exp. Psychol. Hum. Learn. Mem.* 1:567–75

41. Hintzman, D. L. 1974. Theoretical implications of the spacing effect. See Ref. 4, pp. 77–99

42. Hintzman, D. L., Summers, J. J., Block, R. A. 1975. What causes the spacing effect? Some effects of repetition, duration, and spacing on memory for pictures. *Mem. Cognit.* 3:287–94

43. Hintzman, D. L., Summers, J. J., Eki, N. T., Moore, M. D. 1975. *Mem. Cognit.* 3:576–80

44. Hitch, G. J. 1975. The role of attention in visual and auditory suffix effects. *Mem. Cognit.* 3:501–5

45. Holding, D. H. 1975. Sensory storage reconsidered. *Mem. Cognit.* 3:31–41

46. Holding, D. H. 1975. A rejoinder. *Mem. Cognit.* 3:49–50

47. Humphreys, M. S. 1975. The derivation of endpoint and distance effects in linear orderings from frequency information. *J. Verb. Learn. Verb. Behav.* 14:496–505

48. Jacoby, L. L. 1974. The role of mental contiguity in memory: Registration and retrieval effects. *J. Verb. Learn. Verb. Behav.* 13:483–496

49. Jacoby, L. L. 1975. Physical features vs meaning: A difference in decay. *Mem. Cognit.* 3:247–51

50. Jones, M. R., Zamostny, K. P. 1975. Memory and rule structure in the prediction of serial patterns. *J. Exp. Psychol. Hum. Learn. Mem.* 1:295–306

51. Katz, S., Atkeson, B., Lee, J. 1974. The Bransford-Franks linear effect: Integration or artifact? *Mem. Cognit.* 2:709–13

52. Katz, S., Gruenewald, P. 1974. The abstraction of linguistic ideas in "meaningless" sentences. *Mem. Cognit.* 2: 737–41

53. Kausler, D. H., Pavur, E. J., Yadrick, R. M. 1975. Single-item recognition following a verbal discrimination study trial. *Mem. Cognit.* 3:135–39

54. Kintsch, W. 1974. *The Representation of Meaning in Memory.* Hillsdale, NJ: Erlbaum. 279 pp.

55. Kolers, P. A. 1975. Memorial consequences of automatized encoding. *J. Exp. Psychol. Hum. Learn. Mem.* 1:689–701

56. Kolers, P. A., Ostry, D. J. 1974. Time course of loss of information regarding pattern analyzing operations. *J. Verb. Learn. Verb. Behav.* 13:599–612

57. Kosslyn, S. M. 1975. Information representation in visual images. *Cognit. Psychol.* 7:341–70

58. Kroll, N. E. A. 1975. Visual short-term memory. In *Short-term Memory,* ed. D.

Deutsch, J. A. Deutsch, pp. 153–79. New York: Academic

59. Kroll, N. E. A., Kellicut, M. H., Parks, T. E. 1975. Rehearsal of visual and auditory stimuli while shadowing. *J. Exp. Psychol. Hum. Learn. Mem.* 1:215–22

60. Landauer, T. K. 1974. Consolidation in human memory: Retrograde amnestic effects of confusable items in paired-associate learning. *J. Verb. Learn. Verb. Behav.* 13:45–53

61. Levy, B. A., Craik, F. I. M. 1975. The co-ordination of codes in short-term retention. *Q. J. Exp. Psychol.* 27:33–45

62. Light, L. L., Berger, D. E. 1974. Memory for modality: Within-modality discrimination is not automatic. *J. Exp. Psychol.* 103:854–60

63. Light, L. L., Kimble, G. A., Pellegrino, J. W. 1975. Comments on *Episodic Memory: When recognition fails*, by Watkins and Tulving. *J. Exp. Psychol. Gener.* 104:30–36

64. Loftus, G. R., Patterson, K. K. 1975. Components of short-term proactive interference. *J. Verb. Learn. Verb. Behav.* 14:105–21

65. Lorayne, H., Lucas, J. 1974. *The Memory Book.* New York: Stein & Day

66. Mandler, G., Worden, P. E., Graesser, A. C. II. 1974. Subjective disorganization: Search for the locus of list organization. *J. Verb. Learn. Verb. Behav.* 13:220–35

67. Martin, E. 1974. Serial learning: A multilevel access analysis. *Mem. Cognit.* 2:322–28

68. Martin, E. 1975. Generation-recognition theory and the encoding specificity principle. *Psychol. Rev.* 82:150–53

69. Martin, E., Noreen, D. L. 1974. Serial learning: Identification of subjective subsequences. *Cognit. Psychol.* 6:421–35

70. Mazuryk, G. F., Lockhart, R. S. 1974. Negative recency and levels of processing in free recall. *Can. J. Psychol.* 28:114–23

71. Moeser, S. D. 1975. The integration of verbal ideas. *Can. J. Psychol.* 29:106–23

72. Moyer, R. S. 1973. Comparing objects in memory: Evidence suggesting an internal psychophysics. *Percept. Psychophys.* 13:180–84

73. Mueller, J. H., Kausler, D. H., Yadrick, R. M., Pavur, E. J. 1975. Encoding strategies in double-function verbal discrimination learning. *J. Exp. Psychol. Hum. Learn. Mem.* 1:55–59

74. Murdock, B. B. Jr., Anderson, R. E., Ho, E. 1974. Effects of presentation order on learning in multitrial free recall. *J. Verb. Learn. Verb. Behav.* 13:522–29

75. Okada, R., Carey, S. T. 1974. Whole-list retention following whole-part learning. *J. Exp. Psychol.* 102:332–34

76. Paivio, A. 1974. Spacing of repetitions in the incidental and free recall of pictures and words. *J. Verb. Learn. Verb. Behav.* 13:497–511

77. Paivio, A. 1975. Perceptual comparisons through the mind's eye. *Mem. Cognit.* 3:635–47

78. Pellegrino, J. W., Battig, W. F. 1974. Relationships among higher order organizational measures and free recall. *J. Exp. Psychol.* 102:463–72

79. Pellegrino, J. W., Salzberg, P. M. 1975. Encoding specificity in associative processing tasks. *J. Exp. Psychol. Hum. Learn. Mem.* 1:538–48

80. Pellegrino, J. W., Siegel, A. W., Dhawan, M. 1975. Short-term retention of pictures and words: Evidence for dual coding systems. *J. Exp. Psychol. Hum. Learn. Mem.* 1:95–102

81. Peterson, M. J. 1975. The retention of imagined and seen spatial matrices. *Cognit. Psychol.* 7:181–93

82. Petrich, J. A., Pellegrino, J. W., Dhawan, M. 1975. The role of list information in free-recall transfer. *J. Exp. Psychol. Hum. Learn. Mem.* 1:326–36

83. Pisoni, D. 1975. Auditory short-term memory and vowel perception. *Mem. Cognit.* 3:7–18

84. Postman, L. 1975. Verbal learning and memory. *Ann. Rev. Psychol.* 26:291–335

85. Postman, L. 1975. Tests of the generality of the principle of encoding specificity. *Mem. Cognit.* 3:663–72

86. Postman, L., Stark, K., Burns, S. 1974. Sources of proactive inhibition on unpaced tests of retention. *Am. J. Psychol.* 87:33–56

87. Potts, G. R. 1974. Storing and retrieving information about ordered relationships. *J. Exp. Psychol.* 103:431–39

88. Powell, G. D., Hamon, T. G., Young, R. K. 1975. Selective encoding interference in paired-associate learning. *J. Exp. Psychol. Hum. Learn. Mem.* 1:473–79

89. Reder, L. M., Anderson, J. R., Bjork, R. A. 1974. A semantic interpretation of encoding specificity. *J. Exp. Psychol.* 102:648–56

90. Reitman, J. S. 1974. Without surreptitious rehearsal, information in short-term memory decays. *J. Verb. Learn. Verb. Behav.* 13:365–67

91. Roediger, H. L. III, Crowder, R. G. 1975. The spacing of lists in free recall. *J. Verb. Learn. Verb. Behav.* 14:590–602
92. Santa, J. L., Lamwers, L. L. 1974. Encoding specificity: Fact or artifact. *J. Verb. Learn. Verb. Behav.* 13:412–23
93. Scholz, K. W., Potts, G. R. 1974. Cognitive processing of linear orderings. *J. Exp. Psychol.* 102:323–26
94. Schulman, A. I. 1974. Memory for words recently classified. *Mem. Cognit.* 2:47–52
95. Shaffer, W., Shiffrin, R. 1972. Rehearsal and storage of visual information. *J. Exp. Psychol.* 92:292–96
96. Shiffrin, R. M. 1975. Short-term store: The basis for a memory system. See Ref. 15, pp. 193–218
97. Small, D. W. 1975. The abstraction of arbitrary categories. *Mem. Cognit.* 3:581–85
98. Sternberg, R. J., Bower, G. H. 1974. Transfer in part-whole and whole-part free recall: A comparative evaluation of theories. *J. Verb. Learn. Verb. Behav.* 13:1–26
99. Thomson, D. M., Tulving, E. 1970. Associative encoding and retrieval: Weak and strong cues. *J. Exp. Psychol.* 86:255–62
100. Till, R. E., Diehl, R. L., Jenkins, J. J. 1975. Effects of semantic and nonsemantic cued orienting tasks on associative clustering in free recall. *Mem. Cognit.* 3:19–23
101. Tulving, E. 1972. Episodic and semantic memory. In *Organization and Memory*, ed. E. Tulving, W. Donaldson, pp. 381–403. New York: Academic
102. Tulving, E., Colotla, V. 1970. Free recall of trilingual lists. *Cognit. Psychol.* 1:86–98
103. Tulving, E., Thomson, D. M. 1973. Encoding specificity and retrieval processes in episodic memory. *Psychol. Rev.* 80:352–73
104. Tversky, B., Sherman, T. 1975. Picture memory improves with longer on time and off time. *J. Exp. Psychol. Hum. Learn. Mem.* 1:114–18

105. Underwood, B. J. 1972. Are we overloading memory? In *Coding Processes in Human Memory*, ed. A. W. Melton, E. Martin, pp. 1–23. New York: Winston-Wiley
106. Underwood, B. J. 1974. The role of the association in recognition memory. *J. Exp. Psychol. Monogr.* 102:917–39
107. Underwood, B. J., Reichardt, C. S. 1975. Contingent associations and the double-function, verbal-discrimination task. *Mem. Cognit.* 3:311–14
108. Underwood, B. J., Reichardt, C. S., Malmi, R. A. 1975. Sources of facilitation in learning conceptually structured paired-associate lists. *J. Exp. Psychol. Hum. Learn. Mem.* 1:160–66
109. Watkins, M. J. 1974. Concept and measurement of primary memory. *Psychol. Bull.* 81:695–711
110. Watkins, M. J., Tulving, E. 1975. Episodic memory: When recognition fails. *J. Exp. Psychol. Gener.* 104:5–29
111. Watkins, M. J., Tulving, E. 1975. Recall and recognition: A reply to Light, Kimble, and Pellegrino. *J. Exp. Psychol. Gener.* 104:37–38
112. Weaver, G. E. 1974. Effects of poststimulus study time on recognition of pictures. *J. Exp. Psychol.* 103:799–801
113. Weber, R. J., Harnish, R. 1974. Visual imagery for words: The Hebb test. *J. Exp. Psychol.* 102:409–14
114. Wickens, D. D. 1972. Characteristics of word encoding. See Ref. 109, pp. 191–215
115. Wickens, D. D., Contrucci, J. J. 1974. The effects of formal and acoustic repetition in the Brown-Peterson paradigm. *Mem. Cognit.* 2:581–84
116. Wickens, D. D., Gittis, M. M. 1974. The temporal course of recovery from interference and degree of learning in the Brown-Peterson paradigm. *J. Exp. Psychol.* 102:1021–26
117. Woodward, A. E., Bjork, R. A., Jongeward, R. H. Jr. 1973. Recall and recognition as a function of primary rehearsal. *J. Verb. Learn. Verb. Behav.* 12:608–17

Ann. Rev. Psychol. 1977. 28:417–59
Copyright © 1977 by Annual Reviews Inc. *All rights reserved*

INSTRUCTIONAL PSYCHOLOGY ♦279

M. C. Wittrock

University of California, Los Angeles, California 90024

Arthur A. Lumsdaine

University of Washington, Seattle, Washington 98195

INTRODUCTION

Since the days of E. L. Thorndike, educational psychology has actively contributed to the construction and testing of theory in psychology. As a part of educational psychology, the study of instruction provides a socially significant context of interest to experimental psychologists studying learning, perception, attention, motivation, and memory, and to differential psychologists studying individual differences in relation to instructional variables and treatments. Instructional psychology also provides opportunities to test the utility and robustness of models and concepts derived from either of these fields of psychology. With its social significance and its broad appeal to psychologists of different specialities, instructional psychology continues to be involved in important developments and shifts in psychological research.

Since 1900, some of the leading discoveries made by behavioristic and cognitively oriented psychologists occurred in the study of the problems of instructing children or adults. The fundamental studies include research by E. L. Thorndike and C. Judd on transfer of learning, by M. Wertheimer on meaningful learning and problem solving, by E. R. Guthrie on temporal contiguity, by B. F. Skinner on operant conditioning, and by J. S. Bruner and D. P. Ausubel on perceptual and cognitive processes in meaningful learning and school curricula. The work by R. M. Gagné, R. Glaser, A. W. Melton, and others on the design of training facilities continued the tradition.

Instructional psychology is now involved in a notable shift of emphasis in psychological research and theory. The shift pervades much of the recent research on instruction and provides a theme for this chapter. Peripheralism and associationism, which were two of the bases of twentieth century behaviorism (Strike 230), were also two of the foundations upon which the study of instruction and the practice of American education were built during the period between 1900–1955. With the

417

addition of a nonintrospective empirical methodology and a carefully restricted lexicon chosen to describe the characteristics of observable stimuli and measurable behavioral responses, associationism fostered behaviorism in America.

The recent shift of interest from behaviorism to cognitive psychology has sometimes been misunderstood as a move away from associationism, empirical rigor, and from much of the data accumulated in the first half of the twentieth century. Instead, the shift of interest is away from the peripheralism of reinforcement theory, which was never a part of Aristotelian associationism nor of nineteenth century British associationism. In his work "On Memory and Recollection," Aristotle (9, pp. 287–313) used imagery as the basis of memory, and associations and order as the bases of recollection or retrieval. The British associationists also described associations in mentalistic or cognitive terms.

The current shift emphasizes the study of central cognitive and affective associationistic and holistic processes by which the learner selects, transforms, and encodes the nominal characteristics of experience into functional, meaningful internal representations. A cognitive perspective implies that a behavioral analysis of instruction is often inadequate to explain the effects of instruction upon learning. From a cognitive perspective, to understand the effects of instruction upon learning and memory one must comprehend how learners use their cognitive processes, knowledge, abilities, aptitudes, and interests to transform the nominal stimuli of instruction into functional ones. These cognitive processes include attention, motivation, verbal and imaginal encoding, storage, and retrieval. The shift helps to bring together experimental psychology and differential psychology.

The shift to greater emphasis on the study of cognitive processes has important implications for changing teaching and instruction. If learning is conceived primarily as a change in behavior due to reinforced practice, instruction would often be designed to provide differential reinforcement of the correct behavior in the presence of the appropriate environmental stimuli. Laboratories, such as those constructed by psychologists and used by the armed forces during and after the Second World War to teach complicated technical skills to nonspecialists, demonstrated one utility of a behavioristic model of instruction.

By contrast, a cognitive approach emphasizes the elaborations which the learner performs on information more than the features of instruction. Cognitive approaches emphasize that one can learn by observing others, by watching a model, by viewing a demonstration, by listening to a lecture, by being told, by reading a book, by constructing images, and by elaborating words into sentences. In brief, cognitive approaches emphasize that one can learn without practice or reinforcement of overt behavior, and that one may learn by actively changing perceptions of experience, by constructing new meanings and interpretations of events.

The recent cognitive shift has been evident long enough now for us to evaluate some of its effects upon the study of instruction. In the following pages we review some of the studies which characterize the research in instructional psychology from 1973 to 1975. See McKeachie's previous review (162) of instructional psychology from 1970 to 1972 and, for additional relevant background, the immediately preceding review of the topic by Glaser & Resnick (90a) and the closely related earlier review by Lumsdaine & May (152a) dealing with educational media.

ATTENTION

Adjunct Questions

Following up earlier studies conducted in the 1950s and reported by May & Lumsdaine (158, Chapters 6 and 7) and by Lumsdaine (150a, Chapter 17–19), research in subject matter or other prose learning frequently has found that questions inserted into instructional material influence its retention. Adjunct prequestions, i.e. ones inserted in the text before the presentation of material containing the answer to the question, often increase learning or retention of the specific kinds of information to which the questions direct the students' attention, but commonly reduce learning or retention of other information presented. Compared with adjunct prequestions, adjunct postquestions may sometimes facilitate learning and retention of related material as well as material specifically asked about. However, on tests of nonverbatim learning, control groups given no adjunct questions may do as well or better than the groups given adjunct pre- or postquestions. In a review of relevant research, Ladas (135) finds little support for the notion that adjunct questions facilitate comprehensive learning (i.e. on material not specifically asked about). See Lumsdaine (152) for a discussion comparing more recent and earlier findings on adjunct questions.

The explanations commonly given in the literature for the different effects of adjunct pre- and postquestions point to differences in how they function. Prequestions would seem to work by focusing attention upon queried aspects of material, while postquestions would work mainly by stimulating, shaping, and reinforcing rehearsal or review of the previously presented material.

The research conducted during the interval reviewed here continues to investigate this attentional hypothesis and the review and rehearsal hypothesis. Swenson & Kulhavy (235) found that with elementary school children adjunct postquestions facilitated retention of the previously questioned materials and of other information in the text. Boker (19) found that postquestions facilitated verbatim and nonverbatim retention of information, while prequestions facilitated learning and retention of material specifically asked about, but depressed the retention of information not specific to the questions asked. Snowman & Cunningham (226) and Bull & Dizney (29) give similar interpretations to their results.

The authors of the studies frequently asked why adjunct questions affect learners in the reported way. With postquestions, the answers are not clear. They did not seem to reduce retroactive inhibition (Walker 247); nor did they appear to increase learning to learn (Voss 245). Rothkopf & Billington (206) report that they found only "an extremely small effect" to support their hypothesis that attempts to recall postquestioned materials result in the retrieval and indirect review of related material.

With prequestions, however, the recent data appear amenable to clearer explanations. Frase (74) explains the effects of prequestions by a selective attention model, which is consistent with his finding that question-specific recall was higher than recall of other information from the passages. Boyd (22) also finds the effects of prequestions to be consistent with a selective attention model. Koran & Koran (131) report that prequestions increased retention only of specific answers to the adjunct questions. In sum, the hypotheses currently advanced to explain the effects of postquestions by retroactive or backward working rehearsal or retrieval processes are not conclusively supported by the data at this time. With prequestions, the studies support a selective attention model.

Within the last several years, studies using adjunct questions other than narrowly factual ones are increasing in frequency in the literature. With broader, more interpretive questions, the effects of adjunct questions may be different from those reported using narrow, factual questions. Rickards & DiVesta (194) found that unlike factual ones, pre- and postquestions involving meaningful processing increased retention broadly. Mayer (160), studying mathematics learning, found that adjunct questions serve to direct attention to the goals of instruction. He found no backward or retrieval effect due to adjunct questions. Not surprisingly, the broader or more comprehensive the questions, the broader was the learning he found. Felker & Dapra (71) found that questions which involved applying a model broadly facilitated learning, while more specific questions about definitions or calculations narrowed learning. They also found that comprehension questions, whether in pre- or in post-position, provided the greatest facilitation of problem solving. Bull & Dizney (29) found that curiosity enhancing prequestions, more than factual prequestions, facilitated retention.

The findings about adjunct questions suggest one hypothesis that is consistent with many of the recently reported studies. The hypothesis is that pre- and post-adjunct questions produce most of their effects upon retention by selectively affecting attention. From this model we might expect prequestions to be more effective than postquestions at directing attention to the exact answers specified in the questions. With factual prequestions, learning would be greatest for the specific, cued information. On the other hand, factual postquestions would not be as effective as factual prequestions at directing attention to the cued facts but, in addition to rehearsing previously presented facts, could influence attention in the paragraphs which follow the embedded questions. The result would be a broader learning, which would include the general class of factual material in the passage. These results are commonly found in the recent literature.

According to the same selective attentional model, if the learner possesses appropriate background knowledge and aptitude, thought-provoking adjunct questions which emphasize comprehension or inference should facilitate meaningful processing of the information relevant to the theme, concept, or organization cued by the question. Adjunct questions given before, rather than after, the relevant materials to be learned could be expected to be better at facilitating learning of the theme, concept, or organization identified by the question. Questions given after the relevant material should direct attention to related material in the subsequent paragraphs, and consequently should again produce broader, more divergent learning of the related materials and less learning of the specific theme identified in the question.

In four attempts to obtain deep or meaningful processing, Anderson & Biddle (8) compared verbatim with paraphrased test questions, which they called adjunct questions. Generally, the authors failed to enhance retention or meaningful processing with paraphrased test questions not embedded in the text. Andre and Sola ("Imagery, Levels of Processing, and Retention of Meaningful Sentences," in preparation) maintained that to facilitate meaningful processing and transfer, Anderson & Biddle's paraphrased test questions or directions should have been embedded in the learning materials so that the learner could have modified the processing of them after the initial test items. In essence, the questions or test items then can function as prequestions, directing later processing. The research supported Andre and Sola's hypothesis. Their embedded paraphrased test items enhanced learning of the concept relevant to the earlier items. Their results agree with a selective attention model.

As a part of the recent evolution toward the study of the internal processes of learning from instruction, most of the research on adjunct questions has contributed to an understanding of the attentional processes in the learning of factual information. In research on adjunct questions, additional studies of the encoding and meaningful processing of themes, concepts, and complex organizations are needed. See Norman's chapter on the role of memory and knowledge in the answering of questions (177, pp. 160–64) for implications for teaching which follow from a model of encoding and retrieval.

Stating Objectives

The giving of precisely defined behavioral objectives to the learner has often been considered appropriate for enhancing many kinds of learning. Recently, however, researchers are beginning to question the value of giving learners very precisely defined behavioral objectives. How do specific and general objectives differentially affect learning? Should we not expect objectives to affect selective attention, somewhat as adjunct questions influence it?

Attention does seem to be influenced by goals or objectives. Samuels & Dahl (214) found that fourth graders and college students increased their reading rate by about 100 or 170 words per minute respectively when their purpose for reading was to learn general rather than detailed information. Objectives also direct attention to information which might be ignored. Duell (61) supported the hypothesis that behaviorally defined objectives function by selectively directing attention to information which would not otherwise be considered important. See also earlier results reported by May & Lumsdaine (158, Chapter 7).

In a comparison of objectives placed before or after a text, reminiscent of the studies on pre- and postquestions, Kaplan & Simmons (125) found that information directly relevant to the objectives was learned well in either condition, but information not directly relevant to the specific objectives was learned better when the objectives came after the text. The above findings agree with a selective attention model in which the objectives orient the students to learn specified material and thereby direct them away from learning other material.

A complex issue in the literature is the relation between the specificity of objectives and the breadth of learning. Specific objectives often increase the learning of information peculiar to them, sometimes without decreasing the learning of related prose material (Rothkopf & Kaplan 208). Kaplan & Rothkopf (124) and Kaplan (123) report that specific objectives increased learning of material directly relevant to the objectives and sometimes of other material as well. Gagné & Rothkopf (86) report that compared with general directions to learn, learning goals substantially increased the learning of material relevant to the goals, provided the material closely followed the goal.

Other studies again show (see 158) that giving objectives reduces the learning of material not directly relevant to them. Frase & Kreitzberg (76) found that precise reference in directions to the words of, rather than to the topics of, the text enhanced the learning of information specific to those words, but reduced learning of other information. Duchastel & Brown (59) found that objectives facilitated the learning of information relevant to the objectives, but decreased learning not specified in the objectives. Rothkopf & Billington (207) found the recall of factual information relevant to the goal to be independent of related but not directly relevant information.

In sum, the findings indicate that stating objectives to students often facilitates the learning of information directly relevant to them. Even that issue is complicated (Duchastel & Merrill 60). The findings about the learning of information not directly relevant to the objectives are inconsistent, sometimes indicating that specific objectives narrow learning to directly relevant information.

The breadth of learning may be different with more complex conceptual subject matter such as mathematics. In a field test of a mathematics curriculum, Ehrenpreis & Scandura (66) found that when children learned only the higher order nonspecific rules, they performed better than the children taught the more specific rules. The higher order rules were better for solving problems involving either the more specific rules or the rules beyond the scope of either curriculum. The background knowledge and information processing strategies of the learner also probably influenced the way objectives function.

It is clear, however, that giving the learner behaviorally defined, specific or narrow objectives has not fulfilled its early promise. Objectives sometimes do not facilitate comprehensive learning, apparently because they are effective at selectively directing attention. They are tedious to construct, and they often constrain teachers to narrow their conceptually oriented instruction to the attainment of measurable but trivial ends.

Although it oversimplifies the complexity of the processes of learning in these studies, a selective attention model explains many of the recent findings about adjunct questions and objectives. To build a deeper understanding of how learners comprehend the information in a text, one should construct comprehensive models of the learning and the recall of prose, such as Frase (75) has developed. We suggest relating the research on prose learning to the research on encoding and to the research in reading. We also suggest further study of prose learning in educationally relevant subject matter areas, such as the areas studied by J. Scandura, F. DiVesta, R. Mayer, and their associates. With conceptually organized subject matter, the effects of questions, objectives, and directions may be different than they are with the texts commonly used in the research studies. See Duchastel & Merrill (60) for a review of related research.

Delay of Gratification

One last line of research colorfully illustrates the effects of selective attention upon children's learning and motivation. Mischel and associates have conducted an interesting series of experiments on the control of the attentional and motivational processes involved in the delay of gratification. They found that preschool children waited longer for rewards they preferred when they were distracted from the rewards (Mischel, Ebbesen & Zeiss 169) or when they imagined that the food rewards were nonedible objects, such as when they pretended that marshmallows were white clouds (Mischel & Baker 168). Their research illustrates some of the instructional implications which one may derive from the recent research on attention. Instructions can also be useful, practical ways to direct the learners' attention, and to help them to transform, elaborate, or reorganize information.

One important implication from the recent research on cognitive processes in selective attention is that learning depends upon the learners' perceptions and interpretations of the events they encounter. Further, instructors can often modify these perceptions and interpretations with adjunct questions, objectives, and instructions which selectively influence attention.

MOTIVATION

The recent research on attributional processes, locus of control, and cognitive reinterpretations of reinforcement theory reports findings important for changing instruction. The instructor's role changes if he perceives himself to be responsible for changing the learner's inappropriate attribution of success or failure. The instructor's role also changes when he realizes he can help the learner to attend selectively to information and to construct meaning from it. The learner's role in instruction changes if he holds himself responsible for learning. The meaning of reinforcement also changes if its effects depend upon its perceived informational and affective qualities, upon whether the learner relates them to his effort, ability, or luck.

Attribution

Attribution theorists such as F. Heider, H. Kelley, J. Rotter, and B. Weiner study perceptions of causality. Weiner (248) states that performance depends upon the perceived causes of success or failure to learn. Success which the learner attributes to his ability, a stable internal cause, will not be reinforcing and will not increase perseverance. Success attributed to effort, an unstable internal cause, will increase motivation to continue to learn. Similarly, failure attributed to unstable external factors will not reduce motivation to learn; but ascription of failure to lack of ability will reduce motivation.

For the improvement of instruction, attribution theory implies that some unsuccessful students may need to learn to ascribe their failure to lack of effort rather than to low ability. Heckhausen (104) trained 12 teachers of fourth graders to teach their underachieving students with high fear of failure to expend more effort at school-work and to attribute their lack of success to lack of sufficient effort. As a result, student scores on the speeded Primary Mental Abilities subtests increased, as did student ascription of failure to lack of effort. Dweck (64) taught elementary school children who had high expectancies of failure to attribute them to lack of effort and to succeed better than a success-only group in difficult situations later.

It is important to remember that increased effort may not be sufficient to enhance achievement. The added effort must lead to success for the attribution training programs to increase learning.

Several studies examined the attributions of student successes and failures made by teachers. In a study of attributions made by female undergraduates as teachers, Ames (5) found that the undergraduates held themselves responsible for student failures, but credited student successes to student ability. In a study of male and female undergraduates teaching fictitious students, the teachers were more self-serving, accepting credit for success but not blame for failure. In the same study, Brandt, Hayden & Brophy (24) also found that female undergraduates classified as having an internal locus of control more frequently held themselves responsible for student learning than did females classified as having an external locus of control. Male undergraduates showed no such difference. Brandt & Hayden (23) report that male and female teachers ascribe motivation differently to successful and unsuccessful over and underachievers.

The differences between the Ames study and the latter two studies may be due to the use of real and fictitious learners. In natural situations, teachers may be less defensive than when they must deal only with data given them by an experimenter. Beckman (13) reports that female teachers and student teachers attributed the deteriorating performance of the child they were teaching to situational factors or to themselves. Increases in student performance were attributed to the teacher, not to the situation. A constant outcome, i.e. no change in the child, was attributed to factors external to the teacher.

Locus of Control

In an area closely related to the studies mentioned above, Rotter's concept of internality, or locus of control, has led to interesting research on the improvement of instruction. DeCharms (50) introduced "origin" training to make origins out of pawns, e.g. to produce children with internal rather than external loci of control respectively. In a field study with 720 sixth graders, deCharms (51) reports that an origin training program increased achievement motivation, increased scores on all scales of the Iowa Test of Basic Skills, and reduced tardiness and absences from school. In a more recent study, deCharms (52) describes an elaborate training program for teachers which increases student achievement by increasing their internal locus of control.

Parent et al (182) found that college students high on internal locus of control learned computer programming better under low-discipline conditions, while students high on external locus of control learned better with highly disciplined conditions. However, Johnson & Croft (120), who also used Rotter's I-E (Internal-

External) scale to measure locus of control in learners, found that in a personalized system of instruction, locus of control was not related to learning. In another study, Gozali et al (94) found that when they were taking a verbal ability test, internals more than externals used time systematically and in relation to the difficulty of items. Apparently, if one perceives outcomes to be affected by one's actions rather than by luck, then time is used more discriminately in relation to the problems. Although it is unrelated to ability, locus of control could be related to achievement for the above reason.

In a Keller personalized instruction class, students with an external locus of control, compared with students with an internal locus of control, contracted for and earned lower grades, showed more state anxiety, and did worse on a final examination. Allen, Giat & Cherney (2) found that in a graduate school of business, locus of control was one of several useful predictors of academic success. But when children determined their own academic standards for reinforcement, learning was no better than it was when yoked children tried to achieve the same standards externally imposed (Nord, Connelly & Diagnault 176).

The role of success and praise in relation to locus of control has been studied recently. MacMillan & Wright (153) induced success and failure among second, fourth, and sixth graders. Failure tended to increase outerdirectedness, which declined with increasing age. Lintner & Ducette (149) found that male but not female elementary school children with an external locus of control were responsive to praise on some tasks.

Paton, Walberg & Yeh (184) noted that with most minority groups other than orientals the data of the Coleman report indicated that variance in academic achievement was significantly correlated with a sense of environmental control, which is akin to Rotter's concept of internality. From questionnaire data, more black students than whites reported that they are capable of learning, but more blacks than whites reported that luck is more important than hard work for attaining success in school.

Intrinsic Motivation

DeCharms (50) proposed that we are intrinsically motivated when we perceive ourselves as the causes of our behavior. When we perceive forces external to ourselves to be the causes of our behavior we are extrinsically motivated. From his model of motivation, he hypothesizes that the addition of extrinsic rewards to intrinsically motivating activities decreases intrinsic motivation. Most of the relevant studies support the interesting hypothesis (e.g. Deci, Cascio & Krusell 54; Lepper & Greene 138; Lepper, Greene & Nisbett 139). Notz (178) reviews 15 of the recent relevant studies and finds support for the hypothesis. However, Calder & Staw (32) are critical of some of the recent studies. In agreement with Notz's summary, Levine & Fasnacht (146) reviewed the recent research on token rewards and concluded that the addition of extrinsic rewards to an intrinsically motivating activity reduces its intrinsic motivation.

When one interprets the above findings, it is important to remember that Deci, Lepper, Greene, and others are studying activities which are intrinsically motivating, while the typical activities encountered in studies of token rewards are not intrinsically motivating. The different findings of the two lines of research do not necessarily conflict with each other.

For instruction, the recent research on intrinsic motivation and locus of control implies that extrinsic rewards should not be added to intrinsically motivating instructional activities. At a deeper level, the research on locus of control and attribution theory implies that instruction should be designed to enable the learners to attribute success or failure to their effort or lack of it, respectively, not to external causes, such as the environment, the instructor, or luck.

The research on attribution theory, locus of control, and intrinsic motivation suggests that profound changes in instruction are needed. To develop learners with internal loci of control, rather than to design the learners' environment to control and to reward their learning, requires fundamental changes in approach to motivation in many instructional contexts. See the recent volume by Deci (53) on intrinsic motivation and the research cited above by deCharms and by Weiner for further discussion.

Reinforcement

The research on reinforcement addressed two different classes of problems. The first problem is the empirical effects of reinforcers upon learning and achievement. The second class of problem is a reinterpretation of the theory of reinforcement.

Research on the effects of reinforcement in instruction continues to yield interesting findings. In some studies reinforcement increased appropriate classroom behavior through a contingency management program (Thompson et al 239) and through a token reinforcement program (Kazdin 126). In other studies token reinforcement brought token learning, that is, a decrease in intrinsic motivation that occurred when extrinsic motives were first added to intrinsic ones and later withdrawn (Levine & Fasnacht 146). As a reinforcer, free time increased accuracy in three academic areas (Marholin, McInnis & Heads 154). Praise did not increase Stanford-Binet IQ scores among disadvantaged children (Quay 189), but reward did increase scores on the Figural Form A of the Torrance Tests of Creative Thinking when taken by disadvantaged learners (Johnson 116). Success feedback led to higher scores on the nonverbal battery of the Lorge-Thorndike intelligence test than did failure feedback (Bridgeman 27). Black or white teachers reinforced other race youngsters more than same race youngsters, male youngsters more than females, and black female youngsters least of all (Byalick & Bersoff 31). Verbalizing reasons to children studying arithmetic was at least as good as praising them for developing resistance to extinction of independent study of arithmetic (Taffel, O'Leary & Armel 236).

Cognitive Reinterpretation of Reinforcement Theory

For a long time, evidence has indicated an advantage for learning when a reinforcer or feedback, which are not necessarily synonymous, immediately follows a response. The animal literature has clearly supported the hypothesis that a delay of reinforcement reduces retention.

More recently, a delay-retention effect, which indicates that retention can be better when feedback following an immediate test is delayed, raises questions about the meaning of reinforcement and feedback as they have been studied in instruction. A fundamental question is the extent to which reinforcement behaves as if it were a cognitive process of providing information, feedback, or approval to be interpreted and stored, or behaves as if it were an automatic process by which behavior is associated to stimuli without information processing or awareness by the learner.

Surber & Anderson (233) built upon a series of earlier studies on the delay-retention effect. They showed that a delay of feedback increased retention. The delay-retention effect was explained by an interference-perseveration hypothesis in which feedback provides information to be processed. After reanalyzing data from several studies to compare the verbal rehearsal hypothesis with the interference-perseveration hypothesis, Sassenrath (217) agrees with Surber & Anderson that the interference-perseveration hypothesis is more clearly supported by the data.

These data together with the data summarized earlier on attribution theory lead to tentative implications about how reinforcement may operate in verbal instruction. It seems to supply affective or cognitive information which is interpreted and encoded by the learner. There may not be a need to posit a separate, automatic *process* of reinforcement in which the onset or termination of an external stimulus automatically increases the probability of a preceding response.

LEARNING AND MEMORY

In the section on learning and memory we examine how the effects of instruction depend upon the processes of encoding, storage, and retrieval of information. We will emphasize research on the instructionally relevant information processing strategies learners use to encode and store information.

Generative Processes of Learning

Wittrock (253, 254) proposed a model in which learning with comprehension is a generative process of constructing meaning from semantic memory and distinctive memory of events. In the generative model, teaching and instruction are designed to help the learner to transfer memories of previous experiences to the comprehension of new information. In support of predictions from the model, instructions to generate associations among randomly arranged or correctly arranged familiar words usually doubled their retention, even when the high frequency words chosen randomly from a dictionary could not be ordered into a hierarchy (Wittrock & Carter 256). In one trial elementary school children learned and remembered the meanings of unfamiliar and undefined vocabulary words by reading them in a familiar story (Wittrock, Marks & Doctorow 259). Comprehension and retention of events in a story were approximately doubled by replacing a low frequency word in each sentence with a synonymous high frequency word (Marks, Doctorow & Wittrock 155). In these studies the model predicted the findings that familiar contexts, words, and stories facilitate the transfer of stored information to the construction of meaning for new events.

In a related approach, Jenkins (111) presents a model of memory which emphasizes the importance of contextual processes in remembering information. Tulving & Thomson's (242) encoding specificity model also indicates the distinctive nature of episodic information coded into long-term memory, as does research by Bransford & Johnson (25) on contextual processes in comprehension.

The importance of specifically relevant background information to the meaningful learning of subject matter has also been shown. With college students learning mathematics, Mayer, Stiehl & Greeno (161) found that specific prerequisite knowledge and skill, but not general intellectual ability, increased learning in meaningful discovery treatments. Egan & Greeno (65) report similar relations between specific background factors and learning from meaningful instruction. Provided the learner possessed the specifically relevant prerequisites, instruction emphasizing the discovery of meaning led to understanding, inferences, and broad transfer. Instruction emphasizing the rote use of formulas or algorithms enhanced computation, regardless of the learner's previous knowledge of mathematics.

The above studies imply that comprehension depends upon the transfer of distinctive, highly relevant past experience to the instructional context. Meaningful learning methods facilitate comprehension and transfer by building upon previous knowledge and skill, a characteristic not shared by rote learning methods. The relationship between the learners' backgrounds and the instruction is important in determining understanding and comprehension (Wittrock 254).

In related studies of proactive processes in instruction, Francis (72) found that a familiar reception method was increasingly better than an unfamiliar discovery method when the task was difficult. Royer & Cable (209) facilitated comprehension of a prose passage with an introductory passage that contained concrete referents for the difficult words in the second passage. Kalbaugh & Walls (122) found proactive and retroactive inhibition to reduce the learning of science materials and biographies. Wittrock & Cook (257) found that motor learning depended upon transfer of specifically relevant previous experience. In sum, a number of recent studies indicate the importance of relevant contextual and background experience in learning from instruction.

Several studies tried to facilitate the generative processes involved in using one's relevant background to construct meaning. Wittrock (255) summarizes two experiments with elementary school children reading stories containing either or both (a) inserted headings for each paragraph or (b) instructions to construct and write for each paragraph a sentence relating their experiences to the paragraph. As predicted, the combination of headings and generated sentences produced the greatest comprehension and retention, followed in turn by generated sentences alone, paragraph headings alone, and last by the control groups. In a related study, Rickards & August (193) compared learner-generated with experimenter-provided underlining of sentences (a) which the learner desired, or (b) which the subject considered structurally important to the passage, or (c) which the experimenter chose to be of high or low structural importance, respectively, or (d) which the learner considered unimportant. From highest to lowest the treatment means were predicted to occur, and did occur, in the above a-to-d rank order. The authors interpret the results to conform to the generative model of learning.

R. M. Gagné's model of learning set hierarchies also implies that learning is dependent upon the transfer of specifically relevant learning, of prerequisite operations, or of learning sets. The model is frequently supported, for example in a study by Mouw & Hecht (171). White (249) also supported Gagné's model and its implication that subordinate skills must be learned before superordinate ones, while information about specific facts need not be learned hierarchically.

Problem Solving Processes

The cognitive processes children and adults use to solve problems, such as word problems in mathematics, are being studied increasingly in instructional psychology. Rosenthal & Resnick (203) studied the transformations children make in solving word problems in arithmetic. Their data were consistent with Suppes' canonical transformation model, but because of limited data about latency, other models could not be eliminated. In a more recent study, Woods, Resnick & Groen (260) studied second and fourth graders solving single-digit subtraction problems. From among five models of the problem-solving process, the latency data best supported the models which predicted that the child either counted up from the smaller digit to the higher digit, or counted down from the higher digit to the smaller one. The data did not support models which involved counting from zero. The older children, who solved problems twice as fast as the younger children, used a more heuristic, less algorithmic approach than did the younger children. With problems involving the discovery of rules, Breaux (26) hypothesized that the processes of discovery used by learners include deduction as well as induction. He cleverly designed deductive-discovery and inductive-discovery treatments, which he compared with deductive utilization and inductive utilization conditions. For an inductive sequence, the utilization condition produced the fewest errors, while for a deductive sequence, the discovery and utilization procedures did not differ in the transfer of previously learned rules.

One encouraging aspect of the above cognitive approaches to the study of problem solving processes is the authors' increasing willingness to state and to test alternative models of cognitive processes involved in learning subjects taught in schools. The shift to the testing of specific alternative models relevant to school learning is a refreshing needed addition to the literature in educational psychology. For further discussion see Greeno's (97) chapter relating memory structures to problem-solving processes.

Imagery in Encoding

In this section and in the following section, entitled *Verbal Processes in Encoding,* we review instructionally relevant studies on two of the elaborative processes of encoding. The use of imagery in instruction has a long and glorious history (Wittrock 255, Yates 262) which dates to the days of ancient Greece and Rome. Interest in research in imagery has recently been revived in America, after about 60 years of reduced attention. Paivio's definitive volume (180) and recent paper (181) on imagery and verbal processes provide part of the reason for discussing imagery and verbal processes separately. However, we do not wish to imply that his dual-process model, or similar models used in recent research on the hemispheric processes of the brain, is best supported by these data. We use the two categories because they represent currently prominent areas of research.

Pictures, instructions to image, mnemonics, and the drawing of pictures sometimes facilitate learning, including verbal learning. Levin (141) found that a visual imagery strategy, but not pictures, helped fourth graders of high or low reading ability with an adequate vocabulary to increase their reading comprehension. Paris & Mahoney (183) found that children used imagery to integrate information and construct relations which facilitate memory. Rohwer & Harris (199) found that with low socioeconomic status black fourth grade children, multimedia methods, especially pictures with an oral presentation, enhanced prose learning. For white high socioeconomic status fourth graders, multimedia methods did not much enhance prose learning. Oral plus printed presentations retarded prose learning; and oral plus picture presentations again facilitated prose learning.

In four experiments, Lesgold et al (140) found that illustrations given to 6-year-old children, or constructed by them from the correct pieces of a design, facilitated recall of the facts and content of the passages. Bull & Wittrock (30) found that vocabulary words were learned and recalled best when children in elementary school drew their own pictures to represent the definitions of the vocabulary words. The learning of verbal definitions produced the least retention. Goldberg (91) found that illustrations facilitated incidental learning of fifth graders. With paired associates, third grade children learned vocabulary items best when the pictures provided an interactive image, i.e. one which included a figural representation unified within the letters of the word (Lippman & Shanahan 150). Raugh & Atkinson (191) used a two-stage keyword mnemonic method to teach Spanish vocabulary to English speaking undergraduates. The method involves constructing an interactive image between the keyword and the English translation. In one experiment the imagery group scored 88% correct, while the control group scored 28% correct. In a related study (Atkinson & Raugh 10) with undergraduates and Russian vocabulary, the same imagery strategy increased retention from 46% for the control group to 72% for the keyword imagery mnemonic group.

Instructions to form images and experimenter given drawings were investigated with college, high school, and elementary school children (Rasco, Tennyson & Boutwell 190). The instructions, the drawings, or both facilitated learning for the college students and for the elementary school students. Educable mentally retarded elementary school children also profited from imagery or sentence elaboration training (Taylor, Josberger & Whitely 237), with overt verbalization sizably enhancing the effect of each type of elaboration training.

Among elementary school children, imagery and vocalization strategies differed in their effectiveness for learning verbal discriminations, with imagery more effective for homonym pairs and vocalization more effective for synonym pairs (Levin et al 145). In a more recent study, however, Levin et al (144) found that imagery with a relevant motor activity facilitated verbal discriminations, but not discrimination among pictures.

In a comparison of an imagery generation strategy with a sentence generation strategy, second and fifth grade children benefited equally from each strategy (Levin et al 142). Apparently even young children can sometimes learn to generate images if motor practice is used (Varley et al 243). Imagery elaboration training also facilitated memory for pictures among educable mentally retarded junior high school children (Bender & Taylor 15).

The above research on imagery as a training technique with children and older students shows interesting results. It indicates that under certain conditions at least some children and adults can use imagery to learn and remember definitions, pictures, and words. An instrument has been developed to classify elementary school children by their ways of learning prose, either by visual imagery or verbal organizations (Levin et al 143).

How imagery functions during encoding continues to stir interest. Paivio (180) explained imagery as a concrete rather than an abstract process. In agreement with Paivio, Anderson (7) found that sentences with concrete imagery increased recall. Also in agreement with Paivio, Wittrock & Goldberg (258) tested and found the so-called "elusive" interaction which Paivio's dual process model predicts between imagery and verbal processes. That is, if imagery and verbal processes are separate but interacting systems, then when a list of words is being processed imaginally, meaningfulness should add to the retention of words of high imagery value, but detract from words of low imagery value. In two experiments, one with junior high school students and one with college students, the predicted interaction was obtained. In the same study a review of the extensive literature on the issue indicated that the elusive interaction had occurred in most studies of it, but it had been overlooked in them.

The recent research on imagery has practical implications for instruction and theoretical importance for understanding how people construct meaning. Some of the findings of the recent research on imagery are reminiscent of Aristotle's, Cicero's, and Quintillian's writings about imagery in memory and in rhetoric (Wittrock 255, Yates 262), especially the instructions to orators regarding the proper use of imagery to remember speeches. The recent research also suggests that more than one process is involved in learning with understanding and in long-term memory. Imagery seems to be one of those processes. For Aristotle, it was the singular process of memory.

Verbal Processes in Encoding

Verbal elaborations, such as the construction of sentences, stories, themes, and hierarchical organizations, facilitated the learning and retention of paired associates, serial lists, prose, and subjects taught in school. Bower & Clark (21) increased retention of serial lists of nouns from 14% correct to 93% correct by having the learners construct stories which maintained the serial order of the words in the list. When time to learn was limited, Royer & Kulhavy (210) facilitated paired-associate learning by encoding the paired associates into sentences whose introductory phrases functioned as thematic prompts.

Sentence elaborations facilitated retention of noun pairs by college students when the stimulus terms were of low frequency value (Klemt & Anderson 130). Frederiksen & Rohwer (77) found that with a pure-list, between-subject design, for middle and lower socioeconomic status (SES) third graders, pictures plus labels were better than pictures alone, which were better than verbal labels alone for the learning of pairs of nouns. With a mixed-test, within-subjects design, the low SES subjects seemed not to elaborate the noun pairs spontaneously, but they did use the experimenter-given elaborations to facilitate their learning.

In 5 weeks of training, 1 hour per week, educable mentally retarded children 6 to 10 years old were taught with stories and games to use conjunctive, prepositional, rhyming, and sentential mediators to help them learn paired associates (Ross & Ross 205). Second graders who were black or Chinese American or Spanish American and others learned to use aural-verbal or visual-pictorial prompts to enhance their recall of paired nouns (Kee & Rohwer 127). The recall of paired-associates, as well as learning-to-learn, occurred equivalently and significantly across all four ethnic groups.

Verbal elaborations often facilitate learning and memory. Children, including mentally retarded children, who have not learned to elaborate information spontaneously can sometimes be taught to construct verbal elaborations and to increase their learning and retention.

Models of Encoding

The recent research on cognitive elaborations of information indicates that learning and recall are facilitated by constructive processes which embed information into semantic or episodic contexts meaningful to the learner. Recent instructionally relevant models of how meaning, meaningfulness, and constructive processes increase comprehension and retention of verbal materials include the following. Johnson (118, 119) discusses meaning in complex learning as a reconstructive and abstractive process. In one study, meaningfulness showed three-to-eighteenfold increases in retention of prose (Johnson 117). Johnson's model of meaning as a referential process is consistent with much of the recent research on imagery and verbal processes.

As an alternative to stages models of encoding, Craik & Lockhart (43) presented a model of levels of processing, which was later modified in terms of spread and depth of processing (Craik & Tulving 44). The model implies that deep processing facilitates retention and transfer of meaning and comprehension. For example, information encoded by acoustic cues or by rhymes should be less well understood and retained than information semantically or conceptually encoded. In addition to the models by Johnson and by Craik & Tulving, Collins & Loftus (39) presented a spreading-activation theory of semantic processing which builds upon Quillian's associative network model of semantic memory.

Retrieval

The recent psychological research on organization in memory has a parallel in the research on the organization and sequencing of instructional materials, which we will review here. We also cite the recent instructional research on measures of retention and understanding.

Bower (20) studied retroactive interference in prose retention. He varied the microstructure, i.e. the details, of biographies while keeping constant the macrostructure, the superordinate levels, of the originally learned passage. Recall decreased for changed details, increased for unchanged details, and remained constant for the superordinate levels of the structure. Scrambling of the content in a college course in data processing reduced the learning of the conceptual structure that involved relations across sentences, but did not reduce learning of information contained in individual sentences (Kissler & Lloyd 129). Short answer inferences were facilitated by the logical organization of the contents. With second graders, logical sequences which held constant the relevant dimensions while varying the irrelevant ones, or varied the relevant ones while holding constant the irrelevant ones, reduced time to learn to identify nouns, adjectives, and verbs embedded in sentences (Stolurow 229).

Organizing paragraphs about countries by the attributes of the countries, rather than by their names or at random, enhanced free recall (Myers, Pezdek & Coulson 172). The organization by attribute facilitated retrieval of the serial order of the information about the countries. However, Frase (73) compared organization by name and by attribute and found that the retention of the text depended upon the objectives for learning, the phrasing of sentences, and the semantic characteristics of the text, which influenced the strategies used by the learners. Organization by attribute or name did affect how the information was integrated. Frase concluded that the effects of organization of the text depend upon the information processing strategies used by the learner. His conclusion again summarizes the importance of transformations which the learners perform on information.

For the study of instruction, one of the most significant results of the extensive recent research on encoding and retrieval has been a reexamination of the types of tests and test items used to measure the information learned from instruction. New, or rather newly rediscovered tests and measures designed to index the storage and retention of organized information have recently been studied. Carver (34) shows some limitations of commonly used measures of reading and of prose learning, such as tests of factual information and cloze tests, for indexing understanding. In his study, understanding was not necessarily measured by the learning of factual information or by the verbatim memory of words in a sentence. Anderson (6) shows how verbatim test items identical to sentences in a text do not measure comprehension of principles. With substantive changes in the test items, comprehension can be indexed. Since the days of C. H. Judd, authors studying transfer of learning have been making essentially the same points.

The recent cognitive research on learning and memory implies that there is more than one process of constructing meaning. If there are multiple cognitive processes interacting with one another to determine learning and retention, instruction should be individualized to complement them. Perhaps learners should be helped to elaborate information in one mode when it has been presented in another mode. We are only beginning to understand the complex processes of encoding and storage and how to build instruction upon them. Even so, some of the recent relevant studies of learning from instruction show encouraging gains in retention and comprehension when the constructive processes of encoding are facilitated.

In sum, the recent study of the cognitive processes of learning and memory helps to bring together research on the conditions of learning, the processes of learning, and the aptitudes and abilities of the learners. The results of the current, relevant studies often indicate that learning and retention are enhanced by the learner's verbal or imaginal elaborations of information. Most importantly, perhaps, in the current relevant studies, comprehension, long-term memory, and transfer are being used to measure and evaluate the multivariate cognitive and affective effects of instruction upon learning. The rich mix of multivariate effects of instruction represents a welcome shift from the narrower interests of laboratory scientists to the more complex reality of teachers in schools.

THE LEARNERS

Lee Cronbach's (45) pioneering attempts to bring together the fields of experimental psychology and differential psychology are succeeding in instructional psychology. We are encouraged by the close relationships which are developing between the study of learning from instruction and the study of individual differences among learners. Because of these developing relationships, a straightforward distinction between research on learning and research on learners is no longer easy nor necessary to make. Cognitive processes, cognitive structures, and individual differences among learners are often studied in each area. Consequently, we have incorporated studies of aptitude-treatment interactions throughout the relevant sections of this chapter.

We will now selectively review the instructionally relevant research which emphasizes cognitive structures, styles, and abilities of the learner, with the understanding that the following section complements and continues the closely related former section.

Cognitive Structure

The clustering of stored and recalled prose was investigated by Meyer & McConkie (167). The probability of recall of an idea was related to its position in a hierarchy of idea units. The higher the idea was in the hierarchy, the greater was its probability of recall, with the superordinate concepts apparently cuing recall of the subordinate concepts. In several studies, S. Johnson's hierarchical clustering technique has been used to measure the content structure of textbooks and the cognitive structure of authors, teachers, and students. Shavelson (219) and Geeslin & Shavelson (88) used directed graphs to map the subject matter and word association techniques to measure the cognitive structures of students. The results indicated that measures of the content structure and cognitive structure provided useful new information not contained in conventional measures of achievement.

Although Johnson's hierarchical clustering technique sometimes produces questionable hierarchies, it has important uses in the study of instruction. The technique provides a way to measure individual differences in cognitive structures among students, teachers, curriculum designers, and authors of textbooks. The technique could have important practical, diagnostic utility for graphically indicating changes in the ways students organize and remember information.

Cognitive Styles and Abilities

The study of the individualization of instruction increasingly attracts attention to the cognitive styles, aptitudes, and information processing strategies of learners. See Cronbach & Snow (46) for a comprehensive and thorough treatment of aptitude-treatment interactions in instruction.

In a study of the structure of cognitive abilities, Das (49) factor analyzed test score data of 9- to 11-year-old children in Canada and in India. He found two information processing strategies, called simultaneous and successive processing, which are reminiscent of the two cognitive styles identified in research on the hemispheric processes of the brain (Bogen 18).

Since Roger Sperry's early papers on the lateralization processes of the human brain, only a few studies have elaborated or explored some of the implications of the research for the improvement of instruction. In one study involving 11 weeks of classroom instruction in Spanish as a second language, Hartnett (102) predicted and found that left-hemisphere dominant college age learners preferred and learned more from an analytic, deductive curriculum, while right-hemisphere dominant learners preferred and achieved better with a holistic, inductive curriculum. Bogen (18) and Wittrock (255) elaborate some of the educational implications of the research on the lateralization processes of the brain.

From another perspective, other cognitive styles were shown to interact with tasks or treatments. Reflective and impulsive children performed equally well on a global task, but reflective children performed better than impulsive children on an analytic task (Zelniker & Jeffrey, "Reflective and Impulsive Children: Strategies of Information Processing Underlying Differences in Problem Solving," in preparation). They suggested that reflective and impulsive strategies may represent, respectively, left and right hemispheric strategies for analyzing information. Ehri & Muzio (67), McKinney (163), and Robinson & Gray (196) studied reflective and impulsive styles of processing information. When the problem to be solved involved analysis or field independence, the reflective children performed better than the impulsive children.

The learners' cognitive styles are sometimes adapted to their majors and occupations. In a comparison of the cognitive styles of children of several ages and of artists, Gaines (85) found the artists to be field independent, flexible in perception and in choice of dimensions of stimuli, and predominately relational in cognitive style, all characteristics directly related to the requirements of an artist's work. Goldman & Hudson (92) found differences in strategies of processing information among subject-matter majors of undergraduates. These differences in cognitive style were independent of differences in ability but were related to success in the subject matter. However, Labouvie-Vief, Levin & Urberg (134) caution against premature conclusions about relations between processes or aptitudes and instruction. They stress the need for a theoretical base for relating aptitudes and processes to instruction. We agree with them.

A theoretical conception of the processes which comprise mental ability is Jensen's Level I–Level II theory. Level I ability consists of rote learning and primary memory, with few mental transformations. Level II ability consists primarily of conceptual learning, mental transformations, and elaborations. Jensen & Frederiksen (115), Jensen (112, 113), and Jensen & Figueroa (114) tested and supported the interaction which the model predicts between levels of intelligence and socioeconomic status or race. The predicted interaction is that Level II abilities differ more greatly than Level I abilities across lower and middle SES, or across black or white groups, with middle SES or white groups performing better than lower SES or black groups.

In related work on group differences in cognitive processes, Nazzaro & Nazzaro (174) found that in paired-associate learning, middle SES second graders were more able to construct meaningful transformations than were lower SES second graders. Meissner (164) found that lower SES second graders could comprehend concepts better than they could express them or communicate them verbally. In another study (Nelson & Klausmeier 175) lower SES children classified stimuli more on the basis of their appearances than upon their defining attributes or concept names. Salomon (211) predicted and found that learners with low aptitudes profit more than learners with high aptitudes when a model presents the operations which they are to internalize. Skanes et al (224) found that learners with low intellectual abilities profited more than learners with high intellectual abilities from practice on the specific strategies useful for solving problems.

The results of the above studies indicate that there is more than one process involved in learning and in comprehension. Comprehension, which often involves the use of strategies or the production of mediators, is more difficult for some children than for other children. The research implies that children with poor conceptual ability profit from instruction when the conceptual organization of the information is made explicit and is given to them. Of much interest are the data which show that children of poor conceptual ability can sometimes be taught to produce mediators and to use strategies that facilitate comprehension. We need to experiment more with these important remedial instructional methods.

The research on the different cognitive processes involved in rote learning and conceptual learning has a parallel in the research on the relation between long-term recall and intelligence. Labouvie et al (133) found that with immediate recall, measures of memory predicted performance, but with delayed recall measures of intelligence predicted performance. Shuell & Giglio (221) found ability to learn to be unrelated to short-term memory. Goulet, Williams & Hay (93) found that different components of ability are involved in the tasks at different stages of mastery.

From these studies, it seems that learning often depends upon the congruence between the task and the learner's ability and cognitive style. For example, when the task involves analysis, the reflective children do better than the impulsive children. When a global or holistic approach leads to success at the task, the impulsive children do as well as the reflective children. A second implication from the above studies is that instruction should be designed in relation to the learner's cognitive style, either to complement it or to compensate for it. On the other hand, because achievement in schools in both verbal and quantitative areas often involves field independence and an analytic cognitive style, field dependent learners with global cognitive styles may need and may profit from training in analytic, field independent approaches to tasks (Kagan & Zahn 121). That is, sometimes the cognitive style, not the task, should be modified.

A perennial problem in research on aptitude-treatment interactions has been a lack of theories and models useful for matching individual differences among learners to different instructional treatments. The models of cognitive processes represent promising theory-based approaches to the study of individual differences in learning from instruction. The current research on cognition helps to bring together research in human abilities and research in instructional treatments.

INSTRUCTION

Modeling

In the research by Albert Bandura, Leonard Berkowitz, and others, the effectiveness of modeling as a way to learn and to instruct has been well established. In instructional psychology the recent research on observational learning concentrated on the nature of the information that can be taught with models and upon the characteristics of effective models and techniques.

The seven volumes of the reports of the Surgeon General's Scientific Advisory Committee on Television and Social Behavior (e.g. Comstock & Rubinstein 40, 234) present field studies and laboratory studies on the effects of viewing television upon children and youth. Cater & Strickland (35) and Liebert, Neale & Davidson (148) discuss the serious problems encountered in the project because vested interest groups were allowed to influence the selection of the scientists and all others on the Advisory Committee, and consequently to influence the final statement of the Committee's recommendations and conclusions. We will therefore confine our review to the project's relevant research studies on learning by observation of televised models.

In a study reported in Volume 3 of the Advisory Committee's report, and also published in the *American Psychologist,* Eron et al (70) used a causal model to analyze naturalistic longitudinal data. They supported the inference that television viewing of aggression in the third grade causes aggressive behavior later. In a laboratory study reported in Volume 2 of the Advisory Committee's report, Liebert & Baron (147) found that the boys and girls exposed to scenes from actual aggressive programs on television at least temporarily engaged in longer attacks on fictitious child victims than did the children exposed to a nonaggressive television program. On the other hand, Friedrich & Stein (84) found that from televised models children learned and generalized the prosocial behavior of helping others. Television was also an effective medium for the control of attention, even when the children's motor behavior indicated otherwise. Five-year-old children watching "Sesame Street" on television learned and imitated nonintended acts such as kissing (Sproull 228), and maintained eye contact 81% of the time with the television screen while they were interacting, talking, moving about, and playing with other children in the group.

Not only were aggressive acts, prosocial attitudes, and nonintended behaviors learned by observing models, but concepts, such as reversal-shifts by college students (Chalmers & Rosenbaum 36) and seriation by 3- to 5-year-old Papago Indian children (Henderson, Swanson & Zimmerman 105) were also learned by observing others. In the former study, observational learning produced less negative transfer from interfering concepts than did the actual performance of the behavior. Models also facilitated problem solving (Mayer 159), divergent verbal responses (Belcher 14), fluency and flexibility (Zimmerman & Dialessi 265), and willingness to report hypotheses that would otherwise be considered unacceptable (Frederiksen & Evans 78).

Models which facilitated performance included teachers who rewarded students frequently (Friedman 83). When behavior was the criterion, white models of the same sex as the child were best; but with the learning of knowledge, female models were better than male models (Cook & Smothergill 42), and same sex models were better than opposite sex models (Garrett & Cunningham 87).

Research on modeling has led to an understanding of the instructional nature of a myriad of everyday human activities and interactions. People learn behavior, attitudes, knowledge, and social skills by observing models. Modeling is a subtle, highly effective cognitive technique, with profound implications for instruction.

Reading

Cognitive and information processing models of reading are reviewed by Williams (251), Silverston & Deichmann (223), Gibson & Levin (90), and Guthrie (99). The volume by Gibson & Levin applies a theory of perceptual learning to the understanding of psychological processes in reading. These processes include how distinctive features or invariants are differentiated, how relations are abstracted, how irrelevant information is ignored, and how attention to relevant information is heightened.

The recent research in reading centers upon the study of the skills, processes, and strategies of readers. Samuels & Anderson (213) hypothesized and found that differences between good and poor readers occurred in perceptual learning, as indexed by visual recognition memory, not in the learning of associations between stimuli and responses. Their hypotheses and results are consistent with Gibson & Levin (90, p. 23), who state that perceptual learning is not an associative process.

Attention, in the sense of visual orientation to the task, was found among beginning readers to be positively related to word recognition (Samuels & Turnure 216). The relationship was not explainable by reinforcement or extinction of academic or school behavior. Denney (55) found that attention and ability to encode visual information into verbal information were positively related to reading ability. Training which increased attention to the distinctive features of letters facilitated the learning of the names of letters (Samuels 212). Word recognition skill and comprehension were increased by training in the construction of whole words from partial words (Samuels, Dahl & Archwamety 215). Reading was also positively related to ability to manipulate phonetic language components in relation to acoustic cues (Calfee, Lindamood & Lindamood 33).

Encoding and comprehension have also been studied recently in research on reading. Pearson & Studt (185) found that high-frequency words were better recognized and comprehended than were low-frequency words. Siegel, Lautman & Burkett (222) enhanced comprehension by reducing the reading level of course materials, but not by reducing the reading level of technical manuals. In some instances reading comprehension was sizably enhanced by using familiar contexts or by increasing the frequency of the words in the sentence (Marks, Doctorow & Wittrock 155; Wittrock, Marks & Doctorow 259).

We are encouraged by the findings and the theoretical developments occurring in the study of reading. The recent research in reading is producing interesting models of the processes of reading. The use of models to direct research in reading is an improvement over the atheoretical and noncumulative studies of reading methods which characterized the field for several decades. As we suggested earlier, the relevant closely related research on attention, encoding, and prose learning should be incorporated with the recent research on the processes of reading. Alternative models of the processes of reading and of prose learning could then be compared with one another to develop a deeper understanding of the interrelated processes of reading and of the teaching of reading.

Algorithmization in Instruction

The book entitled *Algorithmization in Learning and Instruction* was originally published in Russian in 1966 and authored by Professor Lev N. Landa of the Moscow Academy of Pedagogical Sciences. In 1974, F. Kopstein, working in close collaboration with the author, edited an English translation of Landa's impressive volume (Landa 136). The notion of algorithmization of learning and instruction is closely linked historically to the concept of cybernetics, which Norbert Wiener defined as a science of control and communication involving effective feedback loops between a communicator, e.g. an instructor, and a receiver, e.g. a student.

For Landa, algorithms are not merely instructional strategies; rather they are fundamental features of orderly cognitive processes which students must learn to use as basic tools of effective intellectual ability. Landa's work on algorithms is closely related to American work on analysis of intellectual tasks (see 90a, pp. 208–19). Landa's approach to instruction is closely related to the concept of programmed learning (PL) in the United States, or more appropriately to programmed tutoring (PT) and the later developed American systems of computer-assisted instruction (CAI) (see 90a, 152a, and 162 for reviews). The term programmed tutoring is too ambitious to use to describe the linear programs developed by many of B. F. Skinner's followers. However, it seems aptly descriptive of the highly contingent sequences characteristic of most CAI systems in which the frequent program branching is determining by the responses of each learner.

Programmed tutoring does not require automation via a computer, as is illustrated in the sequences for elementary reading developed and extensively field tested by D. G. Ellson and associates. [See Hawkridge & DeWitt (103) for a review of the results of the studies.] In Ellson's programmed tutoring, branching sequences were mediated by a teacher's aide, who thus substituted for a computer in the instruction.

The aide followed a carefully developed program of contingent instructions, e. g. "If the pupil says 'yes', skip to paragraph 23." Variations of Ellson's promising system have been used in "third world" countries (Ellson et al 69a).

Closely related to Landa's concept of algorithmization is the concept of algorithms in instruction which appears in several recent studies conducted in the United States. Durnin & Scandura (62) found that an algorithm-based technique for assessing behavior potential was a better predictor of test errors than were item form technologies. Ehrenpreis & Scandura (66) used an algorithmic approach to mathematics teaching. They compared two sets of rule-based instructional materials. One set employed 300 lower-order rules only, while the other set used 40% fewer lower-order rules and 5 higher-order rules. The latter instructional materials produced greater learning than the former materials (see also Scandura 218).

In summary, the concepts of algorithmization and algorithms have led to interesting and productive research studies in Russia and in the United States. Landa's approach to instruction emphasizes algorithmic control of contingencies based on a learner's moment-to-moment progress through logically analyzed instructional programs. Although it is adaptable to a computer-assisted instructional system, Landa's technique is not dependent upon it. In his book, Landa illustrates his technique with a human tutorial arrangement similar to Ellson's programmed tutoring system. Translated 10 years after their original publication, Landa's concepts are contemporaneous with the related but independently developed concepts of Ellson. Landa, however, has developed his conceptual system extensively, while Ellson has developed and field tested practical, useful curricular materials. Consequently, Landa's system may diffuse slowly but pervasively into instructional theory and practice. His own vision of the character and scope of his influence is reflected in the final paragraph of his volume, which is quoted here:

A structural-operational analysis of general methods of thinking as well as of the actual methods of instruction is the prerequisite for the creation of the kind of theory of instruction which will make it possible to introduce elements of precise calculation and prediction into the design of the teaching process. It will equip the teacher with the means for making a valid determination, design, and selection of the most efficient and effective methods of instruction. Herein lies one of the basic tasks of didactics and pedagogical psychology (136, p. 615).

Evaluation of Instructional Programs

The evaluation of instructional programs, or program evaluation, is a category of research on educational policy which is receiving increased attention. The availability of the recent review on program evaluation by Perloff et al (186) has permitted us to deal with this area of applied research much more briefly than we could otherwise have done. Program evaluation studies range from modest efforts to estimate roughly the main effects of short, provisional, instructional sequences, up to comprehensive and rigorous research efforts conducted to ascertain accurately and in detail the effects of major programs of instruction. A historic example of the latter type of study is the series of comprehensive experiments by Hovland, Lumsdaine & Sheffield (107) for ascertaining the effects on soldiers' knowledge, opinions, attitudes, and motivation that were produced by the army orientation film series in World War II. Incidentally, an even earlier study of film effects on soldiers was performed by Karl S. Lashley and John B. Watson (137) on the effects of a World War I film on venereal disease.

More recent examples are the studies dealing with the "Sesame Street" programs produced by the Childrens' Television Workshop for the Public Broadcasting System. The volume by Cook et al (41) is an exhaustive post hoc analysis of data which measure the effects of a reproducible, videotaped, widely disseminated instructional program. Much of Cook et al's reassessment of the initial quasi-experimental evaluation of "Sesame Street" by Ball & Bogatz (12, 17) was concerned with the adequacy of their corrections for selection artifacts. However, this major secondary evaluation went beyond the study of validity of the imputed effects of the program to the study of the worth of the outcomes, including their cost-benefit balance. A recent example of a large-scale evaluation study in which a true experimental design was used is the evaluation in Mexico of the Spanish language version of the television program "Plaza Sesamo" by Diaz-Guerrero & Holtzman (56). See also the interesting nonexperimental evaluation study by Abelson, Zigler & DeBlasi (1) of a 4-year follow through program for economically disadvantaged children.

While the focus of any given program evaluation study is limited to decisions concerning the particular program(s) studied, the methodological and policy implications of evaluation studies may be of wide compass. Some of the methodological problems encountered in evaluation studies clearly transcend those which frequently occur in research in learning and instruction (Lumsdaine 151). In particular, evaluation studies must deal with the value of the results in relation to their costs. Evaluation studies also must deal with questions of the comparative validity, feasibility, efficiency, and cost of quasi-experimental and randomized designs.

The massive two-volume *Handbook of Program Evaluation,* edited by Elmer Struening and Marcia Guttentag (231, 100) under auspices of the Society for the Psychological Study of Social Issues, is a major reference work on the methods and concepts of program evaluation relevant to the above problems. The first volume (231) contains three papers on policy and strategy in evaluation research; six papers on approaches, conceptualizations, models, and designs of evaluation studies; eight papers on measuring instruments, data collection, data analysis, and the communication of results; and several papers which deal with the psychological and socioeconomical context and ramifications of evaluative studies. The second volume (100) contains two papers on politics and values in evaluation research, two on cost-benefit approaches, and ten papers, comprising some 500 pages, on the evaluation of mental health and related programs.

A more concise work is *Evaluation and Experiment: Some Critical Issues in Assessing Social Programs,* edited by Bennett & Lumsdaine (16). It includes a landmark paper by J. P. Gilbert, R. J. Light, and F. Mosteller which examines 28 randomized field trials and a number of nonrandomized studies designed to assess the impact of social and medical programs in industrialized societies. Their delineation of crucial perspectives for the conduct of field experiments deserves to be widely read. A more narrowly focused chapter by E. Hilton and A. Lumsdaine deals with studies on the impact of family-planning programs in developing nations. In most of the latter experiments the units of random assignment to experimental conditions are entire population units such as villages, townships, or counties; the authors point up the importance of such a design for preventing contamination effects in large-scale socio-educational experiments. In a third paper of this volume D. T. Campbell and R. F. Boruch discuss problems encountered in the interpretation of quasi-experimental designs for assessing the impacts of treatments. Their conclusions, calculated to temper prevalent enthusiasm for such designs, reinforce the importance, stressed by Gilbert, Light, and Mosteller, and also by Hilton and Lumsdaine, of employing random assignment of treatments in field experiments.

While experiments are thus seen to provide the best source of data on program or treatment impacts, the need is recognized for a rationale and procedure to integrate impact data with the utilities of multiple outcomes of an instructional program. A chapter by W. Edwards and M. Guttentag (16, Chapter 6), and a complementary paper by Edwards, Guttentag & Snapper (231, Chapter 7) elucidate the application of decision-theory approaches to the integration of impact data and subjective utility estimates. These chapters are lent added perspective by Daniel Katz's insightful discussion (16, Chapter 7) of ways in which evaluation data provide feedback to institutional decisions and operations (see also 231, Chapter 20). For further discussion of related issues in the evaluation of programs, see Wortman (261), Mosteller & Moynihan (170), and the recent review by Perloff et al (186).

Two other major recent publications on program evaluation must be briefly noted. The first of these publications is *Social Experimentation,* edited by Riecken & Boruch (195). This book, written collaboratively by members of a committee of the Social Science Research Council, contains papers instructive for administrators and laymen as well as behavioral scientists on experimentation as a method for measuring program impacts, on experimental and quasi-experimental design and analysis, and on operational, institutional, political, and human values in social experimentation. An interesting additional feature is an appendix of brief abstracts of controlled field experiments on programs in law and corrections, mental health, economics, fertility control, and special education and communications.

The other volume to be noted is *Evaluation in Education,* a compendium edited by W. J. Popham (188) for the American Educational Research Association. Among its nine chapters are two dealing with evaluation perspectives and approaches (Michael Scriven, Daniel Stufflebeam), two on tests and measurements (Gilbert Sax, Jason Millman), one each on summative and formative evaluation methods (Peter Airasian, Eva Baker, respectively), and one each on data analysis (Richard Wolf), cost analysis (Emil Haller), and matrix sampling (Kenneth Sirotnik).

TEACHING

After nearly 70 years of concerted empirical research, the largely atheoretical study of the relations between the characteristics of teachers and the effectiveness of teaching is producing some interesting, nonintuitive findings. The recent research emphasizes the cognitive and affective characteristics of teachers and their effects upon students.

Effects of Teachers upon Students

In a valiant effort to find significant relations between teaching and student achievement, Rosenshine (200) reviewed 51 correlational studies which used classroom observational systems or student ratings to characterize the classroom activities of teachers. With one exception he found no significant relation between student achievement and any teacher affective variable, including warmth, praise, and use of student ideas. Student achievement was also insignificantly related to some teacher cognitive variables, including organization, difficulty, use of open-ended questions, use of factual questions, and amount of student-teacher interaction. One teacher-affective behavior, i.e. teacher's strong disapproval of students, was negatively related to student achievement. He found several significant positive relations between achievement and cognitive behaviors of teachers, including achievement orientation, clarity of instruction, structuring of instruction, and variety of classroom materials, variety of teachers' cognitive behavior, opportunity to learn, and teachers' expectations of student achievement.

Teachers' self-ratings were consistently and positively significantly related to student achievement in the three studies which reported relevant data. Student ratings of teachers produced inconsistent results. The ratings were significantly positively correlated with achievement in six of the 12 studies, and not significantly correlated with achievement in the remaining six studies.

His findings are interesting, especially those which disagree with common sense about teaching. For example, with the exception of sharp criticism, none of the affective variables but a large number of the cognitive variables of teaching correlated with achievement. Another interesting finding was that teacher self-ratings related to student achievement more consistently than did student ratings of teaching. As we shall see later, student ratings of teaching more often correlate with the characteristics of the personalities of teachers than with student achievement or with the cognitive behaviors of teachers.

Several different ways to use nonexperimental data to estimate the causal effects of teaching upon student achievement have appeared recently. Veldman & Brophy (244) predicted the effects of teaching upon students by using 115 elementary school teachers as the predictor variable. Residualized gain scores on a standardized achievement test indicated that most of the teachers significantly affected student learning, especially with economically disadvantaged children. Another way to estimate the causal effects of teaching upon students is to contrast the student achievement attained by schools that have different numbers of days of instruction in the school year. In a series of studies, Wiley & Harnischfeger (e.g. 250) found that the quantity of schooling is positively related to student achievement.

Another ingenious way to tease causal relations about teaching and learning from nonexperimental data is to relate the productivity of the careers of former graduate students to characteristics of their graduate teachers. Chambers (37) showed that teachers of doctoral students in chemistry or psychology enhanced creativity largely by the encouragement they provided the students outside the classroom. He eschewed student ratings of teacher effectiveness by currently enrolled students, which often had not previously produced important findings, and measured instead the creative accomplishments of the students in later life.

The more creative students characterized their teachers in graduate school as hard driving, dynamic, intellectually demanding teachers who encouraged out-of-class discussions with them on class-related matters. In classes, these enthusiastic teachers emphasized the understanding of general principles and learning on one's own. Sometimes they were poor teachers in the classroom but excellent teachers out of it. Direct reinforcement of creative student behavior was not a behavior pattern used by these models of creativity. These teachers were more interested in doing research, devoting at least 40 hours per week to it, than they were interested in teaching or administration. Chambers concluded that to improve the teaching of creativity to graduate students one should encourage and facilitate creative research by faculty members, and we would add, by graduate students as well. Ironically, it would also seem that to improve creative teaching, faculty members and graduate students should be selected for their interest and ability in creative research perhaps even more than for their interest in teaching. Lastly, Chambers' research indicates that evaluations of classroom teaching may miss an important part of creative teaching in graduate schools which occurs out of class in the context of research. Creative teaching and excellent classroom teaching are not necessarily synonymous with each other. Creative teaching occurs outside the classroom as well as in it.

A few experimental attempts to study the effects of teaching upon learning have appeared. Notable among them is a study by Wagner (246), who compared a cognitive discrimination training procedure, which taught the teacher to distinguish between appropriate and inappropriate types of teaching for given situations, with a practice teaching procedure which provided practice and reinforcement of appropriate teaching behaviors. In student-centered teaching, the cognitive discrimination group outperformed the reinforced practice teaching group and a control group. As a way to induce changes in teaching, learning to discriminate between appropriate and inappropriate teaching behavior was sufficient, and more effective than reinforced practice of appropriate teaching behavior. The study has implications for the design of teacher training according to cognitive principles of learning and teaching which emphasize the understanding of a discrimination rather than the performance of a behavior.

In sum, after a long period of disappointing results, several interesting and nonintuitive relations between teaching and student achievement are beginning to emerge, perhaps because, in some areas of research, more useful and appropriate multivariate models of teaching are replacing the simplistic ones used earlier. In a recent review of research on schooling, Averch and co-workers (11, pp. 73–74) attribute the present meager understanding of teaching to the influence of the psychology of behaviorism, which they find to be inadequate for application to human learning. Strike (230) reached the same conclusion. Research in the deceptively simple in appearance but actually complicated area of teaching could profit from greater use of tests of sophisticated models of teaching and from the comprehensiveness and explanatory power of research designs based upon causal models for nonexperimental data. To increase the productivity of research on the effects of teaching upon student learning, we suggest more conceptually oriented studies that compare and test models and theories of teaching which specify how the *learners* transform the nominal stimuli of instruction into functional stimuli which predict and explain their behavior.

Teacher Expectations and the Teacher Expectancy Effect

Teacher expectations and the teacher expectancy effect are different from each other. Teacher expectations are the inferences or predictions teachers make about students. The fulfillment of teacher expectations indicates only that teachers are good at predicting what students will achieve, or that student achievements cause teacher expectations.

The teacher expectancy effect occurs when the teacher's expectations cause differential, often inappropriate treatment of children by teachers, which then causes the achievement of the students to fulfill the expectation of the teacher. The Rosenthal effect, or the Pygmalion effect, is a type of teacher expectancy effect upon the intellectual development, mainly IQ, of children. The effect was originally experimentally induced by bogus information to 18 elementary school teachers, 3 in each of the grades 1–6, about the late blooming intellectual ability of 20% of their students. Of the 18 teachers, the first and second grade teachers showed an expectancy effect one year later (Rosenthal & Jacobson 204).

The recent data continue to indicate almost no support for the Pygmalion effect, mixed support for any teacher expectancy effects, and substantial support for the ability of teachers to predict the achievement of many of their students as well as for teachers to alter their expectations in response to information about their students. The lack of support for the Pygmalion effect may mean the effect is not real, or it may mean that more careful research is needed to establish the two-stage causal hypothesis.

Since Merton's paper (166) on the self-fulfilling prophecy, the phenomenon has interested sociologists and psychologists. After reporting a number of interesting studies on the experimenter bias effect, Rosenthal turned to the study of teaching. He and Jacobsen (204) published a study which reported a teacher expectancy effect, which they called the Pygmalion effect.

Nearly all attempts to replicate the Pygmalion effect have failed, and only about one-third of the attempts to show any teacher expectancy effect have succeeded. Brophy & Good (28) report that in some areas most studies do not support a teacher expectancy effect. However, in the natural school setting with credible information, they find that some teachers show an expectancy effect with some of their children. In another recent extensive review, Skilbeck (225) found support for the teacher expectancy effect only in natural situations with expectations based on credible information, or in short-term analog studies with induced expectations.

We find that the latest studies agree substantially with the previously reported findings. With predominantly low-ability students, Mendels & Flanders (165) and Alpert (4) found no support for the Pygmalion effect. In several studies (Dusek &

O'Connell 63; O'Connell, Dusek & Wheeler 179; Yoshida & Meyers 263) attempts to manipulate teacher expectations had no effect upon student achievement, but teacher expectations did help to predict student achievement.

Several recent studies examined teacher expectations and how they might be altered, but did not examine their possible effects upon achievement. Alpert (3) found that teachers' expectations favored poor readers. Several investigators lowered teacher expectations or evaluations with bogus psychological reports about children (Mason 157), with rare, unpopular, and unattractive children's first names, especially boys names (Harari & McDavid 101), and with bogus diagnostic labels for mental health problems (Herson 106).

The bases that teachers used to construct their expectations were also studied. The simulated classroom performance of the children (Brandt & Hayden 23), the type of classroom, traditional or open (Solomon & Kendall 227), the perceived social distance of the teacher from the pupils (Jaeger & Freijo 110), and the speech of the child (Crowl & MacGinitie 47) affected the teachers' expectations and sometimes their evaluations of the children. Teacher attitudes toward children depended more on their personal relations with the children than upon the achievement of the children (Willis & Brophy 252).

In sum, teacher expectations are related to student achievement. However, the teacher expectancy effect is found infrequently, which implies that the effect is not occurring, or that student achievement may cause teacher expectations, or that more incisive models and theories of the cognitive processes thought to be mediating the expectancy effect, and appropriate research methods, are needed to test the two causal links of the hypothesis. For example, the cognitive processes should be indexed independently of the results they are hypothesized to produce. Especially when the teachers' first-hand experience with the children disagrees with the bogus information given to the teachers should these independent indexes be obtained. Secondly, the data (Brophy & Good 28) imply that if the teacher expectancy effect exists, the best place to find it is in the natural classroom, at the dyadic level, involving a teacher and individual students, not the teacher and the classroom as a whole.

Student Ratings of Teachers

Whether they originally were thought to be useful to reinforce teachers or to transfer some control of teaching to the students, student ratings of teachers continue to be of interest to many researchers who study teaching. The latest studies help to understand some of the meanings of student ratings, which were not well understood several years ago.

Before reviewing these studies, we would like to note several methodological and conceptual problems with the research. The widely differing systems of ratings used in these studies encompass a number of different, sometimes noncomparable dimensions of teaching and student reactions. Correlations involving student ratings are also difficult to compare with one another because some of them were obtained within a class taught by one instructor while other coefficients involved multiple classes and multiple instructors. Last of all, the consumer models used in some of the studies often confuse teaching effectiveness with student ratings of teachers. Teaching effectiveness and student ratings of teachers are not synonomous with each other. Nor are they necessarily related to each other, unless one accepts a consumer or industrial model of teaching in which the goal is to please the student. An industrial model is more appropriate for the entertainment industry or for the production of inanimate consumable goods than it is for teaching or learning, where learners might be said to construct rather than consume meaning.

In an excellent review of the recent studies of student ratings of teacher characteristics in higher education, Kulik & McKeachie (132, p. 219) summarize the studies as follows: "Relations are small or nonexistent between (student) rated teaching effectiveness and teacher knowledge, ability, research productivity, or scholarly traits. . . . The highly rated teacher is verbally fluent and strikes his peers as cultured and sophisticated. He is expressive and enthusiastic. . . . The good teacher is a good talker."

Kulik & McKeachie's summary is a good introduction to our review. We find results quite similar to theirs, with additional data which indicate that the ratings commonly measure the attitudes and affective processes of students and the nontask personal characteristics of teachers. More specifically, the data indicate that the student ratings measure satisfaction, social attitudes, and popularity of teachers, more than student intellectual achievement or understanding of basic concepts and issues.

Remmers (192) found correlations between traits of instructors and student ratings to range from -.86 to +.89. He also found an average correlation of +.07 between grades and student ratings. Elliott (68) found a negative relation between the instructor's knowledge of chemistry and student ratings of teachers. Isaacson, McKeachie & Milholland (108) found high positive correlations between student ratings and the teacher's general cultural rating, agreeableness, and enthusiasm.

Rodin & Rodin (198) found a high negative correlation (-.75) between achievement and student ratings of teaching assistants. Gessner (89) found a high positive relation between teaching and achievement, but unfortunately, as Kulik & McKeachie (132) also indicated, his design leaves something to be desired. In contrast to Rodin & Rodin, Frey (80, p. 84) found positive correlations (+91 & +.60) between student ratings of the teachers' presentations and regressed final examination scores. Unfortunately, Frey's research design is also less than ideal, because the student ratings were obtained after the grades were known by the students. See Rodin (197) and Frey (81) for further discussion.

In a victory of charisma over substance, Naftulin, Ware & Donnelly (173) instructed Dr. Fox, an actor completely ignorant of the subject matter, to teach "charismatically and nonsubstantively," and to use double talk, neologisms, nonsequiturs, and contradictions in this teaching. He was rated favorably by all four groups of his students who consisted of psychologists, psychiatrists, social workers, and educators, none of whom detected the farce. They concluded that style was more important than substance in attaining high student ratings, and that student satisfaction and even the feeling of having learned reflect little more than illusions.

Zelby (264) taught sections of engineering courses either by (a) a highly structured method which closely followed the textbook stressing a "how-to-do-it" approach to textbook problems, or (b) a method which stressed understanding and transfer to new problems not always discussed in the textbooks. The students rated more highly the "how-to" approach than the method which stressed understanding, although the latter method produced greater learning, according to the author. His conclusion was that student evaluations might inhibit educational experimentation and development, especially if they are used to decide teacher salaries and promotions. Jaeger & Freijo (109) found that student ratings of the quality of the process of instruction were unrelated to their perceptions of the worth of the outcome of the instruction.

A few studies report that student ratings correlate with student achievement. Frey, Leonard & Beatty (82) found that ratings of clarity of presentation, organization, and accomplishments, but not GPA nor mathematics aptitude, correlated positively with scores on examinations. Doyle & Whitely (58) found student ratings related to student achievement, as did Sullivan & Skanes (232), and Marsh, Fleiner & Thomas (156). Several studies report that student ratings correlated with teacher personality traits or classroom behaviors that were relevant to instruction (French-Lazovik 79, Grush & Costin 98, Tobias & Hanlon 240).

Other studies report small or no relationships between student ratings of task relevant characteristics of teachers or of teaching and student achievement (Rosenshine 201). He suggests that student ratings and student attitudes have overlapping meanings.

Student ratings of teachers are often related to so-called nontask-relevant characteristics of teachers and students. These characteristics include the "warmth" of the instructor (Elmore & LaPointe 69), his popularity (Coats, Swierenga & Wickert 38), his personality (Sherman & Blackburn 220), his bogus reputation (Perry, Niemi & Jones 187), and his enthusiasm (Rosenshine, Cohen & Furst 202). These nontask-relevant characteristics related to student ratings also include the attitudes of the students, especially toward the entertainment of the course (Granzin & Painter 95), the characteristics of the students' personalities (Cunningham 48, Tolor 241), the differences between the grade expected and the grade received (Kennedy 128), the students' frames of reference (Grasha 96), the values and the life style of the student (Di Marco 57), and the needs of the student (Tetenbaum 238). Several of these studies will be described further.

In the Tetenbaum study (238), with simulated styles of teaching, the ratings of the 400 graduate students reflected their social psychological needs. The highest ratings were given to teachers who were supportive, gregarious, and facilitative of interpersonal relations, while the lowest ratings were given to teachers who encouraged competitiveness, assertive leadership, and who were ascendant. Based on their findings, the author suggested a moratorium on student ratings.

In a factor analytic study, Coats, Swierenga & Wickert (38) obtained ratings from over 40,000 high school students. One factor, the popularity of the teacher, accounted for 61% of the variance among the ratings. The other two factors each accounted for less than 10% of the total test variance. Sherman & Blackburn (220) obtained a multiple R of .77 between undergraduate student ratings of teacher effectiveness and teacher personality traits. They suggest that student ratings of teachers depend more on teachers' personality factors than on classroom procedures. Granzin & Painter (95) found that student attitudes best predicted course ratings, with required courses rated lower than courses which the students rate as relevant or important. Interesting and entertaining courses received the highest ratings. They write, "Jokes, theatrics, and simply well-chosen materials and well-delivered lectures are of major importance in achieving high course ratings . . . In any case, [to get higher ratings] an instructor should make his a course students enjoy attending" (95, p. 122).

Most research on student ratings of teachers does not indicate that the ratings measure the effectiveness of teaching, good teaching, intellectual achievement, nor understanding of basic concepts. The ratings appear to be measuring student satisfaction, the attitudes of students toward their teachers and classes, the psychosocial needs of the students, and the personality characteristics, popularity, and speaking qualities of the teacher.

Several implications about defensible uses and indefensible uses of student ratings of teachers are suggested by the finding that many of the ratings measure student attitudes and satisfactions, but not necessarily learning or achievement. A first implication is that student ratings can defensibly be used by a teacher as information for his own use about the attitudes of his students.

A related implication is that the data do not offer support for using student ratings as a measure of teaching effectiveness in deciding to employ, promote, demote, or dismiss teachers or to raise or to lower their salaries. Such questionable uses of student ratings may tend to divert teaching from long-range educational purposes to more immediately gratifying activities which can promote enjoyment rather than learning, as suggested by the comment of Granzin & Painter (95) quoted above.

A third consideration to be noted is that there are serious conceptual problems in relying on consumer or industrial models of learning and teaching, as has been done in recent studies of student ratings. One problem is that the consumer model has sometimes led to misguided attempts to decide essentially nonempirical issues by investigating empirical relationships between achievement and student ratings of teachers. The extent to which student ratings are correlated with achievement does not as such imply how large a role students should be given in the determination of curricula, courses, and the careers of teachers. Another difficulty with consumer models is their possible connotation of the learner as a passive consumer of information and knowledge. At a minimum models are needed which distinguish between teachers and entertainers, and between students and consumers of products. More useful models of teaching and learning might focus on the active constructive role of the learner, his attitudes, experiences, and abilities, in learning and in teaching, as do the psychological models of learning reviewed in this chapter. Such models could facilitate productive research on the effects of teaching upon the constructive processes of learners, which determine student achievement.

SUMMARY

We are encouraged by many of the empirical findings and conceptual developments which occurred in the study of instructional psychology during 1973, 1974, and 1975. They were productive years for the field.

In the study of attention, motivation, learning, memory, and instruction we found several lines of research that evidenced sizable effects upon learning, retention, perseverance, and transfer. Frequently these effects were attained with subject matter taught in schools, such as mathematics and reading, or with instructionally significant psychological processes, such as teaching students to attribute successes and failures to their own efforts. A closer unity between experimental psychology and differential psychology is also developing in the study of instructional psychology. The study of cognitive processes of learners has apparently contributed to the emerging unity. We also noted an increased interest in the measurement and study of comprehension, transfer, and understanding. These criteria help to direct the study of instructional psychology to some of the centrally important problems of teaching and learning.

The recent emphasis upon the construction and testing of models and theories of how learners perceive and interpret instruction has helped the individual studies we reviewed cumulate into productive sequences of research. Several examples are the study of the delay-retention effect, attribution theory, locus of control, intrinsic motivation, modeling, mental elaborations, and cognitive structures.

Several lines of research seem less productive than others, primarily because of inadequate understanding or measurement of the mechanisms hypothesized to be involved in learning from instruction. For example, mediating processes, such as the teachers' perceptions of children, need to be more clearly shown to be altered by the treatment, the bogus information about the students, in order to test the hypothesis that teachers' perceptions affect student achievement.

An encouraging aspect of the research we reviewed is its implications for instruction and teaching. Implications for instruction and teaching follow primarily from the conceptualization or model which emerges from the research, more than from each individual research study. The conceptualization which emerges from much of the research is as old as a teaching technique used in ancient Greece and Rome (Yates 262) to instruct orators in the art of memory. The conceptualization emphasizes the constructive, elaborative perceptual and cognitive processes of the learner, as they are influenced by instruction. Although the conceptualization is over 2000 years old, the recent research in instructional psychology has contributed several useful concepts to the understanding of instruction, to educational psychology, and to the unity of experimental psychology and differential psychology.

Literature Cited

1. Abelson, W. D., Zigler, E., DeBlasi, C. L. 1974. Effects of a four-year follow through program on economically disadvantaged children. *J. Educ. Psychol.* 66:756–71
2. Allen, G. J., Giat, L., Cherney, R. J. 1974. Locus of control, test anxiety, and student performance in a personalized instruction course. *J. Educ. Psychol.* 66:968–73
3. Alpert, J. L. 1974. Teacher behavior across ability groups: A consideration of the mediation of Pygmalion effects. *J. Educ. Psychol.* 66:348–53
4. Alpert, J. L. 1975. Teacher behavior and pupil performance: Reconsideration of the mediation of Pygmalion effects. *J. Educ. Res.* 69:53–57
5. Ames, R. 1975. Teachers' attributions of responsibility: Some unexpected nondefensive effects. *J. Educ. Psychol.* 67:668–76
6. Anderson, R. C. 1973. Learning principles from text. *J. Educ. Psychol.* 64:26–30
7. Anderson, R. C. 1974. Concretization and sentence learning. *J. Educ. Psychol.* 66:179–83
8. Anderson, R. C., Biddle, W. B. 1975. On asking people questions about what they are reading. In *Psychology of Learning and Motivation*, ed. G. Bower, Vol. 9. New York: Academic. 336 pp.
9. Aristotle, 1964. *On the Soul (de Anima); Parva Naturalia; and on Breath.* English transl. by W. S. Hett. Cambridge: Loeb Classical Library, Harvard Univ. Press. 528 pp.
10. Atkinson, R. C., Raugh, M. R. 1975. An application of the mnemonic keyword method to the acquisition of a Russian vocabulary. *J. Exp. Psychol.: Hum. Learn. Mem.* 1:126–33
11. Averch, H. A., Carroll, S. J., Donaldson, T. S., Kiesling, H. J., Pincus, J. 1974. *How Effective Is Schooling?* Englewood Cliffs, NJ: Educ. Technol. Publ. 258 pp.
12. Ball, S., Bogatz, G. A. 1970. *The First Year of Sesame Street: An Evaluation.* Princeton, NJ: Educ. Test. Serv. 333 pp.
13. Beckman, L. 1973. Teachers' and observers' perceptions of causality for a child's performance. *J. Educ. Psychol.* 65:198–204
14. Belcher, T. L. 1975. Modeling original divergent responses: An initial investigation. *J. Educ. Psychol.* 67:351–58
15. Bender, N. N., Taylor, A. M. 1973. Instructional treatments based on learn-

ing strategies and the recognition memory of retarded children. *Am. Educ. Res. J.* 10:337–43
16. Bennett, C. A., Lumsdaine, A. A. 1975. *Evaluation and Experiment.* New York: Academic. 554 pp.
17. Bogatz, G. A., Ball, S. 1971. *The Second Year of Sesame Street: A Continuing Evaluation.* Princeton, NJ: Educ. Test. Serv.
18. Bogen, J. E. 1975. Educational aspects of hemispheric specialization. *UCLA Educator* 17:24–32
19. Boker, J. R. 1974. Immediate and delayed retention effects of interspersing questions in written instructional passages. *J. Educ. Psychol.* 66:96–98
20. Bower, G. H. 1974. Selective facilitation and interference in retention of prose. *J. Educ. Psychol.* 66:1–8
21. Bower, G. H., Clark, M. C. 1969. Narrative stories as mediators for serial learning. *Psychon. Sci.* 14:181–82
22. Boyd, W. McK. 1973. Repeating questions in prose learning. *J. Educ. Psychol.* 64:31–38
23. Brandt, L. J., Hayden, M. E. 1974. Male and female teacher attitudes as a function of students' ascribed motivation and performance levels. *J. Educ. Psychol.* 66:309–14
24. Brandt, L. J., Hayden, M. E., Brophy, J. E. 1975. Teachers' attitudes and ascription of causation. *J. Educ. Psychol.* 67:677–82
25. Bransford, J. D., Johnson, M. K. 1972. Contextual prerequisites for understanding: Some investigations of comprehension and recall. *J. Verb. Learn. Verb. Behav.* 11:717–26
26. Breaux, R. 1975. Effects of induction versus deduction and discovery versus utilization on transfer of information. *J. Educ. Psychol.* 67:828–32
27. Bridgeman, B. 1974. Effects of test score feedback on immediately subsequent test performance. *J. Educ. Psychol.* 66:62–66
28. Brophy, J. E., Good, T. L. 1974. *Teacher-Student Relationships: Courses and Consequences.* New York: Holt, Rinehart & Winston. 400 pp.
29. Bull, S. G., Dizney, H. F. 1973. Epistemic-curiosity-arousing prequestions: Their effect on long-term retention. *J. Educ. Psychol.* 65:45–49
30. Bull, B. L., Wittrock, M. C. 1973. Imagery in the learning of verbal definitions. *Br. J. Educ. Psychol.* 43:289–93

31. Byalick, R., Bersoff, D. N. 1974. Reinforcement practices of black and white teachers in integrated classrooms. *J. Educ. Psychol.* 66:473–80
32. Calder, B. J., Staw, B. M. 1975. Interaction of intrinsic and extrinsic motivation: Some methodological notes. *J. Pers. Soc. Psychol.* 31:76–80
33. Calfee, R. C., Lindamood, P., Lindamood, C. 1973. Acoustic-phonetic skills and reading—kindergarten through twelfth grade. *J. Educ. Psychol.* 64: 293–98
34. Carver, R. P. 1973. Understanding, information processing, and learning from prose materials. *J. Educ. Psychol.* 64:76–84
35. Cater, D., Strickland, S. 1975. *TV Violence and the Child.* New York: Sage Found. 167 pp.
36. Chalmers, D. K., Rosenbaum, M. E. 1974. Learning by observing versus learning by doing. *J. Educ. Psychol.* 66:216–24
37. Chambers, J. A. 1973. College teachers: Their effect on creativity of students. *J. Educ. Psychol.* 65:326–34
38. Coats, W. D., Swierenga, L., Wickert, L. 1972. Student perceptions of teachers —A factor analytic study. *J. Educ. Res.* 65:357–60
39. Collins, A. M., Loftus, E. F. 1975. A spreading-activation theory of semantic processing. *Psychol. Rev.* 82:407–28
40. Comstock, G. A., Rubinstein, E. A., eds. 1972. *Television and Social Behavior I: Media Content and Control.* Rockville, Md: Natl. Inst. Mental Health, HEW. 546 pp.
41. Cook, T. D., Appleton, H., Conner, R. F., Shaffer, A., Tamkin, G., Weber, S. J. 1975. *"Sesame Street" Revisited.* New York: Sage. 410 pp.
42. Cook, H., Smothergill, D. W. 1973. Racial and sex determinants of imitative performance and knowledge in young children. *J. Educ. Psychol.* 65:211–15
43. Craik, F. I. M., Lockhart, R. S. 1972. Levels of processing: A framework for memory research. *J. Verb. Learn. Verb. Behav.* 11:671–84
44. Craik, F. I. M., Tulving, E. 1975. Depth of processing and the retention of words in episodic memory. *J. Exp. Psychol.: Gen.* 1:268–94
45. Cronbach, L. J. 1975. Beyond the two disciplines of scientific psychology. *Am. Psychol.* 30:116–27
46. Cronbach, L. J., Snow, R. E. 1976. *Aptitudes and Instructional Methods.* New York: Irvington. In press
47. Crowl, T. K., MacGinitie, W. H. 1974. The influence of students' speech characteristics on teachers' evaluations of oral answers. *J. Educ. Psychol.* 66: 304–8
48. Cunningham, W. G. 1975. The impact of student-teacher pairings on teacher effectiveness. *Am. Educ. Res. J.* 12: 169–89
49. Das, J. P. 1973. Structure of cognitive abilities: Evidence for simultaneous and successive processing. *J. Educ. Psychol.* 65:103–8
50. deCharms, R. 1968. *Personal Causation: The Internal Affective Determinants of Behavior.* New York: Academic. 398 pp.
51. deCharms, R. 1971. From pawns to origins: Toward self-motivation. In *Psychology and Educational Practice,* ed. G. Lesser, 380–407. Glenview, Ill: Scott, Foresman. 580 pp.
52. deCharms, R. 1972. Personal causation training in the schools. *J. Appl. Psychol.* 2:95–113
53. Deci, E. L. 1975. *Intrinsic Motivation.* New York: Plenum. 324 pp.
54. Deci, E. L., Cascio, W. F., Krusell, J. 1975. Cognitive evaluation theory and some comments on the Calder and Staw critique. *J. Pers. Soc. Psychol.* 31:81–85
55. Denney, D. R. 1974. Relationship of three cognitive style dimensions to elementary reading abilities. *J. Educ. Psychol.* 66:702–9
56. Diaz-Guerrero, R., Holtzman, W. H. 1974. Learning by televised "Plaza Sesamo" in Mexico. *J. Educ. Psychol.* 66:632–43
57. Di Marco, N. 1974. Life style, learning structure, congruence and student attitudes. *Am. Educ. Res. J.* 11:203–9
58. Doyle, K. O. Jr., Whitely, S. E. 1974. Student ratings as criteria for effective teaching. *Am. Educ. Res. J.* 11:259–74
59. Duchastel, P. C., Brown,B. R. 1974. Incidental and relevant learning with instructional objectives. *J. Educ. Psychol.* 66:481–85
60. Duchastel, P. C., Merrill, P. F. 1973. The effects of behavioral objectives on learning. A review of empirical studies. *Rev. Educ. Res.* 43:53–69
61. Duell, O. K. 1974. Effect of type of objective, level of test questions, and the judged importance of tested materials upon posttest performance. *J. Educ. Psychol.* 66:225–32
62. Durnin, J., Scandura, J. M. 1973. An algorithmic approach to assessing be-

havior potential. *J. Educ. Psychol.* 65:262–72

63. Dusek, J. B., O'Connell, E. J. 1973. Teacher expectancy effects on the achievement test performance of elementary school children. *J. Educ. Psychol.* 65:371–77

64. Dweck, C. S. 1975. The role of expectations and attributions in the alleviation of learned helplessness. *J. Pers. Soc. Psychol.* 31:674–85

65. Egan, D. E., Greeno, J. G. 1973. Acquiring cognitive structure by discovery and rule learning. *J. Educ. Psychol.* 64:85–97

66. Ehrenpreis, W., Scandura, J. M. 1974. The algorithmic approach to curriculum construction: A field test in mathematics. *J. Educ. Psychol.* 66:491–98

67. Ehri, L. C., Muzio, I. M. 1974. Cognitive style and reasoning about speed. *J. Educ. Psychol.* 66:569–71

68. Elliott, D. N. 1950. Characteristics and relationships of various criteria of college and university teaching. *Purdue Univ. Stud. Higher Educ.* 70:5–61

69. Elmore, P. B., LaPointe, K. A. 1975. Effect of teacher sex, student sex, and teacher warmth on the evaluation of college instructors. *J. Educ. Psychol.* 67:368–74

69a. Ellson, D. G., Chiam Tah Wen, Le Thi Kim Hai. 1973. The TECH Programme: a self-instructional programme for English listening comprehension. *SEAMO, INNOTECH Project, Final Rep. TP-FR/73*

70. Eron, L. D., Huesmann, L. R., Lefkowitz, M. M., Walder, L. O. 1972. Does television violence cause aggression? *Am. Psychol.* 27:253–63

71. Felker, D. B., Dapra, R. A. 1975. Effects of question type and question placement on problem-solving ability from prose material. *J. Educ. Psychol.* 67:380–84

72. Francis, E. W. 1975. Grade level and task difficulty in learning by discovery and verbal reception methods. *J. Educ. Psychol.* 67:146–50

73. Frase, L. T. 1973. Integration of written text. *J. Educ. Psychol.* 65:252–61

74. Frase, L. T. 1973. Sampling and response requirements of adjunct questions. *J. Educ. Psychol.* 65:273–78

75. Frase, L. T. 1975. Prose processing. In *Psychology of Learning and Motivation,* ed. G. Bower, Vol. 9. New York: Academic. 336 pp.

76. Frase, L. T., Kreitzberg, V. S. 1975. Effect of topical and indirect learning directions on prose recall. *J. Educ. Psychol.* 67:320–24

77. Frederiksen, J. D., Rohwer, W. D. Jr. 1974. Elaborative prompt effects in children's paired-associate learning: Design and population comparisons. *J. Educ. Psychol.* 66:83–89

78. Frederiksen, N., Evans, F. R. 1974. Effects of models of creative performance on ability to formulate hypotheses. *J. Educ. Psychol.* 66:67–82

79. French-Lazovik, G. 1974. Predictability of students' evaluations of college teachers from component ratings. *J. Educ. Psychol.* 66:373–85

80. Frey, P. W. 1973. Student ratings of teaching: Validity of several rating factors. *Science* 182:83–85

81. Frey, P. W. 1975. Student evaluation. *Science* 187:557–58

82. Frey, P. W., Leonard, D. W., Beatty, W. W. 1975. Student ratings of instruction: Validation research. *Am. Educ. Res. J.* 12:435–47

83. Friedman, P. 1973. Student imitation of a teacher's verbal style as a function of natural classroom reinforcement. *J. Educ. Psychol.* 64:267–73

84. Friedrich, L. K., Stein, A. H. 1975. Prosocial television and young children: The effects of verbal labeling and role playing on learning and behavior. *Child Dev.* 46:27–38

85. Gaines, R. 1975. Developmental perception and cognitive styles: From young children to master artists. *Percept. Mot. Skills* 40:983–98

86. Gagné, E. D., Rothkopf, E. Z. 1975. Text organization and learning goals. *J. Educ. Psychol.* 67:445–50

87. Garrett, C. S., Cunningham, D. J. 1974. Effects of vicarious consequences and model and experimenter sex on imitative behavior in first-grade children. *J. Educ. Psychol.* 66:940–47

88. Geeslin, W. E., Shavelson, R. J. 1975. An exploratory analysis of the representation of a mathematical structure in students' cognitive structures. *Am. Educ. Res. J.* 12:21–39

89. Gessner, P. K. 1973. Evaluation of instruction. *Science* 180:566–70

90. Gibson, E. J., Levin, H. 1975. *The Psychology of Reading.* Cambridge, Mass: MIT. 629 pp.

90a. Glaser, R., Resnick, L. B. 1972. Instructional psychology. *Ann. Rev. Psychol.* 23:207–76

91. Goldberg, F. 1974. Effects of imagery on learning incidental material in the classroom. *J. Educ. Psychol.* 66:233–37
92. Goldman, R. D., Hudson, D. J. 1973. A multivariate analysis of academic abilities and strategies for successful and unsuccessful college students in different major fields. *J. Educ. Psychol.* 65:364–70
93. Goulet, L. R., Williams, K. G., Hay, C. M. 1974. Longitudinal changes in intellectual functioning in preschool children: Schooling and age-related effects. *J. Educ. Psychol.* 66:657–62
94. Gozali, H., Cleary, T. A., Walster, G. W., Gozali, J. 1973. Relationship between the internal-external control construct and achievement. *J. Educ. Psychol.* 64:9–14
95. Granzin, K. L., Painter, J. J. 1973. A new explanation for students' course evaluation tendencies. *Am. Educ. Res. J.* 10:115–24
96. Grasha, A. F. 1975. The role of internal instructor frames of reference in the student rating process. *J. Educ. Psychol.* 67:451–60
97. Greeno, J. G. 1973. The structure of memory and the process of solving problems. *Contemporary Issues in Cognitive Psychology: The Loyola Symposium,* ed. R. L. Solso, pp. 103–34. New York: Halsted. 348 pp.
98. Grush, J. E., Costin, F. 1975. The student as consumer of the teaching process. *Am. Educ. Res. J.* 12:55–66
99. Guthrie, J. T. 1973. Models of reading and reading disability. *J. Educ. Psychol.* 65:9–18
100. Guttentag, M., Struening, E., eds. 1975. *Handbook of Evaluation Research: Vol. 2.* Beverly Hills, Calif: Sage. 704 pp.
101. Harari, H., McDavid, J. W. 1973. Name stereotypes and teachers' expectations. *J. Educ. Psychol.* 65:222–25
102. Hartnett, D. 1975. *The relation of cognitive style and hemispheric preference to deductive and inductive second language learning.* MA thesis. Univ. California, Los Angeles. 35 pp.
103. Hawkridge, D. G., DeWitt, K. M. 1969. *An evaluation of the programed tutoring technique.* Palo Alto, Calif: Am. Inst. Res. Rep. No. A102–822–3/69–FR
104. Heckhausen, H. 1975. Fear of falling as a self-reinforcing motive system. In *Stress and Anxiety,* ed. I. G. Sarasen, C. Spielberger, Vol. 2. Washington, DC: Hemisphere
105. Henderson, R. W., Swanson, R., Zimmerman, B. J. 1975. Training seriation responses in young children through televised modeling of hierarchically sequenced rule components. *Am. Educ. Res. J.* 12:479–89
106. Herson, P. F. 1974. Biasing effects of diagnostic labels and sex of pupil on teachers' views of pupils' mental health. *J. Educ. Psychol.* 66:117–22
107. Hovland, C. I., Lumsdaine, A. A., Sheffield, F. D. 1949. *Experiments on Mass Communication.* Princeton, NJ: Princeton Univ. Press. 345 pp.
108. Isaacson, R. L., McKeachie, W., Milholland, J. E. 1963. Correlation of teacher personality variables and student ratings. *J. Educ. Psychol.* 54:110–17
109. Jaeger, R. M., Freijo, T. D. 1974. Some psychometric questions in the evaluation of professors. *J. Educ. Psychol.* 66:416–23
110. Jaeger, R. M. Freijo, T. D. 1975. Race and sex as concomitants of composite halo in teachers' evaluative rating of pupils. *J. Educ. Psychol.* 67:226–37
111. Jenkins, J. J. 1974. Remember that old theory of memory? Well, forget it! *Am. Psychol.* 29:785–95
112. Jensen, A. R. 1973. Level I and level II abilities in three ethnic groups. *Am. Educ. Res. J.* 10:263–76
113. Jensen, A. R. 1974. Interaction of level I and level II abilities with race and socioeconomic status. *J. Educ. Psychol.* 66:99–111
114. Jensen, A. R., Figueroa, R. A. 1975. Forward and backward digit span interaction with race and IQ: Predictions from Jensen's theory. *J. Educ. Psychol.* 67:882–93
115. Jensen, A. R., Frederiksen, J. 1973. Free recall of categorized and uncategorized lists: A test of the Jensen hypothesis. *J. Educ. Psychol.* 65:304–12
116. Johnson, R. A. 1974. Differential effects of reward versus no-reward instructions on the creative thinking of two economic levels of elementary school children. *J. Educ. Psychol.* 66:530–33
117. Johnson, R. E. 1973. Meaningfulness and the recall of textual prose. *Am. Educ. Res. J.* 10:49–58
118. Johnson, R. E. 1974. Abstractive processes in the remembering of prose. *J. Educ. Psychol.* 66:772–79
119. Johnson, R. E. 1975. Meaning in complex learning. *Rev. Educ. Res.* 45:425–59
120. Johnson, W. G., Croft, R. G. 1975. Locus of control and participation in a

personalized system of instruction course. *J. Educ. Psychol.* 67:416–21

121. Kagan, S., Zahn, G. L. 1975. Field dependence and the school achievement gap between Anglo-American and Mexican-American children. *J. Educ. Psychol.* 67:643–50

122. Kalbaugh, G. L., Walls, R. T. 1973. Retroactive and proactive interference in prose learning of biographical and science materials. *J. Educ. Psychol.* 65:244–51

123. Kaplan, R. 1974. Effects of learning prose with part versus whole presentations of instructional objectives. *J. Educ. Psychol.* 66:787–92

124. Kaplan, R., Rothkopf, E. Z. 1974. Instructional objectives as directions to learners: Effect of passage length and amount of objective-relevant content. *J. Educ. Psychol.* 66:448–56

125. Kaplan, R., Simmons, F. G. 1974. Effects of instructional objectives used as orienting stimuli or as summary/review upon prose learning. *J. Educ. Psychol.* 66:614–22

126. Kazdin, A. E. 1973. Role of instructions and reinforcement in behavior changes in token reinforcement programs. *J. Educ. Psychol.* 64:63–71

127. Kee, D. W., Rohwer, W. D. Jr. 1973. Noun-pair learning in four ethnic groups: Conditions of presentation and response. *J. Educ. Psychol.* 65:226–32

128. Kennedy, W. R. 1975. Grades expected and grades received—their relationship to students' evaluations of faculty performance. *J. Educ. Psychol.* 67:109–15

129. Kissler, G. R., Lloyd, K. E. 1973. Effect of sentence interrelation and scrambling on the recall of factual information. *J. Educ. Psychol.* 64:187–90

130. Klemt, L. L., Anderson, R. C. 1973. Effects of sentence elaboration and frequency of usage on noun-pair learning. *J. Educ. Psychol.* 65:25–27

131. Koran, M. L., Koran, J. J. Jr. 1975. Interaction of learner aptitudes with question pacing in learning from prose. *J. Educ. Psychol.* 67:76–82

132. Kulik, J. A., McKeachie, W. J. 1975. The evaluation of teachers in higher education. In *Review of Research in Education*, ed. F. N. Kerlinger, 3:210–40. Itasca, Ill: Peacock. 305 pp.

133. Labouvie, G. V., Frohring, W. R., Baltes, P. B., Goulet, L. R. 1973. Changing relationship between recall performance and abilities as a function of stage of learning and timing of recall. *J. Educ. Psychol.* 64:191–98

134. Labouvie-Vief, G., Levin, J. R., Urberg, K. A. 1975. The relationship between selected cognitive abilities and learning: A second look. *J. Educ. Psychol.* 67:558–69

135. Ladas, H. 1973. The mathemagenic effects of factual review questions on the learning of incidental information: A critical review. *Rev. Educ. Res.* 43:71–82

136. Landa, L. N. 1974. *Algorithmization in Learning and Instruction.* V. Bennett; scientific ed., F. F. Kopstein. Englewood Cliffs, NJ: Educ. Technol. Publ. 713 pp.

137. Lashley, K. S., Watson, J. B. 1922. *A Psychological Study of Motion Pictures in Relation to Venereal Disease Campaigns.* Washington DC: US Interdep. Soc. Hyg. Board. 89 pp.

138. Lepper, M. R., Greene, D. 1975. Turning play into work: Effects of adult surveillance and extrinsic rewards on children's intrinsic motivation. *J. Pers. Soc. Psychol.* 31:479–86

139. Lepper, M. R., Greene, D., Nisbett, R. E. 1973. Undermining children's intrinsic interest with extrinsic reward: A test of the "overjustification" hypothesis. *J. Pers. Soc. Psychol.* 28:129–37

140. Lesgold, A. M., Levin, J. R., Shimron, J., Guttman, J. 1975. Pictures and young children's learning from oral prose. *J. Educ. Psychol.* 67:636–42

141. Levin, J. R. 1973. Inducing comprehension in poor readers: A test of a recent model. *J. Educ. Psychol.* 65:19–24

142. Levin, J. R., Davidson, R. E., Wolff, P., Citron, M. 1973. A comparison of induced imagery and sentence strategies in children's paired-associate learning. *J. Educ. Psychol.* 64:306–9

143. Levin, J. R., Divine-Hawkins, P., Kerst, S. M., Guttman, J. 1974. Individual differences in learning from pictures and words: The development and application of an instrument. *J. Educ. Psychol.* 66:296–303

144. Levin, J. R., Ghatala, E. S., DeRose, T. M., Wilder, L., Norton, R. W. 1975. A further comparison of imagery and vocalization strategies in children's discrimination learning. *J. Educ. Psychol.* 67:141–45

145. Levin, J. R., Ghatala, E. S., Wilder, L., Inzer, E. 1973. Imagery and vocalization strategies in children's verbal discrimination learning. *J. Educ. Psychol.* 64:360–65

146. Levine, F. M., Fasnacht, G. 1974. To-

ken rewards may lead to token learning. *Am. Psychol.* 29:816–20

147. Liebert, R. M., Baron, R. A. 1972. Some immediate effects of televised violence on children's behavior. *Dev. Psychol.* 6:469–75

148. Liebert, R. M., Neale, J. M., Davidson, E. S. 1973. *The Early Window: Effects of Television on Children and Youth.* New York: Pergamon. 193 pp.

149. Lintner, A. C., Ducette, J. 1974. The effects of locus of control, academic failure, and task dimensions on a student's responsiveness to praise. *Am. Educ. Res. J.* 11:231–39

150. Lippman, M. Z., Shanahan, M. W. 1973. Pictorial facilitation of paired-associate learning: Implications for vocabulary training. *J. Educ. Psychol.* 64:216–22

150a. Lumsdaine, A. A., ed. 1961. *Student Response in Programmed Instruction.* Washington DC: Natl. Acad. Sci.

151. Lumsdaine, A. A. 1963. Instruments and media of instruction. In *Handbook of Research on Teaching,* ed. N. L. Gage, pp. 583–682. Chicago: Rand-McNally. 1218 pp.

152. Lumsdaine, A. A. 1971. Some comments on strategy and tactics in research on instructional materials. In *Verbal Learning Research and the Technology of Written Instruction,* ed. E. Z. Rothkopf, P. E. Johnson, pp. 356–67. New York: Teachers Coll., Columbia Univ. 367 pp.

152a. Lumsdaine, A. A., May, M. A. 1965. Mass communication and educational media. *Ann. Rev. Psychol.* 16:475–534

153. MacMillan, D. L., Wright, D. L. 1974. Outerdirectedness in children of three ages as a function of experimentally induced success and failure. *J. Educ. Psychol.* 66:919–25

154. Marholin, D. II, McInnis, E. T., Heads, T. B. 1974. Effect of two free-time reinforcement procedures on academic performance in a class of behavior problem children. *J. Educ. Psychol.* 66:872–79

155. Marks, C. B., Doctorow, M. J., Wittrock, M. C. 1974. Word frequency and reading comprehension. *J. Educ. Res.* 67:259–62

156. Marsh, H. W., Fleiner, H., Thomas, C. S. 1975. Validity and usefulness of student evaluations of instructional quality. *J. Educ. Psychol.* 67:833–39

157. Mason, E. J. 1973. Teachers' observations and expectations of boys and girls as influenced by biased psychological reports and knowledge of the effects of bias. *J. Educ. Psychol.* 65:238–43

158. May, M. A., Lumsdaine, A. A. 1958. *Learning from Films.* New Haven, Conn: Yale Univ. 357 pp.

159. Mayer, R. E. 1975. Different problem-solving competencies established in learning computer programming with and without meaningful models. *J. Educ. Psychol.* 67:725–34

160. Mayer, R. E. 1975. Forward transfer of different reading strategies evoked by testlike events in mathematics text. *J. Educ. Psychol.* 67:165–69

161. Mayer, R. E., Stiehl, C. C., Greeno, J. G. 1975. Acquisition of understanding and skill in relation to subjects' preparation and meaningfulness of instruction. *J. Educ. Psychol.* 67:331–50

162. McKeachie, W. J. 1974. Instructional psychology. *Ann. Rev. Psychol.* 25:161–93

163. McKinney, J. D. 1975. Problem-solving strategies in reflective and impulsive children. *J. Educ. Psychol.* 67:807–20

164. Meissner, J. A. 1975. Use of relational concepts by inner-city children. *J. Educ. Psychol.* 67:22–29

165. Mendels, G. E., Flanders, J. P. 1973. Teachers' expectations and pupil performance. *Am. Educ. Res. J.* 10:203–12

166. Merton, R. K. 1948. The self-fulfilling prophecy. *Antioch Rev.* 8:193–210

167. Meyer, B. J. F., McConkie, G. W. 1973. What is recalled after hearing a passage? *J. Educ. Psychol.* 65:109–17

168. Mischel, W., Baker, N. 1975. Cognitive appraisals and transformations in delay behavior. *J. Pers. Soc. Psychol.* 31:254–61

169. Mischel, W., Ebbesen, E. B., Zeiss, A. R. 1972. Cognitive and attentional mechanisms in delay of gratification. *J. Pers. Soc. Psychol.* 21:204–18

170. Mosteller, F., Moynihan, D. P. 1972. *On Equality of Educational Opportunity.* New York: Vintage Books. 570 pp.

171. Mouw, J. T., Hecht, J. T. 1973. Transfer of the "concept" of class inclusion. *J. Educ. Psychol.* 64:57–62

172. Myers, J. L., Pezdek, K., Coulson, D. 1973. Effect of prose organization upon free recall. *J. Educ. Psychol.* 65:313–20

173. Naftulin, D. H., Ware, J. E. Jr., Donnelly, F. A. 1973. The Doctor Fox lecture: A paradigm of educational seduction. *J. Med. Educ.* 48:630–35

174. Nazzaro, J. N., Nazzaro, J. R. 1973. Associative and conceptual learning in disadvantaged and middle-class children. *J. Educ. Psychol.* 65:341–44

175. Nelson, G. K., Klausmeier, H. J. 1974. Classificatory behaviors of low-socioeconomic-status children. *J. Educ. Psychol.* 66:432–38

176. Nord, W. R., Connelly, F., Diagnault, G. 1974. Locus of control and aptitude test scores as predictors of academic achievement. *J. Educ. Psychol.* 66: 956–61

177. Norman, D. A. 1973. Memory, knowledge, and the answering of questions. In *Contemporary Issues in Cognitive Psychology: The Loyola Symposium*, ed. R. L. Solso, pp. 135–66. New York: Halsted. 348 pp.

178. Notz, W. W. 1975. Work motivation and the negative effects of extrinsic rewards. *Am. Psychol.* 30:884–91

179. O'Connell, E. J., Dusek, J. B., Wheeler, R. J. 1974. A follow-up study of teacher expectancy effects. *J. Educ. Psychol.* 66:325–28

180. Paivio, A. 1971. *Imagery and Verbal Processes.* New York: Holt. 596 pp.

181. Paivio, A. 1974. Language and knowledge of the world. *Educ. Res.* 3 (9):5–12

182. Parent, J., Forward, J., Canter, R., Mohling, J. 1975. Interactive effects of teaching strategy and personal locus of control on student performance and satisfaction. *J. Educ. Psychol.* 67:764–69

183. Paris, S. G., Mahoney, G. T. 1974. Cognitive integration in children's memory for sentences and pictures. *Child Dev.* 45:633–42

184. Paton, S. M., Walberg, H. J., Yeh, E. G. 1973. Ethnicity, environmental control, and academic self-concept in Chicago. *Am. Educ. Res. J.* 10:85–99

185. Pearson, P. D., Studt, A. 1975. Effects of word frequency and contextual richness on children's word identification abilities. *J. Educ. Psychol.* 67:89–95

186. Perloff, R., Perloff, E., Sussna, E. 1975. Program evaluation. *Ann. Rev. Psychol.* 27:569–94

187. Perry, R. P., Niemi, R., Jones, K. 1974. Effect of prior teaching evaluations and lecture presentation on ratings of teaching performance. *J. Educ. Psychol.* 66:851–56

188. Popham, W. J., ed. 1974. *Evaluation in Education.* Berkeley, Calif.: McCutchan. 585 pp.

189. Quay, L. C. 1975. Reinforcement and Binet performance in disadvantaged children. *J. Educ. Psychol.* 67:132–35

190. Rasco, R. W., Tennyson, R. D., Boutwell, R. C. 1975. Imagery instructions and drawings in learning prose. *J. Educ. Psychol.* 67:188–92

191. Raugh, M. R., Atkinson, R. C. 1975. A mnemonic method for learning a second-language vocabulary. *J. Educ. Psychol.* 67:1–16

192. Remmers, H. H. 1928. The relationship between students' marks and student attitude toward instructors. *Sch. Soc.* 28:759–60

193. Rickards, J. P., August, G. J. 1975. Generative underlining strategies in prose recall. *J. Educ. Psychol.* 67: 860–65

194. Rickards, J. P., DiVesta, F. J. 1974. Type and frequency of questions in processing textual material. *J. Educ. Psychol.* 66:354–62

195. Riecken, H. W., Boruch, R. F., eds. 1974. *Social Experimentation: A Method for Planning and Evaluating Social Intervention.* New York: Academic. 339 pp.

196. Robinson, J. E., Gray, J. L. 1974. Cognitive style as a variable in school learning. *J. Educ. Psychol.* 66: 793–99

197. Rodin, M. 1975. Student evaluation. *Science* 187:555–57

198. Rodin, M., Rodin, B. 1972. Student evaluations of teachers. *Science* 177: 1164–66

199. Rohwer, W. D. Jr., Harris, W. J. 1975. Media effects on prose learning in two populations of children. *J. Educ. Psychol.* 67:651–57

200. Rosenshine, B. 1971. *Teaching Behaviors and Student Achievement.* Windsor, England: Natl. Found Educ. Res. in England and Wales. 229 pp.

201. Rosenshine, B. 1973. Teacher behavior and student attitudes revisited. *J. Educ. Psychol.* 65:177–80

202. Rosenshine, B., Cohen, A., Furst, N. 1973. Correlates of student preference ratings. *J. Coll. Stud. Personnel* 14:269–72

203. Rosenthal, D. J. A., Resnick, L. B. 1974. Children's solution processes in arithmetic word problems. *J. Educ. Psychol.* 66:817–25

204. Rosenthal, R., Jacobsen, L. 1968. *Pygmalion in the Classroom: Teacher Expectation and Pupils' Intellectual Development.* New York: Holt, Rinehart & Winston. 240 pp.

205. Ross, D. M., Ross, S. A. 1973. Storage and utilization of previously formulated mediators in educable mentally retarded children. *J. Educ. Psychol.* 65:205–10

206. Rothkopf, E. Z., Billington, M. J. 1974. Indirect review and priming through questions. *J. Educ. Psychol.* 66:669–79

207. Rothkopf, E. Z., Billington, M. J. 1975. A two-factor model of the effect of goal-descriptive directions on learning from text. *J. Educ. Psychol.* 67:692–704

208. Rothkopf, E. Z., Kaplan, R. 1972. Exploration of the effect of density and specificity of instructional objectives on learning from text. *J. Educ. Psychol.* 63:295–302

209. Royer, J. M., Cable, G. W. 1975. Facilitated learning in connected discourse. *J. Educ. Psychol.* 67:116–23

210. Royer, J. M., Kulhavy, R. W. 1973. Encoding behavior while learning thematically prompted paired associates. *J. Educ. Psychol.* 64:39–45

211. Salomon, G. 1974. Internalization of filmic schematic operations in interaction with learners' aptitudes. *J. Educ. Psychol.* 66:499–511

212. Samuels, S. J. 1973. Effect of distinctive feature training on paired-associate learning. *J. Educ. Psychol.* 64:164–70

213. Samuels, S. J., Anderson, R. H. 1973. Visual recognition memory, paired-associate learning, and reading achievement. *J. Educ. Psychol.* 65:160–67

214. Samuels, S. J., Dahl, P. R. 1975. Establishing appropriate purpose for reading and its effect on flexibility of reading rate. *J. Educ. Psychol.* 67:38–43

215. Samuels, S. J., Dahl, P., Archwamety, T. 1974. Effect of hypothesis/test training on reading skill. *J. Educ. Psychol.* 66:835–44

216. Samuels, S. J., Turnure, J. E. 1974. Attention and reading achievement in first-grade boys and girls. *J. Educ. Psychol.* 66:29–32

217. Sassenrath, J. M. 1975. Theory and results on feedback and retention. *J. Educ. Psychol.* 67:894–99

218. Scandura, J. M. 1974. Role of higher order rules in problem solving. *J. Exp. Psychol.* 102:984–91

219. Shavelson, R. J. 1974. Some methods for examining content structure and cognitive structure in instruction. *Educ. Psychol.* 11:110–22

220. Sherman, B. R., Blackburn, R. T. 1975. Personal characteristics and teaching effectiveness of college faculty. *J. Educ. Psychol.* 67:124–31

221. Shuell, T. J., Giglio, J. 1973. Learning ability and short-term memory. *J. Educ. Psychol.* 64:261–66

222. Siegel, A. I., Lautman, M. R., Burkett, J. R. 1974. Reading grade level adjustment and auditory supplementation as techniques for increasing textual comprehensibility. *J. Educ. Psychol.* 66:895–902

223. Silverston, R. A., Deichmann, J. W. 1975. Sense modality research and the acquisition of reading skills. *Rev. Educ. Res.* 45:149–72

224. Skanes, G. R., Sullivan, A. M., Rowe, E. J., Shannon, E. 1974. Intelligence and transfer: Aptitude by treatment interactions. *J. Educ. Psychol.* 66:563–68

225. Skilbeck, W. M. 1975. *Effects of participant involvement on expectational influence: An investigation of experimenter bias.* PhD dissertation. Univ. California, Los Angeles. 203 pp.

226. Snowman, J., Cunningham, D. J. 1975. A comparison of pictorial and written adjunct aids in learning from text. *J. Educ. Psychol.* 67:307–11

227. Solomon, D., Kendall, A. J. 1975. Teachers' perceptions of and reactions to misbehavior in traditional and open classrooms. *J. Educ. Psychol.* 67:528–30

228. Sproull, N. 1973. Visual attention, modeling behaviors, and other verbal and nonverbal meta-communication of prekindergarten children viewing Sesame Street. *Am. Educ. Res. J.* 10:101–14

229. Stolurow, K. A. C. 1975. Objective rules of sequencing applied to instructional material. *J. Educ. Psychol.* 67:909–12

230. Strike, K. A. 1974. On the expressive potential of behaviorist language. *Am. Educ. Res. J.* 11:103–20

231. Struening, E., Guttentag, M. 1975. *Handbook of Evaluation Research: Vol. I.* Beverly Hills, Calif: Sage. 704 pp.

232. Sullivan, A. M., Skanes, G. R. 1974. Validity of student evaluation of teaching and the characteristics of successful instructors. *J. Educ. Psychol.* 66:584–90

233. Surber, J. R., Anderson, R. C. 1975. Delay-retention effect in natural classroom settings. *J. Educ. Psychol.* 67:170–73

234. Surgeon General's Scientific Advisory Committee on Television and Social Behavior 1972. *Television and Growing Up: The Impact of Televised Violence: Report to the Surgeon General.* Washington DC: USGPO. 279 pp.

235. Swenson, I., Kulhavy, R. W. 1974. Adjunct questions and the comprehension of prose by children. *J. Educ. Psychol.* 66:212–15

236. Taffel, S. J., O'Leary, K. D., Armel, S. 1974. Reasoning and praise: Their effects on academic behavior. *J. Educ. Psychol.* 66:291–95

237. Taylor, A. M., Josberger, M., Whitely, S. E. 1973. Elaboration instruction and verbalization as factors facilitating retarded children's recall. *J. Educ. Psychol.* 64:341–46

238. Tetenbaum, T. J. 1975. The role of student needs and teacher orientations in student ratings of teachers. *Am. Educ. Res. J.* 12:417–33

239. Thompson, M., Brassell, W. R., Persons, S., Tucker, R., Rollins, H. 1974. Contingency management in the schools: How often and how well does it work? *Am. Educ. Res. J.* 11:19–28

240. Tobias, S., Hanlon, R. 1975. Attitudes toward instructors, social desirability, and behavioral intentions. *J. Educ. Psychol.* 67:405–8

241. Tolor, A. 1973. Evaluation of perceived teacher effectiveness. *J. Educ. Psychol.* 64:98–104

242. Tulving, E., Thomson, D. M. 1973. Encoding specificity and retrieval processes in episodic memory. *Psychol. Rev.* 80:352–73

243. Varley, W. H., Levin, J. R., Severson, R. A., Wolff, P. 1974. Training imagery production in young children through motor involvement. *J. Educ. Psychol.* 66:262–66

244. Veldman, D. J., Brophy, J. E. 1974. Measuring teacher effects on pupil achievement. *J. Educ. Psychol.* 66: 319–24

245. Voss, J. F. 1974. Acquisition and nonspecific transfer effects in prose learning as a function of question form. *J. Educ. Psychol.* 66:736–40

246. Wagner, A. C. 1973. Changing teacher behavior: A comparison of microteaching and cognitive discrimination training. *J. Educ. Psychol.* 64:299–305

247. Walker, B. S. 1974. Effects of inserted questions on retroactive inhibition in meaningful verbal learning. *J. Educ. Psychol.* 66:486–90

248. Weiner, B. 1977. An attributional approach for educational psychology. In *Review of Research in Education,* ed. L. Shulman, Vol. 4. Itasca, Ill: Peacock. In press

249. White, R. T. 1974. The validation of a learning hierarchy. *Am. Educ. Res. J.* 11:121–36

250. Wiley, D. E., Harnischfeger, A. 1974. Explosion of a myth: Quantity of schooling and exposure to instruction, major educational vehicles. *Educ. Res.* 3 (4):7–12

251. Williams, J. P. 1973. Learning to read: A review of theories and models. *Reading Res. Q.* 8:121–46

252. Willis, S., Brophy, J. 1974. Origins of teachers' attitudes toward young children. *J. Educ. Psychol.* 66:520–29

253. Wittrock, M. C. 1974. A generative model of mathematics learning. *J. Res. Math. Educ.* 5:181–96

254. Wittrock, M. C. 1974. Learning as a generative process. *Educ. Psychol.* 11:87–95

255. Wittrock, M. C. 1975. The generative processes of memory. In *Education and the Hemispheric Processes of the Brain,* ed. M. C. Wittrock. *UCLA Educ.* 17:33–43

256. Wittrock, M. C., Carter, J. 1975. Generative processing of hierarchically organized words. *Am. J. Psychol.* 88:489–501

257. Wittrock, M. C., Cook, H. 1975. Transfer of prior learning to verbal instruction. *Am. Educ. Res. J.* 12:147–56

258. Wittrock, M. C., Goldberg, S. I. 1975. Imagery and meaningfulness in free recall: Word attributes and instructional sets. *J. Gen. Psychol.* 92:137–51

259. Wittrock, M. C., Marks, C., Doctorow, M. 1975. Reading as a generative process. *J. Educ. Psychol.* 67:484–89

260. Woods, S. S., Resnick, L. B., Groen, G. J. 1975. An experimental test of five process models for subtraction. *J. Educ. Psychol.* 67:17–21

261. Wortman, P. M. 1975. Evaluation research. *Am. Psychol.* 30:562–75

262. Yates, F. 1966. *The Art of Memory.* London: Routledge & Kegan Paul. 400 pp.

263. Yoshida, R. K., Meyers, C. E. 1975. Effects of labeling as educable mentally retarded on teachers' expectancies for change in a student's performance. *J. Educ. Psychol.* 67:521–27

264. Zelby, L. W. 1974. Student-faculty evaluation. *Science* 183:1267–70

265. Zimmerman, B. J., Dialessi, F. 1973. Modeling influences on children's creative behavior. *J. Educ. Psychol.* 65:127–34

AUTHOR INDEX

SUBJECT INDEX

A

AB error
  in infant representation
    studies, 272
Abstraction
  of ideas
    in learning and memory
      studies, 402-4
Acetylcholine
  and neuronal mechanisms
    of learning and memory,
      98-103, 105
Acetyltransferase
  and neuronal mechanisms
    of learning and memory,
      102
Achievement
  and effects of teachers, 443-
    46
  ethic
    recent changes in, 182,
      185
  and fear of success
    in sex-role development,
      309-11
  meaning of
    in personnel studies, 181-
      83
  motivation
    in females, 126
    in instructional psychology,
      424-25
    and personality, 120
  pressure
    sex differences in, 312
  and student ratings of teach-
    ers, 446-49
Actinomycin
  and neuronal mechanisms
    of learning and memory,
      102, 105
Actor-observer differences
  in attribution studies, 128
Acupuncture
  and placebo effect
    in pain research, 43-46
Adaptability
  and mental health, 332
Adjunct questions
  in learning studies, 419-21
Adolescence
  and aggression
    related to TV violence,
      157-58
  development of death cogni-
    tions in, 232-33
Adulthood
  development of death cogni-
    tions in, 232-33

Affective role-taking
  and personality development,
    297
  sex differences in, 312
Age
  and empathy development,
    299
  and locus of control
    in personality studies, 118
  and motivation changes
    in personnel studies, 186
  old
    death cognitions in, 233
    and patterns of mass media
      use, 142-44
    relocation of elderly
      and psychological death,
        238
Agenda setting
  effect of mass media, 152-
    53
Aggression
  and auditory communication
    in birds, 70
    in fishes, 65
  disinhibition of
    as mass media effect, 157-
      60
  and empathy
    in children, 299
  and exposure to erotica,
    162
  and media violence, 123
  and modeling behavior
    viewing of, 437
  and personality studies, 123-
    25
  sex differences in, 311
  and suicide, 240
  and TV violence
    effects of, 156-60
Aging
  disengagement theory of
    and death cognitions, 233
Alcoholism
  and locus of control
    in personality studies, 118
Algorithmization
  in instruction, 439-40
Altruism
  and empathy, 299, 307
  and equity
    in children, 308-9
  and helping
    in personality studies, 129-
      31
  and personality development,
    306-7
Americans
  native

and community interven-
    tion, 329
Amnesia
  infantile
    and learning and memory
      studies, 87, 90
Analgesia
  hypnotic
    and pain research, 43-46,
      52-54
Anamnia
  auditory physiology of, 65-
    68
    in anurans, 67-68
    bioacoustics of, 65-66
    general, 65
Androgeny
  and behavioral flexibility,
    126
  and personal adjustment,
    313-14
Anger
  as stage of dying, 241
Animate-inanimate concepts
  and death, 232
Anisomycin
  and neuronal mechanisms
    of learning and memory,
      103
Anonymity
  and aggression, 124
Anurans
  auditory communication in,
    67-68
  auditory physiology of, 67-
    68
  bioacoustic behavior of,
    67
Anxiety
  and death fear, 233-36
  and ethnicity
    in pain research, 45-46
  and health care delivery,
    203
  and job enrichment studies,
    187
  and learning and motivation,
    425
  and locus of control
    in personality studies, 118
  and stress
    in personality studies, 131-
      32
Arousal
  activation
    and imitation of TV violence,
      159
  -level hypothesis
    and aggression, 123-24
  sexual

CUMULATIVE INDEXES

CONTRIBUTING AUTHORS VOLUMES 24-28

499

CHAPTER TITLES VOLUMES 24-28